THE MEDICI

THE

MEDICI

BY

Col. G. F. Young, C. B.

THE MODERN LIBRARY · NEW YORK

The leader's deeds and hard won glory live;
This remains; this alone survives the funeral fires . . . OVID

Not to know the events which happened before one
was born, that is to remain always a boy . . . CICERO

Random House IS THE PUBLISHER OF

THE MODERN LIBRARY

BENNETT A. CERF · DONALD S. KLOPFER · ROBERT K. HAAS

Manufactured in the United States of America

Printed by Parkway Printing Company   Bound by H. Wolff

To

MISS MARY JOSEPHINE ALLEN

OF BOSTON, U.S.A.

TO WHOSE

ENTHUSIASM FOR THE REMARKABLE FAMILY

WHOSE HISTORY IS HERE TOLD

THIS BOOK OWES ITS

ORIGIN.

"The little present must not be allowed wholly to elbow
the great past out of view."—ANDREW LANG.

PREFACE

THERE are in English several histories of three or four of the more important members of the Medici family; but there is none, either in Italian or English, of that family as a whole, the history of no less than nine out of thirteen generations having remained hitherto unwritten.

The history of the Medici is a deeply interesting story; while, besides its intrinsic interest, it helps us to acquire much knowledge about the re-birth of Learning and Art, about the history of Europe in perhaps its most important period, about the birth of Science, and about the great collections of Art possessed by Florence. For without referring largely to all these subjects no true picture of the Medici can be given.

My aim has been to write of them *as a family*—their rise, their "course upon the mountain-tops of power," and their decline and end—and to keep the parts always in subordination to the whole. It may perhaps be thought that more might have been said in the case of one or two members of the family; but to have gone into greater detail regarding individuals would have had the effect of obscuring the general view, besides making the book far too long.

This history takes a somewhat different view of the Medici from that which has hitherto generally obtained. It is a strange fact that in their case the violent partisanship which swayed the historians of their time has been carried on into our own, and writers about them, whether belonging to their age or ours, are banded into two furiously opposing camps; [1] making it very difficult to arrive at a true estimate. Those on the one side can see no faults, and give a picture which one feels to be untrue to life by reason of its successive eulogy;[2] while to those on the other the name of Medici appears to act like an intoxicant, rendering them incapable of seeing what the very facts recorded by themselves demonstrate, and making even facts telling strongly in favour of those concerned appear to such writers only to show a subtle policy towards a nefarious end. And it is those of the latter type who have been best known,[3] and have consequently been followed by writers who, in guide-books on the art and history of Florence, have had occasion to allude to the Medici. There have been Florentines of note (now passed away), well read in the archives of their country, who have said that if only the world at large could study those archives it would discover that the time-honoured view of the Medici which has thus grown up was to a very large extent unjust, and far from the truth; but their voices have not been generally heard.

To "whitewash" historical characters is as great an offence to history as to traduce them, and the view to which I have gradually been led regarding the Medici has not been due to any original bias in their favour. On the contrary, I began this study entirely imbued with the time-honoured theory I have mentioned, and was only brought by degrees to a different opinion by coming to see that the admitted facts refused over and over again to square with the view of this family usually presented to us. I have therefore preferred to judge those concerned by their acknowledged deeds, rather than by comments thereon which (emanating from writers violently biassed against them) are found uniformly attributing good actions to ignoble motives, or distorting those actions until they become full of impossibilities.[4]

Avoiding any attempt to make out the Medici as either this or that, I have endeavoured, eschewing all "legends," to detail simply the facts for which we have evidence. No crimes attributed to them have been omitted or slurred over. If the result is to show the Medici in a better light than hitherto has been the case, that is not due to any desire to "whitewash" them, but is simply the consequence of a want of any evidence for a large proportion of those crimes which have furnished the darker shades in the traditional picture of this family. I have also endeavoured to leave the facts to speak for themselves as far as possible, to narrate rather than to explain, leaving readers to form their own conclusions; as I am confident that in this way what the Medici were and did is likely to be more forcibly appreciated.

As regards the elder branch of the family, this book relates for the first time the histories of Giovanni di Bicci, Piero il Gottoso, and Lorenzo (Duke of Urbino); brings to notice certain points not previously known with reference to Cosimo Pater Patriae, the manner in which that title was given him, and his singular tomb; and throws some new light on the character and deeds of Lorenzo the Magnificent. It takes a different view from that hitherto held regarding Pope Leo X, Catherine de' Medici, and Pietro the Unfortunate. And it discloses for the first time the inner history of Pope Clement VII, the scheme which he formed, the manner in which he carried it out, and the motives underlying his (hitherto imperfectly understood) political manœuvres with Charles V, Francis I, and Henry VIII.

As regards the younger branch of the family, this history is the first that has been written. In this portion of the subject the most notable points are: The various important achievements of Cosimo I and Ferdinand I; the character and importance of Eleonora di Toledo; the history of Anna Maria Ludovica, a member of the family who has been practically unknown, though most deserving of record; the solution of a problem long unsolved connected with the feeling regarding the Medici in their own city; the unveiling (through the results of recent research) of many misconceptions regarding Cosimo I and his sons; the exposure of such errors as the common one of supposing that the palace known as the Pitti Palace was built by that family instead of by

the Medici; the demonstration of the unique connection of
the Medici with the birth of modern Science; and the dis-
closure of the immense gift made by the last of the Medici
to Florence. In the absence of any history of this portion
of the family, it has not been recognised that the deeds of
the younger branch in the domain of Literature, Art, and
Science were, though different in character, of scarcely less
importance than those of the elder branch. The elder branch
advanced Learning and Art by the liberal expenditure of
their wealth in that cause, their enlightened patronage, and
their artistic taste; their art collections, however, being swept
away. The younger branch did for Science what the elder
branch had done for Learning; while it was they who collected all those artistic treasures [5] which now form the attraction of Florence. Thus this portion of the history necessarily furnishes a large amount of information which was
hitherto entirely wanting regarding the artistic possessions
of Florence.

Lastly, as regards Art, this book explains for the first
time the meaning of certain pictures, hitherto misunderstood,
but whose true meaning a complete study of the Medici history reveals. The chief of these are:—Gozzoli's frescoes in
the Riccardi Palace (the Medici Palace), to which frescoes
an entire chapter has been devoted; and the true meaning
of Botticelli's pictures, *"The Adoration of the Magi," "Fortitude," "The Birth of Venus,"* the *"Primavera,"* and *"Calumny."* It also brings to notice a hitherto unknown statue
by Gian da Bologna, called *"The Genius of the Medici"*; a
hitherto unknown portrait of the celebrated Clarice Strozzi,
of whom it had been supposed that no portrait existed; and
a hitherto unknown portrait of the Princess Violante Beatrice, of whom also it had been supposed that no portrait
existed; and gives the first reproduction of a lost portrait
of Maddalena, eldest daughter of Lorenzo the Magnificent,
of the recently discovered portrait by Raphael of Giuliano,
third son of Lorenzo the Magnificent, which had been lost

for three hundred and fifty years, and of nine other portraits
of members of the Medici family which have not previously
been known. And it demonstrates that the recent theories
put forward regarding several of Botticelli's most important
pictures are erroneous.

In the chapters relating to the earlier members of the family short notices have been introduced of the prominent
artists of the time, not merely in order to show to how large
an extent the Medici were concerned in their steady advancement to greater achievements, but still more because
this is essential if the Medici are to be shown in their proper
"setting." The favourite method of separating the history
of the time from the history of its art would in this case
have been exceptionally destructive; for it would have excluded from the biographical sketch of each head of the family that which in the case of many of them was their chief
interest in life; and even to place such notices at the end
of the chapter would have caused a similar separation. The
course adopted preserves better that close touch with the
world of Art which is here essential, while it also assists to
maintain the due sequence of events in regard to Art. These
notices cease after the time of the "Interregnum" (1494-
1512); to have continued them beyond that point, when
the Tuscan school, which had so long led the way, began to
merge into the larger field of Italy, would have had the effect of obscuring the history of the Medici with matters in
which they had ceased to be any longer an important factor.

In the earlier chapters short abstracts have been given
from time to time of contemporary events taking place in
other countries, as this course, though unusual, is I think in
the case of a history of this kind helpful, by keeping it in
touch with general history as it proceeds. The need for such
abstracts gradually decreases as the history of the family
advances.

In regard to the vexed question of references to authorities
I have endeavoured to steer a middle course between quoting

chapter and verse for every statement (a method as much
loathed by the general reader as it is liked by scholars) and
quoting no authorities at all. Either method is, of course,
open to criticism from one side or the other, but I think the
middle course adopted is that likely to be preferred by most
readers.

In the notices on contemporary artists I have freely used
extracts from other writers in detailing the special characteristics of the art of various painters and sculptors; as on
such a subject it has seemed to me preferable to quote the
words of others whose opinion must necessarily have far
greater weight than my own.

I desire specially to acknowledge my indebtedness to Mr.
F. A. Hyett's *Florence* in regard to the characters of Cosimo
Pater Patriae and Lorenzo the Magnificent, to Mr. E. Armstrong's chapter in vol. iii of *The Cambridge Modern History* in regard to the administration of Tuscany under Cosimo
I, to his *Lorenzo de' Medici* in regard to the character and
writings of the latter, and to Count Pasolini's *Life of Catherine Sforza* in regard to that remarkable ancestress of the
later generations of the Medici. Also to Miss Hope Rea's
Donatello, Mrs. Ady's *Fra Angelico*, Mr. Langton Douglas's
Fra Angelico, and Dr. Williamson's *Perugino*, in regard to
the art of those masters.

Original research has been carried out chiefly (though of
course not entirely) with regard to that portion of the history relating to the last six generations of the family. And
here a very large part of the information has, even more
than from books and manuscripts, been gathered from what
buildings and tombs, pictures, statues, and monuments have
to tell, these having proved as valuable a mine of information as the records of the archives. Added to this, I am also
indebted to the researches of the late Professor G. E. Saltini
for much valuable information in regard to this portion of
the history of the family.

This book is written primarily for the general reader, but

not exclusively so, and I trust that scholars may find in it not a little that is new to them, both in the domain of History and of Art. At the same time, it does not pretend to be more than a very inadequate memorial of this interesting family; and none know its imperfections so well as myself.

G. F. Y.

FLORENCE, 12th October 1910.

CONTENTS

CONTEMPORARY HISTORICAL EVENTS

See Note 16, Chapter III, at end of book.

AUTHORITIES CONSULTED

HISTORY

Florentine History, by H. E. Napier.
Histoire de Florence, by Perrens.
History of the Commonwealth of Florence, by Adolphus Trollope.
The First Two Centuries of Florentine History, by Professor Villari.
History of the Popes, by Ranke.
History of the Papacy, by Dr. Mandell Creighton, Bishop of London.
Histoire des Papes, by Dr. Louis Pastor.
The Cambridge Modern History, Vols. II and III.
Italy and her Invaders, by Professor Hodgkin.
Lectures on Mediæval Church History, by Archbishop Trench.
Florence by F. A. Hyett.
La Diplomatie Vénitienne, by M. Armand Baschet.
Lettres de Catherine de Medicis, edited by Le Comte de la Ferrière.
La Jeunesse de Catherine de Medicis, by A. de Reumont.
Venetian State Papers (1202-1607).
Spanish State Papers (1558-1603).
Foreign State Papers—London (1558-1580).
Histoire de France, by Michelet.
Le Istorie Fiorentine, by Niccolò Machiavelli.
Istorie della Citta di Firenze, by Nardi.
Storia Fiorentina, by Varchi.
Storia Fiorentina, by Guicciardini.
Ritratti d'huomini illustri di Casa Medici, by Ammirato.
Histoire des Républiques Italiennes, by Sismondi.
Storia della Repubblica de Fierenze, by Gino Capponi.
Archivio Storico inguardante la Storia d'Italia; Firenze.
Storia del Granducato della Toscana, by Galluzi.
Serie d'Autori risguardante la celebre famiglia Medici, by Moreni.
Celebri famiglie Italiane, by Conte Pompeo Litta.
Firenze dai Medici ai Lorena, by Giuseppe Conti.
Fatti e Aneddoti di Storia Fiorentina, by Giuseppe Conti.
Firenze Citta Nobillissima, by Migliore.
Notizie Istoriche della Chiese Fiorentine, by Richa.
Le Ville Medicee, by Baccini (1897).
Tragidie Medicee, by G. E. Saltini (1898).
Nota e Informazione della Signoria di Firenze, by G. E. Saltini.
Gli Ultimi dei Medici, by Emilio Robiony (1905).
Gius Pubblico Popolare dei Toscani, e Storia della R. Famiglia dei

xix

Medici, by il Cav. Comm. S. L. Peruzzi.
Life of Lorenzo the Magnificent, by William Roscoe.
Life of Leo the Tenth, by William Roscoe.
Lorenzo de' Medici, by Professor E. Armstrong.
Life and Times of Savonarola, by Professor Villari.
Life and Times of Niccolò Machiavelli, by Professor Villari.
Lucrezia Borgia, by Gregorovius.
The Age of the Condottieri, by Oscar Browning.
Private Life of the Renaissance Florentines, by Dr. Guido Biagi.
Florentine Life during the Renaissance, by Walter Scaife.
Cosimo de' Medici, by Miss Ewart.
Beatrice d'Este, by Julia Cartwright (Mrs. Ady).
Isabella d'Este, by Julia Cartwright (Mrs. Ady).
Life of Catherine Sforza, by Count Pasolini.
Life of Charles the Fifth, by William Robertson.
Charles the Fifth, by Professor E. Armstrong.
The Civilisation of the Renaissance in Italy, by **Burckhardt.**
The Renaissance in Italy, by J. A. Symonds.
Florence, by C. Yriarte.
The Makers of Florence, by Mrs. Oliphant.
Giovanni delle Bande Nere, by Adolphus Trollope.
Jean des Bandes Noires, by M. Pierre Gautier.
Autobiography of Benvenuto Cellini.
Life of Benvenuto Cellini, by J. A. Symonds.
Marie de Medicis and her Court, by Louis Battifol.
Women of the Valois Court, by Imbert de Saint Amand.
Women of Florence, by Professor Isidoro Del Lungo.
Milan under the Sforza, by Miss C. M. Ady.
The Medici Popes, by H. M. Vaughan.
Etudes de Critique et d'Histoire Religieuse, by Dr. E. Vacandard.
Man and Manners at the Court of Florence (Horace Mann's Letters
    to Horace Walpole), by Dr. Doran.
Siena, by Langton Douglas.
Echoes of Old Florence, by Leader Scott.
Walks in Florence, by the Misses Horner.
The Palaces of Florence, by Mrs. Ross.
The Châteaux of Touraine, by M. H. Lansdale.

ART

The Lives of the Painters, Sculptors, and Architects, by Vasari.
Modern Painters, by Ruskin.
The Renaissance, by Walter Pater.
Sketches of the History of Christian Art, by Lord Lindsay.
History of Architecture, by Fergusson.
History of Architecture, by Professor Banister Fletcher.
The Cathedral Builders, by Leader Scott.
Mornings in Florence, by Ruskin.
The Principles of Art, by W. White.

Tuscan Sculptors, by Perkins.

The Appreciation of Sculpture, by Russell Sturgis.

Italian Painters, by Morelli.

The Florentine Painters of the Renaissance, by Bernhardt Berenson.

The Painters of Florence, by Julia Cartwright (Mrs. Ady).

Brunelleschi, by Leader Scott.

Fra Angelico and his Art, by Langton Douglas.

Fra Angelico, by G. C. Williamson.

Donatello, by Hope Rea.

Donatello, by Lord Balcarres.

Verrocchio, by Miss Cruttwell.

Antonio Pollajuolo, by Miss Cruttwell.

Luca e Andrea della Robbia, by Miss Cruttwell.

Luca della Robbia, by the Marchesa Burlamacchi.

Botticelli, by Steinmann.

Botticelli, by A. Streeter.

Botticelli, by Julia Cartwright (Mrs. Ady).

Sandro Botticelli, by H. P. Horne.

Leonardo da' Vinci, by Edward M'Curdy.

Life of Michelangelo Buonarotti, by J. A. Symonds.

Life of Michelangelo, by Harford.

Piero della Francesca, by W. C. Waters.

Perugino, by G. C. Williamson.

Raphael, by H. Strachey.

Andrea del Sarto, by H. Guinness.

Pinturicchio, by March Phillips.

The Dominican Church of S. M. Novella at Florence, by the Rev
    J. Wood Brown.

THE MEDICI

THE MEDICI

PROLOGUE

In the fifth century storm upon storm out of the dark North swept away in a great deluge of barbarism all the civilisation of the western half of the Roman Empire. From the Atlantic to Constantinople, and from the Rhine and Danube to the deserts of Africa, all that was learned and cultivated, all that was artistic and beautiful, was overwhelmed in an avalanche of ruin in which not only the triumphs of architecture, literature, and art, produced by many centuries of a high civilisation, but also those who could create such things afresh, were involved in one general destruction.

Then after a night of thick darkness, obscuring everything in Western Europe for two hundred years, during which these barbarian races are battling over the dead corpse of the Roman Empire, comes in the eighth century Charlemagne, creating a brief light for forty years. But on his death the darkness settles down again, wrapping all in gloom; and again we read, "Barbarism and confusion reigned throughout Western Europe for a hundred and fifty years." Meanwhile, from Arabia another deluge, that of the Mahomedans, sweeps in succession over the fair countries forming the eastern half of the Empire, creating there also a similar desolation. Gradually all that is left of the art and letters of the Roman Empire takes refuge in Constantinople, where it remains shut up, surrounded west, north, east, and south by the barbarian flood.

At length in the twelfth century the re-civilisation of the West is begun by the discovery in Italy of the code of the

Roman law. Then come in the thirteenth century Niccolò Pisano, and in the fourteenth century, Dante, Giotto, and Petrarch, to arouse men again to a sense of the beautiful and the cultivated; and Art and Literature begin to flow back to their long-deserted Western home. And so, out of the very grave of that old civilisation of Rome, buried deep nine centuries before, comes the new inspiration, the Re-birth.

But as yet there was none with power to make these efforts produce their full fruit; none with power to unearth the treasures so long buried, to spread a knowledge of them throughout the West, and to make the voices of those long dead begin again to speak. While after these four fathers of the Renaissance [1] had passed away Art and Literature threatened again to die, and the movement thus inaugurated to become but local and temporary.

And then, in the city which had produced three of these men, arose a family who, with the power of wealth, and with a great love for these things, lifted Learning from its grave, spread a knowledge of it through Europe, gave Art the encouragement it needed in order to advance to its highest achievements, and made that city the Athens of the West.

CHAPTER I

FLORENCE

"O Foster-nurse of man's abandoned glory,
　Since Athens, its great Mother, sank in splendour,
　Thou shadowest forth that mighty shape in story,
　As Ocean its wrecked fanes, severe yet tender;
　The light-invested angel Poesy
　Was drawn from the dim world to welcome thee."
　　　　　　　　　　　　　　　　　　—Shelley.

Standing on the hill of San Miniato, and looking down
from thence, as so many belonging to bygone generations
have done, at the city spread out at our feet, we see before
us a city such as none other ever can be to a large portion
of mankind, one in which things have had their birth which
now form the life-blood of all the intellectual existence of
Europe. As Yriarte says: "We must dearly love Florence,
for she is the mother of all those who live by thought."

Her outward beauty is palpable to all. The domes and
spires of a smokeless city bathed in sunshine, the slopes of
the Apennines, extending almost to its walls, covered with
vineyards, olive plantations, gardens, and numberless luxurious villas, the silver thread of the river Arno winding
away in the distance through the beautiful Val d'Arno, the
"tender" colouring which in Tuscany is so marked a feature
of the distant landscape, all these together make up a whole
which is a dream of beauty.

But there is more to be seen than this, and Florence's
charms are not confined to her outward beauty. For this is
the city which produced the Renaissance,[1] an achievement
which will ever surround Florence with an unfading glory.
The influence she has thus exercised has secured for her a

3

world-wide interest. Undoubtedly the main attraction of
Florence for the modern world is as a place where there
breathes a stiller, higher atmosphere than that of the hurrying, striving twentieth century; a place where, if we will,
the history of the past is made to rise before us, and where
the masterpieces of Art strive to draw the mind upwards
from the low level of the trivial, the ignoble, and the commonplace. It has been said, "The arts are the avenues by
which the mind of man soars to its highest limits." If that
be so, then in Florence if anywhere in the world must the
truth of those words be felt. For in this city of Dante and
Petrarch, of Ghiberti, Brunelleschi, Donatello, and Michelangelo, of Giotto, Orcagna, Masaccio, Fra Angelico, Botticelli, and Leonardo da Vinci, not only one of those avenues,
but no less than four of them, have been followed as far
as the mind of man has ever penetrated along them.

We are going for a little while to be occupied amidst scenes
instinct with the spirit of these men. Therefore, in looking at
beautiful Florence let us try to think chiefly, not of her
outward beauty, but rather of all the deep interests which
she is able to unfold to us—in art, in history, in literature—
bound up with the name of Florence for all time. To consider the high-souled *thoughts* which gave their birth to all
that we go there to see: produced by minds which were able
to make their city pre-eminent among all cities in painting,
in sculpture, in architecture, and in poetry, and at the same
time pre-eminent also in learning, and in the science of their
age.

Thus, as we look down upon Florence from San Miniato
we shall be drawn to think of the high aspirations of those
who first planned to build that mighty dome,[2] and who directed their cathedral to be designed *"so as to be worthy
of a heart expanded to much greatness"*; to think of the conceptions of him who, while he was the father of all painting,
could also be so great in architecture as to design that beautiful bell tower by its side;[3] of the strong character of

those freedom-loving Florentines who erected that solidly-built city fortress [4] to guard their supreme council from the effects of their own turbulent spirit; of all that lies collected under that small pointed spire in the background,[5] telling of the dawn of the Renaissance of Art; or, again, of what a world of high-souled thought is represented in the line of statues in that colonnade [6]—Florence's "Valhalla"—extending from the river to the fortress; that galaxy of the great, in poetry, in art, in learning, and in science, all produced by this single city, and containing, even though Brunelleschi, Ghiberti, Masaccio, Fra Angelico, and Botticelli are not there, at least twelve great names of which any *one* would suffice to make any other city famous. And as they look down upon us from their niches, they invite us to walk their streets in spirit with them—with Dante, and Giotto, and Orcagna, and Donatello, and Leonardo, and Michelangelo, and Galileo —and to be uplifted into the world where their thoughts dwelt, so that we too may be, if but for a moment, "among the immortals."

Lastly, we shall be drawn to think of that family who for so many generations took a chief part in all that interests us in Florence; whose care for Learning and Art produced such wide effects; who preserved to the world most of those treasures of art which we now visit Florence to see; and who all lie buried in that church of San Lorenzo [7] which is marked by the smaller dome in the distance, where as their line came near its end they erected tombs which are those of crowned heads, tombs visited by all the world for their masterpieces of art and their magnificence.

The city is what those who once lived in it have made it. And as we look at the memorials of themselves which they have left behind them (and which still belong to their descendants) we must not omit all thought of the race which made these men what they were. For this is Etruria, a country which has always, from the earliest times, led the way

in Italy, and from whence in the Middle Ages there came
forth (as leaders of the movement which we call the Renaissance) a great succession of men of whom it has been said,
"The dazzling light of their genius shines on through the
centuries to show to future generations what man can be
and do." [8] So that these memorials of Florence's past are no
dead records of a bygone time, but afford the strongest inspiration to us of the present day.

And since the Signoria of Florence, when starting at the
end of the thirteenth century to build their cathedral, declared, in the document conveying their instructions to its
architect, Arnolfo di Cambio, that the desire which animated
them was that it "should be designed so as to be worthy of a
heart expanded to much greatness, corresponding to the
noble city's soul, which is composed of the souls of all its
citizens," the great dome of Florence (whose construction
was thus inspired by an aim so different from that which
later on called into being its rival at Rome) may well,
whenever from far or near it strikes upon the eye, act as a
clarion-call to high and noble aims. The men who, in a mere
government document ordering a great public work, could
reach such a level were no common men. And in commenting
on their words, Mr. Walter Scaife justly asks:—"Has the
much-vaunted progress of civilisation during the six centuries
that have since passed carried us so far beyond either the sentiments or the work of these men?"

But there is yet another attraction which Florence possesses
for the modern world. And that is the vividness with which
the past is there made to live before us; the way in which the
twentieth century is enabled to look at the fifteenth even
with the outward eye, and as if four swiftly-flowing centuries
that have intervened were rolled back. The massive strength
of the Bargello, of the Palazzo Vecchio, and even of ordinary
buildings in every direction, forces upon us the recollection
of the fierce fighting which these narrow streets have time
after time witnessed. And while other cities have preserved

little round which interest connected with men eminent in History, Literature, or Art who passed their lives there can gather, Florence, which has held a leadership in Art and letters equalled by no other city except Athens, teems with memorials of those who gave her that leadership. The dome of the cathedral brings to our minds Brunelleschi, its nave re-echoes with the thundering eloquence of Savonarola, its beautiful campanile recalls to us Giotto; the Loggia de' Lanzi reminds us of Orcagna, the Baptistery bears record of Ghiberti, the Torre del Gallo still keeps alive the memory of "the starry Galileo." We see the house where Dante lived; we pass the shops where Giotto, Botticelli, and Andrea del Sarto worked; we follow the same streets by which Verrocchio, Ghirlandajo and Michelangelo went to their daily tasks; we stand before church doorways made beautiful by the art of Luca della Robbia; we listen to Donatello's voice as we gaze at the statues surrounding Or San Michele; we pace the corridors and cloisters of San Marco accompanied by the spirits of Fra Angelico and Savonarola. And in many an old fresco the faces, dress, and manner of life of the men and women of the Renaissance are brought before us with startling vividness.

But the full effect of this vivid realisation of the past which Florence forces upon us is best seen by comparing her with her great rival Venice. Mrs. Oliphant, speaking of Venice, says: [9]—

"After the bewitchment of the first vision a chill falls upon the enquirer. Where is the poet, where the prophet, where the princes, the scholars, the men whom could we see we should recognise wherever we met them, with whom the whole world is acquainted? *They are not here*. In the sunshine of the Piazza, in the glorious gloom of San Marco, in the great council chambers of the Ducal palace, once so full of busy statesmen and great interests, there is scarcely a figure, recognisable of all, to be met with in the spirit—no one for traces of whom we look as we walk, or whose individual foot-

steps are traceable. Instead of the men who made her what
she was, and who ruled her with so high a hand, we find
everywhere the great image of Venice herself. . . . In her records the city is everything, the individual nothing. Venice
is the outcome, not great names of individual Venetians."

Mrs. Oliphant's subsequent remarks show that the root
of the reason why Venice produced no prominent men was
the inordinate love of money. A race with whom money-making and money-spending is the one serious interest cannot
penetrate those "avenues by which the mind soars to its
highest limits." Florence also loved money, but it was not
her chief interest. And so we have this significant result:
Florence, with Art and Learning as her passion, and with
her long line of immortal names in every branch of these,
the city which led the way in producing the civilisation of
Europe; and, on the other hand, Venice, producing next to
nothing of the kind,—no great poet, no great scholar, no
great sculptor, no great statesman known to all the world,
no great painter, even, until her rival had been leading the
way in that particular for a hundred and fifty years, and
had produced a host of such,—and leaving nothing behind
her but her own exalted name, nothing still able to elevate
mankind after her own glory had passed away.

It is a great contrast. And just as it is the lack of the
human interest in the case of Venice that causes that "chill"
to fall upon the enquirer, so on the other hand it is the
abundant possession of the human interest that gives Florence her great attraction. The seed from which the fruit
grew was, in the one case, the love of money, in the other,
the love of Art.

CHAPTER II

THE MEDICI

WE turn from this glimpse of the city to those who were for over three hundred years its most prominent citizens.

The history of the Medici covers three and a half centuries (1400-1748), two of those centuries, the fifteenth and sixteenth, being the most interesting period of any both in History and in Art. It is a period which covers the change from mediæval to modern history (which may be held to commence with the long triangular duel between Francis I, Charles V, and Henry VIII); it covers the time when the conditions changed from those consequent on the feudal system and small, isolated states, to those brought about by regular armies and powerful countries with cla ing interests; it covers the time when the chief political power in Europe shifted from the great independent states of Italy (Venice, Milan, Florence, and Naples) to the northern countries, France, England, and Germany; it embraces the Reformation, with all that brought it about and that followed from it; and it includes the extinction of the (Christian) Eastern Empire and establishment of the (Mahomedan) Turkish Empire in its place, the discovery of a new world in America, the expulsion of the Moors from Spain, and in general the settlement of the different nations of Europe, after centuries of transition, in the localities they now occupy. As regards Art the period is even more important; for with the year 1400 there began that wonderful fifteenth century which saw the birth of the Renaissance in Art, and produced a galaxy of great men in every branch of Art, such as the world had never seen before, and is never likely to see again.

9

The gradual rise of the Medici from comparative obscurity, and not by military conquests, to so high an eminence is one of the most remarkable things in history. From simple bankers and merchants they rose, in spite of much opposition and many vicissitudes, until they became the most powerful family in Europe, and indeed until there was a Medici on the throne of nearly every principal country.[1]

They are interesting from several very different points of view:—

The important place which they took in history makes their story at times almost that of Europe. Cosimo Pater Patriae, Lorenzo the Magnificent, Pope Leo X, Pope Clement VII, and Catherine de' Medici, not to mention others, have made the name of Medici occupy a larger place in history than was probably ever taken by any other family.

Their patronage of Learning and Art. In this domain the Medici have never been approached by any others among the rulers of mankind. The Rothschilds of their time, their immense wealth was lavishly expended on the revival of Learning and the encouragement of Art. In painting, Fra Angelico, Lippi, Gozzoli, Ghirlandajo, Botticelli, Lorenzo di Credi, Leonardo da Vinci, and Raphael; in sculpture, Ghiberti, Donatello, Verrocchio, and Michelangelo; in architecture, Brunelleschi, Michelozzo, and Bramante; with a host of lesser names, all owed much to their assistance. As regards Painting this had specially important results; and just as the age of Pericles in Athens became the "classic period," or period of highest development, of the art of Sculpture, so the age of the Medici has become the classic period of the art of Painting.

Their connection with the Reformation. In this great movement which convulsed all Europe throughout the greater part of the sixteenth century, the two Popes who belonged to this family [2] were those chiefly concerned—namely, Leo X, Luther's great antagonist, and Clement VII, the Pope in whose pontificate England repudiated the claim

of the Church of Rome to exercise supremacy over the
Church of England. Naturally this again adds much interest
to the story of the Medici.

Lastly, owing to an exceptional many-sidedness they
touched life at so many points. In statesmanship and financial capacity, in learning and artistic taste, in civil administration and sympathy with the feelings of the people, in
knowledge of commerce and agriculture, in all these different directions did the Medici evince an unusual ability. And
this was joined to qualities of courtesy, agreeableness of
manner, absence of arrogance, and a free and generous disposition, which much enhanced their power of influencing
those with whom they were brought in contact. They were
not, however, assisted by any attractions of personal appearance, their portraits showing that they were by no means a
handsome family, their only good feature being their fine
eyes, which were proverbial. These various characteristics
make them an interesting family apart from the other aspects of their history.

Two grave charges have been preferred against them:
first, that they by a long course of duplicity deprived their
country of its liberty, and exalted themselves into despots
over it; and, second, that there is to be attributed to them
an evil pre-eminence in crimes of murder. How far these
charges are just will be best seen as we follow the course of
their history; but regarding the second some general remarks are called for.

The charge is a strange one in view of the contemporary
history of other countries. For the history of this family embraces thirteen generations, and out of this number there
are no less than ten generations to whom no such crimes
have been even *attributed*. It is not until we reach the seventh generation that we have the first murder committed by
a Medici; and even that was committed by one who had no
legitimate right to the name.[3] While it is not until we reach

the eighth and ninth generations that we meet with that series of these accusations which has been the main cause of the reputation which has been given to the family.[4] Such a charge against a whole family involves comparison; and when we compare even the whole of the cases attributed to the Medici with those authenticated as committed by other contemporary ruling families, not only in Italy, but also in France, England, and Spain, it becomes evident that the popular belief ascribing to the Medici an evil pre-eminence in such crimes can only be due to a lack either of information or of the sense of proportion. Among ruling families of the time there are few to whom there have not been attributed more crimes of this nature than to the Medici. Nor do we stigmatise the whole line of the sovereigns of England or France because three out of thirteen generations may have committed crimes of this character.

Some writers, while admitting the injustice of this graver charge, and while ready to allow that the Medici were capable, intellectual, and patriotic, assert that nevertheless they were grasping, cruel, intriguing, and stained with vices which were rampant in their times. It is hoped that this history will demonstrate convincingly that the Medici were decidedly not either grasping, or cruel. To say that they were intriguing is merely to say that they were men of their age. Regarding the fourth point, while they certainly were not free from the vices rampant in their times, the indictment in the manner it is made is an exaggeration, implying as it does that the Medici were worse than others, whereas all evidence tends to show that they were distinctly better in this respect than other contemporary families. This general statement, on a point to which modern histories do not consider it necessary to allude except in general terms, will perhaps suffice; but it will be found to be borne out by various facts in the lives of many members of the family as these are followed.

Symonds makes a complaint against the Medici that they

were *"bourgeois." Of course* they were *bourgeois:* it is the very pith of their story: and instead of giving ground for a gibe to be cast at them it contributes much to their honour. It is the essence of their history that they belonged entirely to the people, that their rise began from their championship of the latter against the nobles, and that theirs was an aristocracy, not of birth, but of talent and culture.

They present to us in following their story the most opposite extremes both of conduct and of fortune. Marvellous as to their rise, pathetic as to their vicissitudes, magnificent as to their liberality towards objects for the lasting benefit of mankind, tragic as to many episodes of their career, despicable as to their ignoble decline and end (except for one last act worthy to rank with those of their best days), their history is like a great drama extending over three hundred years, and played out on the widest of stages.

CHAPTER III

GIOVANNI DI BICCI

Born 1360. Died 1428

In the year 1400 the Medici were an ordinary middle-class family in Florence. The family can be traced back as far as the year 1201, when Chiarissimo, eldest son of Giambuono de' Medici, and a member of the Town Council, is noted as being the owner of various houses and towers in the Mercato Vecchio; but the only branch of it with which we are concerned is that which made so great a name in history, and was destined to run an eventful course of nearly three hundred and fifty years.[1]

Of this branch Giovanni de' Medici was at this time the head. For some reason or other his father, Averardo de' Medici, was nicknamed by his companions "Bicci." Among the Medici the same Christian names recur so frequently that each is in history known by some addition or sobriquet, and Giovanni, the founder of the historic branch of the family, is always known as Giovanni di Bicci (*i.e.*, Giovanni, the son of Bicci). He was at this time a man of forty years of age, and highly respected for his character and business ability.

The family were bankers [2] and already possessed of considerable wealth, which Giovanni by his financial ability increased. Several of his ancestors had taken part in public affairs. His great-grandfather Averardo, who had begun the prosperity of the family by successful trading operations, had been Gonfaloniere in 1314; his grandfather Salvestro had been one of the envoys of the Republic deputed to conclude the treaty with Venice in 1336 and two of his father's first cousins had been Gonfaloniere in, respectively, 1349 and 1354.

But Giovanni di Bicci de' Medici [3] came of a family which had signalised themselves in another way than this. For they had on several occasions taken a prominent part in the struggles of the people against the nobles (*grandi*). A distant cousin of his father (also named Giovanni) had, in 1343, been seized and put to death by the tyrant of Florence, Walter de Brienne, Duke of Athens, as one of the most dangerous of the citizens (*popolani*). And when Giovanni di Bicci was eighteen years old, he had seen, in 1378, a distant cousin of his grandfather (another Salvestro), by his powerful words in the Signoria, bring about the riot known as that of the Ciompi (the weavers, dyers, and minor workmen of the guild of wool), which riot, we are told, "broke the power of the nobles, and destroyed the oligarchy of the 'Parte Guelfa' "; while another cousin of his father's, Vieri, had pacified the rebellion of 1393. Thus the family had as its tradition antagonism to the nobles and championship of the cause of the people. Giovanni di Bicci was destined to go far in the same course, as well as to found a family whose influence was to spread far beyond the sphere of the petty politics of Florence.

Let us first see what, in this year 1400, were the conditions surrounding him, (i) in his own city, and (ii) in the larger world beyond it.

(i) Florence, after fierce struggles between rival factions for a hundred and fifty years, had at last settled down with the most democratic government on record. In 1260 the banished Ghibellines, under Farinata degli Uberti, had at the battle of Monteaperto defeated the Guelphs and re-entered Florence in triumph. The Ghibellines had thereupon proposed to raze Florence to the ground; against this Farinata degli Uberti had "raised his single voice," [4] and

prevailed; for which act he has obtained lasting honour in
Florence, and his statue (the only Ghibelline one) has received a place among those of Florence's greatest men in
the Uffizi colonnade. Then had succeeded in 1289 the battle
of Campaldino, giving the final victory to the Guelphs; whereupon the community had been divided into guilds (*arti*),
whose representatives formed the governing body, the Signoria. In 1298 had begun the building of the cathedral, and
of the Palazzo della Signoria, the order for the latter to
Arnolfo di Cambio, the architect, stating that it was required "for the greater security of the Signoria in this city
so given to sudden and violent tumults."

But the internecine strifes did not cease even though the
Ghibellines had been driven out; the same fierce conflicts
as before broke out under new names—Cerchi *versus* Donati,
White Guelphs *versus* Black Guelphs, and so on. At length,
in 1343, Walter de Brienne, a foreigner whom the city had
made its governor, was driven out, when a time of anarchy
and frequent revolutions followed; during which occurred,
in 1348, the great plague described by Boccaccio, and in
1378 the above-mentioned riot of the Ciompi. As a result
the Signoria was reconstituted and composed of representatives ("Priors") from each of the twenty-one guilds, instead
of from the more important ones only; these were directed
to be chosen every two months (afterwards extended to a
longer period); while it was ruled that no noble should be
eligible as a member of the Signoria. The president of the
latter body was the Gonfaloniere, chosen from among the
members of the Signoria, and elected for a similar short period. Nor did even this satisfy Florence's fiercely democratic
instincts. Although all power was vested in the representatives of the various guilds, yet on any large question the
great bell, "the Vacca," in the tower of the Palazzo della
Signoria,[5] summoned the whole male population into the
square below, when the question was decided (ostensibly,
at any rate) "by popular acclamation." This form of gov-

ernment continued for a hundred and fifty years; it had been established about twenty years at the time our story begins.

Passionately indeed was Florence enamoured of freedom. In a struggle of some two hundred years she had first gradually shaken herself free from subordination to the emperors, then fought against and thrown off the power of the nobles, and lastly had established "the most republican republic the world has ever seen." And in deep dread of being brought again under the yoke she had developed so great a jealousy of any action, either by an individual or a family, tending, however remotely, to threaten her independence, that this feeling had become a mania. There was a very short shrift in Florence for any one suspected of harbouring an intention of exalting himself into any position of authority above that of an ordinary citizen.

Florence was at this time at a high level of power, ruling over various subject cities, and constantly increasing her territory by little wars with neighbouring states. Republics such as Florence were of a peculiar kind, since only the citizens of the capital city possessed any political power. None others were allowed any voice in the policy of the state. This complete subjection to the capital city accounts for the fierce struggles of Pisa, Prato, Pistoia, Volterra, and other cities gradually conquered by Florence, against being subdued by her. It is also. no doubt, the reason why history at this period always speaks of "Florence" to denote that state which at a later period we speak of as "Tuscany."

As regards trade and commerce, Florence was at this time the most flourishing state in Europe. Her citizens owned banks in all countries, and the golden florin [6] had become the general European standard of value; marking the leading position in commerce held by Florence.[7] Macaulay, speaking of the revenue about this time, says:—

"The revenue of the Republic amounted to three hundred thousand florins: a sum which, allowing for the depreciation of the precious metals, was at least equivalent to six hundred thousand pounds sterling: a larger sum than England and Ireland, two centuries later, yielded to Elizabeth." [8]

The chief trade was in wool and woollen cloth, both that produced by Florence itself and that sent there from other countries to be dyed and refined by a secret process, and re-exported: a trade memorialised in the still existing names of two celebrated streets in Florence, the "Calimala" (or Calimara) [9] and the "Pelleceria." And the guild of the wool merchants was the most important in Florence; so much so that to this guild was committed the work of building the cathedral. [10] The principal part of the trade of Florence was with England.

(ii) Turning now to the larger world outside Florence we find the other states in Europe situated as follows:—

Venice, a republic of a very different kind and ruled by an oligarchy of nobles, was rapidly advancing to the height of her power, having in 1380 crushed her maritime rival Genoa, and was year by year extending her territories by fresh conquests.

Milan, an imperial duchy, was under the rule of her great Duke, Gian Galeazzo Visconti, the most capable of that family, the builder of the cathedral of Milan and the Certosa of Pavia. He had conquered almost all northern Italy (extending his dominions even as far as Perugia and Spoleto), was at this time only resisted by Florence, and was in full expectation of shortly subduing Florence also, when he would make himself King of Italy.

Naples-and-Sicily, a kingdom, but of the feeblest kind, was in its usual state of anarchy, the bone of contention between the rival houses of Anjou and Aragon, as it had been for a hundred and fifty years.

The Papacy. The situation of the Papacy at this time was most deplorable. There had in 1378 begun "the great schism," with rival Popes at Avignon and Rome: a state of things which had brought down the Papacy to the very dust. For there was here no case of an anti-Pope; both Popes had been duly elected, and each had an equal right to be considered the true Pope. On the side of the French Pope were France, Scotland, Spain, Portugal, Savoy, and Lorraine; on the side of the Italian Pope, were England, Germany, Italy, Denmark, Sweden, and Poland. Whereas salvation was held to depend on being in communion with the true Pope, none during all this period could feel sure that he was so; while it was at any rate certain that one-half of Europe was not. The position was intolerable; and its results during the forty years it lasted were such as to degrade the Papacy to the utmost depth of humiliation.

As regards the remaining countries of Europe:—in England Henry IV had just usurped the kingdom from Richard II, whom he had murdered; in France Charles VI was king, but was mad, and the country in the greatest disorder; Germany was a mass of insignificant states, and the Emperor almost a cypher, the seven princely "electors" invariably choosing as emperor some prince of small dominions and power who would be unable to oppose their own assumption of independence; in the Eastern Empire Constantinople was being closely pressed by the Ottoman Turks; Spain was not as yet one country, Aragon and Castile being still petty independent kingdoms, while all the southern half of Spain was held by the Saracens, or, as they were called, the Moors.

The above is an outline of the general state of Europe before those great changes began in which the Medici were to play so large a part.

The Florence in which Giovanni di Bicci passed his life, though very different in aspect from that with which we are acquainted, nevertheless contained a good deal which we should still recognise. The Baptistery, then already many hundred years old, was much the same as now. So also the Bargello, built about a hundred and fifty years before this time; and close to it the Badia, built in 1330. The Palazzo della Signoria (known to us as the Palazzo Vecchio), built in 1298, was, as to the front portion, much as we see it, but did not extend at the back down the Via de' Gondi, while along the front ran a raised platform, the *ringhiera,* from which proclamations were made. The Loggia de' Lanzi had lately been completed. The cathedral,[11] which had been building for over a hundred years, was still unfinished; and its great dome had not even been begun, while many doubted whether so vast a space could ever be covered in this way. Its beautiful campanile, "Giotto's tower," was finished. The Ponte Vecchio, with its shops (though not then jewellers' shops), was as now; except, of course, for the "Passaggio" on the roof of the shops, constructed long afterwards. Of the two chief churches, Sta. Croce and Sta. Maria Novella, the latter was completed, except for its façade, while Sta. Croce was approaching completion. The city was surrounded by its ancient and picturesque walls, which are now gone, but its main streets still follow the same course as then, and many of them present much the same general appearance. Or San Michele, the curious square church, built by the guild of the wool merchants, was nearly finished; and behind it stood as now the guildhouse of this celebrated "Arte della Lana." As we look at this old house of the great guild of wool (with their emblem of the lamb over the door), and think of the many works in which this guild were then occupied in Florence, we cannot but be impressed with the thought of how many other things besides money-making engaged the attention of this enlightened body of merchants, and of how much in Florence's after-glory has had its birth in that now little-noticed old building.[12]

And it was in connection with these things that a movement was about to begin which was soon to be the paramount question in Florence. For in our review of the Florence of 1400 we have also to think of the existing state of things in regard to Art and Learning. These, though in the previous century roused from their long sleep by Dante, Giotto, and Petrarch, appeared to have sunk back again into slumber. Dante, whose "swanlike dirge of the departing middle ages" had inspired all mankind for a time, had died eighty years before, and no successor to him had arisen. Giotto,[13] the shepherd-boy whose kiss had aroused the sleeping beauty, Art, from her nine centuries of slumber in her Byzantine palace, had died sixty-three years before; his great pupil Orcagna had died thirty-two years before; and the painters of the time (the Giotteschi) had no idea beyond that of a slavish copying of Giotto, and so had sunk into a conventionalism almost as complete as that Byzantine tradition from which Giotto had rescued Art. Lastly, Petrarch, the great scholar who had led men to study the long-buried writings of the classic age, had passed away twenty-six years before, and no other like him had arisen.[14] Thus, when the year 1400 dawned it seemed as though the movement which had begun in the time of Dante and Giotto was merely a passing phase, already moribund, if not defunct.

It was, however, not so. There was soon to be a fresh movement destined far to surpass all that had gone before. And the latter half of Giovanni di Bicci's life, with which we have to do, the period from 1400 to 1428, is the time of this "morning" of the Renaissance; of that extraordinary outburst of Art in every branch, which, felt in some degree in other cities of Italy also at this time, seemed in Florence to permeate the whole people with its throbbing life, producing results the influence of which was, before another hundred years were over, to be felt to the utmost bounds of Europe.

———————

Giovanni di Bicci, with his wife, Piccarda Bueri, and his two sons, Cosimo and Lorenzo (who in the year 1400 were boys of eleven and five), lived first in an old house in the Via Larga, and then in one which still stands in the Piazza del Duomo; and the familiar view which daily met Giovanni's eye from the windows of his house must have been that of the slowly-rising walls and dome of the cathedral, begun so long before, and intended by Florence to be grander than any yet built.

By the year 1400 Giovanni di Bicci was a man in middle age, gracious in manner, retiring in disposition, and much respected by all around him. He has received very little notice from historians, but he was the author of various important works for the benefit of his countrymen and for the encouragement of art. He was distinguished for his ability as a financier, and for his "prudence" (the quality always specially admired by the Florentines), and had made himself highly popular with the people by the liberal way in which he spent his wealth for the public benefit, and by his constant readiness to be their champion in the never-ceasing struggle against the nobles. Being regardless of fame or notoriety, it is only here and there in the history of the time that notice of him is to be found. Moreover, during his lifetime the chief influence in Florence was possessed by the Albizzi family,[15] who, notwithstanding the law affecting the nobles, managed (chiefly by influencing the elections) still to exercise power. Meanwhile Giovanni was laying the foundations of a family which was ere long to obliterate all memory of the sway of the Albizzi.

The first occasion when we find him specially mentioned is in the year 1401. In the picture of the Florence of that age one point has still to be noted without which that picture would not be complete, namely, the terrible outbreaks of the plague which again and again devastated the city in those days, keeping the thought of death and the hereafter ever present in the minds of all men. And our story opens in the midst of one of these awful visitations; and again, as in 1348 and so many other occasions, large numbers of all classes were being daily carried off by this terrible disease. In this distress Florence determined on a costly

votive offering to be placed in her oldest and most highly
venerated church, San Giovanni Battista (better known as
the Baptistery), and that this offering should take the form
of two pairs of very elaborate bronze doors. An international
competition was instituted to settle who should execute this
work, and Giovanni di Bicci, as a leading citizen and a great
patron of art, was appointed one of the judges in this competition. It is an interesting and significant coincidence that
the first mention we have of the first of the Medici should be
his taking a prominent part in an event which has always
been held as the "birthday" of the Renaissance in Art.

During the next seventeen years (1402-1418) the chief
notices which we have of Giovanni are those showing his
quiet but steady advancement in public affairs. In 1402 we
find him elected by his guild, that of the bankers (Arte del
Cambio), as its "Prior," which made him a member of the
Government; and we find him again thus elected in 1408
and in 1411. It is specially recorded that he kept aloof from
the many political intrigues of the time, and that these and
subsequent higher honours were forced upon him unsought.

In 1417 Florence suffered another of those terrible visitations of the plague which afflicted her on so many occasions. This time it carried off 16,000 of the inhabitants.
Giovanni did his utmost to relieve the many sufferings of
the people, while we are told that he "did not confine his
help only to the poor, but was no less ready to alleviate the
misfortunes of the rich."

We must now glance at what had been going on in Europe
during these eighteen years.

The first eighteen years of the fifteenth century were years
of various great events in Europe, all of which closely affected Florence and its Signoria.[16]

In 1400 the Emperor Wenceslaus was deposed by the
"electors" for his worthless, savage, and drunken character.
In his place they chose Rupert, Palatine of the Rhine.

In 1401 the Turks, under Bajazet, having at last come to

the final stage of the long campaign of centuries against the eastern half of the Roman Empire, and having reached and begun to besiege the capital itself—Constantinople, the Eastern Emperor, Manuel Paleologus, who had in 1391 succeeded his father, John Paleologus (John VI), like him visited Italy, Germany, France, and England to try to rouse them to aid in saving Constantinople, and prevent such a dire calamity to all Europe as its fall into the hands of the Turks. He was received everywhere with impartial honours and much sympathy; but as regards Italy, the Papacy was paralysed by the great schism, and also would do nothing unless the Eastern Church would agree to acknowledge the supremacy of the Church of Rome, while the other Italian states were at almost constant war, and threatened at the moment with extinction by Milan. Germany was in chaos, the Emperor having just been deposed. In France the King was out of his mind, and the country in the utmost confusion. And in England the King was a usurper, threatened with civil war. So the Emperor Manuel Paleologus had to return as unsuccessful as his father had been. Help, however, came to Constantinople from an unexpected quarter. The Turkish dominions were suddenly invaded by the Tartars under Timour (or Tamarlane), which called away the Sultan Bajazet from his attack on Constantinople; and at the battle of Angora in the following year he was defeated and taken prisoner by Timour. This defeat shattered for a time the power of the Ottoman Turks, and gave Constantinople a last lease of life for another fifty years.

In 1402 Gian Galeazzo Visconti, Duke of Milan, suddenly died in the midst of his schemes of conquest, relieving Florence of her most formidable enemy, and enabling her four years later to conquer and annex a part of his dominions, Pisa. This conquest of Pisa extended Florence's territory to the coast and gave her a seaport.

In 1409, in Florence's new subject city, took place the Council of Pisa. The effects of the "great schism," with half the countries of Europe recognising one Pope and the other half another, became at length so intolerable that all Europe began to cry for "a reformation of the Church in head and members," a phrase constantly on men's lips all through this fifteenth century; and this was the first of three attempts to that end. The cardinals of both the rival parties deserted their Popes and summoned a Council of the whole Western Church at Pisa to solve the difficulty. To this Council there came about 200 bishops, nearly 300 abbots, over 400 doctors of theology, and the representatives of most of the sovereigns of Europe.

The primary point to be fought out was whether a Council was supreme over a Pope, and therefore able to reform errors in the Papacy, or whether a Pope was above a Council. The sixth century would have been amazed that such a question could be debated, the supreme authority in the Church throughout the early centuries having been a General Council of equal and independent bishops, each himself under the authority of such a Council. But since then one bishop had exalted himself step by step, until the time had come that such a question could be debated.

However, the Council, by the mere fact of assembling on its own authority, and in defiance of two Popes, virtually declared itself the highest power in the Church. Moreover, it at once proceeded formally to lay down the same. And this done, it deposed both the rival Popes for their crimes. Then the Council made the mistake which nullified all its work: instead of proceeding to reform the abuses in the Church, and only after this had been done electing a fresh Pope, it elected a Pope (Alexander V) before attempting to carry out reforms. The natural result followed: Alexander V promptly found means to adjourn the Council, nominally for three years, practically for an indefinite period.

This futile conclusion of the first attempt to reform the Church left matters worse than before. The two deposed Popes refused to accept the sentence of the Council; so that the only result was that there were now three rival Popes instead of two. And so the "great schism" continued. Florence, for allowing that detested thing a Council to assemble in one of her subject cities, was, on behalf of one of the three Popes (Gregory XII), attacked by King Ladislas of Naples, and while the Council was sitting, had to protect its deliberations and her own territory by force of arms. With the result that the Florentine army captured Rome.

In 1410 Pope Alexander V died, and was succeeded by Pope John XXIII. And in the same year Sigismund, King of Bohemia, the younger brother of Wenceslaus, was elected Emperor.

In 1413 in England Henry IV died, and was succeeded by his brilliant son, Henry V. And in 1415 the latter invaded France, because that country would not give him Catherine, the King's third daughter, and with her Normandy, Maine, and Anjou. Then followed the great battle of Agincourt, with its crushing defeat for France.

In the same year as this great battle between France and England there took place the Council of Constance, the second attempt to reform the Church. This Council was summoned by the Emperor Sigismund, that holder of the imperial dignity whom Carlyle sarcastically calls "Sigismund super grammaticam." [17] The widely representative and authoritative character of this Council may be judged by the list of those who composed it. It included 27 archbishops, 300 bishops, 20 cardinals, 300 abbots and doctors of theology, and 14 deputies of various universities; while there also attended its deliberations 26 princes, 140 counts, and about 4000 priests. It sat for over three years at Constance, whose chief fame it has made. It was purposely held out of Italy, whose bishops could not be depended upon to give an independent opinion. And since these latter outnumbered those of all other countries put together, it was ruled that to prevent their having an undue preponderance the voting should be by nations. [18]

This Council put an end to the "great schism," which for more than a generation had been the scandal of Christendom. Having met and appointed the Emperor Sigismund to preside, and having formally declared its authority over all ecclesiastics, the Pope included, it deposed all the three rival Popes; and this time they were unable to refuse obedience. Pope John XXIII was in addition on account of his crimes imprisoned for three years in the castle of Heidelberg. But the Council then made the same mistake as that of Pisa, and before proceeding to reform the abuses in the Church, elected a fresh Pope, Martin V. He at once used all his power to prevent any real reforms being passed, concluded separate *concordats* with each national party, and terminated the Council as soon as possible. And so this Council, like the former one, failed to achieve that reformation of the Church which all good men throughout Europe desired.

One other thing this Council did which has brought upon it and the Emperor Sigismund lasting infamy. This was the burning of John Hus and Jerome of Prague for teaching the opinions of Wickliffe in Bohemia, and notwithstanding that they were at the Council under the Emperor's own written safe-conduct. The disgraceful and only too well-known argument was employed (here, perhaps, for the first time) that faith need not be kept with those who were heretics. Sigismund thus dishonoured his word because he feared that otherwise the Council, to bring about which he had laboured earnestly, would break up. They were burnt at Constance (1416) with every circumstance of odious cruelty; and all else achieved by this Council is for ever blackened by this detestable deed. This action provoked such indignation in Bohemia that it caused a furious war, in which priests were burnt in pitch, whole towns destroyed, commerce ruined, the death of King Wenceslaus caused, and the Emperor Sigismund three times defeated, and finally driven out of the country.

These years (1400-1418) are also those of the extensive

conquests made by Florence's powerful rival, Venice. Between 1400 and 1414 Venice conquered Verona, Padua, Vi-
cenza, Belluno, and Feltre; also Lepanto and Patras; also
Guastalla, Casalmaggiore, and Brescello. In 1416 Venice
gained a great naval victory over the Turkish fleet at Gallip-
oli; and in the next few years subdued all the towns on the
Dalmatian coast, besides waging successful war against Hungary. Venice was at this time at the height of her glory,
growing richer and more powerful every year, with annual
exports valued at 10,000,000 ducats, while the wealth and
magnificence of her governing class was unbounded.

Meanwhile Florence was in these years laying the basis of
a very different kind of glory, the results of which were to be
of much more permanent importance to the world at large.
And this wondrous morning of the Renaissance in Art, which
shone forth in his time, and with which he was intimately
connected, must ever be the main interest in looking at the
life of this first of the Medici; especially since owing to his
retiring disposition we only see occasional glimpses of him
among events at that time forming all the principal life of
Florence.

The fifteenth century started from the very beginning on
its wonderful career in this respect. In the first year of the new
century occurred that event already mentioned, the competition for the execution of the bronze doors of the Baptistery.
The work being a votive offering on the part of the entire
city was intended to be of the very best description, for which
reason this competition to determine by whom it should be
executed was instituted "among artists of every country."
The subject fixed was a bronze panel representing the sacrifice of Isaac.

It is impossible to describe the rivalry and enthusiasm
called forth by this competition: it was a time when the
stirrings of Art were felt throughout the entire population of
Florence, and the excitement over the matter was intense.

When the models were sent in, three of them were considered superior to all others, those of Ghiberti, Brunelleschi, and Jacopo della Quercia, the two former being Florentines and the third a native of Siena.[19] They were all quite young men, Jacopo della Quercia being twenty-seven, Ghiberti twenty-three, and Brunelleschi twenty-two. After further consultation the panel by Ghiberti was judged the best, and the construction of the bronze doors was given to him. The models by Ghiberti and Brunelleschi are preserved in the museum of the Bargello, and there is no doubt that the decision of the judges was correct. Brunelleschi in disgust went off to Rome, declaring that he would learn another art in which Ghiberti should not be able to excel him. This he did, and became the great architect of his time.

Ghiberti began his work at once, and was occupied on the first pair of doors (which represent scenes in the life of Christ) for the next twenty-two years. The labour expended on this work, which was more perfect than anything seen in Art up to that time, and which to this day has never been surpassed, was incalculable. Again and again the panels were recast, Ghiberti always striving after something more perfect, and his patience and determination being so great that he again and again destroyed the results he achieved, being resolved not to desist from his labours until he attained the ideal after which he strove. And very wonderful was the aim which he set before himself. In Ghiberti's hands bronze reliefs became in reality pictures in bronze,[20] even the clouds being represented, and the effect of distance being marvellously rendered. Ghiberti himself tells us (and what he says, while simple enough to us all now, is most interesting when we remember that this is in the early days of Art) as follows:—

"In modelling these reliefs I strove to imitate nature to the utmost. . . . I sought to understand how forms strike upon the eye, and how the theoretical part of sculptural and pictorial art should be managed. Working with the utmost care and diligence I introduced into some of my panels as many as a hundred figures; these I modelled upon different planes, so that those nearest to the eye might appear larger, and those more remote smaller in proportion."

As this work proceeded its influence on Art in general was extraordinary. Ghiberti had to employ a number of assistants, and these pictures in bronze, with their life-like figures and excellent relief, became, as the details of their execution were followed out, a perfect school of Art, in which all who had either the sculptor's or the painter's instinct learnt valuable lessons. Besides the effect thus produced on the Art world generally, two at least of the assistants employed by Ghiberti in this work learnt therein that which enabled them afterwards to attain fame exceeding even his, the painter Masaccio and the sculptor Donatello.

Then followed in 1412, while the above work was still in progress, another event likewise contributing to help forward the outburst in Art. This was the completion by the guild of the wool merchants of their church of Or San Michele, and the decision to adorn the outside of the walls with statues of Apostles and Saints, each statue to be given by one of the principal guilds. Hence fresh emulation, each guild desiring its statue to be the finest, and all the best sculptors vying with each other in the production of these statues; Or San Michele thus becoming another centre of Art inspiration. In this way there were produced during the next few years:—

In 1412 Donatello's statue of St. Peter.
In 1413 Donatello's statue of St. Mark.
In 1414 Ghiberti's statue of St. John the Baptist.
In 1415 Ghiberti's statue of St. Stephen.
In 1416 Donatello's celebrated statue of St. George.
In 1418 Ghiberti's statue of St. Matthew.

Statues by other masters followed in subsequent years.

Life in Florence in Giovanni's day was a very different thing from that which it became two generations later. Anything in the direction of luxury was condemned by plain-living Florence as a sign of degeneracy. And when Giovanni, in order to give assistance to struggling artists, had the whole of the walls of his house decorated with frescoes (a form of decoration hitherto confined to churches), we may be sure that this action was looked upon by many as a questionable innovation betokening a reprehensible tendency to voluptuousness.

For very austere indeed was the style of living then customary. The palaces of even the most wealthy were furnished with a plainness which scorned all idea of either beauty or comfort. Heavy tables and straight-backed wooden chairs covered with leather; bare stone floors, desperately cold in winter; whitewashed walls, only covered with tapestry on state occasions; a huge *credenza* containing vases, glass, majolica, and silver, for use at banquets; wide, hard, comfortless beds, and great chests containing linen and clothes: such were the surroundings, and such the only furniture considered necessary even in the palaces of the noblest families.

As to dress, there was the same austerity; and here Florence enacted very strict laws to check undue extravagance. These laws laid down with the most minute exactness what a lady's dress might be like, and what it might not be like; and the same as regards the men. No lady might have her dress made of other material, nor of greater length or breadth, than was laid down; nor wear any of numerous forbidden ornaments. While for the men was prescribed, for all above the class of artisans, the plain garment, buttoned straight down the front and looking like a priest's cassock. We do not hear much about the ladies of this period; it was not until a generation or two later that they began to come forth from the seclusion considered correct in Giovanni's time; but they evidently fought vigorously against these laws about dress. They evaded them in numberless ingenious ways, and waged an untiring warfare with the authorities on the subject. In this contest, which went on perpetually between the ladies and the officials charged with seeing that these sumptuary laws were obeyed, for which thorny task "foreigners" (*i.e.*, non-Florentines) were purposely appointed, the officers concerned had evidently no pleasant time. One of them reports as follows:—

"When, obeying the orders ye gave me, I went out to seek for the forbidden ornaments of your women, they met me with arguments such as are not to be found in any book of laws. There cometh a woman with the peak of her hood fringed out and twined around her head. My notary saith, 'Tell me your name, for you have a peak with fringes.' Then the good woman taketh this peak, which is fastened round her hood with a pin, and, holding it in her hand, she declareth that it is a wreath. Then going further he findeth one wearing many buttons in front of her dress, and he saith unto her, 'Ye are not allowed to wear these buttons.' But she answers, 'These are not buttons but studs, and if ye do not believe me, look—they have no loops, and moreover there are no buttonholes.' Then my notary goeth to another who is wearing ermine, and saith, 'Now what can she say to this? Ye are wearing ermine,' And he prepares to write down her name. But the woman answers, 'Do not write me down, for this is not ermine, it is the fur of a suckling.' Saith the notary, 'What is this suckling?' And the woman replies, 'It is an animal.' " [21]

No wonder that the authorities remark, "We do but knock our heads against a wall"; and that in the next generation these sumptuary laws were gradually allowed to become a dead letter, the ladies having gained the victory.

In 1418 we hear of Giovanni giving a large sum of money to assist one whose "deservedly incurred misfortunes," we are told, "roused his pity." In conjunction with the chief of the party of the nobles, Niccolò da Uzzano, he obtained after strong efforts the release of the deposed and imprisoned Pope John XXIII, on condition that a ransom of 38,000 ducats should be paid; and the whole of this sum Giovanni himself gave. Pope John on being released came, broken down and destitute, to Florence, and was given an asylum there by Giovanni, who, when the deposed Pope died in the following year, erected to his memory the beautiful monument which is to be seen in the Baptistery.[22]

In 1419 we find Giovanni at his own cost erecting and endowing an important charitable institution which remains to the present day, the Foundling Hospital of Florence, the "Ospedale degli Innocenti." And in carrying out this charitable work he also managed to help forward the cause of Art. Brunelleschi had by this time returned to Florence, having in the intervening years carried out his determination to learn another branch of art in which Ghiberti should not be able to rival him; but he had not yet obtained any opportunity of displaying his powers. Giovanni gave him this opportunity by entrusting the construction of his new hospital to him. Though afterwards eclipsed by his other achievements, the Foundling Hospital remains notable as being the great architect's first prominent work.

In 1421 Giovanni received the highest mark of esteem which his country could confer. In spite of the opposition of the nobles, who urged that it was unsafe to allow one so wealthy and so popular to hold that office, he was, without any seeking for it on his part, elected Gonfaloniere.

In 1422 Florence entered on a four years' war with Milan, whose Duke, Filippo Maria Visconti, the cowardly and treacherous son of Gian Galeazzo, was threatening to absorb all northern Italy. Giovanni di Bicci was against this war, feeling that Florence was not strong enough for it, and could not afford the cost. And in it Florence suffered no less than six serious defeats within a space of about two years. Nevertheless she gained in the end the object for which she fought; after four years of war Venice joined her against Milan, with the eventual result that the designs of the Duke of Milan were frustrated, and he was forced to conclude a peace the

terms of which were honourable to Florence. Thus twice during twenty-five years had Florence stood in the breach and
prevented two successive Dukes of Milan from subduing all
Italy. These two wars are said to have cost Florence a sum
equal in our present money to £6,000,000 sterling.

In 1426 Giovanni succeeded in effecting, in spite of every
kind of opposition from the nobles, the chief political measure
of his life. This was his celebrated *catasto,* the new form of
taxation devised by him. The main tax on the people had
hitherto been an irregular poll-tax, which bore very unfairly
upon them, and gave unlimited opportunities to the nobles
to exercise oppression. It was consequently hated by the
people. Giovanni worked out a scheme to substitute for this
a fixed tax on property, which would be regular in its in-
cidence and prevent the nobles from evading their due share
of the general taxation, and by his weight and influence in
the Signoria succeeded in getting this measure passed. And
this, notwithstanding that it increased very largely the
amount he would himself have to pay. The nobles were, of
course, furious, and accused him of all sorts of ulterior motives; but Giovanni having no such motives went on his
way undisturbed; and for this immense boon which he had
procured for them, the people looked on him as their saviour
and benefactor, and were ready to do anything for one who
had fought thus strenuously on their behalf.[23]

In 1427 Giovanni performed his last act as a champion of
the cause of the poorer classes. A number of the nobles,
headed by Rinaldo degli Albizzi and Niccolò da Uzzano,
held a secret meeting [24] to devise means for reducing the
power of the people in the government. The plan they
eventually settled upon was to put forward a suggestion to
the Signoria to reduce the number of the inferior guilds, and
also to remove the prohibition against members of the *nobili*
being eligible for election to the Signoria, using the argument
that the time had passed when such a prohibition was
necessary.

Having elaborated the details of their plan, the *nobili* on a suitable occasion submitted their suggestion to the Signoria for discussion. The proposal in the manner in which it was put forward was a specious one, while its real object was kept carefully veiled. But Giovanni, ever on the watch to defend the cause of the people, fathomed its real intention. He exerted the whole weight of his influence to oppose the measure; and entirely through his vigorous opposition it was defeated. By this, the last act of his public life, he increased still more his popularity with the people. The wrath of the nobles was proportionate; and all the more so since they could not openly show it without disclosing to all what their object had been. Giovanni on this occasion showed the sagacity to detect, the courage to oppose, and the sound judgment to foil without an open conflict, a dangerous attempt to revolutionise the Government.

The chief events outside Italy during these years were the following:—

In 1420 Henry V of England having by this time conquered all France north of the Loire, the Treaty of Troyes was executed. By this treaty the crown of France was secured to him (to the exclusion of the Dauphin Charles) whenever the mad king, Charles VI, should die; and meanwhile Henry was made Regent of France, and at last married to the French King's daughter, Catherine.

In 1422 Charles VI and Henry V both died, and the latter was succeeded by his six months' old son, Henry VI, the Earl of Bedford being appointed Regent of France on his behalf during his minority.

In 1425 the Emperor Manuel Paleologus died, and his son, John Paleologus (John VII), succeeded him as Emperor of the Eastern Empire, by this time reduced to little more than its capital city, Constantinople.

In 1428 the regent Bedford, having gained several victories

over the Dauphin Charles, crossed the Loire, and began his
memorable siege of Orleans, the key to the south of France.

The years 1418 to 1428 were years of still further developments in that outburst of new life in the world of Art taking
place in Florence.

In the year 1418 the cathedral, begun by Arnolfo di
Cambio a hundred and twenty years before, and which when
finished would be the largest then existing, was approaching
completion. But it still wanted its dome, and all concerned
were in despair as to how a dome was ever to be thrown over
so vast a space. At length Brunelleschi, who was then building the Foundling Hospital, came forward and offered to do
it, but would not say how. There was great opposition to
giving the task to him, and the reason is important as showing the conditions from which Art had gradually to emancipate
itself.

Every citizen of Florence who aspired either to have any
political rights, or to take any part in the important public
works from time to time being executed, had to belong to
one or other of the twenty-one guilds. The seven major guilds
were (1) wool merchants, (2) dyers of foreign cloth, (3)
silk merchants, (4) furriers, (5) bankers, (6) judges and
lawyers, and (7) doctors and apothecaries. There was no
special guild for the workers in art; the painters had to
belong to the guild of apothecaries; [25] the architects and
sculptors either to the guild of the wool merchants, or to
that of the silk merchants. The fourteen minor guilds were
simply those of the various trades, and had lesser privileges.[26]

Up to the time when Brunelleschi made the above refusal
to announce his plans, every great public work such as this
was done *collectively,* under the auspices of some particular
guild, and anything like independent working in such matters was unprecedented. And the whole work of erecting the
cathedral was carried out by a Board of Works acting under
the orders of the guild of the wool merchants. Brunelleschi,

being of an independent character, detested this system, which hampered all artists much, but especially architects. Since his disappointment over the bronze doors he had spent nearly twenty years in studying architecture, more especially the ancient buildings at Rome, and was now confident that he knew a way of building the great dome, and without using any scaffolding, this point being the chief difficulty. But if he succeeded in building it, he desired that it should be *his*, and not that of the Board of Works; and did not want to tell his secret only to have it appropriated by a corporate body, who might also modify his designs. But this was just what the Board wished to be able to do; such novel independence was in their opinion most objectionable, and required putting down; and so there was a tremendous contest.[27]

However, eventually Brunelleschi prevailed, simply because all knew by this time that he was the only man who could construct the dome; the work was given to him, and the construction began in 1420. And though even after this there were constant battles, still by degrees the great dome slowly rose on his designs and under his superintendence.

It was built without any scaffolding, and on a principle Brunelleschi had learnt from studying the roof of the Pantheon at Rome. He tells us that managing while at Rome to get on the roof of the Pantheon, and to take off some of the outer stones, so as to inspect the ribbing of the vault, and discovering the way the blocks of stone were dovetailed into one another so as to be almost self-supporting, this gave him his ideas for the dome of Florence; while it also led him to conceive how to utilise cross-beams to gird the ribs together, and how a second dome within the first would strengthen the whole. The dome is built on this principle, one dome within the other and the two bound together so as to support each other, with a space between sufficient for a staircase, and each dome resting on a "drum." It was the first of the kind ever constructed, was considered the

wonder of the age, and is the largest double cupola in
Europe.[28] Domes had, of course, been a feature of Byzantine
architecture, but the great change made by the Renaissance
was that caused by lifting the dome on a "drum," the dome
thus becoming the chief feature of the building. It is interesting to notice how, as it had been with Learning, and as it
had been with Sculpture, so here again with Architecture we
have a resurrection of the long past; and Brunelleschi receives his inspiration from the Pantheon, built by Marcus
Agrippa fourteen hundred years before.

In 1425 Giovanni di Bicci gave a commission to Brunelleschi which resulted in one of the three chief works [29] for
which the latter has obtained fame, the church of San
Lorenzo, now so famous on account of its tombs of the
Medici family. This church, one of the most ancient in Italy,
having been consecrated [30] by St. Ambrose himself in 393,
was in 1423 falling into ruins. Giovanni now undertook to
rebuild it, devoting thereto a large amount of his fortune; [31]
and after his time it was when completed endowed by his
descendants, and became the family church of the Medici.

On this church Brunelleschi lavished all his talent, and it
is one of his finest creations. Symonds, speaking of it,
says: [32]—

"Not a form or detail in the whole church is at variance
with classic precedent, and yet the general effect resembles
nothing that we possess of antique work. It is a masterpiece
of intelligent Renaissance adaptation."

Following as he did the sobriety and correctness of the
classic style, the keynote of which is *harmony*, Brunelleschi's
buildings are remarkable for this latter characteristic. They
never give one that jar which, like a discordant note in
music, is produced by a falsity in architecture, and whose
effect we feel even though perhaps unable to point out wherein
it lies. His churches of San Lorenzo and Santo Spirito are both

of them examples of this characteristic of harmony, and to it is undoubtedly due their indescribably peaceful effect.[33]

In 1424 the first pair of bronze doors on which Ghiberti had so long been at work were at last finished. They had taken him twenty-two years. The enthusiasm when they were set up was tremendous; nothing like this in Art had been seen before; all Florence crowded to see them; and the Signoria, who never quitted the Palazzo della Signoria in a body except on the greatest occasions, came in state to applaud the work and do honour to the artist. When we think of all that this work had called forth in every branch of Art during the long years he had been employed on it, of the genius which had created this wonderful new departure, and of the determined perseverance by which alone the work was brought to such perfection, we are led to feel [34] that Ghiberti deserved any honour which his countrymen could confer upon him.

Ghiberti, by this time a man of forty-five, at once set to work on his second pair of doors, which were destined to take him still longer, and to surpass even the first pair in excellence.

In 1423, seven years after Donatello had produced his statue of St. George, three years after Brunelleschi had begun to construct his dome, and one year before Ghiberti finished his first pair of bronze doors, Painting showed that same new burst of life which had already been shown by Architecture and Sculpture. For in that year Masaccio, afterwards so famous, and destined to advance the art of Painting by so immense a step that he became the leader of all painters after him, began his frescoes in the Brancacci chapel of the church of the Carmelites,[35] the Carmine.

The influence of Ghiberti's work of the bronze doors is in the case of Masaccio directly traceable. Born in the year of the competition of 1401, he worked as a boy under Ghiberti on the panels of these doors, and there learnt the knowledge of form, effect of light and shade, and other secrets which he afterwards elaborated in his paintings. In these, by a proper use of light and shade, he gave roundness to the limbs; was the first to give to figures natural attitudes and a life-like appearance, and to drapery natural folds; improved the drawing of heads and hands; and, as Vasari says, "improved everything."

But this was not recognised until after his short life had ended. He was crushed with poverty,[36] burdened with the maintenance of younger brothers, always ready to do a good turn to others but careless about his own affairs, and, entirely absorbed in his painting, was almost unknown. Dying at the age of twenty-seven, only four years after he began painting these frescoes, his life was so short, and he was so hampered by debt, that he has left very few works; except for two small unimportant pictures at Berlin, and one in the Accademia at Florence, no picture of Masaccio's is in any of the galleries of Europe, and all his fame rests on the frescoed walls of one small chapel in Florence.[37]

Nevertheless, with him Painting entered on a new epoch, and the Brancacci chapel has become sacred ground to all painters, since there almost all the great masters after him, including, Vasari tells us, Perugino, Leonardo da Vinci, Raphael,[38] Michelangelo,[39] Andrea del Sarto, Fra Bartolommeo, and many of lesser genius, have studied and copied the works of one who is the inaugurator of all that we understand by modern painting.

> "In this chapel wrought
> One of the few, Nature's interpreters,
> The few, whom genius gives as lights to shine,
> Masaccio.
>
> .   .   .   .   .   .
>
> Look around
> And know that where we stand stood oft and long,
> Oft till the day was gone, Raphael himself;

Nor he alone, so great the ardour there,
Such while it reigned the generous rivalry;
He, and how many more, once thither drawn,
Anxious to learn of those who came before,
To steal a spark from their immortal fire
Who first did break the universal gloom,
Sons of the morning." [40]

Giovanni di Bicci, in his readiness to befriend struggling
artists, assisted the poor youth who was then so little known,
and Masaccio introduced a portrait of him into his fresco
picture of the consecration of the Carmine church in 1422,
but this fresco was destroyed when the greater part of that
church was burnt in 1721.

At some time during the year 1427 Masaccio ended his
painting for the Carmelite community and went off to Rome,
none know for what purpose (for of such an insignificant
person nothing was at that time recorded), but presumably
in order to obtain work; and there in the following year
he died in poverty and obscurity, unknown to fame until
after he was dead, when the world awoke to the knowledge
of what a genius had been living in that obscure corner of
Florence where he had worked. [41]

_____

Giovanni died in 1428, at the age of sixty-eight, and at
his death left an immense fortune to his two sons, Cosimo
and Lorenzo. He died deservedly esteemed by his countrymen, beloved by the humbler classes of the people, who had
so often found in him a defender and whose welfare he had
consistently promoted, remembered with gratitude by all
who, struggling to rise in some branch of Art, had never
failed to receive from him a helping hand, and respected
even by some amongst the *nobili* who, though always opposed
by him, had never found him other than an honourable
antagonist. Machiavelli, describing his character, says:—

"He never sought the honours of government, yet enjoyed them all. When holding high office he was courteous to all. Not a man of great eloquence, but of an extraordinary prudence."

Giovanni had assisted at the birth of the movement in which Ghiberti, Brunelleschi, Donatello, and Masaccio were the leaders; he had helped its onward course, and he died as its "morning" ended with the death of Masaccio and began to pass into full noon. Thus the chief interest connected with his life will always be that memorable outburst in Art which took place between the years 1400 and 1428, burning with such ardour among the Florentines that it threw even politics into the background, and formed the prominent feature in the life of Florence during his time. He lies buried with Piccarda, his wife, in the "Old Sacristy," [42] in the church of San Lorenzo, the only portion of the rebuilt church which was finished at the time of his death. Their fine tomb,[43] richly ornamented with figures of *putti* and garlands of flowers, stands in the centre of the sacristy with a large marble table over it. The tomb is interesting from the fact that isolated tombs like this, though common in other countries, were very rare in Italy.

Such was the founder of this family which was destined to have so momentous a history. He laid the foundations of the family solidly, not so much by the popularity which he won through his steadfast championship of the cause of the humbler classes, as by the principles of magnanimity, generosity, courtesy, and care for the people which he taught his sons, and caused to become an unwritten law in this family for three generations after him. As we look at the kindly and sensible old face in his portrait we feel how well it was for Florence in after years that Giovanni di Bicci de' Medici possessed the character that he did. It will be seen how, on his death, the party of the nobles took steps to destroy his work, as well as to prevent these "upstart Medici" from rising any higher.

PART I

PART I

GIOVANNI DI BICCI'S two sons were Cosimo and Lorenzo. Cosimo's branch, which includes all the greater Medici, eventually in the seventh generation died out, when the succession passed to Lorenzo's branch, which carried on the family through six more generations, attained that crown which the elder branch had striven for and made possible, and at last in its turn also died out in 1743.

As the best way of avoiding confusion the history follows the elder branch right down to its end (Part I), before returning to take up (Part II) the story of the younger branch, from its commencement with Lorenzo downwards. This is rendered the easier since the first few generations of the younger branch have scarcely any independent history of their own, theirs being almost entirely merged in that of the elder branch; so that the period when the younger branch has an independent history is a comparatively short one.

CHAPTER IV

COSIMO (PATER PATRIAE)

Born 1389. (*Ruled* 1434-1464.) *Died* 1464

WHEN Giovanni di Bicci died his eldest son Cosimo was forty years old. Up to that time we have only one episode recorded of him, viz., that when in 1415 the Council of Constance was assembled and Pope John XXIII, forced by the Emperor Sigismund, very reluctantly proceeded to it, Cosimo de' Medici, then twenty-six years old, who had known him before he became Pope, went with him at the risk of his life to help to defend him; and had to fly in disguise when Pope John was deposed and imprisoned by the Council.

Cosimo had shortly before this adventure been married to Contessina de' Bardi; [1] and his eldest son, Piero, was born (apparently in the Bardi palace) while Cosimo was absent at the above Council. The Bardi were in the fourteenth century the richest banking family in Florence. Though they themselves have disappeared their oldest palace [2] still stands in the street which was all once their property, and still bears their name, the Via de' Bardi, always to us reminiscent of "Romola." But they had fallen on evil days before Cosimo's marriage to the eldest daughter of the house, having been gradually ruined owing to the loss of a large sum of money which, lent by them to Edward III of England, had never been repaid. [3] By this marriage the Bardi palace came into the possession of the Medici family, and Cosimo appears during his father's lifetime to have lived there, his arms (with eight red balls [4]) being still to be seen in some of the rooms.

Cosimo had been educated at the celebrated school attached to the Camaldolese monastery of Sta. Maria degli
Angeli in the Via degli Alfani.[5] He knew Greek, Latin, Hebrew, and Arabic, besides several modern languages, and
was passionately fond of both Learning and Art. He also
possessed all the qualities which distinguished his father,
and on becoming head of the family soon showed that he
would be likely to play a more prominent part in Florentine
affairs than his father. The family were by this time growing
enormously wealthy, owning banks in as many as sixteen
capital cities in Europe;[6] and Cosimo's great wealth,
courteous demeanour, ability, and tact, all joined as it was
to a generous disposition, made him fully as popular with the
people as his father had been.

In Cosimo de' Medici the party of the nobles (the *Grandi*),
then headed by the powerful family of the Albizzi, saw a
formidable opponent. They already detested this wealthy
family who were rising from the class of the *Popolani* and
gaining such influence, and they saw in its new head one
who aroused their bitterest jealousy. They therefore determined that the Medici must be entirely rooted out of
Florence. This, however, was not easy to accomplish,
Cosimo's popularity being so great; moreover, the most
respected of their number, the aged Niccolò da Uzzano, was
against any such design. Machiavelli tells us that when the
other nobles consulted him regarding their proposed action
against the Medici he warned them that in a trial of strength
the latter would win; that if Cosimo were put to death as
they desired, Florence would be in danger of having Rinaldo
degli Albizzi as a despot, and that if either was to prevail,
of the two he preferred Cosimo; "but," he added, "God deliver this city from private usurpation." So that for the
present the nobles were forced to bide their time.

In 1430, two years after his father's death, Cosimo began
to carry out a project which he had had under consideration
from the time he succeeded his father, that of building a

new palace for the family. For this he chose a site in the Via Larga,[7] the widest street in the city, at the corner where it was joined by a short street, the Via de' Gori, which ran down to the church of San Lorenzo, then being rebuilt with the family money, and which when completed he purposed to endow.

This palace Cosimo intended should be a model of architectural art, and should surpass anything of the kind up to that time seen. Brunelleschi was now the foremost architect of the age; his dome was approaching completion, he was also building the church of San Lorenzo, and in this same year [8] began his other church of Santo Spirito. So Cosimo had at first proposed to employ him in designing his new palace. But on seeing Brunelleschi's plan he considered it too grand in character, and instead of it accepted a less pretentious one by Michelozzo, an architect then coming into notice, and who (chiefly through this work) became recognised as second only to Brunelleschi. For the adornment of the *cortile* of the palace, when it should be completed, Cosimo gave various commissions to Donatello, by this time acknowledged as the leading sculptor. These included the bronze statue of *David* (now in the museum of the Bargello), the bronze statue of *Judith slaying Holofernes* (now in the Loggia de' Lanzi) and the medallions copied from antique gems, still to be seen over the arches of the *cortile*. The first of these works, the *David*, was an epoch-making statue in the history of Art, having probably a greater influence than any other single statue ever executed; [9] it was finished within the next three years (before Cosimo's exile [10]), the other commissions being completed later.

In 1432 Niccolò da Uzzano, for so many years the respected leader of the *nobili* (though latterly thrown into the shade by Rinaldo degli Albizzi), died. He was one of the best statesmen Florence had ever possessed, consistently employing his influence to check the party rivalries of his countrymen.[11]

His restraining influence being removed, the nobles proceeded to carry out their resolve to get rid of these Medici
who were becoming such formidable champions of the people.
Complete success in this object required, they considered,
the death of Cosimo himself and the banishment of the rest
of the family, including his brother Lorenzo and their first
cousin Averardo; in the case of a family of bankers such a
banishment, particularly if they were dispersed, would soon
cause their ruin. With the Albizzi family at their head the
nobili now took steps to effect these objects. And the new
palace, so much superior to any hitherto built in Florence,
assisted them in their design, now that the walls began to
attain sufficient height for the general style of the building
to be appreciated, and particularly the novel and expensive
rustica style of the lower storey.

Having by a skilful manipulation of the elections of the
year 1433 obtained a Signoria considerably under their influence, the Albizzi party accused Cosimo to the Government
of scheming to exalt himself above the rank of an ordinary
citizen (the worst charge possible in Florence), and pointed
among other things to the new palace as being too grand for
a simple citizen, denoting an ambition dangerous to the
Republic. Whereupon Cosimo was suddenly arrested, and
consigned to a cell in the tower of the Palazzo della Signoria,
while arrangements were made for his speedy judicial murder. But the temper of the populace when they heard what
was going on became so formidable that that plan had after
a day or two to be abandoned. The nobles then attempted
to employ poison, and commissioned two of their number
to effect this; Cosimo had from the first expected that this
method would be employed, and for the first three days of
his imprisonment would eat nothing; but this second plan
also failed, as Cosimo's jailer, Federigo Malavolti, refused to
be corrupted. So the nobles had to be content with his banishment; but Cosimo had a narrow escape. In due course a
sentence of banishment was passed by the Signoria, a regular

decree of ostracism, in the Greek style, being drawn up; the whole of the Medici were exiled, Cosimo and his family to Padua,[12] his brother Lorenzo to Venice, and his cousin Averardo to Naples; and they were escorted under a guard to the frontier. The decree declared that the Medici were banished from the city and state of Florence "being dangerous to the Republic by reason of their wealth and ambition." The sentence of exile, and the reasons for it, were published in all other states, so as to make their disgrace as public as possible. And the nobles, though they had failed to secure Cosimo's death, were satisfied that they had nevertheless achieved the ruin of the Medici.

Thus were the Medici for the first time cast forth in ignominy by Florence as foes to her Republic. It was an experience they were to undergo three times in the course of their history. On this first occasion it occurred solely to satisfy the desire of the nobles to get rid of the one family that stood in the way of a return to that state of things wherein the power had been in the hands of the nobles, an object the latter had never ceased to work for since the reform of the constitution which had placed all power in the hands of the people. It is often asserted that the germs of an aim to destroy the Republic and erect a despotic monarchy in its place, existed in the Medici from the first. But so far, at all events, as this first banishment is concerned the statement is proved in the most practical manner to be untrue. For whereas suspicions of this nature when once aroused have, if there be any basis for them, a tendency to grow stronger in the absence of the accused (and certainly would do so in such a city), yet in this case the very reverse occurred; and Florence by her action a year afterwards conclusively proved that there were no grounds for the charge.

By Cosimo's exile the work on the Medici Palace was brought to a standstill, and as neither Michelozzo nor Donatello desired to remain in a city which had cast him out they also went into exile, Michelozzo accompanying Cosimo and

Donatello proceeding to Rome [13] to study such remains of the classic sculpture as were to be found there, though these were at that time extremely few,[14] the Popes not having begun to collect such things, and all the treasures now to be seen in the sculpture galleries of the Vatican and the Capitol then lying buried under the ruins of the devastated city.

The chief events during the first five years after Cosimo became head of the family were the great change which at this time came over the long struggle between France and England (known as the "Hundred Years' War"), and the assembly of the Council of Bâle, the third of the attempts of the fifteenth century to reform the Church. Also, on a smaller stage, Florence's two wars, against Lucca and against Milan.

Regarding the first of the above events, it has been noted how in 1428 the English, then masters of all northern France, advanced southwards and laid siege to Orleans. Then came Joan of Arc, and in three years (1428-1431) changed the whole aspect of affairs in France. The details of her career, ending in a death which was to the lasting disgrace of both English and French, are well known. The English power in France never recovered the blow dealt it by her victories, and from this time forth the English were steadily driven backwards.

In 1431, the same year that Joan of Arc was burnt at Rouen, the Council of Bâle was assembled. In that year Martin V, the Pope who had been elected at the Council of Constance, died. He had revived the autocratic view of the Papacy which had been maintained by the Popes of the thirteenth century, had ruled that archbishops and bishops are merely the delegates of the Pope, and had endeavoured to prevent all further assembling of councils to reform the Church by ruling that Popes were superior to councils. It was a strange outcome of the work of such a Council as that of Constance. However, on his death his rulings were ignored, and a third attempt to reform the Church was made by the assembly of the Council of Bâle. It was convened (like that of Constance) by the Emperor Sigismund. The new Pope, Eugenius IV, having failed in his endeavour to prevent its meeting, or to get it dissolved as soon as the preliminary proceedings were concluded, was, through fear of being deposed, at length forced to acknowledge that a Pope is subject to a council, and sent four cardinals to represent him at it. This Council was sitting at Bâle from 1431 to 1438. It passed various decrees of reform which the Pope accepted; then as it proceeded to deal stronger blows at the Papacy the Pope tried to remove it to Italy. The Council, however, refused to be removed. Its subsequent dealings with Pope Eugenius IV will be noted hereafter.

During the years 1429 to 1433 Florence was dragged into two small wars which brought her much discredit. The Albizzi, wielding the chief influence, first persuaded the Government to enter on an unjust aggressive war against Lucca, and then prosecuted this war with such an utter want of ability that it was no wonder that it was completely unsuccessful; and Florence in this attempt to conquer Lucca reaped nothing but expense, failure, and loss of prestige. This war produced one with Milan, which languished on undecisively until 1433, when a temporary peace was patched up. These two wars, whose only result was an increased expenditure, brought much disfavour upon the Albizzi, who were entirely responsible for them.

The first exile of the Medici lasted only for one year. The large majority of the population loved this munificent and gracious family, and by the time a year had passed saw that they had been made a catspaw to assist the manœuvres of the nobles, and that while there was no ground for the accusation against the Medici, there was every ground for suspecting the motive of the nobles. For the Albizzi and their party, when once they had got rid of the people's main supporter, proceeded, by their scarcely concealed plotting against that democratic form of government which Florence had gained through so many struggles, to give the people good reason for such fears. So in September 1434 the decree of banishment against the Medici was annulled, and messages were sent inviting their return. The Albizzi thereupon flew to arms, assembled their adherents to the number of about eight hundred, and made an attempt to seize the Government before Cosimo should return; but the Signoria obtained troops from Pistoia, and the attempt failed. On the 6th October Cosimo re-entered Florence with a public triumph almost like that given to a conqueror, and in the midst of a rejoicing populace. Machiavelli says:—"Seldom has a citizen returning from a great victory been greeted by such a concourse of people, and with such demonstrations of affection, as was Cosimo on his return from exile." And Cosimo's unassuming demeanour, even on the occasion of so honourable a triumph over his enemies, increased still further his popularity.

His subsequent conduct did him equal honour. In any other state in Europe at that time of the world's history such a return to power would assuredly have been followed by the putting to death of those whose enmity had caused what had been endured. Cosimo and his whole family had been treated with the bitterest animosity by the nobles, and with the greatest ingratitude by those members of the Signoria whom the nobles had induced to do their will; the humiliation of himself and his family had been made known in all the surrounding states; they had been put to much fear, inconvenience, and loss; his own life had been attempted, and nothing had been omitted to secure the total ruin of his family. Yet, when thus triumphantly brought back by the will of the people with ample power to retaliate, we find Cosimo firmly refusing to allow any of those who had caused

these things to be put to death. On the other hand, that some
should suffer banishment on account, not of what had been
done to the Medici, but of the attempt which had been
made, before their return, to overthrow the Government, was
inevitable; the Albizzi and their party could not expect to
get off unpunished after such an endeavour. Those writers
who are anxious to find cause against the Medici have accused
Cosimo of a "vindictive policy" on this occasion; but this
is unjust. The Signoria, terribly frightened at the attempt
(which had nearly succeeded) of the Albizzi and their party
to seize the Government by force of arms, passed a sentence
of exile against some eighty of them.[15] It was not an unnatural result of their conduct. But in any case there is no
evidence that this and other repressive measures against the
Albizzi party, some of which measures had been already
taken before his arrival, were instigated by Cosimo at all.[16]

A few months after the above triumphant return Cosimo
received from his city the most practical demonstration it
could give of its entire revulsion of sentiment towards him,
and regret for the treatment which he and his had received.
He was elected Gonfaloniere, and held that office for the
next two months.

Meanwhile Pope Eugenius IV had become involved in
many troubles, mainly through his continued opposition to
the Council of Bâle. The Emperor Sigismund at length being
determined to force the Pope to submit to the reforms which
the Council was striving to pass, but which the Pope's delegates were obstructing, proceeded to Italy, being invited
thither by Filippo Visconti, Duke of Milan, who hoped that
the Emperor would assist him in the war he was then carrying on against Florence and Venice. After staying for some
time with the Duke of Milan, and after being crowned with
the iron crown of Lombardy, the Emperor, avoiding Florence's
territory, proceeded by way of Lucca and Siena to Rome,
where he was crowned by Pope Eugenius in St. Peter's

(1433). Thence he started on his way back to Bâle, apparently less ready than he had hitherto been to support the Council against the Pope. But immediately afterwards Fortebraccio, commander of the Milanese troops, marched upon Rome, while at the same time Francesco Sforza, also in behalf of the Duke of Milan, seized a large part of the Papal territories in Romagna, declaring that he was authorised to do so by the Council of Bâle. The eventual result was that Pope Eugenius was, in 1434, forced to fly from Rome in disguise and in danger of his life, the people of Rome joining with his other foes in expelling him. He took refuge at Florence, arriving there just at the time of Cosimo's recall from exile. And at Florence this Pope resided for the next eight years, while Rome remained in possession of his enemies.

———————

Cosimo at the time of his recall from banishment in 1434 was forty-five years of age, and thenceforth became the acknowledged leading citizen of the Florentine Republic. But knowing well the fickle nature of popular favour and the peculiar temperament of his countrymen—their habit of constant change, their tendency to fall a prey to one faction after another, and above all their jealousy of any individual who seemed inclined to exalt himself—he saw that an immense task lay before him if he was to retain that position.

It has generally been assumed that Cosimo was actuated solely by personal ambition; but he had other motives than this. Apart from all question of personal or family ambition, he desired to retain that position for two reasons eminently honourable to him. The poorer classes were ground down under a crushing burden of taxation, due to the heavy cost to each individual citizen of wars so constantly undertaken by a state whose population was comparatively small. This evil he desired to remedy by so guiding foreign affairs as to make such wars less frequent. Again he saw that the same cause was severely hampering Florence's commerce, while as a banker on a wide scale he felt that if he could create peace, he would be able considerably to extend Florentine markets and increase the commercial wealth of the Florentines. Feeling that he possessed in himself the ability to do these things, it was in every way natural that he should wish to show that he could do them. Ambition of this kind is not a fault, but a virtue.[17]

But to do all this he must be Florence's leading citizen, no matter who might from time to time be Gonfaloniere. And in order to retain permanently this position—one which could never be more than tacitly granted—two things would be necessary: first, to make all foreign countries recognise that he, and he alone, was the motive power in the Florentine state; and, second, to convince his own countrymen that no one else could so satisfactorily manage their affairs, and in particular their foreign affairs, so that they should be glad to leave all such matters in his hands. And both these things must be done in such a way as never to arouse in the Florentines that peculiar jealousy of any kind of authority which they were so apt to develop. Such was the task before Cosimo, one at which any man might have quailed, in view of the temperament of the Florentine people of his time, as well as the conditions of perpetual intrigue in the midst of which it must be carried out. Yet, as will be seen in the sequel, he accomplished with complete success this difficult task.

But it was not only in the political sphere that Cosimo won renown. Many and varied were the matters which he took in hand for the advancement of Learning, the encouragement of Art, and the assistance of charitable institutions. Before all else he was a deep scholar; one of those who loved learning for its own sake. He maintained a regular staff of agents always employed in searching in the East for rare and important manuscripts, which became the nucleus of the great library which he founded; he instituted the celebrated Platonic Academy for the study of the rediscovered Plato, of whose writings he was an enthusiastic

admirer; no scholar applied to him in vain, and the ways
in which he promoted the cause of Learning were numberless.
Gibbon says of him:—

"Cosimo was the father of a line of princes whose name and
age are almost synonymous with the restoration of Learning.
His credit was ennobled into fame; his riches were dedicated
to the service of mankind; he corresponded at once with
Cairo and London; and a cargo of Indian spices and Greek
books were often imported in the same vessel."

To Art he gave similar assistance; he was a liberal patron
to the painters Fra Angelico and Lippi, to the sculptors
Ghiberti and Donatello, and to the architects Brunelleschi
and Michelozzo; he collected objects of art of every kind;
and he made his collections open to all artists. No less lavish
were his charities; he gave large sums for the rebuilding of
many churches and monasteries, including the Badia of
Fiesole, the monastery of San Marco, and the church of San
Lorenzo, built a hospital at Jerusalem for sick and infirm
pilgrims, and bore a large part in every charitable work undertaken in Florence. Such was the man who in 1434 became
the leading citizen of the Florentine Republic, and set forth
on the political task which has been mentioned.

In 1435 Francesco Sforza, the celebrated *condottiere* commander, visited Florence. During this visit he developed a
great liking for Cosimo, and thus began that friendship between them which in after years had important political
results.

In 1436 Brunelleschi completed his dome, and the cathedral,[19] begun a hundred and thirty-eight years before by
Arnolfo di Cambio, was at last finished.

This completion of the great work upon which four generations had laboured was a notable event, and a ceremony
worthy of the occasion was arranged. Pope Eugenius IV was
at this time residing at the monastery of Santa Maria Novella,

and the cathedral was solemnly consecrated by him on the Feast of the Annunciation, 25th March 1436. "A raised passage, richly carpeted and decorated with tapestry, damask, silk, and flowers, was constructed from the door of Santa Maria Novella, and passing through the Baptistery, to the western door of the cathedral." Along this an imposing procession, consisting of the Pope, thirty-seven bishops, seven cardinals, the Signoria, and the envoys of foreign powers, passed from Sta. Maria Novella to the cathedral. The consecration ceremony occupied five hours, after which the procession was re-formed and returned in the same way. A tablet on the wall of the cathedral commemorates this event. Brunelleschi, more fortunate than Giotto,[20] lived to see the completion of his great work and to take part in the above ceremony. The completion of the dome and the consecration of the cathedral serve to mark the beginning of Cosimo's rule in Florence.

In 1437 Cosimo set about rebuilding at his own expense the afterwards far-famed monastery of San Marco in Florence. This monastery of the Dominican Order had at this time in its community two men who will ever live enshrined in the memory of men as representing all that was best in the spirit of that age, and as counter-balancing much that was evil, Giovanni of Fiesole, called Fra Angelico, and Antonio Pierozzi, called Antonino, afterwards Archbishop of Florence.

Situated near the new palace which he was building, its Prior a man so justly beloved,[21] this monastery seems to have been looked upon by Cosimo as a well-beloved retreat to which he could retire for rest and congenial companionship when harassed by the cares of State and the vexations of political life. And with his usual liberality in all that he undertook he spent money upon it "with a generosity which the modesty of the friars had to restrain." The rebuilding of it cost him 36,000 ducats, in addition to which sum he gave it a large endowment. He had a special cell set apart for his own use, and thither often resorted for converse with the Prior and others of the community; he gave as a nucleus for the monastery library over four hundred valuable manuscript books; and it was at his expense that the walls of the monastery were decorated with those frescoes by Fra Angelico which all the world now visits San Marco to see.

The effect of having at the head of the State a man like Cosimo showed itself at once in the impetus given to all branches of Art. As a result we find Art taking great strides during these first five years of Cosimo's supremacy in Florentine affairs, and artists at work all over the city whose names have since become famous throughout the world. Ghiberti was employed on his second pair of bronze doors; Brunelleschi was engaged on his two churches of San Lorenzo and Santo Spirito,[22] besides several palaces; Michelozzo was at work on the Medici Palace and the monastery of San Marco; Donatello, having returned from Rome, was busy in San Lorenzo and on his various works for Cosimo's new palace; the dead Masaccio's name was earning great fame, for by this time men had recognised his genius, and all painters were eagerly studying his works in the Brancacci chapel; Luca della Robbia was completing his marble screen of the *Cantoria;* Fra Angelico was beginning his frescoes in San Marco; Lippi was painting pictures for Cosimo, in which he was to show the world the lessons which Masaccio had taught; Andrea del Castagno, Domenico Veneziano, Paolo Uccello, and many other artists were at work in Florence, most of them brought thither directly by Cosimo to execute various works for him, while he was besieged with letters by others at a distance importuning him for commissions.

From 1434 to 1436 Florence was again at war with Milan, Filippo Visconti, Duke of Milan, being stirred up to attack Florence's territory by the banished Rinaldo degli Albizzi and his party, "who urged the Duke to make war on Florence, promising to aid him with a contingent of *fuorusciti*, and by fomenting insurrection within the city." At length, however, in February 1437, Florence gained a victory over the forces of Milan at the battle of Barga, which for a time put a stop to Milan's efforts; whereupon Florence again attacked Lucca, but without any success. Milan, however, renewed the war in 1438, and it dragged on, with varying success, for several years, without definite result.

In the year 1437 the Emperor Sigismund died; and immediately upon this Pope Eugenius IV came to an open breach with the Council of Bâle, and summoned a fresh council to meet in Italy, the place chosen being Ferrara. Its main object was to consider proposals made at this time by the Eastern Emperor. The Emperor John Paleologus, following the example of his father and grandfather, proposed making a personal visit to the West to solicit help against the Turks to save Constantinople, which must otherwise fall. The Pope invited him, together with the Patriarch and bishops of the Eastern Church, to a conference, holding out hopes of such aid if the breach between the Churches of the East and the West could be healed.

Upon this action on the Pope's part of convening on his own authority a fresh council to meet in Italy (a step he had never been permitted to effect so long as the Emperor Sigismund lived), the Council of Bâle, refusing to be thus broken up, declared Pope Eugenius deposed. But the feeling of Europe was against the creation of another schism, and by degrees the Council of Bâle dwindled away and came to an end, after having sat for eight years and effected practically nothing towards that reformation of the Church for which it had been assembled. Thus again did the last reforming Council—for it was the last—fail as completely as the two which had preceded it.

Meanwhile the Emperor John Paleologus and his retinue, together with the Patriarch of Constantinople, Joseph, and a numerous body of bishops and theologians, sailed from Constantinople, and in due time arrived at Venice. The Emperor was received with great pomp by Doge Francesco Foscari, and entertained at Venice for a month; after which he proceeded to Ferrara, where Pope Eugenius having also arrived, the Council began its sittings (5th January 1438).

Cosimo, in that task which has been mentioned of gradually bringing foreign nations to recognise in him the motive power of the Florentine state, and also gradually convincing his countrymen that their interests were best served by leaving foreign affairs to him, had had to exercise much patience. He had a matter to effect which necessarily moved but slowly, and during the first few years he had been forced to be content with a very partial control, and often been obliged to acquiesce in action which he was as yet without the power to direct as he would wish. But by the end of the year 1438 he was beginning to have this power, foreign affairs being more and more left to him to manage in his own way. And he now took the first independent step, one which had very important results to Florence. He proceeded to Ferrara, where the Council between the Eastern and Western Churches had been sitting for nearly a year, and so used his influence with Pope Eugenius IV that he got the Council transferred to Florence; whereby he obtained for his city increased political influence, brought to it much added trade, and secured for it additional advantages in the advancement of the cause of Learning. Accordingly the Council removed in February 1439 from Ferrara to Florence, which thus became the centre of interest in this great historical event.

This Council is one of the most interesting assemblages of this kind that ever took place. A gathering which included an Emperor of the East and his retinue, a Patriarch of Constantinople, the principal authorities of the Eastern Church, a Pope of Rome, the principal authorities of the Western Church, and all the most learned men of both East and West, had never before been seen. Moreover, it was the last occasion on which such an assemblage was possible; fourteen years later the fall of Constantinople swept away all that formed its peculiar interest, making it impossible for such a gathering ever to occur again.

This occasion gave Cosimo a great opportunity, both in the political sphere and with regard to the cause of learning. Nor did he allow the cost of entertaining these distinguished visitors to fall upon the State, but made them all his own guests, an action which gained him universal commendation. Residences were provided for them such as they could not have obtained in any other city. The Patriarch of Constantinople was lodged in the Ferrantini palace in the Borgo Pinti; the Pope and his suite in the extensive range of buildings at that time attached to Sta. Maria Novella; while to the Emperor and his retinue were given the whole of the Peruzzi palaces [23] then surrounding the Piazza de' Peruzzi, a group of palaces in which the Eastern Emperor and his suite were more splendidly lodged than they could have been in the dwelling of any prince in Europe. The Council began its sittings on the 2nd March. It sat in the cathedral, beneath Brunelleschi's glorious dome, at that time the wonder of Italy, and worthy to be first used on so unique an occasion.

This gathering gave an immense impetus to what was beginning to be called the "New Learning." It brought to Florence the most learned churchmen of Eastern Christendom, such as Bessarion, Bishop of Nicæa, and also the most learned scholars of the East, such as Gemistos Plethon, whom Cosimo induced to settle permanently at Florence; it brought many rare manuscripts, most of which found their way into Cosimo's library; and, above all, it created personal contact and friendliness, destined to have large results when a few years later this Greek learning should find itself driven from its home in Constantinople. The effect of all this was to advance Florence still further on that path of unearthing the long-buried literature of the past on which Cosimo's efforts had already been long engaged.

And this "New Learning," among many results which it was to have in the future, was to have one result of which men little dreamed, and least of all those most occupied in fostering the cause of learning. For it was destined in time to produce that great convulsion extending over all Europe which we know as the Reformation.[24]

The "New Learning" operated in two different ways to produce this result. First, in its work of increasing a knowledge of the ancient literature it opened up large tracts of history till then scarcely known. It made scholars acquainted with writings belonging to the centuries preceding the dark period before the time of Charlemagne, writings hitherto accessible, if at all, only to ecclesiastics, and able to be read only by a few even of the latter. A large number of these writings referred to Church matters, and had been written by eminent bishops of that period.[25] And these soon disclosed to scholars that during at least six centuries of the Church's earliest life its constitution had been very different from what they now saw it, and with no supremacy of one See over all others; while such writings also made them acquainted with the proceedings of the six great General Councils of the Church which had taken place in those centuries, some of which Councils had given decisions bearing on this very point.

And to this new knowledge of the history of the Church the gathering in Florence added considerably. For it enabled the dignitaries of the Eastern Church to converse face to face, and in their own language, with enquirers on such subjects belonging to the West. And since the Eastern Church prided itself on never deviating by one hair's-breadth from what was held at the beginning, and since the special point upon which the discussions of the Council were taking place was this very one of the claim of the Church of Rome to a supremacy which the Eastern Church maintained did not exist at the beginning, the Eastern bishops and theologians gathered at Florence would be certain to corroborate any discoveries on the above point which the "New Learning" might reveal to the eager scholars of Florence. And what scholars learnt in one generation all mankind would, through them, learn in the next.

Pope Eugenius, therefore, in bringing the bishops [26] and theologians of the Eastern Church into contact with the hot-bed of learning which was growing up in Florence, had done the most fatal thing he could to the cause of the Papacy. Moreover, the time was soon to come when one of these scholars of the Renaissance, poring in some dim library over the documents of the eighth century, would make the amazing discovery that the so-called *Donation of Constantine*, and the celebrated *Decretals* (now known as *The Forged Decretals*), upon which the whole claim of the See of Rome to a supremacy had been based, were nothing less than a series of immense forgeries. As the general result of all this the "New Learning," which now received so strong an impetus, was bound, as soon as it should spread to Germany and England, and as soon as the invention of printing should come to aid it in doing so, to produce the Reformation. The process would take time, but the effect was certain. Where the Councils of Pisa, Constance, and Bâle had failed, the "New Learning" would assuredly not fail. It was a train of gunpowder laid, in an ever-widening circle, from Florence as a centre; though the man was not yet born whose hand would, eighty years later, far away in Germany, eventually set fire to the train.

The second way in which the "New Learning" tended to the same result was of a different kind. It gave a strong impulse towards the study of Plato and other non-Christian thinkers of the classical age, and a tendency to look at all religions from their standpoint. And here also this gathering in Florence had much effect. We are told that Cosimo, always a great admirer of Plato's philosophy, formed the idea of his celebrated Platonic Academy from conversing with the Greek scholar Plethon, the most learned of the Greeks who came to the Council. This famous Academy became the home of the richest intellectual life of the century, and though many of its members made endeavours to reconcile Platonism and Christianity, its general tendency was against the existing order of things in religion. Its influence became later on very widespread, and Symonds says that it would be impossible to over-estimate the influence upon European thought which this Platonic Academy came to exercise about the time of the Reformation—in Italy through Marsilio Ficino and Pico della Mirandola, and in Germany through Reuchlin and his pupil Melanchthon.[27]

This great gathering of 1439 in Florence had its effect also on Art. We are often inclined to wonder where such painters as Fra Angelico, Benozzo Gozzoli, and Gentile da Fabriano got the idea of the gorgeous robes and strange-looking head-dresses which we see in their pictures of Eastern subjects. It was all taken direct from the life of Florence of this year. During that summer the inhabitants of Florence saw a perpetual succession of grand processions and imposing functions in which these visitors from the East appeared in every kind of magnificent and strange costume. Vespasiano da Bisticci and other writers of the time dilate upon their rich silken robes, heavy with gold, and their fantastic-looking head-dresses, regarded with deep interest by the learned on account of their ancient character. And the painters reproduce these before us in pictorial records which are valuable to us on that very account, and because this was the last occasion on which these costumes were destined to appear.

As regards the objects with which the Council of Florence was assembled, no results followed. The venerable Patriarch of Constantinople, Joseph, died in Florence one month before the Council came to an end.[28] After his death an agreement between the Greek and Latin Churches was made by the Council and published with much ostentation by the Pope.[29] But the basis of it was that submission of the Eastern Church to the Church of Rome which had been an aim of the Papacy ever since the tenth century; and the failure of any agreement from that standpoint was a foregone conclusion. The Emperor on the termination of the Council returned at once to Constantinople, and as soon as the terms of the agreement he had made became known, it was violently repudiated by the entire population, and a tumult so great arose that the agreement made at Florence was forthwith dropped and never heard of again.[30] Thus the Emperor John Paleologus, the third in succession to strive to get help from the West to save Constantinople, was no more successful than his father and grandfather had been. It was evidently vain to hope that the nations of Europe could be induced to lay aside their mutual dissensions even to protect themselves from a danger which threatened them all, and the days of the great capital of the Eastern half of the Roman Empire, which had blocked the path of Mahomedan conquest for eight hundred years, were now plainly numbered.

———————

In 1440, shortly after the above concourse had dispersed and Florence had returned to her normal conditions, the palace in the Via Larga which Cosimo had begun to build in 1430 was sufficiently completed for occupation, and he moved into it. The members of the family who were thus the first to take up their abode in this palace to which so much of the after history of the Medici attaches, were Cosimo and his wife, Contessina, and their two sons, Piero and Giovanni, then respectively twenty-four and nineteen years old. A few years later both the latter were to marry and bring their wives also to live in the family palace, which, before Cosimo's death, echoed to the childish voices of yet a third generation. Cosimo's brother Lorenzo died just as this change of residence of the elder branch took place.

In the same year the long and desultory war with Milan was brought to a conclusion. The Milanese army, under

Piccinino, after threatening Florence, retired into the Casentino, where, being followed by the Florentine army, it was
defeated at the battle of Anghiari, by which success Florence
gained the fertile district of the Casentino, and Venice, her
ally, gained Peschiera and Bergamo.

In the following year (1441) there occurred an incident
out of which has originated an accusation against Cosimo
of the gravest kind—to the effect that he instigated the
murder of Baldaccio d'Anghiari, commander of the Florentine
infantry. The crime was an atrocious one, but there is not
a particle of evidence that Cosimo had anything to do with
it. During the war with Milan in 1440 a Florentine named
Orlandini was in command of the troops which had been
stationed to hold the important pass of Marradi, on the
Faenza road, a strong position covering Florence on the
north, and between which and Florence there were no other
troops. The Milanese army, under Piccinino, having failed
in their attack on the pass of San Benedetto, then attempted
to force that of Marradi, where they should have been still
more easily repulsed. But on the approach of the enemy
Orlandini had ignominiously fled, ordering his troops to do
the same, thereby leaving the road to Florence open to the
enemy, who advanced and occupied the heights of Fiesole,
placing Florence for a short time in great danger. And
Baldaccio d'Anghiari being a brave soldier, had boldly
denounced Orlandini's cowardice which had had such serious
results. In 1441 Orlandini became Gonfaloniere, and while
holding that office sent for Baldaccio, "under the garb of
friendship," to come and discuss some military affairs at
the Palazzo della Signoria. The latter accordingly went to
the palace, was received by the Gonfaloniere with every sign
of friendship, and conducted by him to his own room, where,
on a sudden, hired assassins, placed in concealment by Orlandini, rushed upon Baldaccio and killed him, throwing his
body into the *cortile* below. His head was cut off and his
mangled remains exposed to the public in the Piazza della

Signoria, where it was proclaimed that he had been put to death by the Signoria as a traitor to the Republic.

The accusation against Cosimo is that Baldaccio on his way to the palace happened to meet him, and asked his advice about going, and that Cosimo treacherously advised him to go: it being declared that Cosimo desired Baldaccio's death because he feared the growing influence of Neri Capponi, whose close friend Baldaccio was. The motive alleged is exceedingly lame, while the whole story of Baldaccio's having met Cosimo at all or received any advice from him is apparently due solely to political animosity. It is only mentioned by one historian of the time, Cavalcanti, whose hatred of Cosimo is well known.[31] And as the story is not mentioned by any other writer, and comes from a source so unreliable in this particular case, it is now rejected by all historians as unworthy of credence. Gino Capponi in similarly rejecting it says that Cavalcanti "always writes in hatred of Cosimo, while wishing to appear not to do so." [32] Some writers have urged that even if Cosimo did not instigate the crime he must be held no less responsible, since he took no action against those guilty of it. But this ignores the fact that the latter were not private individuals, but the government of the country; that at the date when this occurred (1441) Cosimo had by no means yet gained the degree of power he afterwards attained; and that any action by him against the Signoria under the circumstances would have been at any rate highly unconstitutional, and would practically have been to head a rebellion against the constituted authority of the State. Lastly, the crime is so opposed to the whole tenor of his life that we are justified in rejecting absolutely the idea that he had any part in it, especially as the charge is entirely unsupported by any evidence.[33] Nor except for the desire to find material for a damning charge against Cosimo does the crime appear to differ from many others common at that time. The facts of the case are amply sufficient to account for Orlandini's deed; while he probably had reason to know that the members of the Signoria were not men likely to refuse to support his action before the people, backed as that action was by the evidence of traitorous conduct which he asserted that he possessed against Baldaccio d'Anghiari.

In the same year (1441) Cosimo arranged the purchase by Florence from the Pope of the town of Borgo San Sepolcro, for a sum of 25,000 florins; while we are told, "Cosimo increased the obligation of the State to him in the matter in that he himself advanced the purchase money."

In 1443 Pope Eugenius IV was at last able to return to Rome. Rome was at this time a ruined city,[34] devastated by the long conflicts between the Orsini, the Colonna, and other great barons, and destitute of all culture or civilising influences; and the contrast was all the more severe to the Pope since Florence, where he had been living for eight years, was in advance of all other cities in Europe.

In 1444 Cosimo founded the celebrated Medici Library, the first public library [35] to exist in Europe, and from the example of which the Vatican Library at Rome was thirty years afterwards formed. This library, housed at first in their own palace, was steadily added to by the Medici family in succeeding generations, and by them in 1524 the building in which it is now located (in the cloisters of San Lorenzo) [36] was constructed, designed by Michelangelo. It contains about ten thousand manuscript books of Greek and Latin classical authors, many of them of the rarest value. Among these it possesses the original copy of the Pandects of Justinian (A.D. 533), the discovery of which in the twelfth century caused so great an influence on the civilisation of Europe, and on which our study of the Roman law almost entirely hinges.[37] Also the best manuscript of Cicero's letters; two manuscripts of Tacitus, one of them being the sole existing copy containing the first five books of the "Annals"; a very ancient copy of the tragedies of Sophocles; a most important manu-

script of Æschylus; a Greek treatise on surgery; the Commentaries of Julius Cæsar; a Virgil of the fourth century; a
Syriac Gospel of A.D. 556; the Bible copied from 690 to 716
by Ceolfrid, Abbot of Wearmouth, and called the Codex
Amiatinus; a Pliny of the tenth century; and numerous
literary treasures connected with the time of Dante and
Petrarch and the Florence of the thirteenth and fourteenth
centuries; the whole representing a vast sum of money spent
by the Medici on this splendid contribution towards the
advancement of Learning. It is the parent of all the great
libraries of Europe, and as such deserves to be duly honoured.[38]

In connection with this library it is curious to note how
little printing, when, six years after this, it appeared, was
at first welcomed. "Those who owned these rare and costly
manuscripts of the past, with their beautiful calligraphy,
looked with no favour on crude and ugly reproductions
thereof by a mechanical process." It is recorded by Gregorovius that Federigo Montefeltro, Duke of Urbino (a
prince who was at this time beginning to follow Cosimo's
example in regard to the encouragement of Learning and
Art) would not have a printed book in his library.

In 1446 a general war broke out in Italy. As usual, Filippo
Visconti, Duke of Milan, was its leading spirit, and he had
as his allies the Pope and the King of Naples. Against this
powerful coalition were ranged Venice, Florence, Genoa, and
Bologna. The latter were entirely successful, especially when
Cosimo at length managed to separate Naples from the
coalition, and this brought about peace.

In the same year Brunelleschi died.[39] Grand funeral obse-
quies were held in the Duomo, where his body lay surrounded
by candles beneath the mighty vault that he had constructed,
and was visited by the whole city. He was buried in the
Duomo, his monument being placed opposite that of Arnolfo
di Cambio, he who began and he who finished thus lying

opposite each other in the building which is their joint creation.

In 1447 Filippo Visconti, Duke of Milan, the last of the Visconti family, and the perpetual enemy of Florence, died; whereupon two years of revolutions in Milan followed. Cosimo now executed his greatest stroke of foreign policy. The perpetual state of war with Milan wasted the revenues of Florence and prevented her development. Cosimo therefore determined to entirely change Florence's traditional foreign policy, and instead of Venice for ally and Milan for enemy, to reverse the position. He was opposed by many in his own state who had less political foresight, but he carried his point. Francesco Sforza, the successful soldier, who ever since his visit to Florence in 1435 had maintained a strong friendship with Cosimo, had since married Bianca Visconti, the late Duke's only child. To him Cosimo now gave both political assistance and liberal supplies of money, and as the result of this aid, Sforza, early in 1450, gained possession of Milan, and became its Duke and Cosimo's fast friend. Venice, of course, was greatly incensed, but Florence had no reason to fear Venice, which was neither so valuable as an ally nor so formidable as a foe as Milan. It proved a most successful stroke of policy, bringing to Florence peace instead of constant wars, and making Cosimo acknowledged as the most powerful force in the politics of Italy.

As regards France and England at this time, the "Hundred Years' War" was still proceeding, devastating all northern France, but with the general result that the English were steadily losing their hold of that country.

In 1440 Frederick III became Emperor. He was destined to hold the imperial title without dignity or influence for over fifty years (1440-1493).

In 1447 Pope Eugenius IV died. As his successor there was elected a man of far greater energy and ability, "the eager little scholar," Tommaso Parentucelli, who was a great

friend of Cosimo, and had acted as librarian to the Medici
Library when it was being formed; and he, on becoming
Pope, having taken part in all the life of Art and Learning
at work in Florence, was burning to inaugurate a similar
state of things in Rome. He took the name of Nicholas V;
"and," we are told, "he determined to make Rome, at this
time so desolate and ruined, the metropolis of the world."
He took active measures at once, both in the domain of Art
and in that of Learning.

In 1450 there was invented at Mayence the art of printing, fraught with greater consequences to mankind than many
other events of this time which then seemed of far greater
importance than this at first obscure invention.

In 1452 the Emperor Frederick III visited Italy, and on
his way to Rome passed through Florence, where he stayed
with Cosimo in the Medici Palace.

In the same year war again broke out in Italy, caused
by Alfonso, King of Naples, who, on the death of Filippo
Visconti, had taken his place as the disturbing factor in
Italy, and who now invaded Florence's territory. In the war
that followed Naples and Venice were ranged against Florence and her new ally, Milan. This was the balance of power
which Cosimo had with much labour striven to create. It
was shown to be thoroughly satisfactory, Venice and Naples
being able to effect nothing against Florence and Milan; and
after a time, discovering this, they became ready to agree
to the peace which through the Pope was proposed and concluded. Pope Nicholas V took no part in the war, urging all
states to abandon their feuds and combine against the Turks
to prevent the fall of Constantinople, then closely besieged;
but none heeded him.

———————

For nearly twenty years Cosimo's administration of foreign policy had given him unremitting labour. But these
efforts had been crowned with success. He had by degrees

brought all foreign countries to realise that he was the motive power in the Florentine state. And he had also (through attaining unvarying success) gradually convinced his own countrymen that no one else could manage their affairs so well. It had required much patient tact to convert his countrymen to an opposite policy from their traditional one of having Venice for friend and Milan for foe, to counteract the ill-favour against him which, in consequence, Venice endeavoured to stir up in his own city, and to do all this without losing his position in the process. But the successful issue of the war of 1452 convinced all that his view was correct, and left none any longer anxious to dispute his administration of their affairs. And so long as he continued in the same course (and at the same time shunned, as he was wont, all ostentation of power), he might do almost what he would.

Not that Cosimo was immaculate. He often employed measures to consolidate his power which were harsh and indefensible; he contrived to obtain the banishment of families opposed to him, or to ruin them by financial methods which his power as a banker enabled him to carry out; and on the other hand he managed to elevate citizens dependent on him or devoted to his family. But such practices were part of the customary politics of the time, nor are they quite unknown in modern political life; while it was much that throughout the long and strenuous conflict which he had to wage to retain his position there was no bloodshed. Above all, the welfare of Florence as a whole was so successfully effected, both in home and foreign affairs, that much could be forgiven regarding measures necessary to maintain Cosimo in power, since by this alone was that general result to the country achieved. And the Florentines evidently saw the matter in that light.

But Cosimo's political labours did not end even when he had achieved this result. He had to exercise a never-ceasing attention in order so to conduct the foreign policy of Florence amidst the intrigues of the time as to maintain a bal-

ance of power among the various Italian states, small as
well as large, and thus secure peace in Italy and preserve
Florence from the wasting effect of petty wars. The manifold anxieties of such a position were enough to break down
any man; and even upon Cosimo they told severely. It was
no wonder that he often sought a few hours' retreat from
such anxieties in the quiet monastery of San Marco; nor
that by the time he was sixty-four his health had already
begun to give way.

In 1453 the "Hundred Years' War" between France and
England came to an end. Between the years 1431 and 1453
the English had gradually lost all that they had conquered in
France, and when at length in the latter year the aged Tal-
bot was killed at the siege of Castillon, this war, which had
lasted a hundred and sixteen years, ended. It left the condition of France utterly wretched. "From the Loire to the
Somme all lay desert, given up to the wolves, and traversed
only by the robber and the free lance."

But a greater event than the conclusion of this long war,
and one whose effects still continue, occurred in the year
1453. This was the fall of Constantinople, bringing to an
end the Eastern Empire of Rome (29th May 1453). It was
an event which struck all Europe with horror. For Constantinople was not merely the storehouse of the ancient
learning and culture of the Roman Empire; it was also the
one great capital city in Europe which had always, from its
very birth, been Christian; a city whose foundation had signalised the adoption by the civilised world of that religion,
and which had come to be called in the East "*the* Christian
city." That such a city should be captured by the Turk, and
be henceforth the headquarters of the Mahomedan religion,
and of Turkish misrule and tyranny over the Christian popu-
lations of the Eastern countries, was hateful in the eyes of
Europe. And it happened solely because the Western nations were too much occupied with mutual dissensions to

combine to prevent it, as three successive Emperors of the
East, in 1361, in 1401, and in 1439 had come in person to
implore them to do.

The Emperor John Paleologus had died in 1448, and been
succeeded by his younger brother, the brave Constantine
Paleologus, the last of the long line of emperors who during
eleven hundred and thirty years sat on the throne of Constantine the Great. It was a strange coincidence that the last
Emperor of Constantinople should have borne the same
name as the first. Of Constantine Paleologus we are told,
"He was in no way inferior to any who ever sat upon that
throne." In this final contest *he*, at any rate, did his part
nobly, thereby throwing into deeper contrast the behaviour
of the Western nations.

Deserted by Europe, with the armies of the Turks all
round him, with none but himself to depend upon, with far
too small a garrison to defend thirteen miles of walls, with
a vast crowd of women and children and other non-com-
batants, the defenceless population of a great city, all looking to him to defend them from the atrocities of the terrible
Turks, with every sort of difficulty to be coped with inside
the city, whose inhabitants saw themselves abandoned by
Christendom, Constantine, solely by his own ability and
strength of character, conducted for a year and a half a
splendid defence, and in such sort that instead of the ignoble
scenes witnessed when Rome fell before Alaric, the manner
of the final fall of Constantinople has been felt to be one
of the most glorious episodes in all her long history.

The immediate consequences of the fall of Constantinople
were four:—

Intoxicated by their victory the Turks, wild to press on
and subdue the whole of Europe (where Mahomed II now
planned to set up at Rome the capital of a world-wide empire), advanced into Hungary. But there the brave John
Hunniades barred their way, like another Charles Martel,
and they got no further.

To the Pope, Nicholas V, who alone had laboured to prevent it, the fall of Constantinople was the cause of the deepest grief. He tried to rouse France, England, Germany, and Venice to retake Constantinople and turn the Turks out of Europe. But what with the incapacity of the Emperor Frederick III and the general disunion between the different countries, he could effect nothing. After two years he died (1455), it was said of grief and horror at the capture of the Christian city by the infidel, and at his failure to rouse the Western nations to retake it.

To Venice the fall of her rival was her doom; she began to decay from that hour, losing territory after territory to the Turks, and her commerce at the same time. It was a just retribution. For it was the crime of her treacherous attack upon and capture of Constantinople in 1204 (committed under the name of a "crusade," and solely to satisfy her insatiable greed of wealth) which so weakened the Eastern Empire that the decline in power wrought thereby ended, after two hundred and fifty years of constant defeat, in the final fall of Constantinople, and brought the Turks into Europe. And it was fitting that on Venice should fall the chief punishment. Her wealth rapidly departed; others, Portugal especially, gained the commerce which she lost; and by the end of the century the decay of the once mighty Republic was fully established.

To Florence the fall of Constantinople was a gain. It scattered westwards all that accumulation of the ancient learning which Constantinople had so long preserved, most of which naturally gravitated to the city where many of the leading men of Constantinople had been hospitably entertained only fourteen years before, and where they knew they would find friends. And this helped forward still further that pre-eminence in Learning and Art which was Florence's greatest glory.

As to what happened to Constantinople itself, that is best told in a single sentence by a traveller of our own day, who writes:—"I have never in all my travels grieved so much as at the sight of the once beautiful city, defiled, squalid, and misgoverned."

We have now to look at Cosimo from a financial point of view: at his general as well as his charitable expenditure, and the financial arrangements made between the two branches of the family.

Cosimo, besides his work in the world of politics, had to administer a great banking business. In this sphere he has, by all writers, been given the reputation of a financier of the first rank. Notwithstanding his immense expenditure (which included private subsidies towards State expenses, the entertainment of distinguished visitors to Florence, large sums given to advance the cause of Learning and Art, and the equivalent of a million sterling given to charitable objects), he more than doubled the fortune inherited from his father, and left his son and successor Piero the wealthiest man at that time in Europe.

Another feature of his financial work is the way in which he made his operations as a banker assist those connected with his position as head of the State. He frequently made his immense banking transactions a weapon with which to force other countries to the course required for the welfare of Florence. Thus by his financial assistance the Venetian Republics were enabled to withstand the united attacks of the French and of Filippo Visconti, Duke of Milan; but on being deprived by Cosimo of this support were unable to do so. Again, in the war of 1452, in which Venice and Naples were allied against Florence, one of the chief means by which Cosimo obtained his success was by calling in such immense debts from those countries that they were deprived of resources for continuing the war. Again during the War of the Roses Edward IV obtained such enormous sums from Cosimo's agent in England that he might almost be considered as the means of maintaining that king upon the English throne.

As regards charities, the *Libro di Ragione* shows that Cosimo's private expenditure on churches, monasteries, and charitable institutions exceeded 400,000 gold florins; [40] and this at a time when the whole income of the Florentine state did not reach more than half that sum.

About the year 1453, as Cosimo was growing old and his brother Lorenzo was already dead, a computation was made of the family income and a resolution come to between the two branches as to the manner in which the profits of their banking business should be divided between them. The share of these profits which thus fell to each branch of the family was equal to about half a million sterling—an enormous fortune in those times.

Cosimo built for his family, besides the Medici Palace in the city itself, various villas outside Florence. The chief of these were, Careggi, about two miles to the north-west of the city, Cafaggiolo, [41] in the valley of the Mugello, and the Villa Medici, on the slope of Fiesole, built by him for his son Giovanni. Careggi was Cosimo's favourite residence, and there he was fond of gathering round him the learned society which he loved.

The chief historical events in other countries during the last ten years of Cosimo's life were the following:—

In England, two years after the "Hundred Years' War" with France had ended, began in 1455 the "War of the Roses." This kept England in a state of civil war during the next thirty years.

As regards the Papacy, on the death of Pope Nicholas V in 1455 the Pope elected was Calixtus III. He died in 1458, and was succeeded by the celebrated Æneas Sylvius Piccolomini (Pius II), the chief episodes of whose life are depicted in the series of fresco pictures by Pinturicchio in the library of the cathedral of Siena. This Pope paid a visit to Florence in 1460, and stayed with Cosimo in the Medici Palace.

In Venice there came in 1457 the end of the long and glorious thirty-four years' rule of the Doge Francesco Foscari, who died in that year. He was the last of her great Doges.

In France, in 1461, Charles VII, the king placed on the throne by Joan of Arc, died; in the same year that in England Henry VI was dethroned in favour of Edward IV. Charles was succeeded by his cowardly and treacherous son, Louis XI, "the royal trickster." Detestable as were his long list of murders, carried out by the most treacherous methods, he brought order out of chaos in France.

The thirty years' rule of Cosimo shows us the new movement in Art advancing with rapid strides to greater and greater achievements through the genius of Donatello, Fra Angelico, Luca della Robbia, Ghiberti, and Lippi.

Donatello, the third in age of the four leaders of the Renaissance in Art, exercised by far the deepest influence of the four. Ghiberti, Brunelleschi, and Masaccio each did their part; but Donatello infused a new spirit into the whole matter, breathing into it the breath of life. Sixteen years old when the new movement in Art began, and living to the age of eighty-one, he exercised for fifty years the leading influence in the world of Art. We have therefore to look at him under two aspects, (i) as a sculptor, and (ii) as a guide to the Art world as to the true aim of Art.

(i) Donatello, the first sculptor "in the round" since the time of Greek art, introduced as great a revolution in sculpture as Giotto did in Painting. The nature of this revolution has been well described by a recent writer of his life as follows: [42]—

"In order to estimate the full significance of the new departure in Sculpture inaugurated by Donatello, that sculpturing of isolated statues which had not been attempted since the last artist of antiquity laid down his chisel, it must be borne in mind that for centuries the accepted form for this art had been relief; while also sculpture had not been used as a prime vehicle *by itself* for conveying the artist's idea, but as an adjunct and ornament to architecture.

"Thus in Orcagna's celebrated shrine in Or San Michele in honour of the Madonna, we find the Madonna sentiment diffused throughout all its parts. Her story is told by a series of reliefs; her character is suggested by a carefully-thought-out arrangement of figures representing the accepted virtues of that character, appropriately placed between those stories which appear to illustrate them; symbols are freely employed; and even the material and colours, the white marble, spangled with precious stones and mosaics, contribute their qualities to aid in the expression of the ideal associated in the mind of the artist with the personality of the Blessed Virgin. This was essentially the mediæval form of Art.

"Now the genius of classic art was exactly the opposite of this. Where the mediæval genius was diffuse, the classic genius was concentrated. Where the mediæval sculptor flew to symbols to express 'the eternal things of the supernal glory,' the sculptor of the classic age, choosing the most perfect form in nature—the human—so refined and idealised it, and so transfused it with the spirit and thought desired to be expressed, that it spoke by suggestion to all who had ears to hear. Donatello's predecessors were mediæval, one and all; he himself was a scholar in their school; yet when only twenty years of age, and twelve years before he was admitted as a master in his guild, we see him turn his back on the entire mediæval method, and choosing the way of antiquity, begin his series of isolated heroic statues."

Thus did Donatello, while still quite young, feel the inspiration of that re-birth in Art which was permeating all Florence; and four years after Ghiberti began his first pair of bronze doors, on which Donatello had worked as an assistant, this youth of twenty made that bold and independent return to earlier principles which marks the true genius.[43]

After various statues representing Joshua, Daniel, Jeremiah, Habakkuk, Abraham, St. Peter, St. Mark, the marble

statue of David, and others, all intended to occupy niches
on the walls of the cathedral, the campanile, or the church
of Or San Michele, Donatello produced in 1416 his *St.
George,* generally considered his masterpiece, which gave him
the position of the first sculptor of his time.

But Donatello was to go further than this. About the year
1432 [44] he executed for Cosimo his bronze statue of *David;*
and this statue introduced a new era in the art of sculpture.
For it was the first isolated nude statue that had been made
for more than a thousand years. Even the *St. George* (besides
embodying no attempt to depict the human form undraped)
had only been made for a niche; but this statue of *David*
was intended to stand in the *cortile* of Cosimo's palace and
be looked at from every side. This "remarkable innovation," as Lord Balcarres justly calls it,[45] advanced Donatello's reputation to a still greater degree than even his *St.
George* had done, having an immediate effect on all the
sculptors of his time, and spreading Donatello's fame far
beyond Italy. Seeing it as we now do in the museum of the
Bargello, surrounded by many others, we are apt to forget
the distinguished position which this statue holds as the leader
of all that followed it in sculpture.

The only others of Donatello's numerous works [46] necessary to notice here are his statue of *Judith slaying Holofernes,*
and his medallions copied from antique gems. The *Judith*
was executed, like the *David,* for the *cortile* of the Medici
Palace, and was finished shortly after the family moved into
the palace in 1440.[47] This statue had an important history
some fifty years later (*see* chap. x). The medallions, which
still remain in excellent preservation over the arches of the
cortile, are copies in marble of eight antique gems, the subjects being Diomede and the Palladium, Bacchus and
Ariadne, Ulysses and Athena, Dædalus and Icarus, and four
others of minor interest. The original gems were in the
Medici collection. Whether these medallions were completed
and placed in position at the time when the palace was first

occupied in 1440 (as seems most probable), or at a later date in Cosimo's life, is a debated point.

(ii) But greater still is Donatello's fame as a guide to the aim which Art should set before itself, a message which he taught to sculptors and painters alike. Hitherto the aim that artists had striven after was the production of as life-like a representation as possible of nature; and this alone they had found difficult enough. Donatello introduced a further step, teaching *that form must be a mere means to an end, that of conveying some deep thought to the mind;* that Art, in fact, must be a language.[48] "The outward rendered expressive of the inward; the body instinct with spirit; the soul made incarnate"; this (which has been said to define truth in Art) was in brief Donatello's message to the Art world; and it produced the great stride forward which Art now took. It was, in fact, the inauguration of the whole difference between classic and modern art, the former aiming no further than to portray absolute perfection of form, the latter aiming (simultaneously with this) at conveying some message to the mind. It is this characteristic of Donatello's genius which has caused him to be called by his countrymen "Il maestro di chi sanno" ("The master of those who know"). His statue of *St. George,* in which the ideal to which he gives expression is that of the flesh under the dominion of the spirit, is the best example of this characteristic in his art.

Donatello also revived a branch of art which had been dead since the time of ancient Rome, that of casting statues, and particularly equestrian statues, in bronze—a difficult work, since all its details had in the course of nine centuries become unknown. In 1453, after many difficulties, he completed for the Venetian Republic the first bronze equestrian statue executed since Roman times, that of the Venetian general, Gattamelata, at Padua.

His works in bas-relief have also certain characteristics of their own, notably that exceedingly low relief called *stiacciato,* which he often used with very beautiful effect.[49]

Perkins draws attention to his treatment of the hair, saying that, "though the ancient sculptors were unrivalled in their treatment of hair in the abstract, no sculptor, ancient or modern, ever surpassed Donatello in giving it all its qualities of growth and waywardness." [50]

To compare Donatello with his great successor Michelangelo is absurd. Donatello's fame is that of the leader, of the man who revolutionised sculpture and taught all who came after him what Art's true aim should be; and no excellences in Michelangelo, or any other successor, can touch the point on which Donatello's fame rests.

San Marco not only possessed learned men among its community, and a Prior who was beloved by all who knew him, but also numbered among its members the greatest painter of the day, Fra Angelico.[51] His earlier paintings are to be seen at Cortona, but in 1437 he began his painting at Florence, being at Cosimo's instance set to work, as soon as any portions of the new monastery were sufficiently far advanced for the purpose, to decorate the walls of the chapter-house, cloisters, and corridors with his frescoes. Amongst these the large fresco in the chapter-house representing *The Crucifixion* (with the saints of the New Testament on one side and the prominent saints of the Middle Ages on the other) was specially ordered by Cosimo, who "gave much helpful advice in regard to the details." It was one of the first of Fra Angelico's frescoes painted in San Marco. Cosimo also made Fra Angelico paint, in the cell which he kept for himself, a fresco picture of the Adoration of the Magi, "desiring to have this example of Eastern kings laying down their crowns at the manger of Bethlehem always before his eyes as a reminder for his own guidance as a ruler."

From time to time we meet with a master who, having made some line in Art specially his own, and perfected it to such a point that it is felt that no further advance in that line is possible to man, remains for all time its solitary exponent. It was thus with Fra Angelico. He reigns supreme and alone in that line which he chose, "wherein he sought only to express the inner life of the adoring soul." At the same time he was an artist who steadily improved in technical skill, and his later paintings show that he had carefully studied the works of Masaccio.

Regarding the general style of his painting, Mrs. Ady says as follows: [52]—

"All the mystic thought of the mediæval world, the passionate love of God and man that beat in the heart of St. Francis, the yearnings of Dante's soul after a higher and more perfect order of things, . . . are embodied in the art of Fra Angelico. . . . The brilliancy of colour and richness which he gives in his pictures of angels and heavenly scenes are marvellous. In his picture at Cortona of the *Annunciation* (Fra Angelico's first version of his favourite subject) the angel's wings are gold tipped with ruby light, and his robe is a marvel of decorative beauty, studded all over with little tongues of flame and embroidered in mystic patterns. . . . His picture of the *Coronation of the Virgin* is one of the glories of the Louvre, and in it he has lavished the richest ornament and the most radiant colour on the angels who stand before the throne, each with a spark of fire on his forehead and glittering stars on his purple wings."

Ruskin, speaking of Fra Angelico's painting from the more technical side, remarks as follows:—

"The art of Fra Angelico, both in drawing and colouring, is perfect, and his work may be recognised at any distance, by its rainbow play and brilliancy, like a piece of opal among common marbles. In order to effect clearer distinction between heavenly beings and those of this world, he represents the former as clothed in draperies of the purest colour, crowned with glories of burnished gold, and *entirely shadowless;* the flames on their foreheads waving brighter as they move; the sparkles streaming from their purple wings like the glitter of the sun upon the sea; while they listen in the pauses of alternate song for the prolonging of the trumpet blast, and the answering of psalm, and harp, and cymbal, throughout the endless deep, and from all the star shores of Heaven. . . . This mode of treatment, combined as it is with exquisite choice of gesture and disposition of drapery, gives perhaps the best idea of spiritual beings which the human mind is capable of forming." [53]

For one other point Fra Angelico's pictures are notable; in them we have for the first time heads full of individual character; while he was the first to begin introducing in his pictures portraits of his friends, thus doing much to help forward another line in Art, portrait-painting, which a generation later became a recognised branch of painting. In this way he gives us in his picture of the *Deposition from the Cross,* now in the Accademia at Florence, a portrait of his friend Michelozzo, the architect who was being employed by Cosimo in the rebuilding of San Marco. [54]

Fra Angelico's period of painting in Florence lasted for nine years (1437-1446). In 1446 Pope Eugenius IV, having seen so much of his work at Florence, summoned him to Rome; but that Pope died almost immediately afterwards (1447). However, his successor Nicholas V was, as previously noted, most anxious to inaugurate a new state of things in Rome as regards Art. One of his first efforts in this direction was (after the example of the monastery of San Marco in Florence) to begin covering the walls of the Vatican with frescoes; and this was the commencement of that long series of renowned frescoes which, added to by Pope after Pope, now form so large a part of the treasures of the Vatican. Nicholas V began with his private chapel, and set Fra Angelico to work to decorate its walls. Thus these frescoes in the chapel of Nicholas V are important both as the first of all the frescoes in the Vatican, and also as being Fra Angelico's last work. They took him the greater part of the next five years (1447-1452); and these frescoes in particular show how greatly he had profited by careful study of Masaccio's works, for while they have still his own grace, and skill in delineating character, they are instinct with Masaccio's power. In them we have from Fra Angelico two portraits of Nicholas V in the two pictures representing Sixtus II (A.D. 257) ordaining the Deacon St. Lawrence, and giving into his charge the treasures of the Church. Fra Angelico died at Rome in 1455.

Simultaneously with the above work in Art, Nicholas V commenced the formation of a library in the Vatican after the pattern of the Medici Library in Florence, and collected a large number of manuscript books, and appointed a librarian; but the whole was dispersed by his successors, and it was not until Sixtus IV revived the institution in 1475 that the Vatican Library began its existence.

Luca della Robbia, born in 1400, was employed as a youth on the bronze doors of the Baptistery. After a time he began working on his own account, and struck out a new line of his own. He executed reliefs in marble, in bronze, and in glazed terra-cotta, devoting himself specially to the varied expressions of the human features; and his works, by their truth to nature, and the deep feeling which they breathe, "have won for him an honoured place amongst those who gave an impulse to the Renaissance." [55] Speaking of his art generally, Miss Cruttwell says:—"He is first of all the imaginative sculptor and poet, who embodied the grandest ideals in forms worthy of Pheidean Greece." [56]

In 1438 Luca produced his beautiful relief of the *Cantoria,* executed for one of the organ lofts of the cathedral,[57] and representing groups of boys and girls singing and little children dancing, which at once placed him among the foremost artists of his time. This relief in marble, from its truth to nature and the grace of movement of its figures, was almost as much a wonder to the time as Ghiberti's first pair of bronze doors had been, and had much effect in helping still further forward both sculpture and painting towards a life-like representation of human figures. It is meant to illustrate the 150th Psalm, each of the panels portraying one of the six verses of that Psalm. Regarding this magnificent frieze,[58] the Marchesa Burlamacchi says:—

"Luca della Robbia's *Cantoria* children live and move, the very action of their throats can be seen as they sing, the soul of music is in their faces. There is a swing in their movements as they dance, a grace of attitude, and an elegance of flowing drapery, that throughout the works of the Renaissance has never been surpassed."[59]

Besides the *Cantoria,* Luca della Robbia's other chief works in marble and bronze were the five panels on the north side of the campanile, executed in 1439, representing the development of man's intellect in the arts and sciences; the tomb of Benozzo Federighi, Bishop of Fiesole, now in the church of Sta. Trinità, executed in 1454, and by some considered Luca's best work in marble; and the bronze doors of the sacristy of the Duomo, completed after many years' labour in 1469. His works in glazed terra-cotta will be considered later (chap. vi).

In 1452, six years after Brunelleschi had died and Fra Angelico's painting in Florence come to an end, Ghiberti at last finished his second pair of bronze doors for the Baptistery. These, which Michelangelo a hundred years later declared "fit to be the gates of Paradise," are considered Ghiberti's masterpiece. They represent scenes from Old Testament history, and Ruskin remarks: "The book of Genesis, in all the fulness of its incidents, in all the depth of its meaning, is bound within the leaf-borders of the gates of Ghiberti."[60] They had taken Ghiberti twenty-eight years. He had begun his first pair of doors at the age of twenty-three; he finished his second at the age of seventy-three; and he died three years afterwards. Excepting his three statues outside Or San Michele and one or two minor works, these two pairs of bronze doors were his life's work. As Alexandre Dumas says: "A whole life spent over this marvellous bronze!"

The pathos of the young Ghiberti beginning this beautiful work of art when full of youth and strength, amidst all the enthusiasm of the first outburst of the Renaissance, and finishing it when he was old and worn with years, and when so many who had seen its commencement had passed away, cannot but touch all who think of it. It was another generation who now saw its completion from that which had seen it begun. Cosimo himself, now sixty-three, had then been only a boy of thirteen, Fra Angelico fifteen, Michelozzo eleven, Luca della Robbia a child of a year old. Masaccio, the boy who had worked under him, had covered himself with glory in another line, and was long ago dead. Brunelleschi, his passionate rival, had had time to learn another art, and to make his name famous therein, and was gone. Of all the band of eager competitors for the work he alone remained.

As we look at these beautiful doors, how many thoughts crowd upon us. The terrible sufferings of Florence from the plague, which caused their construction; the celebrated competition with its intense and passionate rivalry; the whole lifetime of work spent in their production; all the art life which surged around them as they lay gradually taking shape in the workshop of Ghiberti,[61] hard by the place where they have now stood for four hundred and fifty years; the school of Art which that workshop became for Florence; the band of eager young assistants, some of whom had since made names which are now famous throughout the world. The final triumph when they were at last completed; the solemn function when they were erected in their place; the grey-haired man of seventy-three, bent with age, who had begun them in his youth, and who, had he had another lifetime before him, would have destroyed even these, and begun yet another effort after something more perfect still; the pride of all who had had a part however humble in their production; the excitement and rapture of a whole city. Lastly, the many things of

which they were the origin and the matrix, the sculpture of
Donatello, the painting of Masaccio, and all that grew from
these; so that as we look at Ghiberti's panels, we see mirrored
in them the triumphs of Raphael and of Michelangelo. It is
thoughts such as these which force themselves upon our minds
as we stand in the crowded modern thoroughfare, with its
trams and tourists and life of the Florence of to-day around
us, and look at Ghiberti's doors.

In 1441 Filippo Lippi, who had been Masaccio's pupil, finished his painting of the *Coronation of the Madonna,* considered his best picture in Florence. A greater contrast could
scarcely be found than that between the two chief painters of
Cosimo's time, Fra Angelico and Filippo Lippi; for Lippi was
in everything the antithesis of his contemporary, Fra Angelico. The orphan son of a butcher, he was left as a boy in
charge of an aunt, who, finding him an idle ne'er-do-well, put
him as a novice into the nearest monastic community, that of
the Carmelites, in whose church of the Carmine Masaccio was
then painting his frescoes. The monks, owing to his laziness,
could do nothing with him, but, watching Masaccio at his
work, Lippi thought this an easier task than learning to read
and write; and Masaccio, finding he could draw, taught him
his art. Lippi was sixteen when Masaccio died, and in the following year, Vasari says, "Lippi boldly threw off the monastic
habit, and took to painting for a livelihood." Though he signs
himself "Frater Filippus," he had no right to the term, as he
had entirely discarded his vows, and owing to his disreputable
conduct no religious community would own him. His life was
a disturbed one, as his drunken character and constant frauds
upon those who employed him caused him to be always in
trouble; after being several times brought up before the authorities for various misdemeanors, at length for a particularly
flagrant case of embezzlement he was flogged.

Lippi's character, however, only affects his credit as a
painter by accounting for the kind of success he achieved. He

had (as was to be expected) no ears for the message which Donatello was at this time teaching, and consequently his pictures on religious subjects have an exceedingly mundane character. Nevertheless, the sweet seriousness of his Madonnas falls in no way short of those of Fra Angelico, and the faces of his children are full of a quaint, mischievous character which is delightful, while in both drawing and colouring he shows the immense advance which had now taken place in Painting. And it is here that Lippi's true claim to fame lies. Masaccio, the only man who up to that time had found out the true methods of the art of Painting, had died too soon himself to be able to make known his discovery, except to the few who could visit Florence and the Brancacci chapel. It was left for Lippi, the rough boy whom he had taught, to show the world Masaccio's discovery. And Lippi did so. Vasari says:— "Taught as he had been by Masaccio, he was a faithful follower of Masaccio's style"; and he adds that he followed the latter's methods so faithfully that it "appeared that the spirit of Masaccio had entered Lippi's body." Thus what Masaccio had done for the art of Painting is chiefly to be seen by a comparison of Lippi's pictures with those of Masaccio's immediate predecessors, the Giotteschi. Lippi's principal picture in Florence is his *Coronation of the Virgin* (painted for Cosimo,[62] and now in the Accademia delle Belle Arti); but his best work is considered to be his frescoes in the cathedral at Prato, painted between 1456 and 1465.

A serious error of the last generation has caused much injustice to Masaccio, and has been widely spread through Robert Browning's poem on Lippi. He makes Lippi speak of Masaccio as a "youngster" then just learning to paint,[63] Lippi saying that after his death this "Guidi"[64] may perhaps rob him of his laurels. This is owing to Masaccio's date being in Browning's time imagined to be later than it really is, so that Lippi was supposed to have *preceded him;* with the result that Lippi, instead of Masaccio, gained all the credit of the great advance in Painting which exists between the Giotteschi and Masaccio. The pathos which throughout attaches to Masaccio is thus still further increased. Not only is he crushed with poverty throughout his life, and his great fame only won after death, but in addition even those laurels are in later times given to the pupil whom he had out of a rough kindness taught for nothing. And then, as the crowning point, this Tommaso Guidi, this great genius, who is the founder of all modern painting, and from whom even Raphael was glad to learn, becomes known to posterity only as "Clumsy Tom." The fuller information now available has put this matter right, and more particularly the registers of the *catasto* tax for the years 1421 to 1428, which give definite and conclusive evidence as to Masaccio's date and circumstances; though even without this Vasari's remark should have sufficed to prevent the mistake. Lippi died in 1469, at the age of fifty-seven.

Though the transcendent genius of Donatello threw all others into the shade, there were various other distinguished sculptors who also flourished at this period, making Cosimo's time specially notable in this branch of Art. The chief of these were:—

Desiderio da Settignano.—A pupil of Donatello, and eminent among the sculptors of this time. Perkins[65] considers his tomb of Carlo Marsuppini in Sta. Croce one of the three finest tombs in Tuscany; while he says of his bust of Marietta Palla Strozzi:[66]—"It would be difficult to point out a bust, which more thoroughly combines those peculiar features of the best *quattrocento* work, high technical excellence, refinement of taste, delicacy of treatment, and purity of design." The beautiful head of St. Cecilia in *stiacciato* (low relief), now the property of Lord Wemyss, which used to be attributed to Donatello, is now said to be by Desiderio.

Bernardo and Antonio Rossellino.—Bernardo Rossellino executed the fine tomb of Leonardo Bruni in Sta. Croce, and the monument of Beata Villana in the Rucellai chapel in Sta. Maria Novella. Of Antonio Rossellino, Perkins says:—"He

possessed grace, delicacy of treatment, dignity, and a rare
feeling of beauty, and sweetness of expression, as we see in the
noble monument of the Cardinal Portogallo at San Miniato,
Florence"; he considers this tomb one of the most beautiful
in Italy.

Mino da Fiesole.—Another still more famous sculptor of
this period who outlived those previously mentioned. His
works show a refined taste, great delicacy of detail, and much
devotional feeling. Regarding his tomb of Bishop Salutati in
the cathedral of Fiesole, Perkins says:—"The bust of the
bishop is certainly one of the most living and strongly characterised 'counterfeit presentments' of nature ever produced in
marble." Mino da Fiesole also executed the beautiful taber-
nacle in the Medici chapel in Sta. Croce, and many busts,
altar-pieces, and other celebrated works during the time of
Piero il Gottoso and Lorenzo the Magnificent.

Antonio and Piero Pollajuolo.—These two brothers were
celebrated sculptors, painters, goldsmiths, and medallists of
the time. Their renown belongs almost entirely to Antonio, his
younger brother Piero producing little notable work. Antonio's principal existing work in Florence is the Silver Altar
of the Baptistery (kept in the Opera del Duomo); and in
Rome his two tombs of Pope Sixtus IV and Pope Innocent
VIII. The fine medal of the Pazzi Conspiracy hitherto attributed to him is now said to be by Bertoldo, the well-known
pupil of Donatello. Antonio Pollajuolo was no less celebrated
as a painter than as a sculptor and medallist. In 1460 three
large and very famous canvases, "five braccia high" (about
nine feet), were painted by him for the hall of the Medici
Palace, depicting the combats of Hercules with the lion, with
the hydra, and with Antæus. Vasari describes them in detail,
and speaks with great admiration of their execution. When
the Medici Palace was sacked in 1494 they were appropriated
by the Signoria, and removed to the council hall of the Palazzo
della Signoria, where they hung for many years, but have since
been lost. Vasari, in mentioning them, states that they were

painted for Lorenzo the Magnificent, but this must be a mistake on his part; for in a letter of Pollajuolo's own he states that he painted them in 1460, and at that date Cosimo was head of the house, and his grandson Lorenzo a boy of only eleven years old; so that they were painted for Cosimo. There are two small panel pictures on the same subject by Pollajuolo, now in the Uffizi Gallery, evidently painted about the same time, and these give us an idea of what the celebrated canvases which adorned the walls of the principal reception room of the Medici Palace in the time of Cosimo, Piero, and Lorenzo were like.

———————

Cosimo grew old very rapidly, suffering severely from gout, and in his later years becoming very infirm, which caused him to leave the home affairs of the State to a very large extent to others; a condition of things under which we first hear of the incapable Luca Pitti, who during the last four years of Cosimo's life thrust himself into a prominent place in public matters,[67] though Cosimo still kept foreign affairs in his own hands. His long labours for his country's welfare had borne their full fruit; none now questioned or attempted to disturb the position he had so deservedly gained; [68] we find the Signoria in an official document (a letter to the Venetian Republic) calling him "Capo della Republica," though he held no official position at the time; and "head of the Republic" he was universally acknowledged to be to the very end of his life.[69]

Cosimo, like his father, had two sons, Piero, born in 1416, and Giovanni, born in 1421. The death of the latter at the age of forty-two is the last prominent incident connected with Cosimo's life. Giovanni had all the family love of learning, and many rare manuscript books collected by him are still in the Medici Library in San Lorenzo. His portrait bust by Mino da Fiesole, who knew him well, gives us a thoroughly reliable

representation of his appearance. As the chronic ill-health of
his elder brother Piero made it unlikely that the latter would
survive their father, Giovanni was brought up as the future
head of the family, was looked on by all as his father's successor, and was Cosimo's favourite son. To a family situated
as the Medici were at this time, it was of the utmost importance that whoever succeeded Cosimo as head of the house
should be both capable and popular; so that Cosimo's feeling
regarding his two sons was not unnatural. Nor did Giovanni
come short of his father's hopes in this respect. His ability,
good sense, tact, and knowledge of men made him highly popular, and he promised to be a worthy successor to Cosimo. So
as Piero's health grew from year to year worse, all the hopes
of the family rested on Giovanni. The latter was married to
Ginevra degli Albizzi, one of that family who had so violently
opposed Cosimo in his earlier years and tried to compass his
ruin and death. Giovanni and Ginevra's only child, a son, then
nine years old, died in 1461.

But alas for human hopes! In 1463, one year before
Cosimo's own death, Giovanni, the hope of the house, died.
The grief into which the family were plunged at this serious
misfortune was very great. Cosimo was broken down, physi-
cally helpless, and his death soon to be expected; Piero was
likely to die any day; and his eldest son, Lorenzo, was only
fourteen years old. So that with Giovanni dead it seemed
that all the prospects of the family were destroyed; for it
was well known that powerful enemies (including all those
other families jealous of the one which was rising to such
eminence) were on the watch for an opportunity to bring its
power to an end. There is the pathetic story of the infirm and
aged Cosimo, after this death of his favourite son, having
himself carried through the rooms of the spacious palace which
he had built (and which had seen two such gaps made in the
family within three years), and several times repeating, "Too
large a house now for so small a family."

Giovanni was buried in the family church of San Lorenzo,

which was then just finished and had been endowed b Cosimo. Giovanni di Bicci and Piccarda had already be buried in the "Old Sacristy," [70] and their grandson, this se ond Giovanni, was now also interred there. And when s years later his brother Piero died, the sculptor Verrocchi Donatello's best pupil,[71] was called upon to design a joi tomb for the two brothers, and executed the very tastef one which stands in the archway between the sacristy and t chapel of the Madonna, consisting of a sarcophagus of pc phyry with bronze acanthus leaves climbing over it. It Verrocchio's earliest important work.

Cosimo died on the 1st August 1464 at his beloved vil of Careggi, at the age of seventy-five. Piero, in relating the grandfather's death to his two sons the following day, sa as follows:—

"He counselled me that, as you had good abilities, I oug to bring you up well, and you would then relieve me many cares. . . . He said that he did not wish any pomp demonstration at his funeral. . . . He reminded me, as he ha told me before, of where he wished to be buried in Sa Lorenzo, and said all in such an orderly manner, and wi so much prudence and spirit, that it was wonderful. He adde that his life had been long, therefore he was well content leave it when God willed. Yesterday morning he had hin self completely dressed; he then made his confession to t prior of San Lorenzo; after which he caused Mass to b said, making the responses as if he were in health. Afte wards, being asked to make profession of his faith, he sa the Creed word for word, said the confession himself, ar then received the Holy Sacrament, doing so with as mu devotion as one can describe, having first asked pardon every one for any wrongs he had done them. Which thin have encouraged me in my hope towards God."

Cosimo's popularity with his countrymen lasted to the ve end, as well as the respect with which he was regarded b the rulers of all other states. He was buried as he had desired without any pomp, and at first in the Old Sacristy of San Lorenzo. The Signoria had planned to give him a magnificent funeral and a very imposing monument, but the Medici family, on the proposal being put before them, refused to have either. The people, however, were determined to give him some special honour. A public decree was therefore passed by the Signoria conferring on him the title of *Pater Patriae,* and ordering that this should be inscribed by the Republic on his tomb. It therefore bears the honourable inscription:—"COSIMUS MEDICES HIC SITUS EST DECRETO PUBLICO PATER PATRIAE." No greater honour could have been done him than that such a title should be thus given him after his death; and by this title of *Pater Patriae* he has ever since been known in history.

But the honour done to Cosimo's memory was not confined to giving him the title of "Father of his country." A further and more peculiar honour was conferred. San Lorenzo, founded in such ancient times,[72] is the "Ambrosian Basilica," having beneath its high altar many highly venerated relics of the martyrs. And an ancient rule [73] of the Catholic Church prohibited, out of reverence thereto, the burial of any persons in such basilicas, only permitting them to be buried in sacristies or chapels attached to the church. And although in special cases persons of importance were allowed to be buried in *the vault* below the church, none so interred were permitted to have a tombstone in the church, but their tombstones were required to be placed in the vault. There are consequently no tombstones in the pavement of the nave of San Lorenzo, except one. This solitary exception is in the case of Cosimo Pater Patriae. Migliore, in his interesting old book entitled *Firenze Città Nobilissima* (1684), in describing the church of San Lorenzo, gives the following account of this matter:—

"And here is to be seen maintained a most laudable disposition of the Canons of the Church, especially at the Council of Bragarense, held in Portugal under Giovanni III; which is, not to allow the burial of the dead in the Basiliche, out of reverence to the relics of the blessed martyrs. And in accordance with this disposition you find at the foot of the altar, in the middle of the pavement, placed to the memory of Cosimo Padre della Patria, the marble memorial in a circle of serpentine and porphyry, with the arms of the Medici at the four sides. But the body is not in the place which is thus represented, but is placed beneath in the vault with all the other personages buried in that church, without any description of them in the pavement above them. This was as a sign of the difference which ought to be maintained between them and him who was like a founder of this church; also as a man who, much separated from the crowd, had no equal in those happy times, when the fame of worthy persons travelled upon the wings of fortune; so that one who well knew his qualities sums up all by saying 'Vir potens, famosus in toto mundo' ('a man most able, famous in all the world'); 'none,' added Il Volaterrano, 'in public affairs of such capacity, nor in learning, wisdom, and knowledge his equal.' "

After dilating on all that Cosimo did for the Republic and for Italy, the account concludes by saying:—

"After his death the Republic conferred on him the honourable title of Pater Patriae, never before conferred on any one in that Republic, and rarely even in that of Rome; and this was accompanied by extraordinary pomp, at the sole cost of the Republic, in transferring his body to this Sepulchre, which brought to mind that given to Fabius Maximus."

And if we penetrate into the vault below, we find in what a peculiar way this special honour to Cosimo was carried out. Evidently the Florentines were determined to do nothing by halves in the matter. For instead of finding, as we should have expected, a sarcophagus with Cosimo's name on it placed in the vault underneath the memorial slab in the pavement of the church, we find immediately below the porphyry slab a large square pillar, of about eight feet on each side, extending right up to the floor of the church above, and having on it only the Medici arms and one short Latin inscription of five words simply stating that "Piero has placed this to the memory of his father." This pillar is Cosimo's tomb; his own name does not appear on it at all; *that* is borne by the porphyry slab above, the whole being thus joined together in one monument. It was an honour never, then or afterwards, accorded to any one else in Florence; and thus is Cosimo after all in reality buried in front of the high altar of San Lorenzo.

An immense amount has been written on Cosimo's character, and as usual in the case of the Medici the most violently opposite views have been enunciated. Those with whom the name of Medici overthrows all balance can see in him no virtues. Thus even a comparatively temperate writer like Symonds (who is far surpassed by others on that side) calls Cosimo "a cynical, self-seeking *bourgeois* tyrant." But Symonds would have found it hard to substantiate his string of epithets out of the facts of Cosimo's life.[74] Other writers declare that every seeming virtue in Cosimo was assumed for some unworthy end. But there are many facts of Cosimo's life which decline to accord with this assertion. Nor had it been true could Marsilio Ficino have written:—"I owe to Plato much, to Cosimo no less; he realised for me the virtues of which Plato gave me the conception." Symonds and other writers accuse Cosimo of having undermined the liberties of Florence.[75] But the changes introduced by him into the form of the constitution were few and unimportant. The truth was that Florence, notwithstanding her republican forms, had never really possessed freedom, and that the people, wearied of perpetual dissensions, strife, banishments, and the losses which these entailed, welcomed the stable and efficient government which Cosimo gave them. Had it not been so, his rule, resting solely on popularity, would promptly have been ter-minated.

There was, however, in Florentine politics a Medicean party and an anti-Medicean party. And the latter put for-ward assertions (quite regardless of whether these had any solid basis) which in later times have formed the ground of unbalanced judgments and exaggerated statements which have been repeated by one writer after another as though they expressed the acknowledged verdict of history.

And at the hands of such writers Cosimo has fared ill indeed. His arduous labours for the welfare of the State and people have been declared due solely to personal ambition. The far-sighted statesmanship by which he managed to con-trol for so long a period the destinies of his country, and to guide her affairs with such success, has been declared to have been merely a crafty plan, pursued with the utmost dissimu-lation, to pave the way towards the destruction of the Re-public. Deeds of his done purely for the benefit of the people have been either dismissed as of little importance, or else attributed to "sinister motives." Lastly, even the title placed upon his tomb by his countrymen has been represented as "a mere empty compliment"; though compliments are seldom thought necessary when the person no longer survives to hear them.

All this, however, involves the assumption that an excep-tionally quick-witted race, specially on the watch against attempts to steal away their independence, should in this one instance, and throughout so long a period as thirty years, have displayed a want of discernment at variance with all their history.

Machiavelli's estimate of Cosimo is as follows:—

"He was one of the most prudent of men; grave and courteous and of venerable appearance. His early years were full of trouble, exile, and personal danger, but by the un-wearied generosity of his disposition he triumphed over all his enemies and made himself most popular with the people.

Though so rich, yet in his mode of living he was always very simple and without ostentation. None of his time had such an intimate knowledge of government and of State affairs. Hence even in a city so given to change, he retained the Government for thirty years."

"Unwearied generosity of disposition" exactly expresses the general idea which is given us by the facts of Cosimo's life as the most prominent feature of his character. And setting aside all testimony of writers on the one side or the other, the indisputable benefits which he conferred on his country, the end which he put to the faction-fighting which sapped Florence's strength, the prosperity and contentment which he secured for the people, the relief from taxation which he brought about by the effects of his enlightened foreign policy, and lastly, the general character associated with his memory in the minds of the common people of Tuscany, all go to refute the unbalanced judgments which have been referred to, and to corroborate those who have considered that the title engraved by his countrymen upon his tomb was justly deserved, and correctly sums up the leading features of his character and conduct.

CHAPTER V

THE MEDICI PALACE

BEFORE taking our next step in the history of the Medici let us look at the house in which they lived, and which is inseparably connected with Cosimo, its builder; for it is a notable one. For this is the cradle in which things which now form all the intellectual life of Europe were nursed and nourished in their infancy, and helped to grow.

The Medici in the course of their history occupied three successive palaces in Florence: the first, that which was occupied by Giovanni di Bicci,[1] connected with their rise; the second, this in the Via Larga, connected with all their greatest time in history; the third, that on the south side of the Arno (the Pitti Palace),[2] connected with their decline and end. But it is this second of the three, their home during all the time of their greatest achievements, which must ever have the chief attraction for those who study their history.

A world of interest gathers round this palace. It is interesting architecturally, as the first to be constructed of all the Renaissance palaces of Florence; it is interesting, historically, from the many important events with which it is associated; and, lastly, it is deeply interesting on account of its connection with Learning and Art.[3]

As regards its architectural interest, the first thing noticeable about it is its date (1430), and its extraordinary advance, in style, spaciousness, and general arrangements, beyond all palaces of like date in France, England, or Germany. We look at it when it has been standing four hundred and seventy-five years, and yet do not find it jar on us by any appearance of inferiority of style, or meanness of proportions. Thus we are apt to forget that it was built when the battle of Agincourt

had only been fought fifteen years, when the Wars of the
Roses had not yet begun, and when Henry VI was only eight
years old. But let it be compared with anything of the kind
elsewhere of the same date, and it will be realised how far in
advance this handsome, spacious, and commodious palace,
erected by the Medici for themselves in 1430, was beyond
even kings' palaces of that date in England, France, or
Germany.

It is built in three orders of architecture, the peculiar style
called "Rustica" on the ground floor, Doric on the second
storey, and Corinthian on the third. The "Rustica" style, with
its grand roughly-hewn stones, a style of construction which
afterwards became so fashionable, was first employed in the
building of this palace. We are told that Michelozzo adopted
it, "because it united an appearance of solidity and strength
with the light and shadow so essential to beauty under the
glare of an Italian sun." It was exceedingly expensive, and
was the principal cause of the new palace being spoken of as
"too grand for an ordinary citizen." The corner of the ground
floor towards the Via de' Gori [4] was originally an open *loggia*.
The windows of the upper storeys are divided by elegant little
columns, with, carved above them, Cosimo's own special device of the three feathers, and the arms of the Medici, the
palle (or balls).[5] On the corner of the palace is the celebrated
fanale, one of the most perfect specimens of the well-known
iron lamps made by Niccolò Caparra, and only permitted on
the palaces of the most distinguished citizens.[6] The solid
character of the ground floor is in accordance with the requirements of the time. In that age the home of an important family
had to be a fortress no less than a palace, and the ground
floor of a Florentine palace was built as solidly as the Bastile,
all decoration being reserved for the upper floors. The entrance
door of such palaces led, through an arched vestibule, into
an open *cortile* (or courtyard), round which the four sides of
the palace were built, with a fine marble staircase leading up
from the *cortile* to the handsome rooms on the first floor.

This palace was deliberately intended by Cosimo to be a
model of Renaissance architecture. It, of course, far surpassed
when built any of the other palaces at that time in Florence,
or in Italy. And it is remarkable that though it was the first
of the kind, and though it was succeeded by numerous others,
many of them of such excellence,[7] it still remains unsurpassed
by any of them; the worthy leader of all the great palaces of
Florence. Professor Banister Fletcher, in his *History of Architecture*, takes this palace as the best example of Renaissance
architecture as applied to palaces; while he also notes that it
gives us both the first and the finest example of two things in
particular, "the solid *rustica* masonry, and the bold and massive cornice (eight feet in height) which crowns the structure,
and considerably aids its impressive effect." [8]

Interesting, however, as this palace is architecturally, it is
still more so as the centre of so much history from the middle
of the fifteenth to the middle of the sixteenth century. This
was the home of the Medici during a hundred years, from
the time of Cosimo Pater Patriae until in 1539 Cosimo I (the
first Grand Duke) moved to the Palazzo Vecchio preparatory
to occupying the new and larger palace which he constructed
on the other side of the Arno.[9] It was thus their home throughout all their greatest time. Here have been entertained emperors, popes, kings, princes, and most of the distinguished
men of that period. Here Cosimo Pater Patriae passed his
strenuous years so full of varied labours; here Lorenzo the
Magnificent gathered round him his brilliant intellectual
coterie; here the future Pope Leo X was brought up; here his
cousin, afterwards Pope Clement VII, devised his deep-laid
schemes for the advancement of the family; here Catherine
de' Medici was born, and lived as a girl. And here nearly all
the most prominent events in Florence's history during her
most important period have taken place.[10] Not many palaces
in Europe have given hospitality to so many notable persons
as have passed through the entrance doorway of this home of
the Medici. Migliore says that owing to the number and high

rank of those entertained there, the Medici Palace was called "the Hotel of the Princes of the whole world." [11] It is now known as the Riccardi Palace, having been, long subsequently, bought from the State by that family; but now that it has again passed into the possession of the State it might well be called by its own name.[12] Though now so little thought of, it is one of the most important buildings in Florence, and should have that importance duly marked.

Greater still, however, is the interest attaching to this palace from the point of view of Learning and Art. The inscription which it still bears [13] designates it as "the nurse of all learning"; and justly so, for it was here that the ancient learning of Greece and Rome was called back to life, and it was from hence that the "New Learning" went forth to change the face of Europe. Entering by the central doorway, and passing through the arched vestibule, one finds oneself in the *cortile*.[14] This court was once adorned with various celebrated statues, among them Donatello's bronze statue of *David* which worked so important an effect in the world of Art; while we still see over the arches his medallions. And here, all round under the arcades, are classical busts, inscriptions, and sarcophagi,[15] recalling the time when the enthusiasm for the ancient learning burnt so strongly here; that time when Marsilio Ficino, the great scholar whom Cosimo treated almost as a son, kept a lamp burning before the bust of Plato as before an altar.

Here also Art was reverenced and encouraged to a scarcely less degree than Learning. The number of objects of art which the Medici collected round them in this palace was extraordinary. A glimpse of it is given us in the remark made by the Duke of Milan in 1471 that he had not seen in all Italy so many objects of art as he saw in this palace.[16] Yet this was before Lorenzo the Magnificent added thereto all the immense collection made by him during his twenty-three years' rule, by which he at least doubled all that had been collected by his father and grandfather. The whole of this great accumulation of art treasures was lost when the palace was sacked by the mob in 1494;[17] while the same plundering of all the art treasures collected in the meantime happened again in 1527.[18] It shows, therefore, what profuse art collectors the Medici were when we find that though all was thus twice over swept away the galleries and museums of Florence still contain paintings, statues, bronzes, gems, and other objects of art, almost all of them collected by the Medici, sufficient to surpass any other collection of such things in Europe.

This passion for collecting objects of art on the most lavish scale was permanent in this family through all changes, and from their rise right down to their end; no differences of character seemed to make any difference in this; and whether they were public-minded statesmen like Cosimo Pater Patriae, or luxurious Popes like Leo X, or iron-handed tyrants like Cosimo I, or incapable occupiers of a tottering throne like the last two Grand Dukes, there is not one of them in the whole three hundred and forty-three years of their course who does not show this strong family characteristic.

In the now deserted court of the palace of the Medici there is to be seen a long Latin inscription which runs as follows. After calling on the traveller to pause and note that this was once the celebrated house of the Medici (*Mediceas olim aedes*), and that here a long list of emperors, kings, popes, and other exalted personages have been entertained, it continues thus:—

"TRAVELLER."

"Once the house of the Medici. In which not alone so many great men, but Knowledge herself had her home. The house which was the nurse of all learning; which here revived again. Renowned also for its cultured magnificence a treasury of antiquity and the arts."

The homes of departed glory are few over which a prouder epitaph could be placed.

And it is in this connection that we may trace the origin of that unique appreciation of Art which the Medici as a family possessed; that second sphere in which they were as notable, though in a different way, as they were in regard to Learning. For they give us an example on a wide scale of the connection between these two things.

All who feel the spirit of Art know that technical excellence is not the chief thing: that there must also be the expression of some thought, some creation of the artist's brain. We see that pictures or statues which lack this, and rely solely on excellence of technique, though they may gain a certain degree of eminence, never obtain the highest and most lasting fame. Hence it is that it has been said of technical criticism that it "can only show us the things that are of minor consequence."

If, then, the real value of a picture lies in the thoughts that it expresses, it is evident that the more knowledge we possess, the more likely we are to be able to read those thoughts and so to appreciate the picture. And this, true everywhere, is doubly so in the case of the great masters of the classic age of Painting, who were many-sided men, learned in many subjects. Ruskin, after long study of an important fresco picture by one of these masters, remarked that he stood amazed at the mass of varied knowledge, in history, science, theology, and other subjects, displayed by the artist; and that, as he realised how much it surpassed his own knowledge on the subjects concerned, and marked that this mass of knowledge on the part of the artist was joined also to perfect drawing and colouring, he felt that he "stood indeed in the presence of a master."

Every picture, in fact (except those belonging to the time of Art's decadence), has *something to say*. Lord Lindsay calls the efforts of the earliest masters, "The burning messages of prophecy uttered by the stammering lips of infants." [19] And whether the execution be crude or not, the true pleasure in Art lies in looking through and beyond it, and deciphering that "burning message," if such be there. Art, therefore, is a universal language; and one in which the artist opens to us a world of high and deep thoughts of which we had before no conception.[20] Thus Learning and Art go hand in hand. For without Learning Art has nothing to say. And Art that has nothing to say will never long hold the attention of mankind.

As, then, we stand in the deserted court of the palace which was "the nurse of all Learning," we can understand how natural it was that the learning of the Medici should lead them to become the greatest patrons of Art that the world has ever seen.

CHAPTER VI

Born 1416. (*Ruled* 1464-1469.) *Died* 1469

PIERO IL GOTTOSO has failed to receive from history the notice that he deserves. He is generally passed over by historians either with no mention at all, or else with merely a few disparaging remarks referring to his physical infirmities. It will be seen, however, that his history and character merit no little attention.

Upon the death of his father, Cosimo Pater Patriae, Piero, then forty-eight years old, succeeded to the headship of the family, and the rule of Florence. From his very boyhood he had been afflicted with gout, and was early in life given the name of "Il Gottoso" (the gouty), by which he is always known. His constant ill health handicapped him greatly throughout life, often making him unable for long periods to take any active part in public affairs, and forcing him instead to devote himself to the retired life of the scholar, while his younger brother, Giovanni, was practically given his place, became his father's favourite, and was looked upon by all as the future head of the family. And the first indication that we get of Piero's character is the fact that we never hear, during all the thirty years that he had to bear this, of any sign of resentment on his part, either towards his father or brother, on this account. Yet he possessed a full measure of the ability of the Medici family, as he both then and afterwards showed. For not only was he recognised as a powerful scholar, but also we find him sent on several occasions during Cosimo's lifetime on various embassies to Venice, to Milan, and to France, and highly thought of by those to whom he was thus sent; and none were more acute judges of character and ability than Doge Francesco Foscari, Duke Francesco Sforza of Milan, and King Louis XI of France. Moreover, in connection with these embassies the character and ability of Piero il Gottoso have received a very unique testimony, one borne to this day by the Medici coat-of-arms. For so high an opinion did Louis XI form of Piero's abilities that he conferred on him, on his becoming head of the family, the very special honour of permission to stamp the lilies of France on one of the balls of the Medici arms, that ball being coloured blue for this purpose. And from this time forward the Medici arms have one blue ball with the French lily (quite different in shape from the Florentine lily [1]) upon it; which thus remains a permanent record of the high estimation gained, in a country outside his own, by Piero il Gottoso.

We do not find that his constant ill health soured Piero's disposition; in every act of his life he showed a disposition the reverse of an ill-tempered one, even though his conduct of business and public affairs had more often than not to be performed from a sick man's couch; while various writers mention that one of his special characteristics was an intense hatred of all quarrels.

But there is a third indication of his character which is more striking. In his case alone we have none of that conflict of opinion among rival historians, giving the most opposite views of character and motives, which has been alluded to as so common throughout the history of this family. Even those most bitterly biassed against the whole race of Medici have nothing to say against Piero il Gottoso; he is the one solitary head of this family throughout their whole history in whose case this feature is absent.

Before considering his history it is necessary to note exactly what was the position to which on his father's death he succeeded. One necessarily speaks of it as the rule over the State, but that term is liable to mislead unless we bear in mind the peculiar position. It must not be forgotten that the governing body was the Signoria, with its president, the Gonfaloniere. Piero was not one of this body, and therefore had, theoretically, no official position. But it had gradually come about, as a consequence of the influence which Cosimo had so long wielded, that every measure passed by the Signoria must be agreed to by the head of the Medici family before it could be carried into effect. Thus the head of the Medici family, though, theoretically, no more than a simple citizen of the Republic, did in actual fact bear the rule over the State, and wielded almost complete authority. But it must be remembered that the continuance of that position rested solely on two conditions—a constantly maintained demonstration by the person in question of an ability greater than that of his fellow-citizens, and a no less constantly maintained popularity. Let either of these factors fail to continue, and the position at once reverted to the theoretical one, wherein the head of the Medici family was only an ordinary citizen, and as liable as any other to be exiled by the Signoria.

When Piero's brother Giovanni died, Cosimo, seeing that Piero's frail life might terminate any day, had advanced the latter's elder son, Lorenzo, giving him practice in every way possible in public affairs, though he was only fourteen. But Lorenzo had only reached the age of fifteen when his grandfather died. He was, however, capable beyond his years; the greatest attention had from the very first been paid by Piero to the education of his two sons; Landino wrote a whole treatise on the education of the two young Medici; and Piero, as soon as Lorenzo was old enough, had appointed Marsilio Ficino (the celebrated head of the Platonic Academy) to be his tutor. When, therefore, Piero became head of the family, he continued the course which Cosimo had begun to adopt, and while he retained foreign affairs in his own hands, left home politics largely in the hands of his capable young son.

For thirty years there had been no further attempts to oust the Medici from that position of power in Florence to which they had attained. Now, however, the attempt was again to be made to get rid of them. A large party of all those jealous of the position this family had come to occupy, saw in the feeble health of Piero and the extreme youth of his eldest son an opportunity for effecting this, and began to stir up a movement against the Medici which was headed by Luca Pitti, assisted by such prominent men as Agnolo Acciajoli, Niccolò Soderini, and even Dietisalvi Neroni, who had been Cosimo's most trusted adviser, and on whom he had specially advised Piero to lean. And since those concerned knew that, owing to the popularity of the Medici, the lower classes of the people would not permit any regular process for their exile, the above movement soon grew into plans for a formidable rebellion by force of arms. The objects which the conspirators set before themselves were the death of Piero and the banishment of the family. The plots for this were being carried on all through 1465 and the first half of 1466.[2] Piero appears to have known that something was going on, but with his habitual dislike of intrigues and quarrels chose to ignore it, and was apparently right in feeling that if it came to a head he had in himself the abilities to defeat it. He knew Luca Pitti's character as a vain but incapable man, and that the others relied too much on the results of his own bad health. Also for some time the conspirators could not agree as to their plan of action. So that for the first two years of Piero's rule no overt action took place.

Meanwhile, the chief events in other states were as follows:—

Pope Pius II died in the same month as Cosimo Pater Patriae, and was succeeded by Paul II.

In France Louis XI was introducing a new era. Cold, measured, crafty, and detestable for his many murders and cruelties, especially for the way in which he in many cases lured his victims to their deaths by treachery, he had gained the name of "the universal spider." At the same time he worked an immense change in France which was for her ultimate benefit. He destroyed the power of the nobles, gradually murdering them in turn until he left none who could be formidable, and quenched all elements of independence; but he converted chaos into order, made France into a strong and prosperous kingdom, and was the founder of her absolute monarchy. During the first six years of his reign (1461-1467) he was occupied in the above struggle, until by the end of this period he had for the time crushed the power of the nobles in France.

In 1466 Francesco Sforza, Duke of Milan, died. Ever since he had gained his throne by Cosimo's assistance he had been a firm friend of the Medici, and the death of this strong ally tended to weaken Piero's position, both as regards foreign affairs and in his own state, as Francesco's son and successor, Galeazzo Sforza, was not so strong a character, nor so surely to be relied upon.

In August 1466 the conspiracy which had been hatching for two years to take Piero's life and destroy the Medici came to a head. The party headed by Luca Pitti assembled their forces in arms a few miles from Florence, and laid plans for seizing Piero, who was lying seriously ill at Careggi. At the same time a force from Ferrara, under Ercole d'Este, Duke Borso's brother, advanced to the frontier to assist them. But the conspirators were completely mistaken in their man; for Piero displayed a resolution and energy extraordinary in one handicapped as he was by severe illness. Getting into a litter, he at once started for Florence; but on the way he had a narrow escape. On this occasion his young son Lorenzo, then seventeen, displayed great coolness in danger, and resource; whereby he saved his father's life. Riding on ahead, he heard of an armed party who were lying in wait for Piero on the ordinary road; with much adroitness he managed to keep their attention occupied while he sent back word to the party who were escorting his father, and caused him to be conveyed by a different route to Florence in safety. Arrived at the Medici Palace, Piero at once set about collecting his adherents, sent to beg the assistance of some Milanese troops who happened to be near the borders of Tuscany, and had soon collected a larger force than his opponents. He marched against them; the conspirators, divided by the vacillations of Luca Pitti and their own dissensions, and confused by Piero's promptness, were unable to fight; their force melted away and dispersed, and the leaders surrendered.[3] A new Signoria just elected promptly passed a sentence of death upon the ringleaders, Luca Pitti, Dietisalvi Neroni, Niccolò Soderini, and Agnolo Acciajuoli; and certainly never did men more deserve it, especially Neroni, who had throughout acted with the basest ingratitude, treachery, and dissimulation.

And now Piero displayed the best side of his character. He utterly refused to have these men put to death, though it certainly would have been to his advantage not to interfere on their behalf, for two of them, Neroni and Soderini, only used their pardon and liberty to stir up Venice to make war upon him. He pardoned Luca Pitti outright, and by his treatment of him converted him into a friend for life; while the others were simply ordered to quit Florence, Machiavelli says:—"It was due to him (Piero) that his partisans did not stain their hands in the blood of their fellow-citizens."

Thus did Piero put down a formidable rebellion without any bloodshed. And this is probably the only instance in those ages of an armed rebellion which aimed at the death of the ruler being suppressed by him *without the loss of a single life:* and even with the conversion of its principal leader into a permanent friend. This one achievement of Piero il Gottoso is sufficient to demonstrate both his ability and the high qualities of his character, and marks him out as one really fit to rule a State. We are told that when Luca Pitti's rebellion

was thus suppressed, the young Lorenzo, commenting to a
friend on his father's action, said: "He only knows how to
conquer who knows how to forgive."

It was conduct and qualities such as this, displayed by the
earlier generations of the Medici, which helped to raise that
family to its high eminence in Florence. And when, sixty years
after this, Clarice de' Medici (become by marriage Clarice
Strozzi) in her impassioned harangue [4] contrasted the behaviour of her ancestors with that of those then representing
the family, and said that it was by magnanimity and clemency
that the former had gained the favour of the Florentines, she
said no more than the actual truth.

The natural effect of the defeat of such a formidable effort
to destroy the family, and especially when so complete a
victory was accompanied by such clemency and kindliness,
was to make the Medici stronger than ever in their peculiar
position in Florence. After this affair their popularity with
the people caused the head of the family to become more than
ever "a king in all but the name."

The above episode was followed in the next year (1467) by
war with Venice. Ever since Cosimo's alliance with Milan,
Venice had waited for an opportunity of revenge upon the
Medici, and this seemed now to have come. Niccolò Soderini
and Dietisalvi Neroni requited Piero for saving their lives by
proceeding to Venice, and persuading the Doge and Council
to attack him, asserting that there was a large party in
Florence ready to take up arms against the Medici. The
Venetian army, therefore, commanded by the celebrated Bartolommeo Colleoni, was in May 1467 despatched against
Florence's territory. Piero's conduct, however, had entirely
won over those who had previously been ready to attack the
Medici, so that the supposed adherents of Venice in Florence
proved non-existent. Piero was also successful in obtaining
as his allies both the Duke of Milan and the King of Naples,
each of whom sent him some troops. The Florentine army

opposed that of Venice in the little state of Imola, where at length a battle was fought in which the Venetian army was defeated. After which, in April 1468, a peace was concluded, as the result of which Florence gained a much coveted addition to her territory, viz., the town of Sarzana and the fortress of Sarzanello. This was followed in August of the same year by a short but very successful campaign, in which Florence, assisted by Naples and Urbino, opposed the Pope and prevented him from seizing upon the small state of Rimini. By these successes Piero still further strengthened the position of his family in Florence.

These various troubles having been overcome, the year 1469, the last year of Piero's life, was one of peace and festivities. His son Lorenzo was now nineteen, and his second son Giuliano fifteen, and in February 1469 these two young Medici organised a splendid tournament which they intended should be the inauguration of a lighter and more festive life than the somewhat sombre one which their father's ill health and the political troubles of the last few years had made customary. It was held in order to celebrate Lorenzo's betrothal to Clarice Orsini, the Roman bride who had been selected for him by his mother, Lucrezia Tornabuoni, whose letters from Rome to her husband Piero describing the young lady's appearance are still preserved. Clarice Orsini, at this time sixteen, also writes letters to Lorenzo conveying various polite greetings; while she complains to a friend that "Lorenzo is so greatly occupied with this jousting" that he does not find time to write to her often enough. By her anxiety and depression for several days "on account of the tilting," and her relief when she heard it was over without mishap to Lorenzo, we are reminded that a tournament was not merely a splendid show, but that wounds and death were always possible in the course of it.[5] It is evident that Clarice's abilities were not of a very high order, and that her education fell considerably below that customary in the family she was about to enter which she considered so far beneath her own. Even Lucrezia Tornabuoni, while praising the appearance of the girl she had chosen for her son, says that she "is not to be compared with Maria, Lucrezia, and Bianca" (her own daughters).

This tournament, which so fully engaged the young Lorenzo's attention, provided Florence with a more gorgeous spectacle than the city had ever before witnessed, and was the first of those great pageants for which Lorenzo's age afterwards became famous. It was immortalised in one of the two most celebrated poems of the fifteenth century, *La Giostra di Lorenzo de' Medici*,[6] by Luca Pulci. Standing in the Piazza Sta. Croce, where (as a substitute for the fierce battles between the citizens of former days) this exciting scene of mimic warfare took place, how vividly does its fantastic splendour, voluminously described in the writings of the time, rise before our eyes:—the reigning beauty of Florentine society, Lucrezia Donati, who was "Queen of the tournament"; the young scions of the Medici, Pazzi, Pucci, Benci, Rucellai, Vespucci, and other principal families, who were the knights, each knight accompanied by his standard-bearer, heralds, trumpeters, pages, and men-at-arms, all wearing his colours, and arrayed in the most splendid fashion;[7] the extravagant *punctilio;* the grandiloquent compliments; the delight of the vast crowd occupying every roof, balcony, window, and other point of vantage round the piazza; and all lit up by Florentine sunshine in February. The knights first appeared in most magnificent dresses for an imposing procession round the piazza accompanied by every sort of display; after which they changed into their armour for the actual combat. We may gather some idea of the dresses from the description of that of Lorenzo. He "had a diamond in the centre of his shield, and rubies and diamonds in his cap; a velvet surcoat, with a cape of white silk edged with red; and a silk scarf embroidered with roses and pearls. For the actual combat he wore another surcoat of velvet fringed with gold, with a helmet adorned with three blue feathers. His horse was draped with red and white velvet, embroidered with pearls." [8] The device on his standard was a bay tree, one half dry and dead-looking, and the other half green, with the motto (worked in pearls), *Le temps revient*, symbolising that a time of youth and joy, after the winter of Cosimo's old age and Piero's ill health, was now to supervene. The occasion was considered of sufficient importance for the King of Naples and the Dukes of Ferrara and Milan to present Lorenzo with horses and armour for it. Lorenzo, in his own writings, mentions this tournament, and says:—

"In order to do as others I appointed a tournament in the Piazza Sta. Croce, with great splendour and at great expense, so that it cost me about 10,000 gold florins.[9] Although I was young, and of no great skill, the first prize was awarded to me, namely, a helmet inlaid with silver and surmounted with a figure of Mars."

Giuliano also, though as yet too young to take so prominent a part as his brother, was splendidly arrayed, and this handsome boy of fifteen, in helmet and armour, and mounted on a fine charger, won the admiration of all. Several busts of him in his armour and wearing the dragon-shaped helmet designed for him by Verrocchio, were executed; and it seems most probable that the terra-cotta bust by Antonio Pollajuolo,[10] now in the museum of the Bargello, and catalogued as an unknown portrait bust, is in reality one of these busts of Giuliano. Miss Cruttwell, in her work on Antonio Pollajuolo, considers that it was executed at about this date, and says:—"It is probably a portrait of one of the Medici, whose type of face and arrogant bearing it resembles closely." Giuliano is known to have specially patronised Pollajuolo, and in the inventory of the collections in the Medici Palace other works by that artist are recorded as being all in Giuliano's room in the palace. Again there was no other youth of the same age at this period in Florence whose bust in this style would have been likely to be executed by Pollajuolo.[11]

But above all it has the well-known lock of hair on the fore-head which was so distinguishing a feature of Giuliano's face, and is often mentioned.[12] So that altogether there seems little doubt that we have in this bust of Pollajuolo's a portrait of Giuliano as he was at fifteen. The bust has been greatly dam-aged,[13] the arms being broken off, as well as the dragon-shaped helmet, leaving only one of the legs of the dragon at one side of the head. But the face, with its "charming boyish frankness," is uninjured, and as Miss Cruttwell says, "seems to fill the room with its buoyant, vivacious life." [14] The details of the armour, representing Hercules fighting with the serpents and with the Stymphalian bird, are as ad-mirably executed as the portrait itself.

In the following June the marriage of Lorenzo to Clarice Orsini took place. On this occasion of the marriage of their eldest son Piero and his wife Lucrezia gave a magnificent entertainment to all Florence. It was a marriage which gave evidence of how the Medici were advancing in worldly es-teem, for the Orsini were one of the greatest families in Italy. But whether the Medici would not have done better for themselves if they had adhered to those Florentine marriages such as they had hitherto made, and which had produced a Cosimo Pater Patriae, a Piero il Gottoso, and a Lorenzo the Magnificent, may well be doubted, looking at the subsequent history.[15] The marriage took place on the 4th June in the family church of San Lorenzo, and the festivities in con-nection with it were on the most profuse scale, the entire city being feasted by the Medici for three successive days. "Feasting dancing, and music continued day and night, until one wonders at the endurance of the people. Some idea of the extravagance of the entertainment may be gathered from such a fact as that there were consumed of sweetmeats alone 5,000 pounds." [16] While the populace were thus regaled all Florentine society was entertained at five immense ban-quets in the Medici Palace.

"At these banquets the loggias and gardens of the palace in the Via Larga were filled to overflowing, separate tables being set out for the young ladies who were the bride's companions,—'fifty young women with whom to dance,' say the records—and for the older ladies forming Madonna Lucrezia's company. In the same way there were different tables for 'the young men who danced,' and for those of maturer years. The feasting began on the Sunday morning, when the bride—mounted upon the splendid charger presented to Lorenzo by the King of Naples—left the house of the Alessandri in the Borgo San Piero (now Borgo degli Albizzi), and entered her new home followed by a train of nobles, the symbolic olive branch [17] being hoisted at the window to the accompaniment of gay music; and the festivities continued until the Tuesday morning, when she went to hear mass at the church of San Lorenzo, bearing in her hand one of the thousand wedding gifts, 'a little book of Our Lady, most marvellous, written in letters of gold upon blue paper, and with a cover of crystal and silver work.'" [18]

But the chief interest of the five years' rule of Piero il Gottoso centres in his prominent connection with the art of the period. He had had greater leisure to pursue the family tastes for Learning and Art than would have been the case had he had better health; and being passionately fond of both, they had for thirty years been the chief interest of his life. A thorough scholar, he was as eager in the collection of rare manuscript books as his father, and made many valuable additions to the Medici Library. Still more important was the unremitting assistance which he gave to Art. Nearly every work of art which remains in Florence belonging to Piero's time was executed either for him or at his instigation, including the one solitary work which the Medici Palace still retains, the frescoes round the walls of the chapel.

In 1466 the great sculptor Donatello died, at the age of eighty-one. In accordance with his dying request to be laid close to his life-long friend and patron Cosimo Pater Patriae, he was buried, at the expense of the Medici family, in the

crypt of San Lorenzo alongside the tomb of Cosimo, almost
the whole city, with every architect, sculptor, and painter
in Florence, following his funeral. He was the last of those
who had assisted at the outburst in Art at the beginning of
the century: Masaccio, Brunelleschi, Ghiberti, and Fra Angelico had all passed away; and besides Lippi, who had left
Florence and died three years after Donatello, the foremost
men in Art now were Luca della Robbia, Leon Battista Alberti, Piero della Francesca, and Benozzo Gozzoli; while
another young painter, Sandro Botticelli, was just coming
forward.

Luca della Robbia is another of those who struck out a
special line in Art entirely his own. His chief work in marble,
the *Cantoria,* and his other works in marble and bronze, have
already been noticed. But the works which have given him
his special fame are the beautiful bas-reliefs executed by
him in glazed terra-cotta (generally white, with a blue background), a method which he gradually perfected and made
his own.

Luca della Robbia's object in adopting this method was
the invention of a form of art which could be employed for
the decoration of churches and other buildings where marble
bas-reliefs from their costliness were impossible. It is believed that the sight of some ancient Greek enamelled ware
gave Luca della Robbia the idea of using the same method
for sculptures in relief. But, however that may be, his actual
discovery, made after profound studies in chemistry and
innumerable experiments, consisted in covering the clay
model with an enamel which is thought to have consisted of
the ingredients of glass mixed with oxide of tin. The exact
method was kept as a family secret.

But the particular method in which Luca della Robbia's
conceptions were given permanence is of far less importance
than the works themselves. As the Marchesa Burlamacchi
says.—

"The joy of life, the sadness of life, the grief of the Madonna, the innocence of childhood, the love of mother for child and of child for mother, the great central lessons of the Redemption, angelic sympathy, all these Luca della Robbia has depicted with a perfection which no other artist has ever surpassed." [19]

His date also is an important item in our appreciation of his genius. Looking at his works one can scarcely realise that he was born in the same year as Masaccio, and long before all that great army of painters who followed in the latter half of the fifteenth century. Yet it is not too much to say that for beauty of expression in the faces of his Madonnas, of his angels, and of his children (including the representations of the Child Christ), it is not until we reach Raphael, born eighty years after him, that we find a painter able to equal him in these respects, while even Raphael does not in these points surpass him. Regarding his relief of the Madonna and Child, with two angels, in a curved lunette (now in the museum of the Bargello), Mr. Allan Marquand, after remarking that there is much of Raphael's manner in the bearing of the Madonna, draws attention to her eyes, and says:— "Luca's ideal of the Madonna was evidently a woman with blue eyes, while to the Child Christ he gives hazel eyes." And in the relief of the Madonna and Child in the Foundling Hospital (in which the Child holds a scroll with the words, "*Ego sum lux mundi*," and the Madonna's hand rests on the inscription, "*Quia respexit Dominus humilitatem ancille suæ*"), Mr. Marquand draws attention to "the eyes marked in lilac, the hairy eyebrows, lilac upper eyelashes and pupils, and a light shade of lilac in place of the usual greyish blue for the iris of the eye." In the relief of the Madonna and Child, with three cherub heads, in an arched niche (now in the museum of the Bargello), the heads of the cherubs are specially beautiful; while his altar-piece in the church of the Impruneta, near Florence, is considered to contain one of the most beautiful figures of St. John the Baptist ever executed.

Luca della Robbia lived to the age of eighty-one, dying in 1482.

Leon Battista Alberti was one of those men of varied genius which the Renaissance so often produced. Nominally he was an architect, and also a painter, but really and chiefly an authority on Art in all its branches. He occupies a similar position in his age to that occupied by Leonardo da Vinci fifty years later, and it was as a universally accepted authority on Art in general, and not for any works of his own, that Alberti gained his fame. Vasari, in speaking of him, enlarges on how necessary learning is to an artist, and speaks of the great aid which Alberti gave to Art by his writings, saying that "such is the force of his writings that he exercised far greater influence by them over Art than many who surpassed him by their works." Alberti was exceedingly versatile; he studied architecture, painting, perspective, sculpture, and Latin; he wrote two treatises on painting, one on architecture, and one on sculpture; he invented a celebrated perspective glass; and Vasari says "was expert in all physical exercises, and in all the accomplishments of a gentleman." Alberti was a Florentine; but he belonged to the party of the *fuori usciti,* or permanent exiles, and spent very little of his life in Florence. He died in Rome in 1472, at the age of sixty-seven.

Piero della Francesca, though he worked first at Florence and learnt his art there, especially studying Masaccio's frescoes, did not belong to Florence itself, but to the small town of Borgo San Sepolcro, which had become part of Florence's territory in 1441.. His great work for Art was the final discovery of the true laws of perspective, that subject on which so many brains in the world of Art had long been busy, and which was the last of the secrets of the technique of Painting

to be discovered. In this achievement he must be coupled to
some extent with Paolo Uccello, and with Alberti; and he
really took up and carried on Alberti's ideas. It was arrived
at by being worked out from a mathematical basis, and not
from any of the empirical methods which had been tried by
many artists in succession. Piero della Francesca's chief work
was his *Treatise on Perspective*, dedicated to the Duke of
Urbino. The most pleasing of his pictures, the altar-piece
now in the Pinacoteca at Perugia, has a long colonnade in
perfect perspective.

Piero della Francesca is also notable for two other things:
we have in his fresco paintings at Arezzo the first real endeavour to paint historical pictures; and in his portraits of
the Duke and Duchess of Urbino (now in the Uffizi Gallery) we have the first regular portraits. In 1469 Piero della
Francesca, then sixty-three, was invited to Urbino by the
Duke in order to paint them. Duke Federigo's is painted
showing the left side of the face in order to conceal the loss
of his right eye, which, together with his broken nose, was
caused by a severe wound received in a tournament. The
likeness, judged by those on coins, is admirable, as also the
perspective of the landscape in the distance. These two valuable portraits hung in the palace at Urbino as long as there
were any Dukes of Urbino. When in 1634 Vittoria della
Rovere,[20] the sole heiress of the last Duke of Urbino, was
married to her first cousin, Ferdinand II, she brought as a
part of her property these portraits of her ancestor and ancestress, thus bringing them into the art collections of the
Medici family. Piero della Francesca died in 1492, at the
age of eighty-six.

Benozzo Gozzoli, pupil of Fra Angelico, is the great illustrative painter of his time. As the teller of a story he is unrivalled. He was a most rapid and indefatigable worker, covering huge spaces with his beautifully executed frescoes in
a wonderfully short time. Thus he has left a mass of paint-

ings which are very valuable historically, bringing vividly before us the manners of the time of the earlier Medici.

Like so many others, Gozzoli began as a worker on the bronze doors under Ghiberti. After a time he began to learn painting under Fra Angelico, working as his assistant at Florence and Rome until 1447, when he first began to paint alone.[21] His three chief works are:—

(i) His frescoes in the church of San Agostino at San Gimignano; a great cycle of frescoes representing the life of St. Augustine from his boyhood to his death, in seventeen scenes. This huge work took even Gozzoli four years.

(ii) His frescoes in the chapel of the Medici Palace at Florence, which are considered his masterpiece (*see* chap. vii).

(iii) His frescoes in the Campo Santo at Pisa. This was a gigantic work. It occupied Gozzoli fifteen years, and was nothing less than covering with his paintings the whole of the north wall of the Campo Santo—"a task," says Vasari, "immense enough to discourage a whole legion of masters." The scenes represent the whole of the Old Testament history from the time of Noah to that of Solomon, in twenty-three scenes. Gozzoli has introduced into these forest scenery, scenes of the vintage in Tuscany, and much that is interesting in the life of the people; also portraits of many prominent men of the time, members of the Medici family, scholars, painters, and other celebrated men. The execution, however, is very uneven, and he was evidently then getting old. He died at Pisa in 1497, and is buried in the Campo Santo he had beautified.

But besides the foregoing, another young painter, Sandro Botticelli,[22] was at this time beginning to come forward. Botticelli is *par excellence* the painter of the time of Lorenzo the Magnificent, but his first period belongs to that of Piero il Gottoso. One of his prominent characteristics is that, being of an unusually receptive nature, he reflects to a singular degree the prevailing mental atmosphere around him; so much so that when the spirit of the time changes, the spirit and character of his pictures change with it. As a consequence, Botticelli's painting may be divided into four distinct periods, with different styles, due to events which caused marked changes in the life of Florence. These four periods are:—

> (I) The period of the rule of Piero il Gottoso—1464-1469.
> (II) The period of the rule of Lorenzo the Magnificent—1469-1492.
> (III) The time of Savonarola's dominance in Florence—1494-1498.
> (IV) The portion of Botticelli's life after Savonarola's death—1498-1510.

Owing to the close connection which his pictures usually have with the events of the time, there is less difficulty than with other painters in determining their date.

(I)

Very shortly after he became head of the family in 1464, Piero began to employ Sandro Botticelli, then a young painter of twenty, in whom he recognised great talent. And the modern world which values Botticelli so highly owes gratitude to Piero il Gottoso for the generous help and encouragement by which he enabled the friendless youth to succeed as he did.[23] Nor was Piero il Gottoso alone in this: his highly-cultured wife, Lucrezia Tornabuoni, was at least as much concerned in the matter as her husband; and in the pictures of Botticelli's first period (when he was between twenty and twenty-five), her influence is clearly traceable. By this talented pair of patrons, Botticelli, only five years older than their eldest son, was taken into the Casa Medici, made almost like a son of the house, and kept continually

occupied in painting pictures for which they gave him liberal remuneration. And Botticelli throughout his life cherished a deep devotion towards Piero il Gottoso and his wife
Lucrezia for the help, affection, and encouragement which
he had received from them in his earliest years.

As regards technique, the chief point for which Botticelli
is always praised is his beauty of line in drawing. His love
of life, dancing movement, and waving drapery is very apparent. Ruskin says:—

"He often appears affected, but would not have been in
accord with the spirit of the time if he had not been slightly
affected; much studied grace of manner, much formal assertion of scholarship, were a part of the spirit of the time."

But he was gifted with another power greater than his
technique. Botticelli was permeated with that spirit which
Donatello had taught as the ultimate aim and highest glory
of Art.[24] Beginning to paint just two years before Donatello
died, Botticelli carried on the latter's message to the world
of Art. He is able, if his subject is a religious one, to make a
single picture convey a whole sermon; [25] if his subject is a
classical myth, to make a single picture bring before our
minds the whole spirit of a period; [26] if his subject is historical, to cause a single picture to relate the entire history
of a long episode. Possessed of such a power, he is naturally
very fond of allegorical treatment, and the suggestion of a
whole train of thought (often giving the entire meaning of
his picture) by some comparatively small detail. Hence, while
his poetry of imagination, his human sympathy, religious
spirit, and beautiful technique cannot but appeal to all, a
mere rapid glance at his pictures will fail to reveal their
depth of thought; while many of his most important pictures
will not be understood at all without a full knowledge of
the history of the period.

All the principal pictures of Botticelli's first period were
painted for Piero il Gottoso.[27] Referring to those which still

remain at Florence, we have four principal pictures belonging to this period, the *Judith*, the *Madonna of the Magnificat*, the *Adoration of the Magi*, and the *Fortitude*, all of them now in the Uffizi Gallery.

Regarding the charming little picture of *Judith* it is remarked by Ruskin that among all the many pictures on this favourite subject this one by Botticelli is the only one that is true to Judith, and that this will be seen if the Book of Judith is studied. His reasons for this opinion, and his remarks on this picture generally are well worth studying.[28]

In the *Madonna of the Magnificat* we have a picture [29] painted for Piero il Gottoso about the year 1465. The influence of Lucrezia Tornabuoni, the deeply religious poetess, is specially apparent in this case; her spirit breathes throughout the picture, which is like a representation in painting of her poems. It is sometimes called the *Humilitas*, in allusion both to the expression on the Madonna's face as she writes her song of praise, and to the fact that the finger of the Child rests on that word in her song. The left hands of both Child and Mother rest together on a bitten pomegranate, the emblem of the Fall.[30] It has been said of this picture that it "expresses a depth of divine tenderness and a deep spiritual feeling such as no other painter, not even Raphael, has reached.[31] It differs in one notable respect from the many other pictures on the subject of the Madonna and Child which Botticelli painted in his third period, namely, in its keynote. For while the keynote of this picture is humility, that of all those of his third period is foreboding sorrow.

This picture was painted for Piero and his wife Lucrezia at the time when their two sons, Lorenzo and Giuliano, were boys of about sixteen and twelve respectively, *i.e.* the year 1465 or 1466. They are the two boys introduced into the picture as angels who are kneeling before the Madonna and Child, and holding the inkstand and the book in which the Blessed Virgin is writing her song, while a third angel bends over them protectingly, resting one hand on the shoulder of

each. Giuliano is the one facing the spectator, with the lock
of hair on his forehead; Lorenzo's naturally darker complexion has been intensified in order to throw all the light
on Giuliano, the favourite younger son of the mother for
whom the picture was painted.

The third picture, the *Adoration of the Magi,* has been
given a name which is somewhat misleading, as it is of course
a *family group picture,* the religious subject being merely
chosen (in accordance with the invariable custom of the
time) as a means by which to portray the members of the
family concerned. It was painted for Piero il Gottoso, about
the beginning of the year 1467, as a votive offering to be
placed in the church of Sta. Maria Novella, in thanksgiving
for the deliverance of himself and his family from the great
danger which had threatened himself with death and his
family with ruin by the conspiracy headed by Luca Pitti.[32]
Though painted with the above intention it appears doubtful whether this was ever carried out, as after being finished the picture would seem to have been retained by the
Medici family, and only to have found its way to Sta. Maria
Novella long afterwards. In it are shown the three generations
of the elder branch of the Medici family up to that time,[33]
surrounded by their principal adherents, including also some
of the eminent literary men whom they had gathered round
them, such as Marsilio Ficino, Cristoforo Landino, the
brothers Pulci, and others.[34] Cosimo, Piero, and Giuliano
represent the customary three kings, one old, one middle-
aged, and one young; Piero having his two sons, one on either
side of him. The following members of the family are
shown:[35]—

On the left side	On the right side
Cosimo Pater Patriae (then dead), *(embracing the feet of the Child Christ).*	Giovanni [36] (then dead), brother of Piero il Gottoso *(standing, in dress of black and red, and with very black hair).*

In the centre

| LORENZO, elder son of PIERO, at the age of seventeen (*standing, holding a sword*). | PIERO IL GOTTOSO (*kneeling, with his back to the spectator*). | GIULIANO, younger son of PIERO (*kneeling, in a robe of white and gold*). |

This picture is highly interesting, not merely (as usually stated) because it shows us the general appearance of the literary coterie whom the Medici had gathered round them, but because it gives the first example of that power which Botticelli possessed of making a picture relate an important incident in contemporary history. For the picture has a special meaning which has passed hitherto unobserved. In it Botticelli refers to the plot against Piero's life which had just been defeated, and to the manner in which that defeat had been brought about. Allusion has already been made to Botticelli's fondness for allegorical treatment and his habit of giving the clue to the meaning of his picture by some single detail which might at first sight escape notice. And he has done so in this case, though the fact has passed undetected; with the result that the meaning of the picture has entirely failed to be understood.

It is the sword held in Lorenzo's hands which gives the clue to the meaning of the entire picture. Whether because the picture was painted in haste to meet a desire on Piero's part to present his offering while the event on account of which he gave it was still fresh in the minds of all, or simply in order that Botticelli might make his meaning more marked, the latter has palpably made scarcely any attempt to give portraits in the case of either Cosimo, Piero, Giuliano, or Giovanni, and has concentrated all his attention on the figure of Lorenzo, who, in consequence of his conduct on this occasion, had become the hero of the hour in the family. This figure he has evidently drawn with great care, the whole attitude and expression being carefully studied, in order by it to indicate the signification of the whole picture. Botticelli

desires to allude to how in this affair Lorenzo by his courage
and sagacity had been the saviour of his father's life, and
indirectly of the whole family from ruin. It will be noticed
that Lorenzo is the only person among all those in the picture who wears a sword; he is given a remarkably large one,
held in both hands, and placed in front of him in a particularly prominent manner, the sword almost obtruding itself
on our notice as we look at the picture. And the point is still
further brought out by the figure standing next him and
pointing at Piero while he looks at Lorenzo, who stands pay-
ing no attention to the gay young companions surrounding
him, but with his gaze steadily fixed upon his father. Thus
does Botticelli make his picture speak, and relate the danger
which had threatened Piero's life, and the part which Lorenzo had borne in warding it off.

The fourth picture, the *Fortitude*, is also very interesting,
both for its connection with the Medici and the manner in
which that connection becomes apparent. For it refers to the
same event as that commemorated in the previous picture;
but in this case our attention is drawn, not to Lorenzo's
conduct on that occasion, but to that of Piero il Gottoso himself.

The first thing noticeable in the picture is that Botticelli,
called upon to paint a figure representing Fortitude, produces one quite unlike the usual conception of that subject. Ruskin, in his comments on the picture, remarks on
this, and how very different Botticelli's treatment of the subject is from that of all other painters. But there is a reason
for this, and although Ruskin was evidently unaware of
such a reason (while he does not show that he even knew
the date of the picture or for whom it was painted), yet the
key to the meaning of all that he notices in the picture is to
be found in the circumstances of the life of Piero il Gottoso.
It is, in fact, an allegorical record in painting of the fortitude,
energy, and resource which Piero had displayed in the event

which was the chief one during his five years' rule, the rebellion of 1466.

This will become apparent if with that knowledge of
Piero's history which Ruskin did not possess we look at his
remarks on this picture. Speaking of this figure of Fortitude,
Ruskin says as follows:— [37]

"What is chiefly notable in her is that you would not, if
you had to guess who she was, take her for Fortitude at all.
Everybody else's Fortitudes announce themselves clearly
and proudly. They have tower-like shields and lion-like helmets, and stand firm astride on their legs, and are confidently ready for all comers. Yes, that is your common Fortitude. Very grand, though common, but not the highest by
any means. . . . But Botticelli's Fortitude is no match, it may
be, for any that are coming. Worn somewhat, and not a
little weary, instead of standing ready for all comers, she
is sitting, apparently in reverie, her fingers playing restlessly
and idly—nay, I think even nervously—about the hilt of
her sword.[38] For her battle is not to begin to-day, nor did
it begin yesterday. Many a morn and eve have passed since it
began; and now—is this to be the ending day of it? And
if this—by what manner of end? That is what Sandro's
Fortitude is thinking; and the playing fingers about the
sword-hilt would fain let it fall, if it might be; and yet, how
swiftly and gladly will they close on it when the far-off
trumpet sounds, which she will hear through all her reverie."

These remarks exactly reflect the circumstances, attitude,
and conduct of Piero il Gottoso in the trial which came upon
him. Thought to be "no match" for those who were preparing to attack him; half absorbed in the "reverie" of a strong
disinclination to turn from the pursuits of literature to meet
quarrelling and strife; feeling the "battle which did not begin
to-day" in the long period of two years during which he had
known this plot to be hatching; the sitting posture (instead
of the usual standing one), which indicated the crippled state
of health that so severely handicapped him; the "worn, and

not a little weary" expression caused both by the long ill
health he had endured and by disgust at the political intrigues around him, including the ingratitude and deception
of Neroni and others; the hatred of strife shown in the fingers that would fain let the weapon in the hands fall; and,
lastly, the resolute character underlying all the weariness
which was demonstrated by the prompt and effective action
taken when the time came—all these are points which show
the true meaning of the picture.

Looking, therefore, at the date when this picture was
painted, at the conduct of Piero il Gottoso in the chief event
of his five years' rule (conduct which had won him much
honour among his fellow-countrymen), and at the character
of the picture, so well brought out in Ruskin's remarks upon
it, there can in my opinion be no doubt that it is to Piero's
conduct in that event that this picture of Botticelli's relates.
And it shows what a master in art criticism Ruskin was, that
although, with his customary want of interest in history, he
was (as is evident) unaware of the circumstances alluded to
by the picture, he should yet have been able so accurately
to gauge its spirit.

Piero il Gottoso, when he was dying in December 1469,
obtained for Botticelli the commission to paint this picture.
The Council of the Mercatanzia had decided to place in their
hall six panels representing the virtues of Prudence, Temperance, Fortitude, Charity, Justice, and Faith, and had
given the commission to Piero Pollajuolo. But Piero il Gottoso, working through Tommaso Soderini, an influential member of the Mercatanzia, got the latter to give the commission
for one of the figures, that of Fortitude, to Botticelli. The
latter painted the picture during the early months of the year
1470, just when he was in deep grief for the death of the
kind and generous patron who had done everything for him,
and one of whose last acts had been to get him this commission; and with his marvellous talent for allegorical design
he contrives to give to his picture of Fortitude for the coun-

cil hall of the Mercatanzia those characteristics which would make it also a remarkable memorial of the character of Piero il Gottoso.

To the above four pictures must also be added Botticelli's portrait of Lucrezia Tornabuoni, now in the Kaiser Friedrich Museum at Berlin, probably the most beautiful portrait up to that time painted, and his picture of St. Sebastian, also now at Berlin.[39] The above were Botticelli's chief pictures during the period that he worked for Piero il Gottoso and Lucrezia Tornabuoni, both of whom he held in highest honour. His second period is best considered in connection with Lorenzo the Magnificent (chapters viii and ix).

Shortly before his death various of his most ardent adherents among the citizens gave Piero il Gottoso considerable trouble. They seem to have been carried away by elation at his uniform success and at the triumph of their party over all who had wished ill to him and his, and, Machiavelli says, gave themselves up to tyrannising over their fellow-citizens and to committing all sorts of excesses. Piero, though he was on his death-bed and unable to move hands or feet, took vigorous action to quell this spirit among his followers. He summoned the most prominent of the offenders to his bedside and gave them a most severe rebuke, promising them that if they did not abandon their course of conduct he would make them repent it, and in order to check the excesses of his own party would take the extreme step of recalling some of their exiled opponents. Nor was this an empty threat; for when he found that, thinking him too ill to interfere, they continued in the same course, he had a secret meeting at his villa of Cafaggiolo with Agnolo Acciajoli, the principal of the exiles, with a view to carrying out what he had said. And had he lived there is no doubt that he would have done it.

But his course was run. He died in December 1469, uni-

versally regretted by all the best of his countrymen, who re-
joiced in his temperate and sympathetic method of ruling.
The life which had been a threatened one ever since he was
a boy, and which had seldom known a day's real health,
nevertheless reached the age of fifty-three. Regarding his
character there is no dispute; even Machiavelli, who was
not the sort of man to appreciate its nobler side, describes
him thus:—

"He was a good man. He hated violence and display. His
goodness and virtues were not duly appreciated by his country, principally because the few years that he survived his
father, Cosimo, were largely occupied by civil discord and
constant ill health. He promptly and firmly put down an attempted rebellion against him without any violence, which
he detested, and managed to turn his enemies into friends.
He took little interest in home politics and faction, but paid
unfailing attention to foreign politics, and was better appreciated at foreign courts than in his own city."

When we consider his energy notwithstanding that he
was so crippled with gout as to be often unable to move hands
or feet, hatred of dissensions and violence, contempt for the
intrigues which made up so large a part of the political life
of Florence in his time, the combination of vigour, sense, and
tact with which he suppressed a formidable rebellion and
dealt with unruly adherents, and, lastly, the clemency he
showed to those who had endeavoured to take his life, we
have apparently just reason to say that Piero il Gottoso had
a fine character, and one which adds not a little to his family's reputation. While it is fully evident from subsequent
events that strong as was the position to which Cosimo had
raised the family, that strength was increased (and by the
most worthy methods) by Piero il Gottoso, even though he
had so few years in which to do it.

Piero was buried in the Old Sacristy in San Lorenzo, in
the same tomb as his brother Giovanni; and over it his sons

placed the graceful monument by Verrocchio already mentioned. It has an inscription round the base saying that his sons, Lorenzo and Giuliano, have erected this tomb to their father and uncle.[40]

Instead of a painted portrait, such having as yet barely come into vogue,[41] Piero, like his brother Giovanni, had a portrait bust of himself executed by Mino da Fiesole, which is now in the museum of the Bargello. It shows a fine and strong face; and as Mino da Fiesole excelled in these portrait busts, and knew Piero well, it is sure to be a good likeness. These two busts of Piero and Giovanni are among the first portraits which were done from life.[42]

The change in the family arms brought about by Piero has already been noted. The number of the balls in the Medici arms varied during their history. In very early times the number was eleven, then nine, then eight, then seven, and at last six. Thus the number of balls is a rough indication as to date. While Giovanni di Bicci was head of the family we generally find *eight*. When Cosimo became head of the family the number changes to *seven;* and that is the number in the arms on the palace which he built. The colouring of one of the red balls blue, with on it the *fleur-de-lys* (or, if in stone, simply on one of the balls the *fleur-de-lys*), is, of course, not found until the time of Piero; so that six red balls and one blue indicate Piero's time. Lastly, in Lorenzo's time we find the number of balls reduced to *six* (five red and one blue), and at this it finally remained. The rule is absolute so far as our never finding seven balls before the time of Cosimo, or seven balls, one of them bearing the *fleur-de-lys*, before the time of Piero, or six balls before the time of Lorenzo, but there are a few occasions where one may find eight balls even in the time of Cosimo, and seven balls without the *fleur-de-lys* even in the time of Piero.

The Medici were great people for heraldic devices with

hidden meanings. Each of them on becoming head of the
family adopted a private crest of his own which he used in
addition to the family one. Thus Cosimo's crest was three
peacock's feathers (intended to signify the three cardinal
virtues he most admired, prudence, temperance, and fortitude); they are to be seen, among other instances, on the
trappings of his charger in Gozzoli's fresco in the Medici
chapel.[43] Piero chose a falcon holding a diamond ring; but
as his time was so short, it is less often met with than the
others; it is to be seen on the *lavabo* in the inner part of
the Old Sacristy in San Lorenzo. Lorenzo assumed as his
crest three (sometimes four) diamond rings interlaced; the
diamond, as not yielding to fire or blows, signifying indomitable strength, and the ring, eternity. And certainly
nothing was more appropriate to Lorenzo's character than a
device symbolising enduring, indomitable strength. His device
is to be seen on the dress of the figure representing himself
in Botticelli's *Pallas and the Centaur*. All three, Cosimo,
Piero, and Lorenzo, used the motto "Semper." It is to be
seen combined with Cosimo's peacock's feathers on the trappings of his charger in Gozzoli's fresco, combined with
Piero's falcon and diamond ring on the *lavabo* in the Old
Sacristy, and round the ornamental border of the chapel in
the Medici Palace. These private crests are important as
often assisting to determine the date of various works, especially in conjunction with the diverse number of balls in
the family arms already noted.

LUCREZIA TORNABUONI

The wives of Giovanni di Bicci and Cosimo Pater Patriae
had not been of any particular note intellectually; in the
case of Lucrezia Tornabuoni, the wife of Piero il Gottoso, it
was otherwise. She was one of the most accomplished women
of that age. She belonged to a family who were formerly
nobles of the name of Tornaquinci, but had changed their

name and arms about two hundred years before in order
to become ordinary citizens and eligible for the Signoria,
and who were notable patrons of Art.[44] She was learned, a
poetess, and a deeply religious woman. She distinguished herself not only as a noted patroness of learning, but also by her
own writings, and Crescembeni is of opinion that she "excelled the greater part of, not to say all, the poets of her
time." Her chief writings were hymns and translations of
Holy Scripture in verse. Both Politian and Pulci speak highly
of her intellectual gifts; and Roscoe remarks that her poems
are the more worthy of praise as being produced at a time
when poetry was at its lowest ebb in Italy.

Dr. Pastor, in his *Histoire des Papes,* couples her with
Cecilia Gonzaga, Isotta Nogarola, Cassandra Fedele, and
Antonia Pulci in detailing the most notable ladies of the
time who came forth from the seclusion in which women had
hitherto shut themselves up, and won for themselves renown in literature and science.[45] Nor was she less notable
in the sphere of religion; and Francesco Palermo states that
the treatise of St. Antonino, entitled *Opera a ben vivere*
("Methods of a good life") was addressed to Lucrezia Tornabuoni.[46] If so, it is high tribute to her devout and sensible
character.

All that we hear regarding Lucrezia Tornabuoni [47] shows
her to have been a woman of exceptionally high character
as well as thus talented. In her eldest son, Lorenzo, the remarkable abilities of the Medici family reached their culminating point, and this was no doubt due to the fact that not
only his father, but also his mother, was so highly gifted.
Lucrezia survived her husband thirteen years, and lived to
see the terrible death of her beloved younger son in 1478,
the war of 1478-1480, and the triumph of her elder son in
1480, dying herself in 1482. And there is no doubt that
during the earlier part of his rule Lorenzo owed much to her
valuable advice. Niccolò Valori says:—

"Lorenzo was most deferential to her, and after his father's death loved and honoured her, showing in all his actions both the affection felt for a mother and the respect given to a father; it was hard to discern whether he most loved or honoured her."

Lucrezia's portrait (in profile), painted by Botticelli, shows a beautiful and intellectual face.[48] She and Piero had five children, two sons, Lorenzo and Giuliano, and three daughters, Maria, Lucrezia (or Nannina), and Bianca. Their three daughters all made notable marriages; Maria married Leopetto Rossi, Bianca married Guglielmo de' Pazzi, and Lucrezia married Bernardo Rucellai, who was himself one of the most distinguished scholars of the time.

By the end of Piero il Gottoso's life the light which Florence had ignited, and had held aloft in Art and Learning for a hundred and fifty years, had begun to show signs of becoming diffused. In Rome a beginning had been made by the efforts of Pope Nicholas V. In Venice the two brothers, Gentile and Giovanni Bellini, and their brother-in-law, Mantegna, were originating a school of painting, destined to become second only to that of Florence. Urbino, under its enlightened Duke, Federigo Montefeltro, was following in the steps of Florence. And both Mantua, under the Gonzaga family, and Ferrara, under the Este family, were beginning to give to Art and Learning a similar encouragement.

CHAPTER VII

THE FRESCOES IN THE CHAPEL OF THE MEDICI PALACE

JUST as the Medici Palace is inseparably connected with Cosimo, so is that which in these days chiefly attracts attention to it connected with Piero.

Of all the mass of art treasures which that palace contained in the time of Cosimo, Piero, and Lorenzo, one alone now remains there, the frescoes painted for Piero il Gottoso on the walls of the little chapel on the first floor by Benozzo Gozzoli. They merit special consideration on the three grounds of their historical interest, their being this painter's masterpiece, and their combining examples of his powers in two different aspects, those on the walls of the chancel being occupied with a religious subject, and those round the body of the chapel with an historical one.

Although a window now exists all authorities state that originally this chapel had no window, and that all these beautiful frescoes were painted by lamplight. If so it increases our admiration of the master's talent. They are still in perfect preservation, though nearly four hundred and fifty years have passed since they were executed. Over the altar, where the window now is, there was originally a picture of *The Nativity*, by Filippo Lippi.[1] All round the chapel at the lower part of the walls runs an ornamental border consisting of Piero's device of a single diamond ring and the motto "Semper."

The chancel pictures.—These give us an example of Benozzo Gozzoli's powers as a devotional painter, the pupil of Fra Angelico. And although this was not the line in which Gozzoli excelled, these pictures show that he can on occasion breathe into his work not a little of the spirit of his master.

On the two side walls of the chancel, covering the whole height of the wall, Gozzoli gives us two pictures representing the world on that night of the Nativity of Christ referred to in the picture which was over the altar. He lays his scene amidst Italian garden and woodland scenery, with groups of angels passing about everywhere singing their song of "Glory to God in the highest, and on earth peace." There are on each wall three groups, one kneeling, another standing, and the third flying; all are turned towards the altar, or rather towards the picture of the Nativity over it.

The kneeling groups (those nearest to that on which the attention of all is concentrated) are, unlike the rest, not singing; they are intently gazing at the great mystery before them of the incarnation in a human body of Him whom they have ever known as the Second Person of the Holy Trinity, that mystery regarding which we are told that "the angels desire to look into it"; and, bowed in awe, are lost in silent wonder and devotion at such transcendent love on the part of God for the human race. The thoughts in their minds are shown in the "glories" round their heads, in which some have the words, "Gloria in excelsis Deo," others "Adoremus," others "Et in terra pax."

The standing groups, a little further back, are occupied in recounting to each other the wonder of this greatest event in the world's history, and, singing loudly, are calling on all to come and see it. The flying groups are hastening up from the distance to see this wonder of God becoming Man, and gazing down at it in adoration.

The spirit of the entire picture may be summed up in the words, "God so loved the world"; while it is made all the more impressive by not containing any representation of that at which all are so intently gazing; seeing as we do only its profound impression upon them, our attention is drawn to concentrate itself on the greatness of the deed which can thus impress even the angels. Probably in the very devotional spirit of this picture is to be seen the influence of Lucrezia Tornabuoni, who no doubt had much to say in regard to its design.

Behind the principal groups angels pick roses in the gardens, a little cherub rests placidly in the top of a tree, bright-coloured birds fly or stand without fear among the angels, and all is happiness and peace. The beautiful peacock wings of the angels, the brilliant colouring of the birds, the exquisitely painted roses, and other details make the picture as deserving of admiration for its execution as it is for its general design. In accordance with the custom of the old masters, and to exemplify that in the things of the spiritual world time and place are non-existent, the background shows us Italian scenery with castles and villages of the Middle Ages.

The general idea of the picture is carried out even in the landscape, its stiffness and formality being due to this cause. Intending that his picture shall breathe throughout it the thought embodied in the singing angels' words, of *peace* brought to a world tortured by sin and sin's results, the master gives to his landscape such characteristics as shall accord with this idea. Ruskin, in speaking of this point, says:[2]—

"In these sort of pictures by masters such as Raphael, Perugino, or Benozzo Gozzoli, whereas all mountain forms are in nature produced by convulsion or modelled by decay, and all forest grouping is wrought out with varieties of growth, all such appearances are purposely banished. The trees grow straight, equally branched on each side, and of such slight and feathery frame as shows them never to have encountered blight or frost or tempest. The mountains stand up in fantastic pinnacles with no fallen fragments; the seas are always waveless; the skies always calm, crossed only by far, horizontal, lightly-wreathed white clouds."

He cites this picture as an example, and points out how "roses and pomegranates, their leaves drawn to the last rib and vein, twine themselves in fair and perfect order about delicate trellises; broad stone pines and tall cypresses over-shadow them; bright birds hover here and there in the serene sky; and groups of angels glide and float through the glades of an unentangled forest."

In this manner has Benozzo Gozzoli in these chancel pictures written his "burning message," and in a language which those of every nationality can read.

The pictures in the body of the chapel.—While the chancel pictures are occupied with the first episode connected with the Nativity of Christ, those in the body of the chapel are concerned with the second episode connected therewith, the journey of the three kings, or *magi* (Il Viaggio dei Rè Magi), to Bethlehem. And here we have an example of Benozzo Gozzoli's powers in his own special line, that of an historical painter; the religious subject being made merely a vehicle for references to the history of the Medici.

In doing this Gozzoli would of course desire to introduce as many allusions as possible complimentary to the family; but the manner in which he has done this is remarkable. The picture is from end to end an elaborate memorial point-ing to all that the Medici had up to that time done for Florence, and for which they had gained honour among their countrymen. But while the whole idea is wonderful conceived and worked out, the empty flattery by which many painters of that age would have spoilt the effect is avoided. Thus we have in this picture far more than merely a "gorgeous proces-sion of the Magi, into which have been introduced portraits of several of the Medici," which is the description it has gen-erally received.[3]

To carry out the above general idea Gozzoli sets to work to make his picture speak of all that had taken place in Florence in connection with this family during the preceding thirty years. Of how the great gathering of 1439 had been invited to Florence at the instigation of the Medici, and hospitably entertained there by them; of how this assemblage had included an Emperor, the successor of Constantine the Great, and a Patriarch of Constantinople the equal theo-retically [4] of the Pope of Rome; of how it had brought to Florence the most learned men of the time, and furthered that revival of the ancient learning which the Medici had, ever since the foundation-stone of this palace was laid, been fostering; of how as a consequence of the hospitality of 1439, learning and culture when driven from Constantinople had taken refuge in Florence; and, lastly, of how the judicious political guidance of the Medici had increased Florence's power and prosperity and advanced her over the heads of other states which had previously been her rivals. Of all this the picture speaks, and the admirable manner in which Gozzoli has worked out this general scheme demonstrates his great talent as an historical painter.

Gozzoli selects for the first of his three kings or wise men, the Patriarch of Constantinople, Joseph. This is the Patriarch who had come to Florence for the Council of 1439, and who died there a month before it ended. He is the old man on the mule, of which half the body has been cut off in order to make a new entrance many years ago into the chapel; as though to show how little splendid frescoes like this were valued at the time this act of Vandalism was committed. Although the Pope of Rome (Eugenius IV) had also been one of the important personages at the Council, Gozzoli in preference to him chooses the Patriarch of Constantinople, both as being an *Eastern* potentate, and also in allusion to those many dealings which the Medici had had with Con-stantinople in their unearthing of the ancient classical lit-erature.

For the second king Gozzoli chooses John Paleologus (John VII), the Emperor of the East. This John VII is the em-peror who had come to the Council of 1439, the last emperor but one before by the fall of Constantinople the Eastern half of the Roman Empire came to an end, as the Western

half had done a thousand years earlier. As the successor of
Constantine the Great (even though his empire had then
shrunk to little more than its capital city), he was theoretically
the greatest of all earthly sovereigns. And though by the
time that this picture was painted his empire had for sixteen
years ceased to exist, Gozzoli nevertheless puts him in as
the second king for the same reason as before, namely, because he wishes to point to the Council of 1439, to Florence
having been the city to which it was transferred, and to the
part which the Medici had had in that transfer, and in giving
its members such royal hospitality there.

For the third king Gozzoli takes the young heir of the
family, Lorenzo de' Medici.[5] By putting him in as one of
the three kings Gozzoli makes the Medici not merely attendants upon the wise men, but "wise men" themselves;
and by the exalted company in which he is placed contrives
a powerful compliment to the family.

Behind the three kings comes their retinue; and here we
find the Medici leading a gathering of all the most learned
men of the time. In the front line we have the two brothers,
Cosimo Pater Patriae (in an embroidered coat, and on his
charger's trappings the Medici arms, with *seven* balls, and
his own private crest of the three peacock's feathers), and on
his right his brother Lorenzo (typically mounted on a quiet
and humble mule); in the left corner Piero il Gottoso (as
usual with bare head[6]); and next to him (on the white
horse) the young fifteen-year-old Giuliano (preceded by a
negro with a bow, in allusion to Giuliano's love of sport).
Giuliano's horse (alone) has a jewel on the frontlet of its
bridle. In each case Gozzoli, ignoring likenesses, has devoted
much care to the dress and general appearance. And then
behind these members of three generations of the Medici
family comes a long procession of scholars and *literati*, extending far into the distance, and including both those Florentines whom the Medici had taught to care for and seek after
learning[7] (such as Marsilio Ficino, the brothers Pulci, and

others), and also those celebrated Greek scholars from Constantinople, whom the Medici had induced to settle in
Florence, and to whom they had given appointments as
professors of classical learning (such as Argyropoulos,
Chalcondylas, and others), or who had come to the Council
c 1439 (such as Bessarion, Plethon, and others), and who
are distinguished from the Florentines by their Greek head-
dresses. The Florentines are all close-shaven, whereas the
Greeks, in the Eastern fashion, wear beards. The man on
foot (with a black cap), immediately behind Cosimo, is
Salviati, a strong adherent of the Medici, and tutor to
Giuliano Amidst the crowd of *literati* Gozzoli has inserted
himself (between two of the learned Greeks), and to prevent
his name being lost, and also, perhaps, because he might
scarcely be expected in such company, has carefully written
his name round his cap.

Throughout the whole picture it is learning, and not
wealth or power, which is exalted. The Pope of Rome was
infinitely more wealthy and powerful than the Patriarch of
Constantinople, and many of the sovereigns of the time than
the Emperor of the East; and, again, those who accompany
the Medici in the retinue of the three kings are, not the
wealthiest Florentines, but the most learned.

In the fore part of the cavalcade, in front of the Patriarch,
is introduced a gorgeously apparelled youth on a handsomely caparisoned horse, on the back of which he carries a
hunting leopard. This is one of those *scherzi* (or jokes) such
as the old masters loved; while it is made at the same time
to serve the general object of the picture. The person represented is Castruccio Castracani, Duca di Lucca,[8] a celebrated and terrible commander, and a formidable enemy of
Florence, who in the early part of the fourteenth century
fought furiously against her, conquered Pisa and Pistoia,
devastated Florence's territory, and carried war up to her
very walls, and, to the indignation of the Florentines, was
nominated by the Emperor Lewis of Bavaria to be imperial

governor of Tuscany. Gozzoli's *scherzo* consists in representing this terrible enemy as a mere youthful hunter, excelling
only in field sports, and contrasted in every way with the
wise and learned Florentines. He is trying to force his pranc-
ing horse through a crowd of them, but they pay little attention to him, excepting one, who holds up his hand forbidding
him to proceed. In all of which we have allusion to the fact
that whereas Lucca had previously been Florence's formidable
rival, and whereas in two wars before the Medici arose
Florence, guided by the Albizzi, had been worsted by Lucca,
she had now been carried by the Medici to a position of
power and importance far beyond that which Lucca possessed,
and had entirely put a stop to Lucca's triumphal career.

Thus in this picture we have brought before our minds,
in one general view, all that the Medici (up to the point in
their career which they had reached in 1469) had achieved
in reviving Learning, in advancing the glory of Florence as
the most cultured city in Italy, and in advancing her in
political power. And what Gozzoli had to say as regards
these achievements of the first three generations of the family
was rendered in such fashion that it could be read by multi-
tudes who could understand no word of Italian; while his
record has proved a lasting one.

The picture possesses much historical interest apart from
its allusions to the deeds of the Medici. The portraits and
dresses of the Emperor and the Patriarch, the dresses and
appointments of the cavalcade, and similar details, are not
imaginary. Thirty years before, when he was about twenty,
Gozzoli had himself seen the Emperor and the Patriarch in
the processions and functions which took place during the
summer of 1439; he had also lately seen the no less splendid
array of the tournament of February 1469; and he takes his
materials from both these, thus reproducing before our eyes
persons, dresses, and customs of which we should otherwise
have but little idea.

The Patriarch of Constantinople is shown in the dress he wore in the processions of 1439. On his head he has the ancient head-dress which he was almost the last to wear; and the chief point noticeable about this head-dress is that while his colleague, the Pope of Rome, had gradually altered his until it had grown into the triple crown, that of Constantinople had been kept as it was at the first.

In the portrait of the Emperor John VII (John Paleologus) we are shown him as he appeared during the processions in 1439. It is highly interesting from the fact that it is probably the sole portrait now existing [9] in the world of any one of all that long line of Emperors, from Constantine the Great downwards, who sat on the throne of Constantinople for eleven hundred and thirty years. His dress and the trappings of his charger are very magnificent. On his head he wears (entwined with his turban) the peculiar crown of the Eastern Emperors of Rome, so different in shape from that which had by that time been adopted by all sovereigns in Western Europe. Unlike the Florentines, he, according to the Eastern fashion, wears a beard. His face is dignified, yet has a melancholy expression; as well it may, as he sees that once glorious empire in its last throes, and knows there is no hope of any assistance coming from the West to save it.

Lorenzo de' Medici's dress is that which he had lately worn at the tournament of February 1469.[10] We note the "rubies and diamonds in his cap," the "velvet embroidered surcoat" (just showing on his arm), and the cape (like a sleeved surplice) "of white silk edged with red," with his sword belt worn over it. He rides the great white charger which had been presented to him by the King of Naples for the tournament, and the trappings of this charger have all over them the seven Medici balls.[11] The mounted pages, heralds, men-at-arms on foot, etc., are also all in the dresses which they wore at Lorenzo's tournament.

The journey of the Magi, always a favourite subject with the old masters on account of its great possibilities for picturesque treatment, has nowhere else been treated on so magnificent a scale. The splendid procession is given every accessory that can add to its picturesque splendour—beautiful youths, gorgeous dresses, fine horses, hunting leopards, greyhounds, falcons, etc.—and winds its way up and down over the rocky paths and wooded slopes of the Apennines, amidst castles, villages, and cypress groves, while all is painted in colours that are almost as fresh as when laid on.

The date of these frescoes is somewhat of a problem. Ruskin states that they were painted between 1457 and 1459; all other authorities say between 1459 and 1463; while both Ruskin and all other authorities say (rightly enough) that they were painted for Piero il Gottoso. The latter, however, did not become head of the family until 1464; while there are also further grounds than this for considering that none of these dates can be correct. In 1457 Lorenzo was a child of only eight years old, and Giuliano only four years old: which makes Ruskin's date at any rate impossible. And even at the latest of the above dates, 1463, Lorenzo was no more than fourteen, and Giuliano only ten: scarcely an age at which fondness for field sports has been developed. Again, all authorities consider that the dresses and appointments of the cavalcade in the procession of the Magi "reproduce the festive pomp and splendour of the pageants of the Medici." [12] Now the earliest of these pageants was that held in February 1469, when Lorenzo was nineteen and Giuliano fifteen; and none can look at the picture with the account of that pageant before him and have any doubt that the tournament of February 1469 formed the model for the dresses and appointments of Lorenzo, the pages, men-at-arms, grooms, and serving men in the picture; while ages of nineteen and fifteen accord with the representation therein of Lorenzo and Giuliano, which ages of fourteen and ten do not. So that the internal evidence of the picture bars all dates earlier than February 1469.

On the other hand, two letters (without date) regarding
the work were written to Piero il Gottoso by Gozzoli while
employed on it,[13] and the tone and expressions used show
that Piero was then head of the family; this would bar all
dates earlier than August 1464, or later than December
1469. While yet a further difficulty (and that which has no
doubt been the chief reason for the dates hitherto assigned
to these frescoes) is introduced by the fact that from 1463
to 1467 Gozzoli was painting his great series of frescoes at San
Gimignano, writing dated letters from thence at that period;
and that in 1468 he signed an agreement for the execution of
his great work in the Pisa Campo Santo, which he is usually
supposed to have begun in 1469, and which was his last work.

In the midst of such conflicting evidence (part of which,
that given by the picture itself,[14] is too strong to be ignored)
the only solution appears to be that these frescoes were
painted neither between 1457 and 1459, nor between 1459
and 1463, but between January 1468 and December 1469,
the chancel pictures, and possibly some portion of the leading part of the procession (including, perhaps, the figures of
the Patriarch and the Emperor) being painted between
January 1468 and January 1469, and the remainder of the
frescoes in the body of the chapel between February 1469
and December 1469, the work at Pisa not being begun until
quite the end of that year. The whole chapel was certainly
painted while Piero il Gottoso was head of the family (1464-
1469); the chancel pictures could only have been begun
upon Gozzoli's return from San Gimignano, i.e., in 1468;
while the details connected with the tournament, and the
ages of Lorenzo and Giuliano, make February to December
1469 the only possible period when the chief part of the
frescoes in the body of the chapel could have been executed
Benozzo Gozzoli was noted for his extreme rapidity of work
and though these frescoes are filled with a multiplicity of
details it was possible for such an artist as he was to execute
them in two years.

CHAPTER VIII

LORENZO THE MAGNIFICENT

Born 1449. (Ruled 1469-1492.) Died 1492

(1) THE FIRST NINE YEARS OF HIS RULE—1469-1478

LORENZO, the elder son of Piero il Gottoso, was only twenty years old when, by his father's death, he became the head of the family, and succeeded to the rule of Florence. Six months earlier he had been married, as already noted, to Clarice Orsini. His three sisters, Maria, Lucrezia (or Nannina), and Bianca, married respectively to Leopetto Rossi, Bernardo Rucellai, and Guglielmo de' Pazzi, were all older than himself, while his brother Giuliano was four years his junior. His mother, Lucrezia, lived during the first thirteen years of his rule over Florence. Having been for several years accustomed to take a large part in public affairs, he was better prepared than most young men of his age would have been for the position to which he was called so much earlier than either his father or his grandfather had been, each of whom had been over forty when he became head of the family.

In Lorenzo the Magnificent the abilities of this family reached their climax. Probably no other man has ever had great talents in so many directions. In statesmanlike insight and judgment; in political wisdom and promptness of decision; in power of influencing men; in profound knowledge of the ancient classical authors; as a poet and writer who bore a principal part in the development of the Italian language; in artistic taste and critical knowledge of the various branches of Art; in knowledge of agriculture, the life and

149

needs of the people, and country pursuits: in all these different directions was Lorenzo eminent. The title of *Magnificent*, which has by common consent been accorded to him, was not due to any ostentation in his private life, for there he was notably unostentatious. "He was so called because of his extraordinary abilities, his great liberality, his lavish expenditure of his wealth for the public benefit, and the general magnificence of his life in which Florence participated." [1] So that his name is intended to bring to our minds, not personal ostentation, but the splendour with which he invested Florence.

Yet while Lorenzo raised Florence to be the most important state in Italy, set her on a pinnacle as the acknowledged intellectual and artistic capital of Europe, and increased the prosperity of her citizens to the highest point, he has (from later ages) received unmeasured condemnation for a far-reaching change which he brought about in her government, and for the creation in this jealously guarded Republic of what was practically an autocracy. It is true that his grandfather Cosimo had wielded an influence in the State such as enabled him to sway public affairs according to his will. But the position created by Lorenzo went beyond this, and was different in kind. In his case it was not an influence, but a rule. Lorenzo, as a matter of fact, had a greater power of statesmanlike vision than even his grandfather Cosimo. He saw that the Florentines were too liable to give way to private feuds to be really fitted for republican institutions, while under an autocratic rule there was practically no limit to the political importance and domestic prosperity to which Florence might be conducted. That he should cherish the desire that his own family should be the one to exercise that rule was not only natural, but justified. The Medici alone among the families of Florence had shown themselves to possess the qualities which could successfully govern the Florentines. Their power had been gained by those means which alone give a just title to rule; [2] while added to all other qualifications, they possessed as a family a positive genius for pouring oil on troubled waters, and getting men to work harmoniously together who under any other rule were ever at enmity. This valuable characteristic (which has passed unnoticed) Cosimo, Piero, and Lorenzo himself all possessed in a marked degree; while it is one which comes out again and again in this family long after their time.

Lorenzo, in carrying out this change, took a unique course. Convinced that an autocratic style of government was the only one of which the conditions of the time admitted, he yet did not follow the example of other rulers around him who in that age were erecting thrones, their methods being force, crime, and treachery. Instead, he solved the apparently impossible problem of combining two things diametrically opposed, an autocracy and a democracy, and contrived to preserve the form of government loved by his countrymen and yet to wield personally an autocratic power. Unsupported by any military force, he yet exercised absolute authority; but only because his countrymen well knew that no one else could produce such happy results. The Florentines saw their city, through his abilities, raised to the leading place among Italian states, made the intellectual and artistic capital of Europe, and daily advancing in a commercial prosperity in which they each individually shared; and they had no desire to kill the goose which laid such golden eggs. They felt that however autocratic was Lorenzo's rule, they had power to end it whenever determined to do so. And the correctness of the view was fully proved by subsequent events.[3]

While, however, Lorenzo wielded an autocratic power, it is necessary to bear in mind, especially in financial matters, that the governing body of the State remained as heretofore the Signoria. The word "rule" or "reign," as applied to the Medici (although it is impossible to use any other), is calculated to lead to the supposition that they received the money raised by taxation, and hence to the idea, when we

hear of large expenditure by them for the public benefit or
amusement, or for the advancement of Learning, that the
money so spent was public money, and that possibly the
people were heavily taxed to provide it—all of which would
be the very opposite of the truth. The money raised by taxation was received by the Signoria and spent by that body
in other directions, and that which the Medici spent on works
for the public benefit, or on pageants and festivities for the
amusement of the people, was given from their own private
fortune derived from their great banking business.

The historian of his time, Machiavelli,[4] speaks of Lorenzo
thus:—

"He governed the Republic with great judgment, and was
recognised as an equal by various crowned heads of other
countries. Though noticeably without military ability he yet
conducted several wars to a successful conclusion by his
diplomacy. He was the greatest patron of Literature and Art
that any prince has ever been, and he won the people by his
liberality and other popular qualities. By his political talents
he made Florence the leading state in Italy, and by his other
qualities he made her the intellectual, artistic and fashionable
centre of Italy."

And in connection with these achievements Lorenzo shows
one notable characteristic. Though he had in him the capacity
to do all this, and was in ability a head and shoulders above
all men around him, yet never throughout his life did he
show any arrogance (that quality in the Uberti, the Albizzi,
the Pazzi, and other chief families of Florence which the
people had always so detested), and to the day of his death,
though so admired by Florence as the source of all her
greatness, remained always singularly free from this failing.
Autocratic sovereign of Tuscany, practically arbiter of the
politics of all Italy,[5] treated by the sovereigns of France and
England as an equal, there is not a sign in him of that arrogant self-assertion which in one belonging to a *bourgeois*

family would with so many have been an inevitable accompaniment of such greatness. Lorenzo did not maintain even the amount of state considered necessary by the President of a modern Republic. No officials guarded the entrance to the Medici Palace. To every citizen of Florence Lorenzo behaved and spoke on all occasions, public or private, as to an equal, while every historian mentions his marked courtesy of manner even to the poorest of the people.

Such was the young head of the Medici family who at so early an age succeeded to the thorny position of ruler over turbulent Florence, without any military force to support that rule, or anything else to rely upon but his own abilities. In his memoirs Lorenzo himself describes the manner of his accession in terms that are almost comical in their diplomatic depreciation of the position to which he was called and his own ability to fill it. He says:—

"The second day after my father's death, although I, Lorenzo, was very young, that is to say, only in my twenty-first year,[6] the principal men of the city and of the State came to our house to condole with us on our loss, and to encourage me to take on myself the care of the city and of the State, as my father and grandfather had done. This proposal being against the instincts of my youthful age, and considering that the burden and danger were great, I consented to it unwillingly; but I did so in order to protect our friends and property; for it fares ill in Florence with any one who possesses wealth without any control in the government."

The contrast in Lorenzo's case between the difficult conduct of public affairs, and the chief outward occupation of his life, particularly during the earlier part of his rule, is very striking. It was a period when the exuberant vitality of the Renaissance was at its height; and the first nine years of his rule, when he was from twenty to twenty-nine, and his brother Giuliano from sixteen to twenty-five, was a time in Florence of constant festivities, of music, art, and poetry, of joy and laughter, and all the bright side of life. It was the fashion of the day to import into all amusements an imitation of the classic times of ancient Greece, and the Florence of that time appears set before us as a city "with youth at the prow and pleasure at the helm," and full of all the life, joy, and pleasure of the old pagan ideal of Greece set in a fifteenth-century dress. Besides all his duties in regard to State affairs, and labours in the founding of institutions to advance Learning,[7] not to mention his own literary work, Lorenzo with his brother led these festivities, organising pageants and other spectacles of the most costly description (permeated with classical learning and poetical allusions) for the popular amusement. Nor are Lorenzo and Giuliano to be considered as the sole authors of such a change from the old "plain living and high-thinking" ideal of Florence; the age was one in which this sort of thing was in the air throughout Italy, and not in Florence alone; it was the way in which that portion of human need which in our age is provided for by theatres and music halls was then supplied. Lorenzo has been charged with thus leading the Florentines into profligacy, but had that been the case there could scarcely have failed to have been evidence of some protest made by his high-minded mother, Lucrezia Tornabuoni whose influence over him was, we know, very great.

The entertainments organised by these two brilliant young Medici took the form, sometimes of grand processions and tournaments, but more often of the most elaborate allegorical masques. Lorenzo and Giuliano themselves designed the various tableaux, into which every kind of classical allusion was woven, while their execution was entrusted to the greatest artists of the day, no trouble or expense being spared to make these gorgeous spectacles, in which the times of ancient Greece were revived before the eyes of the Florentines, as perfect and dramatic as possible. The costumes and chariots were designed by the most celebrated painters; the groups were arranged by renowned sculptors; the speeches were prepared by the foremost classical scholars, such as Marsilio Ficino, Luigi Pulci, and Politian. Horses were dressed up in the skins of lions and tigers; beautiful women posed as the goddesses of pagan divinity; and poets wrote elaborate compositions in verse describing the meaning of the different tableaux in the processions. •

Nor were the young people of the time very unlike those of our own day in devising pastimes of a yet lighter kind. Not to mention midnight tournaments in which fireworks took the place of more deadly weapons, and magnificently arrayed processions by the young men to serenade the young ladies they desired to honour, we have, in a letter to Lorenzo the year before, a midnight snowballing match related. The heroine of this particular adventure was Marietta Palla Strozzi, the daughter of Lorenzo Palla Strozzi, the young heiress who, both her parents being dead, was thought unduly emancipated because she "lived where she liked and did what she would," and whose features are immortalised by Desiderio's beautiful bust of her [8]—half princess, half wayward child, with saucy chin and wilful hair. Writing in Latin to Lorenzo, then absent at Pisa, his friend, Filippo Corsini, detailing the latest doings of Florentine society, says:—

"And whilst I am writing to thee almost the whole city is covered with snow—tiresome for many, and obliging them to stay within, but for others a cause of much merriment and pleasure. Thou must know that there were together Lottieri Neroni, Priore Pandolfini, and Bartolommeo Benci"—Marietta's betrothed [9]—"and they did say, 'Let us seize upon the occasion to make some fine diversion.' And immediately, at about two o'clock of the night, they did present themselves before the house of Marietta Strozzi, followed by a great multitude assembled from every part, to make sport with her at throwing snow. They gave her a portion, and then they began. Ye immortal gods, what a spectacle! How can I describe it unto thee, my Lorenzo, in this feeble prose—the innumerable torches, the blowing of trumpets, the piping of flutes, the excited and cheering crowd! And what a triumph when one of the besiegers did succeed in flinging snow upon the maiden's face, as white as the snow itself! But what do I say—flinging snow? It was truly a veritable shooting at a mark, and by most expert marksmen! Moreover, Marietta herself, so graceful and so skilled in this game, and beautiful, as all do know, did acquit herself with very great honour. But the noble youths would not take leave of her until they had bestowed most generous gifts upon her for a remembrance of them. And thus, to the great contentment of all, this pleasant sport came to an end." [10]

Well might Lorenzo write in his poems:—

> "Quant'è bella giovinezza
> Che si fugge tuttavia.
> Chi vuol esser lieto, sia;
> Di doman non c'è certezza." [11]

But Lorenzo was not always planning pageants and festivities, or engaged in State affairs. Many other things also occupied his attention. Around his villa on Fiesole he gave small villas to the most celebrated literary men of the time, thus gathering round him a society of *literati* of whom we are told that "their readings, recitations, and discussions revived a knowledge and love of classical learning for which posterity has the utmost reason to be grateful." [12] In his villa at Fiesole, and in his beloved villa of Careggi, Lorenzo read with them the ancient authors, wrote Latin verses and poetry in the language of Tuscany, and took an active part in musical entertainments. A feast was held at his villa of Careggi every 7th November to commemorate the birth of Plato, and remarkable indeed must have been one of these gatherings of all the most brilliant scholars of the time. [13] Lorenzo found time also for field sports, of which both he and Giuliano were passionately fond—rising, he says, at earliest dawn, when "the east is already red and the tops of the mountains appear to be of gold." And the remarkable thing is, that notwithstanding pageants, classical studies, literary work, social gatherings, and field sports, there was no neglect of public affairs, but that, on the contrary, these were most ably administered.

In 1470, soon after his father Piero's death, there came (as on each occasion that the family gained a new head) another attempt to destroy the Medici. Dietisalvi Neroni [14] and the others exiled with him thought they saw an opportunity for doing this now that Piero was gone, and in view of Lorenzo's youth and inexperience. Accordingly, having collected a force they seized Prato, the nearest of Florence's subject towns, and hoped by means of concurrent intrigues in Florence and assistance from Ferrara to succeed in the above object. But Lorenzo was equal to the occasion: the intrigues in the city were foiled by his tact, troops were sent from Florence who retook Prato, and the rebellion was put down.

In 1471 the Duke of Milan, Galeazzo Sforza, came with his wife, Bona of Savoy, and two daughters, and a great retinue, to visit Lorenzo, the latter having himself twice been entertained at Milan, once in 1465, when at the age of sixteen he was present at the marriage of Ippolita Sforza to the Duke of Calabria, and again in 1469, when he went to represent his father as godfather to Galeazzo Sforza's infant heir. On the occasion of this visit to Florence [15] the Duke of Milan, desiring to overawe and impress his two young hosts, as well as the people of Florence, came with a great display of his wealth and importance. We are told that his retinue included "councillors, chamberlains, courtiers, and vassals; twelve litters covered with gold brocade, in which the ladies of the party travelled; 50 grooms in liveries of cloth of silver; numerous servants all clad, even the kitchen boys, in silk or velvet; 50 war horses with saddles of gold brocade, gilded stirrups, and silk-embroidered bridles; and 500 couple of hounds, with huntsmen, falcons, and falconers, together with trumpeters, players, and musicians. Also a bodyguard of 100 knights and 300 infantry.

But all this did not have the effect he intended; he stayed in the Medici Palace, which taught him a valuable lesson. For desirous as he had been to display to the Florentines how much greater was the wealth and splendour of Milan, he was forced by what he saw around him to acknowledge that Art was superior to mere costliness; while we find him declaring that in all Italy he had not seen so many pictures by the first masters, statues, gems, bronzes, beautiful vases, medallions, and rare books, as he saw collected in the palace of the Medici. The result was that he departed at the end of his visit with a greatly increased respect for the Medici, and more inclined than he had previously been to maintain the alliance with Florence. From this time forward we find Milan following in the steps of Florence, and its Duke constantly writing to Lorenzo asking him to send him the foremost artists, and endeavouring in every way to make Milan also a centre of Learning and Art.

In July of this same year Pope Paul II died, and was succeeded by Sixtus IV. On the election of the latter the Signoria of Florence sent an embassy to Rome, in accordance with the usual custom, to congratulate him: Lorenzo formed one of the representatives of Florence,[16] and says in his memoirs that he was received by the new Pope "very honourably." These satisfactory relations, however, did not last long; Sixtus IV soon became a Pope whose crimes caused mankind to loathe the very name of the Papacy; and before many years were over he was forming a formidable plot against Lorenzo's life and the independence of the Florentine state.

In June 1472 took place an event in regard to which Lorenzo's conduct has been so grossly distorted by his detractors that the episode has to receive notice. Volterra, the most turbulent of Florence's subject towns, had raised a revolt in connection with some local disputes, and on the

matter being referred to Florence had refused to submit to
the decision of the Government; riots occurred in which many
lives were lost, and the Florentine envoy only just escaped
from the city with his life. Subsequently Volterra sent to
Florence offering submission. Some were for accepting it,
but Lorenzo was against this, on the ground that the offence
had been serious, that it was not the first occasion of the
kind on the part of Volterra, and that the city ought to
receive punishment. It may have been an error of judgment,
but even this cannot be known; while, even if it were so,
it must be remembered that Lorenzo was at this time only
twenty-three years old. Eventually, a force was sent against
Volterra commanded by the Duke of Urbino (neither
Florence nor Venice allowing their armies to be commanded
by one of their own citizens), and after a month's siege the
town surrendered, and opened its gates. Then occurred the
lamentable event in question. As the force entered an affray
accidentally took place between some of the troops and the
populace, and this rapidly spreading grew into a sack of the
town. The Duke of Urbino did everything possible to restrain his troops; he rode among them protecting the women
and children, and he hanged on the spot several of the
soldiery who were foremost in inciting the rest. But on such
occasions a mediæval force was practically uncontrollable,
and in spite of all his efforts the unfortunate inhabitants were
for some hours subjected to outrage and plunder as though
the town had been taken by assault. Lorenzo at once proceeded to Volterra, and did his utmost to mitigate the
sufferings which had been endured. He has been severely
condemned for this sack of Volterra; but certainly not with
justice. It was the result of an accident which he could
not have foreseen; and he showed by his subsequent conduct
how much he deplored it.[17]

In 1473 we find Louis XI writing to Lorenzo, asking him
to effect a marriage between the Dauphin and Leonora of
Arragon, the eldest daughter of King Ferrante of Naples.

Louis XI writes to Lorenzo quite as an equal, and this with
the request itself show what a position the latter had by this
time made for himself, though as yet only twenty-four years
of age. But the King of France was too late in his request,
for the Princess Leonora [18] had already been betrothed elsewhere; and on the 22nd June a very grand cavalcade, scarcely
less imposing than that of the Duke of Milan two years
before, arrived at Florence escorting her to Ferrara to be
married to Ercole I, Duke of Ferrara, who had succeeded
his brother Borso in 1471. She was accompanied by two
brothers of Duke Ercole, the lords of Carpi, Mirandola, and
Coreggio, the Dukes of Amalfi and Atri, and a number of
other nobles. Entering by the Porta Romana this brilliant
cortège rode through the city, Leonora "dressed all in black
velvet, adorned in front with numberless pearls and jewels,
with a cape, and a little black hat with white feathers."
They crossed the Ponte Vecchio and rode up to the Palazzo
della Signoria, where Leonora, without dismounting, received an address from the Signoria, and then rode on to
the Medici Palace, where she stayed during her visit, and at
dinner was waited upon by her two young hosts, Lorenzo
and Giuliano. She stayed with them several days, during
which various festivities were arranged for her amusement.
Among these was a dance on the 24th June at the Palazzo
Lenzi, near the Porta Prato. In those days of inferior artificial light and small rooms, such dances generally took
place during daylight and in the open air, as was the case
with this one, which was given on the "Prato," or open
stretch of grass beside the city gate, between the palace and
the Arno. Probably those who took part in it were dressed
much in the same way as is related of a dance which took
place on a previous occasion in the Piazza della Signoria,[19]
in which the young men were all dressed "in rich green cloth,
with kid boots reaching up to their thighs, and the younger
ladies in splendid dresses high to the throat, and adorned
with jewels and pearls." Leonora also witnessed the annual

horse-race (the Corso) which took place on the same day, the starting-point being the "Prato," and the course being from thence, by the Via della Vigna, the Mercato Vecchio, and the Corso, to the Porta alla Croce. After these and other festivities Leonora departed for Ferrara, much pleased with the two young Medici.

In 1475 there took place a more than usually grand tournament, the most splendid of all the spectacles during those joyous nine years. It was called specially Giuliano's, as that in 1469 had been called Lorenzo's. And from the elaborate preparations made for it, the interest it aroused far beyond the limits of the Florentine state, the number and importance of the visitors invited by the two young Medici to be their guests for the occasion, and the extravagantly magnificent pageant which it presented, this tournament became the event of the time. It was held in the Piazza Sta. Croce, the usual place for these grand spectacles, which piazza, though it now looks so cold and grey, has seen more brilliant and gorgeous displays than perhaps any other place of the kind in Europe. Lucrezia Donati was again the "Queen of the tournament," and the beautiful Simonetta Cattaneo, who had lately been married, at the age of sixteen, to Marco Vespucci, and, though a Genoese by birth, was now the acknowledged belle of Florence, was the tournament's "Queen of Beauty." [20] The splendour of the dresses and appointments on this occasion exceeded even those of the tournament of 1469; Giuliano, now twenty-two, wore a suit of silver armour, and his entire dress is said to have cost 8,000 florins; his and Lorenzo's helmets were designed by Verrocchio, who also painted Giuliano's standard. Giuliano's handsome looks and gallant bearing won all hearts, and whether as the result of his skill in the combat or his good looks he was awarded the prize.

This notable tournament, having formed so prominent an event, was immortalised both in poetry and in painting. And since nothing accorded with the spirit of the age which did not contain profuse allusion to classical literature, both arts clothe what they have to say in classic dress. Poetry speaks first, by the mouth of the youthful prodigy Politian; and just as the tournament of 1469 had been immortalised by Pulci's poem thereon, so was this one of Giuliano by the still more celebrated poem of Politian,[21] entitled *La Giostra di Giuliano de' Medici*. Roscoe says:—

"These two tournaments are chiefly notable because they called forth two of the most celebrated poems of the fifteenth century, *La Giostra di Lorenzo de' Medici*, by Pulci, and *La Giostra di Giuliano de' Medici*, by Politian. The latter poem contains about 1,400 lines, and has been uniformly allowed to be one of the earliest productions in the revival of letters that breathes the true spirit of poetry."[22]

Still more widely known, however, is the record by which Painting has commemorated this tournament. For no less than three of Botticelli's chief pictures refer to this celebrated tournament, and are simply his way of recording in painting the same matters which had been spoken of by Politian in poetry; though Botticelli, *more suo*, expresses what he has to say with such a wealth of allegory that this has not always been fully recognised. These pictures are: his *Birth of Venus* (now in the Uffizi Gallery, Florence), his *Mars and Venus* (now in the National Gallery, London), and his *Return of Spring* (now in the Accademia, Florence); all three pictures being painted for Lorenzo the Magnificent.

Politian, in his poem, following the classical fashion of the day, in allusion to the tournament's Queen of Beauty (Simonetta), describes the birth of Venus. And Botticelli does the same in painting, following exactly Politian's words. How closely he has done so is well described by Mrs. Ady, who says:—

"The composition (of the picture) was evidently derived from Poliziano's poem of the *Giostra*. In a passage adapted from one of the Homeric hymns the poet tells us how the new-born Aphrodite was blown by the soft breath of the Zephyrs, on the foam of the Egean waves to shore. Heaven and earth, he sings, rejoice at her coming. The Hours wait to welcome her and spread a star-sown robe over her white limbs, while countless flowers spring up in the grass where her feet will tread. All this exquisite imagery is faithfully reproduced in Sandro's painting. He has represented his Venus Anadyomene laying one hand on her snowy breast, the other on her loose tresses of golden hair—a form of virginal beauty and purity, as with feet resting on the golden shell she glides softly over the rippling surface of the waves. He has painted the winged Zephyrs hovering in the air linked fast together, blowing the goddess to the flower-strewn shore, and the shower of single roses fluttering about her form. Only, instead of the three Hours of Homer's hymn and Poliziano's poem, he shows us one fair nymph, in a white robe embroidered with blue corn-flowers, springing lightly forward to offer Venus a pink mantle sown with daisies. In the laurel groves along the shore we see a courtly allusion to the 'Laurel who sheltered the song-birds that carolled to the Tuscan spring'; [23] while in the background the eye roams across long reaches of silent sea to distant headlands sleeping under the cool grey light of early dawn." [24]

The picture charms us by its delightful mixture of the spirit of ancient Greece with that of the Renaissance, as well as by its life and movement, and its sensation of the free air of nature. As Steinmann says:—"We seem to hear the tremulous rustle of the laurel grove, and the gentle plash of the waves." [25]

Following this we have the second picture. The tournament is over; Giuliano has carried all before him and rests from his fatigues, basking in beauty's smiles. Politian, in his poem, alluding to Giuliano as the victor in the tournament, had told the story of Mars and Venus, and described Venus, reclining in a woodland glade, robed in gold-embroidered draperies, watching Mars with limbs relaxed

lying asleep on the grass, while little goat-footed satyrs
played with his armour. This scene Botticelli takes for his
second picture, and as before follows closely Politian's
words.

And then, having devoted one picture to the tournament's
Queen of Beauty, and one to the victor in its mimic warfare,
Botticelli makes his third picture (the most important of the
three) relate to Lorenzo and his part in all this, gathering
up in one view the whole subject of these pastimes.[26] This
Botticelli does with great talent, and in a manner all his own.
He takes for his text the celebrated standard which had
been borne in front of Lorenzo at both his and Giuliano's
tournaments, with its motto of *Le temps revient*, its device
of the bay-tree which had appeared dead again putting forth
its leaves, and its allusion [27] to the new era of youth and
joy which Lorenzo had inaugurated, and had likened to the
return of spring after the gloomy months of winter. Making
the leading thought of his picture the theme on Lorenzo's
standard, Botticelli paints for him his beautiful picture, the
Return of Spring (the Primavera), perhaps the most widely
admired of all Botticelli's pictures. As before, Botticelli con-
nects his picture with the recent tournament by introducing
Giuliano and Simonetta; but he wishes to refer not only to
this one tournament, but to all these pastimes; to their
having been inaugurated by and taking place under the
fostering care of Lorenzo (the laurel [28]); and also to the
latter's talents as a poet, in which domain he was already
beginning to earn a great reputation.

And so Botticelli depicts for us a scene of light-hearted,
youthful joy, representing the return of spring, and by his
great talent contrives that the entire picture shall speak of
Lorenzo, and breathe the very spirit of the poems in which
the latter had sung of the joys of May-time in Tuscany.
Shielded from rough winds and scorching sun by a grove
of orange trees, backed by the ever-present laurel, Queen
Venus [29] (Simonetta) stands presiding over the return of

spring to Tuscany; the Graces dance before her; from out
a laurel grove at her side the three spring months, March,
April, and May (or it may be Zephyr, Fertility, and Flora),
come bringing flowers of every hue; Mercury (Giuliano)
scatters the clouds of winter; and the little blind god of love
aims his arrows recklessly around. Lorenzo's tournament
motto of *Le temps revient* could be written below the picture
as its name, so beautifully does Botticelli bring it, the occasion on which it was used, the meaning which it had, and
Lorenzo's talent for poetry describing the beauties of nature,
all in one glance before our eyes. Some consider this picture
Botticelli's masterpiece, while others would give that honour
to his *Madonna of the Magnificat*. The verdict will depend
chiefly upon the temperament of the observer. But whether
the *Return of Spring* be considered his masterpiece or not
none can fail to praise what has been well termed its "rhythmic
grace," as well as the surpassing art with which Botticelli
has made it speak of Lorenzo, his acts, his poetry, and the
motto by which he signified the introduction of a brighter
era.

But dark clouds were coming up on the horizon which were
ere long to overcast all these bright scenes of joy, putting
an end for ever to Lorenzo's youth, and all the happy times
which he and Giuliano had enjoyed together. In April 1476,
before Politian had finished his poem, or Botticelli had even
begun to paint his three pictures,[30] the tournament's poor
Queen of Beauty, Simonetta de' Vespucci, whose lovely face
looks at us so wistfully in Botticelli's *Birth of Venus*,[31] and
of whom Politian says that she "was so sweet and charming that all men praised her, and no women abused her,"
was dead, being carried off by rapid consumption after a
few weeks' illness. Lorenzo, who was then at Pisa superintend-
ing his new university, and had sent his own physician to
attend her and to furnish him with daily bulletins, when he
heard the news,[32] "went out into the calm spring night to
walk with a friend, and as he was speaking of the dead lady

he suddenly stopped and gazed at a star which had never before seemed to him so brilliant. 'See,' he exclaimed, 'either the soul of that most gentle lady hath been transformed into that new star, or else hath it been joined together thereupon.' " [33] Then followed in December 1476 the murder of the Duke of Milan, Galeazzo Sforza, which upset the balance of power in Italy, and changing all political relations involved Lorenzo in serious anxieties. And soon afterwards came the terrible Pazzi Conspiracy, and the bright, handsome Giuliano, Lorenzo's constant companion in work and play, and on whose sound sense he had grown greatly to rely, was foully murdered, and Lorenzo himself plunged into a serious war and many troubles.

The celebrated conspiracy which had these results originated at Rome with Pope Sixtus IV and his nephews of the Riario family. They gained as their accomplices the Pazzi, at this time the leading family amongst the nobles in Florence, and the conspiracy has taken its name from them, though they were not the chief authors of the plot.

Sixtus IV, the first of three Popes who in this age attained an evil pre-eminence, was a fisherman by birth and took the name of the Della Rovere family. His sister married a Riario. Of him it has been said that he "was the first Pope who for the sake of founding a family, sacrificed every interest of the Church, and waded deep in crime and bloodshed for this purpose." The chief political feature of his pontificate is a constant struggle to rob all, right and left, of their possessions to enrich his rapacious nephews. He made himself hated in Rome, above all, for his cruel treatment of the Colonna family, whom he pursued with relentless ferocity, and of all his crimes his atrocious murder of the head of that family, the Protonotary Lorenzo Colonna, in order to wring from them the surrender of their estates, has made his name for ever odious. [34]

Sixtus IV, urged on by Girolamo Riario, the most evil of

his nephews, desired to seize upon Florence in order to give that state to Girolamo. That this involved the murder of the two Medici brothers was a mere detail. The Pazzi, on the other hand, though they desired to exterminate the Medici, had no intention of allowing the Riario to obtain Florence afterwards. Thus did these two bands of criminals combine for the common object of a treacherous double murder, each of them determined to outwit the other when that should have been effected.

The arrangements took some time, but eventually the two parties hatched at Rome, early in 1478, the plot known as the Pazzi Conspiracy, certainly with the full cognisance [35] of the Pope, even though it may be true that he did not know all the details; for these he left to his nephew, Girolamo Riario, the chief originator of the plot, and did not desire to know them so long as the result, the removal of the two Medici, was achieved. In fact, without the Pope's full concurrence Girolamo Riario would never have undertaken an affair involving so many risks, which might, without that support, bring him no profit. Troops, under Niccolò da Tolentino and Lorenzo Giustini, were sent to occupy points on Florence's frontiers at Todi, Città di Castello, Imola, and near Perugia, and arrangements made for their marching upon Florence while that city should be in the state of confusion and helplessness which would result from the murder of the two Medici. As has been remarked, "For such extensive movements the Pope's assent and co-operation were essential." [36]

The principal movers in the business were Girolamo Riario, who was to obtain the state of Florence; Francesco Salviati, Archbishop designate of Pisa, who was promised that he should be made Archbishop of Florence if the attempt succeeded; the young cardinal, Rafaello Riario, the Pope's grand-nephew, who was sent to Florence to represent Girolamo; and the Pazzi family. The latter were very numerous; Jacopo de' Pazzi, who was head of the family, had two brothers, and between them they had ten grown-up sons, besides many daughters. Cosimo, foreseeing the enmity of the Pazzi, had arranged a marriage between one of these nephews of Jacopo de' Pazzi and his grand-daughter, Bianca, Lorenzo's sister; but when the time came this did not protect Lorenzo from the Pazzi. When all the plans of the conspirators were ready the Archbishop Salviati came to Florence bringing with him Montesecco, a mercenary soldier in the Pope's employ, who was to play the chief part in the murder, and other conspirators. At the same time the young cardinal, Rafaello Riario, also came to Florence, ostensibly on a visit to Jacopo de' Pazzi. The cowardly Girolamo Riario, though he was the chief author of the plot, and was to be the person to benefit by it, took care to remain out of harm's way in Rome.

Lorenzo and Giuliano were at the time staying at the charming Medici villa a few miles out of Florence, on the slope of the hill of Fiesole.[37] Rafaello Riario and his retinue stayed with Jacopo de' Pazzi at his neighbouring villa of Laveggi. They were invited by the two Medici brothers to a grand banquet to take place at the Medici villa on Saturday, the 25th April. And the first plan formed by the conspirators was to poison the two brothers at this banquet. The entertainment took place, but Giuliano being indisposed was unable to be present; so the plan fell through. The Pazzi then told Lorenzo that the young Cardinal Riario was anxious to see the treasures of the Medici Palace; upon which Lorenzo invited him and his retinue to stay with him there for the Sunday, when the cardinal intended being present at High Mass in the cathedral. Whereupon the conspirators laid the plan that after attending Mass and returning to the Medici Palace for dinner, their two young hosts should be murdered as they rose from the table. In accordance with the above invitation the party removed to the Medici Palace, but on the Sunday morning it was found that though Giuliano would be at Mass he was still too unwell to be at

the midday dinner; so again another plan had to be formed.
Nor could any delay be allowed, since on that evening the
troops of Niccolò da Tolentino and Giustini would be at
the gates of the city. It was therefore hastily decided that
the murder should take place at the service in the cathedral,
where it was known that there would be a great crowd,
which would facilitate the escape of the murderers. Montesecco, however, declined to take part in this plan, as he
"refused to add sacrilege to murder"; so in his place were
substituted the two priests who were among the conspirators,
Antonio Maffei and Stefano da Bagnone, who had no such
scruples. Meanwhile in the Medici Palace every preparation
was made for the banquet. The rare silver, majolica, and
precious vases were brought out, and the *cortile* which Donatello's medallions and statuary adorned was arranged for
the entertainment of so distinguished a company.

It shows somewhat of the general estimation in which
the Medici were held in Florence that though for several
days danger of this kind, either by poison or dagger, had
been all around Lorenzo and Giuliano, both they, their family, and their numerous retainers should have been so entirely without the smallest suspicion of any danger. And it
was this entire absence of suspicion on the part of the two
brothers which caused the plot to come so very near to succeeding.

Towards midday on the Sunday morning (26th April)
Lorenzo left the Medici Palace, walking with his guest, the
young cardinal, Rafaello Riario, to the cathedral. After a
short interval Giuliano followed, accompanied by Francesco
de' Pazzi and Bernardo Bandini. As they walked Francesco
de' Pazzi in pretended affection put his arm round Giuliano's
waist to ascertain whether he wore a coat of mail under
his clothes; which he found he did not. Giuliano on that day
was entirely unarmed, not even wearing a sword, having
hurt his leg in an accident.

The moment which the conspirators had fixed upon to carry

out this diabolical murder during High Mass of the two young men whose hospitality they were enjoying was that of the elevation of the Host; "this moment," says an historian of the time, "being chosen both by reason of the impossibility of mistaking it, and also on account of the bending attitude of worship which it is the habit of every one in the church to assume at that solemn moment in the service." It was this which had caused the mercenary soldier, Montesecco, to draw back from the plot, he being "appalled, ruffian as he was, at the blasphemy of choosing such a moment for so great a crime." And this was the actual cause of the failure of the plot; for his part had been that of murdering Lorenzo, and the two priests substituted in his place being unused to arms bungled in their work, where those told off to do the same for Giuliano (Bernardo Bandini and Francesco de' Pazzi) succeeded only too well.

In the crowded cathedral the brothers were, according to the plan, separated. At the fatal moment Giuliano, unarmed, was standing at the northern side of the choir,[38] not far from the door leading to the Via de' Servi, while Lorenzo was standing at the south side of the choir. Giuliano, furiously attacked by Bernardo Bandini and Francesco de' Pazzi, fell dead at once where he stood, his body being stabbed again and again as it lay on the ground until it had nineteen wounds.[39] At the same time Maffei and Stefano attacked Lorenzo, but being less prompt than Bandini only succeeded in giving him a wound on the neck. Lorenzo, with much presence of mind, immediately threw off his cloak, wrapped it round his left arm as a shield, and drawing his sword beat off his assailants. He then leaped over the low rail which encircled the choir, and running across in front of the high altar took refuge in the sacristy. Bandini, having slain Giuliano, rushed towards the sacristy to attack Lorenzo, killing on the way with one blow Francesco Nori, a devoted adherent of the Medici, who interposed to prevent him from reaching Lorenzo. Politian, who with one or two others of his friends had followed Lorenzo, closed the heavy bronze doors of the sacristy in Bandini's face; while Antonio Ridolfi sucked Lorenzo's wound lest the weapon should have been poisoned.[40] The whole church was at once in an uproar, the people when they knew what had happened being ready to tear in pieces those guilty of the crime; for the moment, however, the latter in the general confusion escaped out of the church; while the young cardinal, Rafaello Riario, took refuge at the high altar. One of Lorenzo's party in the sacristy climbed up into the organ loft, and saw Giuliano's body lying dead at the north side of the choir, and that the conspirators had fled (this being the first intimation that Lorenzo had of what had happened to his brother); and after a little time Lorenzo, wounded and in deep distress at his brother's cruel fate, was escorted home by his friends.

Meanwhile the other and larger portion of the conspirators were occupied at the Palazzo della Signoria. The plot as arranged was a most formidable one, eminently calculated to paralyse Florence and render her powerless to resist the troops of Niccolò da Tolentino and Giustini, who should in a few hours be entering the city. For the plan had been that while those told off to that work carried out the murder of the two brothers in the cathedral, the principal band of the conspirators, headed by the Archbishop Salviati, should proceed to the Palazzo della Signoria, and having gained admittance to the council chamber, should seize the Government, killing all members of the Signoria who resisted. But on the entrance of the Archbishop and his following the Gonfaloniere, Petrucci (who in this crisis showed himself a decidedly strong man), suspected something wrong. He therefore kept the Archbishop and his party in play for a short time, detaining the Archbishop in his own private room while he quietly sent out to ascertain if there was anything unusual going on in the city. In a few minutes came the news of the tragedy which had occurred in the cathedral; and with it the gathering noise of the furious people, who, while Jacopo de' Pazzi and others of that family strove to rouse them to rise against the Medici, and rode through the streets crying out *"Libertà!"* were refusing to shout as instigated *"Abasso le Palle!"* [41] but instead were shouting furiously *"Vivano le Palle!"* The Gonfaloniere, with great resolution, seized the Archbishop, and promptly hanged him from the corner window on the north side of the Palazzo della Signoria (the corner window of the great council hall), and with him, from the adjacent windows, five of his fellow-conspirators, while the rest were slain on the staircase. "Within half an hour twenty-six bodies were encumbering the staircase of the Palazzo della Signoria, and half a dozen more were dangling from its windows."

The remainder of the conspirators were hunted through the city by the enraged people, whose hatred against them was beyond all bounds, and none who fell into their hands were spared even to be handed over to the Signoria for execution. They had not only killed Giuliano, and attempted to kill Lorenzo, but they had also made a formidable endeavour by force of arms, and with the aid of foreign troops, to seize Florence by a *coup de main,* and all these acts together roused the people to frenzy. They surrounded the Medici Palace and clamoured to see Lorenzo. Wounded as he was, he came out and addressed them, assuring them that he was only slightly hurt, and exhorting them not to execute private vengeance on the perpetrators of this deed, but to reserve their animosity for those foreign enemies of their country who had instigated it. But they paid no heed to his admonition, and all suspected of complicity in the plot were pursued through the streets and slaughtered wherever captured, their mangled remains being dragged about by the infuriated mob, whose rage was not satisfied until about eighty persons had been massacred. Nor was the feeling confined to the city; for days afterwards the country people flocked into Florence, coming, they said, to protect Lorenzo.

But in the Medici Palace was deep and bitter mourning

for the bright and justly loved Giuliano, the idol of his family; and mournful preparations for the solemn public funeral to be held in the family church of San Lorenzo.

Nor when the Florentine people had had time to recover from their first excitement did the popular wrath abate; it became less wild, but more determined. Jacopo de' Pazzi had escaped to the village of Castagno, but was seized and brought back by the villagers, and executed by the Signoria. The same fate met Francesco de' Pazzi, one of the two murderers of Giuliano, his cousin Renato de' Pazzi,[42] Montesecco, and the two priests, Maffei and Stefano. Guglielmo de' Pazzi, brother of Francesco and husband of Lorenzo's favourite sister Bianca, would probably also have lost his life had not Lorenzo, on his sister's account, intervened on his behalf; in consequence Guglielmo was merely banished to a short distance from Florence. The remaining seven of the ten sons or nephews of Jacopo de' Pazzi were sentenced either to imprisonment for longer or shorter periods, or to banishment. "Vespucci also richly deserved hanging, but was let off with two years' imprisonment."[43] Bernardo Bandini, the other murderer of Giuliano, escaped to Constantinople; there, however, he was seized by the Sultan, and sent back in chains to Florence; on his arrival the Signoria at once ordered him to be executed in the Bargello. The indignation of the people, not all of it on account of the attempt against the Medici, but also on account of the effrontery of such an endeavour to seize upon their state "as if a mere spoil of war," caused them to seek for every possible method which they could devise to brand with deserved infamy those who had perpetrated this deed. By a public decree of the Signoria the name and arms of the Pazzi family were ordered to be for ever suppressed. Their palace,[44] and all places in the city named after them, were given other names. All persons contracting marriage with any of that family were declared prohibited from all offices in the Republic. The ancient ceremony on Easter Eve of conducting the sacred fire to the house of the Pazzi was abolished.[45] An artist was employed at the public expense to represent on the walls of the Bargello the bodies of the traitors to the Republic suspended, as a mark of infamy, by the feet. And a medal [46] was struck, by order of the Signoria, representing the choir of the cathedral, the heads of Lorenzo and Giuliano, and the attacks made upon them.

While the fury of the Florentines was thus at a white heat against those who had perpetrated this crime and come so near bringing their country under such a yoke as Sixtus IV had intended, Lorenzo showed in the midst of the frenzy of his city one trait which is deserving of notice; and it was an inherited one. Whether he felt that, notwithstanding the part in the matter which the one member of the Riario family who had come to Florence had played, the latter had been only a tool in the hands of older men, or whatever the cause, it was to Lorenzo that the young cardinal, Rafaello Riario, entirely owed the saving of his life. When the uproar in the cathedral took place the young cardinal took refuge, as already noted, at the high altar, whence he dared not stir. Lorenzo, on reaching home, sent a party of his retainers to protect him, and to conduct him to the Medici Palace, the sole place in the whole city where he could be in safety; there he kept him hidden for some days until the violence of the people had cooled down, and then sent him away in secrecy to Rome. Lorenzo showed similar magnanimity in saving the lives of Rafaello Maffei, the brother of the priest who had attempted to murder him, and of Averardo Salviati, a near relation of the Archbishop who had taken so prominent a part in the plot.

Such, then, was the Pazzi Conspiracy. It differs in no way from the most brutal highway murder and robbery except in its consummate treachery and the high position of its authors. Yet it will scarcely be credited that some writers have styled it a praiseworthy act. Thus, for instance, we find Sismondi crediting the chief actors in the Pazzi Conspiracy with "noble motives." He sees in the conduct of Sixtus IV (whose motive is well known to have been solely the desire to seize Tuscany for his greedy nephew) "elevation of sentiment and a desire for the independence of Italy"; [47] and he regards the Pazzi as "noble patriots striving for the liberty of Florence." The Medici have quite enough faults to answer for without their history being distorted in this preposterous fashion. The judgment of a more balanced writer is as follows:—

"The Pope and his nephew attempted to overthrow the Medici rule because it was a bar to enlarging the temporal authority of the one, and to the personal ambition of the other. The Pazzi were perhaps unconscious that they were being used as tools for the attainment of these ends, and had, no doubt, their own ideas as to the future government of Florence, but there is not a tittle of evidence that they were actuated by a love of liberty. Their conduct throughout seems to have been purely vindictive. It was the Medici, and not the Pazzi, who in the past have been on the side of free institutions. The supposition that the Florentines would have preferred the rule of the Pazzi to that of the Medici is ridiculous, or Jacopo de' Pazzi's shouts of *Libertà, Libertà* would not have been answered with the *Palle, Palle* of the multitude. In truth, there has seldom been a conspiracy which was instigated throughout by meaner motives." [48]

Thus did this celebrated conspiracy fail, and the Medici were more popular than ever, and had weathered the fourth and most formidable attempt to destroy them; [49] while Lorenzo, as the result of this attempt, gained much additional strength for the war which was now before him, in the knowledge that he had a united people at his back. But Lorenzo's youth ended with the death of his much-loved brother; there are no more pageants and festivities, but henceforward war, politics, and literary labours, with field sports as the only relaxation

GIULIANO

Born 1453. *Died* 1478

Giuliano, the youngest of the five children of Piero il Gottoso and Lucrezia Tornabuoni, was, unlike his brother, Lorenzo, exceedingly good-looking; he was gifted with considerable abilities, and for his many endearing qualities was greatly beloved, not only in his own family, but also by the people of Florence. Before his early death he had already shown on several occasions that he possessed plenty of political capacity, and could give valuable advice to his brother. Mr. Armstrong, describing his character, says:—

"He was the darling of high and low, the most attractive of all the Medici. His passion was the chase; he was a bold rider, a skilful jouster, eminent in jumping and in wrestling. Yet he was no brutal athlete. He loved pictures, music, and everything that was beautiful; he loved poetry that told of love; he composed verses in his mother tongue, full of weight and sentiment. He talked brightly and thought soundly, delighted in witty and playful company, but hated above all men those who lied, or bore a grudge for wrongs. Faithful and high-minded, regardful of religious forms and moral decencies, he was ever ready to render service or perform a courteous act. In his relations to his brother, whom he worshipped, there was no sign of jealousy. After the terrible tragedy of his murder at High Mass in the cathedral the city long missed the well-known figure, tall and well proportioned, the olive-tinted features lighted by bright eyes, the long lock on the forehead, and the shock of black hair thrust back upon his neck. He had a grand public funeral in the great church of the Medici family, San Lorenzo, and there was no hypocrisy in the great grief manifested by the people." [50]

The relation which existed between these two brothers is one of the pleasantest things in the history of the Medici. At that epoch jealousy between two brothers placed in such

a position as Lorenzo and Giuliano were was the normal
state of things. That it was entirely absent in their case
speaks well for both of them. And it is an indication of Lorenzo's character, and of what his conduct in the minor relations of life must have been, that he should never have given
cause for any feeling of jealousy in a younger brother so
nearly his equal in ability, and his superior in good looks,
and that, on the contrary, the latter should have "worshipped"
him; or, again, that Lorenzo from his side should never have
felt jealousy at the admiration and popularity so universally
bestowed upon Giuliano, and much exceeding that accorded
to himself.

Giuliano was twenty-five at the time of his death. He left
an illegitimate son, born just at that time. Lorenzo took the
child [51] and brought him up with his own sons; and this
child became in the next generation the well-known Giulio
de' Medici, afterwards Clement VII.

Giuliano, like all previous members of the family except
Cosimo, was buried in the Old Sacristy in San Lorenzo;
but about eighty years afterwards his remains were removed
to the New Sacristy, which had by that time become the
principal burial-place of the family. It has always been felt
suitable that these two brothers, between whom so strong
an affection existed in life, should be buried together; when
Lorenzo died his body was laid in the same grave with Giuliano's, their remains were subsequently removed to the New
Sacristy together, and there they still lie in the same tomb.

When in October 1895 Lorenzo's and Giuliano's tomb was
opened [52] the reason why the latter was so instantly killed
became for the first time apparent. The accounts of the
murder had always mentioned that his body received a large
number of wounds, most of them given after he was already dead, but no mention of a wound on the head was
made in any of the accounts. When, however, the tomb was
opened more than four hundred years afterwards it was at
once observed that Giuliano's head had an enormous sword-

cut extending along the whole of the top of the skull: thus fully accounting for his falling dead at once where he stood.[53] Evidently Giuliano at the elevation of the Host had adopted "the bending attitude" on which the plot relied, and the murderer, Bandini, had taken full advantage of the opportunity it gave, and struck Giuliano down, without his having a chance of defending himself from the blow, by a stroke delivered with great force on his bare head.

CHAPTER IX

LORENZO THE MAGNIFICENT

Born 1449. (*Ruled* 1469-1492.) *Died* 1492

(2) THE LAST FOURTEEN YEARS OF HIS RULE—1478-1492

SIXTUS IV was furious at the failure of the conspiracy. It added fuel to the flame that Florence should have dared to hang his subordinate, the Archbishop Salviati, and put to death his hired agents, Montesecco and his companions. He promptly declared war against Florence, and induced the King of Naples [1] and other states to join him. He confiscated the Medici bank in Rome, and sent an envoy to the Florentine State to demand that Lorenzo should be surrendered to his vengeance. The reply of the Signoria is significant:— "You say that Lorenzo is a tyrant, and command us to expel him; but how are we free if thus compelled to obey your commands? You call him tyrant: the majority of the Florentines call him their defender."

But the Pope did more than declare war: he excommunicated the entire Tuscan State. The document drawn up by Sixtus IV on this occasion is a curiosity in this kind of literature.[2] In it he anathematised, not only Lorenzo (whom he styled "the child of iniquity and the nursling of perdition"), but also the Gonfaloniere and all the members of the Signoria of Florence. The complete unrighteousness of the act is manifest. Because his criminal attempt had failed, and because the Government of a neighbouring State had executed those who had murdered their ruler's brother, attempted to murder himself, and endeavoured treacherously to seize their country, therefore the people of that country were to be visited with a penalty in spiritual affairs. It was a travesty of the whole meaning of excommunication.

Thus was the greater part of Italy [3] stirred up to attack Lorenzo, who justly remarked that his "only fault was that he had not been murdered." But the temper of the Florentines was thoroughly roused; no submission was thought of and Florence prepared herself for a serious war against the whole power which the Pope was able to bring to bear. And here occurred a remarkable incident, interesting as showing how the temper of men's minds was changing, and as a forerunner of the Reformation, now fast approaching in the next generation.

At the period on which we are now entering corruption and vice were being spread over Europe from Rome as a centre. The Church at large cried out against it, but none could see from whence any reform could come. Thus we find a preacher of the Order of St. Dominic, preaching in the year 1484, saying:—"The world cries out for a Council; but how can one be obtained in the present state of the heads of the Church? No human power avails any longer to reform the Church through a Council, and God Himself must come to our aid in some way unknown to us." But in a way un dreamt of by the preacher that aid was already on the road. The "New Learning" was slowly but surely leading men up to that great movement which was to reform the Church.

Writings of the long past, unearthed chiefly through the labours of the Medici in the cause of Learning, were beginning to be the common property of all men. And the result was like a revelation to the men of that age. They learnt when and how the claims of the Papacy had originated; how often and how effectively they had in the early centuries been repudiated by the Church; how those claims themselves had gradually become far more wide and sweeping in character than when at first tentatively put forward; and how in many instances they had only made their way owing to the political circumstances of Europe.

But men learnt more even than this. As these researches
f scholars into the writings of the past proceeded it began
ɔ be seen that an immense falsehood had been perpetrated.
There loomed before men's eyes the most gigantic fraud
hich the world has ever seen." [4] In the latter half of the
fteenth century, men gradually learnt that, whereas these
apal claims had for centuries been based upon three great
istorical documents, these were all of them from end to
nd colossal forgeries, concocted in the Roman Curia during
ʒe darkness of the eighth and ninth centuries—the forged
Donation of Constantine, the forged *Donation of Pepin,* and
ʒat which has obtained in history the name of *The Forged
Decretals*—all three now acknowledged by all Europe (in-
luding the Church of Rome itself) to have been what the
cholars of the Renaissance found them out to be, viz., for-
eries. None, in fact, possessed of any scholarship could
ɛad them without at once seeing that they were so, their
istorical errors and inconsistencies being so gross; but they
ad sufficed for their purpose during an illiterate age. This
uge fraud had misled the whole of western Europe from
ʒe eighth to the fifteenth century, and the entire Papal
difice was erected thereon.

"And then," says a modern historian, "came a scholar of
ʒe Renaissance, Laurentius Valla,[5] and uttered a few words
f caustic comment, . . . and pricked the bubble which had
ɛfooled the world for seven centuries, and the Djin shrank
ack into the bottle, and was hurled into the depths of the
ɛa." [6]

It was as though—nay, far more than as though—Magna
'harta were found to be a forgery.

The pricking of this great "bubble," joined to all the other
nowledge which the "New Learning" supplied, was bound,
ʒhen time had elapsed for the information to spread over the
ountries of northern Europe, to bring about the Reformation.
'or as soon as it became known to most educated men that the

entire Papal claim was based upon a colossal fraud, the revolt
of other national Churches from the usurped supremacy of
the Church of Rome was a certainty. But that time was not
yet; as yet we are only at the stage when these things were
becoming known to a considerable number of men in Tuscany, and at an incident which was but a local and temporary forerunner of the great convulsion. It is an incident
little known, but whose importance is shown by the strenuous efforts subsequently made by the Church of Rome to
destroy all trace of it. On receipt of the Pope's bull of excommunication the whole of the Tuscan bishops assembled
in council in the cathedral of Florence, justified the action
of the State, and not only appealed to a General Council
against the interdict, but *excommunicated the Pope*.

Nor was there anything irregular in this action of the
Church of Tuscany. It was an action which went back to
the times when, had any bishop acted as Sixtus IV had done,
the Churches of other parts of Christendom would have
refused to hold communion with him, or with his Church,
until it had purged itself of such a bishop. And it was only
from the long ignorance which had reigned in these matters
that the bold action of the Church of Tuscany took men's
breath away. And if we enquire where the Tuscan Church
got the idea of action which had been unknown in Europe
for more than eight centuries, the answer is plain. It was undoubtedly Tuscany's "New Learning" which emboldened
the Church of Tuscany to take the course it did, strong in
the knowledge that it was on solid ground in taking action
which any appeal to the early centuries of the life of the
Catholic Church would substantiate.

But the Church of Tuscany did not stop here. It made use
of the newly-discovered art of printing,[7] and printed its sentence of excommunication of the Pope, and distributed copies
thereof to the other national Churches of Europe. This to a
world accustomed to tremble at a Pope's censures seemed a
still more terrible act of lawlessness. But nothing daunted

Tuscany. The whole of the clergy held with their bishops, and the Papal excommunication was treated as a dead letter throughout that State.[8]

In the war which followed Florence was greatly over-matched. She had to face a powerful combination including not only Rome and Naples, but also both of her two ancient rivals, Siena and Lucca, besides Urbino and other minor states, the Pope exerting all his power to make all states join him. Florence was repeatedly defeated in the field, and lost town after town. At length, after nearly two years' fighting, the position being most gloomy, Lorenzo took a remarkable step. Leaving the conduct of affairs in the hands of the Gonfaloniere, Tommaso Soderini, he set out by himself for Naples, to try diplomacy instead of force of arms: thus putting himself into the hands of his enemy in the hope of thereby saving his country. It was a dangerous step, for the Pope was as vindictive as ever, and all knew the unreliable character of King Ferrante of Naples.[9] On his way to Pisa, Lorenzo wrote to the Signoria, explaining his object thus:—

"In the dangerous circumstances in which our city is placed it was more necessary to act than to deliberate. ... I therefore mean, with your permission, to proceed directly to Naples, conceiving that as I am the person chiefly aimed at by our enemies, I may, by delivering myself into their hands, perhaps be the means of restoring peace to my fellow-citizens." [10]

In reply he received from the Signoria a letter conferring on him official authority to negotiate with the King of Naples.

Sailing from the little port of Vada, in the Maremma, Lorenzo reached Naples on the 18th December. There his charm of manner, combined with the masterly sketch which he set before the King of the politics of Italy—showing him the precariousness of Ludovico Sforza's position at Milan, the unreliability of Venice, the changing policy of the Papacy

which varied with each new Pope, and that the friendship of
none was so valuable to him as that of Florence—soon
worked so great a change that the enmity of King Ferrante
was turned into friendship.[11] And the final result was a treaty
in which Florence regained her lost territories. Lorenzo returned in triumph to Florence in March 1480 with a perfect
ovation, the people embracing each other for joy, the citizens declaring that his tact and personal influence had
proved stronger than all the military force of the enemy, and
that all that had been lost in war had been recovered by his
wisdom and judgment. The Pope raged furiously and did
his utmost to continue the war, but one ally after another
withdrew from him, and eventually he had to give in, remove
his interdict, and make peace with Florence.[12]

This return in triumph, bringing "peace with honour"
where all had been so gloomy when he went away, was always
considered by the Florentines the chief event of Lorenzo's
life. And just as Botticelli had immortalised the roseate joys
of those earlier years, before the tragedy of the Pazzi Conspiracy put an end to them and brought storm and trouble,
so now the same painter immortalised the triumph of these
sterner years. This Botticelli (always allegorical) does by
his picture of *Pallas subduing the Centaur*, now in the Pitti
Palace, one of the most admired of his pictures. The centaur,
emblem of crime and war, and typifying the iniquitous Pazzi
Conspiracy and the unrighteous war brought upon Florence
as its result, cowers before the victorious Goddess of Wisdom,
who, with Lorenzo's private crest of the interlaced diamond
rings covering her dress, and wreathed with *laurel*, turns her
back on the bay of Naples, and setting her face towards the
hill country of Tuscany leads the spirit of war captive;[13] thus
representing the triumph of wisdom and peace in the person
of Lorenzo, and the honour accorded to him by a grateful
country.[14]

In this manner did Lorenzo weather the storm which came
upon him when he was thirty years old, through the double

trial of the formidable conspiracy to murder him and the disastrous war which grew out of it. We get a glimpse of how severely it had tried him from his words when apologising for turning to literature as a relaxation in the midst of much trouble of mind. He writes:—

"I shall therefore only say that my sufferings have been very severe, the authors of them having been men of great authority and talents, and fully determined to accomplish, by every means in their power, my total ruin. Whilst I, on the other hand, having nothing to oppose to these formidable enemies but youth and inexperience (saving, indeed, the assistance which I received from Divine goodness), was reduced to such an extreme of misfortune that I had at one and the same time to labour under the excommunication of my soul, and the dispersion of my property,[15] to contend with endeavours to divest me of my authority in the State,[16] to meet attempts to introduce discord into my family,[17] and to sustain frequent plots to deprive me of my life;[18] insomuch that I should at one time have thought death itself a less evil than those with which I had to contend. In this unfortunate situation it is surely not to be wondered at if I endeavoured to alleviate my anxiety by turning to more agreeable subjects of meditation."

This great diplomatic victory was the turning-point in Lorenzo's career. Up to this time he had not gained that autocratic power which he sought;[19] but from this moment it was entirely his. The Florentines were ready to accord any honour to the man who had first defended their country from seizure by an unscrupulous Roman despot and from subjugation to the latter's tyrannical rule, and then, though overmatched in strength, had foiled all that enemy's attacks and restored peace without any loss of territory. Lorenzo might undoubtedly, if he would, at this juncture have made himself sovereign ruler of Florence in name as well as in fact. But he knew his countrymen too well to do so, knowing that his popularity would wane if he adopted that position; and he had the wis

dom to be content with the power, without the insignia, of
sovereignty. The kind of rule which he established—that
combination of an autocracy with a democracy—will always
be held in disfavour by political theorists; but the practical
results proved its entire correctness. The prosperity and
power of Florence went up with a bound; every state desired
alliance with her; while foreign courts eagerly sought Lorenzo's advice and assistance. Even the Sultan was impressed
by his importance, and sent him costly presents, among other
things a giraffe, which must have been somewhat of an embarrassment in Florence. At the same time Florence's commerce immensely increased, her ships, built in her port of
Pisa, trading to the Black Sea, Asia Minor, Africa, Spain,
England, France, and Flanders. And with the spread of her
commerce increased also her influence as the centre of Art and
Learning.[20] The pride which the Florentines took in all this is
brought home to us when we find Giovanni Rucellai, in
detailing in his memoirs a long list of personal benefits for
which he desires to offer up thanks to the Almighty, amongst
them thanking God that he "was a native of Florence, the
greatest city in the world, and lived in the days of the magnificent Medici."

During the first eleven years of Lorenzo's rule the chief
events in other countries were as follows:—

In France from 1468 to 1477 Louis XI was mainly occupied
in a long struggle with Charles the Bold, the great Duke of
Burgundy. The latter was in every way the reverse of his
mean and crafty antagonist, and a far nobler spirit, while his
wise reforms for the good of his country, and his strong and
enlightened government, made him the leading ruler of his
time. The struggle between him and Louis XI continued with
varying success until in 1477 Charles the Bold was killed at
the battle of Nanci. He left an only child, Mary of Burgundy,
who inherited all her father's immense territories. Meanwhile
Louis XI, having exterminated all the greater nobles in

France, had destroyed the feudal system in that country, and in its place had established a standing army. This was the first standing army created in Europe, and its possession in an age when nothing of the kind existed in any other country greatly increased Louis XI's strength.

In Germany the Emperor Frederick III succeeded in 1477 in arranging a marriage between his son Maximilian, Archduke of Austria, and Mary of Burgundy, the sole heiress of Charles the Bold, by which Austria gained an accession of territory extending from Holland to Switzerland. This marriage caused a great change in the state of Europe; to it is due the rise of the house of Austria, and we are told "it begins the era of the larger politics of modern times." In this matter Louis XI entirely overreached himself. The rich and extensive territories which Mary of Burgundy inherited stretched along the most exposed frontier of France. By a continued course of elaborate intrigues, Louis, while amusing the young Duchess with a proposal for a marriage with his son, the Dauphin, which he never intended to carry out, sent troops into her country, corrupted its leading men and then betrayed them to execution, played every one false in turn, and was rapidly seizing her whole territory. To save themselves from him, the states of Flanders secretly negotiated with the Emperor for the above marriage between their young sovereign, Mary, and his son; and in 1478, six months after her father's death, Mary of Burgundy gave herself and all her wide territories to the young Maximilian, and Louis XI, to his great disgust, had to disgorge.

In England the Wars of the Roses still continued, debarring that country from taking any part in the politics of Europe.

In Spain in 1469 (the year that Lorenzo's rule in Florence began) took place the marriage between Ferdinand, King of Arragon, and Isabella, Queen of Castile, whereby for the first time Spain entered as one country into European politics, this marriage uniting the northern half of that country, though the Moors still held the southern portion.

In Milan, after the death in 1476 of the Duke Galeazzo Sforza, his Duchess, Bona of Savoy, governed for a time on behalf of her young son. In 1480, however, her late husband's brother, Ludovico Sforza (commonly known as "Il Moro," owing to his swarthy complexion), managed to banish her, placed her twelve-year-old son Gian Galeazzo, on the throne, and proceeded to govern in his name. And as Il Moro failed to continue the policy of his father and brother in maintaining a close friendship with Florence, this made a material difference to Lorenzo the Magnificent in his labours to preserve the balance of power in Italy.

In southern Italy in 1480, just after Lorenzo had concluded his treaty of peace with Naples, Mahomed II, who after his capture of Constantinople in 1453 had subdued in succession Servia, Bosnia, Albania, and Greece, proceeded to extend his conquests to Italy, and attacked and captured Otranto, massacring the inhabitants. This capture of Otranto by the Turks created great consternation in Italy, and was a principal inducement to Sixtus IV to conclude the peace with Florence already noted. Florence agreed to maintain a fleet of fifteen galleys for employment against the Turks until they should be expelled from Italy.

For the next four years after his peace with Naples and the Pope, Lorenzo was continuously occupied in striving to create a general peace in Italy. Sixtus IV, still endeavouring to seize upon various states for his nephew Girolamo, kept Italy in a constant state of war, in which Milan, Venice, Ferrara, and Naples were all involved; but Lorenzo succeeded in keeping Florence out of it, though for some time his labours to bring all states to peace were without success.

In 1482 Lorenzo's mother, Lucrezia Tornabuoni, died. She had lived to see her elder son's triumph over the cruel enemies who had slain her younger son, and to witness the former's growing power as "the needle of the Italian compass." In the many troubles and anxieties of the previous four years Lorenzo had received much counsel and support from her, and he felt her death greatly. Speaking of it, he says:—"I have lost not only my mother, but my one refuge from many of my troubles, a comfort in my labours, and one who saved me from many of those labours."

In 1483 Lorenzo's second son, Giovanni, though only seven years old, was admitted to minor orders with a view to training him for high office in the Church. And at the same time Louis XI, with whom Lorenzo's influence had now become great, conferred on Giovanni (in accordance with a bad, though not infrequent, custom of the age) the Archbishopric of Aix in Provence. It is curious, and illustrative of the prevailing views on such points, in reading Lorenzo's own account of the matter in his memoirs, to note how he evidently saw nothing incongruous in the matter. He says:—

"On the 19th May we received the intelligence that the King of France had presented to my son, Giovanni, the abbey of Fontedolce. On the 31st we heard from Rome that the Pope had confirmed the grant, and had rendered him capable of holding a benefice, he being now seven years of age. On the 1st of June Giovanni accompanied me from Poggio a Caiano to Florence, where he was confirmed by the Bishop of Arezzo in the chapel of our family,[21] and received the tonsura; and from thenceforth was called 'Messire Giovanni.' The next day we returned to Poggio. On the 8th June arrived advices from the King of France that he had conferred upon Messire Giovanni the Archbishopric of Aix in Provence."[22]

In 1484, all states except the Pope being weary of the war, Lorenzo's efforts were at length successful, and a peace was concluded at Bagnolo between Naples, Milan, and Venice. The news of it greatly enraged Sixtus IV, who was then seriously ill; we are told that on hearing of it he "became speechless with fury"; and (it has been said owing to this cause) on the following day, to the relief of all Italy, he died.

He was succeeded by Innocent VIII (Giambattista Cibò);
and this caused a great improvement in Lorenzo's position.
For, whereas Sixtus IV had been the bitter enemy of the
Medici, with Innocent VIII it was exactly the reverse. He
was much impressed with the political influence of Lorenzo,
and considered it very desirable to keep on good terms with
the powerful ruler of Tuscany, a policy which he steadily
maintained throughout his eight years' pontificate.

In 1481 the united power of the states of Italy, with the
Kings of Arragon, of Portugal, and of Hungary, was put
forth to retake Otranto from the Turks; and upon the receipt
of news, while the siege was proceeding, of the death of Mahomed II Otranto capitulated.

In Spain Ferdinand and Isabella began in 1481 to drive out
the Moors from the southern half of the country, a war which
was to last for the next eleven years.

In England in 1483 Edward IV died, the boy Edward V
was murdered by his uncle Richard, Duke of Gloucester, and
the latter became king. Two years later Richard III was himself killed at the battle of Bosworth, and Henry VII gained the
throne, putting an end to the long period of civil war which
England had endured for thirty years.

In France Louis XI also died in 1483, and was succeeded
by his son, Charles VIII. The latter was a boy of thirteen, of
weak health and small capacity. Louis XI, however, when
dying entrusted to his eldest daughter, Anne of Beaujeu (married to the Duke of Bourbon), the guardianship of her young
brother and the rule of the kingdom during his minority; and
for the next nine years she governed in his name. She displayed
a high intelligence and many remarkable qualities, her nobility of character, justice, and prudence gradually overcoming the ill-will of her brother, the opposition of the French
nobles, and the schemes of Maximilian of Austria, and
obtaining for her the name of "Madame la Grande." Under
her wise methods of government the prosperity of France

greatly increased; while it was she who enabled Henry VII to gain the throne of England.

From the year 1480 Lorenzo the Magnificent remained for the rest of his life undisturbed by dissensions in Florence, and was able to devote himself, especially after the general peace in Italy brought about in 1484, to those arts of peace which were so much more congenial to him than war. Not that his beloved studies were neglected even in the midst of war or the most pressing anxieties. In a letter to Ficino, he says:—

"When my mind is disturbed with the tumults of public business, and my ears are stunned with the clamours of turbulent citizens, how would it be possible for me to support such contentions unless I found a relaxation in Learning?"

Ammirato says:—

"Being now completely free from foreign disturbances, and having perfect quiet at home, he devoted himself to the pleasures and elegancies of peace, occupying himself in the patronage of literature, in book-collecting, in beautifying the city, in bringing into cultivation the surrounding country, and in all those pursuits and studies which have made that age remarkable."

And notwithstanding all the accusations of "despotism" made against Lorenzo, it is impossible not to notice that at no other time in Florence's history was she not only so respected abroad, but also so peaceful, prosperous, and contented at home. Which clearly shows that the form of government established by him was that which ensured the maximum of happiness to the greatest number. It has also been remarked that "the civil equality to which we are accustomed in modern states, but which was quite unknown to the Europe of that age, was by no means unknown to Tuscany in the time of Lorenzo the Magnificent": which seems sufficiently to show that any "despotism" on his part could scarcely have been of a very stringent character.[23] Nor did political affairs, literature, and art absorb the whole of Lorenzo's attention, for under his rule "all industries, commerce, and public works made enormous progress." [24] And in after times the Florentines always looked back to the time of Lorenzo the Magnificent as the happiest and most prosperous period of their history. Nor was this confined only to Florence. Guicciardini commences his celebrated history with the remark that the time of Lorenzo was a season "prosperous beyond any other which Italy had experienced during the long course of a thousand years"; and after a long panegyric on its then happy state, says that this "was by general consent ascribed to the industry and virtue of Lorenzo de' Medici." At the same time in the wider field of European politics Lorenzo became recognised by all sovereigns as the leading man in Italy, and in the Florentine archives may be seen letters to him from Henry VII of England and Louis XI of France, in which both of them address him as an equal, and in the style of a reigning monarch.

But the task of maintaining the peace of Italy, which had devolved upon Lorenzo, was one which taxed all his powers, and it is hard to understand how he found time as he did for all those pursuits which Ammirato mentions. Naples, the Pope, and Milan were only kept from war with the greatest difficulty. Nor was this all. Among the smaller states there existed a chronic condition of feud which required incessant watchfulness on Lorenzo's part in order, by skilful intervention, to prevent it from developing into actual war. He watched over the smallest matters in the politics of other states which might affect, however remotely, the welfare of Florence. Conflicting interests, mutual distrust, and veiled animosity made Italian politics of that time a perfect labyrinth of intrigue. And nowhere is the consummate statesmanship of Lorenzo more apparent than in those portions of his correspondence showing the masterly manner in which he

dealt with the complex situations called forth by these conditions, and demonstrating the successful results which he
achieved.[25] But all this was not done without a strain upon
his powers of mind and body which told severely upon him.
So that we can well understand the wish that he expressed
that he could bury himself for six months in some place
where no rumour of Italian affairs could reach his ears.

In 1484 Florence was drawn into a desultory war with
Genoa, and took Pietrasanta; and in 1487 Lorenzo himself
conducted an expedition against Sarzana (which had been
captured from Florence during the war of 1478-1480), and
retook that town: an act which still further increased his popularity, as the loss of Sarzana had been deeply felt by the
Florentines. In August 1487, while Lorenzo was absent at the
baths of Filetta, whither he had gone owing to his increasing
attacks of gout, his wife, Clarice, died, at thirty-four. She
died somewhat suddenly, and he heard of her death before he
knew that she was ill.

In 1488 Pope Innocent VIII, impressed with Lorenzo's
growing importance, desired a marriage between one of his
sons,[26] Francesco Cibò, and one of Lorenzo's daughters: a
significant sign of the extent to which this citizen family
were rising in worldly estimation. Lorenzo gave him his
eldest daughter, Maddalena. They were married on the 20th
January 1488. An episode in connection with this marriage
gives us a glimpse of the simplicity of the domestic life in the
Medici Palace. It is related that when Francesco Cibò came
with a very grand retinue from Rome for this marriage [27] he
and his suite were splendidly lodged and luxuriously entertained in a separate palace; but after three days Cibò himself
went to stay at the Medici Palace with his future father-in-
law. There, astonished at the simple style of living, so different from what he had been accustomed to in the Papal
palace at Rome, as well as from that which his own retinue
were receiving elsewhere, he thought that an insult was being
put upon him. It was then explained to him that it was no

insult, but the very reverse; that the luxurious entertainment was kept for those who were guests, but that now he was admitted, no longer as a guest, but as one of the family.

In the same year Lorenzo married (22nd May 1488) his eldest son, Pietro, then seventeen,[28] to Alfonsina Orsini, another of that same proud Roman family from whom his own wife had come. Judging from their after results, as represented in Clarice Orsini's son Pietro, and Alfonsina Orsini's son Lorenzo, these two Roman marriages were not at all advantageous to the Medici family.

In 1489 [29] Lorenzo attained a desire which he had much at heart. Though only forty, his health was already failing from hereditary gout. His eldest son, Pietro, showed signs of a careless and arrogant disposition, which did not promise well for his success as a ruler of Florence. Lorenzo was therefore anxious to create a second prop to the family fortunes, so that if Pietro should fail, Giovanni, his second son, might be able to retrieve the failure. If he could get the latter made a cardinal the family wealth and influence would probably, eventually, carry him to the Papal throne: when the family fortunes would be assured. It was therefore a great satisfaction to Lorenzo when by his influence with Innocent VIII he, in this year, though Giovanni was only thirteen, succeeded in getting the latter created a cardinal, the youngest there had ever been.[30]

In 1490 there began in Florence the preaching of the man who was in a few years to become the chief power among the Florentines. Savonarola, a native of Ferrara, had taken up as a special mission the task of recalling the inhabitants of the cities of Italy from their luxurious and profligate ways. He had preached this message first at Florence, as the most important city at that time in Italy; but, unable to get the Florentines to listen to his exhortations, he had departed for several years to preach the same message at Brescia, Reggio, Genoa, and other places. And it was Lorenzo who, in this year 1490, recalled him to preach again his message of reform in

Florence. And this fact should be borne in mind as counter-balancing the baseless statements so often made as to Lorenzo having led the Florentines into profligacy. Nor even when Savonarola's preaching was aimed against himself did Lorenzo resent it. Preaching against the prevailing licentiousness of the times, Savonarola, in predicting the downfall of the various states of Italy before a foreign conqueror, unless a general reformation of morals took place, included among the dynasties who were thus to fall, not only the King of Naples, the Sforza at Milan, the Este at Ferrara, and the occupant of the Papal throne, but also the Medici at Florence. Yet Lorenzo showed no resentment, and took no steps to stop this preaching, though his paramount influence with Pope Innocent VIII would have enabled him at any moment to procure Savonarola's removal. In the following year Lorenzo gave a further example of worthy command over himself. In that year Savonarola was elected prior of the monastery of San Marco, the monastery which had been entirely built and endowed by the Medici. It was consequently customary for the prior on being elected to pay a complimentary visit to the head of the Medici family. Yet when Savonarola, deeming this a worldly and unseemly custom, declined to observe it, Lorenzo treated the discourtesy with dignified forbearance, only saying with a smile: "See now! here is a stranger who has come into my house and will not deign even to visit me." Nevertheless he showed good-will to the prior, often attended his services, and gave as liberally as heretofore to San Marco.

During these two years, 1490 and 1491, Lorenzo was greatly harassed by the quarrel between the King of Naples and the Pope, and by the strenuous labour it involved on his part to keep them from coming to an open rupture. King Ferrante persistently evaded compliance with the terms of the treaty which he had made with the Pope in 1486, and Lorenzo had to exert all his powers of persuasion with Innocent VIII to prevent him from endeavouring to enforce it. At length, however, in February 1492 Lorenzo's efforts to bring them to a better understanding were successful, and they agreed to a mutual settlement of their differences, which set this matter at last at rest.

This completed Lorenzo's work for the maintenance of peace in Italy. He had in twenty-two years perfected that which his grandfather had begun, and created between Venice, Milan, the Pope, and Naples, a firm balance of power which so long as his influence watched over it would keep Italy at peace. But Lorenzo had done more than this, and to protect Florence from the miseries of war had created a more permanent safeguard, one undreamt of by Cosimo. Instead of the chronic enmity with her neighbours which had hitherto always been Florence's condition, Lorenzo—a master in conciliatory action—had in the course of twenty-two years gradually established friendly relations with Siena, Lucca, Bologna, Faenza, Ferrara, Rimini, Perugia, and Città di Castello: thus encircling Florence with a ring of friendly states—a more lasting guarantee for her peace than even a general balance of power. These achievements had brought Italy to that condition referred to by Guicciardini as the most prosperous experienced for a thousand years, and had made Lorenzo recognised even beyond the Alps as the leading statesman of his age.

———————

But Lorenzo the Magnificent has a greater claim to fame than any which is derived from his achievements in the political sphere. It is in the domain of Learning and Art that his chief honour will ever rest; and the former especially was the main interest of his life.

However much controversy may rage round the deeds of the Medici, there is one cause in regard to which it will be difficult to deny that they have deserved unstinted honour and gratitude from Europe at large—that of the *resuscitation of Learning*.[31] And in particular for their rescue, at great cost to themselves, of a mass of invaluable literary treasures

belonging to the classic age, just in time before the spread of
Turkish misrule over all the eastern countries of Europe after
the fall of Constantinople had time to work its natural effects.
For a very few decades of Turkish dominion over these countries would have caused all those treasures to disappear for
ever. Carried out by four generations, there were in this
matter two stages. The time of Lorenzo, notwithstanding all
the enthusiasm of the brilliant *coterie* he gathered round
him, can scarcely be called "a time of learning," such as that
which followed it in the time of Leo X, Erasmus, and the
Scaligers; it was too early for that result. In the case of the
first three of the four generations, the resuscitation of Learning has reference to the splendid work done in unearthing and
making known the materials by which alone later generations
were enabled to become times of learning. Cosimo, Piero, and
Lorenzo did this portion of the work; it remained for
Lorenzo's son, Leo X, to conduct his age to the further step of
becoming a time of learning through the labours of those who
had gone before.

The assistance which Lorenzo gave to this work was unbounded. Large as had been the amounts which his father and
grandfather had given to this object, that which Lorenzo
gave was still larger. It has been computed that in the thirty-
five years, from the recall of Cosimo in 1434 to the death of
Piero in 1469, the family, over and above what they spent in
the search for and rescue of manuscript books from the East,
had given from their private fortune for the public benefit in
the shape of institutions to assist Learning and similar objects
a sum equal, in our present money, to nearly £3,000,000
sterling. To this Lorenzo's own expenditure on the same
object has to be added; and some idea of its extent may be
formed from the amount which he gave annually for books
alone. Mr. Walter Scaife says:—

"Allowing for the difference in the value of money, Lorenzo's annual expenditure *for books alone* amounted to from
£65,000 to £75,000 sterling. He sent the celebrated Giovanni

Lascaris twice to the Orient for the express purpose of discovering and purchasing ancient manuscripts. On his second voyage Lascaris brought back two hundred Greek works, as many as eighty of which were not up to that time even known." [32]

But this was only one item in the process. Not only had such manuscript books to be searched for in Eastern countries, but to be of any use in the spread of Learning, copies of them had to be multiplied; and so an army of copyists [33] were maintained by Lorenzo for this purpose and kept constantly at work. Then, again, there were colleges and other similar institutions to be founded for the assistance of those who had the scholar's instinct but could not afford the necessary books, or the expense of their own maintenance while studying. Among other institutions of this kind, Lorenzo founded the University of Pisa, which, by his liberality to it, he made the most celebrated university of that time in Europe, except that at Florence. When he was only twenty-three (during the time when he and Giuliano were chiefly renowned for their splendid pageants and festivities) he went, at the latter end of 1472, to Pisa to found this university, and stayed there a long time employed on this work, himself taking the direction of the new university. The State gave an annual grant to it of 6,000 florins, but as this was altogether inadequate, Lorenzo gave, to supplement it, more than double that amount out of his private fortune, and by this means obtained for its professors some of the most eminent scholars of the age. But his work at Florence in this direction was still greater; it was at Florence, and in the cause of the Greek language and literature, that the labours of Lorenzo on behalf of Learning culminated. Roscoe tells us that, "while the University of Pisa was for the study of the Latin language and those branches of science of which it was the principal vehicle, it was at Florence only in all Italy that the Greek language was taught, and that there was established a public academy for Greek by means of which the knowledge of the

Greek tongue was extended, not only through all the rest of Italy, but through France, Spain, Germany, and England, from all which countries numerous students attended at Florence who diffused the learning they had there acquired through Europe."

To this Greek academy at Florence Lorenzo gave lavishly, and for its welfare laboured persistently, establishing as its professors such celebrated men as the eminent Johannes Argyropoulos, Theodorus Gaza, Demetrius Chalcondylas,[34] and others. The celebrated William Grocin (afterwards Professor of Greek at Oxford) and Thomas Linacer,[35] the first English scholars who learnt Greek, acquired it at Florence under these great teachers.

All this gives us some idea of how great was the cost of such a work as the resuscitation of Learning. And when joined to Lorenzo's large expenditure on the encouragement of Art, and on State expenses other than those for which he was reimbursed,[36] it caused even the Medici wealth to be heavily reduced; so that Lorenzo the Magnificent died a very much poorer man than his father. But it was money well spent; and his own speech on becoming head of the family, made in reference to the large amount which his father and grandfather had drawn out of the family funds to spend on works of public utility, may be made applicable to himself:—"Some would perhaps think it would be more desirable to have a part of it in their purse; but I conceive it to have been spent to the great advantage of the public, and am therefore perfectly satisfied."

And to the very last Lorenzo's ardour in this cause of spreading a knowledge of learning remained unabated. "The ruling passion strong in death" gained another example in his case. As the two closest of his friends, Angelo Poliziano and Pico della Mirandola, stood weeping by his bedside as he breathed his last, his dying words were:—"I wish that death had spared me till I had completed your libraries."

But Lorenzo's assistance to the cause of Learning did not end here, or with help which he shared with his father and grandfather. The honour which literary men gave to him was not merely that given to a great patron whose wealth was ever at the service of Learning, but was in even greater degree the honour paid to one who was himself an author of literary work, a leader in their own sphere. It is only in recent years that it has become appreciated how high is the place taken by Lorenzo in this respect. Modern opinion, however, credits him with having more of the poetic spirit than any other man of his time, and with having been the leading poetic influence of his age. Thus the most recent authority on the subject says: [37]—

"His (Lorenzo's) sonnets and odes (*canzoni*) are of finer quality than any similar verse since the death of Petrarch; and one seems to catch in them at times an echo of the less highly finished, but also less self-conscious, work of the pre-Petrarchian age, the *dolce stil nuovo* of the expiring thirteenth century. Both he and his friend Politian had felt something of the invigorating influence of the racy Florentine folk-songs; and if Lorenzo had lived free from the entanglements of politics and state-craft, the course of *cinquecento* poetry might have taken another turn. Unfortunately the fashion was left to be set by the courtly poets by whom it was led downwards to the depths of *seicentismo*, with its conceits, its false taste, its insincere sentiment and general lack of all masculine quality."

All Lorenzo's efforts as a writer were employed to put an end to the depreciation of the Italian tongue as compared with Latin. As a boy of seventeen he had declared his belief that this was practicable. In a remarkable letter written by him in 1466 to his friend, Federigo of Naples, he defended what was then the vulgar tongue, declaring that the Tuscan language possessed all the necessary qualifications for literary use, and proving his point by examples from Dante, Petrarch, and Boccaccio; and he urged that the language of Tuscany, so

graceful in its youth, might be made to attain still greater
perfection in its maturity if only the Florentines would earnestly strive to this end. All his writings were intended to
assist this object, and it is chiefly due to these efforts of his
that the Italian language occupies the position it now does,
instead of the lower plane on which it stood in his day.

Lorenzo's poetical writings covered a wide range. He was a
devoted lover of nature and of a country life, and all the best
of his works deal in some form or another with such topics.
He wrote the well-known poem of the *Ambra,* a mythological
poem on the building of his much-loved villa at Poggio a
Caiano, the poem being named after a little island in the
adjacent stream of the Ombrone, and being a description of
the joys of country life and of the delightful spring-time in
Tuscany; *La caccia col falcone,* the doings of a hawking party;
La nencia da Barberino, on Tuscan peasant life, which Symonds styles "a masterpiece of true genius and humour"; *I
Beoni,* a burlesque; and many other poems. "Also numerous
sonnets and love-songs (poems of his youth), mostly inspired
by his romantic but unimpassioned love for Lucrezia
Donati." [38] Nothing came amiss to his muse; he could write
with equal ease pastorals and devotional poetry, sonnets and
carnival ditties, hunting songs and poems on stars and flowers;
and all showing true poetical feeling. [39]

Lorenzo's writings, occupied so largely with that country
life of which he was so fond, open up the pleasantest side of
his character. While here, at all events, we have the satisfaction of being on ground where controversy cannot enter,
since whatever a man's writings show of himself is definite and
incontrovertible. Speaking of how Lorenzo's love of nature,
and sympathy with the feelings and life of the country people,
show themselves in his poetry, Mr. Armstrong says as
follows: [40]—

"As examples of this may be taken the stages in the rose-
bud's life, from his poem *Corinto;* or, a wider theme, the

annual migration of the flocks to the upland pastures. The
flocks pass bleating up the mountain paths, the young lambs
trotting in their mothers' steps; the one just newly born is
carried in the shepherd's arms, while his fellow bears a lame
sheep upon his shoulders; a third peasant is riding the mare
with foal, carrying the posts and nets to guard the flocks from
wolves; the dog runs to and fro proud of his post as escort to
the party. Then comes a little touch of nature unidealised: the
flock is shut within the nets, the shepherds fall to their meal
of milk rolls and biscuits, and then fall fearlessly asleep and
snore all night. Equally well can the poet describe a winter
scene:—the crackling of the leaves beneath the hunter's feet,
his quarry vainly seeking to hide its tracks; the fir tree standing green against the white mountains, or bending its branches
beneath its load of snow; the laurel standing young and joyous
amid the dry leafless trees; the solitary bird that still finds a
hiding-place in the stout cypress which is doing battle with
the winds; the olive grove on a balmy, sunny shore, whose
leaves show green or silver according to the setting of the
wind. Lorenzo finds his materials in the troubles of life as in
its joys; he enters keenly into the sufferings of the peasant
and of animals; he describes one of the woodland fires common
in mountain districts—a chance spark of the flint catching
the dry leaves, then spreading to the brushwood, and then
gaining on ancient oak and ilex, destroying the shadowy
forest homes, the pleasant nests, the lairs where generations of
wild things had stalled themselves, and then the wild rout of
terror-stricken creatures bellowing and shrieking down the
echoing dale. At another time we see the Ombrone in flood,
with its turbid yellow waters grinding stone on stone, bearing
along the plain its mountain spoil of trunk and bough; the
peasant's wife is just in time to free, with trembling hand, the
cattle from the stall. She carries pick-a-back her weeping
little son; behind her is her elder daughter with the poor
household store ... the old shed floats bobbing on the water's
crest. ... It is the close observance of nature which makes
Lorenzo's poetry ever fresh, whether he is describing ants or
bees, or a line of cranes stretching across the sky towards a
sunny spot, or the hunted deer taking its last desperate leap
and the straining eyes of the baffled dogs, or the oxen strug-

gling with their load of stones and logs, or the tired bird falling into the sea because it fears to light upon a ship."

Every one who is conversant with a sportsman's life will feel how these writings of Lorenzo call up scene after scene which has come before his own eyes in the wild life of the mountains, how he is brought in sympathy with the writer, and how none but a man who was an ardent lover of nature, of animals, and of the country people, could observe and write like this.

But no picture of Lorenzo the Magnificent would be complete without notice of that brilliant inner circle of literary men who were his closest friends. Among these the chief were:—POLITIAN, who, before he was eighteen, was already renowned for his translation of the *Iliad* into Latin, at twenty-six was lecturing to students from all countries in Europe on the Greek and Latin classics, and who, though he died at thirty-nine, was the greatest poet of his time;[41] MARSILIO FICINO, who, born in 1433 and trained by Cosimo Pater Patriae, translated Plato and many other works of the ancient writers into Latin, and became the head of the Platonic Academy; LUIGI PULCI, whose celebrated epic poem, *Il Morgante Maggiore,* is said to have been written at the request of Lucrezia Tornabuoni, Lorenzo's mother; and PICO, Count of MIRANDOLA, the most brilliant of the whole band, and celebrated throughout Europe—young, handsome, clever, lofty in character, with graceful bearing and golden hair, knowing twenty-two languages, including Latin, Hebrew, Arabic, and Chaldee, and whose many attainments were the marvel of mankind. He was the most distinguished literary man of the age; Politian calls him "the Phœnix who rested in the laurel" (Lorenzo). "To him," we are told, "all knowledge and all religions were a revelation of God." Savonarola revered his memory, and in his *Triumphus Crucis,* written after Pico's death, declares that "by reason of his loftiness of intellect and the sublimity of his doctrine he should be numbered amongst the miracles of God and nature." Sir Thomas More translated his letters and held him to be a saint. Lorenzo's two closest friends, Politian and Pico della Mirandola, both died soon after him, Politian at the age of thirty-nine, Pico at that of thirty-one, both of them dying in 1494.[42]

To the above four must also be added the celebrated scholar, CRISTOFORO LANDINO, who in his *Disputations* (first published about 1475) relates certain notable discussions of this group of brilliant intellects which took place when on one occasion they were gathered at Camaldoli; and VESPA-SIANO DA BISTICCI, "the last of the master-copyists and the first of professional copyists in Europe, whose book, the *Lives of Illustrious Men,* is a mine of information regarding many important historical characters of the time, written by one who knew them personally.

Such were some of the men who were the chief lights in that distinguished society which Lorenzo the Magnificent created around him, a literary *coterie* probably the most brilliant in intellect which has ever been gathered together at one time and place. With such men as its members, and with such a leader, the Platonic Academy attained a brilliancy which has preserved its renown ever since. The gatherings of this society at Lorenzo's villa of Careggi, or sometimes at the Badia of Fiesole, or at the monastery amidst the forests of Camaldoli, produced discussions and recitations which not only revived the love of classical literature and added much to philosophical thought, but also gave birth to that Neo-Platonism, that religion of love and beauty, which absorbed into itself many diverse minds in that epoch, and was also destined to colour all the poetical literature of the succeeding centuries, so that its voice would be heard long afterwards in the poetry of Shelley and Byron, no less than in that of Ariosto and Spenser.

In regard to Art, Lorenzo's encouragement was almost as great. He more than doubled the art collections [43] of the

Medici Palace, and there was scarcely a contemporary painter or sculptor who was not assisted by him; while to his liberal patronage he added a universally valued critical knowledge.

The unerring *taste* in Art which the Medici as a family possessed is evidenced by the fact that no painter or sculptor of that age is to be found whose work is recognised now as of high excellence yet who was not appreciated by the Medici. They never made a mistake in such matters. To this unerring taste on their part Florence owes it that while the art collections of Rome, accumulated by the Popes, are greater in quantity, those of Florence—almost entirely the private collections of the Medici—surpass those of Rome in quality. And no member of his family possessed this sound critical knowledge and infallible taste to so great a degree as Lorenzo the Magnificent.

As had been the case with his father, Piero, the leading artists of the day did most of their work for him, and nearly every work of eminence in painting or sculpture belonging to Lorenzo's time remaining in Florence, was commissioned by him. Verrocchio did almost all his work for him; that sculptor's graceful tomb in San Lorenzo over Lorenzo's father and uncle, his bronze *David*, and his fountain of *The boy with a dolphin*, were all executed for Lorenzo. Botticelli he made his family painter as well as friend, and all the pictures of Botticelli's second period were painted for him. It was Lorenzo who caused Ghirlandajo's frescoes in Sta. Maria Novella and Santa Trinità to be painted; and it was he who selected and sent Leonardo da Vinci to Milan to become Il Moro's great painter. Among others he also gave commissions to Filippino Lippi, Signorelli, Baldovinetti, Benedetto da Majano, Andrea del Castagno, and the Pollajuoli. The Medici Palace became, Symonds says, "a museum, at that period unique in Europe, considering the number and value of its art treasures"; and these he made available to all young artists for purposes of study. There being at that time no school for sculpture, Lorenzo formed one in his garden near San Marco, collected

there casts from many antique statues, placed the school in
charge of Donatello's pupil, Bertoldo, and invited all young
sculptors to study there. Among those who did so were Lorenzo di Credi, Michelangelo, and many others afterwards
famous. Vassari says that every young man who studied in
this garden distinguished himself. Lorenzo had an eagle eye
for detecting genius, and when Michelangelo was fifteen
years old [44] Lorenzo, chancing to see in his garden the mask
of a grinning faun which the boy had sculptured, made him
an inmate of the Medici Palace, where he was treated as one
of the family, and, Vasari says, was given an allowance of
five ducats a month and resided there for four years; which
would mean until the Medici family were driven into exile
in 1494.

And it was an important time for such encouragement to
Art. For the Renaissance in Art was now approaching the
full blaze of its zenith. Every one of the great masters, except
Tintoretto, was living in the time of Lorenzo the Magnificent.
And although of these Luini, Fra Bartolommeo, Michelangelo,
Giorgione, Titian, Palma Vecchio, Sodoma, Andrea del
Sarto, and Raphael were as yet children, the following were all
at work, viz.: Verrocchio, Botticelli, Ghirlandajo, Perugino,
Leonardo da Vinci, Filippino Lippi, and Lorenzo di Credi;
besides the Bellini and Carpaccio at Venice,[45] Mantegna at
Mantua, Francia at Bologna, and Pinturicchio at Perugia.

Verrocchio, "the true eye," whose real name was Andrea
di Cione, was the chief pupil of Donatello. He executed
many works for Lorenzo the Magnificent, but whether owing
to the subsequent commotions when the Medici were driven
out and their palace plundered, or other cause, very few
of his works remain. Among these are, his tomb of Giovanni
and Piero de' Medici in San Lorenzo; his bronze statue of
David, now in the Bargello Museum; the group of *Christ
and St. Thomas* outside Or San Michele, which has been said
to be the most beautiful head of Christ ever executed; and

his fountain of *The boy with a dolphin,* made for Lorenzo's villa of Careggi, and now in the courtyard of the Palazzo Vecchio. One writer calls this statue "the little boy who for ever flits across the court, while the dolphin struggles in his arms, whose pressure sends the water spurting from its nostrils." And Perkins says:—"Like a sunbeam which has found its way into these gloomy precincts, it brightens them by its presence." Verrocchio's last work was the splendid equestrian statue in bronze of Colleoni at Venice, the second equestrian statue executed since the times of ancient Rome,[46] and superior to that of Gattamelata by Donatello at Padua. Verrocchio only lived to complete the model in clay (of both horse and man) and the casting was completed by Leopardi. Still less of Verrocchio's work as a painter remains. Besides the *Baptism of Christ,* now in the Accademia at Florence, only one other of his pictures is in existence, that of the *Madonna adoring the infant Christ,* now in the Ruskin museum at Sheffield. But Verrocchio's chief fame as a painter is that he was the master of Lorenzo di Credi and Leonardo da Vinci. Verrocchio died in 1488.

When to the graver atmosphere of the time of Piero il Gottoso there succeeded all that season of youthful joy and light-heartedness which marked the first nine years of the rule of Lorenzo the Magnificent, this change in the spirit of the time caused a corresponding change in Botticelli's painting; so that we find him painting in this his second period [47] all those pictures which are so permeated with the spirit of that time. To these have to be added, in the latter half of this period of his painting, his fresco pictures at Rome.

(II)

The chief pictures of Botticelli's second period are the *Birth of Venus, Mars and Venus,* the *Return of Spring,* and *Pallas subduing the Centaur,* pictures in which contemporary events are memorialised under the symbolism of classic myths clothed in a fifteenth-century dress. We have already seen [48] how the first three of these refer to the tournament of 1475, to the brighter era which Lorenzo had inaugurated, and to his work in the domain of literature; and how the fourth refers to the deliverance of Florence by Lorenzo from the war and peril following on the Pazzi Conspiracy.

Soon after the war was ended Botticelli was summoned (in 1481) by Pope Sixtus to Rome to assist, with Perugino and Ghirlandajo, in painting the celebrated series of frescoes covering the walls of the newly-erected Sixtine chapel. His portions of this work consist of the frescoes representing the early life of Moses, the destruction of Korah, the purification of the leper, the temptation of Christ, and the portraits of the seven martyred bishops of Rome. These important frescoes gained Botticelli added renown and he returned to Florence with a great reputation. For the next few years he was, in consequence, in great request among the owners of important villas near Florence, all desiring to have frescoes painted by him in their villas. Amongst others he painted at this time for Lorenzo Tornabuoni an important series of frescoes in the villa of the Tornabuoni family (now Villa Lemmi) at Rifredi, representing events in the history of that family.[49] Also (apparently) a series of frescoes in the villa of Castello, painted for Giovanni di Pier Francesco, of the younger branch of the Medici family. Then came the death of Lorenzo the Magnificent and the expulsion shortly afterwards of the Medici, and Botticelli found himself in a Florence the whole atmosphere of which was completely changed under the influence of Savonarola. So again Botticelli's style changes, and we have the pictures of his third period, which will best be considered in connection with the events which caused this entire change in the life of Florence.[50]

As in Cosimo's day, so also was it in that of Lorenzo. There could scarcely be a greater contrast than exists between the two chief painters of his time, Botticelli and

Ghirlandajo; the former so full of that spirit of speaking to the mind through the eye that every one of his pictures is replete with deep and original thoughts; the latter absolutely without a vestige of this power. Ghirlandajo, though his drawing and colouring are perfect, is constantly called "commonplace" and "prosaic," while it has even been said of him, notwithstanding all his powers of technique, that he is "without the art faculty"; and this feeling regarding his work is undoubtedly caused by this entire absence in him of imagination and originality of thought. Thus in his pictures we find our attention ever drawn to the accessories of the subject rather than to the subject itself; while of all such accessories he is a most careful and prosaically accurate delineator.

But each of the great masters has his own excellence; and Ghirlandajo's lies in this very direction. Ruskin, being noticeably without the historic faculty, could see no excellence in Ghirlandajo, and severely condemns his work on all occasions, calling it the mere handicraft of the mechanic. But those who are interested in what the men and women of this time in Florence looked like can forgive Ghirlandajo his want of the art faculty for the sake of the results on the historic side, results which, had he not given them to us, we should have looked for in vain elsewhere. Ghirlandajo's want of originality led him to be a most careful copyist in every dirction to which he turned his powers. And as he introduced into his pictures on religious subjects representations of the persons of note around him (carried out with a careful accuracy which rendered him quite incapable of flattering them),[51] together with many details of everyday life in Florence, we obtain from him a valuable record of the appearance and manner of life of the men and women of the time of Lorenzo the Magnificent. In this way Ghirlandajo gives us in his frescoes in the choir of Santa Maria Novella portraits of Politian, Marsilio Ficino, Cristoforo Landino, and Demetrius Chalcondylas;[52] of the painters Baldo-

vinetti, Mainardi, Ghirlandajo himself, and his brother; of
the bankers Sassetti and Ridolfi; of the members of the
Tornabuoni family; of the reigning Florentine beauty of
the day, Giovanna degli Albizzi, who in 1486 married Lorenzo Tornabuoni; of the well-known dealer in arms and
armour, Niccolò Caparra; and others. Again in his frescoes
in the church of Santa Trinità we have portraits of Maso
degli Albizzi, Palla Strozzi, Agnolo Acciajuoli, and of Lorenzo himself. And in the church of Ognissanti, in his fresco of
the Vespucci family he has given us a portrait (painted about
1474) of Amerigo Vespucci, who gave his name to America.
Ghirlandajo's best picture is the *Adoration of the Shepherds*,
painted for the Sassetti chapel in Santa Trinità, and now in
the Accademia delle Belle Arti.[53] Ghirlandajo died in 1494,
and is buried in Santa Maria Novella.

In Lorenzo's time the four principal villas possessed by the
Medici were the villa of Careggi, the Medici Villa at Fiesole,
the villa of Cafaggiolo [54] in the valley of the Mugello, originally built by Cosimo and largely added to by Lorenzo, and
the villa at Poggio a Caiano, about twelve miles to the
north-west of Florence, built by Lorenzo.

———————

Lorenzo only lived for two months after effecting the
reconciliation between the King of Naples and the Pope.
He had for years suffered (like his father and grandfather)
from gout, and all through the year 1491 his health was rapidly failing. In consequence he had begun to entrust part of
the public affairs to his eldest son, Pietro. In giving the latter
advice regarding his future conduct as head of the State,
Lorenzo specially warned him never to forget that his position was simply that of a citizen of Florence, telling him
that his own success had been mainly due to his uniform care
on this point.

In February 1492 Lorenzo's attacks became so severe

that he was unable to attend to any business. Early in March
the three years expired during which his son Giovanni's appointment as a cardinal was to be kept secret, and it was
publicly announced. He was formally invested with his new
rank in the Badia of Fiesole, and a grand banquet was given
at the Medici Palace in honour of the occasion; but Lorenzo
was only able to be carried in on a litter to see the brilliant
company assembled to do honour to his son. Giovanni, now
sixteen, had forthwith to leave for Rome to take his seat
in the Sacred College; and on the 12th March he left Florence for the Papal city. Nine days later Lorenzo had himself carried to Careggi and prepared for his end, gathering
around him several of his closest friends, and making them
read to him portions of his favourite authors. From his death-
bed he wrote to Giovanni a long letter of advice and farewell.[55]

This letter to his young son is a very remarkable one.
Striking as it is for its evidence of calm equanimity and
mental vigour unimpaired even by severe illness and approaching death, it is yet more so for the light it throws on
Lorenzo's character. For to a large extent it contradicts forcibly the view of him which a long succession of writers
resolutely biassed against him have made the prevailing
one. Not remarkable, perhaps, had it emanated from some
other source, it is so to us solely because of the false impression of the man which has been given us.

Lorenzo died on the 9th April 1492, at the age of forty-
three, at his villa of Careggi, that much-loved home of his
leisure hours, where Plato and Homer, Virgil and Horace had
been worshipped, and the Muses revered. His two closest
friends, Politian and Pico della Mirandola, were with him
to the last. As his end approached he sent for a priest, who
administered to him the last sacrament; he got out of bed
to receive it kneeling, but was too weak and had to lie down
again. He had already sent to ask Savonarola to come to
him; and it says much for Lorenzo that he should have de-

sired an interview with the uncompromising friar. After it was over a crucifix was held before Lorenzo; he raised himself up to kiss it, fell back, and died.[56]

There are two very different accounts of what took place at the interview with Savonarola. On the one hand we have the account (written at the time) by Politian, who was present,[57] and who simply states that Savonarola exhorted Lorenzo to hold fast to the Faith, to resolve to amend his life if spared, and to meet death, if it was to be so, with fortitude; that he then prayed with him and gave him his blessing. The other account (which appeared long afterwards) is the well-known story that Lorenzo confessed to Savonarola three sins which lay heavy on his conscience—the sack of Volterra, the bloodshed after the Pazzi Conspiracy, and the misappropriation to his own use of some of the Dower Fund; [58] that Savonarola required from him a promise to restore the money thus misappropriated, to which it is said Lorenzo assented; that Savonarola then required that he should restore the liberties of Florence, to which Lorenzo made no reply, and that thereupon Savonarola left him unabsolved.

This picturesque story bears on its face evidence of its falsity. It did not appear until fifty years after Lorenzo and Savonarola were both dead, and admittedly rests on hearsay evidence, whereas Politian wrote as an eye-witness and within a few weeks of the event. Supposing the story true, then it must have been related either by Lorenzo or by Savonarola, for it expressly states that none other was present when Lorenzo made his confession. Burlamacchi, who put it forward, declared that he had the story from Savonarola's own lips. "But," says Bishop Creighton, "we may be pardoned for sparing Savonarola's fame the supposition that he made political capital for his own glorification out of the secrets of the confessional; still less probable is it that the tale was revealed by Lorenzo in an agony of remorse after Savonarola's departure and just before his death." [59]

Moreover, a still more conclusive fact has failed to be observed, namely, that (no matter what may or may not be the truth about them) the three things represented as weighing on Lorenzo's conscience could not have done so *from Lorenzo's point of view*. For the sack of Volterra he was so remotely responsible, and had made such efforts to ameliorate the sufferings caused, that he could not have felt the matter weighing on his conscience; for the slaughter in connection with the Pazzi Conspiracy he was not only not responsible, but had remonstrated with the infuriated people against it, and had saved some of those implicated in the crime; while as regards the Dower Fund the charge would, for the reasons already stated, have appeared to him merely absurd. And still more so since Lorenzo's just dealing in all money matters is very noticeable; not only just, but liberal, dealing in money matters was a marked feature of his character.[60] The so-called misappropriation has been explained above, but in this connection it may be remarked that when four years afterwards Savonarola was himself the ruling power in Florence, exactly the same use (or misappropriation) of the money of this Dower Fund was continued; which completely stultifies any such charge as specially applicable to Lorenzo. Lastly, the final request attributed to Savonarola would have meant the return to a state of things which to Lorenzo represented everything most harmful to Florence's welfare; while it is inconceivable that Savonarola should have required from the dying man that which he was in any case at that moment powerless to perform.

This story has probably played a greater part in creating the mental picture generally formed of Lorenzo the Magnificent than any of the authenticated facts of his life. The artifice of pretending that certain things weighed on his conscience is a much more effective way of instilling in us a belief that he had been guilty of those things than a plain statement to that effect would have been. The story has had a great vogue, both on account of its sensational character,

and of the opportunity it furnishes for calumniating the
Medici, but since the careful analysis of it made by Bishop
Creighton [61] its complete mendacity has been fully estab-
lished. Roscoe's remark is justified:—

"A story that exhibits evident symptoms of that party
spirit which did not arise in Florence until after the death
of Lorenzo, and which is entirely contradictory to the account
left by Politian, written before the motives for misrepresentation existed, is rendered deserving of notice only by the
necessity of its refutation."

Lorenzo the Magnificent and Clarice Orsini had seven
children:—

> Pietro, who succeeded his father.
> Giovanni, afterwards Pope Leo X.
> Giuliano, afterwards Duc de Nemours.
> Maddalena, who married Francesco Cibò.
> Lucrezia, who married Jacopo Salviati.
> Maria, who died unmarried in 1487.
> Contessina, who married Piero Ridolfi.

Lucrezia's husband was a great-grandson of the Jacopo Salviati who was Cosimo's friend, and was a cousin of the Archbishop Salviati hung in the Pazzi Conspiracy. Lorenzo made
the match to re-establish cordial relations between his family and their old friends, the Salviati.

In appearance Lorenzo the Magnificent was unprepos-
sessing. At the same time the portrait of him by Vasari,[62]
painted more than fifty years after Lorenzo's death by a man
who never saw him, would seem not to give a true likeness
of him. It neither accords with the descriptions of his appearance given by contemporary writers, nor with the portraits of him on medallions by contemporary medallists, and
would almost seem intended to degrade his memory by giving him as sinister an appearance as possible and surrounding him with the attributes of a buffoon.[63] Niccolò Valori,
speaking of Lorenzo's appearance, says:—

"He was above the common stature, broad-shouldered, and solidly built, and second to none in athletic exercises. . . . His complexion was dark, and although his face was not handsome, it was so full of dignity as to compel respect."

It is well known that medallions of this period are as a rule much more reliable than painted portraits; and the two which exist of Lorenzo by the celebrated contemporary medallists, Bertoldo and Pollajuolo,[64] show a plain but very powerful face, with something of the look of his father, Piero il Gottoso. The portraits on these medallions also receive strong corroboration from the terra-cotta cast of Lorenzo's face taken after death, and now the property of the Società della Columbaria. So that we may conclude that these portraits, and not Vasari's picture, give us the true representation of Lorenzo. Speaking of the concentrated power of his face, Miss Cruttwell says:—

"In the best portraits that exist of him—that of the Pazzi medal and the superb death-mask of the Confraternity of the Columbaria—the face, with its compressed lips, stern brow, and powerful jaw, might serve as the embodiment of physical and intellectual force." [65]

If, however, Lorenzo's outward appearance assisted him little, his manner more than restored the balance. It is said to have been so extraordinarily fascinating that it caused his plain face and harsh voice to be entirely forgotten. This statement of contemporary writers is fully borne out by various episodes in Lorenzo's life, which make it evident that he had an unfailing power of charming all, both high and low, who were brought in contact with him.

Speaking of Lorenzo in his social capacity, Mr. Armstrong [66] says:—

"Of his qualities as a host and companion there can be no question. . . . He was the soul of courtesy and kindliness, always ready to aid talent, to oblige a friend, to grant a petition, to perpetrate a job, to be button-holed in the public street. The simplicity and friendliness of his letters to his embassadors fully account for the devotion with which they served him. For scholars and artists he kept open house; whoever came first, whatever his age or rank, took his seat at the host's side. His conversation, as his character, has the fascination of variety. At times his tongue had a rough edge. To a cousin who boasted of the copious supply of water at his villa, he says: 'Then you might well afford to keep cleaner hands'; to a Sienese who condoled with him on his indifferent eyesight and added that the air of Florence was bad for the sight, Lorenzo retorts: 'And that of Siena for the brain.' To one who adversely criticised the character of the musician Squarcialupo, Lorenzo said: 'If you knew how hard it is to obtain perfection in any art, you would overlook shortcomings.' "

His achievements have already been detailed. But that a man who died at the age of forty-three should have been able to do all that he did, in raising Florence so high in political power and commercial prosperity, in maintaining the peace of Italy and converting chronic enmity with surrounding states into friendship, in making the Tuscan language the general language of Italy by his works as an author, in carrying forward to so great an extent the resuscitation of Learning, and in helping so largely the advancement of Art, is extraordinary. It did in very truth require that "enduring indomitable strength" which he symbolised by his crest of the three diamond rings to achieve such results in so comparatively short a life.

Lorenzo the Magnificent has been acknowledged by the united voice of Europe to have been one of the most remarkable men who ever held the rule of a State; and his character has always interested mankind, though perhaps it is only in these days that his greatness in a larger sphere has come to be fully appreciated. He was a leader in an age which abounded with great men. And he has been recognised as being one of the chief inspiring forces of the fifteenth century. He is the most important man of all those whose story we are following, and it is therefore worth while to examine that much-debated character in more detail than can be devoted to others.

The violently contradictory opinions common in regard to the Medici culminate in the case of Lorenzo the Magnificent. With writers belonging to the one camp he has every virtue, with those belonging to the other every vice; with the former all his actions are attributed to the noblest motives, with the latter even the most ordinary actions are, in order to show base motives, distorted until they result in statements which are glaringly incompatible.

Apart, however, from this point, another difficulty lies in the versatility of his character, a quality of many-sidedness which he shared with many of his family, but which was specially prominent in him. Speaking of this characteristic in Lorenzo, and the difficulty which it creates, Mr. Armstrong says as follows: [67]—

"It is the prize, or the penalty, of a versatile receptive nature to be regarded as a mystery. The slower mind cannot follow with sufficient speed the workings of so sensitive an instrument, though the eye marks the multiplicity of results. The reality is that the action and reaction of circumstances and character are peculiarly rapid, but the observer believes that the outward manifestations are artificial and dramatic, having little relation to the inner life. This forms a real difficulty in the appreciation of the south European character by Anglo-Saxons, who are seldom genuinely versatile. They have an inborn, deep-seated distrust for such natures; the few English public men, for instance, who have been so gifted have been regarded, at the best, as problems, but more often as impostors, or as characters abnormally weak and changeable.

"Thus it is that Lorenzo the Magnificent has been so often called a mystery.... Really, however, there has seldom been a nature less mysterious. He was completely natural, singularly open to the influence of circumstances. As his in tellect was versatile, so his character was receptive. He possessed in abundance that quality of 'give and take,' that power of impressing others and of receiving their impression, that gift of *simpatia* which to the Italian expresses so much more than its English representative. . . . Lorenzo was equally natural and unaffected whether he were planning a comic novelty for the Carnival, or critically examining the last new manuscript that his agents had brought or forwarded from Greece or elsewhere. At table he would give grave advice to young Michelangelo, throw a rhyme or epigram across the board to Pulci, or discuss the problem of unity in plurality with Marsilio Ficino. He would give audience to an ambassador, or a horse trainer, or a popular preacher; hold a party *caucus* in the Via Larga, attend a critical meeting of the Government, and then ride off to Careggi or Caiano to play with his children, and rise with the lark to ride to hounds, or fly his favourite falcons. Lorenzo's versatility is the frequent theme even of his contemporary countrymen. . . . A lover of the country rather than of the town, whenever he could he would escape to Poggio a Caiano or more distant villas. He was fond of the country people, their manners, their songs, and their pleasures. . . . His family life was extremely simple; he romped with his children, joined in their music, wrote a religious play for them to act. . . . In Lorenzo's career it is impossible to draw a hard and fast line between diplomacy and politics, art and literature, religion and philosophy, domesticity and public life, country sports and city functions. It is difficult to analyse so manifold a character."

Among the charges which a later age found to make against Lorenzo, that of profligacy and of corrupting the Florentines gives most evidence of the virulent partisan spirit which has been mentioned, owing to the entire want of ground for the accusation. So far as his private character is concerned no facts have been brought forward to support the charge. Judged by the standard of his day he was not an immoral man. His conduct in this respect was superior to that of contemporary sovereigns, our own in England not excepted. It is also noticeable that no illegitimate children are ascribed to him: almost a unique instance in that age. But it is in his public capacity that the charge is chiefly made, alleging that he debased the popular taste by the introduction of licentiousness into Art and Literature: an accusation utterly without foundation, and levelled against one most of whose poetry was of an elevating character. In support of this charge his Carnival songs are often cited; but here again the standard of the age must determine the point. And judged by that standard the verdict will be conclusive. Nothing can be said against Lorenzo's poetry in this respect which cannot be said with much greater force against, for instance, Shakespeare. Roscoe remarks:—

"In the poem of Brandolini, the attention of Lorenzo to the dictates of morality is the particular subject of praise, and that by a contemporary writer. Had the conduct of Lorenzo been notoriously licentious, *such praise would have been the severest satire.*" [68]

The accusation that the profligacy of the time among the Florentines is to be laid on Lorenzo's shoulders receives strong contradiction from the contemporary records of Milan, Venice, Ferrara, Mantua, and many other capital cities of Italy, since we there find at this period exactly the same state of things, and the same tendency to sensuous amusements and licentiousness. replacing a severer style of life. It was a general result of the bursting forth of the Renaissance, and had no special manifestation in Florence; in fact, rather the reverse. Lorenzo, as regarded his own private life, was better than his time; while the idea that a ruler should endeavour to elevate his people was one which did not dawn on Europe till many generations later, and it is not likely that it ever crossed his mind. By other writers, again, this corruption of the Florentines is declared to consist in a deterioration from their former strength of character, and the charge which these writers make against

Lorenzo is that of having exercised "an enfeebling influence."
But we do not find this supposed enfeeblement borne ou
by the history of the time, or find the Florentines at the end
of Lorenzo's rule any feebler in character than at its com
mencement. The Florence which in 1494 did not quail befor
the threats of a Charles VIII showed itself no less strong
than that which in 1478 braved the wrath of a Sixtus IV
It was another kind of enfeeblement of which, after the exile
of the Medici, the Florentines had to complain—that due to
their own faction-fighting, and not to any action on the par
of Lorenzo.

Another charge which shows no less animus is that which
asserts that Lorenzo enriched himself at the expense of the
public funds. Various circumstances afforded opportunity
for this charge. Not only was Lorenzo expected to provide
royal hospitality in the Medici Palace to distinguished visitors
to Florence (expenditure which was seldom refunded to him
by the State), but also he frequently had to advance from
the Medici bank the war expenses of the State, and this was
sometimes refunded to him and sometimes not. He had also
in the conduct of foreign affairs constantly to disburse large
sums as secret subsidies to foreign states; these sums were
either advanced or reimbursed to him by the State, but the
secret nature of their expenditure naturally left it open to
any one to suggest that he spent the money on himself. Those
to whom every act of the Medici has an evil aspect have not
failed to take advantage of such an opportunity, while it
seems forgotten that *"secret service money"* is a regular item
of expenditure of every modern government, and is (necessarily) never accounted for by the high official to whom its
expenditure is entrusted. Hence we find these transactions
called "peculation" and "embezzlement" on Lorenzo's part
Such a charge, made against one who had spent his private
funds on the public behalf to so large an extent that even the
immense fortune left him by his father was severely reduced

hereby, gives us a measure of the length to which the partisan spirit against the Medici can go.

At a meeting held three days after Lorenzo's funeral the Signoria officially placed it on record that "he always subordinated his own interest to the advantage and benefit of the community; shrank neither from trouble nor danger for the good of the State and its freedom; and devoted to that object all his thoughts and powers, securing public order by excellent laws." [69] Are we then, on the one hand, to hold this as the correct view of Lorenzo's character and conduct, and that Hallam, Burckhardt, and Gregorovius are right? Or, on the other hand, was Lorenzo "a usurper who aimed only at his own interest," and embezzled the public money; one in whom the enslavement of Florence "was the hard work of his manhood"; and one who for this end "deliberately led the Florentines into profligacy," as alleged by Sismondi, Perrens, Symonds, Villari, and Trollope? [70] Examining the conflicting evidence, and more particularly the facts of Lorenzo's life admitted by all, it would appear that the charge of being a "usurper" cannot be maintained especially in the face of the high authority of Hallam; [71] that the charge of having "enslaved" or made himself a "tyrant" over Florence is utterly irreconcilable with the fact that he had no military force and that his power rested solely on the will of the people; that the charge of "embezzlement" is, for the reasons already given,[72] one which only prejudice can assert; and that the charge of profligacy and of debasing the public taste by introducing licentiousness into Art and Letters is without an atom of foundation.[73]

But, after all, the best evidence as to which side in this controversy is right is furnished by the people of Florence themselves, those who lived under Lorenzo's rule, and who if his actions were such as his detractors have asserted, had to bear the results of them. Did the Florentines as a whole during his lifetime regard Lorenzo with pride and approbation, and sorrow for his death as a national loss; or did they look upon that death as a joyful release to them from the tyranny of a usurper who embezzled the moneys of the State and enriched himself at their expense? It is incontestable that the former, and not the latter, was the view they held; and the evidence which such a fact supplies is absolutely conclusive upon the whole matter.[74]

Lorenzo's funeral was, in accordance with his own instructions, an unostentatious one. He was buried, like his great-grandfather and father, in the Old Sacristy in San Lorenzo, in the same tomb with his brother Giuliano. From thence, however, his and Giuliano's remains were, sixty-seven years afterwards, removed to the New Sacristy, which had by that time been added to the church. Lorenzo and Giuliano lie buried under the end wall of this sacristy, that opposite to the altar.[75]

It is, however, strange to record that no monument marks the grave of the great Lorenzo the Magnificent; while we see that the absence of such a monument actually in course of time caused a doubt as to where he was buried. Michelangelo was to have executed a monument for his tomb, but left Florence without doing so; and so matters have remained ever since. Probably this is chiefly because none have since liked to propose the erection of a monument which by its situation would challenge comparison with the only two other tombs in the chapel, the masterpieces of Michelangelo. No doubt the difficulty is a considerable one; at the same time it seems, from a national point of view, a great pity that it should work such a result. If one may venture to suggest, possibly the difficulty might be met by placing on the wall over the tomb a large black marble slab, perfectly plain, with simply the name *Lorenzo il Magnifico* on it, and year of birth and death, without any other words; it would rely for impressiveness solely on its size, massiveness, and absolute plainness.[76] Such a monument would avoid all clashing with Michelangelo's masterpieces, while it would be in accord with Lorenzo's own sentiments (shown in the instructions as to his funeral), as well as with the spirit of those earlier generations of the Medici to which these two brothers belonged.

Mr. Armstrong's words on the absence of any monument in Florence to Lorenzo the Magnificent are as follows:—

"Florence has not repaid the generous recognition to Lorenzo which he himself gave to others.[77] With or without her wish the fame of the Medici will for ever be linked with hers. In Lorenzo's own words, *'The house goes with the State.'* After four hundred years she might well lay the ghost, if such there be, of political antipathy, to honour with a fitting monument the most national, the most gifted, representative of that many-sided culture for which the city of the Arno is still famous."

Several very important events in the history of Europe took place in the same year as the death of Lorenzo the Magnificent.

Spain.—The consolidation of Spain, begun in 1469 by the marriage of Ferdinand, King of Arragon, with Isabella, Queen of Castile, was in 1492 completed. Ferdinand and Isabella (joint sovereigns), after having between the years 1474 and 1481 created peace and order in their previously troubled dominion, resumed in the latter year the war against the Moors. Their arms met with a wonderful succession of victories, and at length, in 1492, after eleven years of war, Granada, which had been the Moorish capital for two hundred and fifty years, was taken, the Mahomedan power in Spain was ended, and they were driven out after eight hundred years' occupation. In the same year there also took place the discovery of America by Columbus, under the auspices of Ferdinand and Isabella, which added still further to the glory of their reign, and to the power of Spain. The year 1492 was truly a great one for Spain.

Rome.—In the same year, two months after the death of

Lorenzo the Magnificent, Pope Innocent VIiI also died. He was succeeded by the notorious Spaniard, Roderigo Borgia (Alexander VI). This caused Giovanni de' Medici to return to Florence, he being one of the cardinals who had voted against Roderigo Borgia's election, and all these having to fly from Rome.

France.—In this year Charles VIII, having attained the age of twenty-two, took over the government of the kingdom from his capable sister, and began to form projects which were ere long to issue in an invasion of Italy destined to usher in a new era in international politics.

CHAPTER X

Born 1471. (*Ruled* 1492-1494.) *Died* 1503

ON Lorenzo's death Pietro, the eldest of his three sons, succeeded to the headship of the family and the rule of Florence. He himself was twenty-one, his brother Giovanni (who returned from Rome two months after Pietro's rule began) was sixteen, and his brother Giuliano a boy of thirteen. Pietro was strong, handsome, and excelled in all athletic pursuits, but he gained almost in boyhood the name by which he is always known. "It seemed merely to require that he should be a party to any project for it invariably to fail of success." This peculiarity his qualities of character did not tend to neutralise. He had a heedless temperament, and was more inclined to occupy himself in sport and amusement than in attending to affairs of State; while he was cursed with a haughtiness of disposition which he took no pains to conceal, and which ill accorded with the sentiments of republican Florence. Pietro was not a fool, as often stated.[1] He was simply an ordinary young noble of his day, without more brains than other people possessed. But the Medici had always had more brains than other people possessed; it was expected of them; and they were not wanted by the Florentines as rulers if they ceased to be thus gifted.

His wife, Alfonsina Orsini, was just of the character calculated to double the difficulties created by his own faults. She had a full share of the Orsini pride, and by her unconcealed contempt for the Florentines had, even before Lorenzo's death, made herself intensely disliked by them Seeing how esentially the Medici rule depended upon popular ity, Pietro was evidently as unfortunate in the character of the wife who had been given him as in other matters.

We now come to an important turning-point in the history of the Medici. Whereas each generation of this family had had to encounter a formidable attempt to crush them— storms which they had weathered—there was now to come upon them one destined to involve them in many vicissitudes.

Within a year of his succeeding to the rule of Florence, Pietro, chiefly from his disregard of republican forms and of that attitude of equality with every citizen of Florence which his father had so scrupulously observed, began to be very unpopular. Moreover, this unpopularity was increased by his cousins of the younger branch, Lorenzo and Giovanni, the two sons of Pier Francesco. The first two generations of the younger branch had evinced no jealousy against the elder branch on account of their more exalted position. But in the third generation we find Pier Francesco's two sons (their father having died in 1476) beginning, even in the time of Lorenzo the Magnificent, to grow jealous of the importance of the elder branch, and to show a marked coolness towards them; and this feeling Pietro contrived to excite still more strongly. Towards the end of the life of Lorenzo the Magnificent, Giovanni, who was four years older than his cousin Pietro, fell in love with a lady beloved also by the latter. This, naturally, did not tend to improve matters; nor did a lawsuit, instigated by Pietro, which was its consequence. Whatever the reasons, these two cousins of his now began a regular course of hostility towards him; they fanned his rising unpopularity, headed the party opposed to him, and declared themselves attached to the liberty of the people, which they said he was trying to destroy.

It was unfortunate for Pietro that he succeeded to the rule of Florence just when a storm was about to burst upon Italy, with which it would have needed all his father's ability to cope. When death removed the influence of Lorenzo men fore-

saw that it would not be long before Italy was again plunged
into war; [2] but they did not foresee that to wars between the
Italian states were now to be added those due to contests
between France, Spain, and Germany, of which Italy would
form the battlefield.

The event with which this state of things began was the
invasion of Italy by Charles VIII of France in order to attack
the kingdom of Naples. Very possibly had Lorenzo the Magnificent been still at the helm of Italian politics he would
have found means to avert this particular invasion, but
sooner or later similar results would have been certain to
ensue. For the growing strength of other countries, occurring simultaneously with a decline in power of the Italian
states, rendered foreign attacks certain eventually to come
upon Italy; and we are now entering on the time when that
change was beginning by which, instead of Venice, Milan,
Florence, Naples, and Rome taking the lead in European
politics, France, Spain, Germany, and England were to become the leading countries of Europe. The commencement
of this new era in European politics is marked by the accession of the Emperor Maximilian I, who in 1493 was elected
Emperor on the death, after an uneventful reign of fifty-
three years, of his father, the Emperor Frederick III.

Milan.—In 1490 the young Duke, Gian Galeazzo Sforza,
came of age. But he being feeble and indolent, his capable
uncle, Ludovico Sforza ("Il Moro"), who since 1480 had
governed the Duchy in his name,[3] refused to surrender the
rule to him. Gian Galeazzo's young wife, Isabella of Arragon,
appealed forcibly and continuously to her grandfather, Ferrante, King of Naples, against this usurpation; but up to
1493 the protests of the latter had produced no effect. Some
writers have held that it was because Il Moro saw himself
about to be attacked by Naples that he invited the French
King into Italy; there was, however, no sign that either
King Ferrante (who died in January 1494), or his son and
successor Alfonso, was preparing any force to attack Milan.

Other writers state that Il Moro, having resolved to compass his nephew's death and make himself Duke, invited the French invasion in order to stir up trouble which would prevent the other Italian states from interfering with him. Whichever was the reason, Il Moro now invited Charles VIII to attack Naples, and promised him the support of Milan.

France.—Louis XI, while he had consolidated France, had by his method of doing so crushed to a large extent the spirit of the French nation. Charles VIII, proceeding to rule on different lines from his hated father, had begun to look out for some opportunity for military exploits, both to assist in reviving the spirit of the nation and to gratify his own youthful desire for adventure. When, therefore, Ludovico Sforza urged him to put forward the old Angevin claim to Naples, and to bring an army into Italy to attack that kingdom, Charles eagerly accepted the proposal. French imagination was fired by the idea of an invasion of Italy; all classes caught it up with enthusiasm; and preparations on a great scale were forthwith made for an expedition which to the French had all the attraction of novelty and romance.

This expedition of Charles VIII has a special importance of another kind. For this was the first exercise of the new power created by *a standing army*, a power destined to produce great political changes in Europe. Hitherto the armies of such countries as France and England had consisted of the feudal levies brought to the standard of the king by the barons, and the necessity of humouring the caprices and ever-recurring jealousies of the latter when such a force was gathered together greatly nullified its offensive power. These conditions tended to prevent wars being undertaken against other countries, since they made the invasion of another country, far from the homes of such levies, a most difficult operation. But the new weapon which had been forged by Louis XI, primarily as a means of crushing the barons and princes of France, had altered all this, and while making the king supreme over his barons, had also put in his hand a formidable weapon against other countries. Thus it is not surprising that we find historians stating that Charles VIII (who had no ability of his own) was at this time the most powerful sovereign in Europe. The reason was because he alone was in possession of this new weapon, which his astute father had had the wit to forge, and which no other country as yet possessed.[4]

There was, however, one other point in which a standing army differed materially from a feudal army, viz., in the item of cost. Charles VIII's army, which included infantry, artillery, and cavalry, did not consist of more than about 20,000 men [5] (though this was a great effort for those times), but so little had the increased cost of such an army been realised that before it had penetrated any distance into Italy Charles found his treasury exhausted, and had to borrow large sums from the merchants of Genoa at the ruinous rate of interest of 42 per cent.[6]

In August 1494 Charles VIII started from Vienna to invade Italy. Crossing the Alps he entered Lombardy, and was entertained at Milan by Il Moro, and at Pavia by the Duke Gian Galeazzo; and there the latter's wife, the beautiful and unfortunate Isabella of Arragon, threw herself at the French King's feet to intercede for her house, which he was marching to attack; but she gained nothing. And a few days later, on reaching Piacenza, Charles received the news that the Duke was dead—poisoned, it was universally believed, by his unscrupulous uncle, Il Moro, who at once imprisoned Isabella and her four children, and, notwithstanding that the late Duke had left a son and heir, proclaimed himself Duke of Milan.

Meanwhile the other states of Italy prepared as best they might to meet this invasion. Naples, against whom the attack was directed, awaited it in her own territory. Rome made no preparations for defence, the Pope hoping tha'

Charles would not molest him. Venice declared herself neutral.
Tuscany (having no particular reason to espouse the cause
of Naples) would no doubt have liked to have done the same,
but lying right in the course of the French King's march
was obliged to defend her territory. And Tuscany was ill
prepared. The many years of peace had worked their usual
effect in a want of preparedness for war. And to Pietro's difficulties on this account were added others. His disloyal
cousins, Lorenzo and Giovanni, seized upon this opportunity,
and at a time when all private feuds should have been sunk,
made their country's need the occasion for gratifying their
private jealousy. They sent secret assurances to Charles VIII
that they would promote his views, and would assist him
with money, of which, as has been seen, he was much in need.
This action of theirs was discovered, and they were arrested
by Pietro's orders. No one could have been surprised if they
had been executed as traitors to their country, or at all
events imprisoned. Pietro, however, followed the example
which his grandfather, Piero il Gottoso, had set, and behaved
very leniently towards them, simply confining them, Lorenzo
to the villa of Cafaggiolo, and Giovanni to the villa of
Castello. They repaid him by escaping thence, going to
Charles VIII (who was then at Vigevano), and assuring him
that the Florentines would ally themselves with him against
Naples if only he would help them to get rid of Pietro.

By this time Charles's army was entering the borders of
Tuscany and laying siege to its frontier fortresses, which
were defended by such mercenary troops as Pietro had been
able to collect; but these troops being quite unfit to cope
with such an army failed to arrest the French. The frontier
fortress of Sarzana,[7] which Charles attacked at the end
of October, was soon captured; and the French King continued his advance. Pietro had now only two courses open
to him. He has been spoken of with contempt by all writers
for his action in this crisis, but whether this view is correct
seems open to question, as it would appear to have scarcely

sufficiently considered the problem before Pietro. On the fall of Sarzana the only two alternatives possible to him were, either to be prepared to sustain a siege of Florence by the French army, or to endeavour by a partial surrender to induce the French King to pass peaceably through Tuscany, avoiding the capital. The first course meant, inevitably, in view of the complete disparity in military power between the organised army which Charles commanded, and Florence's mercenary levies,[8] the assault and sack of Florence by foreign troops.[9] Had the French King been attempting to conquer Tuscany the matter would have been different, and Florence would have been bound to resist to the end and to fall with honour. But this was not the case; the French King had no special quarrel with the Florentine State; so that the sack of the city would have been endured on behalf of another State which had no claim upon Florence for such a sacrifice, and which, though principally concerned, had sent no force to join with her in opposing the French King.

Pietro, therefore, chose the second course, and in order to persuade Charles VIII to accept terms and pass without further aggression through Tuscany by the coast road which avoided Florence, went off in person to the camp of the King of France to try and achieve this by a personal interview. He there saw for the first time what a regular organised army was like, and, if he had not done so before, must have realised at once how futile would be any opposition which Florence could offer to such a force, and that it could only have a result which he was bound at all costs to prevent. The French King agreed to pass peaceably through Tuscany, but would not consent to avoid the capital, and required, as the condition on which Florence should be spared from assault and her territory from devastation, that Pisa, and the fortresses of Sarzana, Sarzanello, Ripafratta, and Pietrasanta [10] should be held by him until the conquest of Naples had been completed. Most of these places were already in Charles's possession, while it was only a question of days before all would be so; and he had power to hold them for as long as he chose; so that Pietro in agreeing to these terms did not make any very great concession.[11]

Pietro returned to Florence on the 8th November in expectation that the citizens would be thankful, under the circumstances, for what he had achieved. But the seed so assiduously sown by his cousins at last bore fruit; the citizens had not seen Charles's army, and did not know their own weakness and the French King's strength; their pride was wounded by the idea of the surrender of fortresses; and the combined result brought matters to a climax. Pietro was met by a storm of indignation; the measure of his unpopularity was now full; and there was a general clamour for his banishment and that of his whole family. The Signoria assembled, and promptly passed a decree banishing the Medici permanently from the state of Florence (9th November 1494).

This banishment was not carried out in the dispassionate manner of that in Cosimo's time. They were driven to fly from the city for their lives; [12] and the Signoria subsequently offered a reward of 4,000 florins for the head of Pietro, and 2,000 florins for that of his brother Giovanni; while the mob were permitted by the Government to plunder the Medici Palace, which we are told "was sacked from roof to cellar." And so, notwithstanding all that the Medici had during a hundred years expended from their private fortune to benefit the citizens of Florence, there were now robbed from them, and scattered to the four winds, all those treasures of art gathered with so much diligent labour by Cosimo Pater Patriae, Piero il Gottoso, and Lorenzo the Magnificent—a greater collection of art treasures than was to be found in any other single building in Europe. The destruction of this invaluable collection is pathetically related by the scholarly Bernardo Rucellai in a long lament over the priceless treasures, both of learning and art, destroyed on this occasion.

In the former category were valuable manuscripts in every language, collected at great expense, and most of them quite unable to be replaced. Not less deplorable was the loss in the domain of Art. Irrespective of pictures and statues which were plundered, many valuable pieces of ancient sculpture, exquisite gems, cameos, vases, and countless specimens of the work of the minor arts were destroyed, sharing in a general ruin which reduced a palace which had been the admiration of every foreign visitor, and the chief ornament of the city, to the condition of one sacked by an enemy's troops. The contemporary French historian, Philippe de Commines, after giving a long list of the valuable things lost in this great act of vandalism computes that, over and above what was carried off, the money value of what was destroyed represented "more than 10c,000 crowns." [13] All that energetic labour and artistic taste had collected in half a century was dispersed or destroyed in a day.

We have a glimpse of one item among these plundered treasures eight years later, viz., the four valuable vases which had belonged to Lorenzo, and which we find in 1502 offered for sale in Florence. Isabella d'Este, Marchioness of Mantua, writes in that year requesting that Leonardo da Vinci, who was then in Florence, would inspect them for her, as she heard they were for sale, and would send her a report on them and the price at which they were valued. Leonardo, having examined them, was in ecstasies over their beauty; he reported that all four had Lorenzo's name engraved in Roman letters on the body of the vase, and as to the prices at which they were to be obtained, said, "the crystal vase, all of one piece and very fine, is valued at 350 ducats; the jasper vase, of variegated colours and encrusted with pearls and rubies, on a gold stand, at 240 ducats; the agate vase, at 200 ducats; and the jasper vase on a silver stand, at 150 ducats." They were evidently too costly an ornament for the Marchioness of Mantua, and she did not buy them. They therefore remained in Florence, and some fifty years afterwards were sought out and repurchased by Cosimo I, and are now in the Gem Room of the Uffizi Gallery.[14]

One of the statues taken from the Medici Palace was made to serve as a monument of this casting forth by Florence, in ignominy and ruin, of the family which had so long made that city's greatness. The Signoria took from amongst the plundered works of art the bronze statue of *Judith slaying Holofernes*, executed by Donatello for Cosimo Pater Patriae, which had always stood in the centre of the *cortile* of the palace, and set it up in front of the Palazzo della Signoria, engraving an inscription round its base declaring it set up "as a warning to all who should think to tyrannise over Florence." [15] The inscription was a fine-sounding one, and helped (as was intended) to justify the action of those who had cast forth Pietro and his family, because he had been unable to protect Florence from a foreign aggression with which they themselves were just as little able to cope. But it gave no real picture of the case. Pietro had in no sense tyrannised over Florence; he had not the power to do so, and he never committed any act which showed that he even had the wish. All that he had done was to offend her republican sentiments by what the citizens called a haughty demeanour. In after years, when a real tyrant came to rule over them, they were to find by most bitter experience how very different a thing "tyranny" was from the matters, chiefly of mere outward behaviour, which had called forth their complaints against the son of Lorenzo the Magnificent. When, with their Signoria abolished, they groaned under the tyranny of Cosimo I, with the utmost joy would they have welcomed back the free and untrammelled existence which they had enjoyed under the rule of Pietro the Unfortunate.

The members of the family who were thus hurriedly driven forth from Florence were the three brothers, Pietro (then twenty-three), Giovanni (eighteen), and Giuliano (fifteen), with their first cousin, Giulio (sixteen):[16] also Pietro's wife, Alfonsina, and their two infant children, Lorenzo and

Clarice. They fled first to Bologna, and thence to Venice, where they obtained a temporary asylum. Pietro's ignoble second cousins, Lorenzo and Giovanni, were not included in the decree of banishment. They gained immunity for them selves by abandoning for a time (to their permanent discredit) the name of Medici, and taking instead the name of "Popolano," erasing the family arms from the outside of their palace.

Sixty years had passed since the Medici had last been cast out with ignominy from Florence. They were now for the second time to suffer the hardships of exile. The sentence passed against them furnished an example of how evanescent is popular favour and the memory of public benefits. All the deliverance of his countrymen from unjust taxation and the tyranny of the nobles effected by Giovanni di Bicci, all the "unwearied generosity" of thirty years which had won for Cosimo the title of "Father of his country," all the prosperity of Florence wrought by Lorenzo, were forgotten as completely as though they had never been. And the edifice founded by Giovanni di Bicci, gradually built up by Cosimo, strengthened by the qualities of Piero, and perfected by the ability of Lorenzo, fell in ruins. The Medici were back again at the point they had occupied before Giovanni di Bicci began to lay the foundations of the family greatness; but with the additional obstacle to their ascending the ladder again, that now, by the combined effect of Pietro's failure to follow the line of conduct laid down by his father, and the disaffection stirred up by his cousins, their popularity was gone, and the citizens were determined to keep them out of Florence for the future.

This second banishment meant the entire ruin which had been aimed at, but not achieved, in the first. The change in their circumstances was most complete; the numerous activities of public life, which for four generations had become the accustomed occupations of this family, their patronage of

Art and Letters, the social pleasures of an exalted station and
great wealth, all were at an end; and, deprived of all their
possessions, they went forth to lead a nomadic and poverty-
stricken existence for eighteen years.

Pietro spent all the remaining nine years of his life in
fruitless endeavours to get himself reinstated in Florence by
force of arms, not seeing that this was just the way to defeat
his object, by setting the Florentines still more against him.
His father, had he found himself in a like position, would
have left no stone unturned to make the Florentines recall him
voluntarily; but Pietro lacked his father's wisdom, and so
turned to those measures which could by no possibility obtain
for him success. He became a pawn on the political chess-
board to be used whenever any state found itself in opposition
to Florence; and in this way various states in turn lent him
troops, with which he made three successive attempts against
Florence, which all proved abortive. In these endeavours the
Medici brothers wandered from state to state in Italy, but
after five years of failure, which rightly or wrongly they
attributed to Pietro's proverbial misfortune, his two brothers
and their cousin Giulio separated themselves from him, declaring that they should never succeed while combined with
him. Having already sought the protection in turn of most of
the states of Italy, and finding themselves becoming regarded
as troublesome refugees, the trio, Giovanni, Giuliano, and
Giulio, determined to abandon Italy for a time, and in 1499
started on a wandering tour "to traverse the principal countries of Europe."

. They went first into Germany, where on reaching Ulm they
were arrested and sent under a guard to the Emperor Maximilian, who, however, released them and treated them well,
complimenting Giovanni "on bearing his adverse fortune with
patience, and on his prudence in employing the time which
was thus at his disposal in gaining a knowledge of foreign
countries." Experiencing various adventures, and being several times detained in custody, they visited during the years

1499 and 1500 most of the principal cities in Germany, Flanders, and France, and desired to have visited England, but were prevented by adverse weather from crossing the sea. Returning through France, they at length arrived at Marseilles, whence they proceeded to Genoa, where they resided with Giovanni's sister, Maddalena Cibò. From Genoa after a time they proceeded to Rome, where Alexander VI, having now cause of offence against Florence, laid aside his previous ill-will and treated them with consideration.

Meanwhile Pietro, finding no more help obtainable elsewhere, had joined himself to the French, and in 1501 received a vague promise of assistance from Louis XII, which, however, came to nothing. Eventually Pietro, unfortunate to the last, accompanying the French army in their campaign in southern Italy, was, during the confusion of the retreat towards Gaeta after their disastrous defeat on the Garigliano, upset in the boat in which he was conveying down the river to Gaeta four pieces of heavy artillery which he had saved from capture by the enemy, and was drowned (December 1503).[17]

Botticelli has painted a well-known portrait of Pietro, which hangs in the Uffizi Gallery, and, as he knew him well, it is certain to be a good likeness.[18] He has dark brown hair, and the remarkably fine eyes which (through many generations) were a noted characteristic of his family, while his face has a melancholy expression, attributable to his invariable ill-fortune. He wears a scarlet cap, and holds in both hands a medallion of his great-grandfather, Cosimo, appealing to the people of Florence, by the memory of him to whom they had themselves given the title of "Father of his country," not to treat his descendants as they were doing. This portrait, always known to be by Botticelli, was formerly thought to represent Pico della Mirandola; while another suggestion has in recent years been made [19] that it represents Giovanni, the son of Cosimo, who died in 1463. As, however, Giovanni died as a

man of forty-two when Botticelli was only nineteen, it is
sufficiently obvious that the portrait (which represents a man
of twenty-four or twenty-five) cannot be that of Giovanni. It
undoubtedly represents Pietro the Unfortunate, and has been
correctly so labelled by the authorities of the Uffizi Gallery.
The medallion held up in the hands and presented to the
spectator (and forming the most prominent feature of the
picture), is by itself sufficient to be absolutely convincing on
the point; for that particular appeal to the memory of Cosimo
Pater Patriae would be quite meaningless as regards either
Pico della Mirandola or Giovanni; it would, in fact, not be
applicable in the case of any one else than Pietro the Unfortunate. The picture was evidently painted a year or two after
Pietro's banishment; either for himself, or one of the exiled
Medici party. Botticelli being the "court painter" of Lorenzo
the Magnificent, and almost living in the family, had known
Pietro from the latter's very childhood, and owing, as he did,
all his career, first to Piero il Gottoso, and afterwards to
Lorenzo, undoubtedly sympathised much with the family in
being driven from Florence, and mourned over the destruction
of all their art treasures and the ruin of this great house. The
feature of the medallion [20] is just such a touch as Botticelli
delighted to introduce in order to make his picture tell its
own story.

———————

Having seen the Medici, in the fifth generation of the
family, banished for the second time from their country, and
before we enter on those eighteen years in which Florence lost
all the power and prosperity she had enjoyed for sixty years,
we may take a brief glance at what this family had achieved
during the first hundred years of their course, and may also
examine how far the two charges which have been referred
to [21] are justly to be made against them, so far as this portion
of their history is concerned.

Looking back at the position in the year 1400 there appear

to be two grounds on which (irrespective of more personal considerations) the Medici justly deserve fame; first, their raising Florence to so exalted a position, and, second, the results they accomplished in the domain of Learning and Art.

From a petty state which did not exceed in power and influence many others around it, the Medici had gradually raised Florence until she had become practically the capital city of Italy, not only exceeding in power the other states (such as Pisa, Lucca, Siena, Mantua, Ferrara, Urbino, and others) which had formerly been her equals, but also, as a city, surpassing in grandeur, prosperity, and intellectual eminence even Rome, Venice, Milan, and Naples; and out of Italy no city at that time could compete with these. When on the banishment of the Medici the army of Charles VIII entered Florence we are told, "They saw a city which immeasurably surpassed any at that time in France, and could not contain their astonishment at the grandeur of its palaces and public buildings,[22] and the culture and refinement of its inhabitants, which they admitted to be far superior to their own."

But the second point is of far wider importance. The Medici have a just right to fame for the permanent benefits which they conferred on mankind at large by their fostering care over Learning and Art, and their readiness to expend a colossal fortune upon these things in an age before men had yet fully learnt to appreciate their value. This liberality was specially important in regard to the resuscitation of Learning, since this was a work which could not have been carried out without an expenditure such as the Medici alone among families of that period could afford.[23] And it was well for mankind that the Medici, through four generations, were ready to shower their wealth, not upon the ostentatious display of riches which was common enough around them, but upon the resuscitation of Learning and the advancement of Art. Europe to-day reaps the result of this their character, and owes them immeasurable gratitude for all that they did, and were, in this particular.

Turning to examine the charge that the Medici deprived

their country of its liberty and exalted themselves into tyrants over it, it would appear that this charge involves considerable wresting from their proper meaning of both the
word "liberty" and the word "tyrant." The only "liberty"
which the Medici took away was the freedom to indulge in
an internecine strife which made life in Florence one perpetual
faction-fight—a state of things under which no previous government had been able to protect the lives and property of
the citizens. With no due degree of liberty did the Medici
rule interfere, and life in Florence in their time was as free
as in any modern state. While as regards the word "tyrant"
it is sufficient to observe that a tyranny cannot exist without
a bodyguard of troops to support and protect the ruler when
his acts are tyrannical or opposed to the will of the people.
Wealth alone cannot create a tyranny; for even should it go
the length of purchasing the suffrages of the majority of the
citizens, its power still remains based upon the votes of the
majority, and the minority (even though they may have
much to say regarding the means by which these have been
obtained) cannot call such a power a tyranny without misuse of terms. The Medici rule rested solely on popularity, and
a rule which rests on that basis has no power to tyrannise.
This was fully proved when, two years after Lorenzo's death,
and simply because the popularity which had formed the sole
basis of his power was lost, Florence with only a word sent
his successor and his whole family into exile.

The usual theory put before us regarding the Medici is
that it was by craft and dissimulation that they rose to power
in Florence. It was not so. Nor amongst a people so abnormally well versed (through two hundred years of political
intrigue) in every form of craft and dissimulation could that
method ever have succeeded; there was no race in Europe
with whom it would have so surely failed. It was by the
display of a pre-eminent ability in the conduct of public
affairs, it was by a large-minded magnanimity constantly
evinced in their dealings with those brought in contact with

them, it was by their defence of the people against the oppression of the nobles, by their freedom from arrogance,
their clemency in victory over crafty and ungenerous foes,
and a generosity which knew no bounds in spending their
private wealth for the benefit of their fellow-countrymen; it
was by *these* qualities that the Medici rose to power in
Florence. And we have this corroborated by Voltaire, who
says of the Medici that "no family ever obtained power by
so just a title": a statement which one such as Voltaire would
certainly never have made had they obtained it either by
force or by craft.

With regard to the second of the two charges, it is truly
a most significant fact when we find that amidst all the
virulent abuse which has been poured forth by so many pens
during three centuries upon these five generations of the
Medici no accusation of murder has ever been made against
either Giovanni di Bicci, Piero il Gottoso, Lorenzo the Magnificent, or Pietro the Unfortunate. So that if we except the
single case of the accusation [24] made by Cavalcanti against
Cosimo Pater Patriae of complicity in the death of Baldaccio
d'Anghiari, which is rejected by all reliable historians, the
whole five generations of the Medici whose lives are covered
by these hundred years are free from any charge of murder.
Yet this is during a period (1400-1503) specially notable for
such crimes, and when the records of almost all other states [25]
show a long catalogue of thoroughly authenticated murders
committed by their rulers. [26]

It is said to be the just penalty of greatness to endure
severer criticism than is applied to others. And certainly
the Medici may be held to exemplify the fact. The history
of that time is full of cases of families [27] who were seizing
upon thrones, and wading through blood to gain them, without any higher object than that of enriching themselves.
Yet the Medici, who took a more patriotic course, while they
certainly evinced (however its degree may be disputed) a

higher aim, have been criticised and condemned as these others have never been. The accusation that they "made themselves despots in order to extract from a down-trodden people wealth to spend upon themselves" has been made of a family whose liberality, in spending their private fortune [28] upon matters for the public benefit, exceeded all that has been elsewhere known in history. It was not the Florentines, but the citizens of London and Paris, Lyons and Bruges, Genoa and Venice, who supplied the income which the Medici spent, to so limited an extent upon themselves, and to so large an extent upon Florence.[29] Nor will the assertion that they "destroyed the liberties of Florence in order to exalt themselves into despots" continue to be tenable when their rule is compared with that set up at this same epoch by Louis XI in France or by Henry VII in England; or when we note that "the citizens of Florence enjoyed under the Medici a far greater degree of representative government than the people of either France or England." Had not the Medici established the kind of rule they did, the Pazzi, the Capponi, the Strozzi, and others would have headed various factions, as the Donati, the Cerchi, and the Albizzi had done before them; and none of that internal peace and prosperity, that national importance and cultured eminence, would have resulted which Florence was so thankful to possess while it lasted, and so proud to look back upon after it passed away.

Nor does a wider outlook fail to give evidence on the same point. Throughout the greater part of the fifteenth century the rule of the Medici, by its suppression of internal strife, the consequent increase of weight in international politics, and the powerful assistance given to Learning and Art, produced results to Florence which were the envy of all surrounding states. And the failure of the latter to advance in a similar way, both politically and in Art, has been directly attributed to the absence of any family with the capacity to do for them what the Medici did for Florence. Thus as regards Art it has often been pointed out that up to the time when the Medici arose, Siena, for instance, was on a level with Florence, but from that time forward could no longer compete with her. While as regards politics it has been remarked by Professor Langton Douglas [30] that Siena, hitherto equal in power to Florence, was left behind by the latter, "owing to that faction-fighting which the Medici rule made impossible in Florence." We see, therefore, that to the very fact for which on behalf of Florence the Medici have been condemned, other states have attributed all Florence's greatness.

ON the same day that Pietro and his family fled from Florence, Charles VIII entered Pisa, and thereupon declared that city "free from the Florentine yoke." The Signoria sent an embassy (which included Savonarola) to the King to protest against this action as to Pisa, and to treat with him, but the only reply they could extract was, "Once in the great city all shall be arranged." Savonarola had prophesied that a foreign invader should come to chastise the states of Italy for their profligate ways; the first of those states was now beginning to discover what forms such chastisement might take. The Republic, though they had exiled Pietro owing to his inability to prevent the French King's advance, found themselves as little able to do so as he had been, and eight days afterwards Charles VIII entered Florence in the style of a victorious monarch entering a conquered city; while the Florentines found themselves required to accommodate in their midst an army of twenty thousand men. And to have a mediæval army of another nationality thus placed was a critical business; at any moment the smallest *contretemps* might produce an explosion and the plunder and sack of the city. It may be judged therefore with what pleasure the citizens of Florence saw this army march into their streets.

As this was the first standing army ever seen by Europe, and as we know something of what standing armies have become during the intervening four hundred years, it will be interesting to have a look at this first one; to stand, as it were, in the crowd at the Frediano gate on that 17th November 1494, and watch this army as it passes into Florence.

It consisted of 3,000 cavalry, "the flower of the French chivalry," 5,000 Gascon infantry, 5,000 Swiss infantry, 4,000 Breton archers, 2,000 cross-bowmen, and a strong train of artillery, the latter drawn for the first time by horses, instead of oxen, a new thing in that age. The general appearance of these troops has been described for us by an old chronicler, who evidently watched them closely that day, and gives a vivid description of this entry into Florence. He says:—

"The King of France entered the city at the Porta San Frediano, riding under a rich canopy borne by four knights, two on either side; and on each side of him rode his marshals. The royal body-guard followed, consisting of a hundred of the handsomest youths of France, and two hundred knights of France on foot, in splendid dresses. Then came the Swiss guard with their brilliant uniforms of various colours, having halberts of burnished steel, their officers wearing rich plumes on their helmets. . . . The centre consisted of the Gascons, short, light, active men, whose numbers seemed never ending. After these came the cavalry, whose splendid appearance was admired by all, and in which there were to be found the most noble young men of France. They had engraved armour, mantles of richest brocade, banners of velvet embroidered with gold, chains of gold, and ornaments of gold. The cuirassiers presented a hideous appearance, with their horses looking like monsters, from their ears and tails being cut quite short. Then came the archers, extraordinarily tall men from Scotland and other northern countries, and they looked more like wild beasts than men." [1]

Guicciardini (who was then a boy of twelve), speaking of the whole procession, says it was "a spectacle in itself very grand, but one for which the spectators had small liking, by reason of the dread and terror with which it filled their minds." As regards Charles VIII himself,[2] the incapable youth who wielded this formidable weapon, Guicciardini says that he was short, ugly, deformed, and altogether uneducated, and in all matters that he took in hand displayed an entire want of prudence and judgment; while Philippe de Commines says that he was "weak, wilful, and surrounded by foolish counsellors." Such was the youth at whose mercy Florence now lay.

The army was quartered about the city on the unwilling inhabitants, and Charles proceeded to the despoiled and dismantled Medici Palace, where he took up his abode. There next day he summoned the Signoria before him to hear the humiliating terms which he intended to impose on the city. But the ancient spirit of Florence was as strong as ever, and when these terms were read out to them the members of the Signoria utterly refused to accept them. Whereupon the King flew into a rage and swore that if the treaty he had dictated were not forthwith signed they should have war; that he would sound his trumpets, call out his troops, and sack the city. Upon this one of the senators, Piero Capponi, gave that answer which has passed into a Florentine proverb: "If you sound your trumpets we will sound our bells." Charles knew what that meant, for he had on the day before seen a brief example of it in connection with a false alarm; he knew that it meant the ringing of the great bell, "La Vacca," which hung in the tower of the Palazzo della Signoria, and which when it sounded out over Florence [3] would call out into the streets the whole male population of the city, armed and ready to fall on the French troops, scattered in their various quarters, and before they could offer any collective resistance. He would find himself in a hornets' nest. Charles reflected for a moment, and then passing the matter off with a bad joke gave in, and Florence was saved.[4] A less humiliating treaty was drawn up and agreed to, though it was not a whit more satisfactory for Florence than that for agreeing to which Pietro the Unfortunate had incurred such a storm of indignation from the same men. Its chief articles were that Pisa, and the fortresses of Sarzana, Sarzanello, Ripafratta,

and Pietrasanta, should remain in Charles's possession until
the conquest of Naples was complete, and that Florence
should pay him an indemnity of 120,0co ducats. And two
days later Charles marched his army out again, and departed
for Rome *en route* to Naples.

On Charles's arrival before Rome, Pope Alexander VI took
refuge in the castle of St. Angelo, but was induced to come
forth, and to give Cæsar Borgia as a hostage; and after
spending a month in Rome Charles marched on towards
Naples. Alfonso II, King of Naples, had no lack of courage
or military ability. His bravery at the battle of Otranto
against the Turks had won him military renown. Nevertheless, he made no endeavour to defend his kingdom on this
occasion. Fearing the strength of the French army he fled
to Sicily; and Charles VIII entered Naples on the 22nd
February 1495 as a conqueror.

But while he spent his time there in triumphs and festivals
a formidable confederacy was formed to crush him, consisting
of the Emperor Maximilian, Ferdinand, King of Arragon, the
Pope, Venice, and even Ludovico Sforza, by whose invitation
he had invaded Italy. Meanwhile his army, wasted by its
excesses in Naples, was rapidly dwindling by disease. Charles
saw no safety but in an immediate march back to France.
Leaving part of his army in possession of Naples, he in the
beginning of June started on his return march, proceeding
by Rome and Siena, and hastening as much as possible. But
the allies assembled a force of 40,000 men to bar his way,
awaiting him on the northern side of the Apennines. Owing to
losses by disease and the detachment left at Naples, Charles's
army was reduced to 9,000 men. He reached Siena on the
13th June, and Pontremoli on the 29th June; from there he
crossed the Apennines by the pass of that name, an operation
which took him six days. The battle which ensued was fought
on the 6th July, on the banks of the Taro at Fornovo, on the
northern side of the Apennines. The French had the greatest
difficulty in transporting their artillery over the mountains,

and most of it arrived too late to take part in the battle,
which, though very short, was the bloodiest that had taken
place in Italy for two centuries. The Italians were entirely
routed, and lost 3,000 men, including their second-in-com-
mand, Rodolfo Gonzaga, uncle of the Marquis of Mantua;
the French only lost, Commines says, about a hundred men,
but the Italian writers say a thousand. Charles showed much
personal courage, and much bad generalship; nevertheless,
the French army succeeded in driving their opponents off
the field, and continued their march towards Asti, though
their long line of baggage, impeded by the difficulties of the
mountains, for the most part fell a prey to the enemy; so
that both sides claimed the victory. Charles reached Asti on
the 15th July, and remained there until October, when he
returned to France. The King of Naples soon after regained
Naples; and the sole results to Charles VIII of his expedition
were the debts he had incurred to meet its expenses.

The superior power possessed by the new engine in war
which was wielded by Charles VIII so inefficiently was very
clearly shown at Fornovo.[5] At that battle the allies had
40,000 men, Charles only 9,000. The latter fought under
every disadvantage; they were weakened by disease, "weary
with long marches, insufficient food, and bad quarters," and
had to fight as they emerged from the difficulties of a mountain pass, proverbially the position in which a force finds it
hardest to bring up its full strength. On the other hand, their
opponents were "fresh and well cared for," [6] and awaited the
French on the banks of a river, the passage of which the
latter had to force. Nevertheless, as the result of the attack
which the French delivered, the Italian force "suffered so
severely that, though they still far outnumbered the French,
no persuasion could make them rally and renew the fight."
Charles's army, though less than a quarter the numerical
strength of their foes, badly commanded, and fighting under
every disadvantage, beat back their enemy, forced the passage
of the Taro, broke through the cordon drawn between them

and their objective, and continued their march; thus gaining
the honour of the day, even though most of their baggage
was plundered in their rear by the enemy. Fornovo was the
first occasion on which a standing army was tested in battle,
and the results showed very distinctly how much greater was
its power than that of the kind of troops hitherto employed.

This expedition of Charles VIII into Italy, although it was
so barren of immediate results, had great ultimate consequences, and was a turning point in the history of Europe.
Michelet says that it "was no less than the revelation of Italy
to the nations of the north." It ushered in that new era already mentioned, in which the northern nations were to oust
the Italian states from the foremost place in the politics of
Europe, a process which was accompanied by a state of almost
constant war in Italy.

During the eighteen years that followed Florence sternly
kept the Medici out of her territories, and foiled all schemes
for their return. It was made death to be found guilty of
attempting to restore that family; and in 1497 old Bernardo
de Nero, who was seventy-two years of age and had been
three times Gonfaloniere, being found guilty of this offence,
was beheaded.[7]

This period (1494-1512), which in a history relating to
the Medici power in Florence it is convenient to call the
"Interregnum," and which covers the pontificates of Popes
Alexander VI and Julius II, was an eventful one in the
history of Italy and of Europe. But Florence, her destinies
no longer swayed by the family which had known how to
make their country strong and powerful, took an altogether
insignificant part in these events, more so than any other
state in Italy; whilst the struggle of contending nations was
taking place all round her she was entirely occupied in
ignoble turmoils over domestic politics. She suffered severely
in consequence, having to endure heavy taxation in order
to pay subsidies now to one and now to another of the com-

batants, and only just missed being captured by Cæsar
Borgia, before whom she had most ignominiously to humble
herself.

So far, therefore, as Florence is concerned, the record of
this period consists of little else than internal discord and
misgovernment. Unceasing turmoils between rival factions,
fresh constitutions formed every few months, an administration utterly corrupt, a total decline in political influence
abroad, and anarchy, injustice, and misery at home, are the
prevailing features of this period. And nothing could better
have vindicated the rule which the Medici had exercised
than the state of things which supervened when it was withdrawn. Some have contrived even here to found a charge
against that family, declaring this due to their having "ener-
vated the Florentines." It was, however, simply the reversion
to those conditions which had obtained before the Medici
arose, and which reappeared upon the removal of the only
power which had ever been able to keep Florence free from
such conflicts.

During the first four years of the above period (1494-
1498) the chief influence in the State was exercised by
Savonarola. Upon the departure of Charles VIII one change
after another in the form of government took place accompanied by constant disturbances, until at length an end to
these was put for a time by Savonarola, who, in accordance
with the cry of the people for a constitution on the lines of
that of Venice, formed the *Grand Council,* comprising every
citizen of twenty-nine years of age who, or whose father,
grandfather, or great-grandfather, had held one of the higher
magistracies; the number of members was limited to 1,000,
with a change of members every six months.[8] Savonarola also
made strenuous efforts to put down the luxury and profligacy
to which the Florentines had become addicted; and for a
while he succeeded. The extraordinary movement [9] which
he brought about is without a parallel; Florence for a time
put on a Puritan garb. And the effect manifested itself in

many differently minded men. Baccio della Porta became a
monk in the monastery of San Marco, taking the name Fra
Bartolommeo. Two of the Della Robbia family became
priests. Lorenzo di Credi spent the rest of his life in the
monastery of Sta. Maria Novella. Botticelli became an ardent
disciple of Savonarola, and would paint only pictures inspired
by his sermons. Cronaca, the celebrated story-teller, would
talk only of Savonarola. Michelangelo to the end of his life
retained a vivid remembrance of the powerful voice and impassioned gestures of the great preacher, and pondered over
his sermons in his old age.

Among the many notable scenes which the Piazza della
Signoria has witnessed none is more remarkable than that
strange bonfire for the destruction of worldly allurements,
the "Vanities," which took place in 1497, at the time of the
Carnival, in the midst of a concourse of the entire city.
Harford, in his *Life of Michelangelo*, says:—

"A pyramidal scaffold was erected opposite the palace of
the Signoria. At its base were to be seen false hair, false
beards, masquerading dresses, rouge pots, cards and dice,
mirrors and perfumery, beads and trinkets of various sorts.
Higher up were arranged books and drawings, busts, and
portraits of the most celebrated Florentine beauties. . . . Even
Fra Bartolommeo was so carried away by the enthusiasm
as to bring his life-academy studies. Lorenzo di Credi, another devoted follower of Savonarola, did the same. . . . The
Signoria looked on from a balcony; guards were stationed
to prevent unholy thefts; and as the fire rose there was a
burst of chants, and the singing of the 'Te Deum' to the
sound of trumpets and the clanging of bells."

But eventually the people got tired of a life bereft of their
favourite "vanities"; and about the same time Savonarola's
preaching, which had hitherto concerned itself with the errors
of Florence, began to thunder against the far greater iniquities of Rome, and to urge for a reformation of the Church.

And it was indeed high time for such a reformation; for the state of things at Rome was arousing universal indignation. Alexander VI (Roderigo Borgia), who was Pope from 1492 to 1503, has been styled by Mosheim "the Nero among Popes," and the conjunction in him of shameless greed, perfidy, cruelty, and licentiousness brought the Papacy to the lowest moral depth it had touched since the dark age of the tenth century. His politics were governed solely by one consideration, that of acquiring, by whatever means, as many of the minor states as possible in order to form a sovereignty for his son, Cæsar Borgia, called by Ranke "a *virtuoso* in crime."

Such being the character of the Pope at the time, an earnest reformer like Savonarola could scarcely fail to give voice to what were becoming the sentiments of all Europe regarding the Papal court. His sermons began to denounce its iniquities and to press for a General Council to reform the Church. Neither Alexander VI nor Cæsar Borgia had the smallest intention of suffering the fate which had overtaken Pope John XXIII eighty years before, and one such sermon delivered in Rome would have promptly ended Savonarola's life. But in Florence he could not be so easily got at. The Pope did his utmost to silence him, and to get him into his power, but for some time unsuccessfully, he being too popular with the Florentines.

But Florence no longer had the strong government and united people which she had possessed when she hung an Archbishop and defied a Pope who attempted to stir up strife within her walls. Her condition now was just the reverse; and in a city torn by so many factions, and with a government become both weak and corrupt, it was easy to create a party hostile to the stern preacher of reform, and ready to perform the Pope's work. So that at length in 1498 Alexander VI was able to send emissaries to Florence, who soon persuaded the Signoria to act as his agents in a crime which has brought permanent infamy, both on the Pope who ordered it, and on the government which carried it out. Meanwhile Savonarola had written letters to various sovereigns pressing them to assemble a General Council; so that the Pope was more anxious than ever to have him put out of life with all speed. It was unfortunate for Savonarola that just at this juncture Charles VIII, on whom he chiefly relied (though it was reliance on a broken reed), was on the 5th April 1498 accidentally killed at the castle of Amboise by striking his head against the top of a low doorway. He was succeeded by his distant cousin, Louis XII.

On the 7th April a challenge by the rival community of the Franciscans to an ordeal by fire, to which Savonarola weakly agreed (and for which elaborate preparations were made, though the Signoria never intended it to be carried out), served the purpose of destroying his popularity with the people, who were furious when at the last moment the ordeal was vetoed. Accordingly on the 9th April Savonarola received a summons from the Signoria to surrender himself into their hands. The friars of San Marco refused to allow him to be taken from them to what all knew meant torture and death, and the church and monastery were furiously attacked by the troops of the Signoria during a whole day, and bravely defended. In the evening, however, on the troops forcing their way into the church, Savonarola refused to allow further bloodshed, and, after taking a sorrowful farewell of the brethren, surrendered himself to the troops. He was taken to the Palazzo della Signoria, imprisoned in the cell called the Alberghettino, and day after day subjected to torture, the Pope sending frequent messages to the Signoria to wring something from him which might serve as a ground for putting him to death.

Nevertheless, this was a difficult task; one, however, to which those who wished to stand well with the Pope, turned all their evil ingenuity; with the result that the so-called trial became a mockery of justice. Seldom has there been a blacker page in the proceedings of any government than that relating to Savonarola's trial and condemnation. The criminal court by which in the ordinary course he should have been tried, the "Eight," not being supposed to be sufficiently hostile to him, had new members appointed to it, though the period of office of their predecessors had not expired. When, however, it became apparent that even this would not suffice to attain the desired result, a special court was constituted composed of seventeen commissioners, all of them Savonarola's avowed enemies. Even one of these, Bartolo Zati, when he learnt the nature of the work expected of him, refused to serve, declaring that he would take no part in a murder.

Savonarola was subjected to successive "trials," and during these, for a period of about sixteen days, was tortured daily; once he was placed on the rack fourteen times in a single day. Nevertheless, nothing could be proved against him or wrung from him, which his judges could twist into an admission of either treason or heresy.[10] So his enemies had to resort to forgery. A miscreant, named Ser Ceccone, a notary who had said to one of the judges, "If no case exists, one must be invented," was employed to take down the victim's replies while under torture. And this change in the arrangements produced the required results. In refutation of the supposition that on this last occasion Savonarola falsified his previous replies, Mr. Hyett says as follows:—

"On the 19th April a document purporting to be a report of Savonarola's replies to the examiners was signed by him. It is probable that his signature was obtained by a trick, but, be this as it may, it is certain that the signed deposition had been falsified, or as one of the judges euphemistically put it, 'for a good purpose somewhat had been omitted from, and somewhat added to it.' On the strength of this garbled report many writers have said that he broke down under torture, and even Professor Villari gives a reluctant assent to this view, and offers an elaborate apology for his hero. But as evidence against Savonarola the document is not worth the paper it was written on. It is in part admittedly fictitious, and which parts of it are additions, and which alterations, or what has been omitted, it is impossible to discover. Everything tends to show that Savonarola, in spite of his physical infirmities, displayed on the rack heroic fortitude." [11]

On the 19th May the Papal commissioners charged with the final proceedings arrived in Florence. Nardi states that their instructions were "to put Savonarola to death were he even another St. John the Baptist." On 20th May and the two following days, Savonarola underwent before them his third mock trial, being examined under worse torture than ever. The results of this final examination were never signed or made public, the trial being thus practically left unfinished. Nothing had been elicited from him proving his guilt of heresy or crime. Nevertheless, on the evening of the 22nd May, after many days of torture, after every kind of fraud and injustice had been put in force, and as the result of a so-called trial not even legally completed, Savonarola, whose only crime was his denunciation of the vices of the Borgian Papacy and his appeals for its reformation, was condemned to death. And also the other two friars of San Marco who had been tried with him, Fra Domenico and Fra Silvestro. On the following morning, 23rd May 1498, the three companions were brought out of the Palazzo della Signoria on to the *ringhiera,* and after being subjected to various insults were conducted to the scaffold. And on the very spot where the bonfire of the "Vanities" had taken place, the reformer, who had a short time before been worshipped by Florence, was hanged and burnt in presence of the whole city.

Thus did Florence show before the eyes of Europe what the rule of the Medici had been to her. Such a crime as the above would have been as impossible under the rule of Lorenzo the Magnificent as under any government of the present day. In this episode we seem to see a totally different Florence from that of twenty years before; and instead of a united people, strong in their sense of justice, defying a Pope even though he was backed by numerous allies, we see a

divided people and a corrupt and subservient government,
ready at a Pope's command to set at naught every principle
of justice, and to employ methods from which every honest
Florentine revolted. The defiance of all law, the disgraceful
frauds, the corruptibility of the judges, and the faction-
fighting through which alone the Pope was able to achieve
his object, all showed how greatly Florence had in only four
years deteriorated through the loss of that rule under which
she had during the previous sixty years made herself great
and respected. The crime of Savonarola's judicial murder
is the strongest possible vindication of the rule which had
been established by the Medici.

———————

That movement which exercised a permanent influence on
so many others, had its effect also on Botticelli. The entire
change in the mental atmosphere of Florence wrought by
Savonarola during the years 1494-1498 caused a no less
radical change in the character of Botticelli's pictures. So
that we have now a third period in his painting.

(III)

Just as Cronaca could talk only of Savonarola, so could
Botticelli now paint only pictures which repeated the impassioned sermons of Florence's great preacher. Henceforth
we have no more pictures from him of graceful Greek goddesses and classic myths, but picture after picture on the one
subject of the Blessed Virgin and Child.

The same train of thought runs through them all. No
longer does Botticelli paint her in all the joy of the Magnificat; it is now the sorrow of the Mater Dolorosa that is
set before us, and with every variety of illustration. And
in this too there is a distinction; it is not as the sorrowing
Mother beneath the Cross that she is depicted, but as the
young Mother with the ever-present sword of a foreboding

sorrow piercing her heart with the knowledge of that which was to come, of which others around her were ignorant, and in which, therefore, they could afford her no sympathy. Sometimes it is the Mother alone who feels this foreboding sorrow, sometimes it permeates both Mother and Child, but whether in her alone, or in both, this is always the prevailing thought. Speaking of these pictures, Steinmann says:—

"A presentiment of coming woe seems to cast its shadow on the Virgin's soul. . . . She embraces the Child with a half-repressed fervour of passionate love, but all the time the shadow of an underlying sorrow makes the flame of joy burn dimly." [12]

All this is in accord with Savonarola's sermons; and here we see Painting able to bring to our minds the words of a preacher dead four hundred years ago.

In doing this Botticelli introduces many touching details by which to bring his point home to those to whom he speaks. As examples the following may be taken:—

The Madonna of the Pomegranate.—This picture (in its original frame)[13] hangs in the Tuscan room of the Uffizi Gallery. The Child Christ holds in His left hand a bitten pomegranate,[14] and looking with a sad expression straight at the beholder, holds up His right hand in blessing. Steinmann says:—"In this picture both Child and Mother are more than ever conscious of bearing the burden of all the sorrow of mankind." He considers this to be Botticelli's best picture. Hanging as it does opposite the *Madonna of the Magnificat*, the two are well placed for comparison, the one painted in Botticelli's earliest years, the other not less than thirty years afterwards; the keynote of the one, humility, of the other, foreboding sorrow.

The Madonna and Child in the Brera Gallery, Milan.—In this case the Child is sitting on the Virgin's knee, and is playing with a rough wreath of thorns and three nails, and looking up at her in wonderment at her sadness.

The Madonna and Child in the National Gallery, London.—The Virgin embraces the Child, who stands on her lap. He looks in her face, seeking for the cause of her sorrow, while her face and attitude express a deep tenderness, penetrated as usual with a profound sadness. This picture has been a good deal damaged in its travels, but the damage has spared the face of the Child Christ, which is particularly beautiful.

The Madonna of St. Barnabas.—Painted for the convent of St. Barnabas, and now in the Accademia delle Belle Arti, Florence. This picture has suffered (through damage in removal and attempted restoration) as regards the face of the Child Christ, which has been quite spoiled, but the rest of the painting is beautiful, and it is one of Botticelli's most admired works. Two angels stand on either side of the Madonna and Child, one holding up before her a crown of thorns, and the other, three nails, while two more angels hold back the curtains of the throne. The Virgin looks straight out before her with a sweet, sad expression. Six saints stand before the throne, representing different types of mankind: St. Michael, manly strength and beauty; St. John the Baptist, asceticism; St. Ambrose, the strong, practical bishop; St. Augustine, theological learning; St. Barnabas, unselfish devotion to the consolation of the miserable and oppressed; and St. Catherine, womanly feeling. Steinmann, remarking on this picture, says:—

"It would seem as if Dante's wonderful characterisation of the Virgin struck the keynote of the whole picture, viz., his words, 'Umile ed alta, più che creatura' ('Humble and high beyond all other created being'). . . . Sitting on her throne under the velvet canopy, affectionately served by angels, venerated by saints, she yet can feel no joy. She gazes straight out before her, with a sad, far-away expression in her eyes—'humble and high,' in truth, yet sighing under the weight of her destiny, and with the sword already piercing her heart."

In one other point, noticeable in all these pictures, Botticelli differs markedly from the artists who were to follow in the next generation, led by Michelangelo. *Botticelli forces our whole attention on the subject, not on the painter.* In looking at them it is not of Botticelli that we think. As Steinmann says:—

"There never was a painter who so entirely forgot *himself* in his subject; and in these pictures he has concentrated his whole thoughts on the character of the Madonna; and there has been none since his day who was so unwearied in inventing new modes of treatment which should both bring the Virgin and Child into human closeness to the beholder, and at the same time arouse his awe and veneration."

(IV)

But a time came when, instead of Florence being swayed by Savonarola's sermons, it condemned him and put him to death; and for those who revered him the only feeling left was horror, both at the crime itself, and at the reign of anarchy and vice which succeeded it. And so now again we have a complete change in Botticelli's pictures, caused by the change in the circumstances around him, and have the pictures of his fourth and last period. In this there are (besides his sketches illustrating Dante's poem) only two pictures, but they are notables ones: viz. (i) *Calumny,* now in the Uffizi Gallery, Florence, its general idea taken from Lucian's account of a picture on that subject by the Greek painter, Apelles; [15] and (ii) *The Nativity,* now in the National Gallery, London. The drawings illustrating Dante's *Divine Comedy* were executed at various times between 1492 and 1497, but were left unfinished; Botticelli, the ardent partisan of Savonarola, being thenceforth entirely engrossed with the tragedy of the latter's end.

The celebrated picture of *Calumny* is thus described:—

"The scene is laid in a stately judgment hall in the classic style, on the decoration of which every resource of art has been expended. Between its lofty arches there is a distant view of a calm sea; life-sized marble figures stand in the niches of the pillars of the hall (like the figures outside Or San Michele), and every vacant space is adorned with richly-gilded sculpture. It is a magnificent Renaissance building, which fancy imagines a place in which wisdom and justice alone would exist, a place of refuge in which poets and thinkers may prepare new intellectual achievements as they walk in this stately portico by the sea. Instead of this we witness a fearful deed of violence. In bitter contrast with the splendid marble all round, in ironical mockery of the solemn statues of justice and virtue on the walls, a noisy throng is dragging the innocent victim of calumny before the tribunal of the Unjust Judge, who sits with crown and sceptre on a richly-decorated throne. Two female figures, Ignorance and Suspicion, whisper in the long ass's ears of the Unjust Judge, while in front of him Envy declaims with imperious force. With his right hand Envy leads on Calumny, who holds a burning torch before her as a treacherous symbol of her pretended love of truth. She dashes impetuously forward, with her left hand grasping mercilessly the hair of her victim, who lies on the ground stripped naked, with his folded hands raised to heaven in assertion of his innocence. Calumny's appearance is plausible and crafty; her clothing is costly, and her two attendants, Fraud and Deception, are busy twining fresh roses in her golden hair. Behind these (as what follows from injustice and cruelty) comes the tormentor, Remorse, a hideous hag clothed from head to foot in ragged mourning attire, who, clasping her trembling hands before her, turns her face round over her shoulder to look at the figure behind her of naked Truth (a slim female figure recalling Botticelli's *Venus*), who gazes upwards and lifts her right hand to heaven in adjuration against the scene of injustice, cruelty, and wrong." [16]

Now what does all this mean? At first sight this picture repels us by its strange scene of grotesque violence; but it has its meaning in the history of the time. For in this picture

Botticelli writes for those who may come after, the story of how Savonarola was done to death. In the stately Renaissance hall, the refuge for poets and philosophers, with its solemn statues of Wisdom and Justice, and its profuse decoration by Art, Botticelli represents Florence as for sixty years *it had been*. In the Unjust Judge, with his ass's ears, seated on a throne with crown and sceptre which he is not fit to bear, and in the scene of violence enacted in front of him, the painter represents the government of Florence as *it had become;* still occupying the localities where such different sentiments had once prevailed. In the figures of Ignorance and Suspicion, Envy and Calumny, Fraud and Deception, he represents the motives and the methods which had prevailed to put to death their victim, Savonarola. While the figures of Remorse and Truth embody Botticelli's prophecy of what shall afterwards follow.[17]

This picture was painted by Botticelli for his friend, Antonio Segni, in the year 1498 or 1499, and it is stated that it was not allowed to be seen by the public eye until after Botticelli's death; if so, this would help to confirm the above theory as to its meaning. It is, of course, deeply interesting both on account of the great preacher himself, and also as the powerful record given by one then living as to the way in which Savonarola's life was taken, and how false were the lies which then, and for many years afterwards, were sedulously promulgated regarding the self-accusations declared to have been made by him under torture.

And then we have another strange picture, *The Nativity,* painted at the end of the year 1500, Botticelli's last picture (now in the National Gallery, London); and this again refers to Savonarola, and to the state of things in Florence after his death. In an inscription written over it in Greek Botticelli explains its meaning thus:—

"This picture I, Alessandro, painted at the end of the year 1500, in the troubles of Italy, in the half-time after the time, during the fulfilment of the Eleventh of St. John, in the second woe of the Apocalypse, in the loosing of the devil for three years and a half. Afterwards he shall be chained, according to the Twelfth of St. John, and we shall see him trodden down as in this picture."

In the centre is the usual group of the Nativity, while right and left kneel the Magi and the Shepherds with angels pointing out to them the miracle. On the pent house roof and in the sky angels sing the Gloria in Excelsis, and dance hand in hand swinging olive boughs and crowns in their joy. In the foreground devils crawl away to hide in the rocks, while rejoicing angels fall on the neck of Savonarola and his two companions, "the witnesses slain for the word of their testimony." The picture not only shows how deeply rooted was the memory of Savonarola in Botticelli's mind, but also it and its inscription testify to what was the condition of crime and vice which ran riot in Florence in these years, when Cambi tells us that "citizens who sought redress in the law courts were frequently stabbed in the street the next night, judges pronounced iniquitous sentences, and there was no reverence for holy things or fear of shame."

After this date Botticelli became too infirm to paint; he died in 1510, at the age of sixty-four, and was buried in his father's vault in his parish church of Ognissanti.[18]

Although Perugino belongs to Perugia he painted for so many years in Florence, where all his best work was done, that he is always classed with the Tuscan school. When he died in 1524 he was almost the last[19] of that great school which had given to Painting its re-birth and had led the way in that art for over two hundred years; Ruskin considers Perugino the culminating point of the Tuscan school of painting.

Having spent three years in Florence as the pupil of Verrocchio (1479-1482), and having executed various works there in the years 1486-1491, Perugino in 1492 set up his studio in that city. Ruskin says:—"It is from this time that we date the great series of pictures in which he seems to carry to their deepest depths the expression of devotion, of self-sacrifice, and of holy grief." Perugino painted regularly in Florence from 1492 to 1498, and again during the greater part of the years 1501 to 1510, after which date he did little notable work. So that all his best work was done during this period of the Interregnum. As all know, he was Raphael's master; and he survived his great pupil by four years.

Perugino has four chief characteristics. First, free open space; regarding which Mr. Bernhardt Berenson says:— "Space composition . . . is not an arrangement to be judged as extending only laterally, or up and down, on a flat surface, but as extending inward in depth as well. It is composition in three dimensions, and not in two; in the cube and not merely on the surface." In this "space composition" Perugino excelled all either before or after him; by regular gradations his distances recede far into the background, giving a feeling of vast and limitless space.

Second, aloofness in his figures. Dr. Williamson says:— "They stand apart from one another, connected by a thread of thought with each other, and with the central feature of the picture, but each of them in every other way self-contained."

Third, his beautiful landscapes, "with distant hills bathed in a blue mist revealing long stretches of fertile land on either side, with single trees silhouetted against the sky. and all bathed in pale golden sunlight."

Fourth, a severe absence of strong action or excited emotion. "Convulsive action was as much an offence to him as was its absence in his works an offence to Michelangelo."

The joint effect of these four characteristics is to produce pictures breathing a wonderful peace. Regarding *The Entombment,* now in the Pitti Gallery, Dr. Williamson says: [20]—

"In this picture space composition is seen in its full vigour. How vast is the space in which the episode is placed, and how wonderful the sense of immeasurable distance produced. How quiet is the atmosphere of the scene; how reverent and tender a mood it creates. The picture is one of the best Perugino ever painted. . . . Each figure is distinct, self-centred, and enfolded in its own grief. . . . It is a picture full of sentiment, yet sober and thoughtful."

And regarding his *Baptism of Christ,* now at Rouen, the same writer says:—

"Around the two central figures are kneeling angels and attendant figures, eight only in number, carefully graduated in size according to position, aloof, serious, and still. Away and away beyond is the rolling landscape with its exquisite hills, and dainty detached trees standing out clear against the sky. On and on the eye travels seeking to reach the limits of this limitless vision, and impressed more and more by the skill that painted in so tiny a compass so vast a scene."

Of Perugino's masterpiece, his fresco of *The Crucifixion,* painted in the chapter-house of the convent of Sta. Maria Maddalena de' Pazzi in Florence, it has been very generally felt that it is the most perfect representation of the Crucifixion ever achieved by any painter; while the whole picture breathes an indescribable spirit of *peace.*

————————

After Savonarola's death Florence became more than ever a prey to anarchy. Three different factions, the Ottimati, the Bigi, and the Frateschi contended unceasingly, and frequent changes in the constitution only produced increased strife. At length after three years of turmoil the citizens were driven to a measure which stultified all their action in abolishing the rule of the Medici. They resolved that the only remedy for the evils of the city was the appointment of a Gonfaloniere for life, as a sort of permanent Dictator. There were various candidates, but, as might have been expected under the conditions which prevailed, instead of a strong man being elected the majority of the votes were given to a weak one whom no party had any reason to fear. Piero Soderini, a well-meaning and generally respected man with no strength or ability, was elected; and he remained permanently Gonfaloniere during the rest of the period of the Interregnum; though owing to his weakness and incapacity this brought little amelioration of the evils under which Florence groaned. The legal tribunals were utterly corrupt; crime of every kind was rife; men of ability kept aloof from public affairs; the Great Council refused to vote money necessary to meet the financial engagements of the State; disputes and riots were incessant; and all writers give deplorable accounts of the condition of the city. Cambi says:—"Justice no longer existed among the citizens through fear of each other"; and Guicciardini remarks:—"It is difficult to imagine a city so thoroughly shattered and ill-regulated as ours was at this time." This condition of things in Florence naturally caused her to sink into a position of insignificance among the states of Italy; her foreign affairs were unceasingly mismanaged, being in the hands of men who were without any talents for such a task.

Yet it was a time when a capable direction of foreign affairs was above all necessary. After Charles VIII's expedition Pope Alexander VI brought about a league between Rome, Venice, Milan, the Emperor Maximilian, and Henry VII of England, against France, a league which threatened the very existence of the French monarchy, and of those states, such as Ferrara, Florence, and Bologna, which clung to the French alliance. Louis XII, on succeeding to the French throne in 1498, set himself to break up this league; and the campaigns which during the next fourteen years he carried on in succession against Milan, Naples, Venice, and the Pope, kept

Italy in a state of permanent warfare and threw all states there into confusion.

In 1499 Louis XII sent against Milan an army which drove out Il Moro, who fled to Innsbruck, to the protection of the Emperor Maximilian. The latter in this year married his eldest son, the Archduke Philip, to Joanna, the eldest daughter of Ferdinand and Isabella of Spain, a marriage which had important consequences in the next generation. In the same year Florence put to death the only man she possessed who had the talents of a general, Paolo Vitelli. The Republic had sent him with a force to retake Pisa (which Charles VIII had never restored), but the attempt failed, and Vitelli was accused of treachery, recalled, and executed, though it is stated by Guicciardini that he was innocent.

In 1500 Il Moro regained Milan, but was soon afterwards captured by the French, and carried off to France, where he was imprisoned in the castle of Loches for the remaining eight years of his life, Louis XII taking possession of Milan. In the same year the combined forces of Spain and France conquered Naples; but this was followed by a dispute over its possession which brought on a three years' war between them. Nor did central Italy fare any better than the north and south. In the endeavour to establish a sovereignty of central Italy, Cæsar Borgia was seizing state after state, thus gaining in succession Imola, Forlì, Urbino, Faenza, Pesaro, Rimini, and Piombino, and making himself the terror of Romagna.

In 1501 Cæsar Borgia, having gained Faenza by causing its ruler, the young Astorre Manfredi, to be murdered, advanced into the Val d'Arno and threatened Florence. The Signoria ignominiously bought him off by agreeing to appoint him Captain General of Florence's forces at a fixed salary of 36,000 florins a year. In the same year Alexander VI, in order to detach Ferrara from the French King, succeeded in bringing about a marriage between his daughter,

Lucrezia Borgia, and Alfonso, the eldest son of the Duke of Ferrara.

In 1502 Cæsar Borgia, who as the result of various crimes had now become "Duke of Valentino, Duke of Urbino, Duke of Romagna, Prince of Andria, and Lord of Piombino," informed Florence that her government did not please him, and that she had better amend it. The Signoria, relying on Louis XII's approaching return to Italy, ordered its envoys to temporise; and other events called off Cæsar Borgia for a time from attacking Florence. He, however, informed her government significantly that the French King would not be always in Italy.

In 1503 Louis XII advanced again into Italy to prosecute his war with Spain for the possession of Naples, but the campaign turned out adversely for the French. This would undoubtedly have brought Cæsar Borgia again upon Florence, but just as this juncture Pope Alexander VI suddenly died, Cæsar Borgia being at the same time taken dangerously ill.[21] Cæsar Borgia after some time recovered, but only to find all his power broken through the death of the Pope. The various states which he had usurped at once reverted to their original rulers, and Cæsar Borgia was eventually arrested by the commander of the Spanish forces in southern Italy, Gonsalvo, and sent as a prisoner to Spain, where four years later he was killed while fighting for the King of Navarre.

In December 1503 the French army in southern Italy sustained a crushing defeat at a battle which took place on the river Garigliano; it managed to retreat in great disorder to Gaeta, but was there forced to capitulate, and to agree to return to France.[22] This brought the three years' war in southern Italy between France and Spain to an end, and Naples and Sicily were annexed by Ferdinand of Spain to the Spanish Crown and placed in charge of a Viceroy. It was in the above battle that Pietro the Unfortunate lost his life; whereby his next brother, Cardinal Giovanni, became head of the Medici family.

Pope Alexander VI was succeeded by Pius III, but he died one month later, and was succeeded by Julius II (Giuliano della Rovere), the celebrated fighting Pope, the destroyer of the old St. Peter's, the founder of the new St. Peter's, and the friend, and antagonist, of Michelangelo. A strong character, with many good points, he was fonder of war than of anything else, and was perpetually in the field, commanding his forces in person. Italy had now become the battlefield on which France, Spain, and Germany fought perpetually for supremacy, and this strong fiery old man [23] seized with avidity the opportunity this state of things gave him to indulge his predilection for war.

From 1503 to 1507 Julius II was chiefly occupied in subduing in succession the various states of Romagna, and forming them into "the States of the Church," which he now founded, and which thenceforward remained permanently the temporal dominion of the Papacy. In 1508 he turned his arms against Venice, and formed the "League of Cambray," a league entered into by Louis XII, the Emperor Maximilian, Ferdinand of Spain, and himself, to crush the power of Venice, and for the partition of her inland dominions.

Meanwhile the fortunes of the Medici family were beginning to emerge from the gloom in which for ten years they had plunged. On Julius II becoming Pope in 1503, and Giovanni (a man whose good-natured and peaceable disposition had always been contrasted with that of his elder brother) becoming in the same year the head of the family, many who had before looked on the Medici with disfavour became ready to help them, including Pope Julius himself. Nor was the same effect unfelt even in Florence. It was Pietro and his wife who were so specially obnoxious to the Florentines, not the Medici family as a whole. And as time went on and the effects of the misrule in Florence became more and more intolerable, the number of the citizens who secretly desired the return of this family, now that it was represented by two such characters as Giovanni and his brother Giuliano, grew constantly greater; though none dared to acknowledge this desire owing to the laws which made it death to urge the return of the Medici.

Giovanni's behaviour and manner of life in Rome was such as to encourage these sentiments. He showed no disposition to interfere in the affairs of the Florentines, though under the incapable rule of Pietro Soderini they continued in their chronic state of discord and anarchy. He lived plainly, having in fact but little means for ostentation, and often finding it hard to keep out of debt; never desponding, always cheerful, animated, and agreeable in his manners to all, and taking great interest in all matters connected with Art and Litera- ture, though he had little money himself to spend upon such things.[24] By this course of conduct, and by the qualities of his character (which made friends where Pietro only made enemies), Giovanni gradually retrieved the downfall of his family, creating a feeling in their favour both outside and inside Florence which led a few years later to their being re- installed in power there.

The whole family, including Pietro's widow Alfonsina with her two children, Lorenzo and Clarice, were now living at Rome. And in the year 1508 Alfonsina managed to arrange at Rome a marriage between Clarice, now fifteen, and Filippo Strozzi, the head of the most wealthy and important Floren- tine family next to the Medici. For thus daring to marry "the daughter of a declared rebel and outlaw" Filippo Strozzi was summoned before the Signoria of Florence, heavily fined, and banished for three years; but the sentence was a half- hearted one, as we find him back in Florence in little more than a year afterwards.

In 1509, as the result of the League of Cambray, there took place the decisive battle of Agnadello, at which Venice received from the allies a crushing blow, from which she never recovered. Her power had been steadily declining since 1453, and was by this defeat completely broken; and as a consequence she lost Verona, Padua, Bergamo, Brescia, Cremona, and Piacenza, and became no longer of importance in European politics. In the same year Florence, after a long siege, recovered Pisa, which had been lost to her for fifteen years. In this year Henry VII of England died, and was succeeded by his son Henry VIII, then eighteen. The latter in the same year married Katharine of Arragon, daughter of Ferdinand and Isabella, and younger sister of Joanna of Spain

In 1510 Julius II changed sides, and allied himself with Spain and Venice against the French, endeavouring to expel the latter from Italy. This brought him into collision with Ferrara and Florence. He first led a successful attack against Mirandola, and then advanced against Ferrara, but was defeated. Meanwhile Louis XII retorted by proposing a Council to depose the Pope, and demanded from his ally, Florence, that she should allow it to assemble at Pisa. Florence was placed in a dilemma; if she consented she dreaded the Pope's enmity; if she refused she would offend Louis XII, and lose the protection of the French alliance. Soderini's government was quite incapable of dealing with such a problem, and by vacillation and endeavours to trim between the two opponents contrived to offend both. Florence agreed to the assembly of the Council at Pisa, but refused to permit a French force to enter Pisa to protect the Council, and did not send Louis XII the troops she had promised. Julius II now determined to put an end to the inefficient government in Florence, and to reinstate the Medici, and only waited until he should first have driven the French out of Italy, as by means of the Spanish alliance he hoped soon to do. In the meantime he appointed Giovanni his representative with the force of Papal and Spanish troops which was then besieging Bologna.

This period of the Interregnum, when war and its miseries raged over Italy, and confusion and anarchy were rampant in Florence, is nevertheless the time when Art reached its

culminating point. It was as though men, seeking an anti-
dote to the violence and turmoil around them, turned to the
pictures of the great masters of the time which breathed an
atmosphere of peace and rest not to be found elsewhere.
The zenith of the Art of the Renaissance falls between these
years, 1494 and 1512, during which period *The Last Supper*, by Leonardo da Vinci, the frescoes on the roof of the
Sixtine chapel by Michelangelo, and the frescoes of the
Camera della Segnatura by Raphael, were painted, works in
which Art reached its highest development.

There now succeeds a great army of painters, all of the
first rank, and all practically contemporaneous, in whose
hands Art, so long associated almost entirely with Florence,
soared forth over all Italy. To mention only the names of the
chief of those who all flourished at this epoch is to call up
before the mind's eye a mass of Art creations such as no
other period has produced. The following were all painting
at this period, besides many others of less note:—

Botticelli (Florence).	Francia (Bologna).
Leonardo da Vinci (Florence).	Pinturicchio (Perugia).
Filippino Lippi (Florence).	Luini (Milan).
Lorenzo di Credi (Florence).	Raphael (Urbino).
Fra Bartolommeo (Florence).	Carpaccio (Venice).
Michelangelo (Florence).	Giorgione (Venice).
Andrea del Sarto (Florence).	Titian (Venice).
Perugino (Perugia).	Palma Vecchio (Venice).

In the year 1505 there were all working in Florence at
one time Perugino, Leonardo da Vinci, Michelangelo, Raphael, Fra Bartolommeo, and Lorenzo di Credi. One may
safely say that never on any other occasion were six such
painters collected together at one time and place. Leonardo
da Vinci and Michelangelo [25] were at work on their cartoons
for the great hall of the Palazzo della Signoria; Perugino
was engaged on his *Assumption* in the church of the Annunziata; and Raphael was painting his *Madonna del Gran
Duca* (Pitti), his *Madonna del Cardellino* (Uffizi), and his
fresco of *The Last Supper,* in the monastery of San Onofrio.

which bears his signature and the date 1505.[26] Botticelli was at this time sixty-one, Perugino fifty-nine, Leonardo da Vinci fifty-three, Michelangelo thirty, and Raphael twenty-two.

Leonardo da Vinci was sent by Lorenzo the Magnificent to Il Moro, as the best among the Florentine painters whom he could recommend to him, in 1487. He remained with Il Moro for twelve years, during which time he founded the Milanese school of painting. He returned to Florence from 1503 to 1506, after which his principal home was Milan until 1516, when, at the earnest invitation of Francis I, who was anxious to inaugurate the patronage of Art in France, he removed to that country, and died there in 1519, at the age of sixty-seven.

Raphael entered the school of Perugino at Perugia in the year 1500 at the age of seventeen. He came thence to Florence in 1504, being then twenty-one, and painted there for four years. He was summoned by Pope Julius II to Rome in 1508, and worked there under that Pope and his successor, Leo X, for the remaining twelve years of his life, dying at Rome in 1520 at the age of thirty-seven.

Michelangelo, whose earliest impulses towards Art had been fostered and directed by Lorenzo the Magnificent (whom throughout his life he never forgot), went to Rome for the first time in 1496. He worked there till 1500, when he returned to Florence, and remained there until 1506, when he was summoned by the Pope to Rome to design an immense tomb, larger and grander than that of any other Pope, which Julius II desired to have constructed for himself; and in 1508 he was given the difficult task of painting the frescoes on the roof of the Sixtine chapel.

But to Michelangelo, grand as was his genius, has been traced the downfall of Art which about two decades later commenced, and which was fully developed long before his death in 1564. Ruskin, carefully tracing out the cause of this downfall, says [27] that so long as artists employed their artistic powers to depict their subject, Art continued to ad-

vance, but as soon as they reversed the process and employed
their subject to display their artistic powers, Art's downfall
began; and that this disastrous change was made by Michelangelo, who practised the latter method throughout his life,
whose unrivalled powers led all to follow him, and who, by
adopting a principle alien to the true spirit of Art, was the
author of its downfall.

It would seem that there was in Michelangelo a false
idealism which was ready to distort to any extent the character of his subject in order to produce a result which would
glorify his powers of execution. This first showed itself in
his *Bacchus* (executed at Rome in 1496, and now in the
Bargello Museum), which statue Shelley, while fully ap-
preciating the great powers of execution that it displayed,
declared to be "a most revolting mistake of the whole spirit
of Bacchus." It showed itself still more in his *David* (1503),
which, astonishing as it is in execution, is false to the true
spirit of Art, in that in order to display the powers of the
sculptor it falsifies the character of the subject, which might
just as well be that of a young Samson or Hercules. The same
thing is no less apparent in his *Moses* and in his statue of
Lorenzo, Duke of Urbino. In each case the subject is treated
as of no importance, and distorted out of all resemblance
to its character, in order to form a vehicle for the display
of certain powers in the sculptor. There is not one of Michelangelo's statues in looking at which we are not forced by the
artist to think, not of the man depicted, but of Michelangelo.
It is no wonder, therefore, in view of Michelangelo's long life
and the leadership which his surpassing genius and the death
of all the contemporaries of his earlier years gave to him,
that Ruskin, after prolonged study of the subject, should have
traced to him that downfall in Art which, not long after
Raphael's death, set in. And if any one should desire to see
how great that downfall was, he has but to walk in Florence
from Or San Michele, which Donatello's statue of *St. George*
adorns, to the Piazza San Lorenzo, where Baccio Bandi-

nelli's hideous statue of *Giovanni delle Bande Nere* (executed in 1540) is an eyesore to the whole locality, or into the Piazza della Signoria, where the same artist's no less hideous statue of *Hercules slaying Cacus* (executed in 1534) disfigures the front of the Palazzo Vecchio.[28]

Before quitting the subject of Art's zenith and downfall, the part which Pope Julius II played in connection with the former must not be omitted. For in the intervals of war Julius II, following the Florentine school of thought in philosophy and religion, formulated a scheme which is set forth in the two final achievements attained by the art of painting, Michelangelo's frescoes on the roof of the Sixtine chapel, and Raphael's frescoes on the walls of the Camera della Segnatura, both works being in the Vatican and both executed for Julius II. These works, by two masters who differ so greatly, have yet underlying them a fundamental idea common to both, which, in view of the place and the circumstances, can only have been furnished by the Pope himself. The Florentine school of thought, under the leadership of Cosimo, Lorenzo, Ficino, and Pico della Mirandola, had endeavoured to amalgamate Platonism and Christianity. Julius II, surrounded by men trained in that school, went a step further, and in the paintings which he caused to be executed by Michelangelo and Raphael in the Vatican propounded that both the Jewish dispensation and the Greek philosophy were "ante-chambers through which the human race was shepherded to Christ."[29] We see this idea first introduced in the frescoes on the roof of the Sixtine chapel, wherein Michelangelo demonstrates it by showing the human race led to Christ through a long line of Pagan Sibyls and Jewish prophets.[30] And we see the same idea elaborated with a still greater wealth of thought in Raphael's frescoes round the Pope's principal official room, the Camera della Segnatura, the first work executed by Raphael on reaching Rome in 1508, frescoes of which the general scheme must have been supplied by the Pope, though the wonderful way in which it is worked out is Raphael's own great achievement.

In the four world-renowned pictures which cover the four walls of this room Raphael (on the text given him by the Pope) preaches his great sermon; and in pictures in which the celebrated scientists, philosophers, and poets of pre-Christian times appear together with those of the Christian epoch, teaches the lesson that the human soul is to aspire towards God *in each of its faculties;* in the exercise of reason and scientific research (*The School of Athens*); in the exercise of the artistic and æsthetic faculty (*Parnassus*); in the exercise of the faculty of order and good government (*Secular and Ecclesiastical Laws*); and lastly in the exercise of the more definitely religious faculty (*Theology,* the science about God). In these pictures, therefore, two lessons are combined; first, that the pre-Christian philosophers and scientists showed in their degree aspirations towards God, and helped to prepare the human race for Christianity; and second, that in man's aspirations towards God his highest intellectual faculties are not to be excluded, but that all his faculties are to be included, and consecrated to God.

The thoughts thus expressed show the standpoint which had at length been reached after nearly eighty years' discussion of these subjects by the thinkers of Florence. We are reminded of Pico della Mirandola's speech long before. "Philosophy seeks truth, theology finds it, religion possesses it." How much of the "sermon" belongs to Julius II, and how much to the great artist Raphael, we can never know. But we could have no grander example of the way in which Art is a language and has deep thoughts to speak to all who will listen to its words.[31]

But there was one event at this time in the world of Art, inseparably connected with Pope Julius II, which by no means redounded to his glory or that of any of those concerned in it. Urged on by Bramante and Michelangelo, he committed the enormous vandalism of pulling down the old St. Peter's (rich with a thousand years' historical associations), because it would not hold the huge and tasteless tomb which he had ordered,[32] and erecting instead the present St. Peter's. Regarding this act and the motives which caused it, Ranke remarks as follows:[33]—

"Was it not profoundly significant that a Pope should himself resolve to demolish the ancient basilica of St. Peter's, the great metropolitan Church, every part of which was hallowed, every portion crowded with monuments that had received the veneration of ages, and determine to erect a temple, planned after those of antiquity, on its site? Both the factions then dividing the jealous world of Art urged Julius II to this enterprise. Michelangelo desired a fitting receptacle for the enormous monument of the Pope which he proposed to complete on a vast scale, and with that lofty grandeur which he has exhibited in his *Moses*. Yet more pressing was Bramante, whose ambition it was to execute that bold project of raising high in the air, on colossal pillars, an exact copy of the Pantheon in all the majesty of its proportions. Many cardinals remonstrated, and it would even appear that there was a general opposition to the plan; so much of personal affection attaches itself to every old church, how much more then to this, the chief sanctuary of Christendom. As Panvinius wrote: 'He had men of almost all classes against him and especially the cardinals; not because they did not wish to have a new basilica erected with all possible magnificence but because they grieved that the old one should be pulled down, revered as it was by the whole world, ennobled by the sepulchres of so many saints, and illustrious for so many great things that had been done in it.' But Julius was not accustomed to regard contradictions; without further consideration he caused one half of the old church to be demolished, and himself laid the foundation stone of the new one."

The year 1512 opened with a new series of military operations. France, Ferrara, and Florence on one side were against the Pope, Spain, and Venice on the other. The French army was commanded by the brave and capable young general, Gaston de Foix, cousin of Louis XII, and only twenty-four years of age. The Spanish forces were commanded by Raimondo da Cardona, Viceroy of Naples, and the Papal troops were placed by Julius II under Cardinal Giovanni de' Medici; and as to rise in favour with Julius II one had to be above all things a soldier, Giovanni could not refuse, though he evidently had no talents in that direction. After several brilliant successes had been gained by the French under the able leadership of Gaston de Foix, a pitched battle was fought on the 6th April 1512 at Ravenna, in which the Papal and Spanish army was totally defeated by the French, who, however, sustained a serious loss, for at the moment of victory their brave young commander, Gaston de Foix, was killed.[34] This battle was one of the bloodiest on record; and while the commander on the French side was killed, Cardinal Giovanni, the Pope's representative, was taken prisoner by the French, and sent, a captive, to Milan.

Pope Julius II was not cowed by this reverse; he rapidly collected a fresh army, the loss of Gaston de Foix seemed to paralyse the French, the tide of victory turned, and within three months the French army was driven across the Alps. Then Julius II turned his arms against Florence, and the troops of the "Holy League" which he had formed were sent against her, Julius II being determined to put an end to the existing state of things in that city, and to visit Soderini in particular with his wrath for having allowed the assembly of the Council at Pisa. Cardona's army of Spanish troops was therefore ordered to advance into Tuscany, and Cardinal Giovanni having escaped from Milan, he, his brother, and his cousin, were sent with it, the Pope informing Florence that the terms he required from her were that she should dismiss the Gonfaloniere Soderini, pay a fine of 100,000 florins, and allow the Medici to return to Florence. These terms Soderini's government declined to accept, and sent an inefficient force, chiefly composed of Machiavelli's newly-

organised militia, to oppose Cardona's army at Prato, about
ten miles from Florence.

Cardona reached Prato on the 28th August, and summoned
it to surrender, which being refused the attack was at once
commenced, and after a feeble resistance the town was taken
by assault on the 29th August. The terrible sack of Prato
which has become proverbial among such events on account
of the atrocities committed by the inhuman Spanish troops
ensued. Mr. Hyett says:—

"The horrors of the sack which followed are without a
parallel in history. For twenty-one days no attempt seems
to have been made by Cardona to control his savage, greedy
and licentious soldiery. Every building was pillaged. The defenceless inhabitants were chased from street to street, and
slaughtered as soon as overtaken. Neither youth, age, nor
sex, neither the sanctity of place nor office, were respected. ...
Mothers threw their daughters into wells and jumped in after
them, men cut their own throats, and girls flung themselves
from balconies on to the paving-stones below to escape from
violence and dishonour. It is said that 5,600 Pratans perished." [35]

A mediæval army was on such occasions absolutely uncontrollable, and it is a mistake to speak of Cardona as
though he wielded a power over his troops of a kind similar
to that possessed by a modern commander, and failed to
exercise it. Discipline as we understand it scarcely existed
in such armies at any time, and in the sack of a city not a
vestige of it remained. From the moment that a town was
taken by assault there was no longer an army, but only a
horde of savage ruffians with arms in their hands, mad with
passion, and ready in a moment to turn their weapons against
those who for the time were but nominal commanders, should
these latter attempt to interfere with their proceedings. The
real cruelty was perpetrated by the weak and incapable governing body headed by Soderini in sending a totally insuf-

ficient force to Prato, not strong enough to meet Cardona's army with any chance of success, but just sufficient to make the result upon Prato which actually occurred a certainty; and this in the case of a town which had no voice in the matter of offering resistance to that army.

The Medici brothers were not present during the whole of these terrible doings at Prato; Giuliano was only there during the first two days, Giovanni for ten days longer. During this time they exerted themselves to do what they could to protect the women and children, among other things getting a guard placed over the great church in which a large number of them had taken refuge. And Jovius states that "if the Cardinal de' Medici and his brother Giuliano had not, at the risk of their lives, opposed themselves to the fury of the conquerors, these enormities would have been carried to a still greater excess."

While these horrors were taking place at Prato, Florence was occupied in carrying out a rapid revolution. Immediately on the news being received that Prato had been taken and that these atrocities were being perpetrated there, a number of the citizens, justly attributing all that had occurred to Soderini's mismanagement, forced their way into his room, made him resign his office, and sent him under an escort to Siena; whence he fled to Castelnuovo, where, that town being under the Turks, he felt safe from Julius II, whose personal animosity against him for the matter of the Council he well knew. The remaining members of the Government hastily signified to Cardona their willingness to allow the Medici to return, and agreed to pay the fine which the Pope demanded; and on the 1st September 1512 the Medici once more entered Florence, after an exile of eighteen years.

Moreover, it was soon evident that the people were glad to get them back again, that it had only been the power of a dominant faction which had kept them out so long, and that the result of the misrule suffered under the government of the latter had sunk deep into the minds of the people. For had it been otherwise the re-establishment of the family in Florence would not have been accompanied by the results which ensued. That they were greeted on their arrival with the old shouts of *"Palle! Palle!"* may not of itself show much. More significant, however, is the fact that the Spanish troops who had escorted them into the city were able within a month to be entirely dispensed with. And this notwithstanding that all laws passed since 1494 were repealed, that the Consiglio Maggiore established by Savonarola was abolished, and that the Government was remodelled on exactly the same lines as in the times of Lorenzo the Magnificent, although a law expressly forbidding this had been passed in 1495.[36] There was no demonstration whatever against these changes, and Professor Villari tells us that "after the Spaniards had left the new Government required no support from foreign troops." [37] Also the writings and conduct of Francesco Valori, Nerli, and Machiavelli fully corroborate the statement made by the latter that "even those who disapproved of the present constitutional changes, soon reconciled themselves to the return of the old order of things." From the above it is clear that although the Medici returned in accordance with terms imposed upon the city by Julius II, yet the people were well content to have it so. They were in fact sick to death of the misgovernment they had experienced for so many years, and ready to welcome a rule which had ever been associated with order, and security to life and property.

And the conduct of the Medici brothers, Giovanni and Giuliano, was worthy of the occasion. They followed the traditions of their house, and the example that had been set by Cosimo Pater Patriae and Piero il Gottoso. Their family had been made to suffer much, they themselves had had to endure for long years the harsh conditions attaching to the life of outcasts and wanderers, they returned to a family home which had been swept bare, all the invaluable collections of their ancestors which it had contained when they left it having been wantonly destroyed, or carried off. Never

theless their father Lorenzo's speech of forty-six years before
was not forgotten by his sons, and they showed that they
knew how to conquer, by showing that they knew how to
forgive. The vindictive policy which among the Florentines
invariably accompanied the return to power of a banished
faction was by the Medici entirely rejected. There were no
executions, prohibitions, confiscations, or banishments, except in the case of Piero Soderini, who had been banished
by the Florentines themselves before the Medici returned.
And even he was afterwards befriended by Giovanni.[38]

In this manner did the Medici once more set up their rule
in Florence; and all things seemed to augur well for its satisfactory continuance, especially as it was decided that that
rule should be placed in the hands of Giuliano, both Giovanni
and Giulio being anxious to depart to Rome, where the election of a new Pope was imminent.

CHAPTER XII

GIULIANO (DUC DE NEMOURS) AND LORENZO (DUKE OF URBINO)

THE Medici when they returned again after so many years to Florence were represented by the two brothers, Giovanni and Giuliano, and their first cousin, Giulio. They had been youths of eighteen, fifteen, and sixteen when driven out from their home; they returned as men of thirty-six, thirty-three, and thirty-four. During the intermediate years they had had many varied experiences, had seen much of life, had had many hard things to endure, and ample opportunities of realising how differently the world treats those who are in a position to grant favours and those who have to seek them. On one of the trio the effect of these experiences had been good, on the other two the reverse.

And the relative characters of these three young men are important in regard to subsequent events. The senior member of the trio, Giovanni, was an easy-going, pleasure-loving man, with a full measure of the ability customary in his family, but ever ready to avoid trouble; while the experiences through which he had passed had left him with few scruples as to the manner in which he attained his objects. With his brother Giuliano it was otherwise; he had a thoroughly good disposition, and one which would not allow him to adopt unworthy methods. But it is with the third member of the trio that we are in this matter chiefly concerned. Giulio was full of energy, and endowed with extreme ability, second only to that of his uncle, Lorenzo the Magnificent, though the objects to which he throughout life devoted his powers were on so much lower a level as to make this less generally apparent. From their very boyhood he had attached himself closely to his cousin Giovanni, becoming his constant companion and adviser, and an agent ever ready to take all trouble off his shoulders; an arrangement which exactly suited Giovanni's ease-loving character.

These conditions were fraught with important consequences. For during the long years of exile Giulio's fertile brain had designed a course of action in regard to Florence, should they ever succeed in regaining power there, which would make an entire change in the traditional policy of the family. No more should there be any of that resting of the Medici power upon mere popularity, which had proved, Giulio considered, such a broken reed; but it should rest, if he could direct events, upon force pure and simple. But the force should be that of the steel hand in a velvet glove, and the despotism thus planned be made as little irksome as possible by the outward form of a republic being still maintained, at all events for a time. For Giulio's far-reaching schemes went further than this, and looked forward to a time when even the form of a republic might be abolished, a despotic monarchy of Tuscany set up, and a crown at length be placed upon a Medici head. All this could, he considered, be brought about (or at all events set in train) if Giovanni would continue to be guided by him, and if only it could be managed that Giovanni should become Pope.

To this member of the trio such feelings as generosity, magnanimity, care for the people, readiness to give unselfish labour for the good of one's country, clemency towards enemies, and other similar motives of action, which had been so long inherent in all the men and women of this family that they had grown to be assumed as matters of course, were completely non-existent. Beneath a handsome exterior and a graceful manner he hid a cold-hearted disposition, a nature able to entertain only ignoble aims, and a character burdened with no scruples whatever.

But Giulio well knew that the younger of the Medici

brothers, Giuliano, would absolutely oppose any such projects, and in the present relative position of the two brothers would be able to do so successfully. Therefore Giulio's plans must be kept for the present to himself. Let Giovanni, however, become Pope, and it should then be seen how differently Florence would be ruled; while it would be easy to provide for Giuliano elsewhere, and to place Florentine affairs in the hands of some more amenable agent.

Such were the plans laid during the years of exile by this base-born scion of the Medici, who, possessing all their ability but not a particle of their other qualities, and scheming to direct the family towards aims, and raise it by methods, which were the only ones he appreciated, became its evil genius. And now the first step necessary to his schemes had been gained, and they were once more installed in power in Florence; and Giulio turned all his attention to the second step, that of getting Giovanni made Pope. The dim crown in the distance which Giulio had set before him as the family aim had advanced one step nearer than it was when they were homeless exiles without power or influence; but he little realised through how many vicissitudes the family were at length to gain that aim after he had passed away.

GIULIANO (Duc de Nemours)

Born 1479. (Ruled 1512-1513.) Died 1516

Giuliano, the third son of Lorenzo the Magnificent, was thirty-three years of age when his family returned to the home from which they had been driven out when he was a boy of fifteen. During the earlier part of their period of exile he had taken refuge with the Duke and Duchess of Urbino, Guidobaldo Montefeltro and his talented wife, Elisabetta Gonzaga (the second greatest lady of the Renaissance),[1] both of whom were very fond of him. And during the years of exile he had shown himself possessed of both general capacity and military ability. On his family being reinstalled Guiliano was placed in charge of the rule of Florence, ruling, that is to say, in the same manner as Lorenzo the Magnificent had done, the ostensible Government being as heretofore the Signoria. And as soon as the new Government had been established Giovanni (accompanied as always by Giulio, his *Fidus Achates*) departed to Rome.

This return after eighteen years' banishment (or rather the election of Giovanni to be Pope, which was almost simultaneous with it) marks the second turning-point in the history of the Medici. Up to this point, great as had been their rise, the position which they had attained was not higher than that of various other rulers of Italian states; now, however, their history enters on a new phase, one in which they were to be among the most important people in Europe, intermarrying with crowned heads, and taking a prominent part in great events of European history.

Giovanni's decision to place the rule of Florence in Giuliano's hands, rather than in those of Pietro's son Lorenzo (who was then twenty, and had returned with his two uncles), was a wise one. For Lorenzo's character was similar to that of his father Pietro and his mother Alfonsina; while to inaugurate again the kind of rule maintained by Lorenzo the Magnificent it was eminently necessary that the power should be in the hands of one who had a conciliatory disposition, and was in sympathy with the feelings of the Florentine people.

Giuliano was in every way calculated to fulfil these requirements. Born just after the conspiracy of the Pazzi, his father, Lorenzo the Magnificent, had given to him the name of the much-loved brother whose murder was so great a grief; and in disposition Giuliano was extraordinarily like the uncle whose name he bore. All writers agree as to his admirable character. He had a generous and sympathetic nature and conciliatory manners, was opposed to bloodshed and violence, was highly accomplished, and a great lover of Literature and Art. At the courts of Urbino and Mantua, and wherever else he had wandered during the years of exile, the young Giuliano de' Medici had been a favourite at all social gatherings; and Castiglione gives us, in his *Il Cortigiano,* an attractive picture of him, describing him as the chivalrous champion of women. Another writer says:—"He was a thoughtful and religious man, of a peaceful and generous nature, revolting from the crimes in those days necessary to the success of worldly ambition." He has been justly called "one of the most attractive personalities the Italian Renaissance can claim to have produced." He showed himself at once, even in his outward actions, desirous of meeting Florentine views; he shaved off his beard [2] in accordance with the fashion among the Florentines (who regarded a beard as the badge of the foreigner), he wore the Florentine *lucco,* and, avoiding all ostentation, bore himself simply as an ordinary citizen.

But Giuliano's rule of Florence was of short duration. In February 1513 Julius II died, and, as his successor, Giovanni de' Medici was elected Pope, and took the name of Leo X. Immediately upon this Giulio's schemes began to work. Giuliano's lenient rule must be replaced by one more adapted to the new Pope's views regarding Florence; so he was made "Gonfaloniere of the Papal forces," an office which necessitated his residence in Rome, and the rule of Florence was made over to his less scrupulous nephew Lorenzo, who was ordered to conduct Florentine affairs in accordance with instructions given to him by the Pope.

Just before this change was made the plot occurred which blighted the political career of Machiavelli. He had been Secretary to Soderini's Government, but had signified his willingness to serve under the new *régime.* Two young men, Boscoli and Capponi, fired with ideas acquired by reading the ancient Roman authors, had concocted an ill-digested plot for the murder of Giuliano and his nephew Lorenzo. They had apparently no confederates, but one of them dropped in the street a paper which disclosed their plot and contained a number of names (presumably of men whom they thought likely to sympathise with them), amongst which Machiavelli's was one; and the finder took the paper to the Signoria. The latter caused Boscoli and Capponi to be executed; but of the rest, while a few were banished, the greater part were set at liberty, it being felt that the plot had no real sympathisers, but was simply a dream of two hare-brained young men. Machiavelli was one of those held to be entirely innocent, but the suspicion which had rested on him for a few days ruined his career, as he could get no further official employment; he retired to his country villa, and took to Literature.[3]

Giuliano on being relieved of the rule of Florence retired to Rome, a change which was not unacceptable to him. "He preferred the charms of private life, literature, and the society of learned men to ambition." And such society, having been driven from Florence by the anarchy of the previous eighteen years, had now gravitated to Rome, which under Julius II, and still more under Leo X, was becoming what Florence had once been, the centre of Art and Learning in Italy.

In 1513 Louis XII again advanced into Italy and attacked Milan, but was repulsed by the armies of Ferdinand and Maximilian, sustaining a decisive defeat at the battle of Novara.

In 1515 Louis XII died (on the 1st January), and was succeeded by his distant cousin, Francis I.

———————

Giuliano, loving a quiet and unostentatious style of life, was averse from the honours which his brother, Leo X, in the desire to aggrandise his family, now thrust upon him. He was made lord of Parma, Piacenza, and Modena, but he thwarted the design which Leo X formed to make him Duke of Urbino by dispossessing its Duke, Francesco della Rovere, who in 1508 had succeeded his uncle, Guidobaldo Montefeltro. When this was proposed Giuliano absolutely refused, "because it would be an injustice to the rightful Duke"; and Leo X had to defer his design to gain Urbino for his family until after Giuliano was dead.

Early in 1515 Giuliano was sent by the Pope as his representative to congratulate the new King of France, Francis I, on his accession. Francis developed a great liking for him, and while at the French court Giuliano was married to the charming Philiberte of Savoy, then seventeen years old, the "Anima Eletta" of Ariosto, the young aunt of Francis I, sister of his mother, Louise of Savoy. The French King at the same time created him Duc de Nemours, by which title he is always known, to distinguish him from his uncle Giuliano, the brother of Lorenzo the Magnificent.

Soon after his return to Rome from France Giuliano accompanied Leo X as commander of the Papal forces to the conference between the Pope and the King of France which was held at Bologna in December 1515; on which occasion there were great festivities in Florence, both on the way to Bologna and during their stay at Florence on their return. But in February 1516 Giuliano, being much out of health, removed to the Badia of Fiesole; and there, on the 17th March, he died at the age of thirty-seven, sincerely lamented by the Florentines, to whom he had greatly endeared himself. Thus the two Giulianos were, each in their respective generations, the best beloved of their family. To the very last Giuliano endeavoured to prevent his brother's design upon Urbino, and Alberi tells us that when Leo X came to see Giuliano at Fiesole in his last illness, the latter begged him almost with his dying breath not to attack the Duke of Urbino. Philiberte of Savoy did not survive him many years; she only lived to the age of twenty-six, dying in 1524.

Giuliano was buried with great ceremony in San Lorenzo, in the New Sacristy then just begun by Michelangelo under the orders of Leo X, being the first member of the family to be interred there. And in after years over his tomb was erected one of the two great masterpieces of Michelangelo.[4] Guiliano

left no child by Philiberte, but left an illegitimate son, Ippolito, born at Urbino in 1509.

The fine portrait of Giuliano by Raphael is particularly interesting because it has only recently come to light after
being lost for three hundred and fifty years. The portrait of
him in the Uffizi Gallery by Alessandro Allori (1535-1607)
had always been said to be a copy of one known to have been
painted by Raphael and mentioned by Vasari as having been
seen by him; but since Vasari's time all trace of this portrait
had disappeared. In 1901, however, a picture which had been
bought by the Grand Duchess Marie of Russia some years
before was brought to Paris by Prince Sciarra-Colonna for
examination by the late M. Eugène Müntz, Director of the
École des Beaux Arts, who after a careful inspection pronounced it to be undoubtedly the lost portrait by Raphael of
Giuliano (Duc de Nemours). And this opinion has since been
confirmed by that of Dr. Wilhelm Bode, Director of the Royal
Gallery of Berlin, and other experts. The picture differs from
that by Allessandro Allori in having in the background a view,
looking from the Vatican, of the castle of St. Angelo, and
showing the corridor leading from the Vatican to the castle. It
was evidently painted in Rome in 1516, either just before, or
more probably just after Giuliano's return from his embassy
to France. He wears the style of cap in vogue there, the French
style of dress, and a beard, as customary in that country.
Over a scarlet vest, and a black doublet, he wears a cloak of
greyish-green brocade bordered with fur, the left sleeve having
on it a narrow strap with a gold ornament.[5] The document
in his hand, and the folded paper stuck into his cap, refer to
his diplomatic mission to Francis I.[6]

LORENZO (DUKE OF URBINO)

Born 1492. (Ruled 1513-1519.) Died 1519

LORENZO, the only son of Pietro the Unfortunate, was two
years old when the family were exiled, eleven years old when

his father died, and sixteen when his sister Clarice was married in Rome to Filippo Strozzi. In consequence of his father's wandering life and early death he was brought up by his mother Alfonsina, and had imbibed from her all those ideas of pride and arrogance which were most repugnant to the Florentines. When he was twenty-one the rule of Florence was placed in his hands as the representative of his uncle, Leo X, the senior member of the family. He was ordered to rule in accordance with detailed instructions which were drawn up for his guidance by the Pope, and which specially warned him against offending the feelings of the Florentines by ostentation in his mode of life, or by any display of that arrogant demeanour to which he was inclined. Leo X and his adviser Giulio were bent upon ruling Florence with a strong hand, but at the same time they had no desire to disturb the excellent relations between them and the people which had been established on their return to power. And for the first two or three years Lorenzo obeyed these wise instructions; though he had little capacity, he refrained from giving offence, and when in 1515 Leo X visited Florence, the enthusiastic reception which the people gave him showed that the Medici rule was still popular.

In March 1516 Giuliano's death removed the obstacle to Leo X's design of seizing upon the Dukedom of Urbino and giving it to one of the members of his own family. The Papal forces were at once sent against Urbino, Lorenzo being put in command; the reigning Duke, Francesco della Rovere, was driven out; and on the 30th May the Papal army entered Urbino. Whereupon Leo X declared Lorenzo Duke of Urbino (by which name he is always known); but he remained so in little more than name, and on Leo X's death five years later the rightful Duke recovered his state.

This new acquisition by the representative of the Medici family charged with the rule of Florence was of doubtful advantage to that State. Lorenzo had not the wit to be a Duke in Urbino and a simple citizen in Florence. He now disre-

garded the instructions he had received, and his insolent bearing, his maintenance of a semi-ducal ceremonial, and his dissolute conduct, soon made him hated in Florence. Moreover,
Lorenzo's new dignity involved Florence in a costly war; for
Francesco della Rovere made strenuous endeavours to regain
his inheritance, and Lorenzo, before his authority over Urbino
was secured, had to undertake a campaign lasting many
months.[7] All this embittered the Florentines; conspiracies to
take his life were frequent, followed by executions which
enraged the people still more against him; and matters were
rapidly tending towards another revolution.

In 1518 Leo X and his adviser Giulio (who had now become a cardinal) succeeded in arranging with Francis I that
Lorenzo should be married to the King's distant relative, the
beautiful Madeleine de la Tour d'Auvergne. The contemporary historian Fleurange remarks that she was "trop belle que
le marié," referring to Lorenzo's dissolute life. Lorenzo went
to France in great splendour, both to represent the Pope at the
baptism of Francis's eldest son, as well as for his own marriage
to the King's relative. He was accompanied by his brother-in-
law, Filippo Strozzi, and other principal Florentines, "all
dressed in crimson velvet and with a numerous retinue." [8]
The court of Francis I was at this time the most brilliant in
Europe; it was now assembled at Amboise, and there, first the
baptism of the heir to the throne took place, followed three
days later by the marriage of Lorenzo de' Medici and Madeleine de la Tour d'Auvergne. Fleurange, who was present,
says that the festivities on the occasion of this marriage were
on a more splendid scale than had ever before been witnessed
in Christendom, and gives a long description of them. The
young King Francis I delighted in the most gorgeous pageants,[9] and no place was more suited to the display of sixteenth century magnificence than the splendid old feudal castle
of Amboise. The festivities lasted a month, after which Lorenzo and his bride returned to Florence, where the Medici
Palace must have seemed to Madeleine a somewhat sombre

abode after the brilliance of Francis I's court. After this marriage Lorenzo added to his other misdemeanours in Florentine eyes by adopting the French custom of wearing a beard, a dire offence in Florence; and the portrait we have of him was evidently painted at this time.

Madeleine only lived for one year after her marriage. She died in the Medici Palace, on the 29th April 1519, a fortnight after giving birth to a daughter (Catherine). And six days later, on the 4th May, Lorenzo, worn out by a dissolute life, also died, at the age of twenty-seven, his death being to the advantage, not only of Florence, but also of the Medici family, to whose name he had brought nothing but discredit.

Lorenzo was buried, as his uncle Giuliano had been, in the New Sacristy of San Lorenzo; [10] and Michelangelo received orders from Leo X to design his monument. This in after years he carried out in the manner which has made this monument perhaps the most generally admired of all Michelangelo's works; and these two tombs in the New Sacristy over Giuliano (Duc de Nemours) and Lorenzo (Duke of Urbino) are probably the best known tombs of any in Europe. [11] Over each sarcophagus sits a statue of the man whose remains it contains; but these statues make no attempt to resemble the man depicted. To Guiliano, [12] who had a fine character, is given a statue representing quite the reverse; while to Lorenzo, the most worthless of the Medici, is given a statue [13] so grand that poet after poet has been inspired to write fine lines about it, attributing to the man the qualities represented by the statue. [14] When this result was foreseen, and it was pointed out to Michelangelo that the figures bore no faintest resemblance to the men represented, he contemptuously asked who would know it in the ages to follow.

The plans of Giulio de' Medici had been much disarranged by the results of Lorenzo's failure to follow the instructions laid down for him. On the latter's death, therefore, Leo X sent Giulio with all speed to Florence to undo the harm to the family interests which Lorenzo had caused. He must have

travelled with great despatch, for he arrived in time to super-
intend the arrangements for Lorenzo's funeral, which was
carried out with much magnificence. Giulio then turned his
attention to the matters on account of which he had been sent
to Florence, and here for the first time gave public evidence
of his great ability; for he was completely successful in his
arduous task. The embittered feelings which the misgovernment of Lorenzo had called forth caused the political atmosphere to be one of seething discontent. The *Frateschi,* led by
Jacopo Salviati, declared the existing method of government
to be too oligarchical; the *Ottimati,* led by Piero Ridolfi,
condemned it as being too republican; while outside these two
parties were many turbulent spirits who merely aimed at
anarchy. Giulio skilfully avoided identifying himself with
either of the opposing parties, and yet contrived to please both
of them, while at the same time keeping the real power in his
own hands. And during the five months that he remained in
Florence he lightened taxation, brought the finances into
order, reformed the administration of justice, and restored to
the elective bodies rights of which Lorenzo had deprived them.
Nardi tells us that both his measures and his demeanour gave
general satisfaction. This five months' work on Giulio's part
was in its way a masterpiece in the art of government.

But Cardinal Giulio had other difficulties than these to
surmount. There were very intricate family politics also
through which a way must be found if his cherished scheme
was ever to bear fruit. By Lorenzo's having died leaving only
a daughter who was a baby a week old, the position of the
family as rulers of Florence had become very precarious, since
Cosimo's branch threatened to become extinct. Lorenzo had
been the only son of Pietro the Unfortunate, and of his two
uncles, Giuliano was dead, and Giovanni was Pope; while
Giuliano's son, Ippolito (then ten years old), as well as
Giulio himself, were both illegitimate. So that this little baby
Catherine was the last legitimate representative of the elder
branch. The succession to the headship of the family (and

with it to the rule of Florence) would, therefore, on Leo X's death, by rights go to the younger branch, either in the person of Pier Francesco, great-grandson of Cosimo's brother, Lorenzo, or in that of the latter's other great-grandson, Giovanni delle Bande Nere, who was now twenty-one years old, and already making a name for himself as a military commander. Not only, however, had the younger branch shown no aptitude for State affairs, but also that branch deserved no consideration from any of Cosimo's branch, seeing that they had been the chief cause of the exile of the family, had discarded the family name during the years of the interregnum, and had acted a mean and ignoble part all through. So that Leo X and Giulio were determined to keep the rule of Florence out of their hands and in those of Cosimo's branch, if this should be in any way practicable; nor were either of them likely to be at all scrupulous as to the methods by which this object might be effected.

But all this—by what schemes under such circumstances the power was to be kept in Cosimo's branch, what was to be done with this baby girl who had become the most important person in the future of the family, and how all was to be combined with that ultimate aim of which he never lost sight —furnished for Cardinal Giulio a problem the consideration of which occupied many more hours of those five months at Florence than even the difficulties of public affairs. Immediately after the splendid funeral in San Lorenzo he took up his abode in the Medici Palace, now tenanted by so small an owner. And we can well imagine the far-reaching dreams and complex projects for a distant future which filled the active brain of Giulio de' Medici as his deep, thoughtful eyes for the first time looked down in her cradle on this last frail scion of Cosimo's branch, a fragile bark to bear so weighty a freight.

CHAPTER XIII

GIOVANNI (LEO X)

Born 1476. (*Pope* 1513-1521.) *Died* 1521

LEO X was by no means so important a character as it has been universally the fashion to depict him. The splendour which surrounded him has caught the popular imagination, and has prevented its being seen how little he merited the exalted view of him which has obtained general acceptance. When, however, he is brought to stand side by side with the other members of his family this inevitably comes out. The combined effect of his desire to take life easily and his unfailing common-sense (which kept him from involving himself in matters likely to lead to embarrassment and disaster) prevented him from becoming, as did his cousin Clement VII, the pivot round which the great events which took place in his time revolved. As a result, in a history of the Medici family (where each individual occupies the place demanded by his own character and deeds) the narrative of Leo's life becomes of far less importance than that of his much less pleasing cousin Clement, who not only played a more important part in the affairs of Europe, but also pursued a course which had infinitely greater effect on the subsequent fortunes of the family.

Giovanni, the second son of Lorenzo the Magnificent, was only thirty-seven when, on the 11th March 1513, he was elected Pope.[1] During the previous twenty years, from the time when at sixteen he had left his home in Florence to take his seat for the first time in the Sacred College, his life had been a chequered one. Returning to Florence after only a

few months in Rome, he had during the two years that followed seen the rapidly increasing unpopularity of his family
under his brother Pietro's unsympathetic rule, had been
driven forth with him into exile, had spent five years in
endeavours at various courts to obtain assistance for his
brother in military enterprises against Florence which invariably failed, and then, departing from Italy for a time, had
wandered through northern Europe, seeing many cities and
the life of many lands. Returning at length to Rome, he had
gradually won for himself and his family a position of favour
with the Pope, had been sent by him on important missions,
had been placed practically in command of a military force,
had taken part in a severely-fought battle and been taken
prisoner, had seen the terrible sack of Prato and done something to mitigate its horrors, and, finally, had re-entered his
native city in triumph, and re-established his family in power
there. All this had given him a wide experience of men and
affairs, but it had not altered his ease-loving disposition.

Leo X gave his name to his age, and his nine years' [2] reign
as Pope has been extolled to the skies by the literary men
of three centuries. His character has in part been already
noted. Apart from his love of Literature and Art, an unusually
strong common-sense and a genial good-nature were his
chief characteristics. Erasmus, who knew him well, praises
his kindness and humanity, his magnanimity and learning,
the charm of his manner, and his love of peace and the fine
arts; and comparing his pontificate with that which had
preceded it, says that "an age of iron was suddenly transformed into one of gold." And even Sarpi states:—

"Leo, noble by birth and culture, brought many aptitudes
to the Papacy, especially a remarkable knowledge of classical
literature, humanity, kindness, the greatest liberality, and
an avowed intention of supporting artists and learned men,
who for many years had enjoyed no such favour in the Holy
See."

While Dr. Kraus [3] says:—

> "Paramount in Leo's character were his gentleness and cheerfulness, his indulgence both for himself and others, his love of peace and hatred of war. . . . But on his personal character the great blot must rest that he passed his life in intellectual self-indulgence, and took his pleasure in hunting and amusement while the Teutonic north was bursting the bonds of reverence and authority which bound Europe to Rome."

On becoming Pope, Leo at once actively began all that encouragement of Literature and Art for which his pontificate is famous, inviting learned men from all parts of Italy to Rome, making plans for founding a great university there for the study of the Greek and Latin authors, corresponding with Aldus Manutius and others about inaugurating a printing press at Rome, commencing research work to obtain lost manuscripts of the classical age,[4] planning schemes for important works to be executed by Raphael and other artists, and setting himself in every way to advance the cause of Learning and Art.

He also set about assuring the future of his family. He created as cardinals his two first cousins, Giulio de' Medici [5] and Luigi Rossi; also his nephews (each a son of one of his three married sisters), Innocenzio Cibò, Giovanni Salviati, and Niccolò Ridolfi. With five cardinals in the family there would be a good probability that one of them would succeed him as Pope. His schemes for securing to the family the Duchy of Urbino have already been noted.

In January 1515, Francis I, on succeeding to the French throne, began to make preparations for an expedition to recover Milan. Leo X endeavoured to oppose this by means of an alliance between himself, Ferdinand of Spain, and the Emperor Maximilian.[6] But Francis gained the victory of Marignano and took Milan,[7] and Leo was forced to come to terms with him, which were settled at a personal conference between them, held at Bologna in December 1515.[8] On his way to this conference Leo stayed three days in Florence, where a splendid reception was prepared for him. Landucci, who was present, states that the grandeur of this reception was beyond description, and that "no other city in the world would, or could, have done the like." The city was decorated in all directions with triumphal arches, imitations of buildings of the classic age, statues, and allegorical devices. In the Piazza della Signoria an octagonal temple was erected by Sangallo; over the unfinished façade of the Duomo the design for it made by Lorenzo the Magnificent himself was executed in wood by Sansovino and painted by Andrea del Sarto; a colossal Hercules for the Loggia de' Lanzi was sculptured by Baccio Bandinelli; various triumphal arches were erected by Montelupo, Rosso, and Granacca—one between the Badia and the Bargello, and another near the monastery of San Marco, being specially fine—and the city gave itself up to welcoming with numerous festivities the first Florentine who had ever sat on the Papal throne.

On his return journey from Bologna, Leo stayed at Florence for more than a month, remaining there till the 17th February 1516, and during this visit he made arrangements for completing the family church of San Lorenzo. He ordered Michelangelo to prepare a design for the façade, and sent him to Carrara to obtain the necessary marble; and for this purpose no less than thirty-four shiploads of marble were subsequently despatched to Florence, though the façade remains to this day untouched. Leo also directed the construction by Michelangelo of the New Sacristy in San Lorenzo, which the Pope intended should form a mausoleum to contain six tombs, those of his father, Lorenzo, and uncle, Giuliano, as well as tombs for the other four members of the family who were then living, viz., himself, his brother Giuliano, his cousin Giulio, and his nephew Lorenzo. But only two of these six tombs were ever completed.

In 1516 Leo X, immediately upon his brother Giuliano's death, seized Urbino, as previously mentioned, in order to form a sovereignty for his nephew Lorenzo. The dissatisfaction caused by this procedure led, in the spring of 1517, to a remarkable episode. A serious conspiracy, headed by the young Cardinal of Siena, Alfonso Petrucci, was formed amongst the cardinals to poison the Pope. This being discovered, Petrucci, who had absented himself from Rome, was invited thither under a safe-conduct, as well as a solemn promise given by Leo to the Spanish ambassador that Petrucci's life would be spared; both of which promises were disregarded as soon as the latter reached Rome, where he was thrown into prison and condemned to death. Further examination proved that a large number of cardinals were implicated in the plot; and Petrucci, with his two chief assistants, a surgeon and a secretary, were cruelly tortured and put to death; the lives of the other cardinals concerned were spared, but they were subjected to various deprivations. These punishments aroused so great disaffection among nearly all the remaining cardinals that the Pope had to be surrounded by guards even when celebrating Mass in St. Peter's. To meet this alarming state of affairs, and finally put an end to this extraordinary episode, Leo X took the bold and unprecedented step of creating in one day thirty-one new cardinals.

At this period just before the Reformation, the plurality of offices held by the higher clergy was scandalous; Roscoe states:—"It is actually and substantially true that the same person was frequently at the same time an archbishop in Germany, a bishop in France or England, an abbot or a prior in Poland or Spain, and a cardinal in Rome." The creation of so many additional cardinals, with the benefices given to them, of course increased this evil; and this large number of important Church offices held by permanent absentees, tending as it did to much corruption and maladministration in the dioceses thus deprived of their proper rulers, helped to increase the dissatisfaction with the Church which was steadily growing in northern Europe.

In 1518 Leo X arranged with Francis I the marriage already mentioned between his nephew Lorenzo and the King's relative Madeleine de la Tour d'Auvergne, this being the second matrimonial alliance with the royal family of France made by the Medici family.[9] When in the following year Lorenzo died Leo sent his cousin Giulio to administer Florentine affairs for a time; the latter remained at Florence from May to October 1519, and on his return to Rome Cardinal Passerini was left in charge of Medicean interests in Florence on behalf of the Pope, and continued in charge for the next two years.

In 1521, Perugia being greatly misgoverned by its ruler, Gianpaolo Baglioni, described as "a monster of iniquity," Leo X determined to put an end to the Baglioni rule there and to incorporate Perugia with the States of the Church. He seems to have considered that against such a criminal any treachery was admissible. Baglioni was invited to Rome under the pretext of consulting with him about political affairs, and given the Pope's safe-conduct; but on arrival was thrown into prison, subjected to torture, and beheaded in the castle of St. Angelo, the Pope taking possession of Perugia.[10] About the same time a similarly treacherous endeavour was made to enlarge still further the States of the Church by seizing Ferrara; but the agents who had been bribed to open the gates on the approach of the Papal forces [11] revealed the plot to the Duke of Ferrara, and the attempt failed. Even Roscoe, with all his admiration for Leo X, remarks that these operations "disclose some of the darkest shades of his character." [12]

And they are to be attributed,[13] if not wholly, at all events to a very large extent, to that action which was the fundamental mistake of Leo X's life. For in order to satisfy his easy-going temperament, and indulge in those pursuits of Literature and Art, convivial pleasures, and luxurious enjoyment, for which alone he cared, Leo surrendered the whole conduct of the political affairs of the Papacy into the hands

of his energetic and crafty cousin Giulio; with the consequences which were to be expected from the latter's unscrupulous character. Leo X must of course bear the full
responsibility for the acts which he permitted to be done in
his name; but while this is so, the political acts of his pontificate are to be ascribed rather to Giulio than to Giovanni, and
in looking at the latter's life and character this requires to be
borne in mind. To him political and ecclesiastical affairs were
a wearisome burden to be got rid of as much as possible, while
as time went on he left them more and more in the hands that
were so willing to undertake them, leaving him free to attend
to those matters which to him were so much more congenial.
It was indeed hard on such a nature that it should be his lot
to have to deal with a movement like the Reformation, and
be expected to divert his attention from the latest reproduction of some classical work brought out by Aldo's printing
press to give heed to the troublesome complaints of a Luther.

It is almost as much a relief to us as it must have been to
Leo himself to turn from his political life to his action in
regard to those matters which were his chief interest. Here we
find another man altogether; and here there is neither apathy,
boredom, surrender of his leadership to others, nor treacherous or underhand dealing. In that world of Literature and Art
which his soul loved, and in his sympathy for all the culture
of his time, he is worthy of that atmosphere of splendour
which has gathered round his name. His great-grandfather
Cosimo and his father Lorenzo had contrived both to conduct
difficult political affairs and also to achieve mighty results
in the domain of Literature and Art. Leo X had none of the
energy of his ancestors, while his abilities were cast in a
smaller mould, so that he found one half of the matter as
much as he could attend to; but in that half his achievements,
though not to be compared to those of his father and great-
grandfather, were considerable. Moreover, he had greater
resources to draw upon. Art had advanced to its zenith;

great stores of the classical literature had by this time been brought to light; printing had come to assist in their reproduction, instead of the slow and laborious process of hand copying; while great as had been the wealth which his ancestors had possessed to assist their efforts in this cause, Leo had the still greater resources of the Papacy.

To detail all that he did in the patronage of Literature and Art would fill a volume. The same effect was produced at Rome as had taken place eighty years before at Florence, when his great-grandfather Cosimo became the leading man in that city. Scholars and artists flocked to Rome, where such a patron was to be found. Leo founded the university of Rome, to which he summoned a crowd of celebrated men, and which had eighty-eight professors as teachers of various branches of learning; and he did not rest until he had, with the assistance of Marcus Masurus and Aldus Manutius, established a press at Rome for printing the works of the Greek authors,[14] which, as they issued, were corrected by the celebrated Giovanni Lascaris himself, who had in his earlier years been employed in the researches of Lorenzo the Magnificent, and whom Leo now summoned to Rome to help him in this work. Ariosto speaks in glowing terms of the gifted company of poets and learned men whom Leo gathered round him. His own classical attainments were considerable, and he was justly acknowledged as a judge on all such matters. "He had a passion for all books and manuscripts, both in the dead and living languages, and these he devoured with avidity, remembering and quoting their contents out of an excellent memory." [15] Towards Art his patronage was unbounded, and great as was his renown, it has been held by many that his protection of, and affection for, Raphael (who died the year before him) "is, and always will be, Leo's best and noblest title to fame."

The above pursuits were combined with all the amusements of an existence frankly given up to enjoying life as much as possible, and never showing from first to last any indication

that a future life was to be expected. This latter is a strange
trait under the circumstances, and one which had very important results. Lorenzo the Magnificent, for all his love of
the Pagan classical literature, and whatever he may or may
not have been in conduct, never displayed this trait; but in
the son whom he had helped to become head of the Church, it
is a marked feature, and various eminent writers have supported the opinion of Mosheim in designating Leo X as an
Atheist. Not that he was by any means wanting as regards
the outward performance of his religious duties; for as to these
he was most scrupulous. But both Europe in that age and
Mahomedan countries in our own can show plenty of examples
that the scrupulous performance of such duties is compatible
with entire unbelief.

So far as one can judge (on so essentially private a matter)
from a man's outward conduct and expressed opinions, Leo
was a simple epicurean Pagan. He was not a coarse volup-
tuary, but his speech on becoming Pope frankly displayed
his mind:—"Since God has given us the Papacy, let us enjoy
it." And he did. Hunting and hawking parties in the Cam-
pagna, pleasant gatherings at his villa of La Magliana, convivial supper parties at Rome, the delights of literature,
poetry, music, and theatrical representations, a "revelry of
culture" as Gregorovius has called it—these things occupied
the greater portion of his time. Unlike most scholars, or any
previous Pope, Leo was greatly devoted to sport, as understood in those days, and often spent a month or more at a
time absent from the Papal city either fishing or pheasant
shooting round the lake of Bolsena, or staying at his favourite
hunting-lodge of La Magliana, five miles from Rome, in the
fever-laden valley of the Tiber, taking part in grand *battues* of
stags, wild boar, and every sort of game, and scandalising
the Papal master of ceremonies by appearing in hunting costume and, worst of all, in long riding-boots.[16] When in Rome
his life was a less healthy one. The Venetian ambassador at
his court has described the ponderous and unwholesome ban-

quets, lasting for hours, and in their lavish profusion and variety of incongruous dishes reminding us of the feasts of the Roman emperors of antiquity. And Isabella d'Este, Marchioness of Mantua, who was the Pope's guest during the winter of 1514, has graphically detailed how she and her maids-of-honour were plunged into a perpetual round of "banquets, balls, processions, hunting-parties, popular festivals, and dramatic performances." [17]

Occupied in this constant succession of festivities, field sports, and literary and artistic delights, Leo led an easy, jovial existence, troubling himself as little as might be with political affairs, and leaving the heavier burdens of the Papacy—whose course was at that epoch becoming from day to day more thickly strewn with rocks and shoals—to be borne by his cousin Giulio.

In 1515 the Emperor Maximilian's grandson Charles, then fifteen, was invested with the government of Flanders, his father, Philip, having died in 1506. His genealogy is important, and was as follows:—

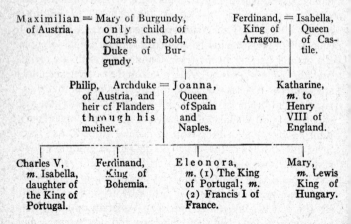

Maximilian = Mary of Burgundy, only child of Charles the Bold, Duke of Burgundy.

of Austria.

Ferdinand, = Isabella, King of Arragon.

Queen of Castile.

Philip, Archduke = Joanna, of Austria, and heir of Flanders through his mother.

Queen of Spain and Naples.

Katharine, m. to Henry VIII of England.

Charles V, m. Isabella, daughter of the King of Portugal.

Ferdinand, King of Bohemia.

Eleonora, m. (1) The King of Portugal; m. (2) Francis I of France.

Mary, m. Lewis King of Hungary.

In 1516 Ferdinand of Spain died, and Charles was invested with the government of Spain and Naples in place of his mother Joanna, who was set aside, being mad. In the same year the eight years' war, begun by the League of Cambray, was brought to an end by the treaty of Noyon between Francis and Charles, which left France in possession of Lombardy, and Spain in possession of Naples and Sicily.

In 1519 the Emperor Maximilian died, and Charles succeeded to the crown of Austria and Flanders. There ensued five months' rivalry between Francis I of France, Henry VIII of England, and Charles of Austria, as to which of them should be elected Emperor. Finally Charles was elected.

Thus Charles V inherited Austria from his grandfather Maximilian, Flanders from his grandmother Mary of Burgundy, Spain and Naples from his grandfather Ferdinand and his grandmother Isabella, and the imperial title (with such dominions as still remained to it) by the election of the German Diet. The result of his election as Emperor was a contest between the three rivals which lasted for twenty-eight years, in which Francis and Charles were always opponents, and Henry sided sometimes with one and sometimes with the other.

In 1520 Charles V visited Henry VIII in England in May, and in June Francis I and Henry VIII held the meeting known as "The Field of the Cloth of Gold," to cement their friendship.

In 1521 Francis declared war against Charles, invading simultaneously Luxembourg from one side of France and Navarre from the other. Henry, led by Wolsey, sided with Charles.

The atmosphere of cultured Paganism which Leo X created around him in the Vatican was unique. And it has been too well described by Ranke to be given in any other words. He says:—

"At that time men sought to emulate the ancients in their own language. Leo X was an especial patron of this pursuit. He read the well-written introduction to the history of Jovius aloud in the circle of his intimates, declaring that since the works of Livy nothing so good had been produced. A patron of the Latin improvisators, we may readily conceive the charm he would find in the talents of Vida, who could set forth a subject like a game of chess, in the full tones of well-cadenced Latin hexameters. A mathematician, celebrated for expounding his science in elegant Latin, was invited from Portugal. In this manner he (Leo) would have had theology and Church history written. . . . It was in his presence that the first tragedy was performed, and also the first comedy produced in the Italian language; and this notwithstanding the objectionable character of a play that imitated Plautus. Ariosto was among the acquaintances of his youth. Machiavelli composed more than one of his works expressly for him. His halls, galleries, and chapels were filled by Raphael with the rich ideal of human beauty. He was a passionate lover of music, and its sounds were daily heard floating through the palace, Leo himself humming the airs performed. . . . Easily does life veil its own incongruities. Such a state of things was directly opposed to Christian sentiment and conviction. The schools of philosophy disputed as to whether the soul were really immortal or whether it were absolutely mortal. Nor are we to believe that these opinions were confined to a few. Erasmus declares himself astonished at the blasphemies that met his ears. Attempts were made to prove to him—a foreigner—by passages from Pliny, that the souls of men are absolutely identical with those of beasts." [18]

Such was the atmosphere in which Leo X passed his life as Pope; and if this mode of life was less objectionable than that which had distinguished some of his immediate predecessors it was not less at variance with the urgent needs of the circumstances of the time.

For a storm was beginning to gather north of the Alps destined in no long time to envelop all Europe, and to give the Papacy other things to think of than light literature and the triumphs of Art. The Papacy had fallen to one who neither outraged the world by crime and immorality, like Sixtus IV and Alexander VI, nor harassed mankind by perpetual war, like Julius II; but the causes which had long been tending towards a revolt from the Papacy were still steadily at work, and, as the results of the invention of printing increased, were ever gathering greater strength. Printing presses did not only reproduce the Greek and Latin works of Pagan poets; and the ancient manuscripts unearthed by ardent research included the writings of Irenæus and Tertullian, Cyprian and Basil, no less than those of Cicero and Pliny, Tacitus and Livy. The work of Cosimo and Lorenzo was now about to produce results which they had never anticipated. The "New Learning" was no longer confined to Florence, or to Italy; it had spread far and wide, carrying with it to Germany, to Flanders, to Switzerland, to France, and to England the knowledge of the fraudulent basis on which the Papal claim to supremacy in the Church rested, the knowledge of a Christian age in which there had been no Papacy and all bishops had been of equal rank and authority, and the knowledge of a pre-existing scheme of Christian doctrine not overlaid by the errors and corruptions which had subsequently grown up in the Church at Rome. And as this knowledge spread, wider and stronger grew the determination to end the existing state of things in the Church, to cast off the usurped supremacy of Rome, and to return to a purer form of Christianity.

Not that the Roman Church is to be justly charged with all that her opponents asserted. The power developed by the Papacy had in its time done great things for religion. During a large part of the earlier Middle Ages the Papacy was the sole authority in Europe which stood for justice and righteousness; and had it not possessed the power it gradually developed it would have been unable to withstand effectively, as it did, the almost universal unrighteousness in high places. But that time was long past, and for at least two centuries the Papacy had only made use of its power for purposes of worldly aggrandisement; with results that caused the condemnation which it incurred to be fully deserved.

The gradual spread of this newly-acquired knowledge, following on the failure of all efforts to obtain reform by means of a General Council,[19] had by degrees made men ready, as soon as opportunity should occur, to fly to arms to obtain that reform which it was evident was to be gained in no other way. This effect had been steadily growing during the pontificates of Sixtus IV, Innocent VIII, Alexander VI, Julius II, and Leo X; but so little did these Popes realise the conditions of the case, that they seemed, by the kind of life they led, bent upon bringing about that appeal to arms. They were bishops of the leading see of Western Christendom; yet anything more opposed to the ideal life of a bishop, whether measured by the standard of the earliest centuries of the Church's life, or by that of our own age, than were their lives it would be hard to conceive. And so the natural result followed in a conflagration which brought cruel wars and innumerable sufferings upon mankind, and tore the civilised world asunder for one hundred and fifty years; but in the end cleansed Christendom.

And here we come upon one of those strange revelations, impossible for any one at the time to have seen, but which History (throwing its light back upon events long past) every now and then shows to those who come afterwards. From the time of Cosimo we see four successive generations of the Medici, the very last family to wish to bring about such a movement as the Reformation, and the very family out of which were to come the two Popes who were the leading opponents of that movement, eagerly engaged in pursuing a course which made them, little as they dreamt it, the chief agents in producing that great revolt from the Papacy. For it was not Luther, but the "New Learning" which pro-

duced the Reformation. A very little consideration will show
that no single individual, much less one placed in so obscure
a position as Luther, could have produced a convulsion which
shook all Europe from end to end. What Luther did was to
set light to materials which were ready to take fire. And this
"New Learning" was created, nourished, fostered, and endowed chiefly by the Medici. It is strange indeed to note
what energy they devoted, and what wealth they expended,
through a period of eighty years, on that which was to bring
upon the Papacy such dire results. And to do so during the
very time that the Papal throne was occupied by the two
members of this family who in turn sat upon it.

Of the five Popes who have been named, Leo X was the
one against whom mankind had by far the fewest accusations
to bring; it was, however, his fate to take the action which
finally precipitated the crisis. The legacy which Julius II
had left him of building a new St. Peter's caused such a heavy
drain on the resources of the Papacy [20] that it became necessary to find some unusual means for raising funds. Accordingly, in 1517 Leo published a bull declaring that the Pope
had the power of granting Indulgences affecting the state of
souls after death; and that this doctrine was an essential
article of belief. And this was followed by the scandalous
measure of the sale of these Indulgences; thus starting a
traffic in holy things which roused northern Europe to a
pitch of indignation such as even the crimes of Alexander
VI had failed to call forth. Obviously one who doubted
whether souls were immortal would find no difficulty in declaring his power to grant such Indulgences, or in selling
them to any one who would give money for them; and it is
very probable that Leo felt astonished at the uproar which
his action aroused.

Upon the issue of this bull by the Pope Luther published,
and nailed up on the door of the principal church at Wittenberg, his celebrated "Theses" against both the sale of Indulgences and all the additions which had been made to the

theory and practice of Indulgences during the thirteenth, fourteenth, and fifteenth centuries, with all that they involved. The system of Indulgences, with the doctrines on which it was based, was no new invention of Leo X; it had existed for at least three hundred years, and Leo only redeclared it. But the "New Learning" had caused the temper of men's minds to change; and the new departure of *the sale* of such Indulgences came just when men were least disposed to endure it.

The conflagration quickly spread. Germany was soon in a blaze, and Flanders and Switzerland showed signs of following suit. Luther proceeded to rouse all men against the iniquities of the Papacy, and to urge the assembly of a General Council to purge the Church; and at length in June 1520 he published his celebrated *Appeal to the Christian Nobility of the German Nation*. Four thousand copies were distributed with the greatest rapidity, the printers working while Luther wrote; and it immediately produced a strong impression throughout Germany. At the same time, from the other side, Leo published in all countries his bull of 1520, condemning the doctrines of Luther, calling upon all princes and peoples to seize him and his adherents, and excommunicating all who might harbour them. This bull Luther (protected by the Elector of Saxony) publicly and solemnly burnt at Wittenberg. And so began a conflict which was to last for generations, splitting countries, nations, and even families asunder, and having far-reaching effects which are still extending.

In the following year Leo, anxious to drive the French out of Italy, deserted Francis and engaged to join Charles in an attempt to regain Milan. The Imperial and Papal forces were commanded by the Marquis of Pescara, and in November 1521 Milan was captured. The news reached Leo at his villa of La Magliana on the 22nd November, and filled him with the greatest joy. But the same evening he caught a chill on returning hot and tired from the chase;

fever set in, he returned to the Vatican, grew rapidly worse, and died on the 1st December. There was, as usual, a suspicion that his death was due to poison,[21] and Castiglione, who was with him at Magliana, at first believed this; but the *post-mortem* examination which was held failed to confirm the suspicion. And in view of the excessively malarious character of the locality of Magliana nothing could be more probable than that malarial fever contracted at the place where he so often resided should eventually be the cause of his death.

Leo X was forty-five when he died. He was buried at first in the Vatican. The result of Julius II's action in regard to St. Peter's was that neither he himself nor any of the next three Popes after him could be buried there; and for several years no tomb was erected to Leo X. But after the death of Clement VII (1534) it was decided that these two Medici Popes should be interred in the church of Santa Maria sopra Minerva; whereupon Cardinal Ippolito de' Medici removed Leo X's remains from the Vatican to that Church, and commenced the erection of the tombs of the two Medici Popes, Leo X and Clement VII, which are to be seen there. After Ippolito's untimely death in 1535, these tombs were completed by Leo X's sister, Lucrezia Salviati.

It would have been hard if the Medici, the greatest of all patrons of Art, and belonging to Art's own special home, Florence, should not have been able to show us a unique succession of portraits of themselves, executed by the leading painters of their day. And in Leo X's case, none other could of course be employed to paint his portrait than his own great *protégé* and favourite, Raphael. And so Raphael has given us one of the most celebrated portraits in existence, that of Leo X with his two first cousins, Giulio de' Medici and Luigi Rossi, which hangs in the Pitti Gallery. And it tells us much of Raphael's own character to note that even though he is entirely dependent upon this great patron, yet he will not flatter him, and we feel that we have the man to the life placed before us. Easy-going, jovial, indolent, luxury-loving, shrewd, and worldly wise, all this he was; and just so does Raphael depict him. His tendency to fat was not altogether his fault; he had it throughout life, and endeavoured to combat it by outdoor pursuits, and it was on the advice of his physicians that he carried these on even after he became Pope, notwithstanding the shock that it gave to the ideas held by the Papal officials as to what was becoming in a Pope. His love of learning is indicated in the picture by the book which he had just been studying; his love of all forms of art, both by the illuminations of the book, and by the highly chased silver bell; and his indifferent eyesight (which was proverbial) by the spectacles and the magnifying glass, which latter Jovius says he used on all occasions. Of the two cardinals shown with him, Giulio is the one standing at the right hand of the Pope, who seems to be listening to his advice—their respective attitudes through life. Giulio's clever and intelligent, yet cold, hard face is probably a much better likeness of him than that afterwards painted by Andrea del Sarto. Luigi Rossi was the Pope's secretary. The picture is not only notable for its portraiture, but also as a wonderful study of the combination of colours, the whole (except the Pope's white robe) being in various shades of crimson and red.

Exaltation to the Papacy is probably the severest trial to character which this world holds. And it was one which Leo was not able to bear. A steady deterioration in his character from the time that he became Pope is the most marked feature in him. Many-sided like all his family, he was a remarkable mixture of good and bad points; but in the end the latter predominated.

CHAPTER XIV

THE TWENTY MONTHS' PONTIFICATE OF ADRIAN VI

1521-1523

ADRIAN VI did not belong to the Medici family, but as his short pontificate of twenty months spans the period between the two Medici Popes, and is important with reference to their history, it is desirable to detail briefly the events of his reign.

On the death of Leo X an unusual amount of discord took place at the conclave assembled to elect a new Pope. Giulio de' Medici, having been the late Pope's adviser in everything, counted on succeeding him, and employed all the arts of which he was a master to get himself elected. But out of the thirty-nine cardinals assembled as many as eighteen wanted the office themselves, and Giulio was only able by all his efforts to get together a party of fourteen. Wolsey was also a candidate, and had for a long time been swaying the politics of England in favour of Charles V in the latter's struggle with Francis I, so as to obtain in return the Emperor's influence on his behalf at this election. With the Emperor's candidate in possession of seven votes, with Giulio de' Medici in possession of fourteen, and with the remaining eighteen cardinals each striving to gain votes for himself, the conclave became a scene of the most disgraceful party struggles, and the discord was so great that it seemed as though no conclusion would ever be reached. At last Giulio's party, merely as an expedient for wearying out their opponents, voted one morning at the daily scrutiny for the most unlikely man they could think of, Cardinal Adrian Dedel of Utrecht, Archbishop of Tortosa, who had been the Emperor's tutor, at that time governing Spain as Charles V's representative. To their amazement and disgust a majority of the other cardinals, seeing that they could not succeed themselves, and in order to defeat Giulio's party, at once voted the same. And to the astonishment of all Europe one who had never been dreamt of by any one for such an office, and had made no candidature for it, became Pope. Thus did "the sad and serious Adrian," an earnestly religious Fleming, succeed to the throne so recently occupied by the cultured epicurean, Leo. If all Europe had been searched, a more startling contrast to the latter could not have been found. The new Pope at once gave evidence of his temperament by declining to follow the custom which had so long prevailed of changing his name, preferring to adhere to the practice of the earlier centuries in this respect.

Giulio de' Medici, having thus failed, departed to Florence and took over the charge of Florentine affairs. The absence of any opposition to his doing so shows that no doubt was felt as to the tacit right of a Medici to control the Government of Florence. And this undoubtedly rested on solid ground, and was due to the instinctive feeling that Florentine affairs only went smoothly when a Medici was at the helm. Passerini's inefficient administration had gradually created considerable discontent, financial affairs were in disorder, and much discord prevailed. But Giulio de' Medici, wanting in so many other respects, had just one good quality, inheriting in full measure that special gift, conspicuous in this family in generation after generation, of a genius for pacifying the angry passions of Florentine political life. By his conciliatory manner, careful attention to public affairs, and knowledge of the feelings of the Florentines, he soon put an end to the prevailing discord, and under his guidance Florentine affairs were satisfactorily administered.

"It was the universal opinion that never since the city had been under the rule of the Medici had it been governed with greater appearance of civil liberty, or more skilful concealment of despotism." [1]

Nardi's remark shows that Giulio was still carefully pursuing his scheme, and biding his time until those of the family who were then children should be grown up, and he himself in a position to adopt a more rigorous attitude towards Florence than that of merely "controlling" her Government.

Meanwhile Adrian VI was showing himself a Pope such as Rome had not seen for many centuries. He was not only virtuous and frugal, humble and pious, a hater of pomp, and simple and straightforward in character, but he also viewed with indignation the corruption which abounded in the Church, and set himself vigorously to the task of reform. There was a prompt end to all the pleasant ways which Rome loved, and a *volte-face* which was in some of its aspects almost comic. Bishops to whom life at a distance from Rome was like banishment to a barbarous country were sent off to their neglected bishoprics; the sycophantic throng of poets, philosophers, artists, and musicians who had surrounded Leo were swept out of the Vatican; the supper-parties, hunting-parties, and convivial gatherings came to an abrupt end. The Pope insisted on living in the simplest fashion, with a very small establishment, and spent a great part of his time in prayer and study. Rome was consumed with an unutterable disgust.

Moreover, whereas it had been a main object with every preceding Pope to aggrandise his family and increase the Papal dominions, Adrian VI refused to do anything of the kind. He restored Urbino to its rightful Duke, Francesco della Rovere, and gave back to the Duke of Ferrara the territories which Leo X had taken from him. Such acts increased his unpopularity. Adrian, however, was unmoved by the indignant wrath of the corrupt community by which he was surrounded. He set before himself three main objects

—the reform of the Church, the restoration of peace in Germany, and the defence of Christendom against the Turks. That he lived too short a time to effect any of these objects does not detract from the honour due to him for having earnestly and by wise methods striven to attain them.

In 1521 the Diet of the Empire was assembled by Charles V at Worms to consider how to check the growth of the new opinions in religion which were causing so much conflict in Germany, with the result that Luther was placed under the ban of the Empire.

In 1522 Charles V again visited England. Henry VIII, urged on by Wolsey (who still hoped for the Emperor's assistance at the next Papal election, which all felt could not be far distant), now deserted the side of Francis, which he had lately been favouring, and took that of Charles. Meanwhile Solyman, the Turkish Sultan, after invading Hungary and taking Belgrade, turned his victorious arms against Rhodes, which, held by the Knights of St. John, had been the bulwark of Christendom against the Turks since the fall of Constantinople. Adrian VI appealed earnestly to Charles, Francis, and Henry to lay aside their quarrels and unite to save Rhodes from the Turks; but they were too occupied with their mutual jealousies, and the story of Constantinople was repeated. After a stubborn resistance of six months Rhodes had to capitulate. Charles gave Malta to the Knights of St. John, and they retired there. In this year 1522 the conquest of Mexico added yet further to Charles's Spanish dominions.

In 1523 Francis I carried the war into Lombardy, and despatched a large force thither under Bonnivet. At the same time, swayed by his vicious mother, Louise of Savoy, he by various insults drove into rebellion the best general that he had, Charles, Duke of Bourbon, Constable of France, who, relentlessly persecuted by Louise because he would not marry her, and deprived of his position in the French army at last in desperation deserted his country, and offered his services to Charles V.

In his endeavours to reform the Church, Adrian VI showed both wisdom and vigour. Not only did he insist on a reform of their ways by the bishops who had so long brought discredit upon their office, but he also set himself with all his power to heal the discord in Germany by searching out the cause of the disease and the remedy required.

For a hundred and twenty years Europe had cried out for a reform of the Church "in head and members." Three great Councils had been assembled, and all the power of the laity throughout Europe put forth to effect this reform; but all had been foiled by the "head," which refused to admit that it needed reformation. Adrian VI for the first time struck a different note. He ordered Ægidius of Viterbo, the learned Principal of the Augustinian Order, and the most pious man of intellect at that time in Rome, to furnish him with his opinions as to the disease and its remedy; in response to which Ægidius drew up the great document in which he showed the disease to be due to "the misuse of Papal power," and that the remedy was "a limitation of the absolutism of the Head of the Church." Adrian VI agreed with the views expressed, and the result was the celebrated set of instructions issued by him in 1522 to the Nuncio Chieregato, in which the Pope declared that the disease had spread from the head to the members, from the Pope to the bishops and cardinals. He wrote, "We have all sinned, there is not one that doeth good," and announced his determination to carry out a radical reform. Had Adrian VI lived longer, widespread results must have ensued from such an edict emanating from such a source. But it was not to be; and when the grave closed over Adrian VI, the last non-Italian Pope, it closed also over all chance of a reform of the head and members conducted by the "head" himself.

Not, however, that Adrian VI took the Protestant side by any means. He was both learned enough and wise enough to see the error of both sides; and he met the fate of all who are able to do this, and are honest enough to let both know it. To the Diet of the Empire, then assembled to discuss the subject, he addressed a most powerful protest against the doctrines of Luther, while in the same document acknowledging candidly, and in the most positive terms, the corruptions of which Luther and his followers accused the Church of Rome, and showing that he was determined to eradicate them. Adrian VI presented the almost unique instance in that age of a man of the humblest birth who had risen in the Church solely through the great respect entertained for his profound theological learning; [2] and this justly-deserved reputation, joined to his candid acknowledgment of the corruptions of the Church, with the stringent measures he was taking to extirpate them, made his protest against the new doctrines, and his demonstration of the ignorance on which they were to a large extent based, far more forcible than that which any other Pope of that time could have made. Whereas others maintained such doctrinal points by appeals to this or that precedent, Adrian did so out of his own knowledge as a theologian. Thus the gentle and humble Adrian condemned Luther's opinions much more sharply than Leo X had ever done; while he also passed severe censures upon the princes of Germany for allowing them to spread owing to their own ignorance and their attaching greater importance to political contests than to religion.

Truly many centuries had passed away since any head of the Roman Church had spoken in this fashion, or been animated by sentiments like these. But in that corrupt age a Pope of this type was obnoxious to all parties. He was obnoxious to the followers of Luther for disagreeing with their doctrines; to the princes of Germany, who, as he rightly said, only paid heed to the matter so far as they could make use of it for a political purpose; to the cardinals, who bit-

terly resented reforms which robbed them of all for which
they cared; and, above all, he was intensely obnoxious to
the Roman people, who loved a Pope who spent money freely
and was troubled with no inconvenient morality. Both of
the two latter parties looked upon Adrian VI and his ways
with a horrified disgust too deep for words; the change from
the one extreme to the other, from the easy-going, lavishly
generous Leo, to the austere reformer Adrian, was too bitter
a contrast. A Pope who admitted that the Church needed a
reform, and was bent on carrying it out, was altogether insupportable. Of course his end was certain; Rome wanted
no Popes of this sort, and would not endure them; that he
existed even so long as twenty months is extraordinary.[3]
At the end of that time he was poisoned; and lest there should
be any doubt of the fact, or of their great relief thereat, the
Roman people on the night after his death adorned his chief
physician's house with garlands, and with the inscription
written over them, "To the deliverer of his country."

Thus ended Adrian VI, who, had his lot been cast in other
times, would have accomplished much for the Church. He
died on the 14th September 1523, and was buried in the
Church of Santa Maria dell' Anima. And the epitaph written for his tomb by his faithful friend and companion, Cardinal Enckenvoert, was certainly suitable:—"Proh dolor!
quantum refert in quae tempora vel optimi cujusque virtus
incidat." [4]

CHAPTER XV

GIULIO (CLEMENT VII)

Born 1478. (*Pope* 1523-1534.) *Died* 1534

(1) THE FIRST FOUR YEARS OF HIS PONTIFICATE

CLEMENT VII has generally been looked upon as a more or less feeble intriguer, humbly carrying out during the pontificate of his cousin Leo X plans originated by the latter, and involved in disasters in his own pontificate owing to want of ability. How far from the truth is the first portion of this view of him has already been shown; while as regards the second portion it will be seen in the sequel that the disasters in question, far from being due to any want of ability, were deliberately incurred for the sake of a single definite object which governed all his actions.

Giulio de' Medici, son of the Giuliano killed in the Pazzi Conspiracy, was tall and good-looking, spare in figure, of agreeable manners, and, except his uncle Lorenzo the Magnificent, was the cleverest of all this able family. Ranke, speaking of him after he became Pope, says:—

"He spoke with equal knowledge of his subject whether that were philosophy and theology, or mechanics and hydraulic architecture. In all affairs he displayed an extraordinary acuteness; the most perplexing questions were unravelled, the most difficult circumstances penetrated to the very bottom, by his extreme sagacity. No man could debate a point with more address, and he manifested a circumspect ability in practice which none could surpass."

At the same time he was, as we have seen, of a cold-hearted and crafty disposition, and absolutely unscrupulous, with none of those qualities of kind-heartedness, magnanimity, and cheerful *bonhomie*, which in the case of his cousin Leo X helped to balance great faults.

In this member of the family we see the Medici reaching their highest importance in the politics of Europe, and their history becoming for a time to a large extent that of Europe. But more than this; we see in him one who turned this family from those aims which his ancestors had followed, who set it upon a path where even success could confer no glory, and who, leading it to strive after an ignoble aim, brought upon the name of Medici obloquy and condemnation where before it had won honour and esteem. This course of action, already steadily pursued by Giulio ever since the family were reinstated in Florence, was now to have a greater development.

Upon the death of Adrian VI the same disgraceful scenes which had characterised the previous conclave were repeated; and this time they lasted much longer. For seven weeks the bribing and intriguing continued, Giulio's two chief antagonists being Wolsey and Alessandro Farnese.[1] At length, on the 19th November, Giulio triumphed and was elected Pope, assuming the name of Clement VII. He was then forty-five years old.

On becoming Pope the first point which Giulio, now Clement VII, had to settle was how to retain the rule of Florence in the elder branch of the family,[2] seeing that he himself could no longer reside there, that Lorenzo's only child was a girl of four years old, and that Giuliano's[3] son, Ippolito, was too young at present to be entrusted with authority. Under these circumstances, Clement decided for the present again to delegate the control of Florentine affairs to Cardinal Passerini as his representative. Accordingly, Passerini was in May 1524 sent to Florence, and for the next three years Florentine affairs were administered by him under orders from Rome, though the Signoria continued to be ostensibly the ruling body.

With Cardinal Passerini Clement also sent Giuliano's son Ippolito, now a handsome, intelligent, and attractive youth of fifteen, who was looked upon by all as destined to succeed to the authority exercised by his father twelve years before with such satisfaction to the Florentines. He took up his abode with Cardinal Passerini at the Medici Palace, assumed the title of "Il Magnifico," and was elected a member of the Government. A few months later there was also sent to Passerini's charge, from Naples, where he had been brought up, another boy, Alessandro, then about thirteen, who now for the first time appears in connection with Florence, and whose woolly hair and negro-like appearance had already caused him to be called "The Moor." [4] This boy's origin was a secret. Born during the time that the family were in exile he was in reality the son of Clement himself,[5] but the latter had hidden the fact, and kept the boy out of sight as long as he could. Subsequently, after Giuliano, Lorenzo, and Leo X were all dead, Clement brought this boy forward as an illegitimate son of Lorenzo. The fact that Clement had not begun to make this claim, and to pass Alessandro off as Lorenzo's heir, at the time when he first became Pope is corroborated by what took place on that occasion. For when Clement on becoming Pope consulted the envoys of Florence as to what he should do with regard to that State, three of them advised him [6] to give the supreme power to a Gonfaloniere appointed from year to year "until Ippolito was old enough to rule." It is significant that it was Ippolito who was mentioned, and not Alessandro, as must have been the case had the latter been declared at this time to be the heir of Lorenzo. It was not until three or four years later that Clement devised the scheme of passing over Ippolito in favour of Alessandro, and giving as a reason that he was Lorenzo's son.

The eleven years' pontificate of Clement VII (1523-1534) was a troubled time in Europe. The triangular duel which Charles V, Francis I, and Henry VIII carried on lasted for twenty-six years, never ceasing until Francis and Henry both died in the same year (1547); and during the first half of this long struggle it was Clement VII who kept this contest alive. The latter during the whole of his reign as Pope was employed in prosecuting vast schemes of "diplomacy," all with the object of playing off Francis against Charles to prevent their combining against himself, and of effecting his own designs while pretending to favour each of theirs in turn. Thus, whereas Adrian VI had striven to create peace between them, Clement's whole aim was to inflame their animosities to the utmost. In this he succeeded only too well; and by their unceasing wars large portions of Europe were laid waste, ravaged by ruthless and undisciplined armies, whose track was like that of a pestilence.

It is curious to note the sanguine expectations which were formed when Clement VII succeeded to the Papal throne, and how strangely they were falsified. It was anticipated that his pontificate would show all that had been best in that of Leo X, while avoiding its defects. Belonging to a family so renowned for their patronage of literary and artistic culture, and being himself fond of art, science, music, and the conversation of learned men, it was confidently asserted that there would be a restoration of that culture which had been put to flight by his predecessor; while from his sober temperament it was presumable that there would be none of that extravagance and luxury which had marked the reign of Leo X. Lastly, of his great administrative ability there was no doubt; he had ruled Rome well in Leo's day; while at Florence he had on two separate occasions put an end to dissensions, re-organised the finances, and given general satis-

faction in the midst of discordant elements. There appeared
therefore every ground for the confident expectation entertained that his pontificate would be an unusually satisfactory
one.

Yet the result was extraordinarily the reverse. The difficulties surrounding him on becoming Pope and the qualities he
possessed for meeting them, are thus described by Trollope:—

"The time was a difficult one for any Pope. But a straight
course along an open road would have been less congenial
to the talents and temperament of Giulio de' Medici than one
where intrigue, craft, and wily policy were necessary, and
the situation was one exactly suited to his talents and disposition. Calm, moderate, unimpassioned, active, vigilant,
astute, with nothing genial, large, or noble about him, but
decorous, correct, and eminently respectable, while at bottom thoroughly unscrupulous, it might have been thought
that Clement was just the man for the occasion, and that
he if any man was bound to rise a winner from the slippery
game of the politics of the time. Yet the result was such that
his pontificate has been called the most disastrous of any
pontiff who ever sat on the Papal throne." [7]

Clement was not long in showing what would be the general
character of his policy. Soon after he became Pope the Emperor, anxious to bring about that reform of the Church
which Adrian VI had not been given time to effect, began to
suggest the assembly of a General Council. Clement professed
entire agreement, but by plausible stipulations contrived to
create difficulty after difficulty in the Emperor's path, hoping
meanwhile that the pressure of war would soon give the latter
other matters to attend to. This result soon followed; and
during the next four years Clement's endeavours to keep the
two great rivals at feud were so successful that widespread war
swept backwards and forwards in turn over Burgundy, northern France, southern France, Savoy, northern Italy, and
southern Italy.

Clement at first took the side against Francis, who was beset with difficulties. Three armies had entered France, a Spanish force advancing into Languedoc, a German one entering France on the north-east, and an English one occupying Picardy. On the other hand, a large French army, under Bonnivet, had, as already noted, invaded Lombardy. Charles's armies in northern and southern France were repulsed by the French; but in Lombardy, where the Imperial army was commanded by Lannoy, Viceroy of Naples, with whom were Pescara [8] and Bourbon, the French suffered serious reverses. All through these wars the Spanish generals were superior to the French; Francis had no good general, and suffered perpetually from the irretrievable loss he had caused himself by having driven from his service Charles, Duke of Bourbon.

In 1524 the French army in Lombardy was at length forced by Lannoy to commence a disastrous retreat towards France, and in this retreat was severely defeated at the passage of the Sesia, where the Chevalier Bayard, the knight "sans peur et sans reproche," who commanded the rearguard of Bonnivet's army, was mortally wounded, and died on the field. The Imperial army, driving the French before it, advanced into southern France, and laid siege to Marseilles. Francis (as though the ordinary miseries of war were not enough) met this invasion by laying waste the whole of Provence, the garden of southern France, in order that the invading army might be unable to subsist; the entire population of the district was made to move elsewhere, villages were razed to the ground, cattle driven off, crops destroyed, and the sufferings of the people were almost as great as though they had been the captives of a hostile force. By this measure the Imperial army, after heavy losses from disease and starvation, was forced to quit France, and retired again into Italy. Clement, who hitherto had encouraged Charles, now began to intrigue with Francis, and in December 1524 concluded a secret treaty with him.

Meanwhile Francis, elated by his success in Provence, pre-

pared, against the advice of his ministers and generals, and
even of his mother, Louise of Savoy, to invade Lombardy with
a large army under his own command. All the flower of the
French nobility flocked to join this expedition. Francis appointed his mother Regent of France in his absence, and
marched for Italy with the most powerful army which had
till then been seen in war.

At first Francis was successful. He took Milan, and then
proceeded to attack Pavia, defended by the experienced
Spanish general Antonio de Leyva. During three months
Pavia sustained a most rigorous siege, everything known to
the engineers of that age being employed to reduce it. Francis
added strong reinforcements to his army, bringing up a large
body of Swiss troops and also receiving troops sent to join
him by Clement, commanded by Giovanni delle Bande Nere,[9]
now the foremost commander of his time among the Italians.
Meanwhile Lannoy, Pescara, and Bourbon were collecting
troops sufficient to oppose the powerful army of Francis, and
at length advanced to the relief of Pavia. A great battle was
fought outside the walls on the 24th February 1525, in which
the French sustained the most fatal defeat known in those
times. The battle of Pavia is the greatest military event of the
sixteenth century. Francis I (who very nearly lost his life
owing to his refusal to surrender to the Duke of Bourbon)
was taken prisoner; nearly the whole of the French nobility
were either killed or captured; [10] ten thousand men of the
French army were killed and the rest surrendered; and in a
fortnight after the battle not a Frenchman remained in Italy
except those who were prisoners in Lannoy's hands. It was a
crushing defeat for France, whose whole military strength
had been collected in this army commanded in person by the
King. Lannoy at once sent news of his victory to Charles V,
who was in Spain, and shortly afterwards escorted Francis I
thither as a prisoner. Clement VII, aghast at the mistake he
had made, deserted Francis, and hastened to make a treaty
with the Emperor; but it was a hollow affair, and Clement's

punishment was only postponed until the Emperor had leisure for it.

For one of Clement's pieces of deception at this time Florence has reason to be glad. After the battle of Pavia Clement in his terror was anxious to propitiate Federigo Gonzaga, Marquis [11] of Mantua, one of the Emperor's chief adherents in Italy. Gonzaga expressed a desire to possess the portrait of Leo X, painted by Raphael, which was in the Medici Palace at Florence. Clement promised he should have it, and wrote from Rome, ordering that the picture should be sent to the Marquis of Mantua as soon as a copy of it, which he at the same time directed to be made by Andrea del Sarto, was completed. Andrea del Sarto made so good a copy that no one could tell the difference; and this copy was sent to Mantua purporting to be the original. Even Giulio Romano, Raphael's own pupil, did not detect the deception until it was pointed out to him years afterwards by Vasari. It is impossible to believe that this fraud was carried out without the secret orders of Clement VII. The result, however, is that the original remained in the possession of the Medici, and hangs with that portion of their pictures which now forms the Pitti Gallery in Florence.[12]

In 1526 Francis I, after thirteen months' captivity in Spain, obtained his liberty on condition that he would restore Burgundy, would agree not to attack Milan again, and would reinstate Charles, Duke of Bourbon, in the estates of which the latter had been robbed by Louise of Savoy. Some writers have maintained that the terms were too severe, but, on the contrary, in view of the crushing victory which Charles had won at Pavia, they must be held to be exceedingly moderate; no indemnity was extorted nor any attempt made to cripple the power of France for the future. Francis I gave his two sons, Francis and Henry, then respectively ten and nine years old, as hostages for this agreement. But as soon as he reached France he repudiated the whole of it, and was absolved therefrom by Clement, who had resolved again to change sides, since Charles was becoming too strong.

Clement now formed an alliance which he called the "Holy League," consisting of France, England, and the Pope, with Venice and Florence, to oppose Charles, to relieve Francesco Sforza, besieged in Milan by the Imperial army, and to set Francis's sons at liberty. Clement expected that Francis would be the life and soul of this league. But Francis, owing to his defeat and imprisonment, had gone through such a time of distress that his spirit was for a time cowed; he desired tranquillity, and for the first time failed to be roused by the Pope's incitements; he delayed doing anything, except to allow certain troops to be engaged for him by Clement in Italy, among them the corps commanded by the latter's relative, Giovanni delle Bande Nere, for whom Clement was, as usual, anxious to find some fighting to do.[13] The forces assembled by Venice and the Pope were placed under command of the Duke of Urbino and advanced against the Imperial army in Lombardy. But the Duke of Urbino (no great friend of Clement) by losing several opportunities gave Bourbon time to bring up reinforcements to the Imperial army. Bourbon immediately took command of the latter and very soon captured Milan, and drove the allied forces to retire on Lodi. It was in these operations that Giovanni delle Bande Nere was killed near Mantua.

While these events were taking place in France and Italy, Germany was in a state of turmoil through the conflict on the subject of religion, which had now developed into actual war. To allay these conditions, which weakened Germany at a time when it was especially necessary that she should be strong, Charles assembled the Diet of the Empire at Speier to consider the religious differences, and this meeting of the Diet granted great toleration to Luther's opinions; so much so that the resolutions passed on this occasion came to form a sort of Magna Charta to the Protestant cause. They had a political object. The Turks were now pouring into Hungary, and the Emperor was urgent to oppose them, but could not do so as long as half his territories were torn by these dissensions. He hoped by the settlement at Speier to get the Protestant princes of Germany to march with him against the Turks. It was, however, already ˙too late, and in August the Turks gained a great victory over Hungary at the battle of Mohacs, in which Lewis II, King of Hungary, was killed.

Though not evident at the time, we can see now that Clement VII by his course of action became himself the chief assistant to the cause of Protestantism. Every time that he induced Francis to attack Charles he made it more difficult for the latter to deal with the rising tide of revolt against the Church taking place in Germany, which needed all Charles's attention, and which he would probably have assuaged, or at all events greatly mitigated, had he not been forced to devote most of his attention to the defence of those parts of his Empire attacked by Francis, attacks in most cases instigated or encouraged by Clement.

Meanwhile retribution was being prepared for the latter. The Emperor thought it time to give him a lesson, and punish him for his various tortuous dealings. In September 1526, therefore, the Emperor drew up a manifesto systematically setting forth the treacherous manner in which the Pope had acted throughout the previous three years.[14] He then instructed his agent, Moncada, to stir up the powerful family of the Colonna, who attacked and plundered the Vatican, drove Clement to take refuge in the castle of St. Angelo, and there made him, as a condition of his release, agree to renounce the Holy League, to withdraw his troops from Lombardy, and to give hostages for his good faith.

But Clement was not to be held firm even by the giving of hostages.[15] As soon as he was again free he repudiated his engagements, collected a force, attacked the territory of the Colonna, razed to the ground fourteen of their castles and villages, and executed a general massacre of men, women, and

children belonging to them; thus filling up the cup of his
misdeeds.

Then the Emperor (always deliberate, and never relin-
quishing any purpose which he had once formed) prepared a
terrible vengeance. He sent, during November and December,
additional troops from Spain to Lannoy, his commander in
southern Italy, and from Germany to Bourbon, his commander
in northern Italy (Pescara having just died), and ordered
Bourbon on their arrival to march upon the Papal States.
The Imperial army in Italy was composed of all the greatest
ruffians from every race in Europe, Spanish and Germans
predominating. They had been for some time deliberately
kept by Charles V without pay, and the state of want to
which they were reduced made these troops almost unmanage-
able except by Bourbon, who from his many qualities as a
general had a wonderful power over them. Nevertheless, his
position was rendered most difficult. Northern Italy, ravaged
by these incessant wars, was almost a desert, and could no
longer support his troops. To increase his difficulty there now
came to join his army, already in arrears of pay, this addition
of sixteen thousand Lutheran troops from Germany, who
had not only been promised their pay on reaching Lombardy
and were bent upon plunder, but also came with a fixed determination to execute vengeance upon the Pope, to whose
faithlessness they attributed all the woes of Christendom; to
his charge were laid the long continuance of war throughout
Europe, the defeats sustained from the Turks, even their
own present state of privation; and they openly announced
their intention of marching to Rome and hanging the Pope.
Their commander, Frundsberg, ostentatiously carried with
him a silken rope for this especial purpose.

In January 1527 Bourbon made over the government of
Milan to Antonio de Leyva, and set his army in motion
southwards. On reaching Bologna, where he halted for a
short time during February, a mutiny of his troops, who were
now in the greatest destitution, was only pacified by his

promising to march upon Rome. Clement, threatened by
Bourbon from the north and Lannoy from the south, and terrified to find the same storm coming upon himself which he had
brought upon so many others, sent urgent appeals to Francis
to deliver him. But Francis had not yet recovered from the
blow to his spirit caused by his own defeat and captivity, while
he himself had certain scores to pay off upon Clement, and
he made no effort to prevent matters from taking their course.
Bourbon's unruly horde continued, therefore, to move slowly
forwards, while Clement clamoured for aid in every direction,
and even offered 100,000 ducats if this would appease the
Lutheran troops. But the latter were obdurate. Clement made
overtures to Lannoy, who came, bringing the above sum of
money to Bourbon; but more than twice that amount was
due for the arrears of pay alone, and Lannoy dared not approach the camp, as the Lutheran troops, bent upon personal
vengeance on the Pope, would not hear of any truce, and
threatened to kill even Lannoy himself, if he interfered with
them; while Frundsberg, their own immediate commander,
was just at this time struck down by apoplexy (April 1527).
They were determined to hang the Pope and sack Rome,
would obey no other general than Bourbon, and would not
obey even him unless he led them towards Rome.

So while Clement, now in the greatest terror, offered every
possible and impossible concession to any who would come
to his assistance, the resistless torrent rolled steadily on
through the valleys of Romagna and Umbria, Bourbon sub-
sisting his hungry and ferocious troops on the country passed
through, whose inhabitants had sore reason to curse Clement
for bringing this terrible visitation upon them. On the evening
of the 5th May the army encamped outside Rome, and the
troops at last feasted their eyes on its palaces, and promised
themselves, as the reward of all their hardships, the plunder
of the Papal city. Next morning Bourbon ("the ferocious
Bourbon," as his enemies called him, fastening upon himself
the chief characteristic of the miserable material given him to

command), whom his many misfortunes had made tired of life, drew up his army for the attack. He led the assault himself, ascended the first ladder placed against the walls, and fell mortally wounded as his victorious troops gained the city, his last act being to have himself covered with a cloak that his soldiers might not be discouraged by seeing his condition (6th May 1527).[16]

Then followed the terrible sack of Rome. As the Imperial army burst into the city Clement took refuge in the castle of St. Angelo, while his troops were being pursued by enemies who gave no quarter, and who were doubly enraged by the death of their adored commander; and Clement was now able to see some of the results of his crafty policy and double-dealing. The pandemonium which followed is indescribable. The Lutheran troops took pleasure in destroying and defiling all that the Catholic world had revered. Robertson says:—

"It is impossible to describe, or even imagine, the misery and horror of the scene that followed. Whatever a city taken by storm can dread from military rage unrestrained by discipline, whatever excesses the ferocity of the Germans, the avarice of the Flemings, or the licentiousness of the Spaniards could commit, these wretched inhabitants of Rome were obliged to suffer. Churches, palaces, and houses were plundered without distinction. No age or character was exempt from injury. Cardinals, nobles, priests, matrons, virgins, were all the prey of the soldiers, and at the mercy of men deaf to the voice of humanity. Nor did these outrages cease, as is usual in towns carried by assault, when the first fury of the storm was over; the Imperial army, unable to be controlled by any general now Bourbon was dead, kept possession of the city for many months, and during all that time the brutalities of the soldiers continued. Their booty in ready money alone amounted to 1,000,000 ducats; what they raised by ransoms and exactions far exceeded that sum. Rome, though taken various times by the northern nations in the fifth and sixth centuries, was never treated with so much cruelty by the barbarous and heathen Huns, Vandals or Goths, as now by this terrible foe." [17]

While these scenes were being enacted Clement, the author of all this, was a close prisoner in the castle of St. Angelo, besieged by those troops who, as he well knew, had often sworn to hang him, and were now uncontrolled by the only general who had had any power over them. On Bourbon's death the command devolved upon Philibert, Prince of Orange; but the troops made no pretence of obeying him, and it was with difficulty that he could even persuade some of them to desist from plunder and invest the castle of St. Angelo. The Duke of Urbino advanced with an army consisting of Venetians, Florentines, and Swiss in the pay of Francis I, strong enough to have overpowered the army of the Prince of Orange. But the Duke of Urbino [18] had an old score to pay off against Clement, since the time when the latter had helped to rob him of his duchy. So to tantalise him by raising false hopes in his mind, he merely brought his army near enough for Clement to see it, and then marched away, leaving him surrounded by the furious enemies who thirsted for his blood. The Emperor courteously expressed sorrow at the Pope's misfortune; but the Imperial army remained where it was. Nor in fact could any power have removed it; for the troops found Rome exceedingly pleasant quarters, and had not the slightest intention of obeying any order to quit the city so long as anything remained to eat or to plunder. Clement continued besieged by them in the castle of St. Angelo for seven months; and his action when, reduced to great straits, he bade Cellini (who was with him there) melt down his tiara, was symbolical of the position to which he had brought himself. At length he contrived to escape disguised as a pedlar, and fled in miserable plight and with only one attendant to Orvieto, where he arrived in a most forlorn state, destitute of everything, a disastrous conclusion to four years of tortuous scheming (8th December 1527). The Imperial army remained

firmly planted in Rome, and seemed likely to take root there
for good; Lannoy succeeded the Prince of Orange in command,
but died of the plague; all the splendour of the Rome of Leo
X was destroyed; and when, after nine months' occupation,
the army, utterly demoralised by its long debauch, was driven
out of the city by the plague, they left it a ruined and desolated
waste.

Meanwhile, as soon as the news arrived of Pope Clement's
disaster, and of his being besieged in the castle of St. Angelo,
Florence, seeing now an opportunity of throwing off the yoke
which he had long been craftily but steadily tightening upon
her, revolted from his authority, and for the third time banished the Medici family (19th May 1527).[19] At the same time
Venice, taking advantage of the opportunity, seized Ravenna
and other places in the States of the Church; and the Dukes of
Ferrara and Urbino resumed possession of those territories
of which the Papacy had deprived them. At this juncture also
Henry VIII of England began to press Clement to grant him
a divorce from his Queen, Katharine of Arragon, the aunt of
Charles V. But Clement was truly not just then in a position
to offend Charles further, or to give attention to such matters.

CHAPTER XVI

CLARICE DE' MEDICI (CLARICE STROZZI)

Born 1493. (*Married* 1508.) *Died* 1528

CLARICE, the second of the two children of Pietro the Unfortunate, and sister of Lorenzo (Duke of Urbino), was far more capable than either her father, mother, or brother. Her uncle, Leo X, used to say that it would have been well for the family if Clarice had been the man, and her brother, Lorenzo, the woman. She had a high spirit and strong intelligence, and frequently saved her husband from disaster by her courage and ability. Her very interesting portrait, taken when she was about seventeen, shows a fine strong, intellectual face, fully in keeping with the character she afterwards displayed.

Clarice's life exemplified the vicissitudes of the Medici fortunes; for during her comparatively short life the family were twice in the highest prosperity and twice in the deepest adversity. Born in the Medici Palace when her family was at the height of the splendour to which it had been brought by her grandfather, Lorenzo the Magnificent, she was, when a year old, carried away from Florence when her parents were exiled; and the whole of her girlhood was passed in the nomadic existence entailed on her family by that exile. Her father died when she was ten years old; and when she was fifteen her mother, Alfonsina, gave her in marriage to Filippo Strozzi, head of the Strozzi family, and a man of much influence both at Florence and at the Papal court. Although her husband was fined and banished for this marriage with her he was suffered to return to Florence about a year later, bringing his young bride with him. Then when Clarice was nineteen came the return of the Medici to Florence, and her uncle, Giuliano, became ruler of the State; and in the following year that rule passed to her brother, Lorenzo.

Clarice was the first mistress of the handsome Strozzi Palace in the Via Tornabuoni, which, begun twenty years before, was first occupied when in 1510 she and her husband were allowed to return to Florence, though it was not finally completed until 1536.

In 1513 her uncle Giovanni became Pope, and being a favourite with him, Clarice was often in Rome during the years of his pontificate. In 1519, when she was twenty-six, her brother Lorenzo died, and her distant relative, Cardinal Giulio de' Medici, whom she cordially detested, came to administer Florentine affairs. And when in 1523 he became Pope, Clarice had opportunities of seeing the gradual working of his policy as regards Florence, and the change of feeling towards her family which it produced.

We hear of her again in Rome in 1524, where for some time she resided, taking charge of her brother Lorenzo's only child, Catherine, then five years old. But in 1525, affairs in Rome after the battle of Pavia becoming unsettled, Clarice returned to Florence, where she had the mortification of seeing that palace which was associated in her mind with all the glory of her family occupied by the two illegitimate scions of the family, Ippolito and Alessandro, and their guardian, Cardinal Passerini, Pope Clement's representative.

In the following year Clarice by her boldness and resource saved her husband's life; not the only occasion of the kind during her life. When in September 1526 the Colonna forced Clement to give hostages as a guarantee of his good faith, the latter gave as a hostage his friend, Filippo Strozzi, who was then in Rome; and when Clement broke his agreement and committed his atrocious attack on the Colonna,[1] Strozzi's life was in the greatest danger. Clarice, who had remained in Florence much out of health, as soon as she heard this news got into her litter, travelled with all speed to Rome (where she declared that Filippo had been "basely and foully sent like an innocent lamb to the slaughter"), and by her energetic action on arrival there eventually obtained her husband's liberty.

Early in 1527 the storm which he had provoked burst upon Clement; he was besieged in the castle of St. Angelo; Florence rose in revolt against the thraldom which had been gradually imposed upon her ever since he had become the ruling spirit of the family; and for the third time in their history the Medici were banished.

On this occasion Clarice gave full evidence of her strength of character and lofty spirit. Filippo, her husband, unable to decide which side to take, remained shut close in his palace, full of doubt and uncertainty. No such feelings oppressed his high-spirited wife. Clarice, justly hating Clement VII, was not at all displeased at seeing him brought to disgrace and disaster; the more pride she took in her ancestors the more wrath she felt at the course being pursued by the existing head of the family; and she eagerly seized the opportunity of dealing a blow at his plans which might be a decisive one. She first advised her irresolute husband to stick to the side of the Republic, advice which he eventually took. Then sallying forth to the Medici Palace, the home of her ancestors, now tenanted by those whom she considered only "half-Medici," unworthy to be the bearers of that once honoured name, she proceeded to eject them in the following fashion. The scene in the Medici Palace on that 19th May 1527, and Clarice's part therein, is thus vividly described by Trollope:—

"In the Medici Palace, after the news had come of the terrible sack of Rome, and that Pope Clement had fled and was closely besieged in the castle of St. Angelo, and while in the Palazzo della Signoria the great Council, hastily assembled, and still only half determined to take the decisive step, discussed a revolution, sat the Cardinal Passerini with his three young charges [2] awaiting the decision of the Council, dismayed and irresolute; while the whole length of the Via

Larga outside presented to one looking on it from the Medicean palace a threatening, billowy sea of heads. To them
thus sitting trembling and perplexed, entered the haughty and
intrepid Clarice, bent on bringing them to a very speedy
resolution. Clarice hated her relative Clement, and burnt with
indignation at seeing the illegitimate Ippolito and Alessandro
made inheritors of her family's honours and pre-eminence. . . .
Entering the room with haughty step and flashing eye, full of
indignation, and raising her voice so loud that it was even
heard by those in the street outside, she bitterly taunted the
trembling Cardinal at having brought his own and his master's affairs to such a pass, contrasting how differently things
were managed 'by my ancestors, who were *true* Medici, and
who with benevolence and gentleness gained the loyalty of
the Florentines, and so found them constant in adversity.³
But *you* (turning to Ippolito and Alessandro) who by your
conduct have betrayed the secret of your birth, and convinced
the world that you are not of the blood of the Medici, and
not you alone but Clement also, unworthy and wrongfully
Pope,⁴ and now most rightfully prisoner in St. Angelo, why
are you surprised that all are this day against you? Now
therefore depart from a house to which you have no claim,
and from a city which has no affection for you. For in this
evil hour the family honour depends on *me*.'"

And this forceful lady wound up her harangue by sarcastically
informing them that the Medici Palace was not built in
order to be "a stable for mules." And promptly depart they
did.⁵ As an old chronicler, commenting on this episode,
naïvely remarks: "The Lady Clarice had great power of
tongue."

But apart from all question of her power of tongue, there is
no doubt that Clarice was abundantly right. She saw plainly
Clement's scheme, and how he was step by step carrying it
out; she saw how, as a result, the whole temper of the people
of Florence was changing towards her family; she knew what
a tool her brother Lorenzo had been in his hands; except for
a girl of eight years old, she was herself the last legitimate

representative of a line of ancestors who had been actuated by far different aims; [6] and she was enraged at seeing a policy so destructive to the honour of her house being pursued by one who, illegitimate himself, was scheming to make a second illegitimate scion of the family continue the same policy. And the speech which Leo X had uttered concerning her was, had he known it, a prophetic one. For had she been in her brother's place, Clement would have found in her a formidable antagonist; she would have found means to make the course upon which he had embarked, and which after her death produced the destruction of the Republic, an impossible one; and the family honour would not have been dragged in the dust by an action which has been the principal cause of all the condemnation bestowed upon their name.

By her conduct on this occasion—conduct apparently impelled by a determination to maintain the honour of her family by showing the Florentines that the "true Medici" had neither part nor lot with Clement and his scheme for the enslavement of Florence—Clarice forced the hesitating Signoria over the Rubicon; for by this expulsion of Ippolito and Alessandro, with the Pope's representative, the die was cast, and it meant war to the knife with Clement.[7] And Clarice's bold endeavour to defend that honour of her family which she had truly said depended only on her, was in its own sphere not unworthy to be set beside Piero Capponi's action in that same room thirty-three years before, when he boldly spoke for the liberty of Florence against Charles VIII.

Clarice's character is a fine one. In every act of her life she showed herself a worthy descendant of those Medici who had gone before, and of whom she was so proud; and in this, the last recorded episode of her life, she showed it most. She died in the following year, on the 3rd May 1528, at the age of thirty-five, while the Republic was still in full power, and while her husband was keeping away from Florence, and endeavouring to remain friends both with the Republic and the Pope. She died at their lovely villa of *Le Selve*, on the heights overlooking the valley of the Arno, near Signa, and is buried in the Strozzi chapel in Sta. Maria Novella, Florence. She had ten children, seven sons and three daughters. In his life of his brother Filippo, her brother-in-law, Lorenzo Strozzi, says that at her death her husband "cordially lamented her, and afflicted himself much"; and Filippo Strozzi in his will provided for a monument to be erected to her memory, "seeing that Clarice, my wife, deserves by her virtues to be honoured by me." And certainly Filippo Strozzi had every reason to honour one who was a most true, faithful, and able helpmeet to him, who throughout her life identified herself completely with his interests and plans, and took by far the larger share of the burden, and who not only worthily upheld the name of Medici, but also brought credit upon that of Strozzi.

CHAPTER XVII

GIULIO (CLEMENT VII)

Born 1478. (*Pope* 1523-1534.) *Died* 1534

(2) THE LAST SEVEN YEARS OF HIS PONTIFICATE

THAT Florence should revolt from him, and for a third time banish his family, is said to have been more intolerable to Clement VII than even the sack of Rome and all his other misfortunes. It was a severe blow to his long-cherished scheme. To his former plans there was now added the desire for vengeance. Meanwhile Florence was jubilant; she had reasserted her independence, and had good grounds for hoping to maintain it. Stronger as a state than Rome, the only thing she had to fear was the Pope's gaining allies; and in the condition to which Clement had brought his affairs this seemed highly improbable. The Emperor's animosity had been thoroughly roused, and he and the Pope seemed now too hopelessly estranged to be ever likely to reunite. Francis I was Florence's ally; and besides this, had, in his contest with Charles, other work for his troops than to employ them on Clement's behalf in the latter's private quarrel with Florence. Henry VIII was also Florence's ally, and incensed against Clement for his evasive replies in the matter of his divorce. Genoa, Venice, and Ferrara were all allied with Florence; while the smaller states were nearly all at enmity with Clement for one cause or another. Lastly, he himself was a fugitive, plundered of everything, and in a destitute condition.

But the Florentines, notwithstanding their long knowledge of him who has been called "the master of craft," had not fathomed the capabilities of that fertile brain for finding a way even through such a tangled web as this. Clement's main difficulty was that while he could not hope to regain power over Florence without the help of one or other of the two great antagonists, if he obtained the assistance of one the other would at once take the opposite side, and so neutralise matters. How to avoid this, therefore, became a problem to the solution of which he turned all his mental powers.

First, however, he had to make his peace with Charles, and "get the Emperor's Spanish, Flemish, and German bull-dogs, which had been so ruthlessly let loose upon him, made to let go from his throat." As the price of this release Charles imposed upon him the most humiliating terms, including the surrender of a large part of the Papal territories and the payment of a heavy fine; to all of which Clement had to submit.

In December 1527, soon after Clement reached Orvieto, Francis again declared war against Charles. Henry sided with Francis, hoping thereby to secure the latter's influence with the Pope in the matter of his divorce. For Clement, now completely in the power of Charles, was secretly intriguing with Francis, and urging on this war, in the hope that it would liberate him from this state of bondage. With France and England the other allies against Charles were Venice, Genoa, Florence, and Ferrara.

Florence made a fatal mistake in the side she took in this war. Before it began the Emperor offered if she would side with him against Francis to secure her against the Pope; and Niccolò Capponi, who was Gonfaloniere, exerted all his influence to induce his countrymen to accept this offer, foreseeing that the Pope would eventually contrive to patch up matters with the Emperor, and that whenever this occurred Francis would prove a broken reed. But the Florentines insisted on clinging to the French alliance, and three years later had bitter reason to repent their mistake.[1]

As before, Italy was the principal battlefield. A French army under De Lautrec advanced against Charles's dominions in northern Italy; a second army, assisted by the Genoese fleet, attacked his kingdom of Naples; and for the next year and a half war raged throughout Italy. In October 1528 Clement, who had moved in June from Orvieto to Viterbo, was at last able to return to Rome. He was horror-stricken on seeing its condition, finding it ruined, half burnt, and the population diminished by one-half. Meanwhile, matters were going against the French. They lost the valuable alliance of Genoa; a few months afterwards the whole French army in southern Italy had to capitulate; and lastly, their army in northern Italy suffered a severe defeat from Antonio de Leyva.[2] Exhausted by so many reverses, Francis was inclined to make peace; and to this end discussions regarding a treaty between the two antagonists went on for months at Cambrai, between Louise of Savoy on the part of Francis, and Margaret of Austria on the part of Charles.

The above position of affairs caused Clement to consider that the time was ripe for carrying out a great scheme, the details of which he had been elaborating for many months. Seldom, surely, has such vast machinery been set in motion to attain such a petty object. Europe was now to see the politics of France, England, Spain, Germany, and Italy all manipulated in order that Clement might compass his aim of regaining power over Florence and exalting a scion of his family to be despot over it. Accordingly, in June 1529, while the endless discussions between Louise and Margaret were still continuing at Cambrai, Clement proceeded to Spain, where Charles then was, and laid before him certain proposals for their combined action. The result of this was a secret compact concluded between Charles and himself at Barcelona towards the end of June, which soon had important results to all the countries then at war; though the arrangements made between Charles and Clement in this dubious plot were not allowed to transpire for some little time, but became apparent by degrees in the terms of the treaty of

Cambrai, and in Charles's proceedings in Italy a few months later.

This compact was followed, in August 1529, by the conclusion of the Treaty of Cambrai [3] between Francis and Charles, in which Francis agreed to abandon his allies England, Venice, Ferrara, and Florence, to pay a ransom for his sons, to withdraw his troops from all Charles's territories, and to renounce all interference in future with affairs in Italy. The last item was the principal one, and was that which Clement had employed all his art to secure. Simultaneously with this treaty between Francis and Charles, Clement gave Henry some encouragement in the matter of his divorce, and the latter, anxious to obtain this, offered no remonstrance against the abandonment of the other allies by Francis, and himself followed the same course. This left of the original allies against Charles only Venice, Ferrara, and Florence, deserted by the rest.

The above treaty, combined with the thraldom in which he held the Pope, made Charles complete master of Italy. He now proceeded for the first time to that country (where his armies had been fighting for nearly eight years almost uninterruptedly) to settle its affairs, and to carry out the remaining provisions of the secret compact which had been made between himself and Clement. Reaching Genoa at the end of August he proceeded to Milan, where he reinstated Francesco Sforza [4] as Duke, and dictated terms of peace to Venice and Ferrara. In accordance with the secret compact at Barcelona, Charles treated Venice and Ferrara leniently, and only required from them the restitution to the Pope of the territories they had seized from him in 1527. This left Florence alone, bereft of all her allies; Genoa, France, England, Venice, and Ferrara had one by one been separated from her. Nor was Florence given any opportunity of making her peace with the Emperor in the same way as Venice and Ferrara had done; for this would have prevented that destruction of her Republic which was the object of all these manoeuvres on Clement's part

Moreover, another item in the Barcelona compact now transpired. For, as the price of his submission on all other points, Clement had stipulated that the Imperial army should be lent to him to enable him to crush Florence; to which Charles had agreed on Clement's pointing out that the eventual result would be to the Emperor's own advantage, since instead of a turbulent Republic there would be substituted a ruler who would be a vassal of the Emperor. Thus had Clement in a course of two years' intricate diplomacy, gradually got the bundle of sticks separated, and also obtained the assistance against Florence of Charles's army (for which Clement agreed to pay), while Francis, under the terms of the Treaty of Cambrai, was debarred from interfering. The sum total was a triumph of that kind of diplomacy in which Clement delighted, and in which he excelled.

Accordingly, in the end of September 1529, the Imperial army was ordered to march upon Florence; and in December (while the siege of Florence was proceeding) Clement and Charles met again, this time at Bologna, to perfect these arrangements, to add certain other clauses to the compact between them, and for Charles to be crowned by Clement with the Imperial crown.[5] This coronation took place on the 24th February 1530, and in April, Clement returned to Rome, having, in the further clauses to their compact added at Bologna, set on foot arrangements concerning a private and domestic scheme which he was elaborating as regards his own family. He had by this time determined to supplant Ippolito by Alessandro, and to give the rule of Florence, whenever that state should be subdued, to the latter; but he kept this carefully concealed from all except the Emperor until the time should come, and until he should find means to dispose of Ippolito in some manner which should prevent him from interfering with this plan.[6]

The terms of the secret compact to which Clement had induced Charles to agree at Barcelona, and which was thus finally completed between them at Bologna, were such as fully showed Clement's unscrupulous character; while in them we see that scheme at last taking shape upon which he had for so many years been bent as regards Florence, and which two years before had seemed as though it would have to be abandoned. The principal items were: (I) that on Florence being isolated from her allies by the arrangements settled upon as regarded France, England, Venice, and Ferrara, the Imperial army should be lent to Clement with which to attack and subdue her; (II) that the independence of Florence should be abolished; (III) that Alessandro (called by Clement, the son of Lorenzo, Duke of Urbino) should be invested by the Emperor with the rule of Florence, holding that state as the Emperor's vassal; [7] and (IV) that Margaret, a daughter of the Emperor, then nine years old, should be married to Alessandro as soon as she should be old enough. But the third and fourth articles were not allowed to transpire until more than a year later, Clement having private reasons for keeping them secret for the present. It may be imagined with what indignation the Florentines heard of this resolution to extinguish their beloved Republic, and with what determination they prepared to fight to the death against it. Regarding this whole matter Ranke's comment is as follows:—

"With astonishment did men behold him (Clement), after so many indignities, again connect himself with the Emperor. He so completely changed his policy that the very army by which the horrors of the sack of Rome had been perpetrated before his eyes, and himself held so long a captive, he now called to his assistance, and launched upon his native city."

Nevertheless Florence did not lose heart, though opposed to the united power of Pope and Emperor. Her field army was placed under Francesco Ferrucci, other troops being enrolled to form the garrison of the city. All round the walls of the city a space one mile wide was ruthlessly cleared so as to afford no cover to the enemy, every tree, including even those of vineyards and fruit gardens, being cut down, and every building, including even churches, being demolished, and not-withstanding the fact that some of these suburbs were almost like towns. The Venetian ambassador, Carlo Capello, writing to his government, comments on the widespread ruin thus caused, the many beautiful villas that had been burnt by their owners, and the "greatness of mind" displayed by the general willingness to suffer all these losses for the sake of liberty. One exception only was made, viz., the monastery of San Salvi,[8] on account of Andrea del Sarto's fresco of *The Last Supper,* "which art-loving Florence had not the heart to destroy."

On the 14th October 1529 the Imperial army, commanded by the Prince of Orange, appeared before Florence and oc-cupied all the high ground on the southern side, at a distance of about a mile from the walls, from near Rusciano, on the east, round to Monte Oliveto, on the west, while another equally large force occupied the country on the northern side of the city. Before the investment was complete Florence sent an embassy to Clement in Rome to appeal to his mercy;[9] but they met only with a cold refusal. Yet the troops whom he had gathered round Florence were the ferocious ruffians of many nationalities whom Bourbon had commanded; and Clement had hired them "with 30,000 florins and the prom-ise of the plunder of Florence"; while we are told that even before this army left Lombardy the soldier's usual oath had become, "By the glorious sack of Florence." There was there-fore no doubt as to what was the fate in store for Florence if this enemy got within her walls.

Florence's struggle in defence of her independence was worthy of her former history. She defended herself for ten months against all that the Imperial army could do, and at one time it looked as though she would win. Michelangelo laid aside his chisel and became his country's principal en-gineer,[10] in particular designing all the defences round San Miniato, the principal point of attack. Francesco Carducci was the Gonfaloniere, and although he had not the ability of his predecessor, Niccolò Capponi,[11] he was a worthy and patriotic head of the Government. But the chief hero of the defence is Florence's noble general, Francesco Ferrucci, who well deserved the niche in Florence's temple of fame which he has gained. Keeping the field, and holding the neighbouring town of Empoli, he managed steadily to pour in thence supplies into Florence, again and again defeating the Imperial detachments with his numerically inferior forces, and hampering the Prince of Orange by the knowledge that there was an army in the field on his flank; and so well did he maintain his country's cause that it became at length evident that the Imperial army would never take Florence so long as Ferrucci remained unconquered.

It would have been well for Florence if her forces within the city had been commanded by a man of like character; but here she had made the fatal mistake of employing a foreigner, Malatesta Baglioni, one of that blood-stained family who had previously ruled Perugia; and this caused her defeat. He was a traitor from the very first, and had sold the cause he was engaged to defend. Gino Capponi states that before the siege began Baglioni received from the Pope a written document promising him the lordship of Perugia, confirming any terms which he might make with the Prince of Orange, and *conveying absolution for all crimes which he might commit during the siege of Florence.*[12] Nevertheless, though the garrison was so badly commanded, the Imperial army failed to gain any success; in the sorties and skirmishes which took place almost daily, and were fought with great ferocity, the Florentines nearly always prevailed; and in December a well-arranged sortie of three thousand men under Stefano Colonna [13] was so successful that the besieging army would probably have been routed had it not been for the treachery of Baglioni, who sounded the retreat when Colonna's forces were carrying all before them.

Month after month the struggle continued, and by degrees one after another of Florence's subject towns were captured,

Volterra, Pistoia, Prato, Lastra, San Miniato al Tedesco, and others being successively taken by the Imperial army. But these losses did not daunt Ferrucci, who harassed the enemy continually, and even recaptured Volterra and San Miniato al Tedesco.

At length, in July 1530, the Prince of Orange, seeing that if he was ever to take Florence it was imperative first to defeat Ferrucci, desired to attack him with the greater part of his army, leaving only a weak force round the city; but he feared lest in his absence the garrison should sally out and defeat the force thus left behind. Baglioni, however, enabled him to effect his object, and to attack Ferrucci with an overwhelming force, by engaging not to make any such sortie during the Prince's absence. Thus assured, the latter marched away with a force more than double the strength of that commanded by Ferrucci, and attacked him. The battle between them decided the fate of Florence. It was fought at Gavinana, in the mountains above Pistoia, on the 3rd August 1530. After a severely contested battle the Imperial army won, chiefly because their brave opponents were nearly all destroyed. The two commanders, the Prince of Orange and Francesco Ferrucci,[14] were both killed. Thereupon Florence surrendered, on condition (agreed to on Clement's part [15]) that the ancient constitution should be preserved and the city ruled by the Signoria, but subject to the Emperor as the supreme power in Italy, Florence agreeing to pay an indemnity of 80,000 florins, while the Pope agreed to treat his countrymen "with affection and clemency, as he had always done." [16]

Nevertheless as soon as the city was in possession of the Pope these terms were entirely ignored. Francesco Carducci, the brave head of the Government during the siege, Niccolò de' Lapi, Fra Benedetto da Fojano (a monk who during the siege had encouraged the citizens by his sermons), and many others, Yriarte states to the number of a thousand, were put to death; [17] while many of the leading citizens were imprisoned. The abolition of the Republic and installation of Alessandro as Duke, Clement thought, even in the beaten condition of the Florentines, would be more safely carried out by successive steps.[18] So for a time he caused the government to be carried on by his representative, Baccio Valori, the Signoria being allowed to continue, but all power being vested in Valori, who lived in the Palazzo della Signoria surrounded by a strong body of the Imperial troops. After this arrangement had lasted ten months Clement took the second step by sending Alessandro from Rome to take Valori's place; he arrived on the 5th July 1531, and took up his abode in the Medici Palace.

But before the final step of declaring the Republic abolished and proclaiming Alessandro sole master of Florence could be ventured upon, a fortress was necessary to contain the troops to support this despotism. Accordingly for the present Alessandro was only called "head of the Republic," while arrangements were made for rapidly building a strong fortress (the present "Fortezza da Basso") at the centre of the northern wall of the city.[19] Clement VII's ancestors are often accused of "despotism"; but *they* had no need of a fortress; now, however, that a despotism is in reality about to be set up, a fortress to support it is felt to be a *sine qua non;* so much so that the proclamation of that despotic rule is even delayed until the fortress is ready. As soon as the latter was sufficiently completed to be occupied by the troops lent by the Emperor to support Alessandro's authority, the third and final step was taken; and on the 1st May 1532 Alessandro summoned the members of the Signoria to the Medici Palace, and read out to them the Emperor's order that the Signoria was abolished, the Republic ended, and he himself to be sole ruler of Florence. At the same time a similar proclamation was made from the *ringhiera* in front of the Palazzo della Signoria, the name of which was henceforth changed to Palazzo Vecchio. Alessandro also caused the great bell, "La Vacca," which hung in the tower of the Palazzo

Vecchio, and had summoned so many generations of Florentines to proclaim their will, to be thrown down and broken to pieces.[20] "The bell of the Council," says Davanzati in his contemporary diary, "was taken from us in order that we should no more hear the sweet sound of liberty."

Thus had Clement at last effected the completion of that project which he had assiduously pursued during twenty years. The further development of converting the ducal coronet into a crown was still unattained, but only one step more remained to reach it. The city, held in subjection by foreign troops, groaned in silence; but rage burnt under the surface at the manner in which its conquest had been effected, at the deliberate breach of the conditions under which it had surrendered,[21] and at the odious tyranny to which it now found itself subjected.

Michelangelo, when the city surrendered, fled for his life, and remained for some time in hiding. But his talents were too valuable to be lost, and Clement wanted him for the completion of the family monuments in the New Sacristy, planned in the time of Leo X. So he was pardoned, and given orders to proceed with the work. It may be imagined with what feelings he returned to the execution of such a task in the midst of the daily humiliations of Alessandro's rule. What memories of a bygone very different state of things in the happy days of his youth under Lorenzo the Magnificent, and what despair at the present degradation of Florence, oppressed his soul as he laboured at these monuments may be seen in his work; and there is no ground for the uncertainty which some have expressed as to what ideas Michelangelo meant to convey in these statues of *Day* and *Night*, *Evening* and *Dawn*, when they are studied in conjunction with the contemporary history and his own words.[22] The great sculptor worked at the task given him full of the bitterest feelings at the ruin of his country, at the "wrong," which had been done to her, and at the "dire disgrace" of such a rule as that of Alessandro; and the statues refer to the "day" which once had been, and the dark "night" which had now settled down upon Florence, one regarding which he despaired of any "dawn." Michelangelo left these monuments unfinished, not on account of any artistic reason (as some have fancied), but because, on Clement's death in 1534, before they were completed, he precipitately fled from Florence, being in fear of the tyrant Alessandro's hate when once the Pope was dead.

Germany.—By the year 1530 Charles V had triumphed in every direction. Spain was reduced to subjection; on France had been inflicted the greatest defeat of the century; all temporal power had been taken from the Pope; throughout Italy Charles's supremacy was complete; while his brother Ferdinand had gained the crowns of both Hungary and Bohemia. But in Germany the contest about religion threatened to produce serious civil war. In 1530 Charles assembled the Diet of the Empire at Augsburg to endeavour to find means of healing the breach; and at this assembly Melanchthon put forward a creed [23] which became a rallying point for the Lutheran party, now for the first time called "Protestant." Every effort was made to find terms of agreement between the rival parties in this assembly, and at one time Charles hoped this had been effected; but the Protestants would yield nothing from their side, and after much discussion they were out-voted, and the Diet passed a decree severely condemning their opinions. As a consequence the Protestant princes of Germany (secretly assisted by both Francis and Henry in order to embarrass the Emperor) formed for their mutual defence the League of Smalkalden. But the Turkish invasion of Hungary had now assumed formidable proportions, and to meet it Charles, after great efforts, managed at the Diet of Ratisbon in July 1532 to arrange a truce on the religious question; whereupon the Protestant princes agreed to march with him against the Turks. Accordingly, in August 1532, Charles led a large army against Solyman, the Turkish Sultan, who, overawed by this great display of force, retreated precipitately without risking a battle, and evacuated Hungary and Croatia. Having thus rescued Hungary, the Emperor returned thence, and passed through Italy on his way to Spain.[24] He had no intention of going to Rome, and ordered Clement to meet him at Bologna, regardless of the rough and difficult journey in which this would involve the Pope, who dared not go by the main road which passed through Florence.[25] They met at Bologna in December 1532, when a second conference between them took place. At this meeting Clement was made to feel more than ever the galling yoke of his bondage to Charles; the latter knew that during his absence in Hungary Clement had been again making overtures to Francis, and intended to put a stop to all such procedure on his part. As a counterpoise, however, Clement had prepared a scheme for the Emperor's discomfiture; [26] while the compact which he had secretly formed with Francis (and which included specific proposals for an attack on Milan) did not prevent Clement's forming at this meeting an agreement with Charles to oppose Francis should the latter again endeavour to take Milan.

England.—For nearly six years Clement had by various artifices been keeping Henry VIII at bay over the question of the divorce which he desired from his queen, Katharine of Arragon, the sister of Charles's mother, Joanna. Clement in his position with regard to Charles desired to retain the valuable aid of Henry as long as possible; at the same time, if forced to choose between the two, it was Charles whom he least dared to offend. And as the latter's power over him grew every year stronger, it became more and more certain that Clement would soon be forced to make that choice, and to break with Henry, however much he desired to avoid it. At last, in 1532, Henry would wait no longer.[27] He first tried to force Clement to his will by making the English Parliament pass an Act abolishing the payment of *First fruits* to the Pope; power being left in the King's hand to suspend the Act until it should be seen whether the Pope would meet his wishes. As this failed to produce the desired effect, Henry then endeavoured to force Clement to a decision between himself and Charles by forming an alliance with Francis against the Emperor. Charles's retort was the meeting to which he summoned Clement at Bologna in December 1532, at which he showed the Pope, with great plainness, that he must not dare to offend him, and must throw over Henry and refuse to agree to the divorce. But the more Charles made Clement feel his bondage to him, the more disinclined was the latter to lose any friendship which might sooner or later prove a help to him to get free from this yoke; therefore in secret he still did not despair of contriving by some means to avoid an absolute rupture with Henry. On the 25th January 1533 Henry was secretly married to Anne Boleyn. In February Clement, ignorant of this marriage, granted, at Henry's request, a bull making Thomas Cranmer Archbishop of Canterbury. In May the question of whether or not Henry's marriage to Katharine of Arragon had been illegal was tried in the Archbishop's Court. And on the 23rd May, both houses of Convocation, several foreign universities, and many of the leading canonists of the day, having given the opinion that that marriage was void from the first, the Archbishop, acting with other bishops, annulled it, and three days later confirmed that with Anne Boleyn. But even this did not cause Clement as yet to break with Henry; Francis was Henry's close ally, and Clement hoped to obtain Francis's influence with Henry to persuade him against a breach with the Pope. Therefore though Clement expostulated and threatened, the final thunderbolt of an excommunication was held in abeyance for more than a year, Clement hoping by persuasion to induce Henry to take back his wife when his fickle nature had had time to grow tired of Anne Boleyn.

Although Clement had succeeded in his scheme as regards Florence, he did not find his own position improved. The Emperor still held him bound in fetters, fetters which were stronger than ever since Francis had been shut out from interfering in the affairs of Italy. And while thus cut off from gaining assistance from Francis, Clement felt that he was now being forced by Charles to break with Henry also; when he would become more than ever the Emperor's bond-slave.

Clement therefore now executed his great and final *coup*. During the latter end of 1532 he managed secretly to arrange a compact with Francis which would bind the latter to him by an actual matrimonial alliance. This was nothing less than that the heiress of the Medici family, Catherine,[28] now fourteen, should be married to Francis's second son,, Henry, Duke of Orleans, now about sixteen. The bait by which Clement won over Francis to this proposal was not only the enormous dower which Catherine would bring with her, but also an agreement on Clement's part to assist the French King to retake Milan. Having secretly settled this with Francis, Clement proceeded in December 1532 to the meeting with Charles at Bologna; and there, in the course of their discussions, Clement mentioned to the Emperor the idea of such a marriage, pretending to ask his advice about it, and carefully concealing the fact that he had had any communications, on that or any other subject, with Francis. Charles, knowing that Francis was again planning to get hold of Milan, and being particularly anxious to prevent a friendship between him and Clement which might assist that endeavour, and never believing for a moment that Francis would agree to such a *mésalliance*, advised Clement to make the proposal, thinking that it would bring upon him a rebuff from Francis, which would produce ill-feeling between them. Whereupon to Charles's astonishment and disgust, the thing was promptly carried out. The Emperor having departed to Spain, Clement pushed on all the arrangements as fast as possible; and in October 1533 the marriage was performed by Clement himself, Francis also being present. As a part of the terms of this marriage it was secretly agreed that on Francis gaining possession of Milan with the Pope's assistance, that Duchy should be given to Henry, Catherine's husband, Clement hoping to gratify his ambition by seeing one of his family in power at Florence and the other at Milan. And Clement returned to Rome in December, feeling much secret satisfaction, not only at having achieved so advantageous a marriage for his family, but also at having outwitted Charles, who had held him so long in chains, and who was left with no power of taking offence at this marriage, since he had been led by Clement into actually himself urging the latter to propose it.

But Clement had not a long time in which to enjoy feelings of satisfaction. Before five months were over there pressed upon him from another direction matters which made the last half-year of his life more disastrous than all that had preceded. For the cloud in the west now grew to greater dimensions than those of a mere personal quarrel with a king; and in the last six months of Clement's life events supervened in England which, in their momentous importance to the Papacy, threw all else into the background. For here was no case, as in Germany, of a certain number of individuals, however powerful, revolting from the Pope; but an entire national Church was casting off his supremacy, and a whole nation by its legislature enacting laws prohibiting obedience to his authority; while a king, instead of restraining these actions, was instigating them. And this nation also was that which had hitherto furnished the largest supplies for the support of the Papacy. If one or two more countries should act in the same manner, there would scarcely remain any Papacy to fight for.

In March 1534, both the Church and Parliament of England separately repudiated the supremacy of the Pope, the

Convocation of the Church of England repudiating that supremacy as opposed to the principles of the Catholic Church and an innovation which had not existed for the first six centuries of the Church's life,[29] and declaring that the Pope "hath no greater jurisdiction in this kingdom of England than any other foreign bishop," and the Parliament of England passing an Act which made appeals to the Pope high treason. Thus the repudiation by the Church of England of the Papal supremacy took place *before* the actual rupture between Henry and the Pope.[30] This latter followed four months later, when, in July 1534, the Pope pronounced a sentence of excommunication against Henry, unless he would take back Katharine of Arragon and put away Anne Boleyn; Clement thus still leaving a loophole, in the hope that a rupture between himself and Henry might even yet, at the eleventh hour, be avoided. Henry, however, refused to do this, whereupon the breach became complete.[31] Thus had Henry's personal quarrel with the Pope led to greater consequences than even a king's excommunication, and had enabled the Church of England to cast off that Papal supremacy which had been wrongfully imposed upon her for five centuries.

The sentence of excommunication against Henry VIII was the last public act of Clement VII's life. He died less than two months afterwards, on the 25th September 1534 at the age of fifty-six.[32] His life ended in the midst of the gloom caused by the darkest of all the storms that had come upon the Papacy, and he died with his name execrated in every country, and unregretted by a single human being. It might have been thought that whatever the northern races might feel, at least in the capital city of that Papacy on behalf of which he had contended so strenuously some reverence might have been felt for him. But it was not so. In a letter to the Duke of Norfolk three weeks after the Pope's death, a Roman Catholic correspondent, Gregory da Casale, writes thus:—

"The joy in Rome was great. The most bitter hatred was felt for the dead Pope by every human being; a hatred which, unappeased even by his death, showed itself by repeated nightly attacks upon his tomb. Once it was absolutely destroyed, and the corpse was found transfixed with a sword. And had it not been for respect to the Cardinal de' Medici (Ippolito) the body would have been dragged through the city by a hook. At length an armed guard had to be set over the tomb, since it was every night broken and defiled with all sorts of filth."

Thus ended Clement VII. By setting before himself ignoble aims, and pursuing them with complete unscrupulousness, he did the greatest harm to his own family, to Florence, to Italy, and to the Papacy.[33] He died leaving half Europe fallen away from the Papacy, Rome a ruined city, the name of his family hated where once it had been honoured, and "Italy, from Milan to Naples, a field of slaughter bathed in blood and tears."

————*————

At first sight Clement VII's pontificate is an enigma. He, one of the cleverest members of an exceptionally able family, who had been the guiding genius of the Papacy throughout Leo X's much praised reign, seems in his own pontificate to be perpetually engaged in the most unsuccessful schemes, and involved in the most grievous troubles, indignities, and losses, all without any apparent necessity, and with a result which has caused his pontificate to be considered the most disastrous on record.

The key, however, to this enigma, and the clue to the whole history of these eleven eventful years, is to be found in the reports of the Venetian ambassador at Rome, Antonio Suriano. The latter immediately after Clement's death set himself to show to his own Government that one single underlying motive was the cause of all Clement's actions, and the key to his otherwise inexplicable conduct. And that this all-dominating motive was *the endeavour to avoid the assembly of a General Council*. Suriano writes two long reports to his Government to prove this point, and draws out in detail the many things which Clement was willing to endure for the sake of this one object; while he states that Clement's dread of a General Council amounted to nothing short of abject terror.

In his first report Suriano points out at great length the many occasions on which this exaggerated terror had impelled Clement to the most strange course of conduct, stating that "this overwhelming dread of the General Council, and this alone, induced the Pope to smother his resentment against the Emperor for the many mortifications received from him, and specially for the never-to-be-forgotten outrage of the sack of Rome. All was, if not forgiven, endured in silence, so long as there was any hope that by keeping Charles in good humour the Council might be staved off. And it was only when the Emperor definitely insisted on its assembly that Clement began again to lean towards Francis, in the hope that the latter would impede it." Suriano states that Clement "would not even suffer the word to be mentioned in his presence," and gives in detail the many cogent reasons he had for dreading it.[34]

In his second report the Venetian ambassador gives a masterly sketch of Clement's whole policy, and again points out that through all his manifold schemes there had been this one motive only.

"For this," says Suriano, "took place the conference with the Emperor at Bologna, and the league between His Holiness, His Majesty the Emperor, and Your Serene Highnesses; for this the cruel and shameful siege and conquest of Florence; for this the marriage between the Emperor's daughter, Margaret, and the infamous Alessandro; for this again the marriage between the 'Duchessina'[35] and the son of the King of France. . . . Again, for the same reason, when the arrest in Hungary of the Cardinal Ippolito de' Medici occasioned the Pope, on account of the indignity, such poignant grief that he wept over it, yet was it all passed over unnoticed. Nor could any circumstance avail to arouse Clement or cause him to quarrel with the Emperor, since His Holiness considered that the friendship of the Emperor secured him from the Council so much dreaded by him."

"For this same cause," pursues the ambassador, "although His Holiness had but little love for the Emperor, who ruled him and led him whithersoever he would, yet he was obliged against his will by necessity to consent to whatever the Emperor chose, without manifesting any resistance; and all this from fear of the Council. Therefore, considering this his painful position, and the slavery, as it may be called, in which the Emperor held him, and still more the danger of the Council, he began to show himself more accessible to the most Christian king (Francis I). And hence the marriage of the Duchessina was planned. His Holiness's idea was that by this alliance of his niece [36] with the son of the King of France he should lay the foundation of two pillars of support for his family and his own affairs, especially in the so-much-dreaded matter of the Council; in the hope that by these means some settlement of the religious questions might be attained, and at least the dreaded Council be avoided." And Suriano sums up by saying, "Your Lordships then may be assured that Clement used all possible means to avoid a Council, and the fear of it tormented the mind of His Holiness to such a degree that by reason of it he even lost the friendship of the Emperor, and of others, and finally his own life."

To which may be added the break with England; for Clement would never have allowed the breach with Henry to occur had it not been for the threat of the assembly of a General Council, which Charles V intimated to him in the plainest terms should be the result of his agreeing to the divorce of his aunt.

But there is something deeper to be seen here; though, strangely enough, it has passed without notice. If we look back through the long roll of the centuries we shall see that

all this means in one word—*Retribution*. And so we see
Canossa at last avenged, and after four centuries and a half,
instead of the scene enacted there which burnt itself into the
memory of Europe, we see the rôles reversed, and behold a
successor of the Emperor Henry IV making a successor of
Pope Gregory VII his abject slave, who trembled before him,
and placed the Papal authority at his entire disposal, to be
used only in accordance with his behests.

CHAPTER XVIII

IPPOLITO, ALESSANDRO, AND MARGARET

(1530-1537)

In following Clement VII's history to his death we have had
to neglect for a time the younger members of the family, who
during the last few years of his life were beginning to play
their parts in the drama of the Medici story.

These present to us a group of four, two young men and
two girls, three of them belonging to the family, while the
fourth entered it by marriage. These occupy a considerable
portion of the stage during the years 1530 to 1537; the two
young men destined to meet with early deaths, the two girls
destined to have long lives and to fill important places in
history.[1] They are—Ippolito, the son of Giuliano (Duc de
Nemours); Alessandro, whose dubious parentage has been
already noticed; Catherine, the only child of Lorenzo (Duke
of Urbino); and Margaret, a daughter of the Emperor Charles
V, who at fifteen became the wife of Alessandro. Ippolito,
as the eldest of the group, must be considered first; while
Catherine, being so important a personage, must be dealt
with separately.

Ippolito, the son of the justly esteemed Giuliano (Duc de
Nemours), appeals to us both on account of his own attractive personality and the sadness of his history. Born in
1509,[2] and only seven years old when his father died, he was
as a child taken charge of by his uncle, Pope Leo X, who was
very fond of him, and watched carefully over his education,
delighting in the ability which from an early age he dis-

played. But Leo died when Ippolito was only twelve years old.

We have seen how when he was fifteen he was sent from Rome by Pope Clement VII to reside in Florence, made a member of the Government, and looked upon by all as intended, when old enough, to succeed to the rule of Florence which had been held by his father. During the next three years he, with Alessandro and the child Catherine, remained at Florence under Cardinal Passerini's charge, living in the Medici Palace, until, when Ippolito was eighteen, the third banishment of the family took place. Ippolito thereupon became for a time a wanderer, but when Pope Clement got back to Rome at the end of 1528, Ippolito also returned there.

Ippolito was by this time twenty years of age, handsome, courteous, good-natured, highly cultivated, possessed of much ability, and a universal favourite. Varchi says of him that he was "gifted with every accomplishment, affable and pleasant in his manner, and most liberal to all who excelled in war or letters or in any of the liberal arts." While another quality which the contemporary writers constantly speak of as possessed by him is that of "royal-mindedness."

Towards the end of the year 1529 Clement VII began to form a plan of supplanting Ippolito, as the future ruler of Florence, by Alessandro. This was the more unpardonable in that Ippolito was eminently qualified for that position, while Alessandro, being uneducated, vicious, and universally detested, was as conspicuously unfit for it. Clement began privately to carry out this scheme when making the secret treaty with Charles V at Bologna in December 1529, the third and fourth items of which treaty provided for this arrangement.[3] These intentions were, however, kept concealed from all concerned except the Emperor until Florence should first be subdued and Ippolito disposed of elsewhere.

In the spring of 1531, after the siege of Florence had ended, but while the Pope's intentions had not yet been allowed to transpire, Ippolito, Alessandro, and Catherine were all once more together in Rome, Ippolito being then twenty-two and Catherine twelve; and the idea of these two becoming united in marriage began by some to be entertained. But their common guardian, Pope Clement, had other plans for both of them; he intended to use Catherine as the bait by which to secure the alliance with the King of France which he desired as a defence against the thraldom of the Emperor; while he had reasons of his own for intending that Alessandro, and not Ippolito, should be Duke of Florence. So, while during the early part of 1531 affairs in Florence were left to be carried on by the provisional government under Valori, Clement completed his arrangements for making it equally impossible for Ippolito to become Duke of Florence and to marry Catherine.

Ippolito's natural bent was towards the profession of a soldier, and he disliked everything connected with the ecclesiastical life, and the ways and modes of thought of the ecclesiastics among whom the greater part of his boyhood and youth had been passed. Clement, however, who managed these young scions of the family like pawns on a chess-board, and had numberless ways of forcing them to conform to his will, now proceeded to carry out his object as regards Ippolito by conferring on him the dignity of a cardinal. Ippolito violently refused to accept the proposed honour, but eventually was forced to submit (though he never would wear the cardinal's dress when he could help it), and, to get him out of the way, was despatched on a political mission to Hungary. This done, Clement sent Alessandro to Florence, where in July he was declared head of the Republic; and ten months later, while Ippolito was still absent in Hungary, the Republic was abolished and Alessandro declared Duke of Florence (May 1532).

———————

Installed as absolute ruler of Florence at the age of

twenty, Alessandro showed all the inherent evil of his nature. There is only one example in Florence of the plain ducal coronet; [4] it is to be seen surmounting Alessandro's name over the door leading into the Ognissanti cloisters in the Via Borgo Ognissanti. And sore reason had Florence to look with hatred on that sign of her subjugation. There followed the five most shameful years of her history. The exaltation of this foul and evil youth to a position of power absolutely uncontrolled showed mankind an example of what human nature is capable of under such conditions. His sycophantic admirer Ceccheregli, in his *Attione et Sentenze,* credits him with wit and wisdom, a fine sense of justice, and judgments which would have done honour to a Solomon. But if this was the case it was combined with other qualities which obliterated all such considerations. An historian of his own time calls him a "creature who would have disgraced even the deadliest epochs of Roman villainy"; while another describes him as "one whose excesses were as controllable by human reason as those of a beast of the forest." None dared offend him, or refuse him anything, lest he should murder those dearest to them. Trollope says:—

"The portraits of this wretched youth which hang on the walls of the Florentine gallery show the lowness of the type to which his organisation belonged. The small, contracted features, the low forehead, and mean expression, are altogether unlike any of the Medici race, in whom, whatever else they might be, there was always manifestation of intellectual power.[5] ... His life was one continued orgy. The ministers to his lawless will were ruffians chosen from among the vilest of mankind; ... and these men were made, not only the ministers to, but the companions of, his pleasures; and the companions also of the young, the wealthy, and the beautiful among the aristocracy of Florence."

What wonder that disgust and indignation at being subjected to such a rule was the prevailing temper of Florence;

or that after three years an appeal should have been made to the Emperor to remove so infamous a vassal. The wonder rather is that any city should have endured such a monster so long, and should not have deprived him of life within the first year instead of the sixth. The experience was a more bitter one to Florence than it would have been to other cities. Others had had tyrannies to endure; Florence had never known the rule of a tyrant.[6] The experience killed her very soul for a time.[7]

In the spring of 1533, when Alessandro had been for about a year Duke of Florence, the fourth member of the group, Margaret, then a girl of twelve, fair and pretty, and engaged to Alessandro in accordance with Clement's compact with the Emperor, passed through Florence on her way to Naples. Born in Flanders in 1521, she had been brought up by her two aunts, Margaret of Austria and Maria of Hungary, and was now sent by her father the Emperor's orders to reside at Naples until the time should come for her marriage to Alessandro. Catherine, two years older, who was then in Florence preparatory to her departure for Marseilles for her own marriage, rode out to meet her at the Medici villa of Cafaggiolo, in the valley of the Mugello, on the road from Faenza. And thence, on the 16th April 1533, these two girls, so different in appearance, and destined to have such very different histories, together rode to Florence. Margaret remained for a few days to be shown by Catherine the principal sights of the city, and then continued her journey.

For the next three years Margaret remained at Naples, and as Alessandro's enormities yearly grew more notorious there began to be doubts, especially after the death of Pope Clement, whether her marriage would take place.

"So iniquitous did such a marriage seem, even in that age, that the *fuori usciti* did not believe in the projected marriage, because they did not believe that the princess could be given to a man so infamous." [8]

However, Charles V evidently thought otherwise, and even Pope Clement's death did not cause him to alter his intention to carry out the marriage which had been settled upon between them.

Although the way he had been treated caused a great change in Ippolito, a permanent sadness coming over a disposition which had before been full of brightness, we do not hear of his showing any resentment. He developed a great liking for the Hungarians and for Hungary, and while in that country was fond of wearing the Hungarian dress; though on one occasion while there he was made prisoner under a mistake, a matter over which Pope Clement suffered much humiliation. On his return from Hungary Ippolito took up his abode at Bologna, and shortly afterwards complied with the Pope's request that he should accompany him to Marseilles to be present at Catherine's marriage. At Bologna Ippolito lived in great style, and an incident connected with his life there gives an example of his character. Clement VII, thinking the number of retainers maintained by Ippolito excessive, remonstrated with him: whereupon Ippolito replied: "No, I do not maintain them because I have need of their services, but because they have need of mine." Ippolito had all the family taste for learning; he wrote various poems, and translated the second book of the *Æneid* into Italian blank verse, a work which has been highly praised and often reprinted.

In 1534, Pope Clement being ill, Ippolito returned to Rome, and was with the Pope when he died in September: on which occasion we hear of his protecting the latter's body from insult; while it was he who thereupon commenced the con-

struction of the tombs in Sta. Maria sopra Minerva to the two
Medici Popes, Leo X and Clement VII.

Perhaps we shall not be wrong in considering that Ippolito
showed the nobility of his character in nothing more strongly
than in never exhibiting any malice towards Pope Clement
for the way in which the latter had cheated him and ruined
his life. Yet he evidently felt it deeply, for Varchi tells us:—

"When he understood that Pope Clement had decided that
Alessandro was to be made the heir to the riches and greatness of the house of Medici, and not himself, a great change
took place in him. He was seized with immense anger and
grief, as it seemed to him that being older, a nearer relation
to the Pope, and better endowed by nature, so rich an inheritance and so brilliant a marriage [9] should rather be his;
either not knowing, or refusing to believe, the secret rumours
that Alessandro was the son of Clement."

It is peculiar to notice how it is assumed as a matter of course
that nearness of relationship *to the Pope,* and not right of
primogeniture (as a grandson of Lorenzo the Magnificent),
is that which should constitute Ippolito's stronger claim.

On Clement VII's death Alessandro Farnese was, on the
11th October 1534, elected Pope in a conclave which only
lasted one hour. He took the name of Paul III, and within
three days after his election he ordered a committee to assemble to draw up a scheme for the reformation of the
Church, and to consider the time, place, and mode for the
assembly of a General Council. In politics also the new
Pope adopted a totally different course from that of his
predecessor, endeavouring to assuage the animosity between
Charles and Francis,[10] and maintaining a position of neutral-
ity between them. The above course of action on the part
of the Pope changed the entire political situation; while it
enabled the Emperor to turn his attention to the affairs of
Germany, and to resisting the formidable encroachments of
the Turks.

In May 1535 Charles V sailed with a great fleet from Barcelona to attack the Barbary pirates, who under their commander Chaireddin Barbarossa had established themselves in Algiers and Tunis, and ravaged the coasts of Spain and Italy. The pirates were defeated, and Charles took their capital, Tunis, and in August returned in triumph to Sicily.

———————

In June 1535, Pope Clement being dead, and Alessandro having in the three years he had been in power so outraged the Florentines that he had driven a large number of them into voluntary exile, these *fuorusciti* determined to send an embassy to the Emperor Charles V, to appeal to him against the atrocities of his vassal, and to petition for his removal. The *fuorusciti*[11] had always been a recognised party in Florentine politics, as whichever party was in power caused a number of the opposite party to quit Florence, either voluntarily for their own safety, or by being exiled. But under Alessandro's evil tyranny they had come to muster unusually strong.

They selected Ippolito as their ambassador to lay their petition before the Emperor, the latter being then at Tunis, on his expedition against the Barbary pirates. Ippolito, who was then at Rome, started upon this journey and got as far as Itri, near Gaeta, between Rome and Naples; but, while waiting there for a vessel in which to embark for Tunis, he was poisoned; and the proof was overwhelming that it was done by Alessandro. The agent employed was one Giovanni Andrea of Borgo San Sepolcro; and besides the universal opinion, and the testimony of other historians, Varchi gives proof which is practically conclusive that he was employed to commit the crime by Alessandro.

Thus died at the age of twenty-six the accomplished and deservedly popular Ippolito, put out of life (like so many others) by the detestable youth whom Clement VII had placed in power in Florence. The assassin, Giovanni Andrea, did not long survive; after effecting his escape from Ippolito's servants, who in their rage would have torn him in pieces, he fled to Florence, and lived for some months in Alessandro's palace, protected by the latter. Thence after a time he went to his own town of Borgo San Sepolcro; but there the people, in an outburst of popular indignation at his crime in killing one so universally admired as Ippolito, seized him and stoned him to death.

As we look at Titian's portrait of this handsome and accomplished grandson of Lorenzo the Magnificent we see his whole character and history laid bare before us. Though a cardinal, he will not be painted in that hated dress, but wears his favourite Hungarian costume, and the sword which he would have liked to bear as a soldier. His chivalrous spirit, high temper, quick intelligence, and that quality of "royal mindedness" which those around saw in him, are well brought out by the painter. The picture was painted after that "great change in him" of which Varchi speaks, and his face may well have that look of permanent sadness since, too wholly in the power of his crafty relative the Pope to resist after the thing was done, he had by various subterfuges had his whole life spoilt.

Titian was at this time at the height of his fame, the greatest portrait painter in Europe, and much in request at all the most splendid courts. He had passed from the patronage of the Duke of Mantua to that of the Emperor Charles V, whose admiration for him was exemplified in his speech (on picking up Titian's brush from the ground), declaring that "a Titian might well be served by Cæsar." In order to give a high relief to the head Titian was fond of using, as in this instance, a black background in his portraits. Ruskin, speaking of them says:—"Both for what they present, and the manner of their presentation, Titian's portraits are among the artistic marvels of the world."

In January 1536 war again broke out between Charles and

Francis, while the latter brought another powerful adversary
into their conflict by concluding an alliance with the Turkish
Sultan, Solyman. The French overran the whole of Savoy,
and took Turin. Charles, then resting at Naples after his
North African expedition, remained there from December
1535 to March 1536. He then travelled northwards to oppose
the French, and in passing through Rome made arrangements with Paul III for the assembly of a Council of the
Church as soon as a state of peace should be obtained; though
it was nine years before the Council [12] was able to assemble.
Having arrived in northern Italy, Charles repulsed the
French, and then invaded Provence, but in September was
forced to retire again to Italy, Savoy remaining the prize
of France, and the territories of its Duke becoming reduced
to the single town of Nice.

Whether or not Alessandro's enormities had become so
pronounced before Pope Clement's death in 1534, they evidently had fully done so by June 1535, when Ippolito's mission took place. It therefore immeasurably lowers our
esteem of the Emperor Charles V (who must have been fully
aware, both of the abominable state of things which had
caused Ippolito to be sent, and of the circumstances of his
death) to find that in April 1536, on his way northwards
from Rome, he stayed in Florence at the Medici Palace with
Alessandro. And on the 19th June in the same year Alessandro
was married in San Lorenzo to the Emperor's daughter Margaret, then fifteen, the last iniquitous step in the compact
made by Clement VII with Charles V at Bologna in 1530.

But all was of no avail. Six months later, on the night of
the 5th January 1537, came the end of Alessandro's vicious
life at the age of twenty-six, and in the way in which it was
bound to come sooner or later. He was assassinated by his
young relative and boon companion Lorenzino,[13] of the
younger branch of the Medici family, then aged twenty-two,

assisted by a hired assassin, Scoronconcolo, in a room in Lorenzino's house adjoining the Medici Palace; to which house
Alessandro had gone late at night imagining that he would
meet there a lady of whom he was enamoured, and who was
none other than Lorenzino's own sister Laudomia, the young
widow of Alemanno Salviati, who, we are told, "was as virtuous as she was beautiful," and who had previously rejected
the Duke's odious attentions with scorn.[14] Lorenzino, however,
was merely deluding him, and, instead of his sister, brought
in the assassin Scoronconcolo, and together they put an end
to the detestable being who had for five years outraged
Florence.[15]

Lorenzino was a strange youth. He was the eldest of the
four children of Pier Francesco (the younger) and Maria
Soderini, and had decided ability and character, while it is
specially recorded of him that he had much culture and literary
talent. But he is said to have acted at times as though seized
with temporary madness. On one occasion, when in Rome, he,
although a great admirer of antiquities, in a sudden freak
knocked off the heads of several fine statues of the Emperor
Hadrian; at which act Pope Clement was furious, threatened
to hang him, and banished him from Rome. He was seventeen
when Alessandro was made Duke of Florence, and from that
time he became the latter's constant associate, and companion
in all his vicious courses. His devoted mother, the widowed
Maria Soderini, did her utmost to lead her eldest son into
better ways, and to get him to break off his connection with
Alessandro, but unsuccessfully; a failure accounted for by
Lorenzino in his defence by his statement that his conduct
had had a deliberate object (*see* below). His sister Laudomia
was a celebrated beauty of the time; her portrait, painted by
Bronzino, is to be seen in the Accademia delle Belle Arti,
Florence.

Leaving Alessandro's body where it lay, Lorenzino forthwith took horse and fled from Florence, riding hard through
the night for Bologna.[16] Next morning the Duke's servants,

finding him absent, suspected foul play. Search was secretly made for him, and at evening they discovered his body lying in the room in Lorenzino's house. His death was kept secret, and the body hurriedly conveyed by night into the little church of San Giovannino, close to the Medici Palace; there it was prepared for burial, and on the following night was carried by a few servants with great secrecy to the church of San Lorenzo, and without any religious service was hurriedly placed in the sarcophagus containing the remains of Lorenzo (Duke of Urbino), neither wife, relative, nor friend of any sort being present at this dishonoured interment.

After halting a few hours in Bologna Lorenzino fled on to Venice, where was then living Filippo Strozzi, who was at this time the leading man among the *fuorusciti*. When on reaching Venice Lorenzino burst into Strozzi's room and related what he had done, Strozzi embraced him, calling him the deliverer of his country, and "the Florentine Brutus." Strozzi's delight was so great that he declared that his two sons should marry Lorenzino's two sisters; which was in a short time carried out, Piero Strozzi marrying Laudomia, and Roberto Strozzi marrying Maddalena.

Lorenzino's act has been the subject of much controversy; by some he has been considered the liberator of his country from an intolerable state of things for which there was no other remedy, since appeals to the Emperor had proved useless; by others he has been called a traitor and a regicide.[17] Possibly it would be necessary for us to have to live under such a tyranny as Alessandro's before we could form a just opinion on the point. Be that as it may, praises were lavished upon Lorenzino from every side, and both the Florentines in exile throughout Italy and those within the city compared him to all the heroes of patriotism in history. There are only three possible motives for his act, personal ambition, the liberation of his country, and the protection of his family from insult. None have considered that he was moved by the first of these motives; he was, it is true, the rightful heir to the position in which Clement VII had placed Alessandro, but he never seemed to care for such a position, and was entirely without any family influence to enable him to profit by Alessandro's death, almost his only male relative being an unknown and equally powerless youth of seventeen.[18] In the detailed defence of his act which he drew up [19] he stated that his whole course of action had been a deliberate plan in order to free his country from a monstrous tyranny which had become insupportable; and this account of the matter is believed by historians to be the true one, even though it involves the possession by Lorenzino of an amount of determination beyond his years. But while the above motive on public grounds was that put forward by Lorenzino, he had a no less powerful private one, even though he, naturally enough, did not wish to state it; for in the circumstances under which Florence was at that time, this youth of twenty-two had certainly no other way by which he could protect the honour of his sister.[20]

As a mark of ignominy Cosimo I, on succeeding to the rule of Florence,[21] caused Lorenzino's house to be entirely destroyed. It has in recent times often been declared that Cosimo, on pulling down the house, opened in the place where it had stood a narrow street or alley connecting the Via Larga (now Via Cavour) with the Via Ginori, and called it the *Strada del Traditore*. But this is disproved by the very rare work, in the State Archives, the *Ricerche alle case di Firenze, Anno 1561,* a record, very carefully compiled, of every house in Florence at that date, carried out block by block, from corner to corner of the four streets enclosing each block. This shows with great exactness, first, that there was no street or alley near the Medici Palace running from the Via Larga to the Via Ginori, and, second, that in 1561 the house of Lorenzino had been, not merely spoilt, but entirely destroyed. This record (in regard to the Quartiere San Giovanni), starting from the corner at the intersection of the Via de' Gori with the Via Larga, mentions first "the house of Lorenzo the Magnificent" (the Medici Palace); and then says that the next house is a ruin, "that which formerly belonged to Lorenzino de' Medici, already entirely destroyed (*rovinato*)"; while it mentions no street or alley running from the Via Larga to the Via Ginori. This proves that there was then, at all events, no *Strada del Traditore;* while it also disposes of another theory which has been held, viz., that Lorenzino's house was that which is now No. 5 Via Cavour. The former site of Lorenzino's house is, in fact, covered by the northern portion of the Medici Palace which was added by the Riccardi family when they bought the palace in 1659, part of which addition has an empty space left on the first floor, in accordance with one of the conditions of the sale, which in giving permission to the Riccardi family to build their proposed extension of the palace on this site laid down the condition that such a space should be left above the ground floor at this spot, as a memorial of the murder of Alessandro, which had taken place in a room similarly situated.

Until the year 1875, though it was always known that Alessandro's body had been interred in the tomb of Lorenzo (Duke of Urbino), it was a debated question which of the two tombs in the New Sacristy was that of Lorenzo and which that of his uncle Giuliano. In that year, however, the Italian Government authorised an investigation to settle the point, and the sarcophagus over which sits the figure called *Il Pensieroso* was opened, in the presence of a representative of the Government and various literary men interested.

"It proved to contain," says the account, "two corpses, which turned to dust as soon as the air was admitted, but not before the figure of Alessandro had been perfectly recognised, both by its mulatto type and by the marks of the wounds, especially those in the face, which he had received from Lorenzino and the hired assassin Scoronconcolo."

Another account denies the turning into dust, and says that there were signs of embalmment, that the two bodies were lying head to foot, and that Lorenzo's was clothed in the usual black garment, but Alessandro's in an embroidered shirt. Mr. Charles Heath Wilson, who was present, remarked that one of the cheek-bones of the latter body bore traces of a stab, and that this corroborated Varchi's account of the murder.

When the tragedy of Alessandro's murder occurred, Margaret, not knowing what might be the consequences to herself of the removal of a husband so justly detested by every soul in Florence, fled at once to the Fortezza, which was held by the troops of her father, the Emperor. Thence she departed first to Prato, and then to Pisa, and after a short time, by the Emperor's orders, removed to Spain. There, eight years later, she was at the age of twenty-four forced to marry a boy of thirteen, Ottavio Farnese, grandson of Pope Paul III, and became in after life a very capable and celebrated woman, who as Margaret of Parma was in 1559 made Regent of the Netherlands by her half-brother, Philip II, and ruled that country well under the most difficult circumstances for eight years. In 1567 she insisted on resigning that rule, because she would not be a party to the inhuman measures which Philip had sent the Duke of Alva to the Netherlands to carry out, her last act being to write to Philip begging him to temper justice with mercy. Amidst general expressions of regret, she retired from the Netherlands to her home in Parma, where she died in 1586.

Margaret was the last mistress of the family palace in the Via Larga. Contessina de' Bardi, Lucrezia Tornabuoni, Clarice Orsini, Alfonsina Orsini, Madeleine de la Tour d'Auvergne, and Margaret herself, had each in turn ruled as its mistress. And when the last of them fled from it in terror, this palace, where so many momentous events in the history of Florence had taken place, ceased to be occupied by the head of the family; [22] giving place to a palace, grander indeed in size, but unable to compete with its predecessor in the magnitude of the associations which the latter gathers round it.

———————

On Alessandro's death Clement VII's scheme for keeping the rule of Florence in the elder branch came abruptly to an end, since all of that branch except Catherine were dead; and the succession passed to the younger branch, as it should properly have done on the death of Leo X. All the falseness, injustice, baseness, and treachery employed in order to seat Alessandro on a throne to which he had no right had produced nothing whatever so far as keeping the younger branch out of power in Florence was concerned. Entirely defeating its own aim, Clement's action had only rendered it more easy for them, both to gain that power, and to make it a despotism.

But before we proceed to take up the history of this younger branch, we have still to follow that of the third member of this group of four young people, that daughter of Lorenzo (Duke of Urbino), and great-granddaughter of Lorenzo the Magnificent, with whom Cosimo's branch ended, and who had the longest and most important history of any of the family.

CHAPTER XIX

Born 1519. (*Married* 1533.) *Died* 1589

(1) THE FIRST FORTY YEARS OF HER LIFE

MODERN history has requirements of which former generations seldom dreamt. In former days the method which as a rule commended itself to both writer and reader was one by which characters in history were labelled as "bad" or "good," and little attempt made at any further discrimination. The fact was lost sight of that, since real characters are more complex than this, such a method produces figures unlike any men or women who ever lived, and so gives us distorted views of history. Again, while much more information is available now than formerly, it is also coming to be seen that actions belonging to a bygone age must be judged upon a different principle to that hitherto in vogue. Thus a writer of our time has pointed out that "while with a former generation it was natural to lavish indiscriminate condemnation upon all characters in history who took a different course to that which would now be taken by any one, modern conceptions of the proper attitude of mind in one who deals with history require him to strive to enter impartially into the feelings of all his characters." [1]

In order to avoid that tendency to create impossible figures which is so severely condemned by the modern view of the matter, and arrive at that more discriminate estimate of historical characters now deemed imperative, probably no requirement is more essential than that we should put ourselves mentally into the atmosphere of the time, and carefully guard against judging such characters by the standards of our own age (in which persons live and act under totally different conditions), instead of in relation to the opinions and conditions of their day. Looked at in the latter way, those who were in advance of the moral standard of their time, and those who were behind it, will both be correctly judged; but neither of them will be so if the standard employed is that of our own age.

The foregoing considerations are more important in the case of Catherine de' Medici than perhaps of any other figure in history. For we have in her case an exceptional combination of incentives to the production of a fictitious character. In the first place, the marriage arranged for her by Clement VII in his scheme for outwitting Charles V produced a rooted prejudice against her from the very first in the minds of the French, who felt that in her person the honour of the nation had received a grievous insult, it being a galling wound to French *amour propre* that the son of their king should marry one of *bourgeois* extraction. This feeling steadily increased among the French people (whose favourite name for her was "the Italian woman"), growing from prejudice into hatred, and causing the contemporary French writers to credit her with numberless crimes; "so that, in fact," says a modern French writer, "it would seem from them that scarcely any crime could be committed in any part of France without its being attributed in some way to Catherine de' Medici." The result has been to make any reliable account of her actions practically unobtainable from them.

But this is not all. The intense prejudice caused by this wound to national pride would alone have sufficed to furnish us with a record from the contemporary French writers calculated to produce a very false picture of the person concerned. But to this were subsequently added two other influences tending in the same direction: viz., the effects of a bitter religious conflict, calling forth animosities which knew no bounds in attributing every crime and evil motive to religious opponents,[2] and the delight in tales of crime felt to an unusual degree by the people of that age. Seldom have three such powerful inducements for the production of a fictitious character been combined in connection with one individual; and this combination of national prejudice, religious animosity, and appetite for sensation produced a result in the case of Catherine de' Medici surpassing anything of the kind to be seen elsewhere. The consequence has been that a character has been presented to us which was a radical impossibility; we were asked to believe that it was possible for a woman to have governed an important State for nearly thirty years, enacted many excellent measures for the better administration of justice, intervened constantly between enemies anxious to destroy each other, been throughout life a peacemaker, saved the lives of persons who were her opponents, been greatly liked by various persons of unimpeachable character, and been at the end of her life sufficiently respected by the people of Paris, even when they were in a state of violent rebellion, to be able to pass unprotected through the barricaded streets when no one else could do so, and yet at the same time to have been a prodigy of duplicity and crime, committing murders wholesale. And such a combination being so completely incongruous, it is not surprising that we find a modern French writer saying:—"Catherine de' Medici has been so greatly disfigured as to make her, so to say, unrecognisable; . . . a phantasmagoric personage." [3]

The gradual publication, however, of the State papers of various countries,[4] including Catherine's own voluminous correspondence, is slowly dispelling the errors which this cloud of misrepresentation has gathered round her; with the result that the traditional view about her is slowly giving place to a more correct estimate of her character and actions.[5]

Three things are necessary in order to estimate the character of Catherine de' Medici correctly. First, to measure sixteenth-century actions by sixteenth-century standards of thought and opinion, and not by those of the twentieth century. Second, to give the same weight to facts which tell in her favour as to those which tell against her; as would be done in a court of law. Third, to look with very close scrutiny at any argument which urges that some action of hers in itself praiseworthy should not be held to be so in her case, since it was merely an artifice of "duplicity"; and to require corroborative testimony of facts in support of all such statements.

The course commonly adopted has been the exact reverse of this. It has been that of measuring her actions by the standard, not of her time, but of ours; of giving full weight to, and even exaggerating, all that tells against her, while giving little weight to actions telling in her favour, on the ground that she was "a mass of indifference," [6] or in some other way devoid of the feelings which ordinarily prompt such actions—all of which is pure assumption; and, lastly, where this course is inapplicable, of declaring such actions to be due to duplicity. All this has been done in order to avoid a certain dilemma which occurs in Catherine's case, caused by the fact that a person whom it is considered necessary to portray as "a villain" [7] has to be credited with a number of actions incompatible with that hypothesis; so that, unless these are explained away, there is produced a figure which is palpably an impossible one.

And yet, after all, this dilemma has not been avoided. Again and again, by writer after writer, we find Catherine called an "enigma," a "paradox," [8] a "mystery," or declared to "unite in her character the most discordant and contradictory qualities." And even writers who have been most painstaking in investigating the details of her life have none the less felt themselves impelled to use these terms in an endeavour to escape from this dilemma. But an impossible character is not made less impossible by calling it an enigma; so that this still leaves the dilemma unremoved.

Catherine de' Medici is an "enigma" only to those who start from the basis that she was a villain, and having taken that as an axiom, then find (however much is explained away) that there remain various qualities in her, and actions done by her, which fit so ill with that axiom that all attempt to reconcile the two has to be abandoned. But those who, divesting their minds of the preconceived ideas implanted by the biassed writers of a time of abnormally bitter conflict, judge Catherine's character as it is now revealed in the fuller light available from the State papers of various countries, who measure her actions in due relation to the conditions and standards of her time, and, lastly, who take equally into consideration the light shades with the dark, will find Catherine de' Medici no enigma at all, but a character, remarkable indeed for energy, ability, and other striking qualities, but yet thoroughly harmonious and easy to understand. Not perhaps so well adapted for sensational methods of treatment, but at all events *real:* a living character, not an impossible phantom.

It is remarkable to see in how many ways Catherine shows herself a true representative of the family of whose elder branch she was the last descendant. The abnormal ability and energy, the love of learning, fondness for field sports, artistic taste, common-sense, power to sway those brought into contact with her, and love of ruling, due to the conscious possession of superior powers, all these characteristics which had been prominent in her ancestors appear again in fullest strength in her. It is also evident that she had much of that same many-sided character which we have seen recorded of her great-grandfather, Lorenzo the Magnificent,[9] and seen described as so difficult for the northern races of Europe to understand, and as often causing him, too, to be styled by them, with as little reason, an "enigma" and a "mystery."

Coming to other points more strictly personal to herself, the first we notice is that she was undoubtedly cold and unimpassioned. And she had need to be so, if she was to survive to the age of seventy in a position of authority in such a stormy time as was hers. In this she is the counterpart of two other prominent women of her age, Queen Elizabeth of England and Jeanne d'Albret, Queen of Navarre. At the same time it may be doubted whether Catherine had as much of this quality as either of the other two, and whether a great part of the appearance which she presented of a cold and unimpassioned nature was not due to her abnormal power of self-control. It is admitted by all authorities that her love for her husband, Henry II, was intense, and that his indifference to her was the great grief of her life; while her affection, in her youth for the nuns of the Murate convent, in middle age for her son Henry, and in old age for her daughter-in-law Louise de Vaudemont and her granddaughter Christine of Lorraine, shows that she was not incapable of such feelings. Many accounts credit her with marked love for her children, but, with the exception of her son Henry, it may be doubted whether these statements are not mere courtly flatteries. She was exceedingly careful of her children's health and training, but there it would seem to have ended, and she at times treated them with great harshness.

But most prominent of all the features in Catherine's character were the allied qualities of prudence and self-control. This self-control was in her developed to a degree which bordered upon the marvellous, being such as has been seen in few other individuals. It is constantly referred to as amazing all around her. With it was combined a no less frequently mentioned "prudence"; by which term the writers of that day implied a good deal more than the meaning which we now attach to it. But in her it was, so to say, a prudence run mad, a prudence which had been allowed to absorb all other faculties. All thoughts, all feelings, all desires were, with an iron will, drilled into subjection to this prudence, this unsleeping, incessant care at all times, in all places, under all circumstances, to look, to do, and to speak only that which would advance the matter in hand. Her daughter, the Princess Marguerite (who stood in much awe of her), speaks of her as, "She from whose soul prudence was never parted, who moderated her actions according to her desire, demonstrating plainly that the discreet person doeth nothing he willeth not to do." This feature in Catherine's character was the outcome (as will be seen [10]) of an unusually severe trial, lasting for many years. She was not always like this. But she grew to be so under the peculiar conditions of her life from the age of twenty to that of forty. And it is this rigid prudence and self-control which makes us feel her to be so unhuman. She appears to have, in one sense, neither faults nor virtues, and to be as flawless, and as unattractive, as a bar of finely-tempered steel. As has been said, it was the force of dire conditions which fashioned Catherine the emotional girl, possessed of "sweetness of disposition" and "amiable ways," [11] into Catherine the prudent (and icy) woman. But though it was her misfortune, not her fault, it gave her a characteristic which is perhaps most of all resented by mankind.

It is, however, a mistake to imagine that Catherine was a person of stone. The best judges of her conduct were, not the French, but the ambassadors of other powers living at the court of France, especially those of Venice; and from the recently published Venetian State Papers, and the very full reports [12] which the Venetian ambassadors in succession furnished to their Government of all these events, we obtain invaluable information by which to judge of all such points. Thus, for instance, on this point of her outward appearance of indifference and want of feeling the Venetian ambassador, Giovanni Correr, in one of his reports to his Government, writes:—

"I know that she hath often been found weeping in her chamber; but she at once dried her eyes and dissembled her sadness; and in order to mislead those who estimated the state of affairs by the expression of her countenance, she wore a calm and joyous aspect when abroad."

Although we find some (even among those Protestant writers who hated her with a rancorous hatred), speaking of her "astonishing evenness of temper," she had in reality a hot (though not revengeful) temper. But her abnormal power of self-control never suffered this to appear when it would interfere in any way with her object. When, however, this was not the case her wrath could show itself in a manner terrifying to those around her. The Princess Marguerite, describing one of these outbursts, says:—"Elle jetait feu, et disait tout ce qu'une colère outrée et démesurée peut jeter dehors." Another trait in Catherine, inherited from ancestors who were Florentine citizens, among whom this quality was, and still is, greatly prized, was a never-failing *bonhomie*— a spirit always ready with a laugh, a joke, and a cheerful countenance even in the midst of hardships and misfortunes. Her attainments were of a high order. She was well read and accomplished; she brought to France that love of learning and art inherent in her family; she took a special interest in science; while evidence of her innate artistic taste was in after years furnished by Fontainebleau, Chenonceaux, the Louvre, the Tuileries, and every other palace which she occupied.

Other qualities which we find constantly mentioned are, her great personal courage, power of enduring physical pain without showing any sign, and agreeable manners. The remaining features of her character will be more conveniently considered when we come to look at her as ruler of France.[13] As regards her appearance, the chief points which we find noted by contemporary historians are, her broad forehead, fair hair, fine eyes, beautiful hands, and tall, graceful figure. Her life divides itself into three well-marked periods: viz., fourteen years of girlhood, twenty-six years of married life, and thirty years of widowhood, during the greater part of which she was the all-powerful Queen Regent of France.

FIRST PERIOD (1519-1533)

Catherine, the only child of Lorenzo (Duke of Urbino) and his young wife, Madeleine de la Tour d'Auvergne, belonging to the Bourbon branch of the royal family of France, was born in the Medici Palace on the 13th April 1519, and at her baptism was given the names of Catherine Maria Romola. She is well called in history Catherine de' Medici, for while she was the last of that elder branch of the Medici which had had such a great career, in her all the mental capacity of her family (which her father and grandfather had failed to show) reappeared as strongly as ever, and in this its latest descendant Cosimo's branch showed no smallest sign of deterioration.

When Catherine was born her father, her mother, her grandmother, Alfonsina Orsini, and her father's aunt, Maddalena Cibò, all lay dying,[14] the two former at the Medici Palace, and the two latter at the villa of Careggi. Catherine's mother died a fortnight after her daughter's birth, and her father six days later, while Maddalena Cibò and Alfonsina Orsini both died shortly afterwards. The orphan baby was thus left without any near relations (except her aunt, Clarice Strozzi, who was in Rome), and she remained in charge of servants, a solitary little scion of the nearly extinguished family in that Medici Palace which had again become "too large a house for so small a family." [15]

Ariosto,[16] touched by the friendless condition of this lonely little flower round which so many rough winds blew, wrote at this time regarding her (speaking as for Florence):—

> "Verdeggia un ramo sol con poca foglia;
>   E fra tema e speranza sto sospesa
>   Se lo mi lasci il verno, o lo mi taglia." [17]

Being the sole heiress of the possessions and claims of the Medici family this baby girl was a small person of much importance. On her father's death her distant relative, Cardinal Giulio de' Medici, came to Florence to take charge of the Government and of herself. We have seen the far-reaching schemes which he formed regarding her future and that of the family, and the use that he would make of this orphan girl to advance the latter. And we have seen in what some of those schemes resulted. But we have now to look at Catherine herself, and at her life from the time when she first looked on the world from the windows of the Medici Palace in the Via Larga, Florence.

Her childhood was passed in the midst of stormy episodes, the rage of furious mobs, the clash of arms, and the sound of guns. When she was six months old she was taken to Rome (a difficult journey for a baby in those days, and performed by her probably in a pannier on a mule's back), and was placed by her great-uncle, Leo X, in the charge of her aunt, Clarice Strozzi. She remained at Rome till she was six, by which time Cardinal Giulio had become Pope Clement VII, and the commotions were beginning which ended in the sack of the Vatican. As, therefore, Rome was becoming too disturbed a residence, she was, in 1525, sent back to Florence to her home in the Medici Palace, where she was placed under the charge of Cardinal Passerini, at that time governing Florence in the Medici interest, and in whose charge were also the two boys of sixteen and fourteen, Ippolito and Alessandro: the former much liked, but the latter cordially detested, by the six-year-old Catherine.

For the next two years Catherine remained amidst these surroundings, lessons in the various subjects then considered necessary for every well-born girl [18] occupying most of her time, varied by frequent battles with Alessandro, the quarrels between the two becoming at last so pronounced that Alessandro was sent away to live at the villa of Poggio a Caiano. Then, when Catherine was eight years old, there took place in Rome the catastrophe of 1527, and news reached Florence that the Papal city had been taken and sacked and awful horrors perpetrated, and that the Pope was being besieged in

the castle of St. Angelo. The consternation in the Medici
Palace was great, especially as it was soon known that the
Signoria had assembled and were debating whether Florence
should revolt from Pope Clement and banish the Medici
family. And that might mean death, or at the least much
danger and hardship, and the palace would almost certainly
be plundered of everything by the mob (as it was), and to
what city could they go, since both Rome and all places in
the Papal dominions and in the Tuscan state would be barred
to them.

These questions Cardinal Passerini sat discussing in much
distress of mind with Ippolito and Alessandro on the 19th
May 1527, and Catherine certainly listened. And then their
deliberations were broken in upon by Catherine's capable and
loud-voiced aunt, Clarice, in the manner which we saw; and
they were bidden to depart without delay from Florence. But
not the little "Duchessina," as Catherine was called; [19] for
while the rest, with their retainers, in the utmost confusion
and terror, packed a few necessary things and made a hurried
departure by the exit at the back of the palace into the Via
de' Ginori, and while the mob, which had been for several
hours collected in the Via Larga, began to pour into and
plunder the palace, she was ordered by the Government to
remain behind, to be kept as a prisoner of the Republic, who
intended to use her as a valuable hostage in the case of future
difficulties with Pope Clement. The terror suffered by a child
of eight thus kept behind in the midst of such a scene of
confusion in order to be immured amongst strangers as a
prisoner, was naturally great; and we see what an impression
it made upon Catherine by her conduct three years later when
bidden to leave the convent of the Murate. Thus did Catherine
begin at an early age her apprenticeship to a trouble-tossed
life.

She was first sent to the convent of Ognissanti, and was
kept there for six months. Thence she was removed suddenly
by night, on the 7th December 1527, to the convent of "Le

Murate," on the opposite side of Florence, at the far end of
the long Via Ghibellina, close under the walls of the city.
The plague was at that time raging in Florence, and we read
how this change of prison entailed on Catherine "a long walk
by night through the plague-stricken streets." The convent
of *Le Murate* ("the walled-up ones") [20] was the most important convent in Florence, being that patronized by all
those ladies of the principal Florentine families who took
the veil; and here Catherine remained for nearly three years,
until she was eleven years old. The chief points insisted upon
in regard to her were that she was to be kept in safe custody,
that there was to be no communication allowed between her
and any friends of her family in the city, and that her education was to be duly attended to. This point of Catherine's
education is one much discussed in the correspondence of the
time, and the nuns of the Murate certainly appear to have
done their part well in this respect, for Catherine, though she
left all compulsory education behind her at fourteen, was
one of the most highly educated women of her day. The
Murate also prided itself on its teaching of deportment and
polite behaviour; and in this respect no less than in learning
Catherine in her after life did the nuns credit, for almost
every historian enlarges upon her pleasing and agreeable
manners.

It is in this time spent at the Murate that we have the
first indications of Catherine's character. We are told, by
various writers who deal with her life as a girl, of her kind and
amiable ways; and this seems borne out by the fact that the
nuns of the Murate (a convent where there were notably
many discords) became extremely fond of her. And long
afterwards we find Catherine on her side still cherishing
kindly remembrances of them, and writing to them constantly
in the most affectionate terms. In her letters, written more
than forty years later, when she was Queen Regent of France,
she delights to recall the daily life of the convent, and the
beautiful garden, with the Arno flowing near it, which she has

not seen for all those years; and lapses into poetry as she
speaks of the view looking up the river, saying:—

> "Monti superbi, la cui fronte Alpina
> Fa di se contro i venti argine e sponda!
> Valle beate, per cui d'onda in onda
> L'Arno con passo signoril cammina!" [21]

Here Catherine spent the most peaceful time of her life,
though even during it there were rough winds blowing round
her outside the walls of the Murate; for it was felt that her
death, as the last legitimate offspring of the elder branch
of the Medici, was eminently desirable in the interests of the
Republic. During nearly the whole of her last year at the
convent the city was being besieged by the army which her
relative the Pope had sent against it; fighting took place
almost daily; and as men's passions grew more inflamed in
this fierce struggle between the Republic and its enemies,
there were not wanting those who made various disgraceful
proposals for getting rid of this heiress of the Medici family,
and she was aware that her death was at any moment possible.
Once during this period a member of the Republican Government proposed that she should be suspended in a basket from
the walls as a target for the enemies' bullets; while another
member,[22] furious at Clement's conduct, suggested an even
worse method of disposing of her.

At last, in the summer of 1530, the Government considered
that Catherine was growing too popular at the Murate, and
that through her presence there a feeling favourable to the
Medici was growing up in this important convent, which
might become a cause of inconvenient intrigues; they therefore decided to remove her to another abode. Accordingly, on
the 20th July, in the middle of the night, the convent was
aroused by a loud knocking at the main entrance, with a
summons to open in the name of the Republic. The door
being opened there appeared three senators, the senior of
whom, Salvestro Aldobrandini, presented an order to the
frightened nuns to make over to them the girl, Catherine

de' Medici. A long parley followed, Catherine feeling certain
that this meant that she was going to be put somewhere
where her death could be effected, and protesting with all her
might against being given up to them. At last it was urged
by the nuns that she should, at any rate, be left alone until
the morning; and this was at length conceded. As soon as
the senators were gone, Catherine cut off all her hair, put
on the dress of a nun of the Murate, and, going to the Mother
Superior of the convent, said: "Will they dare now to remove
me when they come in the morning, and to appear before the
eyes of the people in the streets employed in the crime of
forcibly carrying off a nun from her convent?" In the morning, therefore, when the senators again arrived, with a horse
for her to ride, Catherine appeared thus dressed before them,
dared them to take her away, and refused to take off the
dress she had assumed. For hours they argued, and every
persuasion was tried without avail; "Catherine was adamant;
the horse brought for her remained standing at the door in
the street; the struggle of wills continued within." At last
they got her as far as the door of the convent, but there the
senators said they could not take her thus dressed, and she
declared that if she went at all she would go thus, and that
nothing should induce her to change her dress. "She refused,"
says Niccolini, "with wonderful firmness and resolution, declaring that all the world should see that she was a nun being
taken forcibly from her convent." In the end she prevailed,
and they had to take her with them dressed as she was. They
escorted her (presumably by the least frequented streets),
to the convent of Sta. Lucia in the Via San Gallo, and this, they
informed her, was to be her new abode. The fact must have
been a great relief to Catherine's mind.

This first recorded action of Catherine's life showed that
she was no ordinary child; of a girl who could exhibit such
force of character at the age of eleven, it might safely be
predicted that if she ever came to a position of independent
power she would manifest an ability and strength of character

equal to that possessed by any of her ancestors. In connection
with the same episode, we are also given a second indication
of her character; for we are told that she felt lasting gratitude
to Salvestro Aldobrandini for his behaviour on this occasion,
and the manner in which, though firm to his purpose, he had
treated her with politeness and consideration. This she never
forgot. More than twenty years afterwards, when their positions were reversed, she being then the powerful Queen of
France and Aldobrandini a proscribed heretic and outlaw,
sentenced to death by the Pope, she exerted her influence
and saved his life. We are told, "He escaped death through
the intercession of the grateful Duchessina." Gratitude preserved so long and acted upon in this fashion is rare.

The Murate still stands, though long since abolished as
a convent, and still bears out its name by sheltering "walled-up
ones"; for it is now the great prison of Tuscany. Its forbidding door in the centre of the high, grim wall remains as
when Catherine and the senators of the Republic had there
that contest of wills, and recalls the strange scene—the horse
which had been waiting before the door for so many hours,
the weeping nuns within the doorway, afraid that their little
charge was being taken away to be murdered, the three
senators striving to induce the latter to doff her offending
attire, and in the midst the small figure in her black dress,
with pale, determined face, whom not all their endeavours
could shake.

Catherine remained at the convent in the Via San Gallo
during the remaining month of the siege, until in August
1530 the city surrendered to the Pope. It does not appear that
in the terms of capitulation the Republican Government
made any use of the possession of this valuable prisoner; or,
if they did so, the result became a dead letter, like so many
other provisions of the treaty. As soon as she thus regained
her liberty, Catherine "flew back to her beloved nuns at the
Murate," and remained there until the spring of the following
year (1531), when, it being obvious that she had better not

continue to reside in a city to which Alessandro was going to be sent as supreme ruler, Clement VII sent for her again to Rome, which city she had left as a child of six. There Catherine again met her cousin Ippolito, by this time a general favourite in Rome; and an attachment began to grow up between the girl of twelve and the young man of twenty-two, which might in time have become something stronger had circumstances permitted it. Describing Catherine at this time in his reports, the Venetian ambassador at Rome, Antonio Suriano, says:—"This child has a very lively disposition, and displays a charming wit. She owes her education to the care of the nuns of the Murate convent at Florence."

The subject of Catherine's marriage now began to be debated at the Papal court. Among the aspirants were the King of Scotland, the Duke of Mantua, and the Duke of Milan, while the mutual regard between Catherine and her cousin Ippolito also led some to talk of this as the best marriage for her. Infinitely better would it have been for Catherine had this been the alliance chosen; but, as already noted, Clement VII had other views; and by December 1532 he had privately concluded an arrangement with Francis I that Catherine should be married to that King's second son, Henry of Orleans. Her appearance at this time, when she was nearly fourteen, is described by the Venetian ambassador at Rome, as "small and slender, with fair hair, thin and not pretty in face, but with the fine eyes peculiar to all the Medici." And he adds: "She has a remarkably kind, gentle, and cordial manner."

The marriage being thus settled, all the arrangements for it were pushed on by the Pope as fast as possible; Catherine was allowed to return for a short time to Florence (where she stayed again at the Murate convent, the Medici Palace being occupied by Alessandro), and was told to be ready to leave there at the end of August to meet the Pope at Nice [23] and accompany him thence to Marseilles, where the marriage was to take place in October. At this time we have

an interesting glimpse of her from the contemporary painter
and historian, Vasari,[24] who, when she was about to leave
Florence never to see it again, writes thus:—

"She well deserves that we should wish to keep her portrait among us on account of her kind and amiable ways.
Her sweetness of disposition cannot be painted, and of that
my brush [25] can secure us no memorial."

These words will seem strange to those who have no other
mental picture of Catherine de' Medici than the traditional
one. But they are written by Vasari in a private letter to an
intimate friend, and she who is thus spoken of was removing
permanently to a distant country where it was not probable
that she would ever meet Vasari again. So that there is
practically no doubt that these praises, attributing to her a
character universally and deservedly liked, represent the
truth. These words of Vasari, written under such circumstances, together with the reports of the Venetian ambassador
at Rome, and the estimation in which she was held at the
Murate, where she had so long been intimately known, leave
no question as to what Catherine's character was like at the
time when she arrived in France to be married to Henry of
Orleans.

Catherine left Florence on the 2nd September 1533, after
giving a farewell banquet at the Medici Palace to all the
noble ladies of Florence, at which as a parting gift they presented her with some splendid embroideries of pearls on cloth
of gold. The banquet being over, she left the city at three
o'clock, and rode to Poggio a Caiano, where the party slept
the first night. She was accompanied to Marseilles by Maria
Salviati (her father's first cousin), Caterina Cibò, Filippo
Strozzi, and Palla Rucellai. The next day they rode on to
Pistoia, and thence travelled to Porto Venere, on the gulf
of Spezia, where they embarked by sea for Marseilles, touching at Nice (where they met the Pope), and reaching

Marseilles on the 12th October. The fleet as it approached the harbour of Marseilles was a picturesque sight; it consisted of sixty ships, that conveying Catherine having sails of purple cloth embroidered with gold, and being followed by that bearing the Pope, which was covered with a tent of cloth of gold, the deck being carpeted with crimson satin. On landing, a procession of unusual splendour took place through the city; it was headed by a white horse with white trappings, bearing the Host, and led by two equerries also dressed in white. Then followed the Pope, conveyed in his chair borne on men's shoulders, and succeeded by a long procession of bishops and cardinals on horseback, wearing their robes; and lastly Catherine herself, dressed in a robe of gold brocade, and riding by the side of her uncle-in-law, John Stuart, Duke of Albany, who had married her mother's sister, Anne. From every balcony hung costly draperies of velvet and embroidery, while across the streets were festooned countless garlands of the deep-coloured damask roses of Provence mingled with the lilies of France. The two palaces occupied by the Pope and the King of France were separated by a street over which was thrown a covered bridge, uniting the palaces, and made to form a large hall, which was hung with costly tapestries. In the Galleria degli Arazzi at Florence are to be seen three rooms hung with rich tapestries depicting the festivities held on the occasion of this marriage of Catherine; these furnish an interesting record of the costumes worn on this occasion.

The marriage of Catherine de' Medici [26] and Henry of Orleans took place on the 28th October 1533, in the cathedral of Marseilles. The Pope himself performed the ceremony, and Catherine, who wore a dress of white silk embroidered with precious stones, and ornaments of Florentine gold filigree-work, had round her all the few relations she possessed,[27] viz., the Pope, Ippolito (lately returned from Hungary, and dignified and courteous as ever, though clouded by that permanent sadness which had come over him), Maria Salviati, and Caterina Cibò. Catherine was at this time in her fifteenth year, and Henry of Orleans sixteen. The latter was a dull, taciturn youth; the long and severe imprisonment which he and his elder brother had undergone in Spain, while it had ruined his brother's health, appeared in Henry to have had the effect of clouding his brains; and he was a complete contrast to his brilliant and energetic father, Francis I, to whom his second son's heavy and inert character was a constant cause of irritation and contempt.

At this marriage Pope Clement presented two notable gifts, both of which have had a remarkable history. To Catherine herself he gave seven splendid pearls of most unusual size; and these appear in her picture, in the front of her crown. Twenty-five years afterwards Catherine gave these pearls to her daughter-in-law, Mary, Queen of Scots, when the latter married her eldest son; and Mr. Cochrane mentions that Mary is represented with them round her neck in a picture at Holyrood Palace. When Elizabeth put Mary to death she not only took her life but also stole her jewels, seizing upon these celebrated pearls which she had always coveted; they thus became part of the English Crown jewels. And after having assisted at many great historic functions, their last public appearance was in the year 1901, when at his coronation His Majesty King Edward VII wore in his crown the celebrated pearls which Catherine de' Medici had worn in hers.

Clement's other present was given to the bride's father-in-law, Francis I, and was the well-known casket, made by Valerio Vicentino, assisted by his daughter, and carved from transparent rock crystal, depicting twenty-four scenes from the life of Christ, and lined with silver, so as to give an appearance of relief to the engraving. It contained the *pyx* in which the Holy Sacrament was placed on the Thursday of Holy Week, the *pyx* being of fine enamel set with rubies. This casket was one of the most valuable presents given on that occasion, and Vicentino was paid two thousand gold crowns for it; while its value is now priceless. In the seven-

teenth century it found its way back to Florence, and now
stands amongst other gems which belonged to the Medici in
the Gem Room of the Uffizi Gallery; though how it got back
to Italy is a mystery. It was placed by Catherine, during her
son Charles IX's reign, in a cabinet in the Louvre; apparently
it was stolen from the Louvre during the commotions in
Paris after the death of Henry III, and the robber, feeling
it unsafe to retain so remarkable an object in France, took it
to Italy, where, after lying hidden for some forty years, it
must have been bought by one of the Medici Grand Dukes—
most probably by Ferdinand II—as it suddenly appears in the
catalogue of the Medici gems in 1635, but without any record
of when or how it had been obtained.[28]

Having thus followed Catherine's history during the fourteen years of her girlhood, we have next to look at her
during the fourteen years that she was the wife of the French
King's son, and the twelve years following them during which
her husband and herself were King and Queen of France.

SECOND PERIOD (1533-1559)

Francis I had many matters of diplomacy to discuss with
the Pope, while there were also various grand festivities to
be got through before either of them could leave Marseilles,
so that it was a whole month before the King and the Pope
parted. Then Clement VII, with all those who had accompanied him, again set sail for Italy, and Francis I, with his
brilliant court and his new daughter-in-law, started by road
for Avignon to return to his palace at Fontainebleau. Catherine now found herself in an entirely new kind of life; it
was Francis's custom to be continually changing his residences, and the Venetian ambassador, Marino Giustiniano,
who was ambassador to France from 1532 to 1535, says:—
"Never, during my embassy, did the court remain in the
same place for more than fifteen consecutive days." Catherine
shared in these constant flittings, and by these journeyings

from city to city, performed always on horseback, she in a very short time saw a large part of France.

We now obtain accounts of what Catherine was like, both in appearance and character, from a new group of observers, viz., from a fresh set of Venetian ambassadors (those accredited to the court of France), and from those French writers who saw her at the court at this time. The former describe her as "full of vivacity, affable, and distinguished in her manners"; while the French writer, Brantôme (who was then at the court), describing the new bride, says:—

"Her appearance is dignified, but at the same time gracious; her expression is pleasing, and her taste in dress excellent; she has a fine figure, a white complexion, small feet, very well-shaped hands, and a particularly beautiful voice."

We are also told that she rode remarkably well, was fond of an outdoor life, and had unusually good health.

Francis I was himself brilliant and cultivated; of him the Venetian ambassador, Marino Cavalli, says:—"Listening to him one recognises that there is neither study nor art which he cannot discuss with much knowledge. . . . His attainments are not limited to war, but include also literature, painting, and the languages."

Francis soon discovered that his new daughter-in-law was of a livelier wit and more highly educated than most of the ladies of his court, and that her *bonhomie* and cleverness made her an agreeable companion; while her love of hunting and other field sports chimed in with his own strong passion for the chase. So he insisted on her accompanying him on all occasions, and Catherine was soon admitted into the charmed circle of his *Petite Bande,* those sparkling and joyous spirits who, like a corps of feminine *aides-de-camp,* accompanied Francis in his progresses from palace to palace: from forest-encircled Fontainebleau to his proud castle of Amboise by the silvery Loire (where Catherine's father and mother had

been married soon after Francis succeeded to the throne),
and from his sumptuous palace of Les Tournelles in Paris to
what is now to us tragedy-haunted Blois, but whose richly
decorated chambers then resounded with the laughter and
espièglerie of the Petite Bande. This friendship on the part
of the King, though a valuable help to Catherine in her new
and difficult position (and especially when three years later
her enemies found a heavy charge to bring against her),
naturally tended to arouse court jealousy. However, Catherine
was wise enough to bear herself with proper humility, knowing
well how many causes for dissatisfaction the French had
against her. We see a glimpse of these latter in the report of
the Venetian ambassador, Giustiniano, about this time which
says:—

"M. d'Orléans is married to Madame Catherine de'
Medici, which dissatisfies the entire nation. It is thought that
Pope Clement deceived the King in this alliance. However,
his niece is very submissive."

But except for the French King himself Catherine had
not a friend in France, and her position was most difficult.
Not only was the marriage highly unpopular with nobles and
people, and she herself hated as a *bourgeoise* Italian long before the French had ever seen her, but added to this her relative, Pope Clement, had increased the feeling against her by
failing to keep his promises. At Marseilles Catherine had been
talked of as bringing to the French Crown "three rings,"
Genoa, Milan, and Naples. But Clement, when once the
marriage was effected and he had got back to Italy, had
done nothing to assist the French Crown to gain any one of
these dominions. And when in the following year (1534) the
Pope died, and Catherine was left without even such support
as he afforded her, the feeling against her became intensified.
Nor was this all; to these misfortunes on public grounds was
added a more private one. Catherine's husband, Henry, at
that time a dull, sheepish, and gloomy youth of whom his

father could make nothing, and who on his return from his captivity in Spain three years before had forgotten his own language, disliked her from the first, her brilliancy and cleverness only making his own want of ability the more noticeable. So that the prospect before Catherine was not a bright one: in a foreign country, disliked by her husband, hated by the French nation, despised as a low-born foreigner, and with enemies all around watching for an opportunity of bringing some charge against her which would enable France to get rid of her.

In 1535, two years after her marriage, Catherine heard of the tragic death of her cousin Ippolito, basely poisoned by the hated Alessandro. It must have been a severe blow to her, as he was not only a cousin to whom she was much attached, but also almost her last living relative. Seldom has any one been left at her age so absolutely alone in the world; her aunt Clarice (her father's only sister) was long since dead; her distant relative, Pope Clement, had died in the previous year; and now her only cousin, Ippolito, being also gone, she had no living relations at all, except her father's first cousin, Maria Salviati, who after Catherine's marriage had practically retired from the world. Catherine's isolated state in this respect naturally much increased the difficulty of her position, as she was thus without that powerful support of influential relations which others in like cases have generally possessed. So that this girl of sixteen, confronted by so many adverse conditions, had nothing but her own ability and strength of character upon which to depend.

In August 1536, when she had been married nearly three years, her husband's elder brother, the Dauphin Francis, who, ever since his harsh confinement in Spain as a boy, had continued in weak health,[29] died suddenly at Tournon. This death of his eldest son was a terrible blow to Francis I, all whose affection was centered on the Dauphin. On hearing at Lyons that he was ill, the King at once prepared to go to him, when, just as he was starting, came the news of his death.

And we have a vivid picture drawn of the King's grief, and of how on receiving the terrible news he knelt at the window of his palace, before the whole people, who deeply sympathised with him, and prayed for his son, for his people, and for himself.

It was, of course, immediately said by almost the whole nation that the Dauphin Francis had been poisoned by "the Italian woman," in order that her husband might become the heir to the throne. There has never been found a single particle of foundation for the charge, and every historian considers it was simply due to the national prejudice against Catherine. The accusation was not even based on unpopularity arising from any conduct of her own; for she had been too short a time in France, and too little prominent publicly, to be much known by the people. However, the charge was investigated; the Dauphin's cup-bearer, Montecuculli, was accused of having been the agent, and was tortured to make him reveal by whom he had been employed to commit the crime asserted; and under torture, so far from implicating Catherine in any way, he declared the Emperor Charles V to have been the author of the crime, and adhered to this even at his execution. It is, however, believed that this was almost certainly equally untrue, and it has been pointed out that "a dubious testimony uttered under the anguish of torture is far less credible than the cause assigned by the most unprejudiced historians, viz., that the Dauphin, who was of a sickly constitution, died of having drunk too freely of cold water after over-heating himself at tennis, and not of poison at all." In any case, there is admitted to have been no ground for the accusation against Catherine. But when a prejudice once exists everything that occurs strengthens it, and even the result of Montecuculli's trial did not cause the people to lay aside their suspicion against her. Francis I, however, in spite of his grief, did not share this view, and after the death of the Dauphin lavished every kindness upon her, as though desiring to compensate for the unjust suspicion of his subjects.

This event changed very materially Catherine's position and prospects. Hitherto she and her husband had had no higher destiny to anticipate than that of becoming Duke and Duchess of Milan or some similar state whenever the contest between Francis I and Charles V should come to an end. Now, however, they would in due course become King and Queen of France. But this, though it promoted Catherine to a higher dignity and greater importance at the French court than hitherto, by no means improved her position in other ways. For the wound given to the French by her marriage, grievous when she was merely marrying the second son of their King, was greatly increased by her now becoming the Dauphine, wife of the heir to the throne.

Each year seemed to bring some fresh increase to the difficulties of Catherine's position and the sorrow of her lot. When in the first year after the marriage Pope Clement, her chief bulwark against French disfavour, died; when again in the following year the cousin she had been fond of was murdered, and she was left alone in the world; and when again in the third year the French people persisted in accusing her of having poisoned her brother-in-law notwithstanding every evidence of her innocence, each of these things added yet another drop to a cup which was an unusually bitter one to be drunk by a girl of seventeen. And now there began a still harder trial, one which was to last for twenty years. About the year 1540, when he was twenty-two, her taciturn young husband, Henry, fell completely under the dominion of Diane de Poictiers, the beautiful widow of the Seneschal of Normandy. She ruled him entirely, becoming the leader of the party of the Dauphin at the court (in opposition to the party of the King, which was led by the Duchesse d'Etampes), while Catherine had to stand aside and see herself put in every way in the background, openly insulted by Diane de Poictiers (who took every opportunity of showing her affronts), and neglected by Henry, who spent most of his time at Diane's great estate of Anet. Catherine bore it in silence and with

excellent tact (which was remarked upon with approval even
by Francis I, who was greatly irritated by his son's treatment
of her); but the way the iron entered into her soul is disclosed by her letters long afterwards to her favourite daughter, in one or two touching allusions to this sorrow borne for
years in silence.

About this time a fashionable craze for Protestantism set
in at the French court. One outcome of this was a passion
for Marot's French psalms, and each person was to be heard
singing his or her favourite one on all occasions. We are told
that Catherine took a particular affection for one beginning
"Vers l'Eternel, des oppressés le Père," which was for ever
on her lips, and no doubt appealed to her in consequence of
her husband's coldness and neglect, and the prejudice against
her evinced by the French people.

The portrait of Catherine, painted at this time, when she
was twenty-one years of age, is that which has always been
the picture of her preserved in her own family. Though not
possessing beauty, she has a fine intelligent face, with the
Medici eyes, a broad forehead, and fair hair, the picture thus
agreeing exactly with the descriptions of her given by Suriano,
Vasari, and others at this time.[30] This portrait of her was
permanently kept by the Medici family with their other
family portraits in their principal villa of Poggio a Caiano,
where it and they still hang. The villa and its contents passed
from the Medici Grand Dukes to their successors, the Austrian Grand Dukes, and from the latter to the King of Italy,
being now the royal villa in Tuscany. Although the painter's
name has been lost, the crown, the historic pearls, the agreement with the descriptions of contemporary writers, and
above all the locality in which the portrait has always been
preserved, leave no doubt as to its authentic character.
Painted for Catherine in France by an Italian artist, it was
most probably sent by her as a present to her relative, Cosimo
I, at the time of his marriage in 1539 to Eleonora di Toledo.

In 1542 another trouble came upon Catherine. Now twenty-three, she had been married for nine years and had no children. This was not only the sorrow it would in any case have been, but also it increased very materially the opportunity of those who had always desired to see her put away, and the slur upon the honour of France removed. Diane de Poictiers did not fail to find here another occasion for wounding the neglected wife whom she hated; this she did by making a sneering allusion to Francis I on the subject in the hearing of those who, she knew, would repeat it to Catherine. This was followed by a sort of family conclave at which the matter was formally discussed; and at this Diane, strange to say, was also present, and deliberately urged upon the King that Catherine ought to be divorced; to which Francis I was reported to have agreed, as being inevitable. At this time only one person showed any kindness to Catherine; moved by pity for the many things she had to bear, Marguerite of Angoulême, Queen of Navarre, Francis I's deservedly beloved sister, wrote to Catherine to comfort her, telling her, "My brother will never allow this repudiation, as evil tongues pretend." Re-assured by this sympathy, Catherine went to Francis I and offered to resign her husband and enter a convent, if he willed it. The Venetian ambassador, Lorenzo Contarini, in his report, says:—

"She went to the King and with many tears told him she had heard it was His Majesty's intention to give his son another wife, and as it had not yet pleased God to bestow on her the grace of having children, it was proper that as soon as His Majesty found it undesirable to wait longer, he should provide for the succession to so great a throne; that, for her part, considering the great obligation she was under to His Majesty, who had deigned to accept her as a daughter-in-law, she was much more disposed to endure this affliction than to attempt to oppose his will."

Francis bade her have no fear, and assured her that he would not allow her to be put away. And in the following year this particular trouble was removed from Catherine by the birth of a son, born at Fontainebleau, who was named Francis after his grandfather. Between 1543 and 1555 she had ten children; three of these died in infancy, but of the remaining seven, four were sons, three of whom (Francis, Charles, and Henry) in turn sat on the throne of France, and three daughters, Elizabeth, who married Philip II of Spain, Claude, who married the Duke of Lorraine, and Marguerite, who married Henry of Navarre.

In 1547, when Catherine was twenty-eight, and had been married fourteen years, Francis I died, and her husband became Henry II of France. This intensified for Catherine both of the evils which she had borne so long in prudent and dignified silence, but with an aching heart. The supposed insult to France in her person, great at her marriage, and greater still when she became the Dauphine, seemed to the French greatest of all now that she was Queen of France; consequently her unpopularity with the people became more pronounced than ever.

But still more than this did Henry's exaltation to the throne increase that which was the chief sorrow of Catherine's life. Henry was now twenty-nine, and no longer dull and stupid as he had been as a youth. Though often given to depression, and fonder of hunting and pleasure than of attending to the affairs of his kingdom, his character had strengthened and improved; and Catherine secretly loved him intensely, though he did not in the least return her affection. It is the opinion of all authorities that the one real passion of Catherine's life was for Henry; but he himself (stated by one of the Protestant writers of the time to be "intoxicated by that baggage, Diane") never either appreciated it, or was even aware of it. And his accession began the great triumph of "Diane de Poictiers, the beautiful huntress, she whom Jean Goujon has sculptured, nude and triumphant, embracing with marble

arms a mysterious stag, enamoured like Leda's swan; Diane
de Poictiers, the wondrous woman of eternal youth, the
elderly Alcina, who, to charm a youthful Roger, has discovered the fountain of youth; Diane de Poictiers, whom
Primaticcio's frescoes at Fontainebleau sometimes represent
as the luminous Queen of Night, and sometimes as a sombre
Hecate surrounded by eternal fires." [31] Henry's accession to
the throne gave opportunity to Diane to show all her power
over him; and this in a manner which in no other age or
country would have been possible. Though she was forty-
eight and Henry only twenty-nine, his infatuation for her was
such that he entirely resigned to her both himself and his
kingdom; a surrender so complete that his contemporaries
credited Diane with the possession of an enchanted ring or
some other magic power.

"We are not in a natural world. This is an enchantment;
and it can only be carried out by violent spells and dramatic
strokes. The Armida of fifty years, who holds a king of thirty
in bonds, must daily use her magic wand." [32]

Henry exalted fidelity to her into a virtue; all his leisure
hours were spent with her; and at her estate at Anet, "In
thickets of myrtle and roses, amidst statues, fountains, and
gushing springs, in the depths of dark and game-abounding
forests, the King leads an enchanted existence."

Catherine had none of those attractions which her rival so
potently possessed. Her charms were those of intellect only;
and though these had been strong enough to greatly please
her husband's capable father, Francis I, they had no power to
attract the duller nature of Henry. Thus there now began
for Catherine a twelve years' torment, self-repression being
her hourly task. Diane de Poictiers, created by Henry Duchess
of Valentinois, practically ruled all things. At Henry's coronation she occupied the chief place; even the special taxes levied
on the accession of a new king were bestowed upon her; she
disposed of all offices, both secular and ecclesiastical; she

absorbed lands and wealth in every direction; while Catherine was left to live at the gloomy castle of Chaumont,[33] Diane's splendid residences of Anet and Chenonceaux were made by her almost regal in magnificence; the Guises (the six sons of Claude, Duke of Guise),[34] at this time her faithful vassals, were promoted to all the chief offices in the kingdom; and no meeting of his council was attended by Henry until he had first discussed with Diane the matters to be brought before it.

While such was the position with regard to Henry and Diane, Catherine the Queen had to lead a retired, self-contained existence, making herself as little obtrusive as possible, careful over every word and look lest she should give opportunity to those who watched for grounds on which she might be accused of some crime and got rid of. She had to see her ability shrouded and given no opportunity for exercise, her rightful position usurped by a woman twenty years older than herself, and far less talented, her birth and family scorned and ridiculed,[35] her advice never sought by her husband, and herself despised and insulted by a court and people who took their cue from him. Moreover, Diane de Poictiers "delighted in devising constant slights and veiled insults [36] against the 'Italian woman.' " While perhaps more galling still was her insisting, when Catherine's children were born, in installing herself as head nurse, and as M. Georges Guiffrey says,[37] "Monopolising the cradles, and settling all questions regarding the newly born," taking entire management of everything, nursing Catherine, receiving letters from the court physicians complimenting her upon her care over the Queen, and from Henry a salary "on account of the good, praiseworthy, and agreeable services she hath rendered to our dear and much loved companion, the Queen." And yet when Catherine's son Charles was born (1550), Henry left the Queen three days after his son's birth, and went to stay at Anet with Diane, an act which even in those days was considered an unexampled breach of royal etiquette.

The above shows us a state of things such as could have

occurred only in France, and at that period. At first sight we
are inclined to wonder how Catherine could have endured all
this. But that which caused its chief bitterness was at the same
time that which enabled her to endure it, viz., that through it
all she had a strong passion of love for her husband. It was
this which caused Catherine to endure all these things without
showing a sign. Strange as this fact may seem, we have it
vouched for by two unimpeachable witnesses, viz., by those
observant onlookers, the Venetian ambassadors, and by her
own letters years afterwards. The ambassador, Contarini,
writes:—

"At the opening of the reign the Queen could not endure
this love of the King for the Duchess; but later, *by reason
of the urgent prayers of the King,* she resigned herself, and
now she bears it with patience."

It was because Catherine loved Henry so strongly, and knew
that the only way by which she could retain even such small
portion of his regard as she possessed, was to endure uncomplainingly all that such a position entailed, that she patiently,
and without ever once reproaching him, bore for twelve years
a combination of exasperating mortifications such as would
have driven most women into furious resentment. In the
latter case the court would have been turned into the same
state of disgraceful turmoil as resulted when, about sixty
years later, the same conditions caused Marie de' Medici to
resent the conduct of her husband, Henry IV.[38] The behaviour of a weak character when placed in such circumstances
is exemplified by Marie, that of a strong one by Catherine;
and severe though the trial was, the latter reaped her reward,
not only in the respect which she earned from many for the
manner in which she bore it, as well as the satisfaction to herself in preserving the court from scenes similar to those afterwards witnessed in Marie's case, but also in retaining a
certain portion of her husband's regard.[39] And there is considerable dignity in the way in which, years afterwards, she

makes, in writing to her eldest daughter Elizabeth, then Queen of Spain, the only direct mention of this trial which she ever permitted to pass her lips; as well as in the terms in which on another occasion she wrote to reprove her son-in-law, Henry of Navarre, for his infidelities to his wife. At the time when the Regency of the kingdom had just devolved upon her, and when she was oppressed by many heavy cares, she writes to her daughter Elizabeth, about two years after the latter's marriage, as follows:—

"*M'amie*, commend yourself very much to God; for you have seen me in former days as contented as you are now, and believing that I should never have any trouble but this one that I was not loved in the way I wished by the King, your father, who doubtless honoured me beyond my deserts; but I loved him so much that I was always afraid of offending him, as you know well enough. And now God has taken him from me. . . . Therefore think of me, and let me serve as a warning to you not to trust too much in the love of your husband." [40]

Writing towards the end of her life to Henry of Navarre, she says:—

"My son, I was never in my life so dumbfounded as when I heard the words which Frontenac has been reporting everywhere as being those which you ordered him to convey to your wife. . . . You are not, I know, the first husband who is young and not too wise in such matters, but I believe that you are the first, and the only one, who after such events would venture on such language to his wife. I had the honour of marrying the King, my lord and your sovereign, whose daughter you have married, but the thing which vexed him most in the world was after he found out that I knew about such doings." [41]

These letters shed a flood of light on Catherine's character; but apart from this, the two allusions to Henry II which they contain show very plainly why it was that Catherine deliberately endured in silence for twelve years the heavy trial which has been mentioned, and at the same time how deeply she felt it, since the memory of it remained with her so many years afterwards.

But Diane de Poictiers did not confine herself to affronts in connection with private matters. From 1552 to 1558 France was at war both in Germany and Italy, and when Henry proceeded on the German campaign Diane contrived a severe public indignity to Catherine by persuading him not to give the Regency during his absence to the Queen, though this course had always been usual in such cases. The insult was the more severe in that Catherine was by far the most capable person at the court; that she felt it severely we know both from her letters and her speech on the occasion; while it did her the greatest harm with the people, lowering her greatly in their estimation and increasing their long-standing contempt for her. Nevertheless when, on Henry's departure to the war, the order communicating this decision was read to her, we are informed by a letter from a friend at the court to the Constable Montmorency that she "only smiled, and said that though it had pleased the King not to give her this authority which His Majesty Francis I gave on a similar occasion to his mother, Louise, and though she would have used it well had he done so, yet it was not her intention to ask him to redress the wrong. Only, she said, she would prefer not to have the order published, 'lest it should lower her reputation with the people.' " No wonder that those who heard her words and saw her receive such an affront in such a manner, marvelled openly at her "wonderful self-control."

Such, then, was the trial which lasted through so large a portion of Catherine's life. And it was this severe ordeal (involving through so many years a daily and almost hourly exercise of self-control) which both tested, and formed, her character. She was only twenty when this trial began, and had shown by her history as a girl that she possessed her full share

of that tendency to emotion natural to one of Italian blood;
thus for her to learn self-control was more difficult than for
women of northern race, like Elizabeth of England or Jeanne
d'Albret of France. Nevertheless, through the long discipline
of twenty years, she grew from an emotional girl into a
woman in whom the power of self-control was so developed
that it amazed all who saw it in exercise. Those who looked
merely on the surface saw only "indifference," or in some
cases duplicity; while it is, of course, possible to argue that
all self-control is duplicity. But to those who saw deeper (as
it is plain from their reports that some of the Venetian ambassadors did) the real character was evident enough. And
the combination of the endurance displayed, the motive for
which the trial was submitted to, and the dignified manner in
which the burden was borne, irresistibly impress us.

It is necessary to notice, in view of the traditional idea regarding her, that during the whole of this portion of her life,
i.e., up to the age of forty, there are no tales of crimes alleged
against Catherine de' Medici. Ground for such a charge was
the very thing for which her numerous enemies watched in order to get her divorced; but they never were able to produce
any. All the charges of that kind [42] relate to the period of her
life after she was forty.

At last, in August 1557, when Catherine was thirty-eight,
she had her first opportunity of showing her abilities. During
the absence of the King in Champagne the main French army
under the Constable Montmorency was totally defeated at
the battle of St. Quentin by Emmanuel Philibert, who in 1553
had succeeded his father as Duke of Savoy. Montmorency
himself was taken prisoner; northern France was left completely defenceless; Spain was jubilant at this crushing defeat of the French arms; and a general panic took place in
Paris. In this time of national emergency it was not Diane de
Poictiers (though her ascendency over all affairs of the kingdom was still continuing) who came to the front, but Cath-

erine, Diane being as helpless in the crisis as every one else.
The disaster was stupendous.

"History has related what were our losses; immense, un-
heard of since Pavia. . . . The first shock of the news was
overwhelming; France was stunned by the blow. Already
Paris believed the enemy within the walls, and the realm
captured. In the capital the citizens packed their possessions
and fled, some to Orleans, some to Bourges, some still further. . . . To stop the flight, to rouse energy, to sound in the
ears of France those words able to arouse the dead, 'The
country in danger,' this was the imperative duty of whoever
governed. But the King was absent; only the Queen was in
Paris. What did the Queen? I leave the Venetian ambassador
to reply." [43]

Giacomo Soranzo, the Venetian ambassador at that time, in
his report of the 14th August 1557, relates that Catherine at
once went to the *Parlement*,[44] urged on them not to lose heart
(as they were ready to do), but to vigorously prosecute the
war, and to vote large subsidies for the defence of the kingdom; and she showed so much courage, wisdom, and ability,
that she was not only completely successful, but received an
immense ovation from the members of the *Parlement*.

"She expressed herself with so much eloquence and feeling that she touched all hearts. . . . And the assembly concluded amidst such applause for Her Majesty, and such
lively marks of satisfaction at her conduct, as cannot be described in words. All over the city nothing is talked about
but the Queen's prudence, and the happy way in which she
acted in this undertaking." [45]

Thus did Catherine, on the first occasion in which she had
an opportunity of showing her powers, overcome (for a time,
at all events) the prejudice which the French people had
nourished against her for so many years.

"Her action gave all the more surprise because it was so little expected. Catherine de' Medici by this act raised the veil of unconcern with politics to which the force of circumstances had until now condemned her. . . . It was the first hour of her initiative, the first evidence of that personality which she was later on to raise to so high a degree. . . . She revealed herself as Queen, and gave evidence to the Parisians that the blood of the nation had become her own blood." [46]

Nor was it only in the French people that Catherine, by the qualities which she showed in this her first public action, produced a change of opinion regarding herself; Henry was greatly impressed with her conduct on this occasion, and after the episode entirely changed his mode of behaviour towards her, henceforth during the remaining two years of his life treating her on all occasions with marked respect.

During the twelve years of her life as Queen, Catherine, shut out from State affairs, found her main occupation in the education of her children. This she undertook almost entirely herself, and the manner in which she performed it was considered by those around her to show a laudable example of devoted attention and good sense. Her sons (who all inherited, in a more pronounced degree, their father's want of ability) soon passed under other instructors,[47] but her three daughters, Elizabeth (born 1545), Claude (born 1547), and Marguerite (born 1553), were taught entirely by Catherine herself. With her three young daughters Catherine also brought up Mary, Queen of Scots, who, born in 1542 and brought to France at the age of five, was the eldest of the four girls. The list of the various translations, essays, and exercises set them by Catherine is still to be seen, and shows how thorough was her teaching and how wide its range. To the little Mary she dictates the following to be translated by her into Latin:—

"The true grandeur and excellence of a prince, my very dear sister, does not consist in honours, in gold, in purple,

and other luxuries of fortune, but in prudence, wisdom, and
knowledge. And by so much as the prince wishes to differ
from his people in his mode and fashion of living, by so much
should he be removed from the foolish opinions of the vulgar. Adieu and love me as much as you can." [48]

It is strange to remember that at the very time that Catherine was teaching Mary these principles, Diane de Poictiers
was taking every opportunity to teach the latter to despise
her as "La fille de marchands."

Catherine's daughters were brought up with exceeding
strictness, Catherine being all her life a very great stickler for
les convenances. It is extraordinary to note from their letters
how greatly her children admired her, and how much they
thought of it when they won her praise. This was not confined
to one, but is common to them all. Her favourite daughter was
the eldest, Elizabeth; the youngest Marguerite (she who
afterwards proved such a thorn to her husband), was the most
troublesome even at that age, and in her letters she tells us so,
and that at times she had even to be beaten. But she admired
her mother just as much as did the rest.

The last year of Henry II's reign was a time of important
marriages, and festivities, pageants, and *fêtes* in connection
therewith such as Henry loved. On the 24th April 1558, Catherine's eldest son Francis was married to Mary, Queen of
Scots, both of them being fifteen years of age. This wedding
was arranged on the grandest scale, with every accessory
that could add picturesque effect. A gallery hung with vine
branches laden with grapes was constructed from the Bishop's
palace to the door of the cathedral of Notre Dame, in front
of which was placed the royal dais; and as the brilliant *cortège* approached the dais, heralds flung gold and silver among
the crowd, until they had to desist owing to the scramble for
it creating so great a disturbance. The young bride, "dressed
all in white and looking like a lily, and wearing a crown blazing with diamonds, sapphires, and emeralds," took her place

under the portico, where the marriage ceremony was performed by the Archbishop of Rouen, the wedding ring being handed to him by the King, who drew it from his own finger. After which Mass was celebrated inside the cathedral, the bride and bridegroom occupying a throne under a canopy of cloth of gold. In the evening there was a ball at the palace of Les Tournelles, combined with "masques and mummeries" in the Palais de Justice, at which the children of the Dukes of Guise and Aumale rode on artificial horses caparisoned with gold and silver trappings and drawing coaches filled with gorgeously dressed pilgrims. These were followed by six ships covered with crimson velvet, and imitating as they moved the rolling motion of the sea, in the foremost of which embarked the King and the young bride, in the next the Dauphin and Catherine, in the third the Duke of Lorraine and the Princess Claude, and so on, the ships then sailing round the great hall, "which was illuminated as much by the blaze of jewels worn by the company as by the torches and cressets." [49]

This was followed a year later by the two marriages, in June 1559, of Henry's sister Marguerite to Emmanuel Philibert, Duke of Savoy, and of his and Catherine's eldest daughter Elizabeth, then fourteen, to Philip II of Spain,[50] this latter marriage being by proxy. The pageants and *fêtes* in connection with these two marriages went on for many days, and concluded with a grand tournament held in front of the palace of Les Tournelles on the 30th June, in which the King himself took part, and which was witnessed by "four Queens" —Catherine, her daughter Elizabeth, Mary, Queen of Scots, and Marguerite. Catherine's celebrated astrologer, Gaurico, had some time before predicted that Henry would be fatally wounded in a duel at the age of forty, and had repeated this prediction a week before the tournament; and Catherine had grave fears about Henry's taking part in the contest, and endeavoured to dissuade him from doing so; but he was bent upon it. As he rode into the lists a boy in the crowd cried out: "Sire, do not tilt"; but no one paid any attention to it, nor did the boy himself, when afterwards interrogated, know why he had been moved to cry out. After several courses in which Henry was victorious he sent Catherine a message that he "would try one more bout for love of her." He did so; his opponent Montgomery's [51] lance pierced Henry's eye; and, to the horror of the whole assemblage, the King fell from his horse mortally wounded. He was at once carried into the Tournelles palace, lingered for ten days in great agony, and then died.

On this terrible conclusion to the tournament the greatest confusion pervaded the court, while, as soon as it was known that the King was in a dying state, all public affairs were thrown into the utmost disorder. In this emergency the Queen came forward as alone having the right to assume the management of affairs. And her first exercise of authority was to order the Duchess of Valentinois to depart to her own house. But Catherine never at any time during her life showed a revengeful spirit, and upon Henry's death she allowed Diane de Poictiers to retain possession of her magnificent château of Anet, contenting herself with forbidding her the court, and requiring Diane to resign her other château of Chenonceaux [52] in exchange for that castle of Chaumont which Catherine never desired to see again.

Catherine's grief at Henry's death was immense. For several days she would not speak, and when the Venetian ambassador came to condole with her, he says that she received him in a room of which both walls and floor were all covered with black, as well as everything in the room, while she herself could scarcely speak to him. From this time forth she always wore heavy mourning and a widow's veil, and adopted a new motto, *Lachrymae hinc, hinc dolor*. Nor was this grief simulated; all writers have considered that in these various signs of grief there was no pretence. She who for so many years had so hidden her feelings that many declared her to have none, could not hide them now; she had lost the one love of her life, a blow felt all the more because the man whom she thus mourned had never known how much she loved him, nor returned her affection; and for a time she shut herself up with her grief in an impenetrable silence.

Thus ended Catherine's married life at the age of forty. We have now to see her in a new rôle, one in which the powers and abilities which had so long been allowed no exercise were at last to have full scope.

CHAPTER XX

Born 1519. (*Married* 1533.) *Died* 1589

(2) THE LAST THIRTY YEARS OF HER LIFE

THE period on which we now enter is a strange one, full of
the most violent contrasts. The latter half of the sixteenth
century in France is a time when all the elements of tragic
drama are at their height. Only the music of a Wagner could
do it justice. Rivers of blood flow. Lives are thrown away for
a bagatelle. "Balls alternate with massacres." At one moment
thunder, lightning, and dark clouds; at the next a blue sky,
the soft sound of music, and sunshine amidst gardens of
roses. Stilettos ornamented with pearls. French gaiety and
wit even in the midst of terror and death. One thing only
stable, a universal courage. Such are the characteristics of
an epoch in which two streams, the barbarism of the Middle
Ages and the refinement of more modern times, met in a
conflict of tossing waves before the former was finally overcome by the latter.

The women of this period are peculiar to their time, differing entirely from those of any other century; and properly
to appreciate any one of them we have to realise the exceptional atmosphere in which they lived, and of which they
formed so prominent a part. Fearless, capable, learned, vivacious, full of energy and common-sense, half Pagan and
half Christian, deeply religious at one moment and at another consulting astrologers and purchasing love potions,
riding like Amazons, fond of danger and dressing, music and

love, assisting at tournaments, accustomed to bloody sights and cruel sufferings at a period when all held their lives by a very slender thread, a mixture of laughter and tears and Stoicism, they are full of contrasts and surprises, while yet at all times intensely human and intensely interesting.

And where such women found themselves placed in positions in which, in an age of fierce conflict and violent passions they were called upon to govern states, they perforce developed the qualities necessary to such conditions. Thus of Jeanne d'Albret, niece of Francis I, and mother of Henry of Navarre, it has been said that she was "a Queen in whom nothing was woman but her sex, a soul wholly given to manly things, a mind capable of great affairs, a heart invincible by adversities"; [1] and the same might have been said of either Catherine de' Medici or Elizabeth of England. All three of them were like women of iron; and had need to be so. It was an age in which, in addition to the greatest ability, the qualities required, in order to obtain for those over whom they ruled the one blessing which is the greatest of all to a country —the blessing of peace,—were a will of adamant, a rigid impassibility, a steadfastness unconquerable. And it is to misunderstand the whole epoch to condemn them for not possessing those qualities which we admire in women rulers in our age, and for possessing those sterner characteristics which were the need of their time if they were to preserve those over whom they were set from the most grievous evils. Such a character, for instance, as that of our deservedly honoured Queen Victoria would in that age have been simply crushed, and would have been of no use to poor passion-tossed France. In stormy weather ships' anchors must be made of iron, not of gold.

And in coming to this third period of Catherine's life we reach a stormy time indeed. M. Imbert de Saint-Amand, referring to the dangers which lay before her on coming to power, says:—

"Never had a more overwhelming burden rested on a woman's shoulders. A Blanche of Castile's force of soul would not have been great enough to struggle against the tempests about to be let loose on France." [2]

The period of Catherine's life which now begins—the thirty years from 1559 to 1589—is that of the reigns of her three sons, who in turn succeeded each other. Her eldest son, Francis II, coming to the throne at sixteen, only reigned for a year and a half (1559-1560). Her second son, Charles IX, succeeded his brother at the age of ten, and reigned for fourteen years (1560-1574). Her third son, Henry III, succeeding his brother at the age of twenty-three, reigned for fifteen years (1574-1589). During the seventeen months of her eldest son's reign, Catherine had little more power than before her husband's death, Francis II being entirely ruled by her opponents, the Guises; but during nearly the whole of her second son's reign Catherine was Queen Regent of France, while during her third son's reign she was, though not Regent, the most important of his advisers, striving to keep his indolent and foolish character from bringing his throne to disaster. Thus during nearly thirty years she was the most important person in France. Before coming to the detailed history of those years it will be well to glance at the task by which she was confronted, the qualities she possessed for coping with it, and the general characteristics of this the most important of the three periods of her life. And although during the first seventeen months of this period she did not obtain the control of affairs, yet this space of time being so short we may disregard it for the moment and look at these thirty years as a whole.

First, then, as to the evidence on which we have to rely. Controversy has raged for three centuries over the events of this period; with the result that the evidence by which we have to judge of Catherine's character and conduct during this portion of her life is to the last degree conflicting. By some she is represented as without ability, discernment, or breadth of view, full of vacillations and shifty compromises, acting as the moment prompted, one whose only motive was a lust for sovereignty, an intriguer working out the tangled schemes of a changeable and baleful policy, and caught in her own snares. According to others she was endowed with an ability and power of discernment seldom seen upon a throne, one who brought to the cause of a distracted country a power of endurance in adhering to a wise but difficult course, an intelligence, and a strength of character worthy of the highest praise. Thus she is by some represented as the ruin, and by others as the salvation of France.

But while writers of the former class are steadily tending to become less credited as fuller information becomes available,[3] they also frequently refute each other. Thus, those who have held her responsible for the massacre on St. Bartholomew's Day are contradicted by so great an authority as the historian Michelet, who in his antipathy to "the Italian woman" will not allow to her ability or importance of any kind, treating her with cold disdain, calling her a "nonentity," and saying:—"Never had she either the idea or the courage required (for such a massacre). . . . Her admirer Tavannes overrates her, I consider, and exaggerates in attributing to her the idea of Coligny's death." [4] To this a later writer, M. Armand Baschet, nourishing an almost equally strong feeling against Catherine, vigorously responds:—"Desiring to be more than true, you are worse than false. . . . To listen to you, one would think Catherine de' Medici knew not even the first word about politics"; pointing out that in thus acquitting Catherine of having caused Coligny's death, Michelet destroys his own argument, by acquitting her of that which is the chief charge against her.[5] Honoré de Balzac, on the other hand, while he praises her living chastely in the midst of the most licentious court in Europe, considers that the enormous crimes and destruction which were being committed throughout France by the Protestants justified even such a massacre as that of St. Bartholomew's Day; thus exonerating Catherine on grounds which admit all that her worst enemies have said. A fourth authority, Brantôme (who lived in the midst of all these events), remarks:—"She has been strongly accused of the Paris massacre. . . . There were at least three or four others who might be more justly accused of it than she"; while he is never tired of praising her goodness, her wisdom, her peace-making endeavours, and "her grief at seeing so many nobles and people perish" in these bitter contests which were rending France. Lastly, a recent writer of her life, after admitting her freedom from prejudice, her tolerance, patience, and self-control, and that she gave no cause for scandal, asserts that none of these qualities in her were deserving of any praise, but were all due to bad motives, adding:—"We shall follow her in these pages with admiration, but with hatred." [6]

The above afford an example of the conflicting opinions on the subject of Catherine's conduct during these thirty years. As before, however, our safest guides will be those dispassionate onlookers, the Venetian ambassadors, who one after another were accredited to the court of France. Their secret reports to their own government, those actions of hers which are admitted by all, and lastly her own letters, will together form a more reliable guide to the truth regarding Catherine de' Medici than the writings of any other authorities that could be produced.

Catherine was now, at the age of forty, at the full maturity of her mental powers, and with an ample sphere for their exercise at last opening before her. The long years of obscurity and repression had disciplined and matured her character, her abilities were at their zenith, and her knowledge and experience had been ripened by her having stood as an onlooker, watching the movements of the political world of France during twenty-six years with the discernment which she so abundantly possessed. There is ample proof in her letters that she intended to undo the harm which incapacity during the previous twelve years had produced, to pacify the passions which had been aroused by unjust and short-sighted methods of government, to bring the country to peace, advance its prosperity, and raise it high in the estimation of other countries. The crest and motto which she had adopted at her marriage was a rainbow with the words, "I bring light and serenity"; and it is admitted on all hands that on coming to power she strove earnestly to carry out this motto.

But unfortunately for Catherine a widespread movement was sweeping over Europe which made all such achievements for the time impossible. The great conflict over religion which had so long been tearing Germany to pieces was now spreading to France; Geneva and Rome were beginning to make that country their battleground.[7] Already during the latter part of Henry II's reign (under the influence of Diane de Poictiers, an ardent opponent of the new religion) there had been cruel persecutions and executions on account of religion. By the time that Catherine became Queen Regent the two hostile forces had become ranged against each other; and soon a religious war—that most vindictive of all wars—raged over France, tearing the country to pieces, devastating its cities, maddening its people, and making permanent peace unattainable even by the wisest administrator until such time as the force of religious animosity had spent itself by the sacrifice of a hecatomb of noble lives. Throughout the whole period covered by the reigns of Catherine's second and third sons did this contest last, and for five years beyond it. Thus it was her ill fate to have to rule France during just that period which the effects of the Reformation would have caused to be the most tempestuous time in that country's history whoever had been on the throne.

However, when Catherine began her task these things were hidden in the future; and the manner in which she endeavoured to cope with it has won praise from numberless high authorities. The difficulties were immense. France was torn by a furious conflict between the Protestants (called in France, the Huguenots) and the Roman Catholics, who plotted and warred ceaselessly against each other, while each endeavoured to get the throne on their side—even by force, if in no other way.[8] In this state of things Catherine's determined policy was to refuse to take either side, and to endeavour to create peace between these implacable foes by compelling them to learn mutual toleration and by holding an equal balance between them. When about eighty years later the same sort of struggle took place in England the King took a side, with results which were disastrous to both throne and country. It was just this which Catherine foresaw, and struggled all the years of her power to avoid; and she shows considerable statesmanship in having set this endeavour before her. Catherine (more successful than Charles I) saved her son's throne, and again and again wrought peace between the two parties by her policy; but she did so at the price, which was inevitable, that both parties in turn abused her as double-minded. Every concession, or even bare measure of justice, to one side was immediately seized upon by the other as an offence, and asserted to be a departure from some previous concession to themselves, and to show dissimulation on her part. Nevertheless Catherine steadfastly maintained her course, though opposed by every sort of difficulty. She had the wisdom to choose as her Chancellor and chief adviser the enlightened and temperate Protestant, Michel de l'Hôpital, and with his assistance she was enabled to steer the course she had elected to follow with at times considerable success; though under the conditions in which France then was no peace brought about could be lasting.

That she was not understood goes without saying; the course she was trying to carry out was many years in advance of her time; she was endeavouring to act as a constitutional sovereign would in these days, and to follow a policy of equal toleration to all which did not come into fashion among the nations of Europe until some two hundred years afterwards. Catherine exhausted every method of reconciliation; she passed measures favouring one side as much as the other; she gave appointments to Protestants as well as to Roman Catholics; she made mortal enemies like the Duke of Guise and the Prince of Condé embrace each other; she had as many Protestant ladies-in-waiting as she had Roman Catholics; whereas in 1555 there had been only one Protestant church in France, six years later there were two thousand. But when a country is in the state in which France was moderate courses are out of favour; the people at such times consider those who act thus to be "lukewarm"; and France was too wild with religious hatred (the fires of which were steadily fanned from Geneva and Rome) to be able to appreciate a tolerant course of action. How little able the age was to understand or value a policy of toleration we may see both from the reports of the (unbiassed) Venetian ambassadors and from those of the (strongly biassed) Spanish ambassador, Chantonnay. The Venetian ambassador, Suriano, writes:—

"It is well known that several of the women who are most intimate with the Queen are suspected of heresy and bad conduct; and everybody is aware that the Chancellor in whom she trusts is an enemy of the Roman Church and of the Pope. We saw, too, how lukewarm were her efforts to protect the Catholic party."

While the Spanish ambassador, Chantonnay, writes to his master, Philip II:—

"Take into consideration that whatever is lawful at Geneva as to sermons, administration of the sacraments, and similar things, may be done with impunity throughout the kingdom, beginning in the King's house."

To this policy Catherine adhered in spite of obstacles which to most would have appeared insurmountable, even sustaining war from Spain rather than abandon it. And it is very significant in connection with the degree of responsibility to be attached to her on account of the massacre on St. Bartholomew's Day in 1572, to find that during the whole of the previous twelve years it was for her *moderation and tolerance* that she was abused by the French, not for conduct of the opposite kind, and that it was contemptuously said of her that she "had the olive branch always in her hand."

Nor do Catherine's own letters (reticent as they are about herself) fail to give corroborative testimony as to what was her endeavour and what her difficulties. Writing after her son Francis II's death to her ambassador in Spain, she says that her endeavour as Queen Regent will be "to rehabilitate by degrees all that the malice of the times [9] has destroyed in this kingdom." While to her daughter Elizabeth she writes that God has taken her brother, "and has left me with three little children and a kingdom so divided that there is not a single person in whom I can wholly trust, and who is not swayed by party passion." [10]

There is no doubt that Catherine possessed all the qualities for a just and wise government of France if only the religious strife could have been put down, or had never arisen; and we have numerous instances given us of the many improvements, even distracted as the country was, which she introduced into the administration. Like all who have greater abilities than their fellows she had a joy in ruling, "un affetto di signoreggiare" as the Venetian ambassador Cavalli calls it. It is a mistake to style this, as some have done, a lust for power; it is a quality which all possess who are fitted to rule. And so far from being a defect in Catherine, it would have shown a culpable want of energy if, endowed as she was with unusual abilities, she had not manifested this love of ruling.

During this third portion of her life, after she had reached the age of forty, Catherine suddenly becomes charged with the wholesale commission of crimes of murder. Regarding this all that need be said here is that the accusation specifies no particular individuals, and that as it begins simultaneously with the religious conflict it is presumable that there is some connection between the two matters. It may also be noted

that it has been held by some well qualified to form an opinion
on such a point, that the ignorance of the science of medicine
at that time precludes the possibility of knowledge of the
subtle poisons which are presupposed in all these cases, and
that on that ground alone these stories should be rejected.
Undoubtedly the people of that age *imagined* that they possessed subtle poisons (and were therefore ready to attribute
death to such methods); just as they thoroughly believed in
witchcraft and the possibility of causing the death of a person
by means of a wax figure transfixed with pins; and just as they
believed in incantations, horoscopes, and the various mys-
teries of their imaginary science of astrology. But they deceived themselves in the one case as much as in the other.
Murders by poison in that age when they did occur generally
show the use of a poison by no means subtle; and any such
murders if committed by Catherine would have been able to
be definitely specified.

In connection with this general accusation almost an entire
literature has gathered round Catherine de' Medici of stories
(based on no foundation, repudiated by historians, and often
directly contradicted by the circumstances) of poisoned
gloves, handkerchiefs, bouquets, and other things of the same
kind.[11] This literature has been preferred to sober history;
but it has been pointed out by Creighton [12] that such stories
"gathered round many prominent characters of that day,
and are a proof, not of the guilt of the person concerned, but
of the low morality of the age." [13] These stories, while they
gratified an appetite for sensation, assisted the endeavours of
political opponents to blacken the character of "the Italian
woman." Among them is the well-known fable of the secret
cupboards in the suite of apartments occupied by Catherine
at the château of Blois, which a later age, in search of sensation, felt sure must have been intended for keeping her
poisons: a story which once passed for history, but has now
been exploded as entirely apocryphal.[14] These ingeniously
contrived cupboards were almost certainly intended for keep-

ing the huge mass of secret correspondence which so prolific a letter-writer as Catherine collected round her, and the copies of those letters which now fill so many volumes of the Secret Records of various countries. There was also another use to which a portion of these cupboards may have been put. Astrology was the fashion of the day, and in connection with it a large paraphernalia of minerals, drugs, and magic substances of many kinds were considered indispensable. Catherine was an ardent votary of this cult, and these cupboards may also have been partly used for this purpose. This taste for astrology surrounded Catherine with an atmosphere of mystery which much assisted the growth round her personality of a literature of the kind mentioned.

Apart, however, from these stories, looked upon by historians in the light of fables, and showing merely the low morality of the age and the bitterness of the religious conflict, there are two murders (and only two) with which Catherine has been definitely charged, one that of Coligny, the other that of Lignerolles, an objectionable associate of her third son Henry who mysteriously disappeared, and was presumably murdered. The former of these cases may be left to be considered when we come to that point in Catherine's history, but the latter may well be mentioned here, since it shows an example of the kind of foundation upon which accusations of this nature were credited in that age and have been handed down to our own.[15] The charge is founded on a single sentence in a contemporary diary, the anonymous writer of which, speaking of Lignerolles's disappearance, curtly states:—"The Queen Mother, with the full consent of her children, had him killed." Knowing as we do that the two parties in France at that time were ready to believe and propagate the wildest stories without any proof, and stuck at nothing in their abuse of a religious opponent, it is impossible to credit any statement of this nature (made by either party) unless it has independent corroboration from State papers or other similar sources. And a single bald statement like this certainly requires it in no ordinary degree. Yet not only is none such forthcoming, but also the statement itself contains its own refutation. For, knowing what we do of Catherine de' Medici, who is there that will believe that she was the sort of person who, intending to commit such a crime, would discuss it beforehand with those daughters (for she could not under the circumstances discuss it with her son Henry himself) about whose character and training she was so abnormally strict; still less that she would obtain from them a "full consent" to this secret murder? Yet this, preposterous as it is, is that which is involved by the statement on which alone this charge rests.

Astrology did not by any means exhaust all Catherine's scientific tastes. She was interested in all branches of science, while both mathematics and mechanics had especially great attractions for her. Another branch of knowledge in which her sound sense is very conspicuous was that of hygiene, in which she was altogether in advance of her time. In opposition to the ideas then prevailing on the subject, she was a strong advocate for plenty of air and exercise, and in her letters to her daughters is found giving them unlimited good advice on this point. She was also much opposed to the conservatism of the day in medical matters, constantly urging the desirability of enquiring into new methods in medicine and surgery, and of taking note of new discoveries in medical science made in other countries

Catherine was a most indefatigable letter-writer. Her letters deal with every imaginable subject, from the most important affairs of international politics down to pleadings on behalf of innumerable *portégés* for whom she desired benefits, and the most minute directions about her children's health and how their clothes were to be made; and all her letters breathe a profound common-sense. M. Armand Baschet says:—

"A just and veracious history of Catherine de' Medici would be impossible without studying her private letters.

Her ability, her penetration, her astonishing facility in over-coming all difficulties, show themselves in all her expressions." [16]

And Michelet himself has said:—

"At the head of the Laubespins, the Pinarts, the Villeroys, and other French secretaries, at the head of the Gondis, the Biragues, and other Italian secretaries, must be placed that untiring female scribe, Catherine de' Medici. If there is no despatch to draw up, she makes up for it by writing letters of politeness, compliment, or condolence, even to private persons." [17]

Reading of this indefatigable letter-writing, which occupied so many hours of each day of Catherine's life, we look with renewed interest at the small *cabinet vert* in her château of Chenonceaux, with her initials carved on the ceiling, which was her boudoir and writing-room, and the place in which the greater part of her mass of letters and minutes on State affairs were written. Her labours were incessant; the Venetian ambassador, Sigismondo Cavalli, says:—

"At table, or while walking, she is unceasingly conversing with some one on affairs; her mind is bent, not merely on political matters, but on so many others, that I do not know how she can endure and go through so much."

M. Battifol [18] states that she was the most extravagant of all the Queens of France; but he adds that she was the one who (owing to her immense dowry) had the richest personal property. Her chief amusement was hunting, of which she was passionately fond, not merely when young, but through-out her life. She had many accidents; on one occasion she broke her leg out hunting, and another time by a severe fall fractured her skull, necessitating the operation of trepanning; but she continued to hunt until nearly sixty years of age. After one of these accidents she writes:—"You ask for news of my fall, so I will tell you that it was a bad and heavy one; but, thank God, I was not much hurt, and am only marked on my nose, like the sheep of Berri." She was the inventress of the side saddle; and it must have required some courage to be the first to attempt to ride a horse in such an entirely new manner. Her son, Charles IX, tells us that she was always very regardless of herself, "for that she was of her nature very slow to complain," and says that she frequently neglected her own health, though so particular about that of her children. She bore pain with the endurance of a Stoic, never complaining. In her old age, when constantly tormented with attacks of rheumatism, she invariably treats the matter with a passing joke at her own infirmities. All writers refer to her unusual courage in danger. When determined to drive the English from France, she insisted, in order to inspire the troops, on taking part personally in the siege of Rouen and entering the battle; and when remonstrated with by the Constable and the Duke of Guise, "only laughed and asked why she should spare herself more than they did." [19]

Her agreeable manners when she came as a bride to France have been already alluded to; on her becoming Queen Regent this characteristic had greater scope, and we find all writers referring to it. Brantôme (always most enthusiastic when speaking of Catherine) expatiates in glowing terms on this point, saying that she was "tall and majestic and of a winning presence," and that "as Queen of France and doing the honours of the court she was most brilliant and magnificent, and nothing ever equalled her." And even Trollope says:—"Catherine the Queen was one of the most graceful mannered women of her time; grave diplomatists were fascinated by her conversation, and learned lawyers charmed by her affability."

Whether it was her fault, or her misfortune, that she acquired a character, among later generations, for exceptional malevolence, and how far the character usually attributed to her has been a just one or the reverse, is a point regarding which the main facts of her life, as they appear in the fuller light now available, are best left to speak for themselves.

Having thus seen what were the chief features of the task before Catherine, and the qualities she possessed for coping with it, we can now glance at the principal events of these last thirty years of her life, and at how she bore herself through the stormiest period of French history.[20]

(1559-1560)

On Henry II's death his eldest son, Francis II, then sixteen, succeeded to the throne. He was sickly in body, and intensely feeble in character, and it might have been thought would certainly have been under the domination of his mother. But the powerful group of brothers, the Guises, whom Diane de Poictiers had placed in the principal offices of the State, were by no means ready to sink into obscurity as she had been obliged to do; and chance now gave all the power into their hands. The feeble-minded youth who had become King was entirely swayed by his young wife, Mary, Queen of Scots, who was now Queen of France as well as of Scotland, and of whom Catherine in her letters at this time writes;—"Our little Scottish Queen has only to smile to turn all Frenchmen's heads." But Mary, herself also only sixteen, cared not at all about politics, and was chiefly bent on amusing herself. She was proud of her two crowns and her beauty, was surrounded by adulation and flattery, and in no mood to be occupied by such dull subjects as affairs of State policy. Therefore she was only too ready to leave the entire management of State affairs to her powerful uncles, the Guises,[21] and the latter almost at once secured complete dominion over the pitiful and contemptible youth, Francis II, using him simply as their tool, and effectually preventing Catherine from having any influence.

Moreover, the religious question helped to strengthen this state of things. Diane de Poictiers had always been the bitter enemy of the new religion, and she and the Guises were determined, now that the latter had complete power, to exercise it by a vigorous stamping out, by the most ruthless methods, of Protestantism in France. And as Catherine was considered to have leanings towards the Protestant party, and at any rate to be exceedingly lukewarm, and certain not to be at all disposed towards the stringent measures which the Guises intended to adopt, they were determined not to allow her to have any control over affairs. So that Catherine, during her eldest son's short reign of seventeen months, though outwardly occupying a more important position owing to the removal from the scene of the Duchess of Valentinois, had practically little more power than she had during her husband's lifetime; and although Francis II began his reign by issuing a decree ordering his mother's authority to be obeyed as if it were his own, this became a dead letter (if it was ever intended to be anything else), and the Guises alone ruled France.[22] To the Duke of Guise Francis by a formal decree gave absolute authority over the whole of the military affairs of the kingdom,[23] and to his brother, Charles de Guise, Cardinal of Lorraine, similar authority over the whole of the civil affairs, while one lucrative office after another was absorbed by them and their brothers. With the entire administration of the kingdom in their hands, the ambition of this family became more unbounded than ever, and they aspired even to set aside all the princes of the blood royal.

Shortly after Henry II's death, Catherine, in her dejection at the loss of the husband she had loved, the incapacity of her eldest son, and the unquiet state of the kingdom, which threatened, under the intolerant rule of the Guises, soon to bring heavy troubles upon the throne, went off to Chaumont, before its transfer to Diane de Poictiers had been effected, to consult her astrologer Ruggieri (who had long lived there in a set of apartments in one of the towers of the castle) as to the future of herself and her sons. And then ensued that strange "Vision of the future Kings of France," of which one

Nicholas Pasquier, son of a member of the States-General, tells us. How that the Queen Mother, being told by Ruggieri to gaze steadily into a large mirror which hung on the wall, when she would see the future Kings of France appear in succession, while each of them would reign as many years as his apparition in the mirror made complete turns, in trepidation did so. First, there appeared a pale and sickly youth whom she recognised as her son Francis II, who slowly made one turn and then faded from her view. Next came her son Charles, who, as Catherine breathlessly watched, made thirteen turns and passed out of sight. He was followed by her son Henry, who rapidly made fifteen turns and then suddenly vanished. Then entered on the scene Henry of Navarre, who, as Catherine (now unable to remove her gaze from this strange pageant) watched as one spellbound, made twenty turns, and likewise suddenly disappeared. Following him came a bright boy,[24] who continued turning again and again until, when he had done so thirty times, Catherine in an agony cried out that she could look no more, and fainted away. So at least runs the legend. And the next day Catherine, much shaken by what she had seen, left Chaumont, and never again saw the château where she had spent so many gloomy years, and the last visit to which had been marked by so weird an experience.

But the residence which she had taken in exchange for it was the delight of Catherine's heart, and became during the rest of her life her favourite abode. Situated on the borders of the forest of Amboise, Chenonceaux, which had originally been a mill, worked by the waters of the river Cher, had been gradually improved by successive owners until it became a charming château, which about the year 1523 was bought by Francis I. Catherine had always coveted it, from the days when Francis I had taken her there on some of their hunting trips together. And it was another of the bitter things she had had to bear that on the latter's death her husband, Henry II, instead of allowing it to become hers, gave it to Diane de

Poictiers. The latter had since enlarged and beautified it, and
Catherine, now that it had at last become her own, was bent
upon improving it still further. For a time, however, she was
obliged to defer these plans until public affairs should become
less troubled. For the condition of these now became most
threatening, and it was evident that at the rate matters were
proceeding the throne would ere long be in serious danger.

For the Guises were not long in embarking on the course
they had determined upon as regards Protestantism. The
Cardinal of Lorraine, especially, was a most baneful character
for any country to be cursed with, being a violent persecutor,
loathed by the people, and bent upon rooting out Protestantism by the most drastic methods. Jeanne d'Albret, Queen of
Navarre, wrote of him that he "would like to set households
by the ears all over France." And he certainly succeeded in
doing so. Under his administration of the country the most
cruel persecution of Protestants at once set in; and when
after a short time Anne du Bourg, a sincere and earnestly
religious man of very temperate views and high character, a
"Moderate," and a leading member of the *Parlement,* was
condemned and put to death by the Guises for being a
Protestant, matters reached a climax. The Protestants
(backed, it is said, by Elizabeth of England) laid a plot while
the court was at Blois to capture and put to death the Guises,
and, if possible, to seize the young King and make him a
Protestant; or, if he refused, to make the Prince of Condé
King. Catherine did not know what they were planning to
do, but she was entirely opposed to the way in which the
Protestants were being treated (as she considered that toleration was the only safe course for the kingdom) and hated the
Guises, though as long as her son was ruled by his wife, and
both of them by the uncles of the latter, Catherine had to
stand aside and look on. But she writes:—

"When I see these poor people burnt, beaten, and tormented, not for thieving or marauding, but simply for up-

holding their religious opinions, when I see some of them suffer cheerfully, with a glad heart, I am forced to believe that there is something in this which transcendeth human understanding." [25]

The Protestants, knowing of this sympathetic attitude on her part, and not knowing how small her power was, appealed to her against what was being done on the King's authority under the administrative powers which had been granted by him to the Guises, and she, unwilling to acknowledge how powerless she was, extracted a promise from the latter to stop the persecutions; but she could really effect nothing, and the persecutions continued.[26] However, after a time she succeeded in getting a decree issued by the King forbidding the persecution of Protestants; but the Guises had no intention of obeying any such decree, and practically snapped their fingers in her face. Catherine consulted Admiral Coligny as to what could be done, and he told her (what she knew already) that the Guises were "hated like the pest, and alone to blame for the disturbed state of the country"; but it was easier to say this than to discover how to oust the Guises, who had become practically kings of France. Meanwhile the Protestants were elaborating their plot, regarding which Calvin afterwards said: "Never was enterprise worse conceived, or more stupidly carried out." The English Roman Catholics were suffered to find it out, and they informed the Duke of Guise; whereupon the latter promptly removed the King, the Queen Mother, and the court from Blois to Amboise (which was a more secure abode), and awaited events.

At Amboise the Guises, who desired to make the matter appear as formidable as possible to the King, so that they might punish with the greater severity those implicated in it, kept the court in almost as complete confinement as though they were in a state of siege, the gates of the castle being shut, and the neighbouring roads patrolled by parties of cavalry. In March 1560 the conspirators made their attempt to capture the Guises and the King, but in such a feeble and desultory fashion that from first to last the so-called conspiracy presented no real danger to those concerned. So much so that there is even an appearance throughout the affair of the Protestants having been deliberately led on by the Guises to make the attempt in order that the latter might be able to destroy as many of them as possible. Whether this were the case or not, the attempt was made in a manner most inadequate for such an enterprise. A few of the conspirators were found by the cavalry patrols lurking in a wood near the castle; a day or two later a larger band were captured; Condé, who had secretly been head of the plot, deserted his followers with their consent, and took his place at court as though he had had no connection with the conspiracy; the rest of the conspirators, instead of thereupon abandoning the enterprise, as they would have been wise to do, foolishly advanced against the castle, though they could never have expected to take it. Their attack, feebly carried out, was easily repulsed; in the retreat the greater number of them were taken prisoners; and the plot collapsed.

The Guises, who headed the Roman Catholic party, by causing the King to place in their hands the entire civil and military administration of the kingdom, were not only able to persecute their religious opponents with impunity, but could also declare any actions of the latter in retaliation to be acts of treason against the King. And it was exactly this making the throne take a side (carrying with it consequences of this kind), which Catherine, when a year later she came into power, refused to adopt. But the Guises, being violent partisans who were determined to root out their opponents, cared for no such considerations, and were governed by one sole aim, that of making their own party triumphant; they therefore now proceeded to punish all those whom they had captured, not as heretics, but as persons guilty of treason against the King. By this means, notwithstanding the King's decree forbidding any further executions on account of re-

ligion, they would be able nevertheless to put to death a large
number of important Protestants.

From the prisoners, under torture, the Guises learnt (if
they did not know it before) that there had never been any
danger to the King, and that the whole plot was aimed at
themselves alone; and their vengeance, inspired, not only by
the desire of the triumph of their party, but also by fears for
their own safety, was cruel and vindictive. Every Protestant
throughout the country round upon whom their soldiers could
lay hands was summarily hanged, drowned in the Loire, or
brought to the castle to be beheaded. These massacres of
their opponents went on for a month; every part of the walls
of the castle was disfigured by heads of the slain; and the
Guises, in order to implicate the members of the court in
their proceedings, forced them whenever they could to witness these executions, even the Prince of Condé being compelled by them to do so. Finally, in order to strike terror into
all who might think of engaging in such plots against their
power in future, as well as to assist in giving the desired
appearance of a condemnation for treason against the King,
the Guises arranged a public execution of the fifty-seven
principal prisoners, and made it as impressive as possible.
They directed that the execution (fixed for the 30th March)
should be carried out in the presence of the whole court, and
issued notices throughout the surrounding country, proclaiming the execution and ordering all to be present at it. In
obedience to this order the people came in crowds, and occupied hill-tops, roofs of houses, and every point from which
the scaffold was visible; while for the members of the court
the Guises arranged seats in tiers round the open space,
as if for a fête. When the whole court, with the young
King and Queen and their attendants, the Queen Mother
and her ladies, and the Princes of the Blood, including
the Prince of Condé himself, had taken their places, the
Duke of Guise placed himself close to the scaffold on horseback, and one by one the fifty-seven gentlemen condemned

to death laid their heads on the block and were beheaded.
Catherine and the whole court were so horrified at this dreadful spectacle that they were thankful to leave Amboise on
the following day for Chenonceaux, where Catherine, "to
get rid of the horror of blood," arranged a series of garden
fêtes to wipe out the effect of the terrible scenes which the
Guises had created for them during the month they had
passed at Amboise. Thus did Francis, Duke of Guise, and his
brother Charles light the fires of civil war in France which
were to rage over that country for more than a generation.

By certain writers Catherine's conduct in connection with
the above episode has been described with every epithet of
condemnation. One French chronicler declares that the Guises
arranged these executions "as a distraction for the ladies, who
were becoming bored at staying so long in one place"; others
state that "Catherine and her ladies were present at the
spectacle," and took pleasure in watching the tortures inflicted on the Protestants; others that these executions "were
witnessed by the cold-hearted Court from a balcony as if
they had been stage-representations"; [27] and again, that
Catherine showed her cruel temperament by finding fault
with the Duchess of Guise when the latter wept copiously at
"the cruel shedding of so much innocent blood" [28]—blood,
by the way, which was being shed by that lady's own husband and his brothers. But the facts do not appear to bear
out this colour which the French Protestant writers have put
on them, though it was one natural enough, perhaps, to the
friends of those who were being put to death. It was not
"Catherine and her ladies," but Francis II and his court (of
which they formed a part), who looked on at these executions.
And it was not as an "amusement," or from a wanton pleasure
in cruelty,[29] that they were there, though the arrangements
made by the Guises no doubt caused it to have that appearance to those whom Francis, Duke of Guise, and his brothers
thus slaughtered. So far from its being any pleasure to the
court to be there, we know that both Francis II, Mary, and

many of the rest were almost fainting from the dreadful spectacle, and that it was just because Catherine and all of them
felt so horrified at it that she arranged for them all to quit
Amboise next day and depart to Chenonceaux. The Guises
(in whose hands Francis was a mere puppet) insisted on the
presence of the King and his whole court at these executions
with a threefold object. First, to have to watch such an
execution would tend to intimidate all at the court who (like
Condé) might be inclined to take part with the enemies of
the house of Guise. Second, the presence of the members of
the court on such an occasion would tend to embroil them
with the Protestants; which was just the effect it had, causing the Protestant writers to declare that they were there as
an amusement, and to inveigh against them for such heart-
less cruelty. Third, any member of the court who refused to
be present at the execution of those who had plotted against
the King's authority and made an organised attack on his
residence, could *ipso facto* be pointed at by the Guises as
being an enemy of the King and a friend of those who had
desired to make him their prisoner. It is not likely, for instance, that Condé would have been present as a spectator
at the execution of those whose leader he had been, and who
still honoured him,[30] if he had not been forced in this manner. Hence, neither Catherine nor any other lady of the court
could be absent; and we see this exemplified in the case of
Anna d'Este, Duchess of Guise, who, when she refused to
go to the execution, was dragged there by the Guises by
physical force; and when subsequently she said that she was
sure God would have vengeance on those who took so many
worthy gentlemen's lives, she endured much rough treatment
and anger from her husband's brothers in consequence. And
if Catherine said anything to her at all on account of her
weeping (which is very doubtful), it was nothing more than
a remark intended to urge her to maintain a due amount of
self-control.

Moreover, Catherine did not remain passive during these

proceedings of the Guises. She made a strong endeavour to save the lives of many of the prisoners, and we are told "tried everything she could, even seeking out these new kings [31] in their chambers, and caressing them"; but without avail, for the Guises were determined to slay them all. It is also noteworthy (as showing that these condemnatory remarks upon Catherine in connection with this episode proceed more from bias than from any solid basis of fact) that although Mary, Queen of Scots, was likewise present at this execution, and as Queen of France occupied at least as important a position at it as the Queen Mother, while also we do not hear of her having importuned her uncles on behalf of the lives of any of these prisoners as Catherine had done, yet none have ever made similar remarks regarding Mary, Queen of Scots, in the matter.

The fact is that these ladies were all of them *women of their time,* and that to look on at an execution of this kind was not the same thing to them as it would be to any one in these days. France was becoming far too much accustomed to such cruel deeds for women to fail to grow more or less callous to such sights. We may also remember that these ladies could both look on at executions, and also bear themselves with calmness and fortitude when their own turn came to suffer in like manner. Their doing the former is no proof of cruelty on their part, as it would be in our days. And we who live in more peaceful times are in error if we impute cruelty to them owing to our judging their actions by a standard which relates to an entirely different set of conditions.

Catherine now succeeded in getting a council on the subject of the religious differences assembled at Fontainebleau; and at this council, notwithstanding the angry frowns of the Guises and their puppet the King, she spoke boldly against the policy which was being pursued regarding the Protestants, and stated that one half the people were Protestants, and asked sarcastically "if it was supposed that the sword could be used against them all." Nevertheless matters did not mend; and throughout the summer of 1560 plots on the part of the Protestants for a general rising throughout the south of France (including the seizure of Lyons), and imprisonments and executions of prominent Protestants on the part of the Guises, continued to take place.

One artifice of the Guises did Catherine much harm in the eyes of the people of France, while it has largely affected the writings of the contemporary French historians who deal with the events of these seventeen months. So long as the puppet King was entirely under their dominion, and so long as the entire civil and military rule of the country was by his decree vested in them, the Guises knew that neither Catherine nor any one else could interfere with them. At the same time they knew how greatly they were hated by the people; [32] and to shield themselves as much as possible from the odium caused by their actions, they made the incapable youth who was their tool, in authorising their proceedings, from time to time quote also his mother's name as he had done in his original decree; thus making it appear as though their actions were done with Catherine's concurrence. And although she opposed them on every occasion at the court, she was powerless to take any action which would right her in the eyes of the country so long as the position remained the same with regard to Francis. However, a time was rapidly approaching when she would be freed from this position, and be able to show all men what her real attitude was.

The Guises now began to fly at higher game, and planned to achieve the death both of the Prince of Condé and his brother, Antoine de Bourbon, King of Navarre, the two leading members of the Protestant party; and were not deterred even by the fact that they were of the blood royal, and next in succession to the throne after Catherine's sons. Condé especially was known by them to have been a party both to the plot which had ended at Amboise, and to that for the seizure of Lyons. Accordingly in September the Guises caused the King of Navarre and the Prince of Condé to be summoned by the King to the court (which was then at Orleans), the King stating that he wished them to come and refute their accusers, and promising them a safe-conduct and a friendly reception. Catherine could not have known what the Guises meant to do, nor would they have dreamed of letting her know it, and she no doubt did not believe that they would dare to take the lives of princes of the blood royal; for when Navarre and his brother showed reluctance to come, she wrote begging them to do so as the King wished it so much, and that she and all the court would receive them hospitably. On their arrival at court Condé was at once seized under the orders of the Duke of Guise, and thrown into prison as a preliminary to his execution for high treason; while for the King of Navarre, who could not be thus accused, the Guises had another plan. So far from Catherine having plotted to take the lives of Condé and the King of Navarre, as has been maintained,[33] her subsequent conduct in this affair completely disproves the assertion.[34]

The plot to which the Guises persuaded Francis to agree, and which they carefully kept concealed from Catherine, knowing that she would find means to frustrate it, was that he should summon Navarre to come to his apartment in a private manner and unattended. The only attendants on the King would be themselves and the Marshal de Saint-André. Francis was to reproach Navarre with the state of the country, and then in a sudden rage to strike him with his dagger, when the other three would assail him as defenders of the King's person, and despatch him.

But Catherine heard of the plot just in time. She hastily sent the Duchess of Montpensier to warn Navarre of it, and told him not to go when an invitation came to him from the King; at the same time she herself went to her son and used all her powers to prevent him from obeying the Guises' commands in this matter. The account of what took place, and of how Catherine had saved his life, was afterwards related by Navarre to his wife, Jeanne d'Albret, who published it in a manifesto in 1568. He told his wife that in accordance with the Queen Mother's warning he disregarded the first invitation he received from the King, but on receiving a second summons, thought it would appear cowardly to refuse, and went. As soon as he entered the room the Cardinal de Lorraine closed the door carefully behind him. The King received him, wearing his dagger, and reproached him bitterly as he had been instructed to do; but Navarre, owing to the warning he had received, replied in so humble a fashion that he gave no opportunity to the King to display any wrath, and after a time Francis allowed him to depart unharmed, to the intense rage of the Cardinal de Lorraine, who, in disgust at the failure of the plot, as he departed burst out with "Voilà le plus poltron cœur que fut jamais." Catherine was overjoyed at having been thus successful in saving Navarre's life, and herself related her part in it to his wife, Jeanne d'Albret.

But the Prince of Condé was still held fast in prison, and the Guises, who knew that he was their chief opponent, were determined that his life at all events should not be saved. Catherine had succeeded in getting his prison changed from Orleans to Amboise, but that was all she could effect; and she writes an ambiguously worded letter, saying how strong the latter place was and how impossible it would be for him to escape thence (apparently with the object of showing that the Guises need have no objection to Amboise as the place of his incarceration), concluding with, "I do not think that there is any place in all France where the Prince could be safer or better looked after." [35] That she intended to save his life if she could is fully proved by what happened immediately afterwards; so that whatever else this letter may mean, it certainly does not mean that she intended to help the Guises to effect their purpose. Nevertheless, the latter

secured Condé's condemnation to death, and got the sentence
of death signed by the King, and the 10th December fixed
as the date of the execution. The Guises would not suffer
even Condé's wife to see him, not even when she begged to
be allowed to do so once before he died "to give him
courage."

Just at this juncture Francis II fell ill; and a few days later
this incapable youth breathed his last, after a reign of seventeen months. He died on 5th December 1560, his name hated
throughout France owing to his surrender of himself and his
kingdom to such a rule as that of the Guises.

(1561-1574)

On Francis II's death Catherine's second son, Charles, a
boy of ten, succeeded to the throne. Catherine was made, during his minority, Queen Regent of France. And the first act
of her power was one which tells directly against the view
ordinarily held of her. The death of the Prince of Condé,
who was marked out as the leader of the Protestant party,
and whom they were already proposing to make King, must
have seemed highly desirable, not only in the interests of
Catherine's sons, but also in the cause of France; since the
death of their leader might be expected to paralyse the
Protestants, and prevent their commencing a civil war, as
they were now proposing to do. Catherine, whose *affetto di
signoreggiare* had at last a chance of being gratified, desired
greatly that scope for showing her ability for ruling which
she would have as Queen Regent on behalf of a boy of ten.
On the other hand, Condé's existence seriously threatened
this; he had already headed two plots in succession which had
as their object to place him on the throne instead of Catherine's son; and he had been openly spoken of by the Protestants as "Louis XIII." Condé, in his prison, was ignorant
of Francis II's death, and supposed that he himself had but
four days more to live; and Catherine had only to let the
law take its course.

This, however, was not the course which Catherine adopted. We are told:—

"Guise saw that his power was at an end, knowing that during the minority of the next King the Queen Mother would be Regent. He at once went to her, and urged her with all his force, for the sake of her own and her son's safety, to allow the sentence of death which had been passed against Condé to be carried out, and also to put to death the King of Navarre." [36]

Catherine flatly refused, countermanded the execution, and ordered Condé to be set at liberty. She then sent for the King of Navarre, told him she had had no hand in the schemes to take the lives of himself and his brother, and offered him her friendship on two conditions; first, that he would forego his claim to the Regency (for which he had small desire and was not fit), and, second, that he would make peace with the Guises so that there should be an end to the strife between the two religious parties which was threatening to desolate France. These terms he accepted, and he also was set at liberty; though Catherine must have had grave doubts whether he would keep the second promise; and she would have been justified, for he very quickly broke it.

Thus did Catherine make her first essay in that long endeavour to be a peacemaker to France which was to continue through so many years. We who have followed the course of the Medici have seen at least three other occasions in which conduct similar to this was displayed by them; and as Condé's prison doors roll back we seem to hear an echo of Lorenzo's speech that "he who knows how to forgive knows how to rule."

Catherine, on becoming Queen Regent, showed at once the line she intended to adopt of endeavouring to maintain on the part of the throne that attitude of toleration towards both the religious parties which she justly considered to furnish the only hope of preserving the country from the horrors of a desperate civil war. Within a month of her being installed in power as Queen Regent she published a royal Edict, dated 28th January 1561, stopping all persecutions in consequence of religion, releasing all who were in prison on that account, and ordering that there should be full liberty given to the Protestant religion throughout France. At the same time she wrote to the Pope demanding that Communion in both kinds should be administered to the laity, that prayers should be said in the vulgar tongue, and that certain other reforms in Church matters desired by the Protestants should be carried out. For the above Edict she was, of course, abused by the Roman Catholic party, who under the *régime* of the Guises had nourished high hopes of seeing Protestantism stamped out in France; and when a little later she similarly granted concessions for which the Roman Catholics asked, she incurred like abuse from the Protestant party; though there were a few among the latter who took a more balanced view, as, for instance, Languet, who wrote that she "sought to moderate all things." And throughout the years that followed we find her always struggling to maintain the same attitude, and incurring odium now from one side and now from the other in consequence; so that among the writings of the day the assertions as to her "duplicity" and "double-mindedness" throve apace. This endeavour to maintain (or recover) peace by holding the balance between the two parties who divided France is the key to all Catherine's conduct. She strove for it earnestly while as yet the two adversaries were only drifting towards war, and when at last they broke into open war she again and again brought about peace by the same method; though only to find her efforts nullified by their inability to live peaceably together. And this long and strenuous effort as a peacemaker to France (notwithstanding that by no fault of hers it failed of permanent success) will ever remain Catherine's chief claim to praise.

But the dark clouds which had gathered over France were not to be dispelled by any such efforts, forcibly as Catherine made them, nor until long-continued storm had poured itself out upon that country. Throughout the whole of the remaining twenty-eight years of her life that storm raged, and during that time France saw no less than eight religious wars follow each other in succession; while the short interludes of peace were each scarcely more than a truce during which the two antagonists collected their strength for a fresh contest. And bitter indeed was this conflict. Mézeray, who wrote about fifty years after Catherine's death, says:—

"If any one were to relate all that took place at this time, in different parts of France, all the taking and retaking of towns, the infinity of small combats, the mutual insults and retaliations, the furies, the massacres, it would take up an immense number of volumes."

Before, however, this great contest began, Catherine, during the year 1561, made three splendid efforts to avert it. With a greater breadth of view than any one else in either France or England at that time possessed, she formed a plan to assemble a National Church Council of the leading Protestants and Roman Catholic authorities in France, and to direct their deliberations herself *"on the lines of studying the institutions of the Primitive Church, investigating how far divergencies from the latter were the cause of the complaints made by the Protestants, and seeking to arrive at a settlement on this basis."* [37] This was a most remarkable proposal; there was no other sovereign in Europe then, or for many generations afterwards, who could have conceived the idea of assembling such a council and of personally directing its deliberations on the lines proposed.[38] And perhaps no other act of Catherine's more strongly brings out the ability and breadth of view which had been brought to the service of France by a Medici coming to occupy that throne. The idea was entirely Catherine's own, and her letters show how much she hoped for from it; and had she been able to carry out her own strong desire to keep the matter a strictly national one, and to prevent all outside interference, it is probable that success might have crowned her efforts, and France have been saved from all the miseries of the most terrible period in the history of that country.

The proclamation ordering the assembly of this National Church Council was issued on the 25th July, and on the 9th September 1561 (three weeks after Mary, Queen of Scots, a widow of nineteen, had bidden a sad adieu to France, and sailed for Scotland), the Council assembled at the monastery of Poissy, near Saint-Germain.[39] On the Protestant side were thirty-two leading Protestant ministers, Jeanne d'Albret (who was looked upon as a host in herself), the Prince of Condé, Admiral Coligny, and a number of Protestant nobles; while on the Roman Catholic side were forty bishops, six cardinals, twelve doctors of the Sorbonne, the Cardinal of Lorraine, and his brother, the Duke of Guise. The Queen Regent, with the boy King and the rest of the royal family, the members of the Council of State, the Chancellor, Michel de l'Hôpital, and other important members of the court, made up one of the most impressive assemblages which France had ever witnessed. Catherine opened the proceedings by a speech expressing a hope that the debates might be so conducted as to bring peace to the kingdom. Fine addresses were delivered by the principal leaders on either side, and at first Catherine hoped for success. But on the 19th September there arrived Cardinal Ippolito d'Este of Ferrara, who held three archbishoprics in France, and also came as legate from the Pope, and with secret orders from the latter to stop the proceedings. And from the moment of his arrival all chance of a settlement between the two parties ended. Frequent scenes and furious discussions brought about an entire failure of this effort by the 26th September; and Catherine's concluding speech, in which she dissolved the Council, said:—"We are sorely grieved that this meeting hath

not produced that fruit we had wished, so needful for the love
of the whole Christian Church."

Catherine then tried another plan, and to avoid the angry
recriminations of a large assembly containing many discordant elements, arranged a smaller conference, consisting
of five of the leading Protestant ministers and five of the principal Roman Catholic clergy who were in favour of reforms.
This conference was successful in arriving at a settlement satisfactory to both parties, and drew up a joint agreement on the disputed points concerning the Holy Communion
(the chief point of dissension), and submitted this agreement
to the bishops for their approval. But the latter, knowing
that the Pope would never agree to it, refused their assent.
Meanwhile, Catherine continued to carry out her broad-
minded reforms with a view to an equal treatment by the State
of both religions; various important posts were given to
Protestants, fresh decrees furthering religious liberty were
continually being promulgated, and Paris, strongly Roman
Catholic, saw appointed as its Governor, a Protestant, the son
of the Constable Montmorency.

But Catherine's difficulties were enormous. Not only were
constant intrigues by both the rival parties to circumvent each
other taking place even while these conferences were being
carried on, but also every country around was eager to take
part in the conflict and make France a general battle-ground
in which the religious question which divided Europe should
be fought out; and Catherine had to strive hourly against
anything being done which would afford a pretext to any of
these adjacent powers for intervening in the strife. Her chief
embarrassments came from the fanatic Philip II of Spain. He
kept at her court as his ambassador Thomas Perrenot de
Chantonnay, a man employed by Philip more in the capacity
of a detective than as the envoy of a foreign power, and who
threateningly told Catherine that he "knew every detail of
her days." Through him Philip II menaced her perpetually
with an armed intervention by Spain on behalf of the Roman

Catholic party in France. While Chantonnay, knowing that France in its present disunited state was powerless to resist such an invasion, treated the Queen with the utmost insolence on every occasion that her policy of tolerance caused her to take any step to the advantage of the Protestants. On the opposite side of France the Emperor was closely watching for some excuse to make war upon Catherine in order to recover Metz; Elizabeth of England was eagerly on the look-out for some pretext for taking arms on behalf of the Protestants; while from the Italian side the Pope and the Duke of Savoy were both anxious to join in the fray.

Catherine also laboured under another difficulty. Unlike her opponent Elizabeth, who was surrounded by a band of exceptionally able and reliable counsellors, Catherine was in this particular unusually ill provided; and, while surrounded by spies who watched and reported to their own governments every word and look of hers, she had not, as she truly said in her letters to her daughter, a single person about her in whom she could trust. At the very time that the conference with a view to a peaceful settlement in religion was sitting, a plot was set on foot by the Protestants to carry off her younger son Henry, and set him up as a rival to his brother Charles; and another proposal was made (even in her Council of State) by one of the Roman Catholic leaders to seize herself and throw her into the Seine in a sack. This latter proposition she had the pleasure of herself hearing through the tube which she had secretly had made from the council chamber to her apartment. Added to these various perplexities she had daily "to exercise blandishments, prayers, and remonstrances" in order to keep the leaders of the two parties from coming to blows even at her court. And when the strain of so many anxieties told visibly even on her strong physique, the ambassador Chantonnay had the insolence to tell her that he believed that her indisposition was merely due to her eating too many melons; to which she replied with some dignity that "it was not the fruits of the garden, but the fruits of the spirit, which

made her ill." Well might one of those acute Venetian ambassadors who watched and reported all these proceedings say
that he did not know what ruler would not have made mistakes under so many difficulties, and express surprise that she
did not give way to one or other of the two parties. Nor did
any termination to this strain appear likely to occur; she had
for a time by her tolerant measures put down the flames which
had been ready to burst forth, but none saw more clearly than
Catherine herself that they were not put out; and what she
said in writing to her ambassador in Spain was only too true:
—"The ashes of the fire which has gone out are still so hot
that the least spark will make them leap up into bigger flames
than we have ever seen."

But Catherine was not yet daunted; and although both her
first and second attempts to avert the impending conflict had
failed, she made yet a third. Paris, violently opposed to her
policy of toleration, broke out into tumults; every Sunday
there was fighting of some sort round the churches; and in
these quarrels lives on both sides were lost. Whereupon Chantonnay had the effrontery to tell the Queen Regent that if she
did not quickly put an end to these heretics his master "would
come to the assistance of her Catholic subjects and would
certainly make war upon her." But Catherine came of a
family who were not to be cowed by threats like this, and she
told him bluntly to tell his master that she "would be mistress
in her own house." Accordingly, in December 1561 she called
a meeting of the States General and made a powerful speech
in favour of a policy of toleration, and then summoned a
third conference between the two parties to meet at Saint-
Germain on the 3rd January 1562, consisting of "thirty Presi-
dents and Councillors chosen from the eight *Parlements*,[40]
and twenty members of the Privy Council including the
Princes of the Blood." The proceedings began with a remarkable speech from the Chancellor in favour of allowing the two
religions to live side by side in France. This was followed by
a most powerful speech from Catherine herself in the same di-

rection. After a debate of twelve days a compromise was at
length agreed upon, which, though not all that Catherine desired, nor completely satisfactory to either party, was more
agreeable to the Protestants than it was to their opponents.

Having thus at last obtained a settlement which an influential body of men representative of both parties could accept,
Catherine drew up an Edict, following their recommendations,
which afterwards became very celebrated under the name of
the "Edict of January." This, though it did not allow the
Protestants to build churches, authorised their assembling
for worship; still more important than this, it gave them for
the first time legal recognition, the State thus acknowledging
two different religious bodies. But when this Edict (containing
such an entirely new departure) was sent by the Queen to
the *Parlement* to be registered and published, they altogether
refused to publish it, and took up a most determined attitude.
Catherine was furious; she at once mounted her horse and
rode at a gallop from Saint-Germain to Paris,[41] "and," says
the account, "in good sooth it seemed as though she would
gallop straight into the Council chamber in order the better
to demonstrate her absolute will and have the Edict registered." She found the President and Councillors obdurate;
they declared that the Edict would do evil to the kingdom,
and dishonour to God, and that nothing should induce them
to register it; and at length the President rose to leave the
hall, solemnly saying to the Queen, "Your Majesty is taking
the road that will lose you crown and kingdom." But Catherine was as firm on behalf of her measure of toleration as the
Deputies were against it. And as we watch her standing alone
before the *Parlement,* determined that they and not she should
give way in a matter which she felt was the last chance of
saving the country from civil war, suddenly before the mind's
eye there rises that scene of thirty-two years before, at the
door of the Murate convent in Florence, when she was a girl
of eleven, and the whole drama seems to have been acted
before on a smaller stage, and we know which side will con-

quer. And so it turned out; for, notwithstanding all the determination of the President and Councillors, Catherine prevailed, and before she left the council chamber she had obtained a promise that the Edict should be published on the following day; which was done. Though in publishing it the *Parlement* themselves attested that her determination had been greater than theirs by adding the words:—

"Published, read, and registered in our Court of Parlement at Paris, by reason of the importunity of those who profess the so-called new Reformed religion. And this only provisionally, while awaiting the majority of the King."

This episode completed Catherine's first year of power. And that year certainly showed no insignificant tale of work. She could not undo the harm which had been done during the years when she had compulsorily been merely an onlooker while incapacity of various kinds (first during her husband's reign, and then during that of her son) steadily drove France towards civil war; but on getting hold of the helm she made a fine effort to save the ship from the rocks even at the eleventh hour. And her Edict of toleration immediately on coming to power in January 1561, her proclamation of July assembling a National Church Council, her broad-minded reforms in the matter of giving appointments equally to those of both religious parties, her second conference in October when the first failed, her third conference proclaimed in December when the second failed, and lastly, in January 1562, her celebrated "Edict of January," which so often formed the basis of peace in the years which followed, collectively made a record of which any ruler of a country drifting towards civil war might well be proud.

But all Catherine's efforts were rendered of no avail. The Roman Catholic party, headed by the Guises, declared her "Edict of January" to be intolerable, and that there could not be two religions side by side in France; the Protestant party declared that her Edict did not go far enough, and clamoured for further concessions; several fights, with the slaughter of opponents, took place, and both parties now prepared openly for civil war. An intercepted letter from a Protestant minister disclosed to the Guises the fact that the Protestants were plotting a wholesale massacre of the Roman Catholics in Paris; the writer of the letter quoted the examples of Gideon and Judith, and said that he "felt in his spirit a God-sent vocation to do this deed." Ten years later (on St. Bartholo-mew's Day, 1572) the Roman Catholics apparently felt the same "vocation." Catherine, knowing that the object of both sides was to get possession of the King, withdrew with him to Fontainebleau, first ordering the Duke of Guise not to bring an armed force into Paris, an order which he promptly proceeded to disobey; whereupon Catherine, determined to keep the antagonists apart if possible, begged Condé to quit Paris, which he did. Guise, with a Roman Catholic force, seized Paris; the Protestants, under Condé and Coligny, seized Orleans and other towns on the Loire and the Rhone; and the First Religious War had begun (May 1562). The Duke of Guise proceeded with a force to Fontainebleau, cap-tured the Queen Regent and the King, and escorted them under a guard first to Paris and thence to Melun, where, though treated with courtesy, they were practically Guise's prisoners, and were not allowed to communicate by letter or other means with the outside world. Elizabeth of England, joining in the conflict, sent over an English force which occu-pied Havre and Rouen; and the war rapidly spread in both northern and southern France. Meanwhile Catherine, who after a time had managed to get free from the power of Guise, was struggling in every way to reconcile the combatants, but for some time without any success. Various battles ensued, in which at length the King of Navarre was killed, Condé taken prisoner by the Roman Catholics, and Montmorency by the Protestants.

In February 1563, while the Duke of Guise was besieging

Orleans, occurred an event which, while it assisted the cause of peace at the time, laid the seeds of still more bitter strife later on. This was the murder of the Duke of Guise, who, as he was riding unarmed back to his house, was shot by Poltrot de Meré, a Protestant who had attached himself to Guise's army in order to execute this crime, and who at his trial stated that it was Admiral Coligny who had employed him to commit the deed, though whether this was true or not has never been made clear. Francis, Duke of Guise, was a noble character, and the most deservedly beloved and hon- oured figure of that time, and his murder by the Protestants was the chief cause of the bitter hatred against Admiral Coligny and the Protestant party on the part of the Roman Catholics which eventually culminated in the massacre on St. Bartholomew's Day ten years later.

This death of the commander on the Roman Catholic side, combined with the other events which had for the moment deprived both parties of the most fiery spirits among their leaders, gave Catherine an opportunity which she at once seized. She forthwith arranged a meeting between herself and the two chief prisoners on either side, Montmorency and Condé, at Orleans, and in a few days had caused them to agree to terms of peace which were almost exactly on the lines of her "Edict of January." And on her return to Amboise, where she was then staying, she was able, on the 19th March 1563, to proclaim, in an edict called the "Edict of Amboise," the peace which she had effected. Thus ended the First Re- ligious War; and Catherine was so delighted at her success that she is said to have "danced for joy." She had a right to feel satisfaction; and her joy was not dimmed by any knowl- edge that seven other wars of the same kind were to follow, in which the most arduous labours in the same direction were often to fail. She promptly carried off her children, Charles IX, Henry, Duke of Anjou, Francis, Duke of Alençon, and Marguerite, together with the Prince of Condé and his wife, the young Henry, now Duke of Guise, the other young Henry,

now King of Navarre, and a brilliant company to Chenonceaux for a happy week of festivities to celebrate the cessation
of the war. These were varied and picturesque.

"Naval battles and water *fêtes* on the Cher were followed
by fireworks and torchlight dances in the long galleries, while
spirited encounters took place in the woods and gardens between troops of gentlemen and ladies of the court disguised
as satyrs and nymphs." [42]

Having been so successful in causing the two parties to
make peace, Catherine's next move was to bind them together
as much as possible by urging that it was the duty of all
Frenchmen to combine to drive the English from French soil.
And entirely owing to her own enthusiasm on this point, she
was able three months later to assemble an army commanded
by the leaders of both parties, which advanced to attack the
English in Rouen, and which she herself accompanied, going
into the battle herself, and saying that she "would never rest
until she had driven the English out of France." The campaign was entirely successful, and in July the English force
surrendered, and France was once more free from foreign invasion. It was the last time for many a long day that the two
parties of Frenchmen were to be found fighting on the same
side.

Peace having been thus brought to France for a time,
Catherine caused Charles IX, now fourteen, to be installed
at Rouen, and then took him on a prolonged tour through
France, both to make him acquainted with his kingdom and
also to keep the court away from Paris, where religious animosity was always ready to break out. This tour lasted
nearly two years, from the spring of 1564 to the end of 1565,
in the course of which the court visited nearly all the principal
places in southern France. The court numbered over eight
hundred persons, accompanied by a huge retinue of servants,
and there are graphic accounts of this immense progress,

which was like a moving pageant. We hear of gaily-dressed nymphs who issued from glittering rocks by the wayside, of shepherds who suddenly appeared and recited long Latin poems, and of various other diversions to beguile the tedium of the march. At Bar-le-Duc there took place the baptism of the Queen's grandchild, Christine of Lorraine, the child of Catherine's daughter Claude. And at Macon Catherine was called upon to settle a fierce sectarian quarrel over the knotty point of whether in processions the children of Protestant parents could be permitted to walk side by side with these of Roman Catholic parents. Though the fires of civil war had been quenched, the ashes still smouldered, and while at Roussillon Catherine found it necessary to issue a further Edict calling upon each of the two parties to respect the religion of the other.

The court reached Bayonne in June 1565, where Catherine had arranged that her daughter, Elizabeth of Spain, was to meet them. There followed three weeks of balls, tournaments, and other festivities to celebrate this happy meeting. Elizabeth was accompanied by the Duke of Alva (afterwards of such evil memory in the Netherlands), who had come to Bayonne with a fixed programme, carefully settled beforehand with his master, Philip II, in accordance with which he intended to extort from Catherine agreement to three main conditions, the exclusion of all Protestants from holding any public office, the prohibition of Protestant services, and the expulsion from France of all Protestant ministers. And the Protestant writers have always maintained that at this meeting Catherine, with the utmost duplicity, made a secret compact with Alva for the extermination of Protestantism in France; [43] and that the massacre which occurred seven years later in Paris was the result of this meeting between the Queen Mother and Alva. But here we have a notable instance of how modern research overthrows long-established errors due to reliance upon the perfectly unscrupulous partisan writers of that epoch. For the above theory in connection with this meeting at Bayonne, a theory which had until recently become so firmly established as to be an accepted fact of history, has now been completely refuted by the publication of the Spanish State Papers, including Alva's secret despatches to his master, Philip II. For these show that so far from anything of the kind having taken place, Alva, by his own admission, entirely *failed* to induce Catherine to agree to anything that he urged for the repression of Protestantism. He tells his master that he was unable to get her to agree to prohibit the Protestant preachers (authorised by her Edict of Amboise); or to dismiss her Chancellor, Michel de l'Hôpital; or to consent to any of the other proposals which he urged upon her; "and this notwithstanding the lofty energy and consummate prudence displayed by the Queen of Spain" to assist his efforts; adding that he found the Queen Mother "more than cold for the holy religion." [44]

The court returned to Paris at the end of the year; and during the following year (1566) Catherine, besides many labours to maintain the existing tranquillity on the religious question, was mainly occupied in getting, with the able assistance of her Chancellor, a large number of very important enactments passed for the better administration of justice throughout France. These swept away numerous unjust practices of the courts of justice, and many abuses in the management of the police which pressed severely on the people, and with which her recent prolonged progress through the country had made her acquainted. Many of the new laws thus enacted obtained a permanent place in the French legal code and were of lasting benefit to France.

These four years (1563-1567) were also a time of much activity on Catherine's part in other directions. Both of what were, until 1871,[45] the two principal palaces in Paris are inseparably connected with her name. The palace of the Louvre, begun a few years before his death by Francis I on the designs of the architect Lescot, was completed by the end of Henry II's reign, and Catherine was the first sovereign of France to occupy it, when she came to power after her son Francis II's death. And in the year 1564 she began building her own palace of the Tuileries,[46] connecting it with the Louvre by a long gallery passing through the crowded quarter of the city which then occupied the intervening space.[47] For this palace she employed the celebrated architect Philibert de l'Orme, who had been ousted from royal favour by the Guises during Francis II's reign, but whom Catherine on coming to power reinstated. Besides this work she was also busy in making extensive improvements at Fontainebleau, Chenonceaux, and others of the royal residences, in collecting objects of art of all kinds, and in patronising literature. And notwithstanding all the storms of war through which France passed during the years of Catherine's rule, they form a notable epoch in French literature, the poets Ronsard, Du Bellay, Belleau, Binet, and other lesser stars having made this period famous by their collective name of "the Pleïade."

Catherine's Edict of Amboise, supplemented by that issued at Roussillon, had kept France free from war for four years. The religious animosities, however, fomented on the one side by the Calvinists in Geneva,[48] and on the other by the intolerant temper of the Guise faction, at length again blazed out, and in September 1567 the Second Religious War was begun by an attempt made by the Protestants to seize the person of the young King while the court was at Meaux. The battle of St. Denis followed, in which the Constable Montmorency was killed. During the next six months severe fighting took place in various parts of France, in the course of which the Protestants took Rochelle, which became their permanent headquarters. Eventually, in March 1568 this second war was brought to an end by the so-called Peace of Longjumeau.

How untiring were Catherine's efforts to maintain peace, and how great the difficulties of the task, is shown in the reports of the various ambassadors. Thus the Spanish envoy Alava,[49] in one of his secret reports to Philip II, informs him that as the Queen was coming one day from the council chamber, and when he, being pressed by her to say why he looked at her as he did, remarked in reply that her eyes were swollen with weeping, "She said: 'It is but too true, but I have every reason, for alone and single-handed I bear the burden of affairs. You would be amazed (so she spake) if you understood what has just happened. I no longer know in whom I can trust.' " [50] Again the Venetian ambassador, Giovanni Correr,[51] reports thus:—

"I do not know what prince would not have made mistakes in such a great confusion; how much more a woman, a foreigner, without trusty friends, frightened, and never hearing the truth from those about her. For my part, I have often been surprised that she did not become thoroughly confused, and give way to one or other of the two parties; which would have been a final calamity to the kingdom. It is she alone who has preserved the remnant of royal majesty still to be found there. For this reason I have always pitied rather than blamed her; and she has often reminded me of it when speaking of her distresses and the woes of France."

Words such as these give a vivid picture of the difficulties which Catherine's policy entailed on her, and of the ability with which she adhered to it. Nevertheless, difficult though it might be, the correctness of that policy is shown by the ambassador's remark that her abandonment of it would have been a final calamity to the kingdom.

The peace made at Longjumeau proved but of short duration. The two parties had no real intention of becoming reconciled, and in August 1568 the Third Religious War began, and was fought with great ferocity on both sides. Two months after it began Catherine heard of the death of her favourite daughter, Elizabeth of Spain, at the age of twenty-four. Catherine's grief thereat was very great, but she had little time to indulge it, as the terrible state of affairs which now supervened in France claimed her whole energies. In March 1569 was fought the battle of Jarnac, in which the Prince of Condé was killed. That which Catherine had long laboured to prevent now occurred,—the participation of other countries in the conflict. A German army entered France to assist the Protestants, and a Spanish one to assist the Roman Catholics; and with the entrance upon the scene of these foreigners the contest took a more savage character. The leaders on both sides gave orders to their troops to give no quarter; city after city upon being taken was sacked; "whole garrisons had their throats cut"; and the war assumed the appearance rather of one between fanatical Hindus and Mahomedans than between people of a civilised race. The time was a terrible one—for both Protestants and Roman Catholics. The various woes suffered were enormous. But all that we are concerned with in this history is Catherine's conduct in connection with them.

The Protestants (who could not be retaliated upon in the same way) delighted in destroying and defiling everything which in the eyes of their opponents was sacred; they demolished churches and mutilated shrines, they dragged crucifixes and relics in the mud, they gave the Holy Sacrament to dogs and cattle and greased their boots with the holy oil, they profaned the sepulchres of the ancestors of the reigning family, "they burnt at Cleri the bones of St. Louis, King of France, and at St. Croix the heart of Francis I," they destroyed the beauty of every building on which they could lay hands, and in short poured out their fury upon everything which to the French people represented refinement, care for religion, and pride in the past history of their race. This conduct roused their antagonists to frenzy; a cry of fiercest wrath and a vow of vengeance went up from all Catholic France; and instead of one massacre of St. Bartholomew's Day, it was more to be expected that there should have been a dozen such in different cities of France. And, in fact, we find contemporary writers after that massacre speaking in this very strain, and saying that it was no more than a due retaliation for all that the Protestants had done throughout France, not only in massacring their opponents, but also in their hateful destruction and desecration of everything revered by the latter. How deeply Catherine felt all this misery which in spite of her strong efforts to avert it had descended upon France can be seen in her letters. She says:—"I do not think there is any one in the world who can feel more pained and horrified at the atrocious evils wrought by the foreign troops than I, who am dying of it on my feet." [52]

The popular feeling of maddened indignation and hatred was most of all rampant in Paris; while second only to the citizens' rage against the Protestants was their wrath against the Queen Mother for her tolerant Edicts allowing to Protestants liberty of worship and prohibiting persecution of them. The Parisians declared her policy to be "like ordering the cats and the rats to live at peace together"; they petitioned for leave to abandon France and go to live in some country where they might practise in freedom the Catholic religion; and when she ordered her Edict of toleration to be read to the people from the pulpits, the priests not only refused to do so, but again and again referred to her in their sermons as "Jezebel." It was no wonder that Catherine wrote: "All the towns in the kingdom would not cause me one half the evils I endure from Paris alone." Nor is it any wonder, with Protestants in such a state that they could commit the enormities which have been mentioned, and with Roman Catholics calling the Queen Mother "Jezebel" because she would persist in allowing their enemies liberty of worship, no record of Catherine's actions emanating from either side is to be relied upon, except where such is corroborated from more trustworthy sources, or by facts admitted by these writers themselves in formulating their indictments against her, as for instance this one of her persistent pursuit of a policy of toleration.

Catherine at this time, feeling Paris an unsafe abode, and knowing, on the other hand, how eager the Protestants were to capture the young King, while southern France was in too great a state of conflagration to afford an asylum, carried him off to Metz, where for some time the court took refuge. She still laboured for peace, and on the same lines of mutual toleration, and writes:—

"If those who started the war had had the patience to let us complete what we had begun at Saint-Germain,[53] we should not be in the difficulties we now are in regard to bringing about a durable peace; which, after all, even when it is obtained, cannot be more satisfactory to both parties than the old Edict of January." [54]

After various important cities had been taken and retaken the battle of Moncontour was fought in October 1569, at which the Protestants, now commanded by Coligny, sustained a severe defeat. More sieges followed, but at length, in August 1570, Catherine succeded in bringing the war to an end by arranging the peace of Saint-Germain-en-Laye in which the terms obtained by the Protestant party were even more favourable to them than those contained in her "Edict of January." Nevertheless, as the result Catherine only reaped abuse from both parties. Philip II, urgently demanding that the war should be continued until the Protestants were completely crushed, was full of wrath at any peace having been made; the Roman Catholic party in France declared that the terms of the peace which the Queen Mother had arranged were far too favourable to their foes, and that "the vanquished had been treated as though they were the victors"; while the Protestant party declared that the terms were not favourable enough, and also that they were only a trap laid for them by the duplicity of the Queen Mother. But Catherine had to consider France as a whole; the country was utterly exhausted by these furious wars, its condition altogether deplorable, and a cessation of this fratricidal strife absolutely necessary. Any peace between two combatants which strikes at all an even balance between them is always considered unfair by both.

That which Catherine had effected at Saint-Germain-en-Laye was of this nature, and M. Lavallée speaks no more than the truth when he says:—"It was another effort to make the two religions live together, and to give some repose to exhausted France." As to the accusation against Catherine of duplicity on this and other similar occasions, while they are only what was to be expected from the state in which France was, they probably gained their chief material from the necessity perpetually laid upon Catherine, if France was not to be invaded by the Spaniards, of outwitting Chantonnay, between whom and herself an hourly duel (on his part in order to discover what were her intentions, and on her part to hide them from him) was ceaselessly fought.

Undoubtedly this peace was a great triumph for Catherine, the second of this kind which she had gained. For the results proved her wisdom. Notwithstanding the wrathful grumbling of the Roman Catholics that the terms were too favourable to the Protestants, and of the Protestants that they were not favourable enough, France quieted down, and the Protestants went to their *prêches* and the Roman Catholics to Mass without molesting each other. Catherine was overjoyed at her success; and though she saw that after so fierce a storm the waves could only be expected to calm down by degrees, she had good hopes of being able to create permanent harmony, "and," as she says in her letters, "make a nation of France." Speaking of those who declared that the miseries of France had all been caused by her refusal to suppress the heretics, she writes:—

"If things were even worse than they are after all this war they might have laid the blame upon the rule of a woman; but if such persons are honest they should blame only the rule of men who desire to play the part of kings.[55] In future, if I am not any more hampered, I hope to show that women have a more sincere determination to preserve the country than those who have plunged it into the miserable condition to which it has been brought."[56]

Catherine now had leisure to turn her attention to other affairs than the miseries of war, and to think of matrimonial projects and artistic concerns. Her palace of the Tuileries was by this time nearly finished, and she delighted in laying out its gardens and in arranging to adorn them with all sorts of examples of the new art in earthenware pottery which had been invented by the celebrated Palissy. She had a year or two before rescued him from extreme poverty, as well as from persecution as an ardent Protestant, and she now established him as superintendent over these various works at the Tuileries. At Chenonceaux also she was busy in laying out new gardens on an elaborate plan, and here too she employed Palissy to assist her; while in many other directions she indulged those artistic tastes which she had inherited.

The marriage of her children also now occupied her attention. The peace between the two rival parties in France enabled her to set on foot three matrimonial projects, all intended to cement the reconciliation and make it permanent. These were, the marriage of her son, Charles IX, now twenty, to Elizabeth of Austria, the daughter of the tolerant Emperor Maximilian II; that of her next son, Henry, Duke of Anjou, to Elizabeth, Queen of England; and that of her daughter Marguerite to Henry of Navarre, the son of the redoubtable Protestant, Jeanne d'Albret. The first of these marriages, that of Charles IX to Elizabeth of Austria, was soon carried out, and they were married in November 1570. The negotiations for the marriage of Elizabeth, Queen of England, to Catherine's son Henry (or failing him, with his younger brother, the Duke of Alençon), dragged on for years, and were eventually dropped. But the third marriage, that of the Princess Marguerite to Henry of Navarre, was also carried out, and took place two years after that of her brother Charles. Elizabeth of Austria, Catherine's new daughter-in-law, was virtuous, wise, and had in every way a charming disposition; having no taste for politics, she occupied her time almost entirely in numerous charitable works, and was looked upon by the people as a saint. She was very sincere in her religion, and when at her coronation, at which she was to receive the Holy Communion, various unforeseen delays caused the ceremony, instead of taking place in the morning as intended, to be delayed until three in the afternoon, she remained fasting the whole day; and although (it being feared that she might faint) authority was given for her to break her fast, she would not do so, "and," says the record, "received the Holy Communion at six in the evening as upright and gay as though it were six in the morning."

The difficulties in the way of Catherine's project for the marriage of her son, Henry of Anjou, with Elizabeth of England were mainly created by the Pope, who foresaw in it a possibility of the Church of France seceding from his authority in the same way as the Church of England had done. But, great as these difficulties were, those which had to be overcome in connection with the project for the marriage of the Princess Marguerite with Henry of Navarre (which marriage was Catherine's main attempt to bind the two hostile forces in France together) were greater still. For not only was the Pope equally opposed to this project for similar reasons, but also Henry's mother, the strong-minded and stern Calvinist Jeanne d'Albret,[57] had great doubts as to whether she could allow her son to marry a Roman Catholic, much as she desired the match from every other point of view. However, having at length made up her mind to agree to it, but to keep her son as much as possible away from Roman Catholic influences, she came, early in 1572, to Paris in order to conduct the negotiations herself, ordering her son to remain in Navarre until she had completed them. Jeanne d'Albret had been in bad health for some time, and the feverish energy with which she threw herself into the preparations for her son's marriage exhausted her remaining strength; finding her health failing, she summoned her son from Navarre, but died in Paris on the 9th June before he arrived. Catherine visited

her on her death-bed, and wrote in admiration of her patient
endurance of her sufferings. It has for three centuries been
a favourite story that Jeanne d'Albret was poisoned by the
Queen Mother by means of a perfume which Jeanne had
bought from Catherine's perfumer. The story, which had its
origin in libels published by the Calvinists at Geneva, has
been repeatedly disproved by the most reliable historians, as
well as by the reports of Jeanne d'Albret's two physicians,
Caillard and Desnœuds, both of them Protestants who had
written many things against the Roman Catholic party, and
would at once have denounced such a crime had it occurred.
But nevertheless the story continues to hold its ground, no
amount of disproof, nor even the fact that Catherine was
scarcely likely to endeavour to overthrow a plan which she
had so long laboured to achieve, having had any weight
against so fascinating a piece of sensational fiction. The most
recent authority on the subject dismisses the story in the
following words:—

"A legend that she (Jeanne d' Albret) had been poisoned
long formed one of the stock charges against the Queen
Mother. There is as little evidence for it as for most of the
similar accusations brought in those days." [58]

Henry of Navarre, accompanied by five hundred Protestant
gentlemen, arrived in Paris a few days after his mother's
death, where Admiral Coligny, the young Prince of Condé,
and a great concourse of the Protestant party, were already
assembled for this marriage which was to heal all wounds
and bind the two parties firmly together. And on the 18th
August 1572 the Princess Marguerite and Henry, King of
Navarre, were married in the midst of a grand assembly of
all the principal men of both parties, and with much magnificence. A ball at the Louvre followed in the evening, and
the festivities continued throughout the next three days.

But this great gathering of the rival parties in a city at all
times so inflammable as Paris had serious dangers for the

preservation of the state of outward tranquillity which had now been maintained for two years. The things which the Protestants had done in desecrating and destroying all that their opponents held dear were not forgotten; and the citizens of Paris, who had so long loathed Catherine's policy of toleration towards their opponents, were roused to a white heat of animosity at seeing the marriage of their King's sister to the leader of the rival community; while many of the attendant circumstances of the ceremony were highly unpalatable to them. On the other hand, the majority of the Protestant party liked the marriage no better, thinking they saw in it a design to entrap their leader, Henry of Navarre, into becoming a Roman Catholic. Neither party, so far as their subordinate members were concerned, took any pains to hide their contempt and hatred of the other, or to avoid offending their religious sentiments. Even the marriage ceremony itself, at which the whole body of the Protestant gentlemen had ostentatiously withdrawn when the celebration of the Mass began and gone to walk up and down outside in the gardens, provided fuel to the slumbering fires. Moreover, there were still deeper causes of enmity at work; Henry, Duke of Guise, the leader of the Roman Catholic party, looked upon Admiral Coligny as the treacherous murderer of his father, Francis, Duke of Guise, a crime which Henry, his mother, and the whole family of Guise were firmly determined to avenge on the first opportunity, Henry's mother being specially urgent with him to take this vengeance. So that this marriage, intended to bind the opposing forces together, had within it all the elements for a fresh outburst of their enmity; hatred and suspicion were rampant on both sides, and it needed but a spark to set all Paris in a blaze.

That spark was soon supplied. On the 22nd August, four days after the marriage, Admiral Coligny, walking from the Louvre to his house, was fired at from the window of a house inhabited by one of the retainers of the Duke of Guise,[59] and wounded in the hand and arm. The King and Queen Mother,

knowing the seething state of Paris, and being in the greatest
anxiety lest anything should be done by either party which
might bring on a conflict and civil war in Paris itself, immediately on hearing of this outrage visited Coligny, expressed the greatest concern at what had happened, and sent
the King's own surgeon, Ambrose Paré, a Protestant, to
attend Coligny, and a guard of their own soldiers to protect
his house; they offered the Protestant nobles lodgings round
their leader; and they promised Coligny that there should
be a strict search for the criminal and his prompt punishment.
The house was at once searched, but the man, whoever he
was, had escaped. These actions were, of course, put down
by the Protestants to "dissimulation" on the part of the
Queen Mother, but there is not a particle of proof to support
the charge. They are just such as would be natural in the
position in which Catherine found herself, placed between
two bitterly hostile parties who could only be kept at peace
from hour to hour with difficulty, while a conflict within Paris
itself threatened to engulf the throne, and would in any
case bring to ruin all that Catherine had striven for and
hoped that she had achieved by the marriage just concluded.

This outrage upon Coligny brought matters to a climax.
All through the 23rd August secret plots were going on, each
party (frightened and suspicious) plotting to massacre the
other; and at early dawn on the morning of the 24th (St.
Bartholomew's Day), the Roman Catholic party suddenly
rushed upon their opponents. Armed bands headed by the
Guises, the Duke of Angoulême, and other Roman Catholic
nobles issued into the streets and roused the only too eager
Paris mob to fall upon the Protestants throughout the city.
The Duke of Guise at once hurried with all speed to Coligny's
house accompanied by a band of his own soldiers, who, over-
powering the guard, forced their way into Coligny's chamber
and murdered him. His party were taken by surprise, the
fanatical hatred of the citizens burst forth like a river long
dammed up, and the Protestants (with the exception of the

Prince of Condé, the King of Navarre, Michel de l'Hôpital, and others whom Catherine protected, either in the Louvre or by sending strong guards to defend their houses) were brutally massacred throughout Paris.[60]

The historian Sully, speaking of this massacre, says:—

"The whole house of Guise had been personally animated against the Admiral ever since the assassination of Francis, Duke of Guise, by Poltrot de Meré, whom they believed to have been instigated to this crime by Coligny; and it must be admitted that the Admiral was never able to clear himself of the charge. If this cruel slaughter was, as many people are fully persuaded, only the effect of the revenge of the house of Guise, ... it must be confessed that no person ever executed so severe a vengeance for an offence as did Henry, Duke of Guise, for his noble father's murder."

The Protestant writers have maintained that this massacre was a long-premeditated scheme, but this view is no longer held by historians, fuller knowledge having shown that the Spanish ambassador, Çuniga, spoke the truth when he reported that, with the exception of the murder of Coligny, the rest was due to sudden impulse. It remains to consider whether Catherine is to be held responsible for this massacre, as, on the authority of the infuriated Protestants, has so long been declared, or whether the charge of responsibility on her part was only another result of their long-standing prejudice against her, one which made French Protestants prefer to lay this crime on the shoulders of "the Italian woman" rather than on any of their own nation. First, as to the murder of Coligny, one of the two murders which have always been charged against Catherine,[61] and both of which accusations are now considered to have been unjustly made against her. The circumstances under which it is now known that Coligny's murder took place, the fact that Catherine is acknowledged to have had no special feeling against him, and, above all, the fact that this murder meant the ruin of a plan to achieve which she had laboured hard for two years, appear sufficient to dispose of this charge.[62]

Catherine's part in the massacre as a whole is a question on which (like that of the guilt or innocence of Mary, Queen of Scots) opposite opinions will probably always continue to be held. And this is inevitable, because the only records of her actions on these three days (22nd to 24th August) are all furnished by persons who were violent partisans of one side or the other, and at a time when none took pen in hand with any other idea than to obscure the truth as much as possible for the advantage of his party. The Protestants desired to show the Queen Mother and her son the King as guilty of the crime perpetrated against themselves; while the Roman Catholics desired to show that in what they did the Queen Mother and the King were on their side. The following fact is eloquent as to the way in which, under such conditions, the history of this affair has been written. It was declared by the Protestants that Charles IX had himself assisted in the massacre by firing at their co-religionists from a window of the Louvre; the very window was pointed out, and so thoroughly was this fact supposed to be authenticated that a tablet to that effect was in after years affixed to the window. This tablet was, however, removed in 1802, *on its being discovered that that wing of the palace was not even built until the reign of Henry IV.*[63] It is from accounts written in this fashion that we have to gather what Catherine's words and actions within the Louvre were at this time.

None know really what went on in the Louvre during the 22nd and 23rd August preceding the commencement of the massacre on the morning of the 24th; and it is upon this that the question of Catherine's part in the matter turns.[64] Two things only are certain: first, that of those around Catherine during these three days *there is not one, either Protestant or Roman Catholic, French, English, or Italian, whose word on the subject we can trust in the smallest degree;* and second, that if Catherine were responsible for this massacre, then it was the only occasion in her life that she resorted to violent measures.[65]

Even the Venetian ambassadors fail us at this point in Catherine's history, and throw no light as regards the massacre in August 1572. There is a long gap in the Venetian State Papers at this part of the sixteenth century, the official despatches of this period having been lost. The regular ambassador at this time at the court of France was Sigismondo Cavalli. In addition to him an ambassador extraordinary, Giovanni Michieli, had just been deputed to that court for a special purpose connected with the proceedings of Spain in Flanders. And in default of the official despatches all that we have is a semi-private account by this Giovanni Michieli, which is by no means equally trustworthy.[66] This purports to give a circumstantial report of the proceedings in the Louvre, charges Catherine with the sole responsibility both for Coligny's murder and for the general massacre, and states that her action was the result of a long-premeditated plan, and that the whole scheme of the marriage of Henry of Navarre and Marguerite had been merely a trap to inveigle all the leading Protestants to Paris. But the remarks made by M. Merimée show how little real value can be attached to this statement of Giovanni Michieli. M. Merimée says:—

"I cannot admit that the same men could have been able to conceive a crime whose results must be so important, and to execute it so badly. The measures, in fact, were so ill taken that soon after the Saint Bartholomew the war began afresh, the reformers certainly winning all the glory of it, and retiring from it with new advantages. In short, is not the assault on Coligny, which took place two days before the Saint Bartholomew, sufficient to refute the supposition of a conspiracy? Why kill the chief before the general massacre? Was not this the way to alarm the Huguenots and put them on their guard?" [67]

Giovanni Michieli, in fact, was not in a position to furnish information of any value. He had only reached Paris a week or two before; he was unable to base his opinion on any observations of his own, as he appears to have had as yet no communication with the Queen Mother (who had only arrived from Lorraine just before the marriage); and he is only able to relate what he had "heard on this subject from persons highly situated who have access to the secrets of the court"; in other words, from just those persons whose evidence, as already noted, is in this case absolutely worthless.

We are therefore left to form such inferences as we may from the surer ground of collateral evidence and from the following considerations:—

(i) If Catherine was responsible for instigating this massacre, then she committed an act which is at variance with the whole of the rest of a policy steadily pursued by her for a long number of years, in spite of the greatest difficulties, and to carry out which she had made formidable enemies; and an act which entirely stultified that policy.

(ii) Again, if she was responsible for this massacre, then one possessing one of the most acute intellects ever seen upon a throne took action which caused all her special efforts of the preceding two years to be absolutely thrown away, and destroyed the effect of a marriage to achieve which she had undergone severe labours, and had incurred much odium from a large part of the French people. Also it is impossible that she should not have foreseen that it would be at once declared that the marriage was a long-premeditated scheme to entrap the Protestants to their destruction.

(iii) As this massacre began the Fourth Religious War, Catherine, who had everything to gain by peace and to lose by war, yet becomes, by the hypothesis, the deliberate originator of that war.

How far the theory that Catherine de' Medici was responsible for the massacre on St. Bartholomew's Day will square with these facts is a point which each must decide for himself.[68] They cannot be slurred over or explained away, but must be faced.

What, however, is probably the truest view of this question was long ago pointed out by a Protestant historian, "the fair-minded Ranke," who stated that the responsibility for this massacre had been unfairly placed by the French people on the shoulders of Catherine de' Medici, whereas it was they themselves who must bear it; for that this massacre was caused entirely by their own state of wild fanaticism and the frenzied hatred by which at the moment both of the religious factions who faced each other in Paris were possessed.[69]

The two parties into which Frenchmen were divided, furiously embittered against each other by many cruel deeds during ten years of conflict, and brought into close juxtaposition in a single city, were seething with animosity, and from the moment that Guise's retainer fired upon Coligny were bent upon massacring each other; it was only a question of hours which should be the assailant, while the knowledge of what their opponents were planning drove each forward. The Protestant party who had marched into Paris in confident strength, had already once before planned to massacre the Roman Catholics in Paris,[70] and it was to a large extent fear of what their opponents might do which caused the rapid resolve of the Roman Catholics to be the first in the field. "The night, the unexpected situation, the thought of having in the Louvre itself thirty or forty of the most redoubtable Protestants, a Pardaillon, a De Piles, the first swordsmen of France," [71] all combined to make Guise and his party rush to massacre their opponents before the latter should do the same to them, and to force the Queen Mother and the King to stand aside while they worked their will upon their foes. Catherine between the two antagonists had only one object, that which she had always had, to preserve the throne from being overwhelmed in the storm. But she was placed in a more difficult position than hitherto, owing to the close proximity of the two foes. Walsingham, the English Minister, afterwards told her that it would have been easy to seize the persons who were plotting on the Protestant side, and so have avoided the explosion; but his argument took no account of the fact that any force with which she could have done so must have been a Roman Catholic one, and that would at once have brought about the same catastrophe. As far as can be judged in the absence of any record that can be trusted, Catherine, for once in her life, was thoroughly frightened (as well she might be), and seeing that a conflict was going to take place which she had no longer any power to prevent, sought only to keep herself and her children and her daughter's husband from being destroyed in it. While the massacre was spreading through the city, she sent her commands to the Roman Catholics to desist, but no one paid any attention to her, and for the time being Paris was as much beyond any control as a city in which a sack was taking place.

The truth is that France had become by this time so maddened by these furious religious wars that such a massacre was likely at any time in any city; and as a matter of fact, as soon as the news of what had occurred in Paris spread, similar massacres did take place in one or two other towns. It is also evident that Queen Elizabeth of England did not attach much credit to the reports of Catherine's responsibility in the matter, for though she thought it politics to express her reprobation of the massacre, she did not break off the negotiations for her own marriage with Catherine's son.

The above massacre ruined all Catherine's plans. During the visit which she and her son had paid to Coligny when he was wounded, Charles IX had said, looking angrily at the Duke of Guise: "It is I who am attacked"; whereupon Catherine had added: "It is all France." And she was right; the flames of war were relighted, destined to cause still greater desolation and misery to France than even that which the country had already experienced. The Fourth Religious War began at once, and raged with great fury for the whole of the next twelve months, until in July 1573 a temporary truce was effected, called the Peace of Rochelle, as before on the lines of Catherine's now celebrated "Edict of January."

(1574-1589)

The Peace of Rochelle proved nothing more than a six months' truce, and in February 1574 the Fifth Religious War broke out. Three months later, in May 1574, Charles IX. died; [72] and as he left only a daughter,[73] he was succeeded by his brother, Henry III, then twenty-three. When Charles IX's Queen, the good Elizabeth of Austria, was condoled with because her child was not a boy, she replied that she was glad of it, since that would only have added yet further divisions to cause affliction to distracted France.

Henry III, Catherine's favourite son, who now ascended the throne, was a strange character, inheriting more of his father's peculiar disposition than either of his brothers, but with all his father's weak points greatly intensified. He had plenty of intelligence, had been made Lieutenant-General of the realm, and taken part with distinction in the various campaigns during the previous five years (including the battles of Jarnac and Moncontour), and had eight months before been elected as King of Poland, where he governed with much success, and won the greatest admiration from the Poles, notwithstanding that they were mostly Protestants. But his abilities were combined with an indolence which caused him, on becoming King of France, to make his mother undertake all affairs that were troublesome, and also with a taste for the most extravagant follies, a taste which became more pronounced as he grew older. On hearing in Poland that he had become King of France he arranged a midnight escape from his faithful Polish subjects in the manner of a conspirator fleeing for his life. Entertaining at this time a violent passion for the Princess of Condé, he poured forth the most extravagant sentiments to her in letters written in his blood; [74] but on hearing of her sudden death, he showed his grief by wearing little silver death's heads all over his dress, even on his shoe ribbons, and after a week appeared completely to forget her, and became entirely occupied in making proposals of marriage to a young lady, Louise de Vaudemont, whom he had chanced to see a month or two before at Nancy. Meanwhile, he went off to Avignon, and while there joined "the flagellants"; [75] and insisted on the ladies of the court, and even his mother, doing so also. His follies and extravagant vagaries were innumerable, each more fantastic than the last. His mother idolised him; she could refuse him nothing; and those who have held that Catherine de' Medici was without the softer feelings natural to a woman have only to study the expressions in her letters wherever the name of her son Henry occurs to discover that this view is far from the truth.

We have a somewhat touching glimpse of Catherine at this period in connection with a visit which, while staying at Lyons, she paid to the studio of the painter Corneille de Lyon. There, looking round the pictures on the walls, she saw one of herself as she had been about five-and-twenty years before, "attired in the French *mode*, with a little cap edged with pearls, and a dress having large sleeves of silver tissue, lined with lynx." After gazing at it sadly for a few moments, recalling as it did the memories of the years of her long trial, in the days of Diane de Poictiers, she turned to the Duc de Nemours and said: "Cousin, you remember well the time and fashion of this picture; and you can say, better than any of those around us, if I was once as I am painted here."

Henry III was crowned at Rheims on the 13th February 1575, and two days afterwards married Louise de Vaudemont. Her father was the Count de Vaudemont, and it speaks well for Henry, as a counterpoise to his many follies, that he thus chose for himself the daughter of a simple gentleman of France (whose family were not even wealthy), rather than any of the royal princesses who had been spoken of as a desirable match for the new King of France. His choice proved an excellent one; Louise had a charming character, her beautiful disposition, modesty, wisdom, and innate goodness being praised by all writers; she shone like a star amidst the corruptions of the court, yet gave offence to none, and was respected by all around her, while her husband invariably treated her with deference and affection. Both Protestants and Roman Catholics had at last found one point at all events on which they could agree, for both of them loved and reverenced "La Reine Blanche," as Louise came to be called. And it is one of the brightest spots in the character of Catherine de' Medici that she was intensely fond of Louise de Vaudemont, and showed it to the last hour of her life.

Meanwhile, the Fifth Religious War continued to rage over France, and an end to the conflict seemed as far off as ever, "though," we are told, "the Queen Mother did not cease to labour for peace tooth and nail." At last, however, in April 1576, a peace was concluded at Beaulieu, again on the basis of Catherine's "Edict of January." And this time France obtained rest for nearly a year.

Nothing could better show how thoroughly the Edict for which Catherine had fought and won her struggle with the *Parlement* in January 1562 provided just that balance between the two parties which the needs of France required than the fact that again and again after war had raged we find the Protestants, in negotiating for peace, stipulating for the terms of this Edict, and again and again find peace between the combatants made on its basis. If only the two parties had been sufficiently ready "to live and let live" to have adhered to it, France would, through Catherine's celebrated measure of toleration, have saved itself many years of misery. Some have held that there was in Catherine's career, as the ruling spirit of France, a Protestant period and a Roman Catholic period, and a complete change from the former to the latter after the year 1562; [76] but this constant attainment of peace on the basis of her "Edict of January" time after time for so many years afterwards entirely contradicts this, and refutes the idea that there was ever this change in her attitude. It was just because her attitude remained always unchanged that the same Edict, published so many years before, was able to form the basis of each peace that she brought about.

This spirit of tolerance and natural attraction for freedom is a remarkable feature in Catherine's character in view of the opinion on that point which was universal in her day. Nothing roused greater wrath and contempt in the men of that age than to note a spirit of tolerance in a ruler; they invariably attributed it to either weakness, lukewarmness, or duplicity. And seeing that, after all, Catherine was a Roman Catholic, and as such necessarily had more sympathy with that side in the contest, that she should so steadfastly have adopted a policy of toleration shows a degree of broad-minded statesmanship of which she had considerable reason to be proud. It was undoubtedly due to Florentine ideas, and to that republican atmosphere in which she had been born and brought up, and which had been traditional in her family. [77] Ideas of freedom in political life lead naturally to ideas of freedom in religion. One outcome of this spirit on Catherine's part was a notable one. For when we remember how terrible were the horrors of the Inquisition, nothing tends more strongly to make us regard Catherine de' Medici with favour than the fact that at a time when the Inquisition was perpetrating its detestable enormities in every other country round—in Spain, in Italy, in the Netherlands, and every other Roman Catholic country—Catherine boldly refused during all the years of her life to allow it to be established in France. This brought upon her the enmity of both the Pope and the fanatical Philip II of Spain, whose vengeance in the defenceless state of France could only be warded off by much diplomacy on Catherine's part, with, as a result, many accusations against her of "duplicity." Nevertheless Catherine was as iron on this point, and the anchor which was the sole protection of many lives from horrible tortures and death was not to be torn from its hold. Repeatedly we find men whose lives were in danger from this cause in the adjacent countries flying to Catherine for protection, and obtaining it. One of the most notable of these was Carnesecchi, a Florentine who, becoming one of the chief of the Protestant reformers in Italy, was pronounced by the Pope a "refractory heretic." Forced to fly for his life from Italy, he was protected by Catherine from the wrath of the Pope; and when after a long residence in France he ventured to return to Florence, Catherine wrote to her kinsman, Cosimo I, urging him to protect Carnesecchi as she had done; the disregard of which recommendation resulted in Carnesecchi's being burnt in Rome by the Inquisition.[78]

The Peace of Beaulieu having once more brought a tranquil state of affairs, Catherine, who had inaugurated the reign of each of her other two sons by a *fête* at Chenonceaux, did the same in Henry III's case. That which she now held for him was on a more splendid scale than any which had taken place before, every effort being employed to make the occasion as joyous as possible, and with the hope that at last the miseries of war were at an end. But what we chiefly hear of in connection with the festivities are the extravagant follies of Henry. He received the guests dressed as a woman, with jewels in his hair, earrings in his ears, strings of pearls round his bared neck, an embroidered collar and high ruff; his youthful courtiers were arrayed in a similar manner, while by his desire the ladies of the court were attired as men, but with bare shoulders and flowing hair.

But the sunshine was only temporary, and the storm-clouds were soon again gathered over France. From the first the Guises had refused to be bound by the peace made at Beau-

lieu, as they declared it to be too favourable to the Protestants.
They therefore now formed the celebrated "League" (with
Henry, Duke of Guise, at its head) for the defence of the
interests of the Roman Catholic party. This League had for
its policy one the exact opposite of Catherine's, being formed
to overturn her principle of a recognition by the State of two
religions side by side in France; and while she laboured
steadily to attain peace by means of this principle, the League
strove to keep up a state of war until Protestantism should
have been crushed, and was the cause of innumerable troubles
to France during the next twenty years. The first result of
the formation of the League was that the Guises were enabled
so to manipulate the elections that the States-General when
assembled consisted almost entirely of deputies opposed to the
principle of the toleration of two religions; and on the 1st
January 1577 this assembly declared themselves in favour of
one religion only, and forced the King to abolish the "Edict
of January." The Protestants at once took up arms, were
assisted with money by Elizabeth of England, and the Sixth
Religious War began. It lasted for nine months, but in September the principle of tolerating both religions was again
agreed to, and a peace was made at Bergerac in September 1577.

Catherine was now approaching sixty years of age, and her
appearance was very different from that which she had borne
in the days of Henry II. Instead of the beautiful figure for
which she had been so admired during all the earlier portion
of her life in France, she was now immensely stout. But she
still danced and rode, played games, and excelled in shooting
with the cross-bow. "Her complexion was fresh; 'she had not a
wrinkle on her full round face,' which was set off by the long,
black widow's veil she always wore, fastened back from her
forehead and falling down upon her shoulders. This was for
indoors; when she went out she put a little woollen hat upon
the top of it. Had we met her, we should have probably

thought her a jolly soul—a little inclined to be cynical. But we should have found her good company; colloquial in her speech, with vivid turns of expression." [79]

At times, however, she could blaze out as fiercely as Queen Elizabeth of England herself; but with more dignity. One who knew her well has said:—"She had these moods not seldom, even with the greatest Princes. . . . And at such times she was possessed by anger, and took a lofty tone. Nor was anything in the world so superb as she on such occasions; for her tongue spared the truth to no one." Her ability for business and power of concentration were marvellous. "Brantôme says that he watched her write twenty long letters in an afternoon. And on one of those uncomfortable journeys in a litter to which ladies were then subjected, she, unconscious of joltings and of stoppings, would read through ten pages of parchment—a dry *procès verbal*—'as if she were a lawyer or reporter,' without lifting her eyes till she had finished. Her style in writing is business-like and terse, illumined here and there by homely wit and racy phrase." [80]

Perhaps nothing better shows Catherine's strong nature and entire freedom from all small-minded vanity than her tolerance of jokes against herself. When she heard that the Protestants called their biggest cannon *La Reine Mère* because it was so heavy and unwieldy that they could not move it—a joke which few ladies of stout figure would relish—she only laughed in the most good-humoured manner at the unflattering jest. "For that of her nature she was jovial, and loved a good repartee." A contemporary writer says:—"She was never gayer than when some one brought her a good satire against herself, the bitterer, ruder, coarser, the better. Once when she and the King of Navarre were standing in the window of a ground-floor room, they listened to two vagrants outside who were roasting a goose, and who, as they did so, talked loudly, telling ugly stories of the Queen, cursing her and giving her foul names for all the evil she had done to them. Whereupon the King of Navarre wished to take leave of her, intending to go and have them hanged. But she only called through the window to them: '*Hé!* What, after all, has she done to you? It is thanks to her that you have that goose to roast.' " [81]

In her letters to her son Henry she often displays the sadness of heart which came over her as she saw him more and more given up to follies, and surrounding himself with others more foolish than himself, whose advice he took instead of hers. She writes to him:—"Give orders for some one to tell me how your affairs are going. I do not ask this because I wish to control them, but because if they go well my heart will be at ease, and if they go ill, I can help your trouble. . . . For you are my all, and whether or no you love me, you do not trust me as you ought. Forgive me if I speak straight out like this. I have no wish to live any longer. I have never cared for life since your father died, excepting as I might serve you and God." In another letter to him she says:—"And this is my request, that you will publish anew the ordinance forbidding swearing and blaspheming, . . . and will punish those who do not keep it, . . and firmly resolve not to give either bishopric, or any benefice with the cure of souls, excepting to learned men of good life." [82]

In August 1578, hostilities again threatening to break out, Catherine (her son, Henry III, having none of the gift which she possessed for reconciling hostile parties) set out on a prolonged tour through the south of France in order to prevent war if possible, the first of those wonderful "journeys of pacification" in which she was engaged during the greater part of the next three years. To Bellièvre, her Intendant of Finance, she writes:—

"It seems to me that one ought to quit everything else, and to employ every means to avert the storm of war. I am determined not to return until I see peace. . . . But if God gives me grace to fulfil my desires I hope that this kingdom will feel the good of my labours, and that enduring peace will reign there." [83]

One gazes in astonishment at this woman of sixty, hampered by bodily infirmities and the difficulties of travel at that period in France, and confronted by such apparently insuperable obstacles in the irreconcilable temper towards each other of the two hostile parties, resolutely setting forth (notwithstanding that it was an acute pain to her to thus absent herself from the son whom she adored) determined to overcome all difficulties, to carry out the motto she had chosen when a girl of fifteen, and to "bring serenity" to her adopted country; and displaying a power of endurance, and an ability to win success even under the most adverse conditions, which have extorted admiration even from those most prejudiced against her. For example, Miss Sichel says:—

"It is impossible not to admire the indomitable spirit with which, as she grew older, she pursued her object in the face of every hardship, every obstacle. Between 1578 and 1581 she knew no repose. Driven by her purpose, she was continually traversing France, amidst perils and discomforts unimaginable. So heavy in person that motion meant suffering, she was always on the move; so rheumatic that acute pain was chronic, she uncomplainingly braved every kind of climate. Now she was carried in her litter under a burning sun; now she was snowed up for weeks, amid all the bodily privations and the difficulties of getting provisions that winter in the country then signified." [84]

The provinces to which Catherine chiefly turned her attention in this attempt to prevent war were Guienne, Languedoc, Provence, and Dauphiné. She received no encouragement from those around her in regard to the task upon which she was bent. All thought, and said, that it was a hopeless endeavour, the hatred between the two factions having grown so implacable, and that she was attempting the impossible. Nevertheless she managed to bring about a conference between the two opposing parties, and so successful was she in allaying their mutual feelings of enmity that she ended by getting articles of agreement which placed the two religions on an equal footing drawn up and signed by both sides at Nérac in February 1579; and war was once more averted.

Catherine's satisfaction at her success was naturally considerable. To the Duchesse d'Uzès she says (in another letter): "You have understood me, and I you, for more than forty years of kindly memories." And to this lifelong friend she now writes:—

"I have finished my labours here, and in my humble opinion have made a great many persons to lie; for I have achieved that which was said to be impossible."

But there were other provinces still to be visited where the difficulties were even greater. Thus in coming to Montpellier she approached a city which was on the verge of an appeal to arms, and known to be inimical to her personally. She writes to her son:—

"I walked the whole length of the city walls and reached the gate, which I found guarded by arquebusiers, as I had been told. But that did not prevent me from going on fearlessly, without showing dread or mistrust, although they were all so near my coach (especially as the road there is narrow) that the butts of their arquebuses nearly touched my carriage. The Consuls in their red robes and their caps, together with a great crowd of people of both religions who followed them, came to meet me with all humility, offering you and me their property and lives, with all the devotion of loyal subjects; and both parties promised me on their honour to live according to my commands. When I got nearly opposite the gate another great crowd of people came out of the town, all showing a more friendly feeling than I had been led to expect. The fact that I had gone among them so freely helped a good deal, I am told, to increase their confidence, and also their certainty that peace was near.... I thought to have managed to sleep here yesterday, so as to escape the risk of the plague by making one day's journey, getting earlier to Provence; but I felt rather tired, as I did full six leagues among the rocks of this district before my dinner." [85]

In the recent troubles every church in the town had been destroyed, except one. And this had become a bone of contention. The Protestants claimed half of it; the Roman Catholics refused to worship under the same roof, and claimed the whole building. She got them to refer the knotty point to her, and, after much acrid discussion, arranged an amicable settlement.

In this manner Catherine travelled hither and thither, smoothing difficulties, overcoming obstacles deliberately contrived to frustrate her purpose, producing smiles where she had been met with frowns, and settling innumerable disputes. Last of all she reached Dauphiné, regarding which province she writes to the Duchesse d'Uzès:—

"Here I am in your land of Dauphiné, the hilliest and most aggravating in which I have hitherto been. Every day there is cold, heat, rain, fine weather, hail. And the characters of the people here are just the same. But God, who leads me, is bringing me to my goal, . . . and in ten days I shall be in my beloved France and in the city where is the dearest thing I have in the world. Report says that you govern him; keep me in his good graces; and tell d'Ecars that since she has sat next to him at dinner I am sure he no longer wishes to die." [86]

Again to the same friend she writes:—

"Were it not for the plague, I would bring you news of your estate, but all the neighbourhood round Uzès is so very much infected that they say even the birds flying past it fall dead. This has made me take the other road, between the lakes and the sea; and there we had to sleep two nights in tents, camping thus in the service of my King, whom I long to see again in good health. As for me, mine is good, excepting that Porte-Sainte-Marie has given me a troublesome catarrh, which, at the moment, has turned to sciatica. However, this does not prevent my walking; not very well, though, so that I am forced to have a little mule to ride upon occasions. I think that the King would laugh if he saw me on it, looking so exactly like the Maréchal de Cossé.[87] But if one goes on living, one must grow old, and truly one is very lucky not to feel it more. *You* have to ride in a carrying chair, *I* upon a mule, because I like to travel farther than you do. Tell me that I shall be welcome when I return." [88]

At length her task was accomplished; peace had been created for a time in Guienne, Languedoc, Provence, and Dauphiné. But scarcely had she returned with a joyful heart to Paris when similar troubles began in the north, and she had to set forth again on a journey in December into Picardy; where also she succeeded for a time in averting war.

But the two religious parties had not yet learnt to live at peace together. Their adherents could never refrain for long from insulting each other's religion, thereby provoking brawls which quickly developed into open war; and in this conduct the Protestants were not a whit behind their opponents, while they had always a strong tendency to invoke foreign aid, a course which enlisted against them every one who had a patriotic feeling for France. As before, therefore, this inherent animosity again produced its natural result, and in March 1580 the Seventh Religious War began. After continuing for eight months this war was brought to an end in November by the Peace of Fleix, the terms of which were almost exactly the same as the agreement which Catherine had got the two parties to sign at Nérac.

This peace, joined to the exhausted state of France, created by wars which had continued almost incessantly for fourteen years, now caused a cessation of the contest for four years (1581-1585); though during these years there were from time to time local conflicts in different parts of France, while the state of general disorder into which the country had been brought by this long and bitter struggle was deplorable. In June 1584 Catherine's fourth son, the Duc d'Alençon, died, which, as Louise de Vaudemont had no children, left Henry of Navarre the next heir to the throne. Catherine's many sorrows, disappointments, and bereavements began to weigh heavily upon her. She writes about this time:—

"I am so much accustomed never to have an unspoiled joy that it does not seem so strange to me as it would to another. . . . That God will be pitiful to me who have lost so many; that He will not let me see any more of them die: that is what I pray of His mercy, and that He will allow me to depart, as befits my age." [89]

Catherine de' Medici praying that because so many of her dear ones are gone she may depart this life as befits her age, is certainly not the picture of her which has been painted for us by a long succession of writers. Yet these are her own written words, unearthed after three centuries by the patient labour of an age which seeks to base its knowledge of history on more sure foundations than those which sufficed for previous times.

In July 1585 the operations of the League caused the commencement of the Eighth Religious War (sometimes called the War of the Three Henrys) between Henry III, Henry of Navarre, and the League, under Henry, Duke of Guise.[90] Catherine was now sixty-six years old, and was wearied with this long struggle to create peace; nevertheless, before this war began she took a toilsome journey into Champagne to endeavour to induce Guise to keep from war; but without avail. About this time also she became so disgusted with the follies of Henry III, and the persistency with which he insisted on invariably choosing the most ill-advised courses of action, that she removed from the Louvre, and gave up taking any part in public affairs. We read of her ordering her attendants to carry her "chair" outside the city walls and to put her down for a while in the green fields, that she might, amid the quiet peace of country scenes, gain some rest of mind and allay her utter weariness of spirit at the political condition of the country and her son's refusal to listen to her advice.

But Catherine had adopted France as her country, and notwithstanding the long abuse she had endured from the French, was as intensely national as if born a Frenchwoman. And when she saw one third of the kingdom occupied by the troops of the League, another third by those of Henry of Navarre, a German army also invading the country, and France threatened with complete dismemberment, she came forth from her retirement to make one more effort to save the country and her son's throne. War now raged over the whole of France, but Catherine, though she was by this time sixty-eight, set out on the last of her many journeys in the cause of peace, one which required no little courage, and, travelling through a large part of France which was in revolt from her son, held a meeting with Henry of Navarre near Cognac. This, however, produced only partial results, while news of the alarming state of affairs in Paris, created by the machina-tions of the League, necessitated her hurrying back to the capital. On her way thither she heard at Mort, in February 1587, of Elizabeth of England having had Mary, Queen of Scots, executed,[91] that daughter-in-law to whom Catherine had set Latin exercises, and of whom she had written twenty-eight years before that she "had only to smile to turn all Frenchmen's heads." Elizabeth had put Mary to death be-cause she was a dangerous rival to her throne, and on account of the plots against herself of which Mary had become the centre. If it did not cross Catherine's own mind it must have crossed the minds of others that Elizabeth's position in the matter was exactly that in which Catherine had been placed in December 1560 with regard to the Prince of Condé, and yet that she had not acted as Elizabeth had done, even though she would have had more excuse, since she had merely to allow (as she was strongly pressed to do) a sentence of death already passed against him by others to take effect.

On arrival in Paris Catherine found a revolutionary government installed there, which, prompted by the League, was intriguing with Spain both to seize the King and also to make over Boulogne to Philip II in order to assist the Armada which he was preparing for the invasion of England. However, these plans were eventually foiled, and after a time Henry III was able to leave Paris in command of an army to attack the Germans and expel them from France.

The war continued during the rest of the year 1587, but at length, in February 1588, a sort of peace was patched up between Henry III and the Duke of Guise. Paris, however, was entirely on the side of the latter, and on the verge of revolution; the King therefore ordered Guise not to come to the capital. This order he disobeyed, pretending not to have understood it, and entered the city on the 9th May, being received in the streets with the usual shouts of "One religion." The King was urged by those around him to have Guise assassinated on his leaving the Louvre, and had determined on doing so; but at the interview between the King and Guise, Catherine, suddenly seeing what her son contemplated, took him aside and spoke to him so forcibly that he allowed Guise (who on entering the Louvre had wondered if he should leave the palace alive) to depart unharmed. Three days later Paris rose in revolt on behalf of Guise and the League; barricades were quickly erected, cutting off the different quarters of the royal troops from each other, the Swiss troops were forced to surrender, and the King, with his wife Louise and his mother, protected by a very small force, were besieged in the Louvre. Henry III's cause seemed ruined, and Catherine must have felt that it was chiefly his own fault, through the many follies he had committed. We are told that as the King, the Queen, and the Queen Mother sat at dinner on the evening that this revolution took place, Catherine, "while her son sat unmoved, silently shed great tears throughout the entire repast." [92] However, next day Henry managed to escape from the Louvre, and fled from Paris, leaving his mother to see what she could do by her well-known gift for reconciliation. Issuing from the Louvre almost unaccompanied Catherine went to seek the Duke of Guise. Her journey across the city was a difficult operation. The streets were everywhere blocked by barricades, and at each of these it was necessary to induce those who guarded them to allow her to pass and to make an opening for her sedan chair. But though the Leaguers were in open rebellion she induced them to do so, "all heads being uncovered to the Queen Mother." Nothing could show better than this the influence which Catherine (once so despised by the French people) had in thirty years gained among them. As so often before, she was successful in assuaging the angry passions raging; and though everything was against her she succeeded in getting Guise to accompany her to Chartres, where the King was, and in arranging terms of peace, though the latter practically left Guise all-powerful in the kingdom (11th July 1588). Within a fortnight after this peace was made in France the Spanish Armada appeared off the coast of Cornwall, and the great ten days' naval battle between Spain and England began in which the maritime power of Spain was utterly destroyed.

But peace was not yet to come to France; and round Catherine's death-bed the storm was still to rage. Henry III was now determined to assassinate Guise, but, remembering what had taken place before, carefully kept his design from his mother. Catherine, worn out by so many labours and anxieties, was by this time in a dying condition, and removed to Blois, that fortified château on the Loire which Francis I had so greatly improved and enlarged. Thither in October the King summoned the States-General to assemble; and there, on the 23rd December 1588, Henry carried out his plot to rid himself of the Duke of Guise.

In the great northern wing, built by Francis I, and afford

ing such a splendid example of French Renaissance architecture, Catherine in her richly decorated range of apartments lay dying. Close by rose the wonderful outside staircase, the *escalier à jour*,[93] which more than fifty years back she had so often seen thronged by the laughing groups of the Petite Bande; but a very different atmosphere now pervaded the castle of Blois, and the gloom of tragedy and death overshadowed the abode which Francis had delighted to see brightened with the smiles of beauty and resounding with laughter and the sallies of wit. Catherine's apartments were on the first floor, while the King occupied the suite of apartments on the floor above; and he had warned all in the plot, on pain of death, not to allow the Queen Mother to know what was going on. The murder was secretly debated by the King and Council after the manner of an execution. It was to be carried out by the "Forty-five," the band of gentlemen which Henry had formed as his personal bodyguard; some of the band were placed in the King's bedchamber, and some in the passage outside it. The Duke of Guise, who had received intimation that there was a plot on foot, but would not attend to the warning, being summoned from the council chamber to speak with the King in his cabinet, was attacked as he went thither by the members of the "Forty-five" stationed for that purpose, and fell dead on the floor of the King's bedchamber. Henry III at once descended to his mother's apartments, and, entering the room where she lay ill, announced to her what he had done, saying that now at last he felt secure on his throne. Catherine, knowing what the vengeance of the League would be, and how this deed would again set light to the fires of war, but too ill to attempt any longer to guide the vessel amidst so many breakers, told him he was much mistaken and would live to repent his act.[94] Weak as she was, she dragged herself from her bed and went to visit the old Cardinal Bourbon in the prison to which he had been consigned by the King's orders; but he only greeted her with the old cry that all these misfortunes were the result of her policy of tolerating two

religions. The injustice of these reproaches, combined with
distress of mind on account of the troubles she correctly foresaw would be the result of her son's deed, threw her into a
high fever, and on returning from the interview, she took to
her bed never to rise from it again. And a few days later, on
the 5th January 1589, Catherine de' Medici ended her long
and storm-tossed life. She was three months short of seventy
years of age when she died.

Two women attended her affectionately throughout her
illness, and were with her to the last—her much-loved daughter-in-law, Louise de Vaudemont, and her favourite grand-
daughter, Christine of Lorraine.[95] To the former Catherine
left as a parting gift her beloved château of Chenonceaux—a
solid boon to Louise, who on her husband's death shortly afterwards was left very badly off. Catherine during her lifetime
had erected in St. Denis a double monument for Henry II
and herself; but when she died the war which at once broke
out again on the murder of the Duke of Guise did not permit of
her body being removed thither, and she was buried temporarily in the chapel at Blois. But in 1609, at the entreaty of
the Duchess of Angoulême, who had always liked Catherine,
her remains were removed by Henry IV to St. Denis, and
buried by the side of her husband. The monument over them
consists of the two recumbent figures of Henry II and Catherine, lying on a bronze couch.

The character of Catherine de' Medici as it stands revealed
to us by the fuller information we now possess, and divested
of that cloud of mystery, fable, and misrepresentation which
has so long been gathered round it by partisan writers, is not
difficult to unravel. That which is its salient feature is the
extraordinary way in which (though always suffering abuse
as an "Italian") she threw herself heart and soul into the
cause of France, and amidst difficulties, dangers, and discouragements enough to have made the stoutest heart abandon

the effort in despair, laboured from the age of forty-two to that of seventy to bring peace to a country devastated by a succession of vindictive wars. Thus one of those Venetian ambassadors who have so often formed our guides in this study of her life, calls her "the great moderatress"; while the highest authority has said of her that "she was an indefatigable worker in the cause of peace in her adopted country." [96]

In the previous history of Catherine's family we have seen that one of their chief characteristics was a unique gift for abating strife, and making those who were at feud lay aside their enmity and live at peace. It was their special talent in this respect which had helped them to rise, and had made their rule of Florence so successful. And in Catherine this family characteristic comes out in even stronger degree than in any of her ancestors. Again and again—at Orleans, at Roussillon, at Saint-Germain-en-Laye, at Beaulieu, at Nérac, at Fleix, at Chartres, and on many other occasions—she proved her peculiar gift for pouring oil on troubled waters and getting bitter foes to make peace. This is the chief characteristic which she shows during the thirty years of her widowhood. The other qualities which she possessed have been successively indicated by the facts of her life as we have followed her long and harassed career from her childhood in the Medici Palace in Florence to her death at gloom-darkened Blois.

And if any indication of character is afforded (as it is) by the persons whom an individual has chiefly liked through life, then it is not without significance that, omitting her husband and children, the persons of whom, at different times in her life, we find Catherine chiefly fond—nay more, the only persons of whom we hear that she was specially fond— are the nuns at the Murate, Maria Salviati, Elizabeth of Austria, and above all Louise de Vaudemont, the three latter all of them women who in a corrupt age were like shining lights in a dark sky.[97] Nor, again, is it without significance that so many notable Protestants should have owed their lives to her, such as Condé, Navarre, De l'Hôpital, Aldobrandini, Carnesecchi, and others; or that one who (in the circumstances of France) had special reason to dread making unnecessary foes, should yet have endured the wrath of the Pope and the King of Spain rather than ever permit the Inquisition to be established in the country she ruled. These things, together with the fact that the two murders of which she has in former days been accused are now acknowledged to have been unjustly laid at her door, necessitate a very different view of the character of Catherine de' Medici from that which has been handed down to us by the biassed historians of an age of bitter conflict, and has so long provided material for the writers of sensational fiction.

It has already been remarked [98] that to those who start from the basis that she was "a villain" Catherine de' Medici will always be an enigma. To look at her with affection is impossible; one might as well feel affection for a hundred-ton gun. On the other hand, those who regard her "with hatred" [99] are not those who can draw a true picture of her; inevitably, under such auspices, stories long since discarded by history are given more or less credit, points which tell against her are painted in unduly strong colours, and those which tell in her favour are belittled and robbed of any weight by the manner in which they are put, until a figure is produced which is an incongruous impossibility, and which has to be declared an "enigma" and a "paradox." Those only will understand Catherine de' Medici who will look at her with a calm dispassionateness.

If, then, we may neither hate nor love, what remains? Admiration for strength, for great ability, for untiring energy, for a self-control which has seldom been equalled, for a wisdom beyond her time (enabling her to see that the only policy which can give peace to a country whose people have taken up opposite views in religion is that of causing different religious bodies to learn to live side by side without conflict), for steadfast determination to do the best for France, for persevering endeavour, through countless discouragements, to be a peacemaker. These are the things, confessed even by her enemies, which we are to admire in Catherine de' Medici; and each fresh record brought to light shows more clearly that they are justly to be attributed to her. She did not succeed: but she splendidly tried. And it is certain that where she did not succeed none other of her time would have done so; for neither in Germany, England, or Flanders was it found possible to prevent the forces let loose by the Reformation from resulting in similar conflicts. While in none of those countries was the attempt made, as it *was* made in France, to attain that mutual toleration which all countries have since found is the only sound policy.

We have surveyed the task; and we have seen the effort which Catherine made to cope with it. Sectarian partisans may continue to battle over her conduct, but the point on which the historian will fix his eye is:—Did Catherine, amidst the terrible woes which came upon the French people through the birth of a new form of religion, by her actions increase those woes, or did she diminish them? This is the sole issue upon which history, as distinguished from religious controversy, will fix its attention and will judge her. And on this issue there is no doubt at all what the verdict will be; in fact it has already been pronounced. Her splendid fight for a hitherto unheard-of principle (that two religions should be allowed to exist, each recognised by the State) was a fight to bring peace to France by what we all now know to be the only means by which peace in such matters can be either obtained or preserved. And, beginning from her three magnificent efforts in the year 1561 by this means to prevent France from drifting into civil war, down to the seventh and last occasion when she brought about peace for a time by the same means, Catherine at each juncture did the most that any one could do to prevent, or to allay, the miseries of France. And just so far as she obtained pauses in the conflict (some of them lasting for several years) did she assuage and diminish the sufferings which that conflict created. With the result that the name given her by the leading modern authority on the subject, in summing up her character and work, is that of *"an indefatigable peacemaker."* And with that verdict the whole issue regarding her conduct is conclusively given in her favour.

Upon this last scion of Cosimo's branch devolved a task severer far than had fallen to the lot of any of her family who had gone before. Even that of her ancestor, Cosimo Pater Patriae, pales before that which fell upon the shoulders of his last descendant, the baby-girl upon whom in her cradle Cardinal Giulio had looked down in the almost empty Medici Palace, and round whose path he wove so many thorny briars.

PART II

WE have done with that elder branch of the family which in the course of a hundred and ninety years, beginning from the humble position they occupied in the time of Giovanni di Bicci, in the second generation had created a new epoch for Florence, in the fourth had directed the politics of all Italy, in the fifth had swayed the destinies of Europe, and in the seventh had seated its last descendant on the throne of a Queen of France, and governed that country through thirty years of a most troubled time. We have now to turn to the descendants of Giovanni di Bicci's second son, that younger branch which carried on the succession after the death of Alessandro, gained the crown which the achievements of the elder branch had made possible, and which had been the long dream of Giulio de' Medici, and after ruling over Tuscany for two hundred years, brought the family to an end in 1743.

Beginning with Lorenzo, the brother of Cosimo Pater Patriae, there are of this younger branch four generations before we reach that which succeeded to the rule of Tuscany after the death of Alessandro. And while the first and second of these have scarcely any separate history from that of the elder branch, with the third and fourth generations it is otherwise; these have an independent history of their own, particularly in the case of Giovanni and his wife, Catherine Sforza, and their celebrated son, Giovanni delle Bande Nere. But although the consideration of their history involves retracing our steps, it has the compensating advantage that the story of their lives often throws a sidelight on that of the elder branch. The time of Giovanni and Catherine Sforza is contemporary with that of Lorenzo the Magnificent, Pietro the Unfortunate, and the "Interregnum"; and the time of Giovanni delle Bande Nere with that of Leo X and Clement VII. Lastly, the reigns of Cosimo I and his son Francis I are contemporaneous with the long life of Catherine de' Medici.

CHAPTER XXI

LORENZO (THE ELDER)

Born 1395. Died 1440

LORENZO, the second son of Giovanni di Bicci, generally called Lorenzo the Elder to distinguish him from his grandson of the same name, took no part in that public life which formed the chief occupation of his brother Cosimo. He was of a retiring disposition, without ambition or taste for public affairs, and was content to be a humble assistant to his more capable elder brother, and to confine himself to the banking concerns of the family. He shared in the banishment of 1433, and in the triumphant return in 1434, and lived for six years after that event, dying in 1440. He thus lived long enough to see his brother exercising the chief influence in the State, though not to see all the subsequent developments of the remaining twenty-four years of Cosimo's strenuous life. We see him in Benozzo Gozzoli's picture in the Medici chapel, riding by Cosimo's side on a mule; and the mutual attitude of the two brothers is undoubtedly correctly represented. Lorenzo married Ginevra Cavalcanti, and left one son, Pier Francesco who was about twenty-five years old when his father died.

PIER FRANCESCO (THE ELDER)

Born 1415. Died 1476

Pier Francesco, son of Lorenzo, generally called Pier Francesco the Elder to distinguish him from his grandson of the same name, was eighteen when the family were banished, and he accompanied his father in their exile to Venice. In the following year they returned, and in a short time his uncle

Cosimo became the chief power in the State; while the death of his father six years later left Pier Francesco head of his branch of the family. Like his father, he preferred a retired life; and though his share of the family wealth, divided between them in 1453, was nearly as great as that of his uncle Cosimo, he lived very quietly, taking little part in public affairs, and confining himself to the banking business of the family. Nor did he nourish any jealousy towards his uncle Cosimo and his cousins, Piero and Giovanni, on account of the more exalted position they had come to occupy in the State. He was fifty when Cosimo Pater Patriae died, and he survived his cousin, Piero il Gottoso, seeing the first seven years of the rule of the latter's son, Lorenzo the Magnificent. Pier Francesco died in 1476 at the age of sixty-one. He married somewhat late in life Laudomia Acciajoli, and left two sons, Lorenzo and Giovanni, aged respectively thirteen and nine when their father died. None of this younger branch possessed the financial talent which distinguished the elder branch, so that their wealth, instead of increasing, gradually diminished; but nevertheless Pier Francesco at his death left his two sons very rich. Bronzino's portrait of him is taken from Filippino Lippi's picture of the *Adoration of the Magi*, painted for Pier Francesco's younger son, Giovanni, in 1496; in which picture Pier Francesco and his son Giovanni are introduced in the same way as Cosimo Pater Patriae, his sons, and grandsons had been in Botticelli's picture on the same subject painted thirty years before for Piero il Gottoso.[1]

LORENZO (The Younger)

COMMONLY CALLED LORENZO "POPOLANO"

Born 1463. Died 1507

Lorenzo the Younger [2] and his brother Giovanni, the two sons of Pier Francesco the Elder, failed to continue the attitude towards the elder branch of the family which had been maintained by their father and grandfather. Their father died while they were still boys, and by the time that they were grown up their second cousin, Lorenzo the Magnificent, had created for himself and his branch of the family a position in Italy of such weight and importance that it resembled that of a sovereign ruler; he was entertaining as an equal the rulers of other states, his children were making exalted marriages, and the whole life of the elder branch was quite different from that of the younger. All this created much jealousy in the minds of the younger branch, who found themselves occupying a very inferior position to their cousins, and they consequently began to exhibit a marked coldness towards the latter. It was in order to allay this feeling that Lorenzo the Magnificent brought about the engagement of his daughter Maria to Giovanni, the younger of the two brothers; but this match was unfortunately prevented from taking place owing to her death in 1487. Lorenzo the Magnificent, however, managed to keep this jealousy from growing stronger so long as he lived, and it did not come to a head until after his death in 1492. Nor did the younger branch fail to participate to some extent in the general exaltation of the family. For in January 1493 we find Isabella d'Este, Marchioness of Mantua, in a letter to her sister Beatrice, mentioning Lorenzo, son of Pier Francesco, as one of the four sponsors of her lately-born daughter; and saying that his brother Giovanni had come to Mantua to represent Lorenzo at the baptism of the child.

Soon after this the two brothers became so incensed against their cousin Pietro the Unfortunate that the jealousy they had long nourished against the elder branch was no longer restrained, and they became, as already noted, chiefly instrumental in rousing the ill feeling against him which culminated in the banishment of the elder branch in 1494; we are told that it was principally owing to their representations that Charles VIII turned aside from Pisa, and instead of taking the coast road thence to Rome, advanced upon Florence. This conduct of theirs, together with their adopting for a time the name of "Popolano" and erasing the family arms from their palace, was never forgiven by the elder branch.

After the elder branch had been thus driven out, Lorenzo, who was a man of very mediocre abilities, became (as the reward for his conduct towards the elder branch of his family) a member of the Government. But the position only served to demonstrate his want of any capacity, and he was merely one among other nonentities who nominally ruled Florence while all the real power was wielded by Savonarola.

And this was undoubtedly the reason why the Pope was able so easily to create a party in Florence antagonistic to Savonarola,[3] and possessing the power to bring him to disaster. Men of the mental calibre of Lorenzo, composing nominally the ruling body of the State, but being thrust into the background by the more able character of Savonarola, resented this and nourished a jealousy of him which made them ready to become the Pope's instruments in order to get rid of him.

Lorenzo and Giovanni took in regard to Savonarola an exactly similar course to that which they had adopted in the case of their cousin Pietro, fanning the ill-feeling against the dominant Prior of San Marco, and endeavouring to derive advantage for themselves by heading the party who were being made use of by the Pope to destroy him. And it appears to have been at their instigation [4] that the attack was made on San Marco which resulted in Savonarola's imprisonment and death. These two brothers are therefore flagrantly associated with one of the most disgraceful episodes in Florentine history; their conduct being all the more to be condemned because they took the ignoble part of instigators to the more prominent actors, they themselves keeping to a large extent out of sight.

Upon his brother Giovanni's death in 1498 Lorenzo appropriated the latter's estate of Castello (three miles from Florence), though it really belonged to the child of a few months old whom his brother had left. He pretended to hold the property as the representative of this child, but, in view of the serious difficulties with the Pope in which the child's mother, Catherine Sforza, had become involved,[5] never intended to surrender it.

Lorenzo's whole conduct with regard to his nephew and the latter's mother, Catherine Sforza, displayed the same meanness of character which he had shown by his action in bringing about the banishment of the elder branch of his family in order to gratify an ignoble jealousy, and by his conduct in becoming one of the Pope's tools for the destruction of Savonarola. He was, however, eventually punished. When his sister-in-law was unexpectedly released from her imprisonment and came to settle in Florence, Lorenzo, much to his disgust, had to surrender to her the custody of her son and the villa of Castello. He had embezzled a large part of the boy's inheritance, and dreaded this being discovered; and the manœuvres he adopted to prevent it showed his character.[6] The lawsuit which followed disclosed what he had done; and the shame of the discovery, together with the mortification at having failed in his object, brought on an illness which caused his death. He died in 1507, at the age of forty-four.

Unlike his brother Giovanni, Lorenzo does not appear to have been to any great extent a patron of art. It is said that Botticelli's drawings illustrating Dante's *Divine Comedy* were executed for him; and Vasari says that one of Michelangelo's early works, "a little St. John," was made for him. He is, however, remarkable as being the only male member of both branches of the Medici family of whom no portrait appears ever to have been painted; and this could scarcely have been the case had he been even to a moderate degree a patron of art. He married Semiramide d'Appiano, and left three sons and two daughters.

Lorenzo's eldest son, Pier Francesco the Younger, was a man of even less note than his father. Almost the only thing recorded of him is his active co-operation with his father in the attempt to rob the boy Giovanni, the son of Giovanni "Popolano" and Catherine Sforza, of his inheritance. Pier Francesco took much interest in the minor arts, especially in pottery. From his father he inherited the estate of Cafaggiolo, and there he founded the Cafaggiolo manufactory which soon became famous, the Cafaggiolo-ware being considered to surpass even that of Faenza. He married Maria Soderini, and was the father of Lorenzino,[7] Maddalena, and Laudomia.[8] Pier Francesco died while his son Lorenzino was still a boy.

CHAPTER XXII

GIOVANNI

Born 1467. Died 1498

GIOVANNI, the second son of Pier Francesco the Elder, is said to have been one of the handsomest and most accomplished of the Florentines of his day. He was eleven years old at the time of the Pazzi Conspiracy, and all his youth was passed in the midst of the splendour of the rule of Lorenzo the Magnificent, and when he was nineteen he was engaged to the latter's daughter Maria, who, however, died before the marriage took place. When Lorenzo the Magnificent died in 1492 Giovanni was twenty-five; and in the following year we find him visiting the court of Mantua in great style at the baptism of Isabella d'Este's daughter. After the leading part which he and his brother Lorenzo took in the banishment of the elder branch of the family, Giovanni took service with the King of France, and was given by Charles VIII a post with an annual salary of two thousand crowns; but this did not last long, as in 1496 he was appointed by the Florentine Republic as their ambassador to Catherine Sforza, the masterful Countess of Forlì.

At Forlì Giovanni soon made himself highly popular, and after a short time the Countess of Forlì (whose political position made it almost imperative that she should marry again) showed so much admiration for her handsome and accomplished Florentine envoy that some began to say that she intended to marry him. Nevertheless it was thought by most to be very unlikely that so great a personage would marry one so much beneath her in rank, and only a simple citizen. It was true that under Lorenzo the Magnificent the family had attained a great position, but with his death and the exile of the elder branch of the Medici all their importance had passed away. The future Pope Leo X was at that time merely a wandering member of a banished family, and all the subsequent developments of that family were undreamt of. However, eventually Giovanni's various attractions prevailed, and in 1497, to the disgust of both Milan and Venice, Catherine Sforza, Countess of Forlì and Imola, married Giovanni de' Medici, called in Florence Giovanni "Popolano." He was then thirty, and she thirty-five. It was by far the most exalted marriage which any member of the Medici family had up to that time made.[1]

Giovanni had much fondness for art, and being both accomplished and wealthy was able to gratify his artistic tastes to the utmost. The sack of the Medici Palace in 1494 had filled Florence with art treasures [2] which those who had plundered them were anxious to sell; and Giovanni was able by this means to adorn his villa of Castello with many of the treasures of art which had belonged to the elder branch. Among other artists he patronised in particular Botticelli and Filippino Lippi. We have seen how in 1496 the latter painted for him one of his finest pictures, his *Adoration of the Magi*, now in the Uffizi Gallery. And the anonymous writer who is quoted by the "Anonimo Gaddiano" tells us that Botticelli painted for Giovanni in his villa of Castello various beautiful pictures. We do not know what these were, but the language used by the writer in question seems to imply that they were frescoes.

Giovanni only survived his marriage a little more than a year. In 1498 he accompanied his stepson, Ottaviano Riario, to Pisa as his guardian and guide in commanding a body of troops; he got ill at Pisa, and, becoming no better, proceeded to the baths of San Pietro in Bagno; there he grew worse, and died on the 14th September 1498, at the age of thirty-one, his wife, Catherine, only arriving a few hours before he died. Their only child was a boy, born five months before his father's death, afterwards the celebrated Giovanni delle Bande Nere.

CATHERINE SFORZA

Born 1462. *Married* { I. GIROLAMO RIARIO, 1477 } *Died* 1509
{ II. GIACOMO FEO, 1489 }
{ III. GIOVANNI DE' MEDICI, 1497 }

Catherine Sforza, who was the ancestress of all the Medici who follow, was regarded by those of her own time as a sort of wonder of her age, a woman of almost superhuman ability, courage, and resolution. Her history before she married into the Medici family is valuable, as, since her first marriage was into the family who were their greatest enemies, it throws a sidelight upon the story of the Medici during the time of Lorenzo the Magnificent, Pietro the Unfortunate, and the "Interregnum."

The Sforza were not, like their contemporaries the Este of Ferrara, of long and noble descent. Catherine's great-grand father, Muzio Attendolo, who was given the name of "Sforza," had been a private soldier, the son of a peasant, but had raised himself to be a renowned commander, and married the widow of the King of Naples. His son, Francesco Sforza, had been a similarly renowned *condottiere* leader, who in 1441 had married Bianca Maria Visconti, and in 1450, by the help of Cosimo Pater Patriae, had become Duke of Milan.[3] His eldest son, Galeazzo Sforza, Catherine's father,[4] had succeeded him in 1466, and two years later had married the good Bona of Savoy, called "the Madonna of Italy," and a very different character from her sister, Louise of Savoy, mother of Francis I.

Catherine Sforza was brought up by her grandmother, the Duchess Bianca Maria Visconti, who in all the early struggles of her husband, Francesco Sforza, was not only a most capable adviser and helper to him, and even on occasion a brave leader of his soldiers in battle, but also was adored by the people as a saint and the protector of the oppressed. She was the peacemaker and comforter wherever enmity, wrongs, or misery existed; and it was under her that Catherine was first shown what governing ought to be like. But she died in 1470, after which Catherine was brought up by her stepmother, the Duchess Bona.

Catherine, in accordance with the custom of the time, had a most elaborate education. We have already seen [5] how in the generation immediately preceding hers (in the time of Lucrezia Tornabuoni) ladies in Italy had begun to come forth from the seclusion previously customary, and to make themselves notable by their attainments. And in Catherine's time this became still more pronounced. The ladies of that age were accomplished to an extent which would now be thought scarcely possible. They were expected to be proficient in classical learning and Latin and Greek composition, to be conversant also with the current literature of their own and other countries, to have a knowledge of the various branches of art and science, to be as accomplished in music, dancing, and the playing of various instruments as their brothers were in the use of arms, and be able to ride well and take part in field sports. Cecilia Gonzaga, Ippolita Sforza (Catherine's aunt),[6] and Catherine herself, with, a few years later, Isabella d'Este, her sister Beatrice d'Este, and their sister-in-law, Elisabetta Gonzaga, all furnish examples of the numerous attainments and wide range of culture of the ladies of this time. We read of Ippolita Sforza, at about twelve years old, delighting Pope Pius II, when he visited her father's court, by reciting a Latin oration composed by herself; of Cecilia Gonzaga reading and writing both Greek and Latin at eight years old; of Catherine herself, at the age of ten, reciting Latin verses of her own composition to welcome Cardinal Riario to her father's court; of Elisabetta Gonzaga singing Virgil's poems and accompanying herself on the lute; and of Isabella d'Este reading Virgil and Cicero when quite a young girl, and continuing her classical studies even when Marchioness of Mantua. While at the same time we read of these ladies dancing all night at balls, taking part in elaborate theatrical performances, and engaging in stag-hunts and boar-hunts in which they at times experienced serious accidents. The age was one in which "it was considered that classical learning was the chief ornament either to man or woman, and that it added a special charm to the latter"; and no difference was therefore made in the education of girls and boys in this particular. Castiglione, in summing up his ideas of the perfect lady, after saying "all inspiration comes from women," adds that it rests with her to inspire men with hope and courage on the battlefield, in the council chamber, in the pursuit of Art and Learning, and in the paths of virtue and religion. And these ladies grew up to be re-nowned for the powerful influence which they exercised on the life of their age, an influence due entirely to the high standard of education which they had received. Mrs. Ady says:—

"By their intellectual attainments, their delicate culture, and their refined taste, these noble women of the Renaissance brought Art into close touch with life; and by their gracious and kindly sympathy and knowledge they cheered on the artist souls that were struggling towards the light, and helped to produce immortal works. Will posterity, we wonder, say as much for the ladies of our own age?" [7]

But in Catherine Sforza's life of activity and stress these matters could only be pursued occasionally, having perforce during long periods to be put aside, and she had more often to exercise her power of ruling men and her courage and skill in war, than her ability to compose Latin verses, to encourage Art, and to enjoy the conversation of learned men.

In 1471, when Catherine was nine years old, her father, Duke Galeazzo Sforza, paid that visit to Florence which has

previously been mentioned,[8] and took with him his wife,
Bona of Savoy, and his daughters, Anna and Catherine, when
the latter for the first time met that Medici family into which
she was long afterwards to marry. They stayed with Lorenzo
and his brother Giuliano and their mother, Lucrezia Tornabuoni, at the Medici Palace; and while they were amazed
at the art collections they saw gathered there, it is evident
that the nine-year-old girl looked with a sort of hero-worship
upon the twenty-two-year-old Lorenzo the Magnificent; for
during all the rest of her life, though she never saw him again,
she always held him in the greatest admiration. Although six
years later she became a member of a family who hated the
Medici with a deadly hatred, nothing ever obliterated from
her mind the memory of this visit, and she all her life felt a
strong attraction for the Medici and Florence.

In 1476 her father, Duke Galeazzo, was murdered, and the
Duchess Bona assumed the rule of Milan on behalf of her
six-year-old son, Gian Galeazzo. Catherine had by this time
been betrothed by her father to Girolamo Riario, nephew of
Pope Sixtus IV, and it was feared that the death of the Duke
might cause this engagement to be broken off. However, it
did not do so, and in April 1477, when she was fifteen,[9] she
was married by proxy at Milan, the small state of Imola, in
Romagna, being given her as a dowry. She journeyed to
Rome in much magnificence; and at Parma, Reggio, Modena,
and Bologna, as well as at Imola and every halting place in
the Papal states, was received with great ovations and festivities. She writes to her sister Chiara describing these recep-
tions, and how "they never cease feasting me." In these letters
she signs herself "Caterina Vicecomes," showing that the
Sforza carried on the name of the Visconti. After travelling in
this way for over a month she reached Rome. Seven miles
from the city she was met by her future husband, Girolamo
Riario, "that ex-custom-house clerk who never became a
gentleman," with a very magnificent retinue; and as they
proceeded towards the city they were joined by cardinals,

prelates, and dignitaries of all sorts, and at last at the Ponte Molle by the Papal court and the ambassadors of Spain and Naples. Thus attended, Catherine made her first entry into Rome. We are told that when as a bride of fifteen she rode in through the Porta del Popolo in the midst of this brilliant assemblage her fine appearance created a great sensation. Her dress was "a cloak of black damask brocaded with gold, a skirt of crimson satin, and sleeves of black brocade"; and she is described as "of a fine figure, having a face to be admired rather than loved, the features of beautiful outline, the face hard and even stern, but full of vigour and intelligence." They rode through the narrow streets to the ancient basilica of St. Peter's (which thirty years later was to be demolished by Julius II), and there the marriage ceremony was again performed by Pope Sixtus IV himself; after which the bride and bridegroom were escorted, amidst burning perfumes and festoons of flowers, to their palace (that now known as the Corsini palace) on the Lungara, in Trastevere. Then followed an immense banquet to about two hundred people with every kind of extravagant magnificence, which lasted for five hours.

The family into which Catherine had married was not an agreeable one. Sixtus IV was the son of a fisherman on the coast near Ancona, and the whole family were exceedingly vulgar, and were hated by the Colonna, the Orsini, and the rest of the ancient Roman nobility. Girolamo Riario was the worst of the Pope's nephews, but had been made by Sixtus IV Captain General of the Papal forces and the richest prince in Rome. He was vulgar, uncultured, violent, and arrogant, was loathed by the people for his crimes, and being an arrant coward, never trusted himself in the streets except when surrounded by a band of his villainous retainers, and Catherine, descended from a race of soldiers, can only have looked on him with contempt. However, her life was not without compensations; Pope Sixtus IV, brutal and vulgar tyrant as he was to others, behaved well towards her, and in a very short time she became so great a favourite with him that she wielded an immense influence. Few in that age, placed in such a position, would have borne the moral degradation of such a court as that of Sixtus IV without being contaminated, but it is acknowledged that Catherine did so, and that personal and family pride kept her from being corrupted.

Amidst these surroundings Catherine lived for seven years, the first four of them the most prosperous and brilliant of her life. During these seven years she saw an immense change wrought in Rome, which when she arrived was mean and half ruined in appearance, but which was transformed by Sixtus IV into a fine city. He organised a department for public works, pulled down houses and widened the streets, and built the Sixtine chapel, various important churches, and many other of the buildings which still exist in Rome. In connection with these operations Catherine saw summoned to Rome every notable artist of the time, including Botticelli, Ghirlandajo, Perugino, Mantegna, Pinturicchio, Filippino Lippi, Melozzo da Forlì, Cosimo Roselli, and Luca Signorelli. At the same time Sixtus IV founded the Vatican Library, of which a memorial exists in the picture [10] by Melozzo da Forlì of the Pope surrounded by his nephews giving to the librarian Platina the foundation statutes of the library. Catherine took part in these activities, while we are told that she did a great deal of reading, and delighted in the society of the numerous cultured and learned men then gathered in Rome.

The year after Catherine's marriage there took place (1478) the celebrated Pazzi conspiracy, headed by Sixtus IV and her husband, Girolamo.[11] After the failure of that conspiracy Girolamo sent an emissary to Florence to poison Lorenzo the Magnificent; but this attempt also failed. Again Girolamo planned with certain Florentines to assassinate Lorenzo, and the day was appointed; but again the plot was discovered, and all the conspirators were executed.[12] Historians are unanimous that Catherine had no part in any of these plots, nor was told of them.

In 1478 the first of Catherine's children was born, a daugh-

ter, whom she named Bianca after her beloved grandmother.
In the following year her eldest son was born, and was given
the name of Ottaviano. During the next two years another
son and a daughter were born.

In 1480 a quarrel between the two branches of the Ordelaffi
family at Forlì, the adjacent state to Catherine's little domain of Imola, was seized upon by Sixtus IV as a pretext
for ejecting the Ordelaffi from their territory (over which
they had ruled with honour for a hundred and fifty years),
and giving it to Girolamo Riario. This junction of Forlì with
Imola made a state of some political importance, especially
as one of the two main roads from the north of Italy to Rome
and Naples ran through it.

In June 1481 Girolamo and Catherine left Rome to pay a
visit to their new state, accompanied by an enormous train
of mules and carts laden with all the wealth which Girolamo
had been able to plunder, and which he thought, as the Pope
was growing old, it was advisable to remove from Rome. For
many days this great baggage train crowded the long rough
road from Rome by way of Orte, Terni, and Spoleto into
Umbria, and thence over the passes of the Apennines and
through Ancona, Pesaro, and Rimini to Forlì. The entry of
Girolamo and Catherine into Forlì was a very grand affair,
with triumphal arches, the streets hung with tapestries, com-
panies of white-clad youths bearing palm branches, a triumphal car full of children who sang Latin verses, bands of
music, and the clanging of innumerable bells. Catherine rode
on a white horse whose trappings of cloth of silver were embroidered with pearls; and over the heads of the pair a party
of young nobles in white and gold carried a canopy for a mile
before the town was reached. Then followed the usual feasting, and in the evening a ball, at which Catherine was much
admired for her magnificent appearance in a dress covered
with jewels, and a veil with the device, worked in silver and
pearls, of a rising sun piercing the clouds.

In September they visited Venice, ostensibly for pleasure,

but also with a political object. In the war of 1478-1480 between Florence and Sixtus IV, Duke Ercole d'Este of Ferrara had sided with Florence, and the Pope now wished to retaliate, and to obtain the help of Venice to enable him to treat the house of Este as he had the Ordelaffi, and take Ferrara for the ever-hungry Girolamo. They were greeted at Venice with a splendid reception; but the Venetians saw no reason why they should assist the Pope to take Ferrara for Girolamo; so, while they overwhelmed him and Catherine with honours and delighted them with gorgeous pageants, they sent them away without having effected anything; and Girolamo and Catherine (avoiding Ferrara) returned to Forlì, and from thence to Rome.

Catherine's portrait by Palmezzano (with the castle of Forlì in the background), shows her as she was at this time, at the age of twenty, and before she had yet demonstrated those extraordinary powers of courage and resolution which she possessed.

After their return to Rome Girolamo's enormities increased to such an extent that he became more detested than ever. At length, in the beginning of 1484, he instigated the Pope, with the help of the Orsini, to attack the Colonna, whose possessions he coveted. The Papal troops sacked the whole quarter in which stood the palaces of the Colonna; whereupon Girolamo perpetrated one of his most odious crimes. In order to save the life of the head of the family, the highly respected Lorenzo Colonna, who had fallen into the Pope's hands, Colonna's mother agreed conditionally to give up part of their estates. Nevertheless Girolamo, falsifying the Pope's most solemn word, basely took the life of Lorenzo Colonna, who was atrociously tortured to death in the castle of St. Angelo on the 30th June 1484. Catherine shuddered at these crimes of her husband, and held herself as much as possible aloof from him, occupying herself with the care of her children, and removing herself and them for a time to Frascati. Her husband's baseness filled her with disgust; but when once or twice she reproached him for the vileness of his crimes, he vented his wrath upon her with such violent brutality that after his death she told the Milanese envoy that she "had often envied those who died."

In the midst of these disturbances Pope Sixtus suddenly died, on the 12th August 1484. Anarchy at once ensued in Rome, and the Riario palace (which Catherine had furnished with great magnificence) was attacked by the mob, and sacked. Girolamo was absent with his troops at Paliano, and Catherine and her children were with him. He advanced with his force as far as the Ponte Molle, while Catherine boldly went on and entered the castle of St. Angelo, which she declared she should hold for Count Girolamo. She was now twenty-two, and here gave the first sign of that military spirit and indomitable will which was afterwards to make her so famous. Rome was like a city given up to be sacked, the mob revelling in the abeyance of all authority. The cardinals sent messenger after messenger to Catherine demanding that she should give up the castle; but she only laughed at them, being determined to hold it until a new Pope had been elected and had confirmed her husband in his estates. They tried various expedients, but without avail. Catherine holding the Pope's castle was mistress of the situation, and the cardinals were afraid even to assemble for the conclave. At length they put such pressure upon her husband that, betrayed by him, she had to yield; whereupon she marched out with the honours of war, and she and Girolamo departed for Forlì, where two months later Catherine's third son was born.

Forlì during the next three years was by no means a bed of roses for Catherine. The people loved the Ordelaffi, and Girolamo Riario's character would have made him detested anywhere. So that there were frequent insurrections, both at Forlì and Imola, and either Girolamo or his Countess had constantly at short notice to hurry from the one place to the other to quell these disturbances. In these labours of a difficult government Catherine took her full share, and it was

only by her able assistance that Girolamo was able to preserve his position. On one occasion, in August 1487, when
they were at Imola, her husband being ill, and only a few
days before the birth of Catherine's fifth son,[13] urgent news
came late in the evening that an insurrection had occurred at
Forlì, and that one of the rebels, Codronchi, had murdered
the *castellane* and seized the castle. Catherine forthwith ordered her horse and rode the sixteen miles to Forlì, arriving
there at midnight, and proceeding to the gate of the castle,
which dominated the town, summoned Codronchi to surrender it to her. He replied insolently, promising to think
about it if she would return in the morning to breakfast.
Catherine, sitting on her horse at midnight before the closed
gates of her castle, was obliged to give in for the time, and
retired to her palace in the town, but laid her plans for the
next day. In the morning she presented herself again at the
castle gate. She was told that only she herself, with one
attendant "to carry her breakfast," would be admitted.
Catherine, against the strong advice of her counsellors, accepted the terms offered, and taking with her Tommaso Feo,
whom she knew she could trust, passed in. What transpired
inside none know, but she brought such power to bear upon
the rebellious Codronchi that after a few hours he delivered
up the castle to her; whereupon she placed Tommaso Feo
in command, sallied forth accompanied by Codronchi, and
rode away back to Imola taking him with her, and Forlì was
saved. On the day after her return to Imola her fifth son,
whom she named Francesco Sforza, was born (17th August
1487).

A few months after this, in April 1488, Girolamo Riario
met the natural end of his many crimes, being assassinated
in the palace at Forlì in an insurrection headed by the Orsi
family. Catherine, with her six children and her sister Stella,
were seized by the conspirators in another room, but not before she had contrived to send off a messenger to her half-
brother, the Duke of Milan, with an urgent appeal to him to

send troops to her assistance. She and her children were ignominiously marched through the crowded streets and locked up in the Orsi palace; thence they were removed in the evening to the fortress of San Pietro, where Catherine, her six children (the two youngest in the arms of their nurses), her sister, and two other attendants were all confined in one small room, and underwent much distress and terror, Catherine being the only one of the party who kept her head. The conspirators ordered Feo to give up the castle, but he refused; and next day by a ruse Catherine, leaving her children in the enemy's hands, escaped to the castle. They threatened to kill her children if she did not surrender, but she dared them to do it, and threatened them with the vengeance of the Duke of Milan, while the castle bombarded the town day and night. At length, after the castle had been besieged for a fortnight, troops came to her assistance from Milan; whereupon the leaders of the rebellion fled, the town made a humble submission, and Catherine had conquered. We see her in this hour of her victory as she is described by Cerretani:—

"Wise, brave, great, speaking little, with a full, beautiful face; wearing a tan satin gown with two ells of train, a large black velvet hat in the French mode, and a man's belt whence hung a bag of gold ducats and a curved sword. And among the soldiers, both horse and foot, she was much feared; for that armed lady was both fierce and cruel."

Those of the ringleaders of the rebellion who were caught were executed; the palace of the Orsi was demolished, and all the men of that family who had not fled were put to death in vengeance for Girolamo's murder; and though Catherine did not show general vindictiveness, she showed herself hard and cruel, not only punishing the guilty with death, but consigning to dark and horrible dungeons their innocent families. On the other hand, she refused to allow the troops from Milan to sack the city, as they had been fully confident of doing, or even to enter it; and though this almost caused a mutiny among them, Catherine was resolute, and showed no less courage on this point than she had in confronting the rebellion. She returned to her palace in the town escorted only by a small picked body of these troops, who, though she had deprived them of the plunder of the city, could not help honouring her for the brave way in which she had fought her battle. "And on the way," says Bernardi, "many of our women embraced her feet, for a woman whose first exercise of power was for the protection of other women had not till then been seen." Girolamo's body was buried at Imola, Catherine declaring that she would never forgive the canons of the cathedral of Forlì for having refused it burial; and during the remaining twelve years of her reign she never forgave them or entered the cathedral. The property of the Orsi family was, however, not confiscated, Catherine refusing to take anything of theirs; and she liberated after a short time the women of that family from their imprisonment.

Catherine was now twenty-six, and sovereign ruler of her state, her eldest son, Octavian, being still a child.[14] In the following year (1489) she married Giacomo Feo, the younger brother of her faithful *castellane*, Tommaso Feo, appointing the latter governor of Imola. Giacomo Feo was, we are told, "a fine handsome young man, courteous and pleasant to all, and skilled in all military exercises." She kept the government of her state in her own hands, he remaining simply the commander of her army. There was much jealousy in Forlì against Giacomo Feo on account of his elevation, and, though he did his best to allay it, this feeling smouldered. They had one son, called after his father, Giacomo.

In 1492 Catherine heard of the death at Florence of Lorenzo the Magnificent. Though he had been opposed through life to Girolamo Riario in consequence of the Pazzi conspiracy and the murder of his brother Giuliano, and so had placed Florence always in political opposition to Forlì, yet Catherine had never lost her regard for him and the Medici family; she had always contrived to maintain a sort of private and personal friendship with Florence outside the arena of politics, and much regretted Lorenzo's death. In the same year Sixtus IV's successor, Pope Innocent VIII, also died, and Cardinal Roderigo Borgia became Pope Alexander VI, in whom she was to find her bitterest enemy.

During the next two years Catherine was involved in a web of difficult policy. Charles VIII was about to invade Italy, and Catherine's whole abilities were called forth to prevent her small state from being ravaged by the two foes, on the one side the French with Milan (her natural ally), and on the other Florence, with Rome and Naples. She trimmed perpetually between the two, but at length declared herself on the side of the latter party. When, however, her castle of Mordano was attacked and taken by the French while the troops of the allies made no attempt to give her garrison any assistance, she renounced the side of Florence, Rome, and Naples, and took that of the French and Milan. Many letters still extant passed at this time between her and Pietro the Unfortunate on the subject of these intricate politics. In 1494 Charles VIII in his march through Italy sent a portion of his troops through her state, but they did her no harm, and were eventually recalled by Charles to meet him in Tuscany. Shortly afterwards Catherine's half-brother, Gian Galeazzo Sforza, died, and her uncle, Ludovico Sforza, proclaimed himself Duke of Milan.

In August 1495 [15] those jealous of Giacomo Feo's advancement laid plans to murder him. Catherine, her husband, and her band of young sons were returning joyously from a hunting party, when at the Bogheri bridge Giacomo Feo, who was riding a little behind, was suddenly set upon by a party of conspirators, and stabbed to death. Catherine escaped to the castle and took a terrible vengeance. When her first husband —a man to whom she had been married as a matter of policy, and whom she loathed—was murdered she merely punished with a stern, hard justice. But her second husband was the man of her own choice, the first love of this vehement strong-willed woman, whose great-grandfather had been given the name "Sforza" on account of his violence and impetuosity, characteristics prominent in all the Sforza. Hence we now have a woman raging with tiger-like fury for the murder of her love, her terrible Sforza nature blazing up in all its awful madness of blind and passionate ferocity. The guilty, the families of the guilty (including women, girls, and even children), all on whom the slightest suspicion fell, were involved in a general destruction; and there followed indiscriminate slaughtering, hanging, torturing, banishment, and ruin. For Giacomo Feo's murder more than one hundred persons, men, women, and children, suffered various degrees of misery, over forty of them being put to death in most cruel ways.

"The beautiful Rosaria Ghetti, the unhappy wife of the principal assassin of Feo, was dragged to the castle of Forlì, and there with her two little children thrown down a spiked well. . . . The dungeons of the castle were turned into abodes of lamentation and death; the hall where the *podestà* examined prisoners rang with the clank of instruments of torture and the desperate cries of the victims." [16]

Truly the Sforza nature was a terrible one when roused; the same qualities which produced such indomitable power to overcome difficulties and such an unquenchable spirit in adversity, produced in the hour of vengeance results at which mankind trembled. Even Catherine's own son, Octavian, then sixteen, was by her consigned to prison because she shrewdly suspected that he had had a share in the crime through his jealousy of Feo, even if he had not instigated it. All Italy shuddered at such a vengeance. Pope Alexander VI, though tolerably accustomed to terrible deeds, ventured on a remonstrance; but Catherine turned a deaf ear; until her wrath had destroyed every one and everything connected with the murder of Giacomo Feo she would listen to nothing.

At length the fury of her wrath was satisfied, and she

turned her attention to other matters. Both famine and pestilence were at this time causing great suffering to her people, and Catherine threw herself into a contest with these evils with a fierce energy which seemed desirous of obliterating the memory of her bereavement by the most arduous labours, buying corn and organising famine relief, establishing dispensaries and hiring doctors from other states, and founding confraternities for the care of the sick and other charitable purposes. Politics also demanded all her abilities. The peaceful times of Italy had passed away, and a time of turmoil had succeeded in which her petty state threatened to be crushed between more powerful neighbours. She was divided between her desire to keep in friendship with her uncle's state of Milan and her ever-increasing sympathy with Florence. This latter feeling was in 1496 strengthened by there coming to her as Florentine envoy Giovanni de' Medici, known in Florence as Giovanni "Popolano."

Catherine wanted a guardian for her inert and effeminate son, Octavian; she also wanted a helper and adviser in her precarious position as the female ruler of a state which every power round her coveted; and she saw that she would have once again to contract a marriage of policy. She had always felt an attraction for the Medici family, while Giovanni was not only handsome and accomplished, but also showed much political ability. So in 1497, about two years after Giacomo Feo's death, she married her Florentine envoy, keeping it secret as long as she could for fear of the wrath of her uncle, Ludovico, Duke of Milan, who was constantly urging upon her to have nothing to do with Florence. When at last he plainly taxed her with intending such a marriage (after it had already taken place), she denied it in the most barefaced way, saying she was pained that her uncle should think it possible she would ever take a husband without first consulting him, or marry one of whom he would not approve. However, eventually she had to acknowledge it, and then managed with such ability to show the political advantages of such an alliance that the Duke of Milan gave his consent.[17]

Soon afterwards the Pope sent her a proposal that her son Octavian should be married to his daughter, Lucrezia Borgia. The advantages that would be hers if she consented were plainly placed before her; the result if she refused would, she knew, sooner or later be war brought upon her by the Pope. Nevertheless, her whole soul recoiled from the idea of intermarriage with the Borgia family, with whose crimes all Italy rang. She therefore refused the proposal, and to keep her son out of the way sent him off to see something of war. She dreaded lest he should grow up with the sluggish temperament of his father Girolamo (as he did); so she despatched him with a body of troops to help Florence in its war against Venice and Pisa, and persuaded Giovanni de' Medici to go with him to instruct him in military affairs. These troops had been trained by herself, and during their absence at Pisa she continued to watch over their management, writing long letters containing minute instructions on all details of their administration.

In April 1498 her son Ludovico was born; she named him after her uncle, the Duke of Milan, to conciliate the latter; but when his father died five months later she changed his name to Giovanni, and by that name he is always known. In August [18] her husband, Giovanni, became ill at Pisa and returned to Forlì, and went thence to the baths of San Pietro in Bagno, in the Apennines. After he had been there a few days she received an urgent summons from him saying he was worse, and begging her to come at once. She rode thither from Forlì in haste, but arrived to find him dying, and a few hours afterwards he breathed his last in her arms. His brother Lorenzo came, and conveyed his body to Florence for burial there; and Catherine returned in deepest grief, a third time a widow, to her desolate palace at Forlì.

Dangers now surrounded Catherine Sforza on every side. Through her alliance with Florence she was brought into collision with Venice on the north and the Pope on the south;

while the latter was bent on punishing her for her refusal of his matrimonial project, and also wanted her state for his son, Cæsar Borgia. Venice demanded a passage through her territories for the troops it was sending against Florence, and thought she was too much plunged in grief to refuse. But war made Catherine herself again directly, and she refused the demand of Venice; and upon the latter sending a force against her she defeated it. At the same time Lorenzo the Younger (Lorenzo "Popolano"), her late husband's brother, demanded the custody of her child, on the plea that she must not expose him to the dangers which threatened herself. Catherine replied that there was nothing which she could refuse to the house of Medici, except her child; and kept possession of him. Meanwhile, foreseeing that she would ere long be attacked, she devoted her whole attention to military affairs. Fortifying passes, repairing her town walls, enlisting fresh troops, providing new arms and immense supplies of ammunition, drilling her troops, sitting up late at night going through the accounts that she might provide funds for the payment of her soldiers, regulating even the discipline and expenses of the body of troops she still kept at Pisa with Octavian, arranging for "all the mules to be sent here"—in these and similar activities she displayed her unbounded energy and resource.

In July 1499 Florence sent to her an envoy, the celebrated Niccolò Machiavelli, to endeavour to obtain her agreement to various arrangements by which Forlì was to give much and obtain little. But not even Machiavelli could outwit Catherine, and we are told:—"The young envoy found more than his match in the woman he had tried, and failed, to circumvent." Apparently Catherine had by this time given up inhabiting her palace in the town, and for greater security had transferred her abode to a new residence which she had constructed in the castle. Tomasini, in his life of Machiavelli, describing "those long-vanished halls that witnessed these interviews of Catherine Sforza and Niccolò Machiavelli," says:—

"Catherine had demolished that part of the citadel which had seen her temporary humiliation by the insurgents, and on the highest part of the walls, which were held to be impregnable, had built herself a new and magnificent abode. She had named this 'Paradiso,' from its beauty and the fine architecture of its lofty rooms, decorated with splendid paintings, and brilliant with gilded goffered ceilings on which were displayed the arms of the Visconti. . . . In these rooms, and amidst those defences where not long afterwards this brave woman calmly awaited the assault of the Borgia and her own ruin, she received the envoy Niccolò Machiavelli, who carried away with him a deep impression of her beauty, her greatness of soul, and the strength of her castle." [19]

All through the year 1499 Catherine was busy in preparing for the attack which was coming upon her from the Pope and his ally, the new King of France, Louis XII. The latter had deprived her uncle Ludovico of his throne and put him to flight, so no assistance could come to her from Milan. The Republic of Florence could not help her, for it was itself at this time trembling before Cæsar Borgia, and (notwithstanding the specious protestations of Florentine friendship which had been conveyed to her by Machiavelli) dared take no action which would bring trouble upon Florence from that quarter. No other states would ally themselves with her against two such powerful adversaries as the Pope and the King of France. Alexander VI issued a bull by which he deposed this "daughter of iniquity," and invested Cæsar Borgia with her territories. And Louis XII addressed a circular letter to the states of Italy stating that he was despatching an army under Cæsar Borgia, Duke of Valentino, to besiege and take the fortresses of Imola and Forlì on behalf of the Pope. Thus the force which Cæsar Borgia was able to bring against her was far beyond anything which she could put in the field; for he had not only the whole of the Papal forces, but also 15,000 French under Ives d'Allègre and 4,000 Swiss.

But nothing daunted Catherine Sforza's stout heart, and she prepared with the utmost energy to resist the united power of the Pope and the King of France, and worked away at her defences as though she had any number of powerful allies, instead of only the strength of her own small state. Though she knew that she was enormously overmatched, and that all her efforts would be powerless to prevail against such a force, she was determined to defend the rights of her children to the last. She cut down all the trees round the town; she burnt down the suburbs; she destroyed even the pleasure-house in her park, and cut down its trees; she erected fortifications in every direction; she sent away her children to Florence; she diverted the streams in the hills and flooded the whole country round the town; and she devoted every spare hour to personally drilling her troops and increasing their efficiency.

In November 1499 Cæsar Borgia's army advanced against Imola; it was furiously attacked, taken by assault, and sacked. This frightened the citizens of Forlì, and the Signoria, after long debate, and "much hustling by Catherine," declined to stand by her against the Pope, and agreed to surrender the town. Catherine, on receiving their message to this effect, sent Landriani to tell the members of the Signoria that they were "rabbits." She withdrew her forces into the castle and there stood at bay; and on the following day Cæsar Borgia with his army entered the town. He did his utmost to induce her to surrender, but without avail; the more desperate her case grew, the more resolute Catherine became. The castle was fiercely attacked, but successfully resisted all the enemy's efforts; it steadily bombarded the town, and especially the palace in which Cæsar Borgia had taken up his quarters, which made him furious. After some time he tried a parley, and advanced to the edge of the moat, and presently Catherine looked down on him from the battlements. He pointed out to her the overwhelming strength of his forces and the uselessness of further struggle, and urged her to yield; but she replied that she "was the daughter of one who knew no fear, and was determined to walk in his steps till death." So the bombardment continued. Again a second time he tried a parley, urging upon her still more forcible arguments, but with the same result. Catherine hoped that her half-sister, the Empress of Germany, would induce the Emperor Maximilian to send her assistance; but the latter dreaded Cæsar Borgia too much to do so, and no help came to the beleaguered castle of Forlì.

All through December 1499 the furious contest went on, the castle being continuously attacked, but successfully beating off all assaults. Damage done to the defences by day was regularly repaired each night, and Catherine's resource seemed inexhaustible; while the high spirit with which she conducted her defence, and encouraged the sinking hearts of her troops as their numbers gradually dwindled, won the admiration even of her foes, and especially of the French, who swore they would like to serve under her command. Catherine at this time wore armour permanently, and there is still to be seen a suit of woman's plate armour said to have been hers, which may have been that worn by her during this siege.[20]

"On the last night of the year she took counsel till late at night with her captains and engineers, and at early morn made a thorough inspection of the entire castle. From the height of the chief tower, which she had climbed to look down on the city, the enemy's camp, and the ravaged and snow-clad plain, she saw the dawn of a new century, and the sun rise on the 1st of January 1500." [21]

Four days later a breach was made in the castle walls which could not be repaired, and the enemy forced their way in. But Catherine retreated to the citadel, and still stood at bay, and her beloved "Paradiso" was defended to the end. "Never," wrote Grunello, "had been seen a woman of such spirit." At length, when the castle was crowded with the enemy, the citadel still remaining hers, Catherine ordered the magazine to be blown up, determined to perish unconquered in the ruins; but it was done ineffectively, and only gave further assistance to the attack. At last Cæsar Borgia demanded to parley with her, and while she spoke with him she was treacherously seized from behind, and the defence of Forlì by its lion-hearted Countess was at an end (8th January 1500).

D'Allègre, the French commander, declared that Catherine was the prisoner of the King of France; but Cæsar Borgia refused to give her up, and on the 23rd of January he marched out of Forlì conveying her as a prisoner to Rome, and treating her with many indignities. Cæsar Borgia reached Rome on the 26th February, and as Catherine once more entered through the Porta del Popolo she must have contrasted this entry with that first brilliant one of hers as a girl of fifteen twenty-three years before. At first she was treated well, but was soon consigned to the dungeons of the castle of St. Angelo on a charge of plotting to poison the Pope, and was there shamefully treated. The Borgia did not dare openly to put to death one whose sister was married to the Emperor and whom the King of France claimed as his prisoner, but they intended that she should die nevertheless; and for a whole year she disappeared from sight. However, in June 1501 the French army returned to Italy and heard of her disappearance into the dungeons of St. Angelo; her gallant defence of Forlì had shed glory on the French arms by their capture of so formidable a castle, and Louis XII refused to allow her to be thus treated, and insisted on her being set at liberty. Cæsar Borgia opposed her liberation with all his might, declaring that she would turn Lombardy and Romagna upside down; but the commander of the French army, D'Allègre, who had tried to protect Catherine from him when she surrendered at Forlì, swore that if she were not set free at once the French army, then approaching Rome, should plunder and sack the city; and the Pope had to submit.

D'Allègre rode himself to the castle of St. Angelo to announce to Catherine her freedom. Then was revealed what she had endured since she had been imprisoned in the Borgia's dungeons.

"The woman who rose to greet Monseigneur D'Allègre bore no resemblance to her whom he had known a year and a half ago. She had spent over a year in the dark, narrow cell into which the Borgia had thrust her. They had expended as little as possible on her, in continual expectation of her death. She was haggard from suffering and scant food, worn by fever, and livid from living in the dark. . . . Every time that her scanty food was brought her she had dreaded poison; every night she had dreaded the Tiber. D'Allègre was horrified; could this be the fiery lady of Forlì, grand even in defeat, whom he had last seen at the close of her gallant struggle to defend her castle? She was so changed that he did not know her." [22]

And now there comes out a new trait in this woman's character; and it is witnessed to by her own letters. These show that her sufferings were no surprise to her; *she felt that she deserved them.* The influences of her earliest years, under her grandmother, Bianca Visconti, and the Duchess Bona, had never deserted Catherine Sforza. And her letters show that while she believed that God would punish the Borgia for their cruel treatment of herself, she believed no less that in her own sufferings, her victims—those innocent ones who had been thrown down spiked wells, or had been tortured to death in her dungeons—were being avenged, and that God had surely punished her who had been guilty of these crimes.

She was liberated on the 13th July 1501, and at once fled from Rome by the Tiber in a boat to Ostia, thence by sea to a point on the coast near Pisa, and thence by road to Florence. She chose this route because she knew that Cæsar Borgia, disgusted at her being set free, had posted assassins on the land route to murder her. At Florence she met all her children, and was received with cordiality by her late husband's brother, Lorenzo the Younger, the Florentines welcoming her with a public ovation; the warmth of which reception much offended the Pope. Yet this woman, who had formerly so fiercely denounced her enemies, whose violence of language when roused had been the terror of Forlì, and who had been betrayed, calumniated, and tortured by the Borgia, never afterwards mentioned them in anger. Of her sufferings she would never speak. Once only to her Dominican confessor she said: "Could I write all, the world would turn to stone."

During the remaining eight years of her life Catherine lived at Florence in much retirement, chiefly at her late husband's villa of Castello; though even here she did not enjoy peace, being much harassed both by the money difficulties and incapacity of her elder sons, and by a long struggle, ending with lawsuit, to protect the property of her youngest son. On the death in 1503 of Pope Alexander VI most of the princes of Romagna whose states he and Cæsar Borgia had seized resumed them again, and Catherine urged her son Octavian to do the same and take possession of Forlì; but he being indolent and incapable, declined to make any such effort. It is remarkable to notice how, notwithstanding all their mother's ability and energy, not one of all her five sons by her first husband Riario, nor her son by her second husband Feo, inherited a particle of her qualities, but were all of them without capacity, energy, or strength of character; whereas in her son by her third husband, Giovanni de' Medici, all Catherine's qualities were reproduced in full vigour, and in him Medici and Sforza were most powerfully blended.

This boy Giovanni was now five years old and Catherine soon found herself involved in an arduous conflict to protect him from the designs of his uncle, Lorenzo the Younger, and the latter's son, Pier Francesco the Younger. The former, while Catherine was in prison at Rome and unlikely ever again to appear, had spent a large part of his late brother's inheritance, and this would be discovered unless they could

get the boy into their hands. Accordingly, after various unsuccessful endeavours to get Catherine to give him up, they
went to law with her over her guardianship of him, and also
over the possession of her late husband's villa of Castello.
All Catherine's fighting instincts were roused by this conduct; Castello became to her another Forlì; she declared
that "they should only get her out of it in pieces." At length,
however, she was obliged to leave it for a time until the result
of the lawsuit, which dragged on interminably, should become
known; and while thus forced to leave her abode, took refuge
at that convent of the Murate where another Catherine was,
twenty-three years later, to live during the dawn of life
instead of its close. Eventually the lawsuit was given in
Catherine's favour, but then Lorenzo contrived to steal the
boy, and she had again to go to law to get him back. Thereupon, considering that his life was in danger, she sent him
to the convent of the Annalena, where she caused him to be
dressed in girl's clothes and kept there in hiding for about
a year. Catherine's portrait by Vasari shows her as she was
at this time in her life.

The loss of the above lawsuit, which had become a *cause
célèbre* in Florence, together with the disgrace which he incurred among his fellow-countrymen on account of the embezzlement of his nephew's property, so preyed on Lorenzo's
mind that he fell ill and died (1507). Whereupon Catherine
returned with her boy Giovanni (now nine years old) to the
villa of Castello, where she spent the remaining two years of
her life in training him in all manly exercises. Catherine delighted in him; he was a true Sforza, "all fire, arms, and
horses," as she writes, and she was for these last two years
of her life perfectly happy. But her naturally vigorous health
had been permanently ruined by her terrible imprisonment.
After two happy years with her fiery little son at Castello,
her health, in the early part of the year 1509, began altogether
to give way, one of her feet especially causing her much
suffering. To be nearer to doctors she moved into the city;

and on the 28th of May 1509 Catherine Sforza, the brave
Countess of Forlì, passed away at the age of forty-seven.
She died at the house in the Via Larga which was then the
next but one to the Medici Palace.[23] She was buried in the
chapel of the Murate convent, where she had spent a great
part of her latter years; but her tomb is not now to be seen,
having been broken up when a few years ago that convent
was converted into the State prison. At her death she confided the charge of her son to Jacopo Salviati, who had been
his tutor, and was also a connection by marriage, his wife
Lucrezia being a daughter of Lorenzo the Magnificent, and
belonging to that elder branch of the Medici family who had
been exiled, and who at this time seemed unlikely ever to
be allowed to return to Florence.

CHAPTER XXIII

GIOVANNI DELLE BANDE NERE

Born 1498. *Died* 1526

THE life of Giovanni delle Bande Nere, the only soldier of
the Medici family, comes like a refreshing wind from another
sphere in the midst of all the diplomacy, craft, and ignoble
scheming of the times of Leo X, Clement VII, Francis I, and
Charles V, which is the period in which his short life was
passed.

The only child of Giovanni de Medici and his wife, Catherine Sforza, he was born in Forlì on the 6th April 1498, and
when about a year and a half old was sent away by his mother
from Forlì (then about to be attacked) to Florence, to the
charge of his uncle, Lorenzo. When he was three years old his
mother arrived at Florence from her imprisonment at Rome,
and Giovanni returned to her care; and his earliest recol-
lections must have been those of the villa of Castello, with its
stiff and formal garden and adjacent woods. When about
eight years old he was sent by his mother to the convent of
the Annalena, where he was kept in hiding, disguised as a girl,
like another Achilles. After about a year he returned to his
mother's care, living with her at the villa of Castello, and being
entirely trained by her. As a boy he cared for nothing but
riding, swimming, and manly exercises, and was difficult to
manage, being fiery and headstrong, though he showed an
affectionate and generous nature. He was the joy of his
mother's heart, as she saw in him one such as her own ancestors had been; and she was never tired of expatiating on

534

his manly spirit and his love of arms, horses, and military exercises. At the same time she knew that strength and valour alone would not enable him to achieve success in that military career for which almost from his very cradle he showed such a strong inclination, and from the time he was nine years old she sought everywhere for the best tutors for him, being determined to make him a man fitted to command armies and rule a state.

His mother, however, died when he was still only eleven years old, and, in accordance with her will, Jacopo Salviati became his guardian; and under the care of Salviati and his wife Lucrezia Giovanni remained until he was seventeen. The charge was not an easy one, for even as quite a little boy he would never obey any one but his mother, so that when she died there was no one who could control him; but in time Lucrezia gained great influence over him, and he always held her in much respect. The Salviati lived in a palace in the Corso in Florence notable as being that in which had lived in the thirteenth century Folco Portinari, the father of Dante's Beatrice, and which the Salviati when it became theirs had restored.[1] Here Giovanni grew up, taking warmly to all things which would fit him for a military career, but averse to books except such as might assist that object.

Pope Alexander VI had been succeeded by Pope Julius II, and under his auspices, when Giovanni was fourteen, the elder branch of the Medici returned to Florence. Giovanni watched their entry into the city, and writes that it was "a fine sight." The government of Florence thereupon passed into the hands of Giuliano (Duc de Nemours), Lucrezia Salviati's brother; and a few months later, on the death of Julius II, her other brother, Giovanni, became Pope Leo X. This changed considerably the position of the Salviati, and henceforth the young son of Catherine Sforza looked forward to obtaining his much-desired military career through Lucrezia Salviati's influence with her brother, the Pope.

In 1515, when Giovanni was seventeen, Leo X sent for

him to Rome, where Giovanni speedily distinguished himself by numerous quarrels and equally numerous deeds of bravery; one of these latter is depicted on the wall of the Sala di Giovanni delle Bande Nere, in the Palazzo Vecchio, showing him, when a band of the Orsini tried to take him prisoner, forcing his way through them with only ten soldiers. During this time we find Lucrezia Salviati writing to him as a mother to her son, and giving him much good advice. In the following year, when he was eighteen, Giovanni at last obtained that which had been the desire of his heart from his earliest years, and was given by the Pope command of a troop of a hundred cavalry, and saw his first campaign, he and his troops being sent as part of the force despatched by Pope Leo to attack Urbino, under the command of the Pope's nephew Lorenzo, who had become ruler of Florence.

In this campaign Giovanni showed so many valuable qualities as a leader that he was soon advanced to a larger command. He manifested from the very first all those qualities which most endear a commander to those whom he leads in war, and in a very short time his soldiers idolised him. And there was some one else who idolised him too, namely, his guardian's sensible and good-hearted daughter, Maria Salviati, who had grown up with him, and knew all his aspirations, and worshipped this fine young soldier who loved her and was so rapidly winning distinction. So in November 1516, when Giovanni came back from his first campaign, they were married, he being then a little over eighteen and she seventeen. By this marriage the two branches of the Medici family were united, Maria's mother being a great-granddaughter of Cosimo Pater Patriae, and Giovanni a great-grandson of Cosimo's brother Lorenzo.

But not for long did Giovanni remain encircled by the silken cords of love. He was soon back again with his troops, and seeking fighting wherever it was to be found. Nor did he even confine himself to land operations; once, when there was no fighting to be done on land, he managed to get three small ships fitted out, and proceeded on a cruise in pursuit of the pirates who infested the coasts of the Adriatic. His rise was tremendously rapid, and we soon find him given by Leo X the command of a force of four thousand infantry and a hundred cavalry, and sent to attack Fermo. A hard-fought battle ensued, in which Giovanni was victorious; his letter announcing his success is to be seen in the State archives in Florence, written in the bold, round style which characterises his handwriting. Meanwhile Maria remained in Florence, living in the Salviati palace, where on the 12th June 1519 a son was born to them whom they named Cosimo, at the request of Pope Leo X, after the latter's ancestor, Cosimo Pater Patriae. It is told of Giovanni that in order to make the child courageous he had him thrown from the first floor of the Salviati palace into the courtyard, where he stood and caught him in his arms; though what Maria thought of such escapades with her child is not related.

In this year 1519, when Giovanni was twenty-one, Lorenzo (Duke of Urbino), the nephew of Leo X, died; and as he left only a daughter, while Giuliano (Duc de Nemours) had left no legitimate heir, it was evident that on the death of Pope Leo X the rights of the Medici to the rule of Florence would pass to the younger branch, of which Giovanni was the most important representative. The latter, however, was rapidly making for himself so great a reputation as a commander in war that he despised all such questions, and gave no attention to the matter. The time was one in which war was becoming the normal condition in Italy, and by the time that Giovanni was twenty-two he commanded a force of his own; and these troops were becoming renowned throughout Italy. From the black armour which they wore they were called the "Bande Nere" (or Black Bands), which gave Giovanni the name by which he is known in history. And so invariable was his success in command of this force that he had already gained the title of "The Invincible," and was one of the most noted leaders in Italy.

In 1521, when he was twenty-three, the long war between Francis I and Charles V began, and Giovanni delle Bande Nere was now to have a larger field for the display of his military talents. So far as Italy was concerned this first campaign between the two great antagonists resolved itself into a struggle for the possession of Milan, which since the battle of Marignano in 1515 had belonged to France. Pope Leo X sided with Charles V, and to assist the imperial army in the campaign in Lombardy against the French commander, De Lautrec, sent a large body of troops of which the Bande Nere formed an important part. In these operations we find Giovanni holding with his force the line of the Adda to the east of Milan, and eventually performing a remarkable feat in swimming his entire force across that river in order to make a rapid advance upon Milan; the result of this was that the city was taken, to the great delight of the Pope, who, however, died a week or two afterwards.

During the short pontificate of Adrian VI the war languished, but in 1523, soon after Clement VII had become Pope, the French again invaded Lombardy, and during this and the following year the fighting in northern Italy was incessant. By the death of Leo X Giovanni delle Bande Nere (failing his cousin Lorenzino, then six years old) had become the only legitimate representative of the Medici claims to the rule of Florence. But Clement VII was scheming in every way to keep that rule from passing to the younger branch of the family; and seeing in this successful soldier a dangerous obstacle to his views, managed to find constant employment for Giovanni and the Bande Nere, hoping that sooner or later he would get killed in battle. And Giovanni, caring nothing for political affairs, and entirely absorbed in his profession, was only too ready to be kept thus employed.

Meanwhile Giovanni's reputation as a great soldier grew continually, his renown spreading even as far as England. He had begun by being looked upon as a uniformly successful leader of a first-rate body of troops; he was now getting to be

considered indispensable wherever large operations were to be
undertaken. His poor young wife Maria saw little of him, and
was for ever imploring him to come home and attend to his
family affairs. For she had thoroughly fathomed Pope Clement's design; and, in a letter to her husband in 1523, shows
how bitterly she felt this crafty plan of the Pope's, and the
certainty that sooner or later Giovanni's life would be sacrificed. But Giovanni was not to be got away from the stirring
life of the camp and the great game of war. For a little time,
however, during a pause in the military operations, he was
persuaded to retire to Reggio, where Maria was delighted to
get him to herself for a few months, and induce him to lead
a quiet life, occupying himself with field sports. It was probably at this time that Titian's portrait of him was painted.
At Reggio, attracted by his fame, there gathered round him
quite a small court of notable men; among these was Pietro
Aretino,[2] a man more in his element in the baneful atmosphere of the court of Charles V than in the wholesomer air of
camps, but between whom and Giovanni delle Bande Nere a
strong friendship soon grew up. But this time of rest at Reggio
did not last long, and Giovanni was soon again in the field.
Shortly afterwards Maria writes to him still more strongly
than before, pointing out Pope Clement's artifices, and how
he was arranging to attack Ancona, and sending Giovanni in
command of the expedition, solely with the object of keeping
him continually employed, and in the hope that he would
eventually be killed in battle. But poor Maria's tender exhortations fell on deaf ears.

Early in 1525 Francis I made his great invasion of Lombardy, and Giovanni delle Bande Nere, in command of the
contingent furnished by the Pope, joined the French King
before Pavia, to take part in the siege. Ten days before the
battle of 24th February, Giovanni, while reconnoitring the
enemy, was severely wounded by a round shot and his leg
broken, and was carried to Piacenza. Then ensued the great

battle, and the destruction of the whole French army. Francis I always declared that if Giovanni delle Bande Nere had been there he would not have lost the day; and the accounts of the battle tend to show that he was probably right. This disaster to the French arms put an end to the war for the time. Meanwhile Giovanni was lying wounded at Piacenza, and his troops were in great destitution, owing to its being impossible to extract their pay from the Pope, who took advantage of their commander being *hors de combat* to withhold it. In this emergency Maria, as usual, proved herself a faithful and capable assistant to her husband. She writes beseeching him not again to attach himself to the Pope's cause, pointing out the duplicity with which Clement was treating him, and saying:—

"There will be no Popes like those that are gone. . . . Will you not cease to be at the beck and call of others, and come home and attend to your own concerns, now that there is time? God alone knows the future; remember Papa Leo, and how suddenly he died."

Ending her letter with the prayer that God will keep Giovanni in safety. And then having written thus, she went in person to Rome, and bravely assailed Pope Clement, demanding the pay of Giovanni's soldiers, and forced him to give her six thousand ducats for them.

But Maria did not get her Giovanni to come home and attend to his own concerns. Even before his wound was healed he was again busy in preparations for the fresh campaign which was impending. He writes to Maria to buy fresh horses, arms, and equipment in Florence to replace those lost in the recent operations, and for the new levies which he was raising. And she, though it strained his resources greatly, complied. And a few months later Giovanni was again at the head of his troops, and the tide of war once more sweeping over Lombardy. Francis I having regained his liberty, there was formed in 1526 the league between France, the Pope, Venice, and Florence against Charles V; and at such a time

Giovanni delle Bande Nere, Italy's foremost commander, could not be absent. His command now consisted of the whole of the infantry supplied by the Pope and Florence, together with a corps of about a thousand cavalry; while the entire army of the allies was commanded by the Duke of Urbino. Various operations took place, in which the Duke of Urbino was completely out-generaled by the imperial commander, the Duke of Bourbon, and the allied army forced to retire.

And then came the end; that end for which Clement had hoped, and which Maria had so long sorrowfully foreseen. On the bank of the Mincio, in the plain of Governolo, eight miles from Mantua, there were in November four days' severe fighting; and on the fourth day Giovanni was struck by a shot from the enemy's artillery in the leg previously wounded at Pavia. They carried him to Mantua, where, though an enemy, he was lodged by Federigo Gonzaga, Marquis of Mantua, in his own palace, and treated with every honour. Pietro Aretino was with him, and was directed to tell him that his leg must be amputated, a terrible operation in those days. They said he must be held by ten men, but he declared that no one should hold him, "and, taking the candle, held it himself throughout the operation, which was performed with great ignorance and roughness,[3] causing indescribable agony." And after all it was useless, for mortification set in a few hours afterwards. He endured intense pain, in the midst of which, however, he sent an affectionate message to poor Maria, and wrote an admirable brief address of farewell to his soldiers; and then, saying he would not die in a sick-bed, had himself placed on his camp bed, and the pain thereupon departing, he fell asleep and so died (30th November 1526). He was buried in his armour, in the church of San Francesco in Mantua; but in 1685 his remains were brought back to Florence, and buried in the family mausoleum. And when the Medici coffins were opened in 1857, more than three hundred years after his death, his body was found still lying in its black armour, and

with the amputated leg.[4] Many of his letters are in the State
archives of Florence, while his most prominent deeds in war
are immortalised in the frescoes on the walls of the Sala di
Giovanni delle Bande Nere in the Palazzo Vecchio. He left
only one son, Cosimo, who was seven years old when his
father died.

The grief of the soldiers of the Bande Nere at their great
commander's death was overwhelming. They wore mourning
for him for the rest of their lives, and, carrying a black ban-
ner, his celebrated corps won added honour even after he was
gone to the name he had made so renowned. And long afterwards they gave a notable proof of their regard for him. Most
of Giovanni's soldiers were recruited from his mother's former
patrimony of Imola. And many years after his death, when
his son Cosimo was ruler of Florence, and a movement against
the latter was being got up in Romagna, we are told that
around Imola it could make no way, the old soldiers of Giovanni delle Bande Nere repressing every whisper against their
revered commander's son.

As regards the character of Giovanni delle Bande Nere as a
soldier, we are told again and again of his extraordinary
bravery, his fortitude amidst dangers and hardships, his
modesty, just dealing, generosity, and unselfishness. The person who knew him best was Pietro Aretino, who thus describes
him:—

"He gave away to his soldiers more than he ever kept
for himself. Fatigue and hardship he endured with the greatest patience. In the battlefield he wore no distinguishing
mark, so that by his conspicuous valour alone could he be sin-
gled out from his men. He was ever the first to mount, the
last to dismount. He esteemed men according to their value,
not according to their rank or wealth. He was always better
than his word in action, but in council he never traded on
his great reputation. He had a wonderful art of governing
his soldiers, now by love and now by fear. Of all things he
held indolence in most horror. There is no doubt that his

disposition was naturally virtuous; his faults were those
only of youth, so that, had it pleased God to give him a
longer life, every one would have been as convinced of his
goodness as I am myself. It is certain that he had a most
affectionate heart. In short, many may envy him, but none
can imitate him."

So died, at the age of twenty-eight, the greatest commander produced by Italy in the sixteenth century; [5] one of
whom it has been said that had he lived longer the history of
Italy would have been altered and the Emperor Charles V
have been shorn of much of his glory; [6] one also who attained
the eminence he did, not, like Gaston de Foix or Charles of
Bourbon, through being related to a king, but entirely by his
own talents. We may well enquire what were the particular
methods, peculiar to himself, by excelling in which Giovanni
delle Bande Nere, in only ten years from the time that he
was given his first troop of one hundred men, made himself
the greatest commander in Italy. There were plenty of conspicuously brave men among the leaders of troops at this
time, but they did not achieve the success attained by him;
so that we must look elsewhere than to his renowned bravery
for the secret of that success. If his history is studied it
will be found that two main lines of action produced the
result, both of them demonstrating unusual insight into his
profession.

As regards the first of these, it is stated that he was the
first commander in war who exercised a personal care over
his troops. This new departure on his part had greater results
than many—at all events at that time—would have supposed
likely. For we find that his care of his men, watchful protection of their interests, generosity, justice, and absence of
regard for himself, when joined to his great courage and
chivalrous character, made his soldiers, notwithstanding his
very strict discipline, ready to make efforts for him which
none other could have obtained from them.

But the second way in which Giovanni delle Bande Nere

struck out a new line for himself is more remarkable, requiring as it did an unusual independence of spirit. In those days (as in many subsequent times) it was considered a finer thing to command men who rode than men who fought on foot. Giovanni delle Bande Nere held another view. It is stated that he was the first commander since Julius Cæsar to realise that since it is the infantry arm which in battle bears the brunt of the fighting,[7] that arm must in all ways be given the chief importance (both in peace and war) by a commander who desires success. Acting on this, which only his unusually ardent love for the soldier's profession enabled him to discern, Giovanni delle Bande Nere, though he had begun as a leader of cavalry, very early in his career changed to being an infantry commander, and remained such for the rest of his life. As a consequence he became, we are told, "the first commander under whom the infantry began to acquire fame since the time of the Roman legions."

The result of these two courses of action was that his infantry became such as no infantry had been for many centuries, and won for him the name of "The Invincible" at only twenty-two, while by the time he was twenty-eight he had become the greatest commander in Italy.

MARIA SALVIATI

Born 1499. (*Married* 1516) *Died* 1543

Maria Salviati, daughter of Jacopo Salviati and his wife, Lucrezia de' Medici, and granddaughter of Lorenzo the Magnificent, is one of the most attractive characters of the age, though she lived in the worst time in Florentine history. Married at seventeen to Giovanni de' Medici (soon to become known as Giovanni delle Bande Nere), who had been brought up with her from the time that she was ten and he eleven years old, she made him a most excellent wife. She was of an exceedingly affectionate disposition; she was a virtuous woman in an age when it was the exception; and she was no less noteworthy for her strong sense, wisdom, and capacity. She helped Giovanni in all his difficulties, and whereas he was from his fiery and headstrong nature always ready to become involved in some trouble, she was ever on the watch from a distance, displaying a wonderful forethought, and sending him sound advice which saved him from many quarrels. Her letters to him, many of which are preserved in the State archives of Florence, are models of sense, wisdom, and the strongest affection combined. Her portrait by Vasari is sure to be a good likeness, as he knew her well.

While Giovanni was absent on his almost perpetual campaigns she remained living in her father's palace in the Corso at Florence, where in 1519 her son, Cosimo, was born. During the next three years, Giovanni, having attained command of a troop, was mounting by rapid steps in his profession, and gaining great distinction owing to his invariable success wherever employed, so that the occasions when he was able to be with her were few. And when in 1523 Pope Adrian VI was succeeded by Clement VII this became still more the case. By this time her young husband, all whose youthful aspirations she had shared as a girl, had become one of the most renowned commanders in Italy, and she saw less and less of him. But this did not in any way prevent his being her one consideration at all times, and wherever we hear of her she seems to have no other care or interest but his well-being. Her life had in it much sadness, for, seeing plainly Pope Clement's manœuvres to oust Giovanni from his rights and to keep him always in the field in the hope that he would eventually get killed, she yet found it impossible to get Giovanni to guard his own interests, while she also lived in perpetual dread of hearing of his death. And the higher he rose in his profession, and the more the cloud of war spread over northern Italy (as it did almost uninterruptedly during the last three years of his life), the more impossible did it become for Giovanni to give any attention to his domestic affairs, or to be with the wife who loved him so devotedly.

Maria Salviati reveals herself completely to us in her letters, and the more we see of her the more attractive she becomes. M. Gautier calls her, "This wife who remained always a lover; a modern woman of passion and nerves, out of place among these suits of armour, these swords, and noises of war." [8] And again and again, after quoting long extracts from her letters, he exclaims: "Such tenderness, such womanly words!" In a touching letter to Giovanni in reference to a quarrel he had got into, she implores him to keep out of such broils, and "not to destroy us both by these frequent quarrels," and signs herself "Your desolate wife, who commends herself to you with face covered with tears." At the same time she is far from being weak; and one knows not which to admire the most, her great love for her warrior husband, her pleading tenderness, her gentle reproach, her ceaseless solicitude for his welfare, or her sagacious wisdom and strong common-sense. The tender pathos of many of her letters is indescribable. She knew that in the years before he was twenty-five he was, while absent at Rome, often unfaithful to her, and that she was supplanted by low rivals. And in her letters written at that time it is the peculiar combination of this knowledge (of which she speaks openly), of tender reproach to him for treating her so, and yet of an unswerving affection, care for his welfare, and sensible advice to keep him out of this or that quarrel, which makes them so singularly touching.

Giovanni spent nearly all his private funds on his troops, and, as previously noted, Maria was continually occupied in providing what he required, though it was often difficult to find the necessary money. And that he thus relied upon her to purchase for him such things as horses, arms, and other military equipment shows how well he knew her sound sense and judgment.

At last the news came which she had all along dreaded, and she heard of his being mortally wounded, which news was followed almost immediately by that of his death. His friend, Pietro Aretino, writes to her of how he had himself put Giovanni's body in its coffin, telling her of his own great grief, which, however, he says, must be far less than hers. He describes the funeral at Mantua, and, with a fine touch of sympathy for the desolate wife, speaks of how "the women gazed from the windows with awe and reverence upon the honoured form of him who was your husband, signora, and my lord." Maria replies by a striking letter, dignified and sensible, saying what a comfort it had been to her throughout the campaign to feel that he was with her husband; and then she urges him to write the history of her husband's life, suggesting that he shall write the history of its last fourteen years, and she, with the help of her father, will write that of the first fourteen years.[9] And she ends by a request that he "will commend myself and my poor Cosimo to the Marquis of Mantua, who has been so kind." Reading these letters of Maria's, it is hard to realise that it is all so long ago; we feel that it might have happened yesterday. Here, as so often, we feel how much closer the sixteenth century is to us than, *e.g.*, the eighteenth.

For the next ten years (1527-1537)—*i.e.*, during the three years of the revolt of Florence from Pope Clement, the year of the siege, and the reign of Alessandro as Duke—Maria Salviati lived in the greatest retirement at Trebbia, in the Mugello, about twenty miles from Florence, devoting herself to the education of her son, Cosimo. The only occasion on which she came out of this retirement was in 1533, when, as Catherine de' Medici's nearest relative, she accompanied the latter to Marseilles for her marriage. Maria lived this retired life for two reasons; not only was she left very badly off, most of their patrimony having been absorbed by her husband's military necessities, but also she lived in constant fear for her son now that the elder branch had no legitimate male descendant, knowing well that both Pope Clement and Alessandro were utterly unscrupulous, and looked with no friendly eye on one whose existence might be supposed to be an obstacle to Alessandro's being ruler of Florence. The only

other male representative of the younger branch besides her
son was Lorenzino; and Alessandro knew that the latter
possessed no influence, and would never set up any claim to
the rule of Florence. But it might be otherwise with a son of
Giovanni delle Bande Nere, to whom his father's name and
reputation would give plenty of adherents. Not that Maria had
any desire at all that such claims should be put forward on
behalf of her son; her gallant soldier's death ended all life for
her; and she felt a complete repugnance for the strivings of
ambition and worldly honours. She became a member of the
Third Order of St. Dominic, giving herself up to charitable
works; and she kept her son out of sight of Florence and its
affairs, training him to take pleasure in field sports and a
country life, and secluding him so effectually as far as Florence was concerned that the mass of the citizens scarcely knew
that such a youth existed.

The poverty to which she had been reduced is shown by a
letter of hers written in 1530 to Filippo Strozzi, the wealthy
banker, and head of the Strozzi family, who was one of her
creditors. She says:—

"Magnificent and much respected Sir,—We are, my son
and I, to that degree impoverished and broken down, not
only by private debts but by those due to the Government,
that we are in a desperate position, unless we can find some
one who will assist us until we can get breathing time. We
therefore suppliantly entreat your magnificence that if the
other creditors press and crush us you will have the more pity
on us; and, as you have had from us two hundred ducats
up to this time, that you will be content to bear with us for
this year. I declare to you on my faith that it is impossible
for us to do more; and I will use every effort to meet you
in such a manner as you will find satisfactory at the end of
the time named. I implore and beseech your excellency, and
with all my heart beg of you, not to deny us this favour. For
should you decide otherwise, and determine on pressing us,
I know of no means of meeting your claim. We will not the
less strive our utmost to put together another two hundred

ducats within this year, if it be any way possible, and if you will not have patience with us for the entire debt. Our gratitude will be greater should you give us one year's time for the whole sum. Yet it will be no less if you will content yourself with the two hundred ducats. I will say no more, save that Cosimo and I commend ourselves earnestly to your magnificence.

> Your cousin and sister,
> MARIA SALVIATI DE' MEDICI."

At length, when Maria had been a widow for ten years, and when her son Cosimo was seventeen and a half years old, there occurred in January 1537 Duke Alessandro's sudden assassination; [10] whereupon her son suddenly, and without consulting her, made his bold bid for power.[11] His mother liked neither the thing itself nor his methods, and endeavoured to persuade him to abandon the course on which he had embarked; which greatly enraged him. And the cruelty which a few months later he displayed against those who had opposed him still more deeply pained his gentle-spirited and high-minded mother, strengthening her strong disapproval of his whole course of action. This caused a complete estrangement between them; from the time he became Duke of Florence he never went near her; and she suffered many things from his harsh and unlovely disposition. On her son becoming head of the State, she removed from Trebbia to the villa at Castello, where her husband had lived as a boy, and there resided during the remaining six years of her life, seldom seeing any one, and devoting herself to religion and good works. Her son's conduct was the last drop of sadness in a life which had been always sad; while we are told that Cosimo displayed towards her "such an utter want of affection that even when she was lying ill at the villa of Castello, and he was shooting in the vicinity, he could hardly be persuaded to relinquish the pleasures of the chase for a single day to visit her on her death-bed." A few days later her gentle spirit passed away.

Maria Salviati died at Castello in 1543, six years after her son became Duke of Florence, and was buried dressed in the habit of the Third Order of St. Dominic. In after years her remains were removed from their first resting-place to be laid beside those of her husband when brought from Mantua.[12] When the Medici coffins were opened in 1857 her body was found unimpaired; her coffin bore only her simple name "Maria." [13] She and Giovanni delle Bande Nere lie side by side in the centre of the crypt of the great family mausoleum, with round them their descendants, the grand dukes and grand duchesses, princes and princesses, of Tuscany.

CHAPTER XXIV

COSIMO I

Born 1519. ⎰ *Reigned,*   1537-1574 ⎱   *Died* 1574
           ⎱ *Created Grand Duke of Tuscany,* 1569 ⎰

WHEN on the 5th January 1537 Alessandro's sudden death
took place, all was for some days in great confusion, since, the
Signoria having been abolished,[1] Florence was left by the
Duke's death without any government. Moreover, there were
none left on whom it devolved to form one. Pope Clement VII,
Ippolito, and now Alessandro, were all dead; no male descendant of the elder branch of the Medici family remained; neither
the Strozzi, Guicciardini, Ridolfi, nor any other family in
Florence felt themselves capable of assuming the place which
had been taken by the Medici; while the reigning Pope
(Paul III) had no particular interest in Florentine affairs.
So that there seemed no reason why Florence should not reinstate her Republic; and as those in charge of the fortresses
were ready to agree to it, everything appeared to point to this
course. It was, however, not adopted. The Council called the
Forty-eight still nominally existed, though under Alessandro
it had had no power; and whilst its leading members were
discussing the situation, and before anything definite had been
decided upon, there appeared in Florence from the district of
the Mugello an almost unknown youth of seventeen, Cosimo,
son of Giovanni delle Bande Nere, accompanied by one or
two attendants. Failing Lorenzino himself, who had fled and
made no claim to the rule, this youth was (supposing a republic was not going to be set up) rightfully heir to the succession; while from one point of view his claim might be
considered superior to any which could be put forward on
behalf of Lorenzino, in that, his mother being a granddaughter

551

of Lorenzo the Magnificent, *both* branches of the Medici united in him.

This youth, by his artful assumption of a humble demeanour, by the little that was known of him seeming to indicate that he was not likely to take a prominent part in affairs of State, and by his promises that if he were appointed to the rule all power should remain in the hands of the Council, induced the chief senators to accept him as the head of the State. We are told that he "concealed his ambition under so humble and submissive a demeanour as to provoke the contempt of his friends." The four principal senators Guicciardini, Strozzi, Valori, and Acciajuoli, were completely taken in, and chose him with the idea that he was a youth of little character, whose interests chiefly centred in shooting and field sports, and that he would be a nonentity, and would leave them to rule the country. Accordingly he was elected as chief of the State, it being definitely laid down that all power was to rest with the Council. A bas-relief showing this episode is to be seen on the pedestal of the equestrian statue of Cosimo I in the Piazza della Signoria, and very faithfully reproduces the unassuming attitude which was adopted by Cosimo. Thus did Francesco Guicciardini, Filippo Strozzi, Baccio Valori, and Niccolò Acciajuoli, in order to obtain their own personal ends, deliver over their country to an iron-handed tyrant; Guicciardini, the chief of them, mainly so acting because he hoped that Cosimo would marry his daughter Lisabetta, and that he (Guicciardini) would rule Florence while the young head of the State amused himself. They all had bitter cause in a very short time to repent their action. Simultaneously with this election a decree was, at Cosimo's request, passed by the Council putting the whole of Lorenzino's branch out of the succession in consequence of his murder of Alessandro, Cosimo pointing out that this was advisable in order to make his position unimpeachable.

No sooner, however, was Cosimo installed as chief of the State than he threw off the mask which he had worn. He cast all these councillors aside, assumed absolute authority, and showed himself in his true colours as an arbitrary tyrant who intended to rule by fear. He soon became the most dreaded man in Florence.

Of course, such an entire reversal of all that had been contemplated was bound to issue in a struggle. Before many months were over Cosimo's tyrannical actions had driven a large number of the citizens into voluntary exile, including Filippo Strozzi and Baccio Valori,[2] and by the end of the summer of 1537 these *fuorusciti* had assembled an army to dethrone him, for which purpose they had also gained the help of a considerable body of French troops. The main portion of their forces consisted of four thousand infantry and three hundred cavalry commanded by Filippo Strozzi's eldest son, Piero Strozzi, already a distinguished soldier. Meanwhile Cosimo had also got together a force, and by representing himself as the successor of the Emperor's vassal Alessandro, had obtained the assistance of the imperial troops in Tuscany. His whole force was under the command of Alessandro Vitelli. The battle to decide the fate of Tuscany was fought at Montemurlo, near Prato, on the 1st August 1537; it resulted in Vitelli's gaining a victory which saved Cosimo, and delivered all his opponents into his hands. Vitelli's success was chiefly due to a fortunate accident. The body of troops attacked by him were in reality only the advanced guard of the enemy's force, their main body under Piero Strozzi being away at a distance in the mountains; but with the body defeated by Vitelli were Filippo Strozzi, Baccio Valori, and all the principal men of the party opposed to Cosimo, all of whom were captured. The main body with Piero Strozzi only heard of the defeat of the troops at Montemurlo, with the capture of all the leaders, when the battle was over and it was too late to do anything; and Piero Strozzi had no course but to retire. The column which stands in the Piazza Sta. Trinità, surmounted by a fine figure of Justice, was erected by Cosimo[3] to commemorate this victory of Montemurlo which gave him his throne.

Of all the buildings in Florence one possesses a more solemn interest than any other—interest of the same kind as attaches to the Tower of London—namely, the gloomy citadel of the Bargello. Terrible have been the scenes which its court-yard (the place of execution) and surrounding cells have witnessed; piteous the cries with which its torture-chamber, now the armoury (where is the only oubliette [4] in Florence), has resounded; heart-breaking the grief endured in the open *loggia* [5] overlooking the courtyard where so many bitter wrongs have had their cruel ending.[6] None can climb its pic-turesque staircase, or traverse its halls, insensible to the tragic memories which cling round this ancient fortress of the Po-destà of Florence, where so many who were notable have taken their last look on life. And the victory of Montemurlo added many to these sad memories which attach to the Bar-gello. For Cosimo had set up a despotism no less severe than that of the kings of England and France of that time; and to be consigned to the Bargello was apt to be as fatal to the per-son concerned as to be committed to the Tower or to the Bastile.

The prisoners taken at Montemurlo were very numerous and of high rank, for there was scarcely one of the leading families of Florence which had not some member among them, or a Florentine student at Bologna or Padua who had not joined Filippo Strozzi and Baccio Valori in this attempt. Many of them were quite young, and not a few were Cosimo's per-sonal friends; but they received no mercy, for in Cosimo that quality was non-existent. The cells of the Bargello were crowded with prisoners of distinction; and when the Bargello could hold no more, the remainder were sent to the Fortezza. The prisoners were executed in batches day after day, while the halls rang with the cries of the tortured; not one was pardoned; all were in turn first tortured and then executed.

Baccio Valori and his son, with young Albizzi, were among
those thus put to death at the Bargello. Filippo Strozzi, confined in irony in the Fortezza, to build which he had provided
the funds, was either put to death there, or committed suicide
to escape further torture, his body being found in his cell
transfixed with a sword. Thus ended the rich, handsome, and
accomplished courtier and banker, Filippo Strozzi,[7] the husband of Clarice de Medici, and the friend of popes and kings,
to whom only seven years before Cosimo's mother had written
that humble petition on behalf of Cosimo and herself for time
in which to pay their debt. Cosimo confiscated the Strozzi
palace in the Via Tornabuoni and the whole of Filippo
Strozzi's possessions.[8] Piero il Gottoso seventy years before
had contrived to put down an armed rebellion against himself
without the sacrifice of a single life; Cosimo I seemed anxious
to create the greatest contrast possible, for of all the enemies
who fell into his hands he did not spare a single life. No
wonder that Maria Salviati, looking with horror on these proceedings of her son which she was powerless to prevent, shut
herself up in deepest seclusion at the villa of Castello.

Cosimo was, in fact, a most unusual character. Neither his
mother nor any of those around him up to the age of seventeen
were in the least prepared for the action which he then suddenly took. The bold stroke by which he seized upon the rule
of Florence astounded Maria Salviati, and was as great a
revelation of character to her as to every one else. How completely he had contrived to hide his real nature from all those
who knew him as a boy [9] is shown by the case of Filippo
Strozzi, who, though he had been on intimate terms with him
and his mother while they resided at Trebbia, was nevertheless as much taken in as the other senators. Cosimo is perhaps
the only instance on record of a boy, hitherto occupying an
obscure position, given up to sport and a country life, and
thought to have little capacity, suddenly casting aside every
boyish taste, undertaking the arduous labours of government,

seizing the rule of his country from her wisest and ablest men, and slaughtering wholesale her leading citizens.

But although Cosimo thus showed himself a cruel and merciless tyrant, in his subsequent history he manifested extraordinary abilities; with results for which his country had every reason to be grateful. It is, indeed, little short of marvellous how one who, silent and taciturn by nature, had in his youth been considered "dull," "timid," and "wanting in character," yet developed the capacity to raise Tuscany to the highest pitch of political importance and general well-being which she ever reached. Tuscany, which ever since the time of Lorenzo the Magnificent, under the successive maladministration of Soderini, Lorenzo (Duke of Urbino), Passerini, the Republican Government of 1527-1530, and Alessandro, had for over forty years possessed little or no political importance in Italy, was by Cosimo I raised to a higher position in this respect among the states of Italy than she had occupied even in the time of Lorenzo the Magnificent. The glory of the leadership in Art and Learning was no longer hers; the joy and brightness of the Renaissance were for ever passed away, overwhelmed in the wars which for more than a generation had raged over Italy; but in so far as the remaining factors of political influence, military strength, and commercial progress were concerned, Cosimo I raised Tuscany, not merely to her former level, but beyond it; so much so that she became under him the only state of first-class importance in Italy. Cosimo Pater Patriae and Lorenzo the Magnificent had gloried in advancing the boundaries of the State, but under Cosimo I Tuscany was almost doubled in size; while at the same time the conditions in regard to the administration of justice, and the general advancement of the country, were changed from those customary in the Middle Ages to those thought necessary in modern times. And Cosimo did all this himself; for his principle was to avoid taking any councillors, and throughout his life those whom he employed to assist him were nothing more

than secretaries, and none were given a sufficient power of
initiative for their names to have obtained any record in history. They were invariably men of a humble station in life,
and always chosen from other parts of the country than
Florence.

As soon as Cosimo had, by the victory of Montemurlo and
the execution of all who had opposed him, firmly secured his
power, he set about arrangements for that gradual advancement of his position which he had set before him. As yet he
had merely been elected by the Florentines as head of their
State; so that his first step was to endeavour to obtain formal
recognition of his position by the Emperor. Representing himself as willing to be the Emperor's vassal, and ready to promote
his cause in every way against the French interest in Italy, he
obtained what he sought, the Emperor issuing a Diploma
which conferred on Cosimo "all the authority formerly borne
and exercised by Duke Alessandro." And though the Diploma
did not categorically confer on Cosimo the title of Duke, the
latter from this time forth always signed himself "Duca di
Fiorenza," to which no exception was taken by the Emperor.
In this connection it is interesting to notice that in the rooms
lately reopened on the upper floor of the Palazzo Vecchio, over
the sixteenth century fireplace in Cosimo's room his title is to
be seen inscribed as "Cosimus Florie Dux II"; showing that
at this time in his life (previous to his obtaining the status of
Grand Duke, making him Cosimo I) he called himself "Dux
II," the second Duke of Florence, the first being Alessandro.

Cosimo's next step was to set about arrangements for a
marriage such as would contribute to the strength of his
position. He first endeavoured strenuously to get the Emperor
to give him his daughter Margaret, Alessandro's young
widow; but this Charles V absolutely refused to do, while at
the same time insisting on Cosimo's making over to Margaret
a very large portion of the Medici property, much to Cosimo's
indignation. This first matrimonial project having failed, the

latter turned elsewhere, and in 1539 succeeded in arranging a marriage for himself with Eleonora, the only child of Don Pedro di Toledo, Marquis of Villafranca and Viceroy of Naples, the most capable and trusted of all the Emperor's lieutenants, who ruled the kingdom of Naples from 1532 till his death in 1553. Eleonora di Toledo was escorted to Florence by Don Pedro himself, and they were met by Cosimo at the villa of Poggio a Caiano, fifteen miles from Florence. The Viceroy of Naples and his suite were lodged during their stay in Florence in the monastery of Sta. Maria Novella,[10] and after many festivities Cosimo and Eleonora were married with much ceremony in the church of San Lorenzo, he being then twenty and she seventeen. Eleonora was very rich, and her wealth, together with the political influence which Cosimo gained by becoming the son-in-law of the Viceroy of Naples, made a considerable difference in his position. The portrait of Eleonora by Bronzino on the wall of one of the rooms in the Palazzo Vecchio shows her as she was at about the age of twenty, two or three years after her marriage. She has a fine broad forehead and a pleasing face.

Up to this time Cosimo had lived in the Medici Palace in the Via Larga; and it was there that he brought home his bride. But shortly after making this marriage Cosimo removed into the Palazzo Vecchio, having the rooms on the second floor, which had been those always occupied by the Gonfaloniere, handsomely decorated for Eleonora's reception. He had several reasons for this change of residence, but his principal one was that the Medici Palace was not a defensible castle, and possessed no accommodation for the bodyguard of troops necessary to protect his person; while his occupation of the Palazzo Vecchio, which for centuries had been associated in the minds of the Florentines with the governing body, not only gave him a more secure abode, but also emphasised the fact that he, and he alone, now wielded the entire power of the State.[11] Other rulers around him, such as the Este at Ferrara, or the Gonzaga at Mantua, each occupied their

"Castello" in the centre of their capital city, and no other residence was in fact suitable for a despotic ruler such as Cosimo desired all men to recognise that he intended to be. Immediately at the door of his palace, and passed daily by him, stood Donatello's statue of *Judith slaying Holofernes,* with the inscription which the citizens had placed on it "as a warning to all who might attempt to tyrannise over Florence"; and this Cosimo suffered to remain as it was, in grim irony at the wide contrast between the sentiment expressed by the inscription and the rule which he had established. His bodyguard of Swiss lancers he placed, during the hours that they were on duty,[12] in Orcagna's Loggia, which tl us acquired the name by which it has always since been known of the "Loggia de' Lanzi." The Palazzo Vecchio was a somewhat restricted and gloomy abode for Eleonora, but Cosimo had other plans for the future, and intended arranging for himself and Eleonora a much larger and grander residence later on when he should feel sufficiently firmly established. Meanwhile, by incorporating the buildings on the eastern side, including the residences of the Esecutore di Giustizia and the Capitano dei Fanti, he considerably enlarged the Palazzo Vecchio; and he and Eleonora lived there for ten years, six of their eight children being born there.[13]

But until he had an army of his own, independent alike of any troops lent him by the Emperor and of Florentine levies, Cosimo could not feel secure. Added to which he had views in the future of extending the boundaries of Tuscany when opportunity should offer, and for this a powerful army would be necessary. He therefore gradually raised a force of Swiss, German, and Italian troops (the latter recruited from other parts of Italy than Tuscany), and soon had a small but strong army, which he steadily increased in numbers. In order to strengthen his hold on Florence he also much enlarged the Fortezza, and augmented the number of troops quartered there.

By the above means Cosimo by the time he was twenty-one had firmly established himself as despotic ruler of Tuscany. Bronzino's portrait of him in the Pitti Gallery (one of the best portraits that Bronzino ever executed), painted, Vasari tells us, when Cosimo was forty, accords closely with the description of his appearance given by contemporary writers; these state that his face gave no indication of the great abilities which he possessed, and that he had "a dark and impenetrable disposition," with a power of fierce and relentless anger, all the more terrible because it burnt under the surface.

For the first ten years of his reign Cosimo was chiefly occupied in strengthening his position as Duke of Florence. The three main factors in European politics were, as before, Francis I, Charles V, and the Pope (Paul III). During the years 1536 and 1537 the latter had continued to labour earnestly to bring about peace between the two antagonists,[14] but for some time without avail. At length in June 1538 he got both Charles and Francis to come to Nice; though they would not meet, and the Pope had to conduct negotiations by personally visiting them alternately. So that much credit is due to him for the success he eventually achieved in getting them to agree to a truce which caused a cessation of the conflict for four years. At the end of that time, however, they were again at war, and Cosimo had to choose his side. Abandoning the traditional Florentine policy of alliance with France, Cosimo throughout his reign threw himself heart and soul on the side of the Emperor, opposing the operations of the French in Italy on all occasions. At the same time, beginning as the Emperor's vassal, he gradually purchased his independence. When the war between Francis and Charles was resumed in 1542, and five separate French armies invaded Charles's territories, the Emperor, to raise troops to meet this attack, borrowed money largely from Cosimo,[15] who in return obtained the withdrawal of the imperial garrisons from Florence and Pisa. The same process was repeated on several subsequent occasions, Cosimo taking a step further in the same direction each time that the Emperor was in need of funds, until he attained entire independence. Nevertheless, after he had done so he still continued the same policy of always siding with the Emperor and against the French, so that he came eventually to be Charles V's mainstay in Italy; while the accessions of territory which from time to time the Emperor helped him to acquire, by increasing Cosimo's power increased also Charles's feeling of security as regards Italy.

In 1544 peace was for a time made between Francis and Charles at Crépy. And in December 1545 the Council of the Church which had been talked of for so many years at last assembled at Trent. It, however, failed to possess the character which had been intended; for instead of the two parties in the dispute being present, only one of them was represented at it, neither the Church of England nor the Protestant party in Germany and France sending any representatives to it. So that it became merely a Council of the Roman Church, and as such lost all interest for Europe as a whole.

In 1546 the Strozzi brothers, who had never ceased to seek vengeance against Cosimo for their father's death, made an attack on him, with the assistance of Francesco Burlamacchi, from Lucca; but the attempt failed. In 1547 the long triangular duel, which had lasted for over a quarter of a century, came to an end by the death in the early part of that year of two of the antagonists, Henry VIII and Francis I,[16] just when Francis was preparing a fresh attack upon Charles. This removal of his two rivals materially increased Charles V's power, as all states in Italy soon felt, and in particular the Pope. The attempt of the latter to introduce the Inquisition (which he had established in Rome in 1542) into Naples was defeated, Charles refusing to allow it. The Pope was also endeavouring to get the Council of Trent removed to some city in Italy, and intriguing for this purpose with the French against Charles; but in this, as in all his undertakings, he found a strong opponent in Cosimo, whose state of Tuscany was rapidly becoming the strongest in Italy. At this time we find Cosimo tendering remarkable advice to Charles V, urging him, in a letter of the 6th February 1547, "to use his power for a complete reform of the Church through the Council, taking away the tyranny of the priests, reducing the power of the Pope to its proper spiritual limits, and restoring the pure faith of Christ without the abuses that had grown up about it." [17] Whilst all those in Italy who were in opposition to the Emperor looked naturally to the Pope for assistance, "in the young Duke Cosimo," says Ranke, "Paul III found the very man best fitted to oppose him." And Cosimo himself, in a letter about this time, says:—

"The Pope, who has succeeded in so many undertakings, has now no wish more earnest than of doing something in Florence as well; he would fain estrange this state from the Emperor, but this is a hope he shall carry with him to his grave."

In this year, 1547, Cosimo managed to remove from his path a danger which had from the first threatened him. The decree which he had obtained at the time of his election, putting Lorenzino's branch of the family out of the succession, still left him with a feeling of insecurity, as it was always open to his enemies to get up an agitation to dethrone him on the ground that Lorenzino was the lawful head of the family and the rightful ruler of Florence. Lorenzino's death was therefore much to be desired, and Cosimo had long tried to achieve it, but without success. Lorenzino, after many wanderings in France, Turkey, and other countries, had eventually settled with his mother, Maria Soderini, at Venice, where he lived in constant fear of his life, knowing that Cosimo was employing the most skilled assassins to dog his steps. Knowing the dangers which were around him in the narrow little streets, he seldom trusted himself anywhere outside his house except in a gondola. At length one night in 1547 he was caught unawares in a narrow street by two hired assassins employed by Cosimo, and murdered. The account of how they killed him was related by themselves, and may be read in full detail in various records of the time. Cosimo's plea for this act was that he was only carrying out a just execution of Lorenzino for the murder of Alessandro. Throughout his life he adopted the same attitude on this subject. The view that Lorenzino's act was inspired by a desire to liberate his country, by creating sympathy with Lorenzino, militated seriously against Cosimo's usurpation of the rule of Florence; while it might inspire others to similar action against himself. And it was in order to excite a feeling against Lorenzino, and to extinguish, if possible, the above view of his act (though no other reason for the deed could ever be produced), that Cosimo on coming to power had the house broken down,[18] and that he and his successors, the Grand Dukes, endeavoured in all ways to heap as much odium as possible on Lorenzino's name. With the result that Lorenzino has been handed down to us, not as he was looked upon by his contemporaries, viz., as "the Florentine Brutus," but as one on whom every abusive epithet may freely be cast.

In 1548 Cosimo succeeded in performing an important service for Charles V. The republic of Siena had revolted from the latter, driven out his representative and the Spanish garrison, and placed themselves under the protection of the Pope. Cosimo offered to mediate between the two parties, which was accepted; and he was so successful that he was able to pacify the Sienese, and arrange an agreement that Siena's ancient form of government should be respected by the Emperor, while a representative of the latter with a Spanish garrison should be admitted.

Both France and the Pope were now preparing to attack the Emperor, and he was strengthening himself in every way in Italy for the conflict. As one measure to that end the harbour of Portoferrajo and the adjacent district in the island of Elba was given to Cosimo, and he in a short time made Portoferrajo the strongest naval station in the Mediterranean. He was also allowed to occupy Piombino for a time

to assist him in defending his own coast line near Pisa, an
gained various accessions of territory along the coast. I
1549 Pope Paul III died; and since his successor, Julius III
adopted a more amicable policy towards the Emperor, thi
tended to create peace in Italy.

In ten years from the time of his marriage Cosimo had s
firmly established his rule that he felt able to occupy
different kind of residence from the Palazzo Vecchio; whil
this change was the more desirable since he and Eleonor
had now seven children, the eldest of them being nine year
old. Accordingly early in 1550 Cosimo, imitating the ancesto
after whom he had been named,[19] set about building a nev
palace for the family, that which is now the royal palace i
Florence; and which, though known to us as the Pitt
Palace,[20] was (except as below) entirely built by the Medici
and was their home during two hundred years.

To carry out this purpose Cosimo bought, with Eleonora
money, the estate covering the northwestern slope of th
Boboli hill, on the southern side of the Arno, together with
at the foot of the hill, the portion of the palace which hac
been begun, more than eighty years before, by Luca Pitti
but which that family had never had money enough to finish
This when Cosimo bought it consisted only of the smal
centre portion of the present building embraced by the thre
centre arches of the ground floor [21] and the seven window
above them; it was only completed up to the top of th
first floor, and was still unroofed, leaving more than half th
building (even as it existed in Cosimo I's reign) to be com
pleted. Except this small nucleus the whole of the palac
as we see it was built by the Medici. Cosimo, assisted by hi
able architect Ammanati, completed this centre portion up
to the roof, but without extending it laterally; which alon
suffices to show that the present central court did not exis
even in his time.[22] The estate and the unfinished buildin

upon it were sold to Cosimo by Buonaccorso Pitti for 9,000 gold florins.

It is generally stated that the Pitti Palace is built on the design which had, one hundred years before, been drawn up by Brunelleschi for Luca Pitti. But this (while of course totally incorrect as regards all the rest of the palace [23]) is an error even as regards the comparatively small portion of it which formed the Ducal palace in Cosimo's time, and which scarcely amounts to one sixth of the whole building. For Buonaccorso Pitti, when selling the property, was unable to supply Cosimo with Brunelleschi's design, this having in the lapse of years been lost. Nor even had it been forthcoming would a building designed to accommodate an ordinary citizen family in 1440 have sufficed, a hundred years later, for the residence of the Duke of Florence and his court. Be this as it may, Cosimo's palace when completed consisted only of the comparatively small central portion of the front block of the present palace. When thus finished by him it was a plain oblong building, three stories high, with seven windows on the front which faces the Via Romana, and without either the central court or the two great wings on either side of the latter (running back at right angles to the façade) which now form the great central block of the palace. Thus in Cosimo's and Eleonora's time the palace had a very different aspect from the immense building to which we are accustomed, including as it did only that portion of the façade which is embraced by the seven centre windows. This is remarkably corroborated by a little known picture occupying a dark corner in the long corridor between the Pitti and Uffizi galleries. It shows the portrait of a lady of the ducal court with, in the background, a picture of the ducal palace, demonstrating very plainly what its dimensions were in the time of Cosimo I. The picture, owing to its background, is labelled "A lady of the Pitti family"; but the background itself refutes this, for the palace is represented as *completed and roofed*, which at once proves that the time is subsequent

to that at which the building had any connection with the
Pitti family, and that we are here shown the palace as it was
after being completed by Cosimo I. The picture consequently
represents, not a lady of the Pitti family, but "A lady of the
ducal court." [24] In the beginning of the year 1553 the work
was sufficiently far advanced to allow of the new palace being
occupied, and Cosimo and Eleonora with their seven children
moved into it.[25]

Cosimo, who was extremely fond of elaborately planned
gardens, and was the founder of the Botanical Gardens at
Pisa [26] and the Giardino Botannico de' Semplici at Florence,
took the greatest pleasure in laying out, with the help of
Tribolo and Buontalenti, the magnificent gardens behind his
new palace, extending up the slope of the Boboli hill and covering an immense area; [27] while to Eleonora and her children
the change must have been great after the confined precincts of the Palazzo Vecchio. And as in these beautiful gardens we traverse the long avenues of cypress, ilex, and stone
pine, or follow the shady pathways amidst banks of roses and
azaleas, or sit on the seats of the amphitheatre overlooking
the back of the palace, it is impossible not to think of those
eight children of Cosimo and Eleonora who were the first of
many families of children to play here, and of their chequered
histories:—Maria, whose sad death at sixteen cast the first
gloom over the family; Francis, unstable and unenergetic,
who succeeded his father; Isabella, destined to die a tragic
death at the age of thirty-four; Giovanni, whose death at
nineteen was so severe a blow to his father's hopes; Lucrezia,
married at fifteen, and dying at seventeen; Garzia, his
mother's favourite son, whose death at sixteen was immediately followed by hers; Ferdinand, capable and full of energy,
who succeeded his brother Francis, and carried on the Medici
line; and Pietro, eight years old when his mother died, and
either justly or unjustly accused of murdering his young wife
when he was only twenty-two.[28] Looking at the palace where

they all grew up one feels that its main interest will always be associated with this first generation of the family who lived here.

But Cosimo did not only lay out gardens in connection with his new palace. He intended that it should have a fortress in close proximity to it as well. Therefore, on the summit of the Boboli hill, at the extremity of the gardens, he laid out the lines of the fort of San Giorgio, also called the Forte di Belvedere. Placed so as to join the line of the city walls, and on a height more immediately overhanging the city than that of San Miniato, it commands the whole of Florence, besides completely defending it on the southern side. And this fort, when completed by his son Ferdinand I, became the stronghold of the Medici family.

Cosimo, soon after he had, by his marriage with Eleonora di Toledo, become rich enough to undertake such a quest, set about a diligent search for traces of the ancient Etruscans, making extensive excavations at Chiusi (the ancient Clusium), Arezzo, and other places in "Etruria" to search for specimens of Etruscan art; while at the same time he purchased all rare Etruscan and Egyptian antiquities which chance threw in his way. These efforts of his had important consequences. For this search for remains of the ancient inhabitants of Tuscany was continued by his descendants, producing an immense collection of most valuable and interesting specimens of the art of the Etruscans and objects revealing their mode of life. And these, combined with the Egyptian antiquities also gradually accumulated, resulted in the two collections which now form the Etruscan and Egyptian Museums of Florence,[29] the former being considered probably the finest Etruscan museum in the world. Among the numerous interesting remains of Etruscan art which Cosimo obtained from these excavations were the fine statue of *Minerva*, found near Arezzo in 1541, the celebrated

Chimaera, found near Arezzo in 1554, and the statue known as *The Orator,* found near the Trasimene Lake in 1566, all being of bronze.[30] The most valuable of these "finds" was the statue of the *Chimaera,* or fire-breathing monster, having the body of a lion, a goat's head springing from the back, and (for the tail) a serpent which is biting the goat's head—a statue contemporaneous with the *Wolf of Rome.* It was, however, held to be inauspicious to Florence,[31] and so was kept by Cosimo in his private room in the Palazzo Vecchio and not exhibited to the public.[32]

From the time that he moved into his new palace Cosimo began to turn his attention to the collection, with the assistance of Vasari and Bronzino,[33] of a gallery of pictures such as that which his ancestors had gathered round them in former days in the palace in the Via Larga. The plunder of the Medici art collections which had taken place in 1494, and again in 1527, had dissipated the collections made by the elder branch, scattering far and wide most of what had not been destroyed, valuable pictures which had been the property of the Medici having even found their way to France and Germany. But some portion of these art treasures were still in Florence, dispersed among different families, or hidden away elsewhere; and Cosimo had search made for these, and bought back as many of them as he could find for the embellishment of his new palace, including portraits of former members of the family, a few statues and busts, and objects of art such as the vases which had belonged to Lorenzo the Magnificent.[34] At the same time he set Bronzino to work to paint (from such materials as existed in the shape of representations on medallions, frescoes, or otherwise) the portraits of all the Medici from Giovanni di Bicci downwards. Bronzino carried out this work with great care and long labour, and the series of portraits of the older Medici which he thus painted for Cosimo, and which are now in the Uffizi Gallery, are among his best works. Vasari, who was also at work for Cosimo in other directions,[35] says:—

"In some small pictures painted on plates of copper, and all of the same size, he (Bronzino) painted all the great men of the house of Medici, beginning with Giovanni di Bicci and Cosimo the elder down to the Queen of France (Catherine) in that line; and in the other, from Lorenzo, brother of Cosimo the elder, down to Duke Cosimo and his children. The which portraits are behind the door of the studio made by Vasari in the apartments of the new rooms of the ducal palace."

The two fine portraits of Cosimo I and Eleonora di Toledo gave Bronzino the reputation of the best Florentine portrait painter of his time.

The years 1551 and 1553 were a troubled time for Charles V, who was harassed with defensive and unsuccessful war against the Turks in Hungary, against France in both Savoy and Lorraine, and against the rising in Germany headed by Maurice of Savoy. And that these troubles were not increased by the war spreading also to Italy was due entirely to the strong position to which Cosimo had by this time brought Tuscany, and to his steady adherence to the cause of the Emperor. Nevertheless in 1552 the peace of Italy was severely endangered by the action of the republic of Siena, which again rose in revolt against Charles V, drove out the Spanish garrison, and accepted a French garrison in its place. Cosimo was, however, able to prevent the revolt from spreading to other states, and in January 1553 a force was despatched from Naples to subdue Siena; but owing to the death of the Viceroy of Naples, Don Pedro di Toledo,[36] Eleonora's father, this force failed to effect anything. For his efforts in the Emperor's cause the latter conferred upon Cosimo the coveted honour of the Order of the Golden Fleece.[37]

The attempt from Naples having failed, Cosimo now proceeded to undertake the conquest of Siena himself, nominally of course on behalf of the Emperor, Siena being an Imperial fief. He had by this time a large and well-equipped army, partly composed of German, Swiss, and other non-Italian troops, and partly of the Tuscan militia inaugurated many years before by Machiavelli, which Cosimo had revived and largely increased; while the numerous fortresses of Tuscany were well armed, strongly garrisoned, and commanded by reliable leaders not belonging to Tuscany. The army which he sent against Siena was commanded by Giacomo Medichino, Marquis of Marignano; while that of Siena, consisting chiefly of French troops, was commanded by the skilful soldier Piero Strozzi, Filippo Strozzi's gallant son, who in his unceasing endeavours to avenge his father's death was always to be found opposing Cosimo wherever any fighting was taking place. The war was a long one, Siena making a splendid fight in defence of her ancient republic. Piero Strozzi added greatly to his laurels by his conduct of the campaign; it was carried on throughout the Sienese territory, the whole country between Siena and Florence becoming a frequently fought-over battlefield. Cosimo introduced great barbarity into the conflict by his cruel treatment of the country people of the districts traversed by the war, which increased the determined resistance offered to him. At length, in August 1554 Strozzi's army sustained a severe defeat at Marciano,[38] which was followed by the investment of the city of Siena, which endured a terrible siege for many months. Everything that a brave people could do in such a case was done, even the ladies of Siena taking an active part in the defence. When, after untold horrors had been suffered, the end drew near, it was decided that Piero Strozzi with a portion of the troops should depart to hold Montalcino (one of Siena's subject cities which was yet unconquered), and the command of the defence then devolved on Blaise de Montluc, Marshal of France, who covered himself with no less glory than Strozzi had done. At length, when out of 40,000 inhabitants only 6,000 remained alive, and when everything edible had been consumed, Siena surrendered (April 1555). The concluding scene is thus described by Trollope:—

"The miserable remnant of the brave garrison marched
out with the honours of war, accompanied by six hundred
families who would not stay to see their beloved city under
a tyrant's rule. They marched out into a desolate country;
for two years no spade had touched the soil, from Montalcino
to Siena, from Siena to Florence, no living thing moved upon
the face of the land. Many died that day, though Montluc
killed his horse to give them food. At Buonconvento Strozzi
met them; at length they reached Montalcino, and there the
remnants of Sienese liberty found a haven. The shadow of
an ancient republic rested for a while on its old grey walls
as faintly as their hopes, but it soon passed over the mould-
ering dial and disappeared for ever." [39]

Thus ended the last of the great Italian republics of the
Middle Ages. It had long been in the power either of France
or Spain. Cosimo, when once he had conquered Siena, did
not treat it badly. He retained almost intact its ancient constitution, and preserved the local customs and traditions of
its government; so that there was less change than had been
the case even in Florence itself; and to this conduct on his
part is due the strong local colour which Siena has ever since
retained. On that State coming under his rule,[40] Cosimo appointed as Siena's first governor his own personal friend
Niccolini, and built on the spur called the Lizza the strong
fort of Sta. Barbara, which is still in use. As soon as the
war was over Cosimo paid a long visit to Siena, and arranged
all these matters himself; and so much to the satisfaction of
the Sienese were the various details settled that Siena never
afterwards revolted from the Medici, and became the most
loyal portion of their dominions; while in after years that
city came to consider it as a right that one member of the
Medici family should always be its governor.[41] And out of
Cosimo's army of 30,000 men, 7,000 of his best troops were
recruited from Siena.

In October 1555 the Emperor Charles V, who had been
the most prominent figure in European history for forty

years, abdicated at an impressive ceremony held at Brussels, resigning Spain, Naples, the Netherlands, and his other hereditary dominions to his son Philip II, and the imperial dignity to his brother Ferdinand, King of Hungary and Bohemia. He retired to the monastery of Yuste in Spain, and died there in 1558 at the age of fifty-eight. In the same year that Charles V abdicated, Pope Julius III died, and was succeeded first by Marcellus II, and after a month by Paul IV.

While Cosimo I, by his conquest of Siena and the other acquisitions of territory which he had gradually gained, as well as by the efficient administration of his military affairs, had doubled the territory of Tuscany and more than doubled her offensive and defensive power, the improvements he wrought in her civil administration were still more important. Cosimo ruled by fear; his government was a tyrannical one, and none dared disobey or evade his commands; but he ruled well. In every department of the State order and the strictest discipline took the place of disorder and corruption. The administration of justice was entirely remodelled; a proper criminal code was drawn up, and rigidly adhered to; magistrates were well paid and forbidden to receive any sort of bribe, and terrible retribution fell upon any who transgressed. The police had to submit daily to Cosimo a list of all crimes committed during the previous twenty-four hours; and they had reason to rue it if any attempt to shoot or stab was not promptly followed by the arrest of the criminal. Cosimo's secret prisons, more dreaded than even those of Venice, were kept for those who failed to obey these orders. For the rest justice had never been so evenly administered; never in the days of freedom had justice been obtainable as it now was under the rule of a tyrant. Heavy taxes had to be imposed, especially after the great expense of the Sienese war, but Cosimo by his care over the commerce of the country enabled the people to bear them.

"He revived the decaying silk and woollen trades. . . . By disobeying Charles V's order to the Italian cities to eschew the fairs of Lyons, Cosimo drew trade away from Genoa and Lucca, while he also captured the lucrative trade in brocades with Sicily and Spain. . . . He set an example in scientific farming and fruit-growing. He took a lively interest in the silver mines of Pietra Santa, the marble quarries near Carrara, and the anthracite discoveries on the upper Arno; concessions were obtained for working the alum of Piombino, and the iron of Elba." [42]

Roads, drainage works, harbours, markets,[43] all the appliances of a modern state, grew up in all directions under Cosimo's hand. Pisa, then a depopulated desert, was revived again into a flourishing city; its sanitation was improved by the draining of the surrounding marshes, and its prosperity increased by the introduction of new manufactures; the harbour was reopened by the construction of new docks; the University was re-established, and Tuscans forbidden to take degrees elsewhere; the Pisa School of Botany was founded, and became afterwards very celebrated; while by frequently residing at Pisa with his family, Cosimo made it a fashionable resort. Leghorn was raised from a neglected fishing village of 700 inhabitants to a busy port, and plans were laid for its development which afterwards bore much fruit under Cosimo's son Ferdinand. Siena had its social and commercial conditions in every way improved, while the Sienese Maremma was drained, and agricultural colonies from Lombardy established there. By these and similar methods carried out all over Tuscany, Cosimo advanced the material prosperity of the country no less than he did its political power.

Naval and military affairs showed the same energetic rule. Portoferrajo was made a strong naval station, and in addition to his extensive works on its harbour Cosimo introduced a seafaring population from Sicily and Greece, while he also began the creation of a fleet of galleys which under his son Ferdinand did good service against the Turks and the pirates of the Mediterranean. His army, thirty thousand strong, was well equipped; while of his militia Cosimo was specially proud, and declared that he could mobilise them in five days. He studded Tuscany with fortresses, fortresses which, constructed with the assistance of his celebrated architect and engineer Ammanati, were monuments of defensive strength. As an example of one of these we have the remarkable fortress of San Martino, on the hill above San Piero a Sieve, laid out under Cosimo's orders in order to defend Florence on the north, which, when its garrison and armament were withdrawn two centuries later by the Austrian Grand Duke Pietro Leopoldo (1765-1790) was ordered by him not to be destroyed, but to be kept "as a monument of the military architecture of the sixteenth century." This fort is a mile in circumference, and the strength of its construction extraordinary. It stands on the spur of a hill at the foot of which on three sides flow the waters of the Sieve, and its lofty keep dominates the whole plain of the Mugello. In the centre of the fort is a capacious reservoir for storing water for the garrison; while, should this be exhausted, a deep staircase in the heart of the mountain enabled the troops to lead their horses, without being seen by the enemy, down to the Sieve for water. In the depths of the mountain are vast subterranean halls where were magazines, armouries, foundries for making every kind of military equipment, and store-rooms for food, so that the fortress was considered able to defy the most formidable enemy. The bastions and walls are of extraordinary thickness and solidity; and they, with the battlements and casemated gateways, are studded everywhere with the Medici arms. Within the walls there is much open space for the movements of troops, which is now cultivated. This fortress was begun by Cosimo I and completed by his son Ferdinand I, with the assistance of the architect Buontalenti.[44]

Nor did fleets, troops, and fortresses, the development of trade, and the improvement of civil administration absorb all

Cosimo's energies. The Medici have written their sign-manual even upon the landscape of Tuscany. Few among the many who look with pleasure on the gentle slopes of the Tuscan hills, covered far and wide with those olive plantations whose soft bluish-green tints add so much to the special beauty of the landscape in Tuscany, realise that this great industry [45] which now forms so large a part of that country's agricultural life is due to Cosimo I, who introduced it as a portion of his measures for improving the agricultural prosperity of the country. Such things last when crowns, castles, and Orders of the Golden Fleece have long passed away.

By these various measures Cosimo gradually welded Tuscany into a well-administered modern state and the leading power in Italy; and they would have made his rule entirely admirable had they not been combined with vindictive conduct towards all who opposed him, and a tyranny which crushed out all independent spirit. It is observable that he was to some extent conscious of his own limitations; tyrant as he was, he would at times endeavour to adopt outwardly something of the *bonhomie* and absence of formality which was customary with his great ancestor, Lorenzo the Magnificent; but the *rôle* was one alien to his character, and let any presume to treat him in return with the freedom with which they would have treated Lorenzo, and they at once found Cosimo lapse into the cold and stiff demeanour natural to one who ruled by fear alone and had no sympathy with republican ways.

Among Cosimo's numerous successful efforts to promote the manufactures of the country none was more important in its results than his introduction of the Tapestry manufacture (*Arazzo*), an industry which had hitherto been confined to Flanders. Being anxious to establish a manufactory for this industry which should surpass all others, he founded the Florentine Tapestry Manufactory, and by means of an abnormally high salary induced two Flemings, Nicholas Karcher and Jean Van der Roost, to enter his service for the charge of it, giving them an annual salary of six hundred gold *scudi*, free quarters, and permission to undertake private commissions in addition to their work of charge of the factory. In return they bound themselves to teach the secrets of their art to a fixed number of Florentines and to keep twenty-four tapestries always on hand as examples. All work done for the house of Medici was paid for separately.[46] The results of this action surpassed even Cosimo's expectations. The Florentine Tapestry Manufactory grew in a short time into great repute, its work being considered fully equal to that of Flanders, and even surpassing the latter in variety of design and harmony of colour. This manufactory had a distinguished career for nearly two hundred years, but came to an end when the Medici passed away, the manufactory being closed in 1737 on the death of the last Medici Grand Duke. We are told, "It prospered and fell with the house of Medici." Of the tapestries made by this factory one hundred and twenty-four had been purchased by the Medici family, and these formed part of the gift to the nation made by Anna Maria Ludovica.[47] They were at that time scattered among the various palaces and villas of the family, but they are now to be seen collected together and forming (with specimens of Flemish and Gobelins tapestry which also belonged to the Medici) the Galleria degli Arrazi.[48] And a comparison between them and the Flemish and Gobelins tapestries is decidedly to the advantage of the Florentine tapestries. They are exceedingly rich, woven in gold and silver thread intermixed with silk and wool, the borders especially being very artistically designed.

Cosimo for the amusement of the people introduced chariot races, after the pattern of those of ancient Rome. They were held in the Piazza Santa Maria Novella, where the marble goals are still to be seen. These were originally of wood, but

Ferdinand I caused them to be constructed of marble and
placed (as now) on bronze tortoises made by Gian da Bologna.

In 1557, four years after they moved into the new palace,
occurred the first death in Cosimo's family, that of his eldest
daughter Maria, who died at sixteen, and whose charming
portrait at about the age of ten, by Bronzino, in the Uffizi
Gallery, is well known. In the following century it was declared that this death of his eldest daughter was due to slow
poison given her by her father, the motive being asserted to
be that, having arranged with Pope Paul IV for her marriage
to that Pope's nephew, Tabriano, Cosimo discovered that she
had fallen in love with another youth, a page at her father's
court. No historians of the present day give any credit to this
story, which made its first appearance more than fifty years
after Maria's death. Moreover the State archives now show
that Cosimo, who was at this time strenuously endeavouring
to establish close political relations with Ercole II, Duke of
Ferrara, had arranged for Maria's marriage, not as the story
relates to the Pope's nephew, but to Duke Ercole's eldest
son, Alfonso d'Este. So that Cosimo would by the crime
alleged have destroyed an alliance he was labouring in every
way to cement, and have made an enemy of the Duke of
Ferrara, whom he was particularly anxious to unite to himself
as closely as possible.

In 1558 great destruction was caused in Florence by an
unusually heavy flood in the Arno, which swept away the
Ponte Sta. Trinità, the Ponte alla Carraja, and all the houses
which were on the Ponte a Rubaconte,[49] the Ponte Vecchio
(built by Taddeo Gaddi in 1334) alone of all the bridges remaining uninjured. Florence became in a few hours a sea
of mud and ruin, some parts of the city being submerged to a
depth of twenty-two feet. It was after this flood that Cosimo
built his two fine bridges to replace the two which had been
destroyed, the new Ponte Sta. Trinità being especially notable.
This beautiful bridge, in its proportions, excellence of con-

struction, and the symmetry of its lines, exemplifies the perfection in such architecture then attained in Tuscany, though now unattainable anywhere.[50] Part of the reason why it pleases the eye so much is that its curve is that technically known as a "catenary," being that taken by a chain suspended from supports at both ends, a curve which is neither that of an ellipse or of any other geometrical figure, but special to that particular case.

In June 1558 Piero Strozzi, the eldest of Filippo Strozzi's three sons, was killed at the taking of Thionville. He had spent a large part of his life in warring against Cosimo and endeavouring to exact vengeance for his father's death, and had become one of the most experienced generals of the time. He had spent many years in France, where he was highly thought of by Catherine de' Medici, and was protected by her against the attempts which Cosimo made on his life. Cosimo constantly tried to have him assassinated,[51] but Strozzi never retaliated in the same way; and at his death Cosimo spoke of him with honour, affirming that Strozzi had ever acted against him *"con la visiera aperta,"* and that "Italy had lost in him one of her principal gentlemen": no small tribute from so vindictive an enemy as Cosimo. In the same year the latter gave his daughter Isabella, then sixteen, in marriage to Paolo Giordano Orsini, Prince of Bracciano, and his daughter Lucrezia, then fifteen, to Alfonso, the eldest son of Ercole II, Duke of Ferrara,[52] instead of her sister Maria, whose untimely death had prevented a similar alliance. In November of this year Mary Tudor died, and her sister Elizabeth succeeded her as Queen of England.

The year 1559 was an important one for Europe. In February (four months before Henry II's sudden death at the tournament in Paris[53]) the treaty of Cateau-Cambresis between Henry II, Philip II, and Queen Elizabeth put an end to the war in which France, Spain, and England had been engaged, and closed the long struggle between the two former

for supremacy in Italy, which, begun by the invasion of
Charles VIII, had lasted for over sixty years. That struggle
ended in a complete victory for Spain; and the final result
was mainly, if not entirely, due to the fact that Tuscany,
the most powerful state in Italy, had sided against France
and with Spain. By the above treaty France formally withdrew from Italy, surrendering all her claims in that country;
Siena, together with Montalcino, was assured to Cosimo;
the Duchy of Savoy, conquered by France twenty-three years
before, was restored to its rightful Duke, Emmanuel Philibert, and erected into an independent buffer state between
Italy and France; Spain remained in possession of both
north and south Italy, while Cosimo held the centre; and
the peace thus created in Italy lasted for over half a century.
In June Philip II married Elizabeth of France,[54] daughter of
Henry II, who, being killed a few days later, was succeeded
by his son, Francis II. In July Philip II quitted the Netherlands, which country during the remaining thirty-nine years
of his life he never again visited. Before leaving he appointed
as Governor of the Netherlands his half-sister, Margaret of
Parma, and held at Ghent the last chapter of the Order of the
Golden Fleece that was ever assembled. In August Pope Paul
IV, who during his four years' pontificate had been a constant
cause of war in Italy, died, and was succeeded by Pius IV.

The new Pope was of humble origin, and though named
Giovanni Angelo Medici (or Medichino), was no connection
of the Medici of Florence.[55] Nevertheless, on becoming Pope
he assumed the arms of the latter,[56] and Cosimo made no
objection, hoping to obtain solid advantages through this
Pope's friendship. For Cosimo was now silently at work upon
a project which he had for some time been secretly nourishing.
We are told that the leading marks of Cosimo's character
were "profound sagacity, deep dissimulation, impenetrable
darkness, extreme caution, patience, resolution, and indomitable perseverance." And the project for which Cosimo was
now, in accordance with these characteristics, secretly work-

ing was nothing less than the realisation of that which had
been the culminating point of the dream of Clement VII. As
a Duke he was theoretically merely the Emperor's lieutenant;
as a Grand Duke he would be a reigning monarch. Cosimo
could not hope to obtain that crown upon which his aim was
set through the regular channel, the Emperor; Ferdinand I
(like his dead brother, Charles V) would not be likely to
entertain for a moment a proposal to place a crown on the
head of one who only a few years ago had been an unknown
youth to whom it had been a great favour to allow him to
become ruler of Florence and the Emperor's vassal. But
future Emperors, further removed from the days of 1537,
might not be so opposed; and in the meantime it might be
possible to obtain the coveted dignity through another channel, that of the Pope. For this object paramount influence at
Rome was all important; and to attain this Cosimo was steadily employing every means at his disposal, though allowing
none to know what was his ultimate aim in doing so. Pius IV
was soon entirely under his domination, and when in 1560
Cosimo paid a visit to Rome, and was entertained by this
Pope, his influence was so powerful that the Pope, sensible
that Cosimo was now by far the most important ruler in Italy,
wished, we are told, to make him a king, or what was practically the same thing, a reigning Grand Duke. But Cosimo
put the suggestion aside as a mere polite piece of flattery,
outside practical politics. It was what he was quietly working
for, but his excessive caution made him feel that the time
for such a step was not now, when the nations of Europe had
just made peace together, or while Ferdinand I was Emperor.
When France and Spain should be again at enmity, when
England should be involved in war with one or other of
them, and when a weaker Emperor should have succeeded
Ferdinand I, and one perhaps allied to his family in marriage, then such a step might be hazarded without danger
of provoking opposition other than that of mere verbal protests. Moreover, his relative Catherine [57] (who hated Cosimo,

and thwarted him on many occasions) began in this year
1560 her long career of power in France, and Cosimo, foreseeing that she would soon be involved in difficulties with
both Spain and England, if not also with Germany, when she
would be unable to offer any active opposition to his design,
preferred to wait until this should be the case. In the meantime he succeeded so well in the preliminary step of establishing a paramount influence at Rome that three successive
Popes were practically governed by them.

Meanwhile, Cosimo adopted measures to establish still
more firmly the position of his family, already much strengthened by the marriages of his daughters, one of whom was
now Duchess of Ferrara, and the other Princess of Bracciano,
the wife of the most powerful prince in Rome. In 1560,
through his influence with Pius IV, Cosimo succeeded in
getting his second son [58] Giovanni, now seventeen, made a
cardinal: thus imitating the course which Lorenzo the Magnificent had so successfully taken with that other Giovanni
who had become Pope Leo X. Cosimo hoped that Giovanni,
who was his favourite son, would achieve similar success, while
his joining the ranks of the cardinals would help to strengthen
that influence at Rome which Cosimo had special reasons for
desiring. He also in 1561 instituted the Tuscan Order of
Knighthood, the Order of Santo Stefano, which afterwards
became very famous in Tuscany, and highly sought after. It
was a naval Order, and its primary objects were laid down
as being (i) to rid the Mediterranean of pirates; (ii) to
liberate the Christians held captive by the pirates and the
Turks, and (iii) to propagate the Christian faith. The Duke
himself was the Grand Master, and, by the Order being confined to the nobility and made the chief Order of Tuscany,
the knights became a sort of permanent body-guard for the
protection of the Duke and his dynasty. Being a naval Order
the knights of Santo Stefano had their conventual palace and
church at Pisa, and the church is hung with Moorish banners
taken by them from the Turks and the Barbary pirates, and

with the figure-heads of Turkish galleys captured in war. The knights won special honour at the battle of Lepanto (1571). The cross of the Order was similar in shape to that of the knights of Malta, but in colour red instead of white.[59] In this same year 1561 Cosimo and Eleonora, who had already lost one of their three daughters, heard of the death at Ferrara of their daughter Lucrezia, Duchess of Ferrara, at the age of seventeen. It was in after years declared that she was poisoned by her husband, on the ground of infidelity; but the statement is considered by the highest authority [60] to be quite untrue, and to have been entirely fabricated by the Florentine *fuorusciti*. e+i\es

And now there fell upon Cosimo a terrible domestic disaster. In October 1562 he started on a tour through Grosseto, the Maremma, and Leghorn to Pisa, to see in person various military and engineering works which he had inaugurated at those places. He took with him his wife Eleonora (who had been suffering from hemorrhage of the lungs for more than a year, and was recommended by the doctors to go for the winter to the milder climate near the seacoast), and his three sons, Giovanni, Garzia, and Ferdinand. A bad epidemic of malarial fever was in that year devastating a large part of Tuscany, and especially the Maremma, and the doctors urged Cosimo not to take with him his young sons; but the latter were eager for the chances of sport on such a trip, and persuaded their father to disregard the advice. The expedition had a sad ending; for within a single month Eleonora, Giovanni, and Garzia all died from malarial fever, Giovanni on their reaching Leghorn, and Garzia and his mother three weeks later at Pisa.

Such an event could not in Cosimo's case fail to form a foundation for a tragic tale of murder. And accordingly we find put forward a highly dramatic one, purporting to convey the true story of these three deaths, and stating that in a quarrel while the two brothers were out shooting near Leg-

horn Garzia had stabbed his brother Giovanni, who died three
days later in consequence; that Cosimo was so enraged at
this death of his favourite son that he drew his sword and
killed Garzia with his own hands; and that Eleonora died of
grief and horror at the double crime.

This account (which has continued to the present day)
was that related by the various historians of that age. The
latter, unable to obtain access to the private documents of
the Medici family, were forced to rely upon information
often felt by them to be dubious; and several of them,
though giving this account, throw doubts upon its truth.[61]
The chief cause of their uncertainty was that however deeply
the subject was probed, in no case could it be discovered
with whom the report originated; added to which every investigation showed that it had no origin in Tuscany, but that
all the different versions of the story had this in common,
that they all emanated from Rome, the principal abode of the
Florentine exiles. From thence, spread by letters and news-
agents to Venice, to France, and above all to the large body
of ecclesiastics assembled at the Council of Trent, the story
soon became the common opinion outside Tuscany, and was
eagerly taken up by every foreign enemy of Cosimo throughout Europe.

But this account of these deaths did not all appear at the
same time. Its Roman authors, whoever they were, brought
it out piecemeal. When on the 20th November Giovanni died
it was stated that he had been killed by his brother Garzia.
When three weeks later Garzia died an addition was made to
the effect that Giovanni when wounded had in retaliation also
wounded Garzia, and that this was the cause of the latter's
death. At this point the story remained for some fifty years.

To this first portion of the story there was, however, added,
more than fifty years later, a further embellishment of it to
the effect that Garzia's death had not been caused as previously
stated, but that Cosimo, enraged at Giovanni's death, had
killed his younger son with his own hands; and that Eleo-

nora's death had been caused by horror thereat. During the
intervening fifty years no single letter, document, or historical writing throughout Italy had ever conveyed even a
hint of this deed. This addition by making the story so dramatic increased its chance of spreading; while since it was
produced long after Cosimo was dead it was evidently aimed,
not so much at himself, as at his family.[62] It rapidly spread,
and soon became the common belief.

The State archives in these days supply the information
which the historians of a former day lacked. And recent research therein [63] has furnished a mass of evidence which
conclusively disposes of both portions of the story, and shows
that the historians who doubted its truth were right. This
evidence includes two letters from Cosimo to his eldest son
Francis (then in Spain) relating the events which had occurred to the family during the latter part of this untoward
trip. In the first of these, dated 20th November 1562, he
tells his son that on the 15th Giovanni had been attacked
by malignant fever at Rosignano, that they had promptly
moved from thence to Leghorn, but that he became worse,
and had died there on the date of the letter; that Garzia and
Ferdinand also had fever, but less severely, and that he was
going to take them next day to Pisa, where it was hoped
they would recover; and that this exceptionally malignant
type of fever was very bad all over the part of the country
that they had been traversing. This is followed by a second
letter from Cosimo to his eldest son, dated 18th December,
written amidst all the grief at the death that day of his wife
Eleonora, in which he tells Francis that Garzia's fever had
increased after their arrival at Pisa, that after a severe illness of twenty-one days he had died on the 12th December,
and that his mother, worn out by her exertions in nursing
him while she was herself also ill, had succumbed six days
later, and giving full details of their last hours.

These letters, together with the other documents in the
State archives already referred to, prove with great com-

pleteness that the story which so long obtained credence
as the history of this episode is a complete fable; one perhaps scarcely expected to be taken seriously even by its unknown authors. It was in fact one of a series which had their
origin in the manner by which Cosimo gained his throne.
From the day of Montemurlo a ceaseless war was waged
between Cosimo and that large number of Florentine families
who had lost near relatives in his ruthless executions after
that battle, and lived in exile; a war in which Cosimo, cruel
and vindictive, slew his enemies with the sword whenever
his arm could reach them, and in which the exiles, no less
vindictive, but poverty-stricken and without the resources
he possessed, responded by attempts to murder him and by a
constant stream of stories of this nature poured forth un-
remittingly on the principle that if enough mud is thrown
some must stick.

The Cambridge Modern History (than which there is no
higher authority) dismisses the entire story in contempt with
the following remark:—

"In the autumn of 1562 he (Cosimo) had lost within a
few days from Maremma fevers his wife and his two sons,
Garzia and Giovanni. A year earlier his well-loved daughter,
Lucrezia, died shortly after her marriage to Alfonso II of
Ferrara. These natural misfortunes were in the following
century caught up by scandalmongers and Florentine exiles, and distorted into dramatic tragedies of adultery and
poison, fratricide, and parricide which have passed muster
as the inner history of the reign." [64]

But even without any such terrible additions to its natural
features this episode was sufficiently tragic. Of the family
party of five who had started for a pleasant trip together only
two, Cosimo and his young son Ferdinand, returned. Cosimo
had lost within a month the devoted wife who had been
his constant companion and adviser for twenty-three years,
and two sons, on one of whom, through his recent creation

as a cardinal, he had built many hopes, while both of them possessed many attractive qualities. All the three bodies were brought back to Florence and buried in San Lorenzo, the funeral of Giovanni being scarcely over before the grave was again opened to receive the bodies of his mother and brother. And in one corner of the crypt of the family mausoleum these four lie buried together—Cosimo, Eleonora, Giovanni, and Garzia, the last three with the following dates of death upon their tombstones: Giovanni 20th November 1562, Garzia 12th December 1562, and Eleonora 18th December 1562.

Bronzino's fine portrait of poor Garzia who is given a charming character by those who knew him, and who, dying at sixteen, has had his name thus defamed for centuries to gratify political animosity against his father, must have been painted only a few months before the family left Florence on the tour which was to end so disastrously. Of her five sons he was his mother's favourite son. "She loved him as her own eyes," says an old chronicler.

This loss was a severe blow to Cosimo; and under it he became more than ever dark, sullen, and impenetrable. It left him with only four children, Francis, now twenty-two, Isabella, twenty-one, Ferdinand, fourteen, and Pietro, a child of eight. Isabella returning soon afterwards from Rome, took charge of her father's household, her husband Orsini being content that she should live in Florence while he remained at Rome.

Eleonora di Toledo, the only Spanish wife whom the Medici ever took (their other matrimonial alliances being all with France or Austria), deserves a much more prominent place in the history of that family than she has received. The very large part which she had in the establishment of Cosimo's power in the years 1539-1549 has failed altogether to be recognised. Yet Eleonora di Toledo might almost be looked upon as a second founder of the family, so great was the assistance which she brought to Cosimo when as a youth of

twenty he was destitute of wealth, family, friends, or influence to support the tottering throne which he had seized,
but which without her he would probably in a very short
time have lost, together with his own life. Many have wondered how it was that at the beginning of his career Cosimo,
so signally without the means to effect such a result, should
have been able so quickly and firmly to establish his power;
the secret lies in Eleonora di Toledo. Cosimo in time himself
became rich by a sound fiscal policy, and by the private trading which he throughout his life carried on; but these sources
of income took time to develop, and his urgent want at the
commencement was money with which to start such operations, and to maintain a military force for his own protection; Eleonora brought him the immediately available wealth
of which he stood so much in need. Cosimo was also without
friends or influence to back him; Eleonora brought him the
powerful support of her father whose only child she was,
and who as ruler over the whole of southern Italy was always
able to put pressure upon the Pope to prevent the latter from
molesting Cosimo, as he was very desirous of doing. Above
all Eleonora had exactly the kind of character which made
her an admirable wife to a man of Cosimo's peculiar disposition. She understood how to treat his dark and gloomy moods,
and to soothe his fierce rage; she was strongly devoted to him,
and never lost her great influence with him during all the
twenty-three years of their married life; she was the only
channel to his favour; and she was throughout her life a most
sensible adviser to him. Though accustomed until she arrived
in Florence to the far greater grandeur of her father's vice-
regal palace at Naples, she never complained at being given
as a residence the gloomy Palazzo Vecchio, until after ten
years Cosimo's circumstances enabled him to provide her with
a more suitable abode. Lastly, the extent and beneficial nature
of her influence is amply demonstrated by the marked deterioration to be observed in Cosimo's character from the time that
death deprived him of her when she was forty years of age.

Eleonora's splendid portrait by Bronzino in the Uffizi Gallery, with her little son Ferdinand by her side, is the finest of all Bronzino's many portraits. Whatever may be the reason, her face has an expression of sadness; and the picture has for its background the night scene of a dreary, marshy landscape with dark, desolate hills in the distance, which accords with this expression. The picture was evidently painted some time in the year 1553, when she was thirty-one, and Ferdinand, then her youngest born, was four years old. She wears a magnificent dress of white satin, heavily embroidered all over with rich black "galloon" trimming of a very marked pattern, on her head a net of gold cord set with pearls, round her neck a string of large pearls, and round her waist a girdle having a large tassel of pearls. This dress had an important subsequent history. Eleonora was the first who was buried in the manner ever afterwards customary in this family, all the members of which from this time onwards were buried dressed in their most splendid costumes, and wearing numerous jewels. And Eleonora was buried dressed as she appears in this portrait. In 1857 a commission was appointed by the State to open and examine all the Medici coffins, which, owing to their having been kept without due security after the Medici passed away, had, in the early part of the nineteenth century, been broken into by thieves for the sake of the jewels they contained, and were in considerable disorder.[65] When this examination took place Eleonora's coffin was one of the few found without any name or inscription either outside or inside. But her remains were at once recognised by this dress, which was familiar to all through Bronzino's well-known portrait. The official report on the examination of the coffins states in regard to hers:—

"The body was recognised with certainty by the rich dress of white satin richly embroidered with 'galloon' trimming all over both the bodice and the skirt, exactly as she is depicted in the portrait painted by Bronzino which is in the Gallery of the Statues,[66] together with the same net of gold cord worn on the hair. Beneath this dress was an under-gown of crimson velvet; and on the feet shoes similarly of crimson velvet." [67]

The string of pearls round her neck and the girdle with the tassel of pearls had, however, been stolen.

Cosimo, notwithstanding the heavy domestic blow which he had suffered, did not relax his pursuit of the aim on which his mind was set. To this end it was highly important to have one son a cardinal, who would maintain a constant watch over Cosimo's interests at Rome; and within a month of the funeral of his wife and sons he obtained from Pius IV the creation as cardinal of his fourth son, Ferdinand, to take the place of the dead Giovanni, though Ferdinand was only in his fourteenth year.

In December 1563 the Council of Trent, which had sat for eighteen years, finished its labours and was dissolved. Pope Pius IV (the Pope who made himself a member of the Medici family) has obtained a lasting memorial in the work of this Council from the fact that it drew up *a new creed*, called by his name, which has ever since had to be accepted in addition to the three creeds of antiquity by all belonging to the Church of Rome. As regards the primary object for which it was convened, the Council of Trent achieved nothing. Abandoning the endeavour to reunite Christendom (to attain which object the convocation of this Council had been so anxiously striven after for so many years before it was assembled) it made no attempt to deal with the evil which Pope Adrian VI had so ably diagnosed as the cause of the disease, or to apply that remedy which he had pointed out as the only one, "a limitation of the absolutism of the Head of the Church"; [68] an attempt which even the Councils of Pisa, Constance, and Bâle had made. On the contrary, this Council turned its whole attention to re-establishing the

Papacy on the footing on which it had stood in the thirteenth
century. So that, instead of uniting, it accentuated the differences between the two parties more than ever. Nevertheless the Emperor Ferdinand I did not even yet give up the
hope of effecting a reconciliation. As soon as the Council had
dispersed after this abortive conclusion, the Emperor (following to some extent the example which Catherine de'
Medici had set two years before in France) caused George
Cassander, a highly learned Belgian theologian, to draw up
a statement of the points of controversy between the two
parties to serve as a basis for a fresh conference on the subject. This Cassander did in a very able and broad-minded
treatise, entitled *"A consideration of the articles of religion
under dispute between Catholics and Protestants,"* which was
duly published. But owing to the Emperor's death no further
result ensued.

In 1564 the Emperor Ferdinand I died, and was succeeded
by his son, Maximilian II, with whom Cosimo hoped to be
able to establish closer relations. In this he was successful,
and in January 1565 Cosimo's eldest son Francis was married
to the Emperor Maximilian's sister, the Archduchess Joanna
of Austria, daughter of the Emperor Ferdinand I, and niece
of the Emperor Charles V. It was another step upwards on
the ladder which the Medici had for so many generations been
climbing, being the most exalted marriage they had ever yet
made; and Cosimo had good reason to hope that it would materially assist him when the time should come for him to put
forward a claim to be, no longer merely Duke of Florence, but
a crowned head. It did not, however, augur well for the chances
of happiness of Francis and Joanna that the former had been
for more than a year passionately attached to the beautiful
Venetian, Bianca Capello, while the Archduchess was not only
plain in appearance and unattractive in manner, but also
made no secret that she considered the marriage one altogether
derogatory to her dignity.

As Cosimo was anxious to do honour in every way to his son's bride, nothing was omitted which could add splendour to the occasion. It was settled that the Palazzo Vecchio should be made over to Francis and Joanna as their residence, and the old castle of the Signoria of Florence was under Cosimo's orders beautified in every way by Vasari to fit it for the abode of an Archduchess. The suite of apartments which had been occupied by Cosimo and Eleonora was entirely re-decorated; round the vestibule of the *cortile* were painted fresco pictures of Austrian towns, so that Joanna should have familiar scenes to look at; [69] the massive pillars of the *cortile* were adorned with stucco ornaments on a gold ground, which still remain, though the gold has disappeared; and in the centre of the court Cosimo placed Verrocchio's beautiful fountain of the *Boy with the Dolphin*, which had been made for Lorenzo the Magnificent's villa of Careggi; while a pipe conducting specially pure water from the Boboli hill was brought over the Ponte Vecchio to supply the water which flows from this fountain. The Archduchess arrived in Florence in January 1565, and the marriage, which took place in San Lorenzo, was a very magnificent ceremony, and was followed by a week of public festivities of the most lavish description.

In addition to these arrangements Cosimo, in connection with this marriage of his son with the Emperor's sister, constructed another work which still remains one of the notable sights of Florence. In imitation of the passage which Homer describes as uniting the palace of Hector with that of Priam (as well as to provide a means of escape for his family in time of disturbance), Cosimo arranged to connect, by a long covered gallery, his own palace with the Palazzo Vecchio, now to be occupied by his son. He therefore ordered Vasari to construct the celebrated *Passaggio*, a corridor of nearly half a mile long through a crowded part of the city, starting from the Palazzo Vecchio, passing over the building known as the Uffizi, or public offices (which Cosimo had built in 1561), over the top of the shops on the Ponte Vecchio, through houses and over streets, until it reached the Ducal Palace. The work must have been executed with great rapidity, for the contract was only signed on the 12th March 1565, and Lapini tells us that the corridor was finished by November. The contract for this work gives some details interesting to those who know Florence in these days. It lays down that,

"There shall be an arch above the street [70] where is the Dogana to the wall of the church of San Piero Scheraggio; [71] and another arch at the house of Signor Trajano Boba; and along the Lungarno a corridor with arches and pilasters, as far as the Ponte Vecchio, thence proceeding onwards above the shops and houses of the said bridge on the side towards the Ponte a Rubaconte,[72] and round the tower of the house of Matteo Manelli by means of stone brackets. From this tower another arch spanning the Via de' Bardi, shall rest upon the tower of the 'Parte Guelfa,' opposite the house of the Manelli. The corridor is then to follow the small ally behind the houses facing the principal street, and to pass above the portico of the church of Santa Felicità, where is to be made a *loggia*.[73] Thence the corridor, supported on pilasters along the whole length of the cloisters of the clergy of Santa Felicità, shall gradually descend to the level of the garden of the Pitti.[74] The said corridor and its adjuncts are to be roofed in, the ceilings plastered, whitewashed, and finished according to the orders, designs, and models given from time to time by the magnificent and excellent master Giorgio Vasari." [75]

The sentence in this contract ordering the corridor to be carried round the outside of the Palazzo Manelli on brackets is interesting. That palace occupies the end of the bridge, and had belonged to the Manelli family for many generations. Its position appeared to make it unavoidable that Cosimo's new corridor should pass through it.

"Accordingly," Mellini says, "Cosimo sent for the owners of the said palace, and asked if they were willing courteously to permit him to make the passage through it. But they strongly objected, pointing out that it would spoil their house; whereupon he (Cosimo) placed it as we now see it on stone brackets, passing by a sharp turn round the outside of the house. Nor did he bear them ill-will, saying that every one was master of his own house."

Hitherto the shops on the Ponte Vecchio had been occupied by butchers; on making the *Passaggio* Cosimo ordered them to vacate, and directed all the jewellers in Florence to inhabit these shops; and this has ever since been the jewellers' quarter.

From the time of his eldest son's marriage Cosimo made over to him the entire control of home affairs, though still retaining in his own hands foreign affairs. In the same year (1565) Pope Pius IV died and was succeeded by Pius V (Michele Ghislieri), the stern old inquisitor, and a pitiless persecutor of the new religion. With such a Pope it was not difficult to see what kind of conduct would be most conducive to the maintenance of that paramount influence at the Vatican which it was Cosimo's earnest desire to retain, and the more so since affairs in France, Spain, and Germany showed that the time was approaching when he would be able to take the step for which he had long been preparing.

The character of the new Pope soon made itself felt throughout Italy; a general stamping out of Protestantism wherever it had taken root began. This placed in danger a man who had long been a firm friend of the Medici family, and who had done good service for Cosimo, in particular, in various capacities. Carnesecchi was a Florentine of good family who had been Protonotary Apostolic to Clement VII, and of so much influence with him that it was said that he rather than Clement was Pope. Some years after Clement's death he came under the influence and teaching of Valdès, became a Protestant, and ere long one of the leading Prot-

estants in Italy. After spending some years in France he
returned to Italy, but in 1557 was pronounced by Pope Paul
IV "a refractory heretic," and had to fly for his life. He fled
to France to Catherine de' Medici, who protected him. On
the death of Paul IV he returned to Florence, where during
the pontificate of Pius IV he remained unmolested, and was
one of Cosimo's most trusted friends and advisers. But the
election of Pope Pius V placed Carnesecchi at once in danger
—danger which was increased by his having recently entreated Cosimo to exert his great influence with the Emperor
to bring about the assembly of a really Œcumenical Council
in the centre of Germany, and to effect the Pope's personal
attendance thereat. Pope Pius V, dreading the effect of
Cosimo's influence if exerted in the manner urged by Carnesecchi, earnestly desired to remove this friend and adviser
from Cosimo's side, and was eager to get hold of Carnesecchi
and hand him over to the Inquisition. Catherine de' Medici,
on the other hand, had written to Cosimo urging him to protect
Carnesecchi in the same way as she had done, and to refuse
the Pope's demand for his surrender. But Cosimo throughout
life ruthlessly sacrificed all who came in the way of his plans;
he was bent upon an object which only the Pope's favour
could obtain for him, and he knew well that Carnesecchi's
life would be the price. Therefore, to his lasting shame, he in
July 1566 surrendered this faithful adherent of himself and
his family to the Pope; and in October 1567 Carnesecchi was
burnt in Rome by the Inquisition. Two years afterwards
Cosimo received his reward. "Carnesecchi was the last of the
chief reformers in Italy, and with his death the reforming
spirit in that country, which at one time had been very strong,
died out." [76]

In 1569, the year of the battles of Jarnac and Moncontour
in France, when Catherine de' Medici's troubles were at their
height, Cosimo considered the time at last propitious for the
step he had long contemplated. France was blazing from end

to end with civil war; Spain was occupied with the contest in the Netherlands, and endeavouring also to take part in the conflict in France; England was embroiled with both France and Spain; and in Germany the Emperor Maximilian had his hands full with similar troubles. None were therefore likely to interfere actively against Cosimo's assumption of regal dignity. Accordingly we are informed that "owing to Cosimo's great influence with Pope Pius V, and his many good offices to the Papal See," that Pope now published a bull creating Cosimo I "Grand Duke of Tuscany." In doing this the Pope was, of course, assuming the prerogative of the Emperor, but Cosimo trusted in time to get the latter to acquiesce in what was a *fait accompli*. Nor was the Pope's action unjustified from the general point of view. Cosimo had raised Tuscany to such a position of power and importance that her ruler was justly to be considered on a level with other sovereign rulers of states not in any way in advance of his in these respects. In February 1570 Cosimo was, with much ceremony, crowned in Rome by the Pope. Spain and Germany refused to acknowledge Cosimo's new rank; France and England, however, did so; and within the next few years the other powers of Europe one by one concurred.[77]

The shape of the new crown was peculiar, and was carefully laid down in the Pope's bull. This ordered that the crown of Tuscany was (unlike the French, Spanish, and other crowns) to be "radiated like that of the Eastern kings, alternate with the Florentine lily." [78] It was a royal crown with the points curving outwards, intended to represent the blades of the iris. In the centre of the front was a large red Florentine lily: [79] thus making the crest of Florence's ancient Republic the chief jewel of the royal crown. The sceptre was also peculiar; it was ordered to be surmounted by the Medici *palle*, and upon this the Florentine lily.

The portrait of Cosimo painted to commemorate this occasion shows him wearing his robes as Grand Duke, with on his head the new crown, and in his hand the sceptre.

Thus had the Medici reached at length the summit of their career, and a crown was at last placed upon a Medici head. One hundred and seventy years from the time that Giovanni di Bicci, the humble banker of Florence, is first heard of, his descendant the head of the house entered the group of European sovereigns. Fate in irony had realised the long dream of Clement VII in a manner far different from his intentions; and had placed the crown which he had schemed to gain in the future for his family upon the head not of a scion of the elder branch, but of the son of that Giovanni delle Bande Nere whom he had striven to keep from succeeding to the honours of the Medici, and had thought finally disposed of on the battlefield of Governolo.

The remaining four years of Cosimo's life were only notable for the general deterioration in his character, which, beginning to set in from the time of Eleonora's death, and increasing year by year, became in these last four years strongly pronounced. Leaving the entire government of the country to the inefficient hands of his son Francis, he lived chiefly in retirement at the villa of Castello with a new wife, not at all in his own rank,[80] named Camilla Martelli, whom he had married about the year 1571, and who was treated as a sort of morganatic wife. This marriage gave the greatest offence to his sons, who refused to recognise Camilla as really their father's wife; while this, and undignified disputes in which he was involved with her relations, caused Cosimo's latter days to be wanting in either peace or dignity. He died at the villa of Castello, on the 21st April 1574, at the age of fifty-five, after a reign of thirty-seven years.

Cosimo, whose tomb bears the inscription "Magnus Dux Etruriae Primus,"[81] was interred with great pomp in San Lorenzo, clad in his robes as Grand Master of the Order of Santo Stefano, and wearing his jewelled crown and sceptre and his Order of the Golden Fleece. The Medici were regardless of expense in the matter of crowns. They objected to wear crowns of which even the jewels ornamenting them had been worn by their predecessors; and each Medici Grand Duke was buried wearing his actual crown, not an imitation of it, and with his jewelled sceptre by his side, an entirely fresh crown and sceptre being made for his successor. As a consequence, when in the early part of the nineteenth century the Medici coffins were plundered by thieves the latter sought chiefly for those of the Grand Dukes. Owing, however, to the darkness of the lower crypt, and the manner in which the coffins on removal thither had been piled together in different parts of it without any system, the thieves were only able to find the coffins of five out of the seven Medici Grand Dukes, those of Cosimo III and Gian Gastone, which had no distinctive marks on the outside, escaping detection. These, however, were the only two in which the crown and sceptre were found when the coffins were opened in 1857 by the Commission appointed for the purpose,[82] that of Cosimo I being among those found entirely plundered.

"The body was dressed in the robes of the Order of Santo Stefano, with under these a doublet of red satin, and hose of the same colour on the legs. His sword was extraordinarily large, and in the velvet lining of the scabbard, hidden by the gilded hilt, were enclosed a small dagger and a number of small *stiletti*, with very sharp points, almost as fine as needles, stuck into the lining of the scabbard as into a needle-case. The robbed and broken coffin did not contain the golden crown, the sceptre, and other ornaments which should have been found there."[83]

In Cosimo I the prominent characteristic is a pitiless ferocity; no sentiment of generosity, magnanimity, or mercy ever stirred his nature. His enmity worked with as little pity, and as little remorse, as a machine. Death, prompt and cruel, ensued for all who failed to obey his will, or thwarted his purposes; the doors of the Bargello closed behind them, and the scaffold in its courtyard saw their end. Or if they escaped from

Florence, then the hired assassin was equally sure. Together with this characteristic there was another, of meanness of character. Among other evidences of this there was in him, the son of the bravest leader of troops in Italy, that want of personal courage which so frequently accompanies a cruel nature. He never ventured into a battle himself, sending other men to risk their lives for his advantage; and he carefully surrounded himself with a body-guard, which his cruelties made a very necessary precaution.

But the defects of a cruel and ignoble disposition must not be allowed to hide his undoubtedly great work for his country. In thinking of Tuscany, we are too apt to regard it as it had become in the beginning of the eighteenth century, and so to lose sight of the prosperous kingdom which Cosimo I created in the sixteenth. It is, indeed, strange to compare the small, misgoverned, and insignificant state which this son of Giovanni delle Bande Nere and Maria Salviati seized by his bold *coup d'état* of 1537—its capital half ruined by the long siege of 1530, its scanty territory devastated by the war, and its whole condition brought to degradation by Alessandro's five years' misrule—with the large and flourishing kingdom which Cosimo, its first Grand Duke, left to his successors. He found Tuscany a small and despised state, dependent on a foreign power, without troops, commerce, agriculture, or resources, with ruined towns, a wasted country, and a poverty-stricken population. He left her a large and independent kingdom, with a powerful army, a rising fleet, flourishing manufactures, wide commerce, sound laws, model public works, a well-ordered administration, and a thriving people. He successfully resisted the most powerful Pope of his time, and governed three others in succession; he saved Tuscany from becoming, like Milan, a province of Spain; and he made her the leading state in Italy. There is probably no other example of so small a state advancing within a period of some thirty years to a position of power and importance scarcely inferior to most of the monarchies of the time.

It is this comparison between what he found and what he left which gives the true measure of Cosimo I. In ability he did not fall far short of those earlier Medici who had advanced Florence over the heads of all her rivals in their time and made her the artistic and intellectual capital of Italy. It would have been well had he shown also those other qualities of character which they, in addition to their abilities, had possessed, of a generous and high-minded spirit, readiness to forgive injuries, mercy to enemies, courtesy of demeanour, and sympathy with the people; but these qualities were foreign to his nature, and his rule was that of an iron-handed tyranny.

It was Florence's own deliberate action which had brought that tyranny upon her. On Alessandro's death she could, if she would, have reinstated her Republic. Completely untrammelled, and under no pressure from any direction, she deliberately of her own will subjected herself to the rule of a tyrant.

But tyrant as he was, the effects of his tyranny did not fall upon the mass of the people. And by his even-handed justice, his strong government, capable administration, sound fiscal laws, and advancement of the material prosperity of the country, Cosimo I made the condition of the inhabitants of Tuscany one altogether superior to any which they had ever known before.

CHAPTER XXV

FRANCIS I

Born 1541. (*Reigned* 1574-1587.) *Died* 1587

THE knell of the Medici fortunes has struck; though muffled
at first, its distant tolling can henceforth be heard in the midst
of all their grandeur. Almost from the very day that the
crown, striven after for so many years, first by Giulio and
then by Cosimo, was gained, this family's deterioration, both
in abilities and character, set in. The crown now set above
the *palle* in the family arms becomes but the signal of departing glory. For one hundred and seventy years we have seen
the Medici steadily climbing upwards; for the next hundred
and seventy years we see them sinking steadily down to their
end. There were pauses in that downward course, but its
general tendency was ever the same. And with Francis I, the
eldest son of Cosimo, that decline begins.

It had begun five years before he actually came to the
throne. Cosimo from the time that he gained the rank of
Grand Duke gave up practically the entire government of the
state to Francis, and, adopting an unworthy style of life, apparently disregarded the fact that his son's negligent rule was
sowing the seeds of serious harm to the administration of the
country. The natural result ensued with extreme rapidity, and
within two years of Cosimo's death misrule and corruption
were rampant in every department of the State. Disorganisa-
tion in the administration of the police, and corruption in the
judicial tribunals, soon produced an enormous growth of
crime; and Francis's reign of thirteen years became a continuous record of bad government and social demoralisation.
So that Tuscany, which under a good government might have

escaped the general tendencies of the time, under a bad one did not fail to exemplify those tendencies.

At that period an intense ferocity appeared to have seized upon mankind. All regard for human life seemed to have disappeared from Europe in the bitter passions which the religious wars and persecutions had stirred up. Men had grown ruthless in their familiarity with torture and death, and wherever we look, whether it be in France, Spain, England, the Netherlands, or Germany, a ferocious and merciless cruelty, with a disregard for all justice, is the prevailing characteristic of the time, with murders and torturings as matters of common daily life. Tuscany, under the misrule of Francis I, had her share of these experiences, and was only so far fortunate in that they were not made still worse by the scourge of war; Italy, though it shared in the general demoralisation of the age, was (owing to the settlement made by the treaty of Cateau-Cambresis) able to look on whilst almost every other country was torn by a strife which seemed to turn the wars of the time into the conflicts of tigers.

One result of this state of things was the view taken regarding the assassination of those upon whom a sentence of death had been passed. Rulers such as Cosimo I and Francis I looked upon hired assassins very much as if they were executioners; and such rulers seem to have seen no difference between this mode of putting out of life a man whose death had been decreed and that of the formal execution of a condemned prisoner. Even escape to another country procured no safety, since such assassins penetrated into all countries in pursuit of their victim. Murder and tragedy were thus ever present; while each event of the kind was multiplied fourfold in the imaginations of the people.

Francis I was thirty-three years old when he succeeded to the throne. The fine portrait of him which was painted by Paolo Veronese, and hangs in the state apartments of the Pitti Palace, shows him as he was at about the age of thirty-five;

he wears the Order of the Golden Fleece, and on his cloak the cross of the Order of Santo Stefano. He possessed much the same character as his father Cosimo, and had brilliant mental gifts, but whereas his father's chief interest had been the advancement of Tuscany, that of Francis was science; and this made all the difference possible to the country, since he refused to be drawn from his favourite pursuit to attend to public affairs, which consequently lapsed into the condition which has been noted. At the same time he inherited his father's tyrannical disposition towards the upper classes; with the result that this, when combined with general corruption in the administration and a defective fiscal policy caused a hatred to grow up against Francis which exceeded even that which had been felt against Cosimo. And this excessive hatred created a fruitful soil for the growth of every story of crime against Francis which fertile brains could originate. One of the latter's minor tyrannies was exercised towards his father's morganatic wife, Camilla Martelli. On succeeding the throne, Francis, as the head of the family, having according to the laws of Italy at that time, powers of life and death over all its members, consigned Camilla to incarceration in a convent; and there she remained for the rest of her life. The high taxes which he imposed on corn were specially disastrous to the agricultural colonies planted by his father to reclaim the waste lands of the Maremma, which colonies as a result were ruined, and these lands again became waste. On the other hand, Francis continued his father's plans for the development of Leghorn; but the chief steps in this work were taken subsequently by his brother Ferdinand, and the great success achieved belongs to the reign of the latter.

In each generation, from the time of Cosimo Pater Patriae in 1428 to that of Francis I in 1575, every new head of the house had to meet an attack led by one or other of the principal families of Florence. That which came upon Francis was dealt with by him with less rigour than his father had displayed in 1537, but nevertheless with a severity which brought him into great odium. In the first year of his reign he discovered a widespread plot to assassinate him, which had been formed by various members of the Pucci, Ridolfi, Capponi, and Machievelli families. When discovered by Francis it was asserted that the plot had been abandoned; and this appears to have been true. Nevertheless he proceeded to deal out the severest punishment. All who had been concerned in the plot who did not make their escape were seized and put to death; many other persons declared to have been privy to it were also punished; and a vigorous confiscation of all property connected with them took place. The result was that a large number of the principal Florentine families were brought to degradation; which created an undying hatred against Francis among all the well-to-do classes of Florence. It was an inauspicious beginning to a new reign.

On the ruler of Tuscany becoming a crowned head, all the ceremonial of the court of a reigning sovereign had been introduced; and Francis, probably chiefly to gratify the desire of his wife, the Archduchess Joanna, kept up a great deal more state than his father had done. The court was maintained almost on the lines of that of Spain, which Francis made in all particulars his model.

"A number of gentlemen, divided in two departments, attended to the various branches of the household; sixty pages from the principal families of Italy and Germany were maintained and educated at the palace in all the accomplishments and depravity of the day, but still without neglecting the arts and sciences, or the use of arms, equitation, and all the various acquirements of a gentleman." [1]

In 1576 the Emperor Maximilian II (Francis's brother-in-law), without making any allusion to the action which the Pope had taken in the matter seven years before, not only formally conferred on Francis the rank of Grand Duke, but created Tuscany a Grand Duchy, which the Pope had been unable to do. A few months later Maximilian II died, and was succeeded as Emperor by his eldest son, Rudolph II.[2]

In the summer of this year 1576, the second year of Francis's reign, two terrible tragedies in his family occurring within one week cast a black pall over the Ducal palace. The family at this time consisted of Francis, with his wife Joanna and their children, his youngest brother Pietro (married two years before to a niece of their mother, named like her Eleonora di Toledo), and his sister Isabella. The latter had continued to live at Florence after her father Cosimo's death, the proceedings of her husband, the Prince of Bracciano, not being of a nature to cause her to desire to make the Orsini palace at Rome her residence. Cardinal Ferdinand, their remaining brother, lived at Rome.

Pietro, the youngest of the eight children of Cosimo and Eleonora, deprived of his mother at eight years old, and disliked by his brothers, had grown up passionate, jealous, dissolute, and without a redeeming quality of any kind, and was now twenty-two. His young wife Eleonora, by this time nearly twenty, was universally pitied when at fifteen she came to Florence, a very beautiful and innocent young girl, to be married to him. This ill-assorted young couple lived in the Medici palace in the Via Larga. Pietro, altogether given up to an evil life, had a distaste for matrimony, and from the first treated Eleonora as badly as possible. He scandalised even the society of that time by his disgraceful orgies, while his young wife was left neglected and an object of pity. The natural results followed. Eleonora, made for love, but cast aside and neglected, fell in love with an agreeable and handsome youth of about her own age, Bernardino Antinori. Not long afterwards one of his friends quarrelled with Bernardino and attacked him in the narrow passage [3] running along the south side of the Strozzi palace; and Bernardino in defending his life killed his assailant. He at once gave himself up to the authorities, and was confined as a prisoner in the palace of his family until the Grand Duke's pleasure regarding him should be known. Eleonora, fearing for his life, was wild with grief, and regardless of appearances drove round and round the Antinori palace [4] in the hope of seeing and speaking with him at some window; but failed to see him. Bernardino was exiled to Elba; from thence he despatched a letter to Eleonora by what he supposed a trustworthy hand, but through a chapter of accidents the letter was taken to Francis, and at once caused Bernardino's condemnation to death. He was brought back to Florence, consigned to the Bargello, given only one hour to prepare for death, and executed on the 20th June. Eleonora's own fate followed quickly. On the 11th July she received a summons from Pietro to meet him at the villa of Cafaggiolo [5] (about fifteen miles from Florence on the Faenza road), leaving her four-year-old son, Cosimo, in Florence. Dreading the worst she embraced her little son again and again in an agony of tears and then set out for Cafaggiolo "plunged in grief and with a trembling heart." She reached there in the evening. Pietro made her sup with him, and then drawing his sword killed her.[6] Her body was at once placed in a coffin, and carried that same night into Florence, where it was buried in the New Sacristy in San Lorenzo. There thirty-two years afterwards it was seen when in 1608 the work on the new mausoleum was being executed. Francesco Settimanni in his diary says:—

"The writer from whom this account [7] has been taken adds that in the year 1608 he saw the body of the said Lady Eleonora on the occasion when it was exhumed from the New Sacristy and carried to the vault; [8] and that she was as beautiful as if living, without the corpse being in the least corrupted [9] or injured, and appeared exactly as if sleeping, and was dressed all in white." [10]

Eleonora's little son, Cosimo, died a few months after his mother, and is buried in one corner of the mausoleum.[11]

This story of Eleonora's murder is that which has always been believed, and it is to some extent corroborated by the fact that there is no tablet to her memory in the family mausoleum. At the same time it must be remembered that the story did not appear until a subsequent generation, and is not authenticated in any way; [12] so that we may be doing both Pietro and Francis a severe injustice if we accept it as undoubtedly true. At the time it occurred her death was declared to have been due to heart disease; while it is noticeable that the writer who describes having seen her body thirty-two years afterwards in so perfect a state of preservation saw no sign of wounds; which is peculiar if she were killed with the sword in the manner which had been related by him. After this episode Pietro was sent by Francis to the court of Spain, where he resided almost entirely for the rest of his life, becoming as much hated there as he was in Florence, and a constant thorn in the side of Tuscany. [13]

Five days after this sudden death of Francis's sister-in-law a second dreadful occurrence took place in connection with his sister Isabella. In this case a Medici was the victim, not the perpetrator, of the crime.

Isabella was the most beautiful of the three daughters of Cosimo I and Eleonora di Toledo. Clever, and highly accomplished, she was also of a kind-hearted disposition, and is said to have been the only one of the family who showed kindness to Bianca Capello. [14]

"Wit, beauty, and talent made her conspicuous among all the ladies of the day, and she captivated every heart but her husband's. Speaking French, Spanish, and Latin fluently, a perfect musician, singing beautifully, a poetess and *improvisatrice* by nature, Isabella was the soul of all around her, and the fairest star of the Medici." [15]

But it was her fate to be involved in, and to be the first victim of, a celebrated fourfold tragedy which caused the ruin of the

great house of Orsini. She was now thirty-four, and had been
for eighteen years married to Paolo Giordano Orsini, Prince
of Bracciano, the head of the most powerful family in Rome,
a race who for generations had made and unmade popes and
intermarried with kings, and who possessed fortresses and do-
mains all over Italy. The tragedy in which Isabella's life
terminated is that connected with Vittoria Accoramboni, the
four persons who all lost their lives in it being Francesco
Peretti (Vittoria's husband), Vittoria herself, Paolo Giordano
Orsini, and Isabella de' Medici.

Vittoria Accoramboni, young, beautiful, vain, and ambitious, had captivated Orsini, who, indolent, pleasure-seeking,
and no longer young, cared nothing for the wife whom he left
to live in Florence while he spent his time in Rome. Vittoria,
fired with the ambition of being the Princess of Bracciano,
practically told Orsini, who was infatuated with her, that he
must kill her husband and his own wife, and marry her. He, as
head of the house of Orsini, with absolute powers of life and
death over all members of his family, saw no difficulty, and
proceeded to carry out her injunctions, by first putting to
death Isabella, and then, as soon as opportunity offered, by
similarly disposing of Peretti.

Isabella, who had some suspicion of danger to herself, had
written to Catherine de' Medici begging her to afford her an
asylum, as nowhere in Italy could she be safe from the far-
reaching power of Orsini; and Catherine had replied agreeing
to do so, and had made arrangements to receive her; but it
was too late. On the 16th July, Isabella, already horror-
stricken at her young sister-in-law's sudden death a few days
before, and made still more uneasy by her husband's unexpected and mysterious arrival at Florence, accompanied him
by his request to their villa of Cerreto Guidi, near Empoli.
She went with great misgivings, which she confided on the way
thither to her friend, Lucrezia Frescobaldi, whom she took
with her. When they retired after supper to their own apartments for the night, her husband Orsini, while pretending to

kiss Isabella, suddenly slipped a noose round her beautiful neck, and after a violent struggle strangled her. He had prepared for this crime by making a hole in the ceiling of the room and stationing four men in the room above, from which a rope with a noose at the end of it was let down through the hole and concealed behind the curtains of the window until the moment came that it was required. The room being intentionally kept rather dark this passed unobserved by Isabella, enabling him to effect successfully his cruel purpose.[16] It was given out that she had died from a fit of apoplexy while bathing her head.[17] This was followed in due time by the assassination of Peretti, Orsini sending a party of his soldiers to seize and kill the latter at the Villa Negroni in Rome, where Peretti was betrayed into their hands by Vittoria and killed.

The sequel is well known. Pope Gregory XIII,[18] "guessing how and why these two had met their deaths," refused to allow Orsini to marry the widowed Vittoria. Orsini defied the Pope, and went through a mock marriage. The Pope then sent troops to arrest the murderer of Peretti, but the Orsini retainers beat them off. Eventually Vittoria was seized and imprisoned in the castle of St. Angelo, but escaped; for four years the struggle went on, Orsini and Vittoria living at Bracciano, outside the Pope's jurisdiction. Then Gregory XIII died (1585); whereupon they came to Rome to be married before another Pope should be elected, and the ceremony was hastily performed in the small family church inside the Orsini fortress. Within a few hours to their horror it was proclaimed that the Cardinal of Montalto, Francesco Peretti's uncle, had been elected as the new Pope; and they had to face the terrible Sixtus V, bent upon exacting vengeance for his nephew's murder. Orsini fled to Venice, was exiled, and then, broken in heart at the ruin of his family, died, after making a will leaving his remaining property to Vittoria, who had fled to Padua. But her husband's nearest relation, Ludovico Orsini, enraged at the property being left to her, suddenly burst into her house at midnight six weeks later with a party of masked men, and she was stabbed to the heart. Venice, however, did not permit such acts of private war, and a week afterwards Ludovico Orsini was himself arrested and put to death; and the ruin of the great Orsini family was complete. They never again recovered their former power.[19]

In 1578 Francis's first wife, Joanna of Austria, died, at the age of thirty-one. She had been married thirteen years, and had not had a happy life. She had no qualities to make her either liked by her husband or popular with the Tuscan people, being plain in appearance, of a cold nature, without personal charm, and imbued with a great deal of Austrian pride; and the first Grand Duchess of Tuscany [20] did not hide her contempt for the Tuscan monarchy, and the Tuscan people. Francis had never shown her the least affection, and during the whole of their married life was devoted to Bianca Capello, with whom he had been in love before his marriage to Joanna, and whom after the latter's death he married; and the unceasing complaints which Joanna addressed to her brother, the Emperor Maximilian, on the subject of her husband's behaviour did not make matters go more smoothly. Joanna's six children were Eleonora (born in 1565), Romola (born 1566), Isabella (born 1567), Anna (born 1569), Maria (born 1573), and Filippo (born 1577); but only two of these, Eleonora and Maria, survived childhood, while Romola and Isabella died before their mother. There is a peculiarity about both the portraits of Joanna in the Uffizi Gallery. In both she is shown with her little son Filippo. He was only ten months old when his mother died; [21] yet in one of these portraits he is represented as a child about two years old, and in her other portrait as about four years old. Unless, therefore, these portraits of her were painted several years after her death (and after Francis had married another wife), which is extremely unlikely, it would seem that the figure of the child must have been added afterwards; though with what object, since he died at the age of five,

ɟs not apparent. Joanna of Austria was buried in the church
of San Lorenzo; and when in 1857 the Medici coffins were
opened her body was found so well preserved by the embalming process employed as to appear only just buried, even
the colour of the face being unaltered.[22]

The year after Joanna's death Francis married Bianca
Capello, whose unvarying lover he had been for fifteen years.
The remaining nine years of his reign were almost entirely
devoid of incident, either political or domestic, and his interests became more and more centred in those studies in
natural science to which he was devoted. Francis had an absolute passion for chemistry and natural science. By far the
greater part of his time was spent in his laboratory; and so
reluctant was he to be drawn away from his experiments that
he would often give audience to his Secretaries of State standing before his furnace, bellows in hand. It was he who first
discovered the method of melting rock crystal, and he became
distinguished for his skill and taste in making vases in this
material, many of which are still to be seen in the Gem Room
of the Uffizi Gallery. He was also the first to achieve the
manufacture of porcelain in imitation of the Chinese, and he
founded the existing porcelain industry of Florence which
has attained much celebrity.

Francis had also the usual Medicean fondness for art and
literature. He gave liberal encouragement to all artists, and
in particular to Giovanni da Bologna (1524-1608), the leading sculptor of the day; and it was for Francis that the latter
executed the well-known statue of *Mercury*, now in the
museum of the Bargello.[23] For Francis was also executed by
the same sculptor the group of the *Rape of the Sabines*, which
now stands in the Loggia de' Lanzi, and the statue of
Abundance, placed at the highest point of the Boboli gardens, facing the palace, and said to represent Francis's first
wife, Joanna of Austria. His desire to promote the cause of
literature resulted in the foundation in 1582 of the celebrated

Accademia della Crusca, which still exists, and which was founded under his auspices by Francesco Grazzini and Leonardo Salviata for the purification of the Italian language, its name *crusca* (bran) referring to the sifting of the chaff from the flour.

But there was another work undertaken by Francis which had more important consequences. He was the first to begin arranging the building which we now know as the Uffizi Gallery to adapt it for a picture gallery, and to begin placing there some of the family collection of pictures. Cosimo had erected the lower part of the building to accommodate the various public offices of the State, and on the second storey had placed ranges of workshops where his skilled workmen engraved, painted, made inlaid tables, executed models for statues, distilled essences and carried on many other minor arts.[24] Above this second floor was an open *loggia,* being part of the *Passaggio* [25] leading from the Palazzo Vecchio to the Ducal Palace; this *loggia* Francis now caused to be enclosed with glass, placing the architect and sculptor Buontalenti in charge of the work, and conveyed there a number of the family pictures scattered among their various villas. Buontalenti at the same time executed the statue of Francis (in the dress of a Roman knight), placed over the portico at the southern end of the gallery, facing the Palazzo Vecchio. Thus was begun a work which after generations of the Medici made one of Florence's greatest possessions. The great naval war between England and Spain, the terrible conflict in France, the battles and atrocities deluging the Netherlands with blood, were the events taking place in other countries while Florence was laying the foundations of her great picture gallery; and the peace which she thus enjoyed made her lot by comparison happy, even though under the tyranny of Francis I.

In 1582 Francis lost his only son, Filippo, at the age of five. This was a serious loss to him, as he had no children by his second wife, and the crown would therefore go at his death to his brother Ferdinand, between whom and himself there was no love lost. In 1583 Francis gave his eldest daughter Eleonora, now eighteen, in marriage to Vincenzo Gonzaga, Duke of Mantua.[26] Eleonora's portrait by Pulzone, in the Pitti Gallery, shows her to have had considerable beauty. Her dress is chiefly remarkable for its splendid example of the well-known Medici collar, which has round its edge a string of small pearls. In the same year Francis's daughter Anna died at the age of fourteen. Thus out of his six children four had died in their childhood, one daughter was married, and there only remained to him his daughter Maria, at this time a child of ten.

Francis I continued his father Cosimo's practice of private trading, and operating on a large scale amassed great wealth; and at his death a vast amount of treasure was found to have been collected by him in the fortress of the Belvedere. He died in October 1587 at the villa of Poggio a Caiano at the age of forty-six,[27] his wife Bianca dying at the same time; and his brother Ferdinand succeeded to the throne.

BIANCA CAPELLO

Born 1543. (Became Grand Duchess 1579.) Died 1587

BIANCA CAPELLO's romantic history and celebrated beauty have made a great impression in Italy; pictures of her are numerous, and her story in various forms is related in every chronicle of the time. And lavish as has been the praise accorded to her beauty, scarcely less so has been the abuse showered upon her name. While she must certainly be held to deserve a portion of this condemnation, by far the greater part has been quite undeserved. Francis loved her with a steadfast affection for twenty-four years, never showing any regard for any one else; and the deep hatred felt for Francis attached itself also to any one for whom he showed any regard, and most of all, therefore, to Bianca Capello. Added to this she was a Venetian. For over a hundred years Venice had been Florence's bitter foe and rival; in almost every war they had been opposed to each other; every enemy of Florence found an asylum out of reach of her wrath at Venice; even in the domain of Art they were rivals; and no Venetian need expect to be received at Florence with a welcome. Lastly, Bianca was throughout life strongly hated by Francis's brother Ferdinand, who succeeded him as Grand Duke, and all who wished to curry favour with the latter had an easy means of doing so by inventing stories against her after her death. These three causes together resulted in the imputation of crimes to Bianca by the Florentines of which her character was altogether incapable. All Francis's tyrannies were by those who suffered from them placed on her shoulders, and the more they hated Francis, the more they attributed the cause of his acts to the Venetian to whom he was so devoted.

Bianca Capello was the daughter of one of the proudest and most illustrious of the nobles of Venice, Bartolommeo Capello, and was brought up in all the splendour and luxury customary in a noble Venetian family of that age. She had in a pre-eminent degree that quality sometimes seen of an inherent and unstudied attractiveness, independent of beauty; while in her case to this was added beauty also. It may be imagined that the combination made her irresistible.

"Grace and fascination hung round her movements, and whether grave or gay, silent or speaking, quiet or in motion, she was always completely attractive; while without any particular regularity of features she concentrated within herself the varied influence of every feminine beauty." [28]

No wonder that Titian desired to paint her portrait, especially as in addition to her other attractions she had hair of that beautiful auburn-red tint only seen in Venice, and so admired of all artists. His portrait of her [29] at the age of twenty-one is one of the most beautiful of Titian's portraits.

About the year 1560, when Bianca was seventeen, she fell
in love with a youth a year or two older than herself belonging to a Florentine family, named Piero Buonaventura, a
gentleman by birth, but whose family were in reduced circumstances, while he himself was a clerk in the Salviati bank,
which was situated in one of the narrow streets of Venice,
exactly opposite the Capello palace. Her family would have
killed her rather than allow such a marriage, and they were
married secretly. But an accident threatened suddenly to
reveal what they had done, and they had at a moment's notice
to fly for their lives. Piero hurried his young wife into a
gondola, they escaped by sea, and eventually reached Florence, where his father and mother were living in great poverty.[30] All Venice was horrified at such an insult to its proud
aristocracy; the Capello family were powerful, and the whole
Venetian nobility vowed vengeance on Piero for his intolerable
audacity; a reward of 2,000 ducats was offered to any one
who would murder him, and his uncle, Giambattista Buonaventura, was thrown into prison and there died. Meanwhile,
in Florence Bianca had no easy lot. Piero's mother was bed-
ridden; his father, unable to support this addition of two
extra members to his family, was forced to discharge their
only servant; and the luxuriously brought-up daughter of a
Venetian noble had to take the servant's place, and become
a household drudge. At the same time fear for Piero's life,
and dread on Bianca's part of falling into her enraged
father's hands, kept them both prisoners. That Bianca bore
uncomplainingly all that this great change must have meant
to her for the sake of her love for Piero (who, after all,
showed himself a worthless creature) speaks well for her
natural good-heartedness. She was despised, hard worked,
condemned by all, and execrated by the whole aristocracy of
Venice, but she cared not so long as Piero remained true
to her. During this time of their poverty a daughter was born
to them, Pellegrina Buonaventura, who afterwards married
Ulisse Bentivoglio.

In the year 1563 Francis, then twenty-two, the eldest
son of the Duke of Florence, crossing one day the Piazza
San Marco, looked up and saw Bianca (whose story all
Florence knew) at a window, and at once fell in love with
her. She was then twenty, and at the height of her beauty.
Soon afterwards she was entrapped into a meeting with him
at the house of the Marchesa Mondragone, the wife of Francis's Spanish tutor, who lived at the house called the Casino,
on the west side of the Piazza San Marco.

"Startled by the Prince's sudden and unexpected appearance in a private room, she fell on her knees, declared herself bankrupt of everything but honour, and implored his
forbearance and protection; and for a time he obeyed, and
left her alone." [31]

Soon, however, he began pursuing her with his attentions;
even fears for Piero's life contributed; while the latter, heart-
less and contemptible, who was tired of her and of their
poverty-stricken life, failed to protect her in any way, and
accepted an office which Francis procured for him at the
court, and allowed a palace to be taken for them in the Via
Maggio, near the Ducal Palace. Piero thus promoted became
proud, insolent, dissolute, and generally detested, and after
a short time was one evening murdered at the corner of the
Via Maggio, near the Ponte Sta. Trinità, by one of the Ricci
family whom he had insulted.

Francis remained Bianca's devoted lover all his life, and
his marriage to the Archduchess Joanna of Austria in December 1564, when Bianca was twenty-one, made no difference
in this. When not at work in his laboratory, he spent most of
his time at Bianca's house in the Via Maggio.[32] The Archduchess Joanna, furious at this neglect of herself in favour
of a rival so far beneath her in rank, wearied her brother the
Emperor with complaints, but without avail. And when she
died in April 1578 Francis married Bianca, who was by this
time thirty-five.

At first, on account of the recent death of Joanna of Austria, they were privately married in the small chapel in the Palazzo Vecchio, but in the following year this was succeeded by a very magnificent marriage in San Lorenzo; while at the same time, strange to say, a grand ceremony in honour of the event took place at Venice. Venice, which had cast ignominy upon Bianca's very name, now hastened to do it honour, and not only received with a stately ceremonial and hypocritical compliments an embassy from Florence on the occasion, but promulgated a public decree in Bianca's honour, while the city of the Adriatic "blazed with countless illuminations." This was followed by a pompous embassy from Venice to Florence to invest Bianca "with the prerogatives of her new rank." Bianca was unlike her predecessor in another respect; she did not care for ostentation and the degree of ceremony attaching to a high position. But Francis was determined on this occasion to show her every kind of honour that he could devise. There followed tournaments, bull-fights, balls, a musical drama, feasts, and every sort of pastime for the people, and finally, on the 12th October 1579, in the great hall of the Palazzo Vecchio, an imposing ceremony took place at which Bianca was first declared by the Venetian ambassador to be "a true and particular daughter of Venice," and then, seated by the side of her husband Francis, was crowned with the crown of Tuscany. After which the whole assembly, led by the Grand Duke and the new Grand Duchess, proceeded in state to the cathedral, where High Mass concluded the ceremony. Francis spent on this marriage 300,000 ducats: equal to about one year's ordinary revenue of the ancient Republic.

Bianca Capello was Grand Duchess for nine years. In that position she continued to be very much the same as she had always been, not showing any exaltation on account of being raised to so high a rank, nor any desire for pomp and grandeur,[33] and preferring whenever possible a country life

with Francis at one or other of their villas, removed from
Florence and its abuse of her. For Francis's tyrannies continued to heap condemnation upon her head; and whatever
untoward event occurred, it was always in some manner
attributed to her. It is almost unnecessary to say that when
Francis's only son Filippo died in 1582 it was declared that
she had poisoned him; and this tale, like others of the kind,
was handed down after her death, regardless of the fact that
had she been guilty of such a thing the suspicious Francis
would certainly have found it out and lost all his affection for
her; as well as of the fact that the one ruling desire which
governed all Bianca's life was to please him.

But the people had another reason for hating Bianca
Capello and readily accepting every story against her. They
believed her to be a *witch*, and openly called her so. The hint
had not improbably been dropped by Ferdinand. But the
only kind of witchery that Bianca knew was that of "woman's
witching ways"; and none ever possessed it in a higher degree. And without making light of the one great fault she did
commit, it may well be noted in her favour that although
possessed of this exceptional power of attraction we never
hear, amidst all the stories against her promulgated after her
death, one single breath charging her with infidelity to Francis: a significant fact under the circumstances. It is also
to be noted that all writers credit her, not only with considerable talent, but also with various good qualities. Her
portrait by Bronzino, in the Pitti Gallery, at the age of
thirty,[34] has a sweet expression. He knew her well and it is
sure to be a good likeness. It must have been the last portrait
that Bronzino ever painted, as he died very shortly afterwards.

The feeling with which Bianca was regarded by her
brother-in-law Ferdinand, who lived at Rome and was on
bad terms with Francis, was a prominent factor in her lot.
The inclination which the Florentines had to attribute to
Bianca every crime committed, or imagined to have been

committed, by Francis, was felt by Ferdinand, "her most
deadly enemy," to a still greater degree; and he over and
over again remonstrated with Francis for having anything to
do with her, and endeavoured to get her banished from Tuscany. The hatred he felt for her amounted to a mania; and
his refusal after her death to allow her body decent burial,[35]
his causing her armorial bearings to be erased, and his speaking of her on all occasions in terms of opprobrium showed
how deep was the feeling which (unappeased even by her
death) was nourished by him for so many years against her.
When he became Grand Duke the time-serving contemporary writers followed suit, heaping upon her memory every
possible vilification, and handing down every tale which a
scandal-loving age could invent to her discredit; and this is
the real origin of the many stories which have passed as the
history of Bianca Capello. The true Bianca was a less exaggerated, and far more natural woman. She had many faults,
but they did not run in the direction of murder and poison,
as a sensation-loving populace (ready to believe anything
against a Venetian) confidently asserted.

After Bianca became Grand Duchess she summoned her
brother, Vittorio Capello, to Florence, and he soon became
a great favourite with Francis, and almost his sole adviser.
This still further incensed Ferdinand, and after a time he contrived to put such pressure upon his brother as to cause
him to dismiss Vittorio Capello again to Venice. Many of
Bianca's letters to her brother, in her clear bold handwriting,
are to be seen in the Florentine archives, and they show both
her character and how highly educated she was. Bianca is
reported to have shown a good spirit towards her brother-in-
law Ferdinand on various occasions, constantly endeavouring
to reconcile the two brothers, and by her amiability at times
succeeding temporarily in doing so; while as a part of these
endeavours she several times persuaded Francis to give large
sums of money to Ferdinand to supply his financial necessities.

these latter being very great owing to his expensive tastes in the collection of the treasures of Greek art.[36]

At last in 1587 [37] came the end, Francis and Bianca both dying together, and at that place which above all they would have chosen, the villa of Poggio a Caiano. Notable on many other accounts, this villa has ever since gained its chief interest as the place where the lives were simultaneously ended of these two, who, whatever else they were, had been unswervingly devoted to each other for twenty-four years.

The villa of Poggio a Caiano,[38] since the days when it had been built by Lorenzo the Magnificent, had been much enlarged and improved by successive heads of the family. Its great hall had, under the auspices of Leo X, been decorated with frescoes typifying the deeds of Cosimo Pater Patriae and Lorenzo the Magnificent—frescoes which had been in succession the work of Andrea del Sarto, Pontormo, Franciabigio, and Allori. The ceiling and walls of its dining-room had been painted so as to give the illusion of being seated in a Tuscan garden; the reception-rooms were hung with portraits of prominent members of the family; the wide-spreading park, with the Ombrone flowing through it, afforded the pleasures of the chase; the well laid-out gardens were an unceasing delight to all who saw them; while from the broad terrace spread out a view exemplifying all the special beauty of a Tuscan landscape.

Poggio a Caiano had always been a favourite residence of Bianca Capello,[39] and she and Francis had spent many days there together, hunting in the park, riding about the surrounding country, and enjoying other outdoor pursuits. In October 1587 they went there to enjoy once more its charms at that beautiful season of the year, and to revel in a country life away from the formalities of the court. But they had also another reason. The sincere endeavours which all writers acknowledge that Bianca constantly made to conciliate Ferdinand and heal the breach between the brothers had once more been successful. A reconciliation had been effected, and to cement it Francis and Bianca had invited Ferdinand to come from Rome, and join them in a visit to Poggio a Caiano.

Accordingly Ferdinand arrived at Florence, was received at the Ducal Palace by Francis and Bianca with every sign of cordiality, and together with the Archbishop of Florence accompanied them to Poggio a Caiano. There they remained for some days in complete harmony, the Grand Duchess and the Archbishop exerting themselves to maintain these cordial relations between the brothers who had so long been at enmity. But this happy state of affairs had a melancholy ending. On the 8th October the whole party went out hunting; during the day the Grand Duke while violently heated sat down by a small lake in the park and caught a severe chill, ending in fever, which he insisted on treating himself, taking for it some of the most unheard-of medicines with which his chemical researches had made him acquainted,[40] notwithstanding that his indisposition steadily grew worse and was accompanied with violent sickness. On the ninth day of this illness his malady took a more serious turn; this was increased by Bianca's inability to nurse him (as she was accustomed to do), she having been herself taken ill on the 13th October of a bad type of fever. Francis became rapidly worse, and, after forty-eight hours of great agony, expired on the 19th October. Meanwhile Bianca, seriously ill at the same time, and unable to go to her husband, was consumed with anxiety about him, and her enquiries for him were incessant. She had always been accustomed to say that "between her death and his, hours, not days, would elapse"; and so it proved. After six days' illness, feeling herself to be dying, and not knowing that her husband was already dead, she sent him her parting words by her confessor, Fra Maranta, weeping as she said: "Give my farewell to my Lord Francesco de' Medici, and say to him that I have always been most faithful and most loving towards him; tell him that my illness is made so great because of his; and beg him to pardon it if I have ever offended him in anything." In order to prevent her hearing sounds from the apartment of the Grand Duke (which was near hers) such as would reveal to her that he was dead, his body was carried down to a room on the ground-floor of the villa.[41] But the unusual trampling of feet in the passages, the agitated and tearful aspect of her attendants, and the noise of carriages and horses in the open space below as Ferdinand and the Archbishop took their hasty departure to Florence, soon awakened her to the knowledge that Francis was dead. For a while she lay silent; then after murmuring a few broken sentences she breathed a very deep sigh and said calmly: "And likewise also it accords with my own wish that I should die with my lord." After which she became too ill to speak, and soon afterwards expired, dying eleven hours after her husband.[42]

Of course it was inevitable under the circumstances that Ferdinand should be suspected of having poisoned them both. The fact that by the death of his brother he succeeded to the throne, joined with his well-known hatred of Bianca, made his guilt apparently certain. He at once ordered a *post-mortem* examination of the two bodies, and the doctors reported that there was no trace of poison in either case, but naturally such a report carried little weight; so that the common theory has always been that Francis and Bianca were poisoned by Ferdinand. Side by side with this theory, however, there has been another. Bianca had been too long a subject of vituperation for an endeavour not to be made in some way to throw the guilt upon her, however difficult in this case to do so. Hence we have the well-known story of the tart supposed to have been prepared by Bianca in order to poison Ferdinand, but eaten by accident by Francis, and that Bianca, seeing this, ate of it also, being determined not to survive him; a story which, notwithstanding its almost palpable untruth, has obtained wide credence.[43]

The account, however, given above of this affair (which

is that disclosed by the State archives unearthed within recent years by the patient research of the late Signor G. E. Saltini) shows plainly that Bianca was not even present when Francis became seriously ill, she having then been for four days ill in bed. And it is now considered certain, not only that Bianca was perfectly innocent (which is almost self-evident), but that Ferdinand was innocent also. All historians are now convinced that it was no case of poison at all, and that Francis and Bianca died from the natural causes assigned by the doctors as the result of the *post-mortem* examination, Bianca from dropsy, from which she had suffered for two years, and which was aggravated by her attack of fever, and Francis chiefly through the absurd remedies which he persisted in taking to cure his indisposition. Moreover, Ferdinand's history during the succeeding twenty-two years as Grand Duke showed very distinctly that he was not the kind of man who could be guilty of such a crime.

Ferdinand, however, inspired by his inordinate hatred of Bianca, was led into conduct which was extremely short-sighted. He not only refused to allow her decent burial, but also ordered the destruction of everything that could recall her memory. He caused her armorial bearings to be erased from the escutcheon of the Medici and replaced by those of Austria, when obliged to mention her name would not give her or allow others to give her the title of Grand Duchess, and even in a public document designated her as "La pessima Bianca." By this conduct Ferdinand used the best means possible for making it supposed that he desired to divert suspicion from himself, and for confirming in men's minds the idea that he was guilty.

The two bodies were together brought back to Florence. That of Francis was embalmed,[44] and buried in the church of San Lorenzo [45] with the ceremonial customary in the case of a Grand Duke; but when the architect Buontalenti asked Ferdinand where the body of the Grand Duchess should be buried, he replied: "Where you please; we will not have her amongst *us*." Her body was therefore wrapped simply in an ordinary winding sheet and buried without ceremony, none know where. And so, among the Grand Duchesses of Tuscany, one, the second, is missing from that great mausoleum where all the rest lie buried; and in its crypt Francis I has by his side the first wife whom he so disliked, and who was Grand Duchess for four years, but not the second wife, who was Grand Duchess for nine, and was the only person whom throughout life he had loved, or who loved him. But to Bianca it mattered nothing to what obscurity her body was consigned; for her memory has lived on notwithstanding all Ferdinand's efforts to obliterate it, while the accusations so freely spread abroad against her have gradually shown themselves to be untrue.

Bianca Capello was forty-four when she died. Undoubtedly, notwithstanding all that can justly be said on the other side, she was a woman who deserved a better record than the distorted picture of her which was handed down to posterity owing to the insensate hatred entertained for her by the brother of her husband who succeeded him as Grand Duke. Regarding her one grave fault it has been remarked that, "thrown while yet a mere girl into temptation, distress, and danger, with a warm heart and strong sensibility, her natural protector false, despicable, and utterly selfish, assailed by unwonted hardship and suffering, reduced from the splendour and refinement of exalted station to perform the menial offices of a starving household, with a youthful prince at her feet, and the glimmer of a throne in the distance, she finally sank under temptation, and became—probably not all that her enemies have described her. In an age of infidelity she was at least faithful to the Grand Duke, and probably would have been faithful to her husband had he taken any pains to keep her so." [46] Bianca Capello, in fact, shows herself as one in whom throughout life love reigned supreme. And the true essence of her character is seen in the girl who abandoned all the grandeur and luxury belonging to a Venetian noble's daughter for the man she loved, and in the wife who felt that it "accorded with her own wish to die with her lord," and when she knew that he was dead had no desire to live any longer.

CHAPTER XXVI

FERDINAND I

Born 1549. (*Reigned* 1587-1609.) *Died* 1609

FERDINAND, the fourth son of Cosimo I and Eleonora di
Toledo, who had been made a cardinal when he was fourteen,
at the time of the death of his mother and his brothers,
Giovanni and Garzia, was twenty-five years old when his
father died and his brother Francis succeeded to the throne.
He and Francis differed violently on every subject; it merely
required that a proposal should emanate from one of them
for it to be opposed by the other; and after a time they kept
altogether apart. During the thirteen years of his brother's
reign Ferdinand resided entirely at Rome, where he became
a strong power at the Vatican. Though a cardinal, he never
took holy orders. Fierce, haughty, bold, and independent,
and at the head of a powerful faction in the Curia, he feared
no Pope whatever. On one occasion he withstood even the
ferocious and tyrannical Sixtus V on the subject of wearing
arms and armour in the Vatican, which he, Ferdinand de'
Medici, declined to abandon.

At another time he by his boldness and resource saved the
life of his friend, Cardinal Farnese. The latter had been condemned by Sixtus V to be executed, and the hour for his
execution fixed. But Ferdinand put on all the clocks in the
Vatican by one hour, and then boldly facing the Pope pe-
tioned for Farnese's pardon, and practically forced the Pope
to grant it, the latter, however, only doing so because he
thought that the hour for Farnese's execution was already
past. Then Ferdinand stopped the execution on the authority
he had extracted from the Pope, and his friend's life was
saved.

At Rome Ferdinand signalised himself in two ways. He showed much capacity in the administration of ecclesiastical affairs, being notable in particular as the founder of the great missionary establishment, the Propaganda; and he was still more distinguished as a great collector of the works of classic art. It was a time in Rome when the greater part of the collections of sculpture of the classic age which had been unearthed and gathered together in the Vatican by Popes Julius II, Leo X, Clement VII, and Paul III, had been scattered by subsequent Popes who cared nothing about art; [1] and in Ferdinand's time the Popes had not yet begun again to take any interest in such things.[2] Ferdinand, on the other hand, inheriting the same tastes as his ancestors, purchased eagerly all such works which he could obtain, and became the chief collector of the time in Rome. He built the celebrated Villa Medici at Rome, and there he collected an immense number of the most priceless works of Greek and Roman sculpture. These included the *Venus de' Medici* (found in the villa of Hadrian at Tivoli), the group of *Niobe* [3] *and her children* (found near the Porta San Paolo in 1583), the *Dancing Faun,* the *Wrestlers,* the *Knife-whetter,* the *Apollino,* and many statues of classic times, busts of Roman emperors, and other works of antiquity, which were all subsequently removed by degrees to Florence by him or his successors, and now adorn the staircases and corridors of the Uffizi Gallery. Thus Ferdinand, before he was Grand Duke, purchased out of his own private funds the six best examples of Greek art which Florence possesses; and, except the *Apollo Belvedere,* the *Laocoön,* and the *Torso of Hercules,* the best which were at that time known. As regards the *Venus* (which being purchased by Ferdinand immediately it was found henceforth received his family name) it is too much the fashion to decry its excellence, solely because a former generation erred in the opposite direction. It has been said that this statue cannot be understood at a single visit; while Byron's well-known words about it remain as true as ever. Of the *Apollino* Shelley said that it was "like a spirit even in dreams."

Ferdinand was thirty-eight years old when his brother Francis died. As the latter left no son Ferdinand resigned his cardinal's rank (together with a good prospect of being the next Pope), and succeeded his brother as Grand Duke of Tuscany. His conduct with reference to Bianca Capello is not to be looked upon as a true indication of his character, but rather as a monomania on that particular point. His whole conduct during the long period of twenty-two years that he was Grand Duke (and as such a mark for the searching hostile criticism of those who watched for any cause of offence in the head of this family) showed him to be a man of high character whose life gave no cause of offence to any. Two Medici Grand Dukes preceded him, and four followed him, but he was superior to them all; for though his achievements, great as they were, did not equal those of his father Cosimo, this high character and exemplary conduct more than restored the balance.

On ascending the throne Ferdinand reversed the previously existing foreign policy of siding with Spain, and began to establish relations with France, thus returning to Tuscany's older policy. Unlike Francis, he had always been on friendly terms with Catherine de' Medici; and before the year 1587 was ended he had arranged with her that her favourite grand-daughter, Christine of Lorraine, then twenty-two, should be given to him in marriage. This was, however, for some little time delayed, first by the sudden death of Christine's father, the Duke of Lorraine, and then by the disturbances in France. Nor did the marriage appear a very propitious one; rumours were rife at the French court which declared that the proposed bridegroom was the murderer of his brother and sister-in-law; while in the existing condition of France it was thought unsafe for Christine at present to take the journey. For it was a troubled time. Spain's great Armada was about to sail to attack England, and Spain was laying plans to obtain possession of French ports; while in France civil war was raging, the League being in possession of Paris, and the King (Henry III), with the States-General, having to take refuge at Blois. Ferdinand sent an embassy, headed by Orazio Rucellai, to escort Christine to Florence, but they had to remain at Blois until March 1589 before it was safe for her to travel; and during this time much occurred. In July 1588 the Armada made its attack on England, and in a fortnight was entirely destroyed. Meanwhile Catherine de' Medici was evidently dying, and Christine could not leave her. In December the murder at Blois of the Duke of Guise threw all the court into confusion and terror. On the 5th January 1589 Catherine de' Medici died, Christine being with her to the last; and in March the latter started from Blois on a somewhat melancholy journey, all the court being sorry to lose one who was universally liked, and she herself being very sad at bidding good-bye to France. She was accompanied for a long distance from Blois by a brilliant cavalcade, including Henry III himself, who showed her great affection at parting. At Marseilles she and her escort found the fleet which had been waiting there for her for months; and in due course she arrived at Florence.

The marriage festivities at Florence lasted a month, and were on the most splendid scale.

"Florence resembled the city of a fairy tale rather than the sober habitation of common men. In the courtyard of the Palace the storming of a Turkish fortress was represented with inimitable talent. A magnificent tournament followed, and this was succeeded by a sumptuous banquet; but after the guests had refreshed themselves they found that the courtyard of the Palace had been converted into a mimic sea, and a spirited naval combat ensued, and made the walls re-echo to its thunders." [4]

Christine of Lorraine made Ferdinand an excellent wife. On the death of her mother she had been adopted by her grandmother, Catherine de' Medici, and entirely brought up by her,[5] and is described on her arrival at Florence as "full of grace, vivacity, and spirit." She survived her husband, Ferdinand I, for twenty-seven years, her son, Cosimo II, for sixteen years, and was appointed by the latter Regent of Tuscany during the long minority of his son, Ferdinand II. She was thus the leading social influence at Florence during the greater part of three reigns and for so long a period as fifty years. Though not possessed of much ability, she was a thoroughly good woman, and she completely reformed the court of Tuscany; henceforth no ground was given for the fabrication of dark tales of crime such as that which the atmosphere of the court had afforded in the reigns of Cosimo I and Francis I; and this one important work done by Christine of Lorraine, and made permanent through the excellent bringing up which she gave her son Cosimo II, is sufficient to render her worthy of the utmost praise. One other thing Christine effected. For by showing herself all that she was in this respect, she did an important service to one who had loved her, whom she had loved, and to whom she owed all her training. For nothing could better vindicate the character of Catherine de' Medici than the results which her training produced in the granddaughter whom she had brought up. In the portrait of Christine in the Uffizi Gallery, taken a year or two after her marriage, she wears her court dress and has her crown by her side; the crown is large and heavily jewelled, and has, below the Florentine lily, two figures supporting a shield; her dress is of a peculiar shape, the lower part of the sleeve being removable and fastened with large buttons to the upper part or cape; and this pattern of dress is to be seen in several other portraits of ladies of this time in the Uffizi Gallery. In another portrait of her, taken about the same time, she wears the same shaped dress, and the crown by her side is a small light one having on it only the Florentine lily. In the case of the Medici, not only each Grand Duke,[6] but each Grand Duchess also, was buried wearing her own crown, an entirely fresh one being made for her successor. In her portrait each Grand Duchess is painted with her crown by her side, always heavily jewelled, and each has a different one.

Ferdinand I reigned over Tuscany for twenty-two years. The crest and motto which he chose on coming to the throne —a swarm of bees with the motto *Majestate tantum*,[6a] by which he intended to signify that his rule should be just and temperate, enabling the people to gather wealth as bees do honey—was faithfully acted up to by him; and while his marriage restored order and morality to the court, his various reforms revived Tuscany from the state of maladministration into which it had fallen under Francis. He had a profound veneration for all the acts and opinions of his father; but the bold spirit which he had shown as a cardinal did not continue to appear in his career as Grand Duke, and he often quailed before the Jesuits, which order, recognised by Pope Paul III in 1543, had in only forty years gained entire domination over the Papacy. On beginning to reign Ferdinand pardoned all who had opposed him, and removed all restrictions as to where Florentines might reside. He put an end to the corruption which had invaded the courts of justice, assisted commerce by many wise fiscal reforms, and gave his entire attention to State affairs and measures for the welfare of the country. Among many other useful works with this object he successfully accomplished for the time [7] the draining of the Val di Chiana, which had been an engineering difficulty for generations; he brought under cultivation the plains of Pisa, Fucecchio, and the Val di Nievole; and he gave Pisa water communication with Leghorn, by means of the canal of the Naviglio, into which a portion of the water of the Arno was turned.

But Ferdinand's greatest achievement was the creation of Leghorn; for it was he who practically created that port through the particular measure which made it so remarkable a success. His father Cosimo had begun the conversion of this small fishing village into an important harbour, but had not had time to proceed far with the project; the one good work of Francis had been the continuation of his father's plans in this respect, but though he advanced them to some extent, by far the greater part of the work still remained to be done when Ferdinand came to the throne. The latter took this matter up vigorously, and it became his chief interest; harbours were laid out and excavated, fortifications planned and thrown up, and sound fiscal regulations made to attract commerce to the new port. But these arrangements alone would not have amounted to more than had often been carried out in other cases without any startling results. To them, however, Ferdinand added a measure which in its broad-mindedness was entirely in advance of the ideas of his age. He published a decree (which from Leghorn's Italian name of Livorno he called the *Livornina*) by which it was ruled that in the new port there should be universal toleration, thus making it an asylum of refuge for the persecuted of all religions and nationalities; Protestants flying from France and Spain, Roman Catholics flying from England, Flemings flying from Alva's atrocities in the Netherlands, persecuted Jews from all countries, were all alike welcomed and protected at Leghorn, and found a safe refuge there; while to the Jews Ferdinand gave also a special charter to protect them from persecution by Tuscans. The result of this broad-minded policy was that Leghorn went up with a bound, and before Ferdinand's reign of twenty-two years was ended had risen from an insignificant fishing village into the leading commercial port of Italy after Genoa. Montesquieu, speaking of this achievement, calls Leghorn "the masterpiece of the dynasty of the Medici." The latter could, however, point to greater achievements than this one (both before and after it), important as it was.

Ferdinand also largely increased the Tuscan navy, and the latter, led by the knights of Santo Stefano, gained much honour in the Mediterranean, both by victories over the Turks, and by sweeping from the seas the fierce pirates of Barbary who were a formidable obstacle to all maritime commerce. Towards the end of Ferdinand's reign the war-galleys of the knights of Santo Stefano were in 1607 sent to attack Bona, on the coast of Barbary, the headquarters of the corsairs; the place was fiercely defended by the latter, but the knights took it by an assault in which they displayed unexampled bravery. In the following year the same galleys achieved a still more brilliant victory over the Turks, attacking and completely defeating the much stronger Turkish fleet, capturing nine of their vessels, seven hundred prisoners, and a store of jewels valued at 2,000,000 ducats. This victory was the final success which closed a long series of similar contests, and placed the Tuscan fleet at the head of naval affairs in the Mediterranean. In the Sala del Baroccio in the Uffizi Gallery is to be seen a table of Florentine *pietra dura,* executed for Ferdinand, in the centre of which is a representation of the harbour of Leghorn, with vessels of all nations floating on a sea of *lapislazuli,* and among them a squadron of six galleys of the Tuscan fleet bringing into the harbour two captured Turkish ships.

In his foreign policy Ferdinand continued to increase those close relations with France which he had begun by his marriage. Six months after Christine of Lorraine left Blois Henry III was assassinated, and there followed four years of war in France, during which Henry of Navarre (Henry IV) was contending for his kingdom against the League, which was assisted by Spain. Ferdinand supported his claims and provided him with money, undeterred by the opposition of Spain and the League, who were appalled at the prospect of a Protestant succeeding to the throne of France, and were determined to prevent it at all costs. And it was practically Ferdinand who at length placed Henry IV on the French throne. The revenue of the Grand Duke of Tuscany was at this period equal to, if not greater than, the entire revenue of France; and the sums which Ferdinand lent Henry to enable him to continue the contest were enormous. Great trains of waggons containing specie, and escorted by large bodies of cavalry and infantry, were continually being sent from Florence to Henry in France. After a four years' struggle, seeing that Henry would never gain that throne as a Protestant, Ferdinand urged him to accept the Roman Catholic faith; he smoothed matters over for him with the Pope, and eventually Henry in 1593 renounced Protestantism, was through Ferdinand's strenuous endeavours acknowledged as King by Pope Clement VIII,[8] and in March 1594 at last gained possession of Paris. This was followed in 1598 by the death of Philip II of Spain, which had the effect of still further cementing Ferdinand's close friendship with France; and in the following year the latter was able to arrange a marriage which bound Henry IV still closer to him.

Ferdinand's niece Maria, Francis's second surviving daughter, had been a girl of fourteen when her father and stepmother died and her uncle succeeded to the throne. She was given a home by the latter, and was now twenty-six, the same age as the Grand Duchess Christine; while for one cause or another various proposals for her marriage had one after another fallen through. At length, however, upon Henry IV and Marguerite of Valois being divorced by mutual consent, Ferdinand succeeded in arranging that Maria should be married to Henry IV. The marriage which thus placed a Medici for the second time on the throne of France was performed by proxy in Florence in October 1600; and a few days afterwards Maria set out on her journey, the Grand Duchess accompanying her as far as Marseilles. She had an immense dowry; great as that of Catherine de' Medici had been, Maria's was even greater; and Sully said that no former Queen had ever brought to France such a marriage portion. As Queen of France, Maria (or, as she was always called in France, Marie de Medici) proved herself a decided contrast to her predecessor. Her blond hair and creamy-white complexion—that beauty which inspired Rubens—at first charmed Henry IV until he found out how devoid she was of brains. She was good-natured and was a moral woman in a most immoral time, but, unlike most of her family, she was entirely wanting in humour, wit, or intelligence, being in this respect remarkably inferior to her sister Eleonora, Duchess of Mantua. Henry IV gave her every inducement to show all her worst points. His infidelities were numerous, and Marie was not inclined to pass these over without resentment. Henry looked on the matter in another light; he wrote to Sully, "Our little disagreements ought never to outlast twenty-four hours," and complained of Marie that when she was offended she "took five days over it." She also objected to his illegitimate children being educated with the Princes and Princesses, and to being forced by Henry to address one of the former as "my son." Under these conditions the court of France became a scene of constant dissension; the quarrels, rivalries, and battles-royal which disturbed the palace were incessant, and Henry's great Minister, the Duke of Sully, was constantly called away from affairs of State to pacify the storms in the royal household. Right was entirely on Marie's side, but she did not adopt the best means of fighting her battle. Once in Sully's presence her wrath was so great that she was about to strike the King, when the Minister was only just in time to dash her hand aside. "Madame," he cried, "are you mad? Do you not know he could have your head off in half an hour?" But Marie's quality of good-nature was of value to her. Richelieu writes:—

"A storm was scarcely over before the King, delighting in the fine weather, treated the Queen with such sweetness that since that great Prince's death I have often heard her rejoice over the memory of her life with him."

In Marie's portrait in the Uffizi Gallery, painted not long after her marriage, her dress is very magnificent. Marie de

Medici spent more on dress than probably any other lady who ever lived. The description of the contents of her wardrobe, and of the numerous garments of richest material from among which she daily selected what dress she would wear, fill pages in the accounts of her life. Among them all she had three special favourites, "a dress of cloth of gold on a ground of columbine, a dress of gold and silver embroidery, and a dress of blue velvet sewn with gold *fleur-de-lys*"; and it is the latter which she wears in this picture. The stomacher is of ermine, covered with groups of large pearls and amethysts, each group of four pearls having an amethyst in the centre, while in front she wears a large cross of amethysts from which hang three very large pearls. The sleeves are similarly covered with groups of pearls and amethysts; while the skirt is heavily embroidered with *fleur-de-lys* in gold. Her crown is also encrusted with amethysts and pearls.[9]

Ferdinand I was no less active in the cause of Art than in that of the development of the country, the perfecting of the navy, and the founding of Leghorn. From the Villa Medici at Rome he gradually conveyed to Florence a great part of the works of Greek and Roman sculpture which he had collected there, and placed them in the new rooms over the public offices, the Uffizi; though some of the chief of the works collected by him at Rome (including the *Venus*, and the *Wrestlers*) were not brought to Florence until seventy years after his death, by Cosimo III, and the *Niobe* group and the *Apollino* not until a hundred years later still.[10] To accommodate the various works of sculpture which he was bringing from Rome, Ferdinand commissioned Buontalenti to construct several additional rooms to this gallery, including in particular the beautiful one called the Tribuna, with its ceiling of mother-of-pearl set in gilded gesso, walls lined throughout with hangings of *moiré antique,* and pavement inlaid with coloured marbles. Thus the Uffizi Gallery was for a long period more noted for its sculpture than for its pictures.

and on this account was, down to quite recent times, called "the Gallery of the Statues." At the same time Ferdinand continued the course which Francis had begun of collecting in these rooms any additional pictures which he acquired. We have an example of the vicissitudes which many of the pictures now in the Uffizi Gallery have undergone before at last finding a resting-place there, from the history of Botticelli's beautiful little picture of *Judith*. Painted for Piero il Gottoso, it originally formed part of the artistic treasures of the Medici Palace. Robbed with their other possessions when the palace was sacked in 1494 it disappeared for ninety years, during which time it apparently passed from hand to hand, until it at last came into the possession of Ridolfo Singatti, who gave it as a present to Francis's wife, Bianca Capello, and so it came once more into the possession of the Medici, and after Bianca's death was placed by Ferdinand in the Uffizi collection. Still more extraordinary have been the vicissitudes of one of the greatest treasures of the Pitti Gallery, Raphael's *Madonna del Gran Duca*. For this picture, painted by him in 1505, and now the most highly valued of all Raphael's pictures in Florence, had in the course of two hundred years dropped out of sight, and passing from hand to hand at last came into the possession of a poor widow who esteemed it of so little value that she sold it to a picture dealer for *twelve crowns*.

But the most important work inaugurated in Florence by Ferdinand I, and begun by him in 1604,[11] was the great family mausoleum, attached to the church of San Lorenzo. The site chosen was immediately behind, and adjoining, the choir of the church, from the back of which a door opens directly into the mausoleum; but this entrance has long been kept closed.

The laying of the foundation-stone of this great work was an impressive ceremony, and is thus described in the diary of Francesco Settimanni, a Florentine citizen of the time:—

"On the 6th April 1604 His Most Serene Highness the Grand Duke, having chosen the place alongside the church of San Lorenzo where he proposed to erect a splendid chapel, at the hour of half-past two on Good Friday, the day of the most holy Passion of our Saviour, came to the place accompanied by the whole court. He gave to the Prince Cosimo, his eldest son, a gold spade for the purpose, with which the latter, digging the site where the foundations were to be laid, dug out a portion of the earth, and with his own hands loaded a small gold basket with it, and then raising this earth began the work of the foundations. This being finished, the Grank Duke concluded the ceremony by saying in a loud voice, *'Here shall be our end.'* " [12]

One wonders how far Ferdinand I, standing in the corner of the Piazza Madonna in the space allotted to the new building, surrounded by his numerous sons and daughters and his magnificent court, in making the speech with which he concluded the laying of the foundation-stone of the great mausoleum, looked forward into the future, as he evidently did look back into the past. He certainly little imagined that the long roll of family tombs, lying some in the Old Sacristy, some in the New Sacristy, and some in the mausoleum which he was founding, would end four generations later with a tomb laid where he stood over one who was the last solitary descendant of the family.

The construction of this huge work, which was intended to be as splendid as size and the decoration of the interior with a profusion of precious stones could make it, occupied more than a hundred years, and called forth various descriptions of art work in Florence, originating in particular one important industry which still flourishes. [13] Begun by Ferdinand I, the construction of this mausoleum continued during the whole of the reigns of his four successors, not being really finished [14] until after the death of the last of them. The design of the building as we now see it completed is an immense octagonal chapel surmounted by a dome, the interior of the walls covered with rich marbles, and round the chapel the sarcophagi of the seven Medici Grand Dukes, each sarcophagus being of highly polished Oriental granite (of the same fine workmanship as the inlay work on the walls), and in a niche over each sarcophagus a colossal statue in bronze of the individual Grand Duke, standing, clad in his robes of state, with crown and sceptre; and on each sarcophagus a jewelled cushion in Oriental granite, with upon this a gilded and jewelled crown.[15] Large slabs of porphyry below each monument bear the name and titles of the Grand Duke to whom it refers. The walls are lined throughout with inlaid marbles, *lapis-lazuli*, and other precious stones, "the richest crust of ornament that ever was lavished on so large a surface," [16] and the inlay work is of an improved description introduced specially for the decoration of this mausoleum. It was intended that the dome should be entirely lined with Persian *lapis-lazuli* (divided into *cassetone*), which would have been in unison with the tone and material of the walls; but after the last Medici died this was given up on account of the cost,[17] and the dome was simply painted with frescoes. Round the lower part of the walls are the coats-of-arms of the various territories ruled over by the Medici, and one after another incorporated in Tuscany. There are sixteen coats-of-arms representing these various territories, viz.,—FLORENCE, FIESOLE, AREZZO, CORTONA, PISTOIA, PISA, BORGO SAN SEPOLCRO, VOLTERRA, SIENA, MONTE PULCIANO, MONTAL-CINO, GROSSETO, MASSA, PIENZA, CHIUSI, SVANIA. These coats-of-arms are executed in *lapis-lazuli*, mother-of-pearl, jasper, agate, chalcedony, and other precious stones, and are of the very finest quality of *intarsiatura* [18] work known. The whole building is estimated to have cost about £1,000,000 sterling.

It is the fashion to decry the mausoleum, and to compare it with the New Sacristy, calling the latter an abode of art and the former an example of mere tasteless magnificence. But this is a short-sighted view and displays ignorance of the conditions. In this work Ferdinand I carried out the traditions of his family by helping forward the artistic talents of the Florentines of his time. Those talents, on the decay in Painting and Sculpture, now ran in the direction of the minor arts, and particularly of inlay work in stone; and it was only in that direction that assistance to the artistic talents of the Florentines could at this time be afforded. And had the interior decoration of the dome been completed in accordance with the original design, instead of being covered with highly-coloured and inharmonious frescoes, the merits of the building would have been better appreciated. In any case it remains a remarkable memorial of the Medici and of the grandeur of their conceptions; while it gave a valuable impetus to every branch of those arts which deal with work in marble and precious stones.

This work called for a degree of excellence in the art of *pietra dura* (or Florentine mosaic) far in advance of anything which had previously been attempted. Ferdinand had already prepared for this by founding the "Royal Manufactory of Pietra Dura"; [19] and this manufactory was now set to work to execute all the inlay work required for the new mausoleum when the walls should be ready to receive it, thus originating that *pietra dura* industry which has since become one of the most prominent minor arts of Florence. [20]

The great change which had taken place in the fifteenth century in regard to architecture, sculpture, and painting was now to be followed by a similar renaissance in a fourth art—music. And Florence was again to lead the way. It is to Florence, and to the encouragement given to this new departure in music by Ferdinand I, that lovers of music owe the opera. Music in this new movement followed exactly the same course which had been taken by the other arts two centuries earlier, Renaissance thought being always a resurrection of classical ideas, but in a new and original dress. Towards the beginning of Ferdinand's reign a few earnest lovers of music, dissatisfied with the older form of music,

formed themselves into a society with a view to bring about
a reform on the lines of what they believed to have been the
method of the Greeks in their dramas. The object which this
society aimed at was to see whether, instead of musical interludes being here and there introduced into dramas, as was
then the custom, it was not possible to combine drama and
music together, making the latter an integral part of the
former, the drama being sung continuously from beginning
to end, in the same manner as the Greeks had done; and at
the same time to arrive at a style of music which should
interpret the drama performed, music and drama being thus
wedded together. This society numbered among its leading
members a Bardi, a Corsi, and a Strozzi, names which had
long been celebrated in Florence; also Jacopo Peri, Emilio
Cavalieri, Vincenzio Galileo, the poet Ottavio Rinuccini, and
others, and held its earliest meetings in the Bardi palace in
the Via de' Bardi. Thinking of all the enchanting scenic effects
and musical beauty of the modern opera, it is strange to
realise that its birthplace was this dark and grim old palace
in one of the narrowest streets of Florence.

After many efforts the first continuous musical drama was
produced, the opera *Daphne,* the music being by Jacopo Corsi
and Jacopo Peri, and the words by the poet Ottavio
Rinuccini. It was performed for the first time in 1597, in the
great hall of the Uffizi (that now occupied by the State
Archives), in the presence of Ferdinand I and his whole
court. As a result various improvements were introduced,
and the second opera, *Euridice,* being the story of Orpheus
and Eurydice, the music by Peri and the words by Rinuccini,
was performed for the first time in the same hall and before
the same audience, in 1600, at the marriage festivities in
Florence of Marie de Medici.[21] Other operas followed, and
the work of the reformers was finally crowned by Monteverde
in his opera *Ariadne,* produced at Mantua in 1607, and his
opera *Orfeo,* produced in 1608 (the words of both operas again
being by Rinuccini), an achievement which completed the

revolution in musical drama, and which causes Monteverde to take the same place at the beginning of the seventeenth century which was 250 years later taken by Wagner.

In January 1600 a great storm threw down the huge bronze ball and cross crowning the cathedral, made and placed in position with much difficulty by Verrocchio in 1471. In falling they did much damage to the roof of the cathedral, while the ball rolled some distance down the Via de' Servi. Ferdinand had a new ball and cross made, considerably larger than Verrocchio's, and these, which now crown the cathedral, were placed in position in 1602, and have stood the storms of three centuries.

Ferdinand also completed the fortress of San Giorgio which Cosimo had begun, and called it the fortress of the Belvedere, from the beautiful panorama to be seen thence. He made Buontalenti, its architect, construct in it a subterranean chamber, for which Buontalenti invented a secret lock only able to be opened by himself and the Grand Duke; and here the Medici treasure was henceforth always kept. The amount of Ferdinand's treasure was very great; it is recorded in a contemporary diary that he showed to Bernardo Buonarmoti, to whom he gave it in charge, no less than five millions in coined gold, seven thousand Spanish dollars, and an immense mass of jewels.[22]

To the Medici villas of Careggi, Cafaggiolo, Poggio a Caiano, and Castello, which had seen so many generations of the family, Ferdinand now added another, the villa of Petraia,[23] which he purchased from the Salutati family. He completely restored this villa, and had its beautiful central court decorated by Volteranno and other artists with frescoes representing the coronation of Charles V by Clement VII, the entry of Cosimo I into Siena, the institution of the Order of Santo Stefano, and other episodes in the history of the family.

Ferdinand also caused the fine equestrian statue of his father, Cosimo I, to be executed by Gian de Bologna, and set it up in the Piazza della Signoria. It has on the pedestal bronze bas-reliefs representing the three most important episodes of Cosimo's career: (i) his being given the rule of the State by the Council of the Forty-eight; (ii) his triumphal entry into Siena on its conquest and incorporation with Tuscany; and (iii) his being given the rank of Grand Duke by Pius V.

Having completed and set up the statue of his father, Ferdinand then set Gian da Bologna to work upon a similar equestrian statue of himself, that which stands in the Piazza S. S. Annunziata. This statue has considerable interest, not only from being that rendered celebrated by Robert Browning's poem of *The Statue and the Bust*, but also on other grounds. It is made from the bronze guns captured from the Turks in the naval victories gained by Ferdinand's fleet, and bears on the pedestal his private crest, the swarm of bees and motto *"Majestate tantum."* The horse very nearly found its way to Paris, and was the origin of a celebrated statue in that city. In 1605 Marie de' Medici was anxious to present to Paris an equestrian statue of her husband, Henry IV, to be set up on the open ground between the two sections of the Pont-Neuf. As there was no sculptor in France capable of such a work, she wrote to her uncle, Ferdinand I, asking that he would allow Gian da Bologna to execute it. And with this request she coupled another. As Gian da Bologna was eighty-one, and the work would take a long time, she asked her uncle to give her the bronze horse which was then ready to receive his own statue, and to let another be made for himself. But Ferdinand declined to accede to this cool request, being quite as much alive as Marie was to the probability that Gian da Bologna might not live to complete another bronze horse. He, however, suggested that the moulds used for casting his horse might be made use of for that which Marie desired. This was done; though owing to Gian da Bologna's death it was nine years before the statue (including both the horse and the figure of Henry IV [24]) was completed. Its transport, by sea from Leghorn to Havre and thence to Paris, was difficult, but after being dropped overboard near Havre and recovered from the bottom of the sea, the statue reached Paris and was in 1614 set up on the Pont-Neuf, to Marie's great delight. Inside the horse (which was a facsimile of that which bears Ferdinand's statue) was placed an inscription on vellum stating that Ferdinand, Grand Duke of Tuscany, had ordered the statue to be executed by Gian da Bologna, and had it finishd by Pietro Tacca in affectionate memory of Henry IV.

For Francis I Gian da Bologna had executed a statue celebrated all over the world. For Ferdinand I he executed one as little known as the other is well known, viz., his *Genius of the Medici*, represented by a handsome boy holding aloft in one hand one of the Medici balls, and clasping under the other arm a small goat signifying Capricorn, the sign of the zodiac under which Cosimo I was born. While that sculptor's *Mercury*, as Perkins says, "has winged its way to the museums and houses of every quarter of the globe," this other fine specimen of Gian da Bologna's art, and one so interesting in its connection with the Medici, has hitherto been practically unknown. It is owing to the diligent care for the records of the past evinced by Signor Cornish, Director of the Pitti Palace, that this beautiful statue has been brought to light,[25] having hitherto been hidden away uncared for in a back courtyard of the palace.

In 1605 Pope Clement VIII died, and was succeeded by Leo XI (Alessandro de' Medici). He did not belong to this family, not being a descendant of Giovanni di Bicci. He was, however, a distant connection, being descended from a brother of the grandfather of Giovanni di Bicci. He was only Pope for a month, when he died and was succeeded by Paul V (1605-1621).

Ferdinand and Christine had eight children: Cosimo who succeeded his father, Francesco, Carlo, Lorenzo, Eleonora, Caterina, Maddalena, and Claudia. They were all quite young at the time of their father's death, Cosimo, the eldest, being nineteen, and Claudia, the youngest, only five years old.

The last six months of Ferdinand's life were chiefly occupied with arrangements for the marriage of his eldest son. Ferdinand arranged that he should be married to the Archduchess Maria Maddalena, daughter of the Archduke Charles of Austria. It was a very exalted marriage, Maria Maddalena's sister Margaret being already married to Philip III of Spain, while her brother Ferdinand soon afterwards became the Emperor Ferdinand II. The Archduchess came to Florence, and she and Cosimo were married in San Lorenzo in June 1608 with most magnificent ceremonies. On her arrival part of the walls of Florence were thrown down and a new gateway opened in them for her to enter at; and on entering she received the crown of Tuscany from Ferdinand himself, while "the city blazed with magnificence."

This auspicious event closed Ferdinand's life; he died on the 7th February 1609 at the age of sixty, leaving the affairs of the family in a most prosperous condition, his eldest son just married to the sister of one soon to be the Emperor, seven other children growing up, and an enormous treasure safely stored in the fortress of the Belvedere. He was buried with all the pomp which Florence learned to associate with the funeral of its Grand Duke, being interred in the New Sacristy of San Lorenzo pending the completion of the mausoleum which he had inaugurated, and to which his remains were eventually removed.[26] In the crypt of that mausoleum there has recently been placed an interesting memorial of his principal achievement. On the 3rd March 1906, being the tercentenary of the founding of Leghorn, the Antiquarian Society of that city visited the mausoleum, and after an impressive oration by the President of the Society conveying the gratitude which Leghorn felt to the energy and ability of its founder, Ferdinand I, hung a handsome bronze wreath on the wall over his tombstone inscribed with the above date. So that Leghorn still cherishes with gratitude the memory of the Medici.

———————

With Ferdinand I a notable change begins in connection with a feeling which had greatly affected the career of this family in the past, and was to have still greater effects in regard to them after that career had ended.

Writers on their history belonging to other countries have universally found an insoluble problem in the fact that even after the Medici have long since become extinct a virulent animosity against them should still continue to exist, and that they should be under a cloud in the city which they made so great. It was felt that political antipathies, however strong, did not suffice to account for such a result; since these could scarcely continue in sufficient strength to have such an effect after the entire conditions which called them forth had for many generations passed away. It is, however, in another direction that the solution to this problem lies.

The Florentines, with all their many admirable qualities, possess one characteristic which is the real cause of this phenomenon. This is, a power of jealousy in degree almost inconceivable to those of northern race—a characteristic which is to be seen in operation throughout all Florentine history. This it was which in reality created the fierce internecine contests which time after time rent Florence during the thirteenth and fourteenth centuries; this it was which in the fifteenth and sixteenth centuries brought upon the Medici the violent attacks which they experienced eight times in succession during one hundred and fifty years; [27] and this again it is which has caused that strange fact which has puzzled so many writers.

The poorer classes felt a fondness for the Medici family throughout their history, and had ample reason for doing

so; while even to the present day they have a regard for
their memory. But it was far otherwise with all those Florentine families who had originally been on a par with the
Medici, but had in course of time been surpassed by them.
That result was due to the effects of intellectual gifts so
unusual that none need have felt moved by resentment at
it; but nevertheless the families thus surpassed did feel the
bitterest resentment, and made no attempt to hide the fact.

Nor was this all. When a despotic monarchy is succeeded
by a republic there is only one family embittered by the loss
of former greatness. But when a republic is succeeded by a
despotic monarchy there are created an hundred such
families; and these also the most influential in the State.
Since the Christian era the former case has occurred often
in history; but the latter case has only occurred twice—in
the case of Rome, and in that of Florence. But whereas
Augustus [28] carefully avoided all appearance of despotism,
and whereas the notable Roman families were not ousted
from public affairs, the course taken by Cosimo I, though
perhaps forced on him by circumstances, was the exact opposite of that pursued by Augustus. We have seen how he
took every opportunity of showing that he wielded the sole
power, how he ruled without any Council, and how he invariably chose men who were not Florentines as his secretaries. Not a single one of the old Florentine families, whose
members had for centuries held the highest offices in the
State, including frequently that of Gonfaloniere, saw any
one of its members employed by Cosimo even as a secretary.
It may be imagined what fierce wrath such a state of things
created; wrath which, though it dared not show itself, was
all the more carefully nourished by those concerned. The
taking away of a "liberty" which had never resulted in anything but internecine strife might in time have been forgiven; but the deprivation of all the power and importance
to which the leading Florentine families had for generations
been accustomed could never be forgiven; it was a rankling

sore which could never be healed. The Medici, like other families, were not faultless; but even had they been angels the embittered feelings (so widely shared) consequent on the bare fact of a republic being succeeded by a despotic monarchy, were alone sufficient to produce all the charges which have been made against them.

When, therefore, overt attacks had no longer a chance of success, the Medici having become crowned heads supported by Emperors and Popes, these other families, while outwardly acquiescing in that which they felt powerless to reverse, nourished, from generation to generation, an intense jealousy at the height to which this family had attained, and vented that jealousy, no longer in overt attacks, but in the secret fabrication of stories of crime to cast disgrace upon the Medici.

It is here that there originated, from the time of Ferdinand I onwards, those various stories of this nature which have "passed for history," and which, eagerly caught up by the sensation-lovers of all ages and countries, have had so large a part in forming the general idea entertained of the Medici, that atmosphere of the dagger and the bowl by which melodrama loves to surround them. In this manner, years after he was dead,[29] were fabricated against Cosimo I the stories that he had poisoned his own daughter and killed with his own hands one of his sons; and against his sons the stories that two of them had killed each other, that another had ordered the murder of his sister-in-law, that a fourth had murdered his wife, and that a fifth had poisoned his brother and instigated the murder of his sister.[30] Thus envenomed jealousy contrived to accuse every one of Cosimo's five sons of the murder of a brother, a sister, or a wife.[31] Even, however, were all these stories true it would still be the case, as has once before been remarked, that to not many among the ruling families of the fifteenth, sixteenth, and seventeenth centuries have so few crimes of murder been attributed as to the thirteen generations of the

Medici.[32] Therefore it is not owing to an unusual excess of crime that the character generally imputed to them has gained its prevalence. This demonstrates the source where its true origin is to be found.

And when at length the Medici passed away this long-standing jealousy bore fruit in a never-ending vilification of their name, in accusations of their having taken away a "liberty" asserted to have existed before they arose, in the repetition of these legends against them, and in endeavours in all possible ways to obliterate their memory.[33] The Medici, attacked by the sword in their earlier career, were attacked still more virulently by the pen when they were no more, and when there remained no one to defend their memory. Such were the results of the ordinary course of history being reversed by a despotic monarchy succeeding a republic, instead of the opposite case.

Since the publication of *The Cambridge Modern History* it is no longer possible for any one pretending to a knowledge of history to treat these tales of abnormal crimes except as stories finally condemned as entirely without foundation. But they show how great was the jealousy of the other principal families of Florence against the one of their number which had surpassed them, a jealousy which, never laid aside, appeared to grow even stronger after the grave had closed over the last member of the family concerned. Now, however, that a better day has dawned it is time that these methods of a bygone age should be repudiated. The methods themselves have, one may well believe, been abandoned; but their effects still live, and will continue to do so as long as stories of this nature against the Medici, though condemned by history as false, are still repeated by a generation which would not itself stoop to invent them, and by whom such methods cannot but be utterly despised.

CHAPTER XXVII

COSIMO II

Born 1590. (*Reigned* 1609-1620.) *Died* 1620

COSIMO II, the eldest of the eight children of Ferdinand I and Christine of Lorraine, succeeded his father as Grand Duke at the age of nineteen. The good disposition which he inherited from his mother, combined with the excellent training which from his childhood he had received, made him a most agreeable character, and his tolerance, dislike of quarrels and oppression, friendly temperament, and social tastes, caused him to be universally liked. In these respects he was fully seconded by his wife, Maria Maddalena; and under this young and agreeable pair, the court gained an attractiveness it had never had before. Sustermans was now the leading portrait-painter of the time, and his fine portraits of Cosimo and Maria Maddalena in the Corsini Gallery, Florence, enable us to realise the appearance of this young couple at the time that Cosimo began his reign.

With Cosimo II the life of this family seems to enter on a new phase, one in which, during his time, youth, brightness, gaiety, and vivacity, joined to cultured tastes, a free expenditure of great wealth, and warm interest in amazing scientific discoveries were the prevailing features. While he himself was nineteen, his wife Maria Maddalena was the same age as his eldest sister Eleonora, namely eighteen, his sister Caterina was sixteen, his brother Francesco fifteen, and his brother Carlo fourteen; [1] all of them were cultured, accomplished, and abounding with youthful spirits; and this band of young people, gathering others of their own age

about them, made the palace, with their constant entertainments, lightheartedness, and genial sociability, in a short
time full of life and animation. It is a pleasant view that we
have of these sons and daughters of Ferdinand I. Cosimo
himself, with his brothers Francesco, Carlo, and Lorenzo,
all showed in their lives both good qualities of character and
good abilities. Again, in regard to their sisters Eleonora,
Caterina, Maddalena, and Claudia, we hear in no case of
any of those scandals which had disgraced the former generation; and while Eleonora and Maddalena had no opportunity of distinguishing themselves, Caterina and Claudia
both showed in their respective spheres the good qualities
and high abilities they possessed.[2]

One effect of these new conditions was that Cosimo now
determined that the Grand Ducal palace must be much
enlarged and improved in appearance. He accordingly set
about extending it to three times its former size, by increasing the length of the façade from seven windows to thirteen,
and erecting two great wings (three stories high) at right
angles to the back of the building, enclosing a large central
courtyard, with a terrace at the back of the latter on a level
with the rooms on the first floor.[3] The work was rapidly
carried out, all the necessary stone being quarried on the site
itself, the solid rock on which the palace stands having to
be cut away in order to get sufficient level space for the
wings added at the back of it. This great enlargement of the
building, together with the costly additions which Cosimo
at the same time made to the furniture and interior decoration, made the Grand Ducal palace a much more splendid
abode than it hitherto had been.

Not content with this Cosimo also built for his wife,
Maria Maddalena, the palatial villa of Poggio Imperiale
(called so in honour of her with reference to her Imperial
descent), on a site which she particularly admired on the
slope of the hill leading down from Arcetri, outside the

southern environs of the city; to which villa he made the truly
royal road, nearly a mile in length and bordered on each side
with a strip of garden and a double avenue of splendid
cypress trees, which ascends to it from the Porta Romana.
The building has for many years been given by the King
of Italy as a Government College for young ladies, but the
reception rooms are kept much as they were formerly, and
these show various reminiscences of the time when this was
the favourite residence of Cosimo and Maria Maddalena.[4]
Each of these later generations of the family had their
favourite villa, which thus becomes specially associated
with them. With Cosimo I it had been Castello; with Francis
I, Poggio a Caiano; with Ferdinand I, Petraia; but Poggio
Imperiale had a longer period of favour, being not only the
favourite villa of Cosimo II and Maria Maddalena, but also
of Ferdinand II and his generation of the family. Moreover
one important fact connected with it makes it one of the
most interesting buildings of Florence.[5]

But Cosimo II was occupied with other matters more important to the world than the enlargment of the Grand
Ducal palace, the construction of the villa of Poggio Imperiale, and social entertainments. His reign began the
demonstration of a fact not always sufficiently realised, viz.,
that Florence did not only lead the world in Learning and
Art, but in Science also; a fact still further demonstrated
in the reign of his son, Ferdinand II.[6] This fresh addition
to Florence's laurels was begun by a step taken by Cosimo
as soon as he came to the throne which proved the most
important act of his reign, signalising it even more than
that of his father had been signalised by the creation of Leghorn, and bringing lasting renown to Florence, as well as to
his own name. This was his act of inviting back, protecting
from persecution, and establishing in honour in his own
country, the great Galileo, who had eighteen years before
been compelled by jealous animosity to leave it. Galileo

Galilei, born in 1564 at Pisa, had at the early age of twenty-three been appointed Professor of Mathematics at the University of Pisa. And it was there that he made his first great discovery, that which resulted in his invention of the pendulum. The late Signor Vincenzo Antinori, Director of the Scientific Museum of Florence, in his notice of Galileo, says:—

"The pendulum, as is already known, was the result of the first observations of our philosopher in Pisa; it was the spark which kindled his genius, the instrument by which he tested the conceptions of his mind, the torch which led him along the path of his discoveries. The pendulum, by proving the resistance of air, served to confirm him in his theory of gravitation; it likewise illustrated his theory of music by the intersection of waves of sound. The pendulum suspended to a fixed centre suggested to him the motion of the earth, with the moon, round the sun. And it is singular to reflect how the two marvellous discoveries with which he so happily commenced his glorious career, the isochronism of the pendulum and gravitation, should have occupied him at its close."

But in 1592, when Galileo was twenty-eight, he had been forced, owing to the machinations of those who were jealous of his fame and abilities, assisted by the Jesuits (who objected to his new theories), to resign his professorship and retire to Padua, where he had for eighteen years been supporting himself by teaching mathematics, and where Cosimo as a youth had for some time been his pupil.

As soon as he became Grand Duke Cosimo invited Galileo, then forty-six years old, to return to Tuscany, and established him at Florence, giving him a villa at Arcetri (not far from where he was building his own new villa of Poggio Imperiale), and creating for him an appointment as "Chief Mathematician to the Grand Duke," with an annual salary of 1,000 *scudi*.[7] And in this capacity Galileo remained for twenty-three years, provided with a maintenance which left him free to prosecute his scientific studies, and shielded, under the personal protection of the Grand Duke of Tuscany, from the machinations of his enemies both at Florence and Rome; during which time he made the whole of his discoveries. And the subsequent history showed that had it not been for this protection on the part of Cosimo II these discoveries would never have been made by Galileo; for nothing but this protection prevented the Jesuits from silencing him in 1610 as they eventually succeeded in doing in 1633.[8]

The above action on Cosimo's part very quickly produced astonishing results. Shortly after his establishment at Florence Galileo invented the telescope,[9] and in the first year of Cosimo's reign began by its means to make those great discoveries which were destined to revolutionise man's knowledge of his place in the universe.[10] The celebrated astronomer, Sir John Herschel, says:—

"It is difficult to conceive what Galileo must have felt when, having constructed his telescope, he for the first time turned it to the heavens, and saw the mountains and valleys in the moon.—Then the moon was another earth; the earth another planet; and all were subject to the same laws. What an evidence of the simplicity and magnificence of nature! But at length he turned it again, still directing it upwards, and again he was lost: for he was now among the fixed stars; and if not magnified as he expected them to be, they were multiplied beyond measure. What a moment of exultation for such a mind as his!"

The villa of Poggio Imperiale gains a new interest when we realise that it must have been there that all these, and the other great astronomical wonders which during the next two or three years successively became known to Galileo, were first narrated to others. For he would certainly convey them first to one who had made it possible for him to make these discoveries, and who, though he was Grand Duke, Galileo knew to be as keenly interested in the matter as himself. We can imagine the enthusiasm with which, after a night spent among the stars, he would hasten down to relate to Cosimo some fresh discovery; as well as the amazement with which the circle gathered in the Grand Ducal villa on the slope of the Arcetri hill first heard the astounding truths which Galileo had to relate, which revolutionised all that had hitherto been believed on such matters, and proved that the earth was not the centre of the universe, but merely a minute planet in the solar system.

Galileo's celebrated tower at Arcetri,[11] from which "in the still midnight of far-off time its master read the secrets of the stars," [12] stands overlooking Florence from the southern hills: as though to be a constant reminder of all that was from thence unfolded to mankind.

> "We hail
> Thy sunny slope, Arcetri, sung of old
> For its green vine; dearer to me, to most,
> As dwelt on by the great astronomer;
> .   .   .   .   .   Sacred be
> His villa (justly was it called the Gem [13]),
> Sacred the lawn, where many a cypress threw
> Its length of shadow, while he watched the stars." [14]

Thus did Florence, which had led the world in Learning and Art, now that the sovereignty in that domain had passed away from her, place on her brows a fresh crown of leadership, and show the way in that new branch of knowledge, Science, which was henceforth to be the chief interest of the intellect of the world. It was fitting that the Medici should be as closely associated with this new leadership as they had been with that of the past. Nor did their connection with this stepping forth by Florence on a fresh path of renown go without a permanent record. The first hitherto unknown stars revealed by Galileo by his telescope in the first year of Cosimo's reign were the satellites of Jupiter. And to these, in gratitude to one who had made it possible for him to carry on such investigations, Galileo gave the name of *the Medicean stars* (Stellae Medicae). Thus the satellites of Jupiter preserve for all time among scientific men a memorial that the Medici helped to bring about the first great discoveries of modern science.[15] And if the founding of Leghorn is to be considered a "masterpiece" on the part of Ferdinand I, far more may action which enabled these great revelations of science to be made by Galileo be considered so on the part of Cosimo II.

In 1610 Cosimo sent an embassy to France to condole with his cousin, Marie de Medici, on the sudden death of her husband, Henry IV, who was stabbed in his coach while proceeding to a State function; whereupon Marie became Queen Regent of France during the minority of her eldest son Louis, then nine years old. It was remarked that her nine-year-old son was as fit to reign as she was. Cosimo's envoy obtained scant attention from her to his message, for Marie could think of nothing but the grandeur of her coronation as Queen Regent, and constantly interrupted the envoy to describe it to him, and how her throne had "had nineteen steps." Marie's children were, Louis XIII of France; Gaston, Duke of Orleans; Elizabeth, married to Philip IV of Spain; Henrietta Maria, married to Charles I of England; [16] and Christine, married to the Duke of Savoy; while her sister Eleonora's daughter Eleonora married the Emperor Ferdinand II.[17] Thus in the eleventh generation from Giovanni di Bicci we see a Medici seated on the throne of each of the four principal countries of Europe, France, Spain, England, and Germany.[18] Marie's subsequent history was a sad one. As Queen Regent, she was entirely ruled by her Minister, Concini, and her powerful mistress of the robes, Leonora Gallegai, whom she had brought from Florence, and who trafficked in all appointments throughout the kingdom. In 1617 Marie's son, Louis XIII, threw off her authority, confined her at Blois (whence she escaped),[19] and eventually exiled her from

France. Advised by Cardinal Richelieu, he refused to make
her any allowance unless she would return to Florence. But
Marie's pride rebelled against becoming a mere appanage
of the Tuscan court after having been Queen Regent of
France, and nothing would induce her to accede to this; so
she took refuge in Holland. After many hardships from want
of any resources, and a fruitless visit to England in 1636 to
her son-in-law Charles I and her daughter Henrietta Maria,
she retired in great poverty to Antwerp, her children being
all either unwilling or unable to make her any allowance.
Soon, however, she was requested by the authorities to leave
Antwerp, and then migrated to Cologne, where the painter
Rubens, who had often been employed by her when she was
Queen of France,[20] gave her a house to live in. There after
many sufferings she died in 1642 in absolute destitution, it is
said in a hayloft.

Cosimo II was the last of the Medici to be a banker. Soon
after ascending the throne he abandoned the practice of
private trading, closed the family bank with its branches in
various capitals, and discontinued all commerce on his own
account, considering that the practice was derogatory to a
reigning sovereign, as well as harmful to the trade of the
country. The step considerably reduced the income of the
family, but their immense wealth made this of less consequence.

In 1614, when Cosimo was four-and-twenty, and had been
reigning for five years, all his life was changed in consequence
of a severe illness, the result of an attack of malignant fever,
and from this time forward he became a confirmed invalid.
This permanent ill-health forced him to give but little attention to State affairs, which had its effect on the country, inducing a general apathy in public matters, under which the
prosperity of the country declined; and it might have had
more serious results had it not been Cosimo's good fortune
to reign during a time when Europe was at peace, and when

Tuscany was blessed with unusually abundant harvests. At the same time Cosimo's temperate and tolerant disposition made him respected and liked by the people, notwithstanding the undesirable results of a weak rule. And though forced to live a very quiet life, he did not shut himself up in gloomy seclusion, but continued to take interest in the amusements of the people and in social festivities, even though able himself to take little part in them. He also encouraged Art and Literature with all the zeal of his race, making various valuable additions to the family collections.

The political events of Cosimo's reign were few. His chief interest was in his navy, and he took every opportunity of adding to its strength and efficiency. In the construction of new ships he received much assistance from Sir Robert Dudley,[21] who had taken refuge at Leghorn and had great talents for shipbuilding. He invented for Cosimo various new descriptions of ships of war; but it was eventually decided that for the Mediterranean warfare the galleys propelled by oars were better adapted than any other pattern of ship. Cosimo sent his fleet, led by the knights of Santo Stefano, to assist the Druses against the Turks, and in this service they won still further renown. On only one occasion was Cosimo involved in a dispute with another country which threatened to produce serious consequences. When in 1617 Louis XIII threw off his mother's authority he caused her chief Minister, Concini, to be assassinated, and transferred the property of the murdered man to his own favourite, De Luynes. Cosimo took up the cause of Concini's son, refused to recognise the confiscation of property decreed by the French courts, and demanded that the murdered man's son should be allowed to inherit it. Much ill-feeling followed between the two countries, and mutual reprisals, which were only brought to an end by the intervention of the Duke of Lorraine. The Thirty Years' War, which began about a year before Cosimo's death, did not affect Tuscany, which was steadily sinking into a position of less and less importance in the affairs of Europe.

In 1614, the same year that Cosimo's severe illness occurred, the first death took place among the eight brothers
and sisters. Francesco, who had taken up a military career,
and had been nominated to the command of the army, died at
Pisa in December at the age of twenty. In his portrait in the
Uffizi Gallery he wears a very splendid dress, consisting of a
coat of mail with lace collar and ruffles, the peculiar wide
padded breeches of the time, profusely embroidered in red
and gold, and long scarlet-coloured stockings. In his hand
he holds the baton denoting his command of the army. It is
curious to note that on the table by his side he is given a
jewelled coronet, having round it the Florentine lily repeated
five or six times, as worn by the younger brothers and sons
of the Grand Duke; this being the first time that this feature
appears.[22]

Three years later, in December 1617, Cosimo's eldest
sister, Eleonora, died, at the age of twenty-six. She had been
engaged to Philip III of Spain, but he broke off the engagement, and it is stated that Eleonora died of a broken heart
in consequence. In her portrait in the Uffizi Gallery she wears
a jewelled coronet, a high ruff, and a very handsome dress
with long open sleeves, though the full padded skirt has
the effect of making her look very short.[23] Earlier in the same
year Cosimo's second sister, Caterina, then twenty-four, was
married to Ferdinand Gonzaga, Duke of Mantua. On being
left a widow in 1626 she returned to Tuscany, and was made
Governor of Siena, dying there of small-pox in 1629, at the
age of thirty-six, with a reputation for great piety.[24] Caterina's
portrait and that of her sister Claudia, as well as others in
the Pitti Gallery of Cosimo's brothers, show what a strong
family likeness existed between all these brothers and sisters,
all of them having the same peculiar nose and mouth (un-
pleasing, but showing much character) which we see in
Cosimo's portrait, and which they evidently inherited from
their mother, Christine of Lorraine. And it is remarkable
to notice that this feature appears again in yet a third genera-

tion, as can be seen by the portraits of Cosimo's children, Ferdinand II, his four brothers, and their sisters Margherita and Anna.

Cosimo's second brother, Carlo, became a cardinal, and rose to importance at the Vatican, living to the age of seventy. His third brother, Lorenzo, who was twenty when Cosimo died, lived to the age of forty-eight. Lorenzo's twin sister, Maddalena, became a nun at the age of twenty in the convent of the Crocetta a few months after her brother Cosimo's death, and died there in 1633, at the age of thirty-three.[25] The youngest sister of all, Claudia, was married in 1620, the year of her brother Cosimo's death, when she was sixteen, to Federigo della Rovere, the only son of the Duke of Urbino, a worthless boy two years younger than herself, who, however, died of his excesses before he was eighteen, when she returned to Florence with one baby daughter, who was the sole heiress of her grandfather, the old Duke of Urbino.[26]

In 1619, Cosimo's brother-in-law, Maria Maddalena's brother, became the Emperor Ferdinand II.[27] Cosimo's health was by this time rapidly failing, and it being evident that he had not long to live, he made a will by which on his death he appointed his mother, Christine, and his wife, Maria Maddalena, joint Regents of Tuscany during the minority of his eldest son, then ten years old. Cosimo died on the 28th February 1620, at the age of thirty, much regretted by the people, after a reign of eleven years. He left eight children, five sons and three daughters. He had an exceedingly magnificent funeral, being buried at first in the New Sacristy pending the completion of the family mausoleum, to which his remains were, two generations later, removed.[28]

Strangely enough, a mistake has been made with regard to the length of the reigns of Cosimo II and his son Ferdinand II, the former being always stated to have reigned twelve years and the latter forty-nine years, instead of eleven years and fifty years respectively, as was actually the case.

This is owing to a mistake as to the date of the death of Cosimo II which has been stated to be 28th February 1621, even Napier making this mistake and so stating that Cosimo II reigned for twelve years and Ferdinand II for forty-nine years.[29] But that this is an error is clearly proved by the report on the examination of the coffins in 1857 (*see* footnote 28), as the 28th February 1620 is the date found on the leaden plate inside Cosimo II's coffin, and also on the two gold medallions discovered therein; which latter fact is conclusive. It may be wondered how an historian like Napier could be wrong on such a point; but the explanation is that Napier's history was written in 1847, and so before the opened coffin came to bear its silent testimony.

CHAPTER XXVIII

FERDINAND II

Born 1610. (*Reigned* 1620-1670.) *Died* 1670

THE fifty years' reign of Ferdinand II saw a long step made on the downward path on which the once great family was now plainly embarked; and the pace of that descent, which had been slow at first, now quickens. Incipient decay, becoming more and more pronounced, is the keynote of the reign of Ferdinand II, even though there were still many things done which were worthy of the family's best days.

Cosimo II's will included very stringent provisions to ensure that the government should be satisfactorily carried on during the minority of his son. While it laid down that the two Grand Duchesses, his mother and his wife, were to be joint Regents, it also ruled that they were to be assisted by a council of four Ministers, who were named. The salary of each of these four members of the council was limited to 2,000 crowns. No foreigner of any sort was to hold any office of State, or even of domestic service in the court. No resident ambassador from any country was to be allowed at Florence, those of France, Spain, and Austria being expressly debarred. All private trade by the Regents was prohibited. And, above all, the opening of Cosimo's treasure-vaults was absolutely forbidden, except to pay the marriage portion of a princess, or to give public aid in a time of national calamity. The penalty for infringing these conditions was deprivation of office as his children's guardians.[1] But these provisions, carefully drawn up as they were, only served to afford an example of how easily all such arrangements can be set aside.

The Grand Duchess Christine was now fifty-six, while her daughter-in-law, the Grand Duchess Maria Maddalena, was thirty. Both were excellent women; but they were without any talent for governing; they were still less endowed with the smallest financial ability; and they were excessively fond of pomp and splendour. Never before had such gorgeous magnificence been displayed by the court as now ensued under their rule. They were accompanied on all occasions by a numerous retinue arrayed in the richest costumes,[2] were surrounded by every accessory which could add to their grandeur, and seem to have considered it incumbent on them to make as splendid a display as possible in order to maintain in proper style the importance of the young Grand Duke for whom they were Regents. Everything was done with the utmost extravagance, money being spent in the most lavish way on every matter which they took in hand. Added to this the Grand Duchess Christine, who took the lead, was intensely bigoted, and ready to fall an easy prey to the numerous ecclesiastics who gathered round her, and who in a very short time had established a strong control over all Tuscan affairs; while every order emanating from Rome, no matter how harmful to the country or disastrous to the fortunes of the family, was received by her with the most abject submission.

The results were those to be expected from such conditions. The provisions of Cosimo's will were ignored; the immense treasure which he had left, and ordered not to be drawn upon except in case of public emergency, was all squandered during the eight years' regency of the two Grand Duchesses; want of administrative talent and subordination to priestly influence produced corruption and misgovernment in every department of public affairs; and under this state of things the country sank more and more into a condition of poverty and misrule; while the only persons who profited were the crowds of ecclesiastics, and the so-called "converts," each of whom on the recommendation of a priest received a pension from the Regents. Sustermans' portrait of the Grand Duchess Christine (who was primarily responsible for these results) shows her wearing the heavy black dress, widow's cap, and immense black veil which she always wore after her husband Ferdinand I's death. In her hand she has a locket with his likeness, no rings on her fingers, and no other ornament except a large gold cross.

The Grand Duchess Maria Maddalena necessarily took only a secondary part in the affairs of the Regency, to which her nomination was perhaps intended mainly as a formality, it being recognised that the chief power would rest with her mother-in-law. Being left at her husband Cosimo's death with eight small children all below the age of ten, she had, in bringing them up, plenty of domestic cares to be added to those of government of the country. Besides her eldest son Ferdinand, her other children were Maria Cristina (twin sister to Ferdinand, born 1610), Giovanni Carlo (born 1611), Margherita (born 1612), Mattias (born 1613), Francesca (born 1614), Anna (born 1616), and Leopold (born 1617). In bringing up her children the Grand Duchess Maria Maddalena showed considerable sense, for her sons were all given a very high class of education, the excellence of which they demonstrated in their after lives; while a broad-minded policy was shown in the fact that notwithstanding the strong ecclesiastical influence which pervaded the court they were all in turn sent to be taught science by Galileo. The portrait of Maria Maddalena [3] shows her in her court dress as Regent, with her crown by her side, the crown being very large and somewhat different from that of her mother-in-law.[4]

Ferdinand, the eldest son of Cosimo II, was a boy of a thoroughly good disposition, his gentle and affectionate nature being conspicuous, while his constant endeavour when he grew up to secure peace in Italy caused him to become noted as a peacemaker. But he had one fatal flaw—a want of strength of character; while the influences by which his grandmother's subordination to priestly domination caused him to be surrounded from a very early age were such as tended to increase this defect. His portrait by Sustermans, in the Pitti Gallery, at the age of fourteen shows him wearing armour, but he did not display any military talents. In 1623, when he was thirteen, his young aunt Claudia returned to Florence as a widow of nineteen with her infant daughter, Vittoria della Rovere, and Ferdinand was forthwith betrothed to this child in order to unite the Duchy of Urbino (which would be her inheritance when her grandfather, the Duke of Urbino, died) with Tuscany. The document drawn up on the occasion of this betrothal specially laid down that Vittoria's dowry was to be the Duchy of Urbino, which was to be incorporated with Tuscany.

But a few months later Pope Gregory XV, who had succeeded Paul V in 1621, died, and was succeeded by Urban VIII (1623-1644), whose main endeavour was to enrich in every way his family, the Barberini. Urban VIII soon after becoming Pope put forward a claim on behalf of the Church to the State of Urbino whenever its aged Duke, Francesco Maria della Rovere II, who was then eighty and in failing health, should die, claiming that it would then be a "vacant fief," and as such would belong to the States of the Church. This claim was the more outrageous in that the Duchy of Urbino not only belonged to the child Vittoria della Rovere as her grandfather's sole heir, but also, supposing she was to be set aside on account of being a girl, it then devolved upon the boy Ferdinand himself. When Christine of Lorraine was betrothed to Ferdinand I, Catherine de' Medici gave her as her dowry 600,000 crowns, a transfer to her of all Catherine's rights in the Medici property in Florence, and also of the latter's claim on the Duchy of Urbino, which had never been annulled even when Adrian VI restored the dukedom to Francesco Maria della Rovere I.[5] Thus Ferdinand II claimed

Urbino on a double ground. First, he claimed it as being the lawful property of his betrothed wife Vittoria, she being the only child of the Duke's only son, and not to be set aside by a Papal "bull of investiture" limiting the succession to heirs male only, seeing that the Dukes of Urbino did not admit that their title to their hereditary Duchy depended on any such bull of investiture. Secondly, if Vittoria's claim was set aside, then Ferdinand claimed Urbino in his own right as inherited from Catherine de' Medici, the daughter of Lorenzo (Duke of Urbino); on the ground that though the Duchy of Urbino had been given back by Adrian VI to Francesco Maria della Rovere, yet the Medici family had never acquiesced in this transfer of Urbino from them; this being witnessed to by the fact that on all occasions Clement VII had styled his relative Catherine "Duchess of Urbino," and that she was even so styled in her formal marriage documents. Moreover, that this fact also proved that there was at that time, at all events, no restriction of the succession to heirs male only. He therefore maintained that the will of Catherine de' Medici made him, Ferdinand, the lawful Duke of Urbino supposing Vittoria's claim was set aside. Nevertheless the Papal troops were marched into Urbino, ready to take possession of it the moment that the octogenarian Duke should breathe his last. All that the Pope would concede was that Vittoria should inherit the movable property of the Duke.

In 1625,[6] when Ferdinand was fifteen, his aunt Claudia, then twenty-one, married again, and this time more satisfactorily. She was married at Innsbruck to Leopold V, Archduke of Tyrol, the brother of her sister-in-law Maria Maddalena and of the Emperor Ferdinand II. Claudia's home henceforth was the Schloss Amras,[7] beautifully situated amidst the pine woods and waterfalls on the lower slope of the mountains overlooking Innsbruck, but with its small rooms and restricted area somewhat of a change from the magnificent

Grand Ducal palace of Tuscany. Claudia did not take her daughter Vittoria with her to Innsbruck, but as the latter was betrothed to Ferdinand left her at Florence in charge of her own sister Maddalena, in the convent of the Crocetta, where Vittoria was brought up until she was fourteen. By her second marriage Claudia had two sons and two daughters. When in 1632 her husband Leopold died, she was appointed Regent of Tyrol on behalf of her young son, and ruled that country well during the most difficult time in its history, showing herself a woman of much ability. She was Regent from 1632 to 1646, and not only greatly improved the administration and resources of Tyrol, but also by her wisdom and watchful care over the defences of the country she saved it from being drawn into the Thirty Years' War in which all the rest of the German empire was involved. In the museum at Innsbruck is to be seen a large picture depicting her sitting on her throne presiding at a meeting of the Landstag on the occasion of an urgent national crisis. Her eldest son, Ferdinand Karl, married his first cousin, Anna de' Medici.[8] Claudia's fine portrait by Sustermans in the Uffizi Gallery shows her as she was at the age of thirty; in her dress there is an absence of the excessive ornament then so much in fashion; she has also dropped the high "Medici" collar, and wears a small plain one. In the corridor between the Uffizi and Pitti Galleries there is also a fine portrait of her husband, the Archduke Leopold, dressed in a tunic of yellow leather much embroidered, long yellow leather boots reaching to the thigh, a wide sash round the waist to keep his sword in its place, and by his side his helmet with a huge plume of blue and white ostrich feathers, which, since the whole structure represents a height of about three feet, must have been highly inconvenient when riding.

In 1627, Ferdinand, being then seventeen, was sent on a tour to see something of the world before beginning to rule on his own account. He went first to Rome, but there the

numerous Barberini family, full of pride, and hating the
Medici owing to the opposition they had experienced on their
behalf in the matter of Urbino, behaved towards him with
great insolence, and he departed thence to Vienna to visit
his uncle, the Emperor Ferdinand II, where, with the love
of peace which was his characteristic, he made an endeavour
to bring to an end the dispute taking place over the succession
to the Duchy of Mantua; in which, however, he was unsuccessful. In 1628 he returned home, and took over charge of
the government; but his feeling for his mother and grandmother would not allow him entirely to deprive them of
authority; so that they continued to exercise a considerable
influence in the government. Shortly after his return his
second sister, Margherita, then seventeen, was married to
Eduardo Farnese, Duke of Parma.[9] This marriage strengthened the position of Tuscany in the politics of Italy, constantly troubled as these were by Urban VIII, Parma and
Tuscany becoming allies; while it was also of considerable
importance in its consequences two generations later when,
the throne of Tuscany threatening to become vacant owing
to Cosimo III having no grandchildren, it was held that after
the demise of Cosimo's daughter the rightful heirs to that
throne were Margherita's descendants belonging to the house
of Parma.[10]

In the following year the quarrel over the succession to
Mantua caused Richelieu, the all-powerful Minister of
France, to send a French army across the Alps which occupied Susa, while the Austrian army seized Mantua; but the
conflict did not spread into Tuscany, though the latter State
had to mobilise its whole military strength and remain in a
state of preparedness for war. Soon afterwards Florence suffered from an outbreak of the plague, which raged with great
violence for many months, and plunged the city into the
utmost misery. In this time of distress the measures taken by
Ferdinand were worthy of his ancestors, the earlier Medici.
Money and provisions were liberally distributed to the poor,

150,000 ducats being given to those of the wool and silk trades alone; and Rondinelli, who was an eye-witness, says that all that was done was wisely directed, "not in mere donations, but also in useful works and agricultural labours." [11] Lazzarettos were organized, and a general quarantine established; the court retired into the fortress of the Belvedere, which, occupying a high eminence, enjoyed fresher air than the Grand Ducal palace at the foot of the hill; but Ferdinand and his young brothers, Giovanni Carlo, Mattias, and Francesco, "nobly disdaining this shelter while the people were perishing, went daily into the city, and with hand and voice administered comfort to the sufferers." [12] The pestilence raged for thirteen dismal months, during which time in and around the city twelve thousand people died. Ferdinand established a Board of Health, and this body issued many wise regulations, while they also forced the inmates of the immense number of monasteries and convents with which the city was crowded both to obey sanitary rules, and also to bear their share in receiving and helping those who were convalescent. But Ferdinand's sound sanitary regulations were denounced by the priests as impious; the Pope demanded that the Board of Health should be censured, and required that a severe penance should be exacted from its members; and Ferdinand, unable to resist the pressure of his bigoted grandmother, was forced, notwithstanding his own and the general indignation, to comply with these arbitrary demands; with the result that the Board of Health was made to do penance for having adopted measures which were in every way right and desirable.

In 1631 the war-cloud departed from Italy to spread instead over Germany, Richelieu brought the celebrated Gustavus Adolphus, King of Sweden, into the contest, and the latter ran his short but brilliant course of victory. Ferdinand's two brothers, Mattias and Francesco (then respectively eighteen and seventeen), were both eager to take part in the great events occurring north of the Alps; and the

Grand Duchess Maria Maddalena being also anxious to visit her brother the Emperor, in order to see whether he could not assist to prevent the Pope from seizing Urbino when its Duke should die, accompanied by her sons Mattias and Francesco on this journey. Unfortunately, however, she fell ill on the way, and died at Passau in November, her body being brought back to Florence by her two sons, and buried in San Lorenzo.[13]

And so passes away another of this family who deserves an honourable record. As a young wife Maria Maddalena, high born, virtuous, sensible, and charming in character and manners, had come to Florence bringing brightness, joy, and animation with her, had helped to keep the life of the court free from scandals, and with her accomplished sisters-in-law had made the Grand Ducal palace and her villa of Poggio Imperiale centres of joyous social amusement and relaxation. When her husband's health failed she had proved herself an efficient helpmeet to him, bearing alone the burden of the court entertainments which he wished still to be kept up, showing herself able to give him helpful advice, and in every way smoothing his life as an invalid. Lastly, when he died and she was left as Regent of the country and at the same time a young mother with a large family of small children, she showed herself gifted with sound sense and courage in the manner she brought them up despite the narrow-minded tendencies by which she was surrounded. And however much she may have been wanting in administrative and financial ability, she deserves high praise for this other portion of her work. Every one of her five sons showed in their after lives the effects of a good bringing up and of a large-minded tolerant spirit learnt in their early years; and while her son Francesco died too soon to evince any special ability, her other four sons all made themselves greatly distinguished not only by their good qualities of character but also by their high attainments. Her daughter Maria Cristina died at twenty-two, but her other two daughters, Margherita and Anna, both showed in after years good qualities and marked ability. When at the age of forty Maria Maddalena died, her son Ferdinand and his sister Maria Cristina were twenty-one, her sons Giovanni Carlo, Mattias, Francesco, and Leopold were respectively twenty, eighteen, seventeen, and fourteen, her daughter Margherita was nineteen, and her daughter Anna fifteen years old. As in the Boboli gardens one sits in the long *pergola* (now so empty and deserted) which is always associated with her memory, it inevitably arouses a vision of the past as one is drawn to think of how different it must have looked in Maria Maddalena's day, when thronged with the gay crowd of young people whom she and her two elder sisters-in-law gathered round them in the first years after her marriage, or later on with the brilliant embroideries and brocades of the gorgeously dressed retinue (pictured for us in the gallery hard by) who followed her in the days of her Regency, or again with the joyous groups of her young sons and daughters and their numerous companions who surrounded her in the last few years of her life.

Their mother's funeral being over, Mattias and Francesco again prepared to proceed northwards, and as Gustavus Adolphus was threatening to cross the Alps and bring the war into Italy, these two brothers in 1632 started from Florence with money, arms, and two regiments supplied by Tuscany to assist against him, and to learn war in Germany under the great Wallenstein. Soon afterwards, however, the whole aspect of affairs was changed by the battle of Lutzen in November 1632, at which Gustavus Adolphus was killed, and Richelieu's pride for a time humbled. In this same year Ferdinand's twin sister Maria Cristina died in August, at the age of twenty-two, at the villa of Poggio Imperiale, the favourite residence of this generation of the family.[14]

Meanwhile Francesco della Rovere II, Duke of Urbino, at length died at the age of eighty-two. The Papal troops at once took possession of Urbino, almost before the breath was out of his body; while the Emperor Ferdinand II was too much occupied with the war in Germany to be able to take up the cudgels on his nephew's behalf and prevent this seizure of Urbino, as he otherwise would have done; and Ferdinand, feeling himself unable to resist a Pope without assistance, and hampered by his grandmother's opposition to such a course, as being sacrilege, had to acquiesce in seeing his and his future wife's inheritance robbed from them. The matter created much bad blood between the Barberini and Medici families; Cosimo II's brother Lorenzo made strong endeavours to get Philip IV of Spain [15] to oppose the Pope's action, but his efforts were unsuccessful, and only recoiled upon himself.[16] The general result of the whole affair was that Pope Urban VIII nourished an undying hatred against the Medici throughout his pontificate, thwarting them on all occasions, making every priest and monk in Tuscany an enemy of the Government, and creating incessant difficulties in the administration of a country in which priestly influence was supreme; while by the weakness which Tuscany had displayed over this question of Urbino it lost all weight in European politics. It was a difficult position for a youth of twenty-two to have to confront; and though a Cosimo I would have met it and overcome the difficulties (no doubt with much bloodshed), Ferdinand II was not cast in so strong a mould.

It was not long before Urban VIII found a means of venting his spleen upon Ferdinand, and in a manner which has had the effect of bringing a lasting slur upon the reign of the latter. Galileo, since his achievements in the first year of Cosimo II's reign, had during the years 1609-1632 made many and marvellous astronomical discoveries, in the course of which he had had to carry on a perpetual contest with the Jesuits, who endeavoured in every way to silence him. In 1611 [17] he had visited Rome, had demonstrated his various discoveries to Pope Paul V, and been well received by the latter. Returning to Florence, and publishing more and more astronomical wonders, he was in 1616 summoned by Paul V

to Rome, where his statement that the earth revolved round
the sun was condemned by the Inquisition; whereupon he
ostensibly acquiesced in the falseness of his theory,[18] and
promised not to republish this doctrine. During the next
seventeen years (1616-1633) Galileo, though still attacked
by the theologians, had lived more or less at peace under the
ægis of the Grand Duke, going again to Rome in 1624, and
being received there with honour by the new Pope, Urban
VIII. He again went to Rome in 1630, on which occasion he
received a "caution" to make his books purely mathematical
and not doctrinal, and with this caution was allowed to publish them. In 1632 he published his *Dialogues*. By this time,
however, the affair of Urbino had occurred, the Pope was
incensed with the Grand Duke of Tuscany, and the weakness
of the latter had been fully displayed. Galileo was therefore
in 1633 charged with having gone back from his promise of
1616, and summoned to appear before the Inquisition in
Rome, to answer for his writings which, in maintaining the
fixed position of the sun and the movement of the earth round
it, propounded a doctrine which was declared by the Pope
to be in flat contradiction to the Bible. The causes for this
arraignment of Galileo are said to have been twofold, the
bitter animosity of the Jesuits against all genuine philosophy,
and the enmity of the Pope against the Medici, whose special
protégé Galileo had been for more than twenty years.

Accordingly commissioners were sent from Rome with
orders to conduct Galileo [19] thither, notwithstanding that he
pleaded illness; and Ferdinand II and his grandmother, the
Grand Duchess Christine, stood far too much in awe of
priestly condemnation to think of offering any opposition to
this arbitrary proceeding. At Rome Galileo, now seventy
years old and broken in health, was threatened with torture
by the Inquisition; his theories were formally condemned, he
was made to recant on his knees his so-called errors, and especially to declare his doctrine as to the movement of the earth
false, and was kept a prisoner until the Pope's will regarding

him should be made known. Ferdinand II has received much execration for having permitted the Pope thus to treat Galileo. For Ferdinand's weakness there is nothing to be said, but it would seem that the blame cast upon him in the matter has been excessive, and that it has not been sufficiently realised that he was still to a very large extent under the domination of his grandmother, the Grand Duchess Christine, especially in a matter which touched religion, and that he had been brought up to consider opposition to a Pope's direct command as a deadly sin which nothing could excuse. He must have changed his nature before he could have withstood a Pope's condemnation on a point of this kind.

Galileo having thus recanted his "errors" was condemned by the Inquisition to perpetual imprisonment, but the Pope commuted the sentence to residence in retirement in the gardens of S.S. Trinità al Monte, and after a short time there he was allowed to remove to Florence, where after residing for a little space under the personal charge of the Archbishop he was permitted, though still a prisoner of the Inquisition, to move to his villa at Arcetri on condition that he lived in retirement and received no visitors; but he never published anything more. In 1634 he lost his only daughter, a, nun, Maria Celeste, who had been his chief comfort in his troubles; and in 1637 was allowed by the Inquisition to move to his house in the Costa San Giorgio,[20] but on condition that he did not go out into the city. There Ferdinand, who had been his pupil as a boy (and who had been aimed at by the Pope together with him), visited the old man and condoled with him on the unjust treatment he had received.[21] Galileo soon afterwards became blind, and when Milton visited him in 1638 was no longer able to see anything more of those wonders of the heavens which he had explored. He retired again to Arcetri, and consecrated to science the last remains of his energies, with a heart full of remembrance of his beloved daughter, "who," he wrote, "calls me, calls me continually; while I wait to change my present prison for that community

august and eternal." But he was comforted, he said, with two
thoughts, "that I have not ever declined from piety and
reverence for the Church, and my own conscience." He died
at Arcetri in January 1642 without any enmity against those
who had spoilt his life.[22]

Ferdinand was anxious to erect a monument to him, but
the Jesuits opposed this, and as usual prevailed, and Ferdinand had to content himself with giving Galileo burial in
the chapel of the Medici family in the church of Santa Croce.
It is, however, pleasant to record that this wrong done by
the Jesuits to Galileo's memory was rectified by the Medici
ere they passed away; and the very last year of their rule
was signalised by the deserved honour to Galileo being at last
given, by the erection in 1737 in the nave of Santa Croce of
the fine monument to him, his remains being removed to it
from the chapel of the Medici. Dean Stanley says that it was
from the burial of Galileo and Michelangelo in this church
that Santa Croce gradually became the recognised shrine of
Italian genius; [23] while Byron, in enumerating those whose
dust makes Santa Croce glorious,[24] makes special mention
of Galileo:—

> "In Santa Croce's holy precincts lie
> Ashes which make it holier, dust which is
> Even in itself an immortality,
> Though there were nothing save the past, and this,
> The particle of those sublimities
> Which have relapsed to chaos:—here repose
> Angelo's, Alfieri's bones, and his
> The starry Galileo, with his woes."

In 1633 (the year that Galileo was summoned to Rome)
the plague again broke out in Florence; and this time there
was no Board of Health, former experience having very
effectually put a stop to any further action of that kind.
Instead, therefore, of wise sanitary measures superstition
reigned supreme, accompanied by religious ceremonies which
in puerility and intellectual abasement surpassed everything
previously seen. The *Madonna dell' Impruneta* was brought to

Florence and carried through the streets, "followed by crowds whose contact gave fresh vigour to the pestilence"; and for many months Florence again became a city of mourning.

In 1634, Vittoria della Rovere being now fourteen, the marriage between her and Ferdinand took place. Brought up in the seclusion of the convent of the Crocetta, Vittoria to a naturally frivolous disposition added an entire ignorance of all the circumstances of ordinary life, together with "a most profound admiration for everything connected with the Church." It was easy, therefore, to see that she was not the sort of person likely to be of much assistance to Ferdinand in the difficulties which surrounded him through the dominance of the Jesuits and other ecclesiastical orders over the country. She brought with her as her dowry the movable property of the Duke of Urbino, and this added many valuable pictures to those already possessed by the Medici. In the Uffizi Gallery the portrait by Piero della Francesca of Federigo di Montefeltro, Duke of Urbino, and his Duchess, of Pope Julius II by Raphael, of Francesco della Rovere I and Eleonora Gonzaga by Titian, the two pictures of the *Reclining Venus* by Titian, and the portrait of Francesco della Rovere II by Baroccio; and in the Pitti Gallery the portrait of Guidobaldo della Rovere II (Vittoria's grandfather) by Zuccheri, the *Magdalen* by Titian, *La Bella* by Titian, the portrait called the *Englishman* by Titian, and the *Martyrdom of St. Agatha* by Sebastian del Piombo, besides many others of lesser note, all formed part of Vittoria's dowry, which also included a valuable collection of majolica and Urbino-ware, most of which now forms part of the treasures of the museum of the Bargello. This marriage was shortly afterwards followed by the death, at the age of twenty, of Ferdinand's manly young brother Francesco, who died, greatly regretted by all, in the camp of the Imperial army before Ratisbon, of the plague. His portrait by Sustermans, which hangs in one of the rooms of the villa of Poggio a Caiano, shows him as he was at eighteen. He wears armour, but it has only to be compared with that of his ancestor Giovanni delle Bande Nere to see that armour is by this time no longer worn for use, but merely for show. And the large lace collar, the lace cuffs, and the sash, not worn round the waist as hitherto, but over the shoulder, all tell the same tale.

In 1636 Ferdinand, ashamed of the many humiliations he suffered from the subordination of the whole country to the Jesuits, and at the state of misgovernment to which it had thereby been reduced, had just resolved to emancipate himself from the Grand Duchess Christine's authority and to rule independently, when in December of that year she died, at the age of seventy-two.[25] Excellent as she was as the mother of a family, and in the social sphere, she was hopelessly incapable of ruling; and the country never recovered from the effect of the clause of Cosimo II's will which entailed upon it sixteen years of the rule of a woman utterly unfitted for such a task. When she died Tuscany had become almost more under the domination of the ecclesiastics than Rome itself; clerics of every kind and degree swarmed throughout the country; nearly every office was in their power; they treated the Grand Duke's officials with insolence, telling them that they would obey no laws and pay no taxes but such as had the authority of the Pope; most of the property of the country was owned by monastic orders, and therefore exempt from taxation; there were over four thousand nuns in Florence alone; the people were crushed by taxation borne by only a portion of the population; trade and agriculture were languishing; and licentiousness, crime, and ferocity (going unpunished for lack of the strong hand), were rampant. The Inquisition held its gloomy court in the cloisters of Santa Croce, the most dreaded place in Florence, whither all who did not please the Jesuits were likely sooner or later to find themselves summoned. Torture, confiscations, and penalties, under the orders of the "Holy Office," became common things to the Florentines; and the dismal pomp of the horrible *Auto-da-fé* threw its lurid glare over that Piazza Santa Croce which once had shone with the joy and brightness of Lorenzo's and Giuliano's tournaments.

Not even when Ferdinand came to rule independently was there at first much change in this latter respect. It was in the year 1641 that in the great hall of the refectory of Santa Croce there took place, in the presence of the Princes of the Blood, the nobility, and the whole of the Ministers and high officials of the Government, the celebrated trial of Pandolfo Ricasoli, a canon of the cathedral, and a man of much learning and respectability, who was accused (whether truly or falsely will never be known) of grave and scandalous immoralities; and he and one Faustina Mainardi, who was asserted to be his accomplice, after first doing penance in the Piazza Santa Croce "in garments painted with flames and devils," were condemned to be walled up alive in one of the dungeons of Santa Croce; which sentence was carried out.[26] It is evident that Ferdinand had strong doubts whether the whole charge was not simply due to bitter animosity on the part of another ecclesiastic. He censured the latter for over-officiousness in the way he brought forward the accusation, and eventually effected his removal from Florence to Rome; thence, however, the same individual was shortly afterwards sent back to Florence promoted to the high office of head of the Inquisition in that city. The insult was one of many which Pope Urban VIII contrived to give Ferdinand in revenge for the opposition which he had encountered from the Medici to his seizure of Urbino.

But though Ferdinand thus failed for a long time to exert any successful opposition to the dominant power of the Jesuits, in other directions he gradually brought about improvements, more especially as his brothers began to grow older and to assist him in public affairs. Moreover, finding it so difficult to bring about a satisfactory state of things in regard to the administration of the country so long as Urban

VIII was Pope, he turned his attention to other matters in which his abilities were better able to find scope. The family now consisted of Ferdinand and Vittoria (he being by this time thirty and she nineteen); Prince Giovanni Carlo,[27] now twenty-nine; Prince Mattias, twenty-seven; the Princess Anna, twenty-four; and Prince Leopold, twenty-three. One sister and one brother were dead, while the third sister (Margherita) was Duchess of Parma. Under the influence of his young wife Vittoria the splendour of the court continued to increase, and in 1640 Ferdinand determined on a further enlargement of the Grand Ducal palace. The enlargement of the palace which Ferdinand now carried out again nearly doubled it in size. Cosimo II's additions had made the palace a large square block, three storeys high, the façade towards the Via Romana having thirteen windows. To this Ferdinand now added two more great wings (two stories high) in prolongation, each way, of the front portion of the palace, thus increasing the façade to its present length of twenty-three windows, at the same time adding the buildings round the two inner courtyards. At the eastern end he constructed a corridor uniting that end of the palace with the *Passaggio*.[28]

These additions gave a magnificent range of State apartments on the first floor, consisting of about sixty rooms, the private apartments being chiefly on the upper floor. As soon as the additions to the palace were completed Ferdinand caused the whole of the apartments on the first floor to be splendidly decorated with ceiling-paintings by Piero Berretini da Cortona, Ciro Ferri, and other artists. The recent discoveries in astronomy made by Galileo were memorialised in these decorations, each of the new rooms being dedicated to one of the planets (or to such subjects as *Prometheus*, the *Iliad*, *Flora*, etc.), and Cortona's splendid ceiling-paintings being made to accord with the dedication.

Thus increased to its present size the Grand Ducal palace of Tuscany became a model which several other sovereigns endeavoured in after years to copy,[29] though without attaining the same result. Fergusson, speaking of it in his *History of Architecture,* says:—

"The façade is 460 feet in extent, three stories high in the centre, each story 40 feet in height, and the immense windows of each 24 feet apart from centre to centre: with such dimensions as these even a brick building would be grand; but when we add to this the boldest rustication all over the façade, and cornices of simple but bold outline, there is no palace in Europe to compare to it for grandeur." [30]

And Taine says:—

"Je doute qu'il ỳ ait un palais plus monumental en Europe; je n'en ai vu qui laisse une impression si grandiose et si simple."

The palace which the Medici had built in 1430 in the Via Larga had surpassed all others of the fifteenth century; but no less did that which nine generations later they built at the foot of the Boboli hill surpass all royal palaces in Europe of the seventeenth century. Some idea of its dimensions is afforded by the fact that the central courtyard (round three sides of which the centre block of the palace is built) is exactly the size of the Strozzi palace in the Via Tornabuoni. It is sometimes said that this was done intentionally, in order to be able to say that the entire Strozzi palace could be placed in the central court of the palace of the Medici; [31] but whether it had any such intention or not, the fact helps us to realise the size of the palace built round this courtyard.

The palace is built directly upon the natural rock; in fact in one of the two inner courtyards the floor of the courtyard is the plain rock, lines having been cut on it to give it the appearance of being paved; and in the same courtyard are (in the walls of some of the ground-floor rooms) ornamental gratings by looking through which the virgin rock may be seen actually forming part of the outer walls of these rooms.

Built on such foundations it is no wonder that the palace presents such an appearance of solidity.

The size and form of the building are not apparent in looking at it from the front, because the two-storied portions added by Ferdinand II, projecting as these do far on either side of the centre block, hide the great wings which extend backwards at right angles to the front on both sides of the central courtyard. Owing to the unusual shape of the palace there is no point from which the whole form of it can be seen; so that from whichever side regarded it always looks smaller than it really is; and it is only by walking all round it, or traversing the interior, that its size can be appreciated. The latter is also more particularly dwarfed in the view of the front of the palace owing to the fact that when looking at the building from that point the projecting corner of the upper storey, while preventing the side wall of the centre block from being seen, also gives the impression that the upper story is only one room in depth; whereas there are more than fifty rooms on that storey.

The interior arrangements of the palace remain at the present day very little different from what they were in the time of the Medici, notwithstanding that it has since been occupied by two other dynasties. The ground floor contains the Grand Ducal chapel, a labyrinth of large vaulted rooms accommodating various offices connected with the palace, and the three rooms (known collectively as the Treasure Room) [32] containing the gold plate and rare china for State occasions and many other valuable heirlooms of the Medici.[33] Beneath one of these halls on the ground floor is to be seen the large swimming bath which was constructed by Ferdinand II at the last enlargement of the palace.[34] The Grand Ducal chapel remains as it was in the time of the Medici Grand Dukes; the high altar, a mass of the finest and most costly kind of *pietra dura* work, was given to it by Cosimo III. The grotto under the terrace at the back of the central court (with marble Cupids swimming on the water of the fountain)

has on its walls the arms of Vittoria della Rovere. Ascending
to the first floor we find the eastern end of the former State
apartments occupied by the picture gallery, in sixteen large
rooms decorated with Cortona's beautiful ceiling-paintings,
with, opening from the end of these rooms, the rest of the
State apartments (twenty rooms) and the fifteen rooms which
were occupied, until Florence ceased to be the capital, by the
late King of Italy. The hall which in the time of the Medici
Grand Dukes was their Throne Room [35] (situated in the
original portion of the palace built by Cosimo I) is entirely
painted, both on the arched roof and walls, with frescoes,
executed in the time of Ferdinand I, by Pocetti,[36] representing
the founding of Leghorn, the battles of Ferdinand's army
and navy with the Turks, the attack and capture of Bona
from the Barbary pirates by the knights of Santo Stefano,
and other deeds of Ferdinand I and his father. In this hall is
now placed the beautiful bronze statue, executed for Ferdinand I by Gian da Bologna,[37] of the *Genius of the Medici;*
also the costly ornamental cabinet presented to Anna Maria
Ludovica by the city of Paris.[38] The rooms which were those
of the Grand Duchess Vittoria della Rovere have on the
ceiling-paintings her motto and family arms, the oak. In the
rooms which were those of the Grand Duchess Marguerite
Louise of Orleans (wife of Cosimo III) are various pictures
by French artists. In another room is to be seen the fine
portrait which Paolo Veronese painted of the Grand Duke
Francis I. And in various rooms are specimens of the finest
work of the Tapestry Manufactory founded by Cosimo I,
and of the Pietra Dura Manufactory founded by Ferdinand
I. On the upper floor are, in the right wing the range of
apartments occupied by the present King of Italy when in
Florence (including the private ball-room and private dining-
room), in the left wing the apartments set apart for guests
of the court, and in the centre, facing the piazza in front of
the palace, the private apartments formerly occupied by the
Grand Dukes of Tuscany. These latter, the finest of the fifty

rooms on the upper floor, have splendid goffered ceilings of the same description as those in the rooms of the Palazzo Vecchio which Cosimo I had decorated for Eleonora di Toledo; and as this portion of the upper floor of the palace formed part of Cosimo's building it is probable that these rooms were thus decorated for her in the same way.

The views from the great windows of the first floor are very fine; but it is upon the upper floor that the best idea is gained of the size and height of the building and the extent of the views from it. Owing to the great height of the palace, and its position on a slight eminence, the views looking from the balcony [39] of the upper floor are splendid, the eye being carried right over the city, and the view embracing the entire valley of the Arno and the mountains surrounding it. Similarly from the back of the palace on the same storey an extensive view is afforded of the whole of the Boboli gardens, sloping up to the Fort of San Giorgio; while from the large centre window of the main portion of the building, as well as from the rooms at the ends of the two wings, sports and pastimes taking place in the amphitheatre situated in this part of the gardens could be as easily watched as if sitting in the amphitheatre.

Such was the palace in which the last three generations of the Medici passed their lives.

Ferdinand's reign witnessed a great activity in regard to the minor arts, and especially in regard to one of them. While at this time various sculptors, in particular Pietro and Ferdinando Tacca (the successors of Gian da Bologna), attained a certain excellence, "the last gleams of expiring genius," the chief direction to which the artistic talent of Florence at this period devoted its energies was that of the Florentine inlay-work, or *pietra dura* industry, which had been started by Ferdinand's grandfather, Ferdinand I. The reign of Ferdinand II is notable as that in which this art made so great an advance that it became a speciality of

Florence. This work was, however, so costly that only the purse of the Grand Duke could bear its expense; consequently almost all the efforts of the art were put forth in connection with the Royal Manufactory of Pietra Dura. The erection of the mausoleum, to meet the requirements of which that manufactory had been started, was steadily proceeding, while the very best work which the manufactory could produce was being prepared for the *intarsiatura* work on the lower part of the walls.[40] In addition to this there was also a constant demand from the Grand Ducal palace, now that it had been so much enlarged, for inlaid tables, cabinets, and numerous other articles in this work.[41] Ferdinand took immense interest in this industry, fostering it to the utmost, and under him it reached its highest development. As a consequence other countries became eager to emulate Florence in this new art, and Florentine artists skilful in it were invited to France and other countries to introduce it there. The chief advance made at this time was in the production of half-tints and shadows, to obtain which search for suitable stones was made in the most distant parts of the world. Describing the difficulty of the art, Baldinucci says:—

"Whereas it is the aim of a good painter to mix and diffuse his colours so as to form an infinite number of half-tints, all differing essentially from the original colour, the artist in *commesso* [42] cannot multiply his material, nor melt one colour into another, but must adopt the stone as nature made it. In order to convey the colour by insensible gradations from the highest light to the deepest shadow, he must seek out the most delicate tints which nature has produced in stone and observe the infinite number of shades discoverable in the hardest gems and other stones."

But though so difficult to execute, it is practically indestructible, and this caused it to be highly valued. The most skilful artist in this new form of the art was Luigi Siriès, a

Frenchman, who settled at Florence, and was appointed by
Ferdinand Director of the Royal Manufactory.[43]

Ferdinand's and Vittoria's first child, a son, to whom they
gave the name of Cosimo, had been born in 1639, but only
lived a week or two. Another child, a daughter, was born in
1641, but also only lived a short time.[44] In 1642, however,
another son was born, to whom again the name of Cosimo
was given, and who lived to succeed his father. This was
followed by the marriage of Ferdinand's remaining sister,
the Princess Anna, to her first cousin, Ferdinand Karl,
the eldest son of her aunt Claudia,[45] he being sixteen and she
twenty-six. In Anna's portrait by Sustermans, taken when
she was about twenty, her likeness to her brother Ferdinand
is very marked. Ferdinand Karl and Anna preferred the
attractions of the splendid court of Tuscany to the mountains
of Tyrol, and were more often at Florence than at Innsbruck. They had one daughter Claudia Felicitas,[46] born at
Florence, who married the Emperor Leopold I.

During the next two years, while the Thirty Years' War
continued to be waged with unabated energy in northern
Europe,[47] and while England was becoming involved in civil
war between Charles I and his Parliament, Pope Urban VIII
kept Italy also in a continual ferment by his endeavours to
seize upon various territories for his family, the Barberini.
On his thus trying to take Castro and Ronciglione from the
Duke of Parma, the latter marched his army through Tuscany into the territories of the Pope, who was greatly alarmed
at this attack. Ferdinand was drawn into the quarrel, both
to assist his brother-in-law and to defend his own State, but
his military operations were feeble, and brought Tuscany
no glory. In fact, the condition of the country was such that
military strength was as impossible as satisfactory civil administration. The swarms of ecclesiastics who exercised a
dominating power in every department of the national life,
who grievously mismanaged everything they touched, and

who acknowledged no authority but that of a Pope whose
object was to obstruct the ruler of the country in every way,
produced conditions which made military efficiency impossible. The domination of the country by an ecclesiastical
hierarchy of this kind produced tribunals which were corrupt
and arbitrary; it created monopolies, privileges, immunities
from taxation, and vexatious, ill-advised laws, under which
agriculture dwindled and trade threatened to expire; and it
made the people in general completely poverty-stricken. It is
remarkable that under such conditions no conspiracies should
have arisen against Ferdinand's rule. We still see the old
names appearing from time to time—Capponi, Rucellai,
Acciajoli, Ridolfi, and others—families whose members had
in former times been ever ready to head such revolts; but
none ever seemed tempted to originate a revolt against Ferdinand. His officials were powerless, his troops contemptible,
both Spain and France exceedingly cool towards him, and
the Pope inimical; so that, except for one consideration, a
revolt against his authority would have been easy to carry
out. But the affection of the poorer classes of the people was
too great to make a rebellion against him practicable, Ferdinand's goodness of heart, liberality, love of peace, and easy-
going ways giving them a strong regard for him. Though the
mismanagement of the country was palpable, and though the
sufferings caused by its subjection to a crowd of insolent and
tyrannical priests and monks were felt in every department
of life, yet nevertheless the people liked Ferdinand. There
must have been much that was good in a ruler who under
such adverse conditions still retained the affection of his
subjects.

At length in 1644 Tuscany was at last relieved from that
which had formed its chief infliction for twenty-one years,
by the death of Pope Urban VIII. He was succeeded by Innocent X (1644-1655), and the new Pope adopted an entirely
different attitude towards Ferdinand, showing much friendliness towards him; and Tuscany soon felt the effect of this in

an end being put to the evils due to ecclesiastical tyranny under which the country had so long groaned. As one outcome of this friendly feeling the new Pope made the eldest of Ferdinand's brothers, Prince Giovanni Carlo, a cardinal.

In 1648 the Thirty Years' War came to an end. And in the same year Ferdinand's uncle Lorenzo, the third brother of Cosimo II, died at the age of forty-eight. His life had been spoilt, partly by his own fault, partly by circumstances. He had good talents, and was anxious to employ them for the advantage of his country, but from one cause or another had been prevented from doing so. Twenty years old when his brother, Cosimo II, died, and his only other brother Carlo, being a cardinal and living always at Rome, Lorenzo had been anxious to take some part in the government of the country, but was not allowed by the two Grand Duchesses to do so. Foiled in this he tried to obtain a command in the Spanish army, but in this also was disappointed, as in consequence of his pressing Spain so persistently to take up his nephew's cause in the matter of Urbino, he fell into ill-favour at the Spanish court and was refused the military command which had been promised him. The result of these failures was that he drifted about, his life alternating between literary pursuits and all kinds of erratic diversions. Fond of learned men, he collected round him a sort of academy out of which he subsequently formed two societies which he called the "Inflamed" and the "Immovable," the latter of which, established in the Via della Pergola, eventually grew into the well-known theatre of that name. Among other peculiarities, he was in the habit of constantly taking all sorts of medicines, and eventually died from a dose of poison given him in mistake for medicine.[48] In the following year (1649) all Europe was horrified at the execution by the English of their King, Charles I. But the event created little stir in Tuscany, which had long ceased to have any commercial or political transactions with England, or to pay much attention to events taking place outside Italy.

Ferdinand II was now a man of forty. In his fine portrait by Sustermans (taken at about that age), though contriving to give himself with the aid of armour and other accessories a formidable appearance, this was no doubt with a view to hide his real disposition, which, as already noted, was kind, good-hearted, and weak. He wears a large cloak over his armour and the cross of Grand Master of the Order of Santo Stefano.

Vittoria della Rovere (whose portrait by Sustermans shows her as she was at about five-and-twenty) proved a most unsatisfactory wife to Ferdinand, and was a disappointment all through. She neither brought him the dowry of the Duchy of Urbino which had been the sole reason for his being betrothed to her as a boy of twelve, nor did she make up for being a portionless bride by any qualities in her own character. She was foolish, vain, ignorant, and utterly frivolous. As the result of her education in the seclusion of the convent of the Crocetta she was entirely ruled by the priests; while, having none of the tolerant spirit in matters of religion which Ferdinand and his brothers possessed, she was a constant cause of discord in the family. She also had a bad temper, and the strife which she created soon became so great that for many years she and her husband were entirely separated, living in different parts of the palace, and never seeing each other except when attending State functions; though this state of things, after continuing for about seventeen years, was brought to an end in 1659, when a reconciliation took place.

But the most lasting harm which Vittoria della Rovere did to the family fortunes was produced by the kind of education which she insisted on giving to her son Cosimo, who was brought up by her from a child with the sort of training more suited to one who was to become a monk than that required in the case of one who was to be the ruler of a State: with results altogether disastrous to himself and to Tuscany. Looking at the way that she was throughout his life a heavy drag upon her husband, hampering his best efforts and increasing that priestly domination which was ruining the country, at the still more fatal effect of her manner of training her son who was destined to rule Tuscany for over half a century, and at the long period during which her pernicious influence was exercised, we may with justice say that if Giulio de' Medici was the evil genius of the earlier generations of the family, Vittoria della Rovere was the evil genius of its last three generations. For to her chiefly was due the despicable character of its decline and end. The portraits of Vittoria are numerous, as she delighted in being painted in various characters; her portrait by Sustermans, in the Pitti Gallery, as a Vestal Virgin, is one of the most notable; in another, also in the Pitti Gallery, she appears as the Blessed Virgin in a group of the Holy Family; and in another, in the Uffizi Gallery, as the Magdalen. Whilst Vittoria della Rovere was Grand Duchess the court was maintained with the utmost magnificence. She had a large number of maids-of-honour, chosen from all the noblest Florentine families, and the whole set of their portraits [49] is to be seen in the long corridor between the Pitti and Uffizi Galleries. Vittoria survived her husband twenty-three years, so that her baneful influence was prolonged also for nearly half the next reign.

It is a far cry from Florence to Agra, from the puny court of the small and decaying state of Tuscany to the magnificent splendour of the court of the Great Mogul, the ruler over two hundred millions [50] of people, and an empire the size of Europe. But even in the days of her decadence Florence, which once had led Europe in Learning and Art, was still able to make her influence reach even to such a far-off region as this, and to write her name in imperishable letters on the palaces of India.

Nowhere in all the world does the sunset of departed glory make us feel its pathos as in the long-silent marble halls of the palaces of Agra and Delhi. In them we are surrounded by the very spirit of Omar Khayyam's words:—

> "The palace that to heaven its columns threw
> And kings the forehead on its threshold drew,
>   I saw the solitary ring-dove there,
> And 'coo, coo, coo,' she cried, and 'coo, coo, coo.' "

But there is something else there besides this. For there we may see, if we look closely, the first faint beginnings of the West to influence the East; the first evidence in India (after the time of Alexander the Great) of a Western hand and brain, guiding Eastern taste into a more perfect expression of its own spirit. It is written in letters of *lapis-lazuli*, topaz, jasper, ruby, and turquoise; and it is the hand of Florence that wrote it.

When we stand in the Diwàn-i-Am [51] of the palace at Delhi, where stood the Peacock Throne,[52] the hall which has round its cornice in gold letters the celebrated inscription—

> "Agar Firdous ba-ru-e zamin ust
>   To wuheen ust, wuheen ust"; [53]

when we visit the beautiful Diwàn-i-Khàs [54] of the same palace, whose windows of delicate marble tracery look out over the blue waters of the Jumna; when we walk through the Diwàn-i-Khàs,[55] or the Khàs Mahàl,[56] or the Saman Boorj,[57] of the palace at Agra, or sit in the quiet garden on the bank of the river while before us rises that "dream in marble," the Tàj; [58] and when we see these beautiful white marble buildings of the Indian Saracenic [59] architecture decorated everywhere, round arch and pillar, doorway and window, with delicate floral tracery of jasper, agate, cornelian, blood-stone, *lapis-lazuli*, ruby, turquoise, and other precious stones, the originals long since picked out of the marble by the sword and bayonet of plundering Mahratta, Jat, or Pathan invader, but replaced in imitation by the reverent care

of later British conquerors; and when we afterwards see
similar work in the inlaid tables of the Medici in Florence,
or in their mausoleum, we are apt to imagine that Florence
copied this art from far-away India. But it was not so. Each
was independent of the other. But though the *munubbut-
kàri*, or Indian inlay work of inserting designs in precious
stones into pure white marble, existed long before it received
any influence from the West, and came originally from Per-
sia, the improvement in the designs which is visible in these
palaces at Delhi and Agra received its inspiration from Florence.[60]

It was in 1627 that the fifth of the Mogul Emperors, the
Emperor Shahjehàn, the great building Emperor, grandson
of "the great and magnificent Akbàr," [61] succeeded his father,
the Emperor Jehàngir, and began that series of beautiful
buildings, first at Delhi, and then at Agra, which made his
reign of thirty years the culminating point of Mogul architecture. In 1629 his beloved wife, Urjummund Bànu (niece
of the celebrated Nur Mahàl), died, and Shahjehàn determined that she should have the most splendid tomb ever
erected over any woman. How well he carried out this determination has been attested by the world at large. It has been
well said:—

"The Tàj is in harmony with that side of Eastern feeling
which regards a white muslin tunic and an aigrette of diamonds as full dress for an emperor" (Keene).
"So light it seems," says Bernard Taylor, "so airy, so like
a fabric of mist and dreams, with its great marble dome
soaring up like a silvery bubble, that even after you have
touched it and climbed it you may almost doubt its reality."

And it is in the Tàj [62] that we first see that change in the
inlay work which denotes the influence of the Florentine
pietra dura artists, a change still further developed afterwards in the inlay work ornamenting the palaces of Delhi
and Agra. In 1648 Ferdinand, as a part of his endeavours

to make the new industry at Florence still more perfect, sent
Austin de Bordeaux, a Frenchman in his service who was one
of the leading workers in the Royal Manufactory, with several other artificers, to the Emperor Shahjehàn [63] to procure
certain *silices* only to be obtained in India. These Florentines
while at the court of the Great Mogul suggested more artistic
designs for the inlay work going on in the decoration of the
new buildings at Delhi and Agra, introducing more delicate
floral patterns; while Austin de Bordeaux, instead of returning to Florence, took service permanently under the Emperor
Shahjehàn for this kind of work, being chiefly employed upon
the ornamentation of the palace at Delhi and the construction
of the Peacock Throne. [64] And from this time forth the inlay
work at Delhi and Agra shows that resemblance which has
been mentioned to the *pietra dura* work of Florence. Thus did
Tuscany, even in her decay, still show power to influence
other countries far beyond her own narrow boundaries, and
left her sign-manual upon one of the most beautiful of the
arts of India.

One of the best arrangements made by Ferdinand II was
the plan which he adopted about the middle of his reign of
associating his three brothers with himself in the government
of the country, and giving each of them one branch of State
affairs to administer with almost complete authority, one
controlling military affairs, one finance, and the third political
affairs. Matters being well administered in each case, the
arrangement was both popular and productive of much good
to the country. Prince Mattias commanded the army and had
the management of all military affairs. He was a good soldier,
and had seen much service in Germany during the Thirty
Years' War, from whence he returned with a high reputation
to command the army of Tuscany. In addition to this office
he was also made Governor of Siena, where he became very
popular, and was more often there than in Florence. His
portrait by Sustermans in the Pitti Gallery shows him as he

was towards the end of his life, which terminated at the age
of fifty-four; he wears a blue scarf over his armour, and a
large white collar in the fashion of the time, and holds in
his hand the baton denoting his office as Commander-in-
Chief of the army.

Cardinal Giovanni Carlo had the control of financial affairs,
which he managed well. On being created a cardinal by Innocent X he had resided for some years at Rome, where after
being employed by the Pope in various capacities he was at
length sent to receive Queen Christina of Sweden, the daughter of Gustavus Adolphus, when in 1654 she renounced her
throne in consequence of becoming a Roman Catholic, and
came to settle in Rome. Innocent X, however, died in the
following year, being succeeded by Alexander VII (1655-
1667), and the new Pope found that "the society of young
prelates and Christina's attractions became so agreeable to
all parties" [65] that he thought it desirable to appoint a cardinal of maturer years as Queen Christina's spiritual director,
and requested Ferdinand to recall Giovanni Carlo to Florence, he being considered by the Pope too young and handsome for such an office. Like his younger brother Leopold,
Giovanni Carlo was a great collector of pictures and other
objects of art, and a keen assistant in every undertaking
entered upon by Ferdinand to promote the advancement of
Science, Literature, or Art. His fine portrait by Sustermans
in the Lucca picture-gallery depicts him in his dress as a
cardinal, and was taken when he was about thirty-three years
old. He has the long hair and curls usually associated in our
minds with the cavaliers of that period in England.

But the most capable of all the five brothers was the youngest, Prince Leopold,[66] who had the charge of political affairs,
but whose talents and enthusiasm in the cause of Art and
Science caused these latter subjects to be his principal sphere
of activity. It is strange that this eminently capable man,

who by his ability and energy produced such important and lasting effects for the renown of Florence, should have been consigned to almost complete oblivion. By most he is, if known at all, only known as the originator of the collection of portraits of the painters in the Uffizi Gallery. His important work of not only founding the celebrated scientific society of the "Cimento," but leading it during the whole of its brilliant career, has won for him no credit, his name even being scarcely mentioned in connection with that society. His valuable work in assisting the cause of Literature has been equally unrecognised. Above all, it is to Leopold that the world chiefly owes the two great picture-galleries of the Uffizi and the Pitti, of which Florence is so justly proud; and for this achievement alone his name deserves to be rescued from the obscurity into which it has been allowed to sink. He was a worthy successor of those earlier members of the family who had done so much for Learning and Art in the fifteenth century. And he was the last of this family who showed that exceptional ability for which it had for nearly three centuries been noted.

Leopold corresponded with all the leading men of science and professors of the fine arts throughout Europe; his critical taste and knowledge in all matters relating to Art and Literature were proverbial; while in Science he had not only been one of Galileo's chief pupils, but also his abilities and ardour in that study made him the natural leader of the band of men who had been influenced by Galileo's researches and were anxious to carry still further the scientific enquiries which the latter had inaugurated. The fine portrait of Leopold depicts him in the dress of a cardinal, and was therefore painted towards the end of his life, as he did not become a cardinal until 1667, by which time he was fifty years of age. He holds in his hand one of the many letters on the subject of Art or Science which he was constantly receiving from his numerous correspondents scattered about Europe.

Ferdinand, who had the reputation of being the most cultured ruler of his time in Europe, took as keen an interest in all scientific, literary, and artistic matters as his brothers, Giovanni Carlo and Leopold. And these three Medici brothers, owing to their eagerness in this cause, and the influence which their position and wealth gave them, were at this period the leading men in Florence in all that pertained to Science, Literature, or Art.

Ferdinand's gradual emancipation from the ecclesiastical domination which had so seriously marred the earlier part of his reign, begins to show itself about the time of the death of Galileo in 1642, about which time we see the initiation by Ferdinand of a movement, due to the seed sown by Galileo, which ere long had great results. Ferdinand and his brothers, who had all been pupils of Galileo, had been greatly impressed, not only by his teaching, but still more by the illogical character of the arguments used in condemning his theories, and they were profoundly anxious to initiate, in opposition to the theories of the scholastic philosophy, a system of deduction of truth from the observation of facts, and of dispersion of error by the force of experimental knowledge. As the first step in this direction, and as a preliminary attack on the tyranny over thought exercised by the ecclesiastics and on the false philosophy which they propounded, Ferdinand, when he was thirty-two, formed, about the time of Galileo's death, the *Conversazione Filosofica* of the Palace,[67] a society which, holding its meetings in the Grand Ducal palace itself, had for its members all the ablest literary and scientific men of the day, including such enlightened men as the celebrated Evangelista Torricelli da Modigliana, Niccolò Aggiunti, Famiano Michelini, Viviani,[68] Marsili, Uliva, and the renowned physician, philosopher, and poet, Francesco Redi. From the brilliant talents of those who formed its members this "Philosophical Society of the Palace" gained wide respect from all interested in literature and science.

This, however, was but the preliminary step to one much greater. In the year 1657, when Ferdinand was forty-seven, there was formed under his patronage by his talented brother Prince Leopold the celebrated *Accademia del Cimento* (Academy of Experiment), *the first society for experiments in natural science ever formed in Europe,* and one which became the model for all those subsequently established in England, France, and other countries; and this new Academy held its first meeting on the 16th June 1657 in the Grand Ducal palace, presided over by its founder, Prince Leopold de' Medici, then forty years old. Truly the Pitti Palace, honoured as it is by all artists for its magnificent picture-gallery, should be no less honoured by all scientists as the building in which originated this notable event in the world of Science. The Royal Society of England was not incorporated until 1663, and the French Academy of Science not until 1666; so that Florence in this matter also, as in former days it had done in Learning, and as it had done in Art, led the way. And prominent as had been the leadership of the Medici as to Learning, and as to Art, in neither of these was it so directly marked as in this case of Science. Prince Leopold, both as an earnest pupil of Galileo, and on account of his own proficiency in science, was chosen by the new society as the proper man to lead it as its President.

And very ably he did so. At its first meeting the society ruled that its fundamental law should be that no special school of philosophy or system of science should be adopted by it, and that it bound itself "to investigate nature by the pure light of experimental facts"; also that the society should be open to all talent, and that the privilege of selecting the experiments to be made should lie with the President. It adopted as its motto, *Provando e Riprovando.* Magalotti was chosen as its secretary; and on the walls of the entrance hall of the present National Library (in the Uffizi building) are to be seen the portraits of the distinguished men who were the first members of this famous society.[69]

Thus took place the first case on record of the formation of a society purely for the pursuit of inductive science, and for the furtherance of that new philosophy which Galileo had inaugurated and of which Bacon was to be the chief exponent. Ferdinand took the greatest interest in the work of the new society, and devised several of the experiments, among others the suggestion of the use of the expansion of liquids for thermometric purposes, instead of the air of Galileo's thermoscope. The results of the experiments made by this society were later on detailed by the secretary, Magalotti, and were published in Florence in 1667, under the title, *"Saggi di naturali esperienze fatte nell' Accademia del Cimento"* ("Results of experiments in natural science made by the Academy of the Cimento"); and a Latin translation of this work was published at Leyden in 1731 by Von Musschenbrock. Regarding these results of this society's work a scientist of our own day remarks:—"Many of these experiments are classics in the history of science."

But Leopold was not only fitted to be the President of such a society through his scientific attainments. His gifts of character enabled him to guide smoothly a community of men of very diverse idiosyncrasies who, however talented they were as scientists, were no freer from the frailties of jealousy and envy, vanity and self-conceit, than commoner mortals. And his gifts in this direction received a remarkable testimony. The new society pursued an energetic and brilliant career for ten years. Then Leopold, his brother Giovanni Carlo having died, was made a cardinal in his place, and had to resign his presidency of the society. The removal of the guiding spirit which had known how to make all the members work together for a common object had immediate results which showed how considerable his gifts were in this respect, no less than in the scientific direction. For the society of the Cimento, which in its short career of ten years had won renown all over Europe, had a sudden and dramatic end.[10] Napier relates that upon Leopold's retirement from the leadership of the society, "the clashing pretensions of irascible genius burst forth, and blew the assembly to atoms; its fragments, still bright and precious, were eagerly gathered up by foreign nations, and made the corner-stones of steadier institutions." [71] *It was an epitome of all Florentine history.* Without the leadership of one particular family which alone of all the Tuscan race possessed a special gift for calming discord and inducing antagonistic natures to work harmoniously together, and whose possession of this valuable quality, demonstrated in many generations of this family for two hundred and fifty years, was here exhibited for the last time, internecine conflict ever robbed the talent and genius of the Florentine race of its crown and flower of success. None but a Medici could ever steer the bark of Florentine genius safe to port and keep it from wrecking itself upon the rock of fratricidal strife.

Ferdinand and his brothers Giovanni Carlo and Leopold were no less active in the cause of Literature than in that of Science. By them was formed with diligent labour the "Palatine Library" (or Library of the Palace), which now forms the chief part [72] of the National Library of the Uffizi, and contains fourteen thousand manuscript books and over two hundred thousand printed books. The treasures of this library, though not so great as those of the older Medici library founded by Cosimo Pater Patriae, are still very considerable. It possesses over three hundred volumes of letters and papers of Galileo and his most distinguished contemporaries, including his celebrated *Discourses and Mathematical Demonstrations*, and his treatise called *The Dialogues* which brought upon him the wrath of Pope Urban VIII; also an interesting letter from his favourite pupil Viviani, proving that Galileo was the first to apply the principle of the pendulum to the clock. Among the illuminated books is a missal, once the property of the Emperor Otho III (983-1002), with his name written in it; also another missal with

very interesting medallions in enamel. A Bible which belonged
to Savonarola has his comments written in the margin, and
in so fine a hand that a magnifying-glass is required to de-
cipher them. A scrap-book of Ghiberti's contains notes and
sketches by himself and other artists of his time. The library
also contains autograph letters of Boccaccio, Politian, Machiavelli, Michelangelo, Tasso, Alfieri, Redi, and many other
celebrated men. Also a valuable manuscript edition of
Petrarch's works; and a copy of Dante's *Divine Comedy*,
written only fifty years after his death, and illustrated with
very curious miniatures and a profile portrait of Dante himself. A copy of the *Anthologia* has a frontispiece of the most
beautifully executed miniatures and small medallions, painted
in 1499. A copy of the Pandects of Justinian, made by order
of the Signoria when the original was removed to Rome by
Leo X, has beautiful illuminations executed by Boccardini.
The Latin Bible of St. Jerome, in two volumes, has a miniature of him on the first page, and in the margins beautiful
little drawings of landscapes with deer. Raymond Lulli's rare
book on alchemy and magic has beautifully painted illustrations with charming landscape backgrounds. Another curious
book is the *Miracles of the Madonna,* a very rare Portuguese
work, with illustrations of an Eastern character. A fine copy
of the Hebrew Bible, printed in 1488, is the first edition
ever printed in that language. The poems of Bellincioni,
printed in 1493, another very rare work, has notes in the
margin by the critical Accademia della Crusca. The Latin
poem of the *Convenevole,* describing the corrupt state of
religion in the fourteenth century, an exceedingly rare work
owing to its censures against the Church causing it to be
destroyed wherever possible, has curious miniatures in which
the angels are represented behind walls with the swallow-
tailed battlements of the Ghibelline party, while the people
are behind square, Guelph, battlements. Another notable
book is the *In tria Vergilii Opera Expositio,* by Servius, being
the first book ever printed in Florence (1477); it was printed

by the Florentine goldsmith Cennini, who cast his own type after seeing the results of printing in Germany, and on the title-page commemorates his invention. The first printed copy of Homer, printed on vellum, and presented by the editor, Bernardo Nerli, to Pietro the Unfortunate at the time of the latter's marriage in 1488, has in it a portrait in miniature of Pietro himself at the age of seventeen. One of the first attempts at printing with movable types is a copy of Durando's *Rationale Divinorum Officiorum,* a work explaining the origin of the various ceremonies of the Church, which went through forty-eight editions. The copy of the *Divine Comedy,* with commentaries by Cristoforo Landino (bound in red and white leather ornamented with Landino's arms), which was presented by him to the Signoria in 1481, has fine miniatures, and among them a portrait of Dante himself. The above give some idea of the many rare and interesting books contained in the splendid library which Ferdinand and his two brothers formed.

But by far the most important memorial of the reign of Ferdinand II was made in the domain of Art. Francis I and Ferdinand I had begun placing some of the family pictures in the rooms constructed by them over the offices of the Uffizi; but as yet there was nothing there which could be called a regular picture-gallery, while the rooms up to this time consisted only of a few opening from the eastern portion of the corridor. But in the latter part of Ferdinand II's reign, at the suggestion of Prince Leopold, the two brothers Giovanni Carlo and Leopold, both of whom possessed very large collections of pictures of their own (irrespective of those which were the general property of the family) besides numerous other objects of art, gave the whole of their collections to form the two galleries of the Pitti and the Uffizi, those belonging to Giovanni Carlo being chiefly made to form the gallery in the Grand Ducal palace itself [73] (the Pitti Gallery), and those belonging to Leopold to form the Uffizi

Gallery. At the same time Ferdinand added to these the general collection of pictures which he had inherited as head of the family, as well as those which he had acquired from Urbino with his wife, Vittoria della Rovere.

To house this great collection of pictures, to which many other objects of art were added by each of the brothers, not even the spacious Grand Ducal palace [74] could give sufficient accommodation, and it therefore became necessary to largely extend the gallery constructed over the offices of the Uffizi. This was nearly trebled in size, the corridor being extended all along the western side, and additional rooms being added on that side. Ferdinand also, among other objects of art, added the whole of the valuable collection of gems, rare vases, and other valuable articles now kept in the Gem Room, which was at the same time constructed for this purpose. Leopold not only originated the proposal for the formation of these two galleries and contributed the largest share of the pictures (other than those already belonging to the family), but he also conducted all the arrangements necessary to form the gallery of the Uffizi. At the same time he began the collection of the portraits of the painters of all nations, which now fills four rooms of that gallery. All the portraits of the oldest masters he obtained, some from the Academy of St. Luke at Rome (among which was the portrait of Raphael), and others as the result of a long and careful search made by him throughout Italy for any portraits of them which could be found; and to these he added those of the chief painters of his own time.[75] Another important item in his contributions to the Uffizi Gallery was the valuable collection of drawings to be seen there, which took him many years to collect. Most of the pictures in the Venetian room he bought through a Florentine merchant, Paolo del Sera, who was settled at Venice.

The above action on the part of Ferdinand and his two brothers is the real formation of the Pitti and Uffizi Galleries as we now know them.[76] Prince Leopold's artistic possessions being much greater than those of his brother, Cardinal Giovanni Carlo, he did not restrict himself only to the Uffizi Gallery, and many of the objects of art to be seen in the Pitti Gallery were also given by him: notably the interesting collection of miniatures of important historical personages of his time made by him in the course of his travels through Europe, now in the "Corridor of the Columns," [77] in the Pitti Gallery, which miniatures Leopold valued so highly that he used to carry them with him wherever he went. He also gave, among other articles of the kind, the rich *Stipo*, or cabinet of ebony, enclosing a small altar, and having its many doors and drawers inlaid with precious marbles and curious and beautiful designs in transparent stones, which stands in the centre of one of the rooms, and which after he became a cardinal he occasionally used when he celebrated Mass in the palace.

It was in this manner that the Uffizi and Pitti Galleries were formed. And it shows what the Medici were in the domain of Art, that they could, even in their decadence, form out of their private collections the two most important picture-galleries in Europe.[78] These two galleries, however, were not as yet public galleries, but simply, conjointly, the private picture-gallery of the Medici family. It was to remain for a later generation of that family to make them the property of Tuscany.[79]

This important work formed the occupation which during the last ten years of Ferdinand's reign chiefly engaged the attention of Leopold de' Medici. And it was fitting that this truly great man, of whom we never hear anything but what is good, and who wherever we meet with him is always engaged either in works of charity, or in some important work in the cause of Science, Literature, or Art, should be commemorated in that gallery whose formation was the last and greatest of his many enlightened labours. His statue has fittingly been placed in the room in the Uffizi Gallery containing the portraits of the greatest masters of painting, where he sits surrounded by the portraits of those of whose works he was the largest and most appreciative collector ever known. Around him hang the portraits of Bellini, Perugino, Leonardo da Vinci, Filippino Lippi, Michelangelo, Giorgione, Titian, Raphael, Andrea del Sarto, Guercino, Tintoretto, Velazquez, Rembrandt, Van Dyck, and many another of "that glorious company." [80]

During the years 1649-1660 the Commonwealth was in power in England, and in the Pitti Gallery there is an interesting memento of this time. When the persecution of the Waldensian Protestants [81] was at its height, Oliver Cromwell sent a message to Pope Alexander VII that if these cruelties were not promptly stopped he would send the English fleet into the Tiber to exact retribution; which message forthwith produced an order from the Pope to the Duke of Savoy to desist. Ferdinand was so struck with admiration of Cromwell's action that he sent a request to the latter that he would allow his portrait to be painted for him by Sir Peter Lely. Cromwell acquiesced, and added that he would himself present Ferdinand with it. And in due time the portrait of Oliver Cromwell, presented by him to Ferdinand, and painted by Sir Peter Lely, arrived, and was placed with Ferdinand's other pictures in the family gallery, where it still hangs.

Ferdinand during his reign initiated various experiments with the object of improving the agricultural and commercial prospects of the country, and one of these, though it did not produce the results he hoped, still survives, and is of considerable interest. This was his endeavour to introduce camels into Tuscany, as being hardier and less expensive to keep than horses. They were imported from India, and tried in various places in Tuscany. Unfortunately, however, it was found that the climate and conditions of the country did not suit them. Only at one place did they continue to thrive, namely, in the Grand Ducal park at San Rossore, about

three miles from Pisa, where they may still be seen, the herd
numbering about two hundred, and being employed chiefly
in carrying wood.

In 1660 [82] (the year that in England Charles II regained
his throne) a second son was born to Ferdinand and Vittoria, eighteen years after the birth of their eldest son,
Cosimo. He was given the name of Francesco Maria. Though
the evil effects of a monkish style of bringing-up were by
this time making themselves strongly apparent in their
eldest son, and though Ferdinand showed that he was fully
aware of the error by spasmodic attempts to retrieve it, yet
he allowed the same style of training to be given by the boy's
mother to this second son, Ferdinand perhaps acquiescing
for fear of again disturbing the comparative domestic peace
which had, after so many years of discord, only so recently
been established. In the case of Francesco Maria the effects
were of less importance, as he was not called upon to rule,
and was from the first intended for an ecclesiastical career.

In 1661 Cosimo, Ferdinand's eldest son, being now nineteen, arrangements for his marriage were taken in hand. Under
the kind of bringing-up which he had received he had developed into a gloomy and disagreeable youth, sunk in
bigotry and superstition, unmanly, awkward, hating all society, shunning as impious everything connected with science
or philosophy, an enemy to all cheerfulness, detesting music,
art, poetry, and the conversation of learned men, equally dis-
liking all manly exercises, sullen and ill-tempered, and only
at his ease in the society of friars and monks. Ferdinand
thought to cure this by marriage; but while it was obvious
that to find a wife suitable for such a youth would be a difficult task, if all Europe had been searched none more unsuitable could have been found than the one who was
selected.

The Princess Marguerite Louise of Orleans, then sixteen,
daughter of Gaston, Duke of Orleans, and first cousin of

Louis XIV (who had succeeded Louis XIII in 1643), had been brought up as the future Queen of France. She was lively, beautiful, clever, highly accomplished, full of French *espièglerie*, brilliant in conversation, fond of riding and hunting, detested all gravity and melancholy, and was, in short, the exact opposite of Cosimo in every particular. To crown all, she was deeply in love with the young Prince Charles of Lorraine,[83] to whom, when the plan of her marrying Louis XIV fell through, she had hoped to be married. Her mother, the widowed Duchess of Orleans, wished it, and was opposed to her daughter being given to Prince Cosimo of Tuscany; but her children were left by Duke Gaston under the King's charge, the schemes of Cardinal Mazarin brought the King's authority to bear,[84] and the unhappy girl was given her choice of this marriage or a convent. After being married by proxy in the chapel of the Louvre in April 1661, she travelled to Marseilles, where she was met by Prince Mattias and escorted by him to Leghorn and thence to Florence, the whole journey from Leghorn to Florence being made a brilliant pageant, all that wealth and taste could devise being employed to give it splendour. But Marguerite Louise had left her heart behind her in France, and hated all things Italian. She was received at Florence with great festivities, the Palace was turned into a scene of enchantment, and every device was put forth to give her pleasure, but under the circumstances this was impossible; her broken heart, and the natural disgust which she felt for the monk-like and unattractive Cosimo, prevented her taking pleasure in anything; despair and a settled melancholy seized upon her, and every proposal for her entertainment was met only by bitter sarcasm. Shortly after the marriage Prince Charles of Lorraine paid a visit to Florence, which made matters worse, and after his departure Marguerite Louise no longer made any attempt to conceal her detestation of her position, of Florence, of the Tuscan court, and of everything in Italy. She refused to learn the Italian language, and sent urgent prayers to the King of France to be allowed to enter a convent rather than remain in Tuscany; and neither the endeavours of her father-in-law to assuage her misery, nor the threats of Louis XIV, nor the efforts of his Ministers to smooth matters, had any effect in producing a change in her conduct. There is an interesting relic still in Florence of these dead-and-gone troubles of the poor cruelly-treated bright French princess, Marguerite Louise. Some years ago two of the silver coins in the collection of coins in the Archæological Museum, which bore the head of Ferdinand II, were discovered to be hollow, and to be in reality boxes; and in one of these was a miniature of Prince Charles of Lorraine in his youth, believed to have been concealed in this manner by Marguerite Louise so that she might wear it without detection; which had been the cause of its becoming lost.

In January 1663 Cardinal Giovanni Carlo died at the age of fifty-two. His death was felt to be a great loss, both to the family and to the country, owing to his ability in public affairs, his varied talents, and his agreeable disposition.[85] In the following year hostilities threatened to break out between France and Pope Alexander VII and to bring war into Tuscany, both sides having assembled their forces on her frontiers; but the dispute was at the last moment settled by a conference which was held at Pisa, presided over by Ferdinand, always at his best as a peacemaker.

But all international politics were thrown into the shade by the quarrels between Prince Cosimo and his young wife, which turned the Tuscan court upside down. A son (who was named Ferdinand) was born to this ill-assorted pair in August 1663, but the explosions and turmoils still went on. At one time Marguerite Louise, wishing herself dead, would neither eat anything nor speak to any one; at another she poured forth volumes of the most cutting ridicule on every one connected with the court, so that none dared go near her for fear of her biting and sarcastic wit. The Duc de Crécquy, Louis XIV's ambassador to the Pope, was ordered on his return journey from Rome to visit Florence and endeavour to bring the Princess Marguerite Louise to a better mind; but after a few days "he gave up the attempt in despair and returned to the less puzzling affairs of State policy." A second special ambassador sent from France met with like success. Then Madame du Deffant, who had been the governess of the Princess, was despatched on the same errand, and after a toilsome journey from Paris arrived at Florence armed with copious instructions from Louis XIV as to the arguments she was to employ. But all were equally scorned by the young French princess who, brought up to admire all that was bright and gay and noble in life, and in love with one who fulfilled these ideals, had been handed over to such a fate as marriage to the gloomy and contemptible Cosimo. The written threats of the King of France, the arguments of French ambassadors, the persuasive exhortations of her governess, even the authority of the Pope, were all alike powerless to make Marguerite Louise more ready to endure her lot. At length she could stand the court no longer and retreated to Poggio a Caiano, whence she sent a message to Cosimo that if he dared to come there he would have a missal thrown at his head. After a little time, however, she repented herself of this move, suddenly reappeared at the Palace, flung herself into her father-in-law's arms, and acknowledged herself in the wrong; and for a time the court had a little peace.

In June 1666 Ferdinand's uncle, Cardinal Carlo de' Medici, the last of Cosimo II's brothers, died at the age of seventy-one. He had lived almost all his life at Rome, was Deacon of the Sacred College, and had long been a person of considerable importance at the Vatican. His body was brought to Florence, and buried in San Lorenzo.[86] In the following year Pope Alexander VII died, and was succeeded by Clement

IX (1667-1670). Both the cardinals of the Medici family having died during the preceding four years the new Pope now made Prince Leopold, by this time fifty years old, a cardinal in the place of his brother, Giovanni Carlo. In this same year (1667) Ferdinand's brother, the successful soldier Mattias, died at the age of fifty-four at Siena, of which city he had for many years been Governor, and where he was much liked. He never married, and was thus the third of Ferdinand's brothers who had died leaving no children. His body was brought to Florence, and buried (like all those at this time) in the New Sacristy of San Lorenzo, waiting until the family mausoleum was sufficiently completed for them to be interred there.[87]

In the same year that Prince Leopold was made cardinal, and that Prince Mattias died, the quarrels between the Princess Marguerite Louise and the monkish and irritable youth to whom she had been married again developed into an open rupture. Sent to the family palace at Pisa, Marguerite Louise was kept there by Cosimo as a sort of prisoner, and prevented from holding any communication with the outside world. Finding her circumstances becoming thus ever more intolerable, and that she could get no help from her relatives in France, she evolved the idea of escape from the contemptible Cosimo by joining a party of gipsies, with whom she was discovered one night settling all the arrangements from a window of the palace at Pisa; whereupon that mode of escape was made impossible. Soon afterwards her second child was born, a daughter, named Anna Maria Ludovica. The wild projects and immoderate behaviour into which Marguerite Louise was drawn have too often formed a subject merely for ridicule. They show to what depths of despair this once bright, clever, and accomplished girl had been reduced by the cruel policy of Louis XIV and Cardinal Mazarin in forcing her to marry one so infinitely her inferior in abilities, knowledge, and every other quality; and her vagaries, laughable as they often were, should rather excite an intense pity, since (in one not by any means wanting in ability) they showed how deep was the misery which she suffered.

The aversion which Marguerite Louise entertained for Cosimo being so great, and travel being the best means for enlarging a mind so narrow as his, Ferdinand in 1667 very wisely sent the latter off to make an extended tour of various countries. It had, at any rate, the advantage of relieving Marguerite Louise of his presence for a considerable time, and during his absence we hear of no more of these vagaries on her part. In this tour Cosimo visited Germany, Holland, Spain, and Portugal; from thence endeavouring to reach England, he was driven by a storm to Ireland, where "he was astounded at the wretched condition of the people, whom he found in far greater poverty and misery than those of Tuscany." From Ireland Cosimo travelled to London, and thence passing through France, returned to Florence in 1669 after an absence of two years. Ferdinand's health had for some time been failing; he only lived a few months after his son's return; and in May 1670 the fifth Grand Duke passed away at the age of sixty, and after a reign of fifty years during which the condition of Tuscany had been one long decline. In larger politics Ferdinand's sincere and successful endeavour to preserve peace in Italy was the distinguishing feature of his reign. He was buried with great pomp in a temporary grave in the New Sacristy of San Lorenzo pending the completion of the family mausoleum.[88]

Ferdinand II furnishes a strong illustration of the fact that the greatest crime of which one placed in any position of authority can be guilty is *weakness;* and that in a ruler neither immorality nor even ferocity produce such an amount of misery to others as this failing. Ferdinand's good qualities are patent in every period of his life; his kind and generous disposition, his unselfishness, desire to do good, love of peace, regard for religion, good abilities, and energy in the cause of Science and Art, all these are conspicuous; but they could not compensate for the one defect of weakness. Cosimo I, with all his murders, cruel tyrannies, and deceitful character, made Tuscany for the mass of the people a happy and prosperous country; Ferdinand II, with all his goodness of disposition and desire to do right, made it the most degraded and misgoverned country in Europe. And the root of these opposite results lay solely in the fact that the former was a strong ruler and the latter a weak one. But the full effect of Ferdinand's weakness was not seen till the next reign.

CHAPTER XXIX

COSIMO III

Born 1642. (*Reigned* 1670-1723.) *Died* 1723

To those who have watched the many illustrious achieve-ments of this family during a course of nearly three hundred years it is deplorable indeed to witness the rapid descent to ignominy, which now set in. Down the steep path from degra-dation to degradation go the Medici; and down with them, dragged at their chariot-wheels, goes Tuscany also. And could Lorenzo the Magnificent have stood again in Florence, he might have inverted the form of his speech and said: *"The State goes with the house."* They rose—and fell—together. The death of all ability, the death of all high and generous sentiments, the death of all strength and force of character:— this is what is set before us in the fifty-three years' reign of Cosimo III. Great things are being done in other parts of Europe: the victories of the great Turenne; the victories of Marlborough—Blenheim, Ramillies, Oudenarde, and Mal-plaquet; the spread of science, literature, and art in other countries; but Tuscany has no part in these things, and leads the way no more to anything but degeneracy and ruin.

Cosimo was twenty-eight years old when he succeeded to the throne. His character has already been noted. His travels had not produced any marked improvement in him, their chief effect having been only to give him an unbounded love of ostentation; with the result that the magnificence and luxury of his court far exceeded that of any previous reign.[1] For the first three years matters proceeded tranquilly; peace for a time prevailed between the Grand Duke and his wife, Mar-guerite Louise; the strong respect which Cosimo entertained for his uncle Leopold's opinion gave promise of wisdom and moderation in the government; while the birth in 1671 of a second son, who was named Giovanni Gastone, was welcomed as rendering more secure the continuance of the family.

But this satisfactory state of affairs did not last long. Cosimo's subordination to priestly influence, together with the constant interference of his foolish mother, Vittoria della Rovere, in all matters, after a time provoked the Grand Duchess Marguerite Louise to demand, in 1674, a share in the government. This being refused, she withdrew to Poggio a Caiano, wrote thence to Cosimo, saying, "You make the unhappiness of my life, and I make the unhappiness of yours," and demanded a final separation and permission to return to France. To this Cosimo, afraid of the strong public opinion which existed in her favour, had to consent. Accordingly, delighted to be able at last to turn her back on the country which had been to her like a prison for thirteen years Marguerite Louise left Tuscany for France, where she took up her abode at the convent of Montmartre, near Paris. This was followed by the death in 1675 of Cosimo's uncle, Cardinal Leopold, who died at the age of fifty-eight; [2] and with him departed all ability and common-sense in the conduct of affairs.

The Grand Duchess Vittoria, the field being thus left vacant, now gained the entire influence. And where she was paramount every folly was a certainty. Ferdinand II's min·· isters were replaced by others of her selection, chosen as a rule from the cloister—men so utterly without capacity or spirit that Magalotti compared them to little children frightened lest they should be sent back to school.[3] "Theology became a substitute for statesmanship," and in a short time universal contempt for Tuscany and its sovereign began to be the prevailing sentiment among other powers; while in home affairs one ill-advised measure after another followed in rapid succession. Meanwhile Marguerite Louise was highly popular at the French court, where her lively sallies and constant ridicule of Cosimo and the Tuscan court greatly amused Louis XIV.[4] This made Cosimo furious, increasing his naturally bad temper almost to madness; he threatened to stop her allowance, but Louis XIV forbade him to do so, and Cosimo stood far too much in awe of the French monarch to disobey.

The history of Cosimo III's long reign of over half a century is one of every evil which a ruler at once vain, weak, tyrannical, entirely wanting in brains, and sunk in superstition and bigotry can create. The record becomes wearisome by reason of the constant repetition of the same enormities and imbecilities, while the condition of the outraged people grew ever more deplorable. Cosimo was his own Minister of Justice. His avarice caused him to overtax his subjects, his bigotry to arraign them for offences outside the scope of all ordinary laws, his weak, yet tyrannical, disposition to inflict upon them punishments outrageous in their cruel severity. And these effects, when combined with the measures to which an earnest but mistaken view of religion led a foolish and superstitious character, produced results which made the condition of the people under the worst of Asiatic rulers more tolerable than that of the people of Tuscany under Cosimo III. Crime, poverty, cruel punishments, and priestly interference in every detail of domestic life reduced the inhabitants to the last stage of wretchedness.[5] Cosimo considered it his mission to dragoon his subjects into morality, and his methods in this particular created untold misery. The most ferocious punishments were daily meted out for the smallest offences, or supposed offences, against morality. "The chain and the lash were in constant requisition." The periodical visits of a Dominican friar who made minute examination into all family matters, and by the royal authority commanded marriages, separations, or imprisonment, destroyed all possibility of domestic happiness. "Dissimulation spread like a pestilence;

priests and hypocrisy pervaded all." [6] Marriage portions given
to girls recommended by ecclesiastics, pensions given to
crowds of so-called "converts," a crushing taxation, laws
conceived in entire ignorance of all commercial or agricultural
affairs, outrageous punishments for trivial offences, these and
similar measures caused many of the inhabitants to take
flight from the country; while those who remained became
idle, false, and bigoted. Thus did Cosimo's early training,
habits, and disposition reduce a high-spirited and intellectual
people to the most abject state of moral and material degradation ever known.

One of the worst features in Cosimo was his dislike of his
sons, whom in the most ill-advised manner he persistently
bullied. Both of them had good natural dispositions and
abilities, but both were in turn ruined through the treatment
they sustained from their father; and this in the end brought
about the most disastrous consequences to the family. A
mixture of extravagance and niggardliness, he kept a tight
hold on his purse-strings where his sons were concerned, employing this means of coercing them to his will.

Prince Ferdinand, the heir to the throne, had as his instructors, Viviani, Redi, Noris, the brothers Lorenzini, and
other distinguished men of the time, and being full of talent
and intelligence promised to offer a striking contrast to his
father whenever he should be called upon to rule. By the year
1680, when he was seventeen, this young Prince began to
find the follies of the Grand Duchess Vittoria insupportable,
and to revolt more and more from her authority. He was prohibited by Cosimo from corresponding with his mother, whose
extravagant conduct in Paris continued, and who openly declared her intention whenever Cosimo's intemperance brought
his life to an end, of going to Florence, "chasing hypocrites
and hypocrisy from the court," discharging all the incom-
petent sycophants who had been promoted by the Grand
Duchess Vittoria, and restoring good government and com-

mon-sense. Ferdinand espoused his mother's side in the quarrel, disregarded the prohibition against corresponding with her, and when his instructors, the brothers Lorenzini, were most cruelly consigned to permanent imprisonment in the dungeons of Volterra for supporting him, threw off his father's authority altogether, and became the centre of a band of well-born young men whose avowed object was to assert themselves in opposition to the monastical atmosphere of the court, to favour music, art, and literature, and to contend against all hypocrisy and dissimulation. This society became immensely popular, all the young scions of the leading Florentine families pressing to join it in their detestation of the rule of the ecclesiastics favoured by Cosimo and his mother; while the society was soon still further strengthened by being joined by Cosimo's younger brother, Francesco Maria, who was only three years older than his nephew Ferdinand. On his uncle Leopold's death Francesco Maria had been made a cardinal at the age of fifteen, but had no taste for the ecclesiastical life. Thus the family was divided into two parties, on the one side the bigoted Cosimo and his still more bigoted mother Vittoria, and on the other his brother Francesco Maria and eldest son Ferdinand, with the Grand Duchess Marguerite Louise watching from a distance and encouraging the latter party.

But the concourse of youthful spirits led by Prince Ferdinand soon, in their revolt from hypocrisy and a monkish style of life, went further than merely favouring music, art, and literature, and developed a taste for pleasure and intemperance which nullified all their good intentions and gave Cosimo an opportunity for applying a thoroughly characteristic remedy. A rigorous family inspection, with a searching investigation into every detail of private habits, was instituted, carried out by friars; and this developed into a regular system of *espionage* and persecution, which soon put down any tendency to gaiety and pleasure, and made the opponents of dissimulation and hypocrisy themselves practise these means of evading ecclesiastical tyranny. All classes were subjected to this system; while at the same time monks were placed over the parish priests, and kept the people perpetually employed in "processions, preachings, and penances"; accusations multiplied, while pardon for imaginary offences was only to be obtained by the payment of large sums of money to the ecclesiastics.

Disgusted with this state of things, Prince Ferdinand, being now twenty-two, desired to be allowed to proceed on a tour to see the world; but was kept for two years before Cosimo would agree to let him go. In 1687, however, Ferdinand was allowed to depart on a tour in northern Italy, after being first betrothed to the Princess Violante Beatrice of Bavaria. In November 1688 he returned, and the marriage was carried out with a most gorgeous display of magnificence. A special gate was opened in the wall of the city near the Porta San Gallo, and through this the Princess Violante was drawn, in a car profusely studded with gems, to a chapel erected for the occasion; there she was crowned by Cosimo with the Grand Ducal crown, and thence was conducted to the Palace in a procession of the most extravagant splendour; after which the marriage was performed in the cathedral.[7]

Prince Ferdinand was the hope of all those who desired to see a better state of things dawn upon Tuscany. High-spirited, full of ability, and fond of art and science, he had become the centre round whom gathered all who were learned [8] and cultured, and all that portion of Florentine society which had no taste for the atmosphere of hypocrisy which pervaded the court. But his father contrived to bring these bright prospects to ruin. Ferdinand was as energetic and resolute as his father was weak and undecided, and being eager to employ his abilities to some useful purpose, desired to take a part in public affairs; but Cosimo refused to permit him to do so. Disgusted at a fatuous style of government which was dragging the country to ruin, forced to be the daily witness of errors and follies which he was not allowed to remedy, and subjected to chronic bullying by a father who hated him, Ferdinand gradually took to a dissolute course of life which before he was forty ruined his health, and brought about his death a few years later. Unfortunately he did not care for the wife whom his father had chosen for him, the Princess Violante, though she was in every way worthy of his affection, and deservedly liked by all classes in Florence. She never reproached him for his neglect, and to the last continued to show her affection for him.[9]

In the early part of Cosimo's reign various important additions were made to the art collections in the Uffizi Gallery. Cosimo's intemperance both in eating and drinking caused him to suffer from frequent illness, as a remedy for which his physician, the celebrated Redi,[10] prescribed regular walking exercise; and Paolo Falconieri, one of the cultured men whom Prince Ferdinand had gathered round him, suggested that this exercise should be taken in the Uffizi Gallery, and that the Grand Duke should for his amusement adorn it with all the best specimens of sculpture belonging to the family. Cosimo took up the idea warmly, removed to the gallery many of the statues hitherto placed in the Boboli gardens, and caused to be brought from the Villa Medici at Rome most of the remaining works of sculpture which Ferdinand I had collected, including the *Venus de' Medici*, the *Wrestlers*, the *Knife-whetter*, and the large number of classic busts and other works of sculpture to be seen in the Uffizi Gallery, then called the Gallery of the Statues.[11] The long corridor between the Palace and the Uffizi Gallery, which formed part of this daily walk of the Grand Duke, was also adorned with many pictures, among them the large collection of over six hundred portraits of notable persons in Europe during the fifteenth and sixteenth centuries, which, though they are of no artistic merit, are of much value from an historical point of view.

Cosimo also now took in hand an important matter in

regard to the family mausoleum. Hitherto the numerous members of the family who had died since it was begun by his great-grandfather Ferdinand I in 1604 had, pending the completion of the mausoleum, been buried temporarily in the New Sacristy. Migliore, writing in 1684, in describing the New Sacristy, says:—

"This chapel also serves for burying the bodies of the Grand Dukes and Princes of the Blood, placed in the ground beneath, with short inscriptions merely for record, and not in the form of elegant eulogy such as they merit and their grandeur would require, pending their being transferred to the mausoleum which is being prepared immediately behind the choir of the church." [12]

He also states that in the Old Sacristy were buried the bodies of Maria Salviati, and Cosimo I with his sons Giovanni and Garzia. Thus in the New Sacristy there had been temporarily buried in this manner some eighteen members of the family, viz., Francis I and his wife Joanna, with two of their children, Anna and Filippo; Ferdinand I and his wife Christine, with five of their children, Francesco, Carlo, Lorenzo, Eleonora, and Caterina; Cosimo II and Maria Maddalena, with four of their children, Maria Cristina, Giovanni Carlo, Mattias, and Leopold; and Ferdinand II. By the year 1685, however, the mausoleum, though still only about half finished, was sufficiently advanced for them to be interred there; Cosimo, therefore, now removed the bodies of all the above from their temporary resting-places to the mausoleum. The remains of Giovanni delle Bande Nere being at the same time brought from Mantua, all were duly placed in the crypt, those of Giovanni delle Bande Nere and his wife Maria Salviati in the centre, and the whole of their descendants ranged round them. [13]

Before the middle of Cosimo's reign was reached his imbecile method of government had begun to produce serious difficulties. In the disturbed state of Europe [14] it was urgently necessary that the country should be placed in a proper state of defence; but all military requirements had been ignored by Cosimo's cloister-trained Ministers of State, and no money for this purpose was forthcoming. Vast sums were squandered on religious ceremonies, votive offerings, the foundation of convents, and similar objects, while gold was lavishly poured forth on the crowd of monkish satellites who surrounded Cosimo and his mother, and on the spies who infested every family circle; and this inordinate expenditure on such purposes while the military defences of the country were allowed to go to ruin caused general exasperation. Public opinion loudly complained of this insane policy, and was led by Prince Ferdinand, who openly condemned his father's conduct, and was backed by public applause which kept Cosimo in continual fear of a revolution.

In 1691 the Princess Anna Maria Ludovica, then twenty-four, the only one of his three children for whom Cosimo had any affection, was married to William, Elector Palatine. At the same time Cosimo was granted by the Emperor the title of "Royal Highness." [15] But the condition of the country allowed him small opportunity for satisfaction at these new honours. The people rose and surrounded the Royal Palace clamouring for bread; the provinces were almost depopulated; and savage bands of marauders roamed over the country in search of a livelihood unobtainable by any other means. Tuscany appeared to be sinking into general anarchy. Fortunately, however, in 1693 the Grand Duchess Vittoria, who had for nearly sixty years been the constant cause of discord to the family and ruin to the country, died at Pisa at the age of seventy-two; [16] and this, by removing the chief influence which had led Cosimo into methods which made all satisfactory government impossible, produced some amelioration in the conditions from which the country was suffering.

Cosimo's second son, known as Gian Gastone, was by this time twenty-two. He was good-looking and highly educated, having the reputation of being the most cultured prince of his time, and being specially devoted to science, antiquarian studies, and botany.[17] It was considered a special proof of his exceptional attainments that among various other languages he even knew English. But unlike his brother Ferdinand he preferred a retired and studious life in company with the distinguished Cardinal Noris,[18] who had been his tutor. His active-minded brother Ferdinand consequently despised him; while his father Cosimo disliked him exceedingly, and with his propensity for always taking the most ill-advised course, gave him a very restricted allowance and ignored him on all occasions, with the result that Gian Gastone lived neglected by the court, being without the means to share in social dissipations. Gian Gastone, however, cared little for being thus isolated from the life of society so long as he was left to pursue his studies in peace. He had a good disposition, loved a country life, was free from any feelings of ambition, and with the learned cardinal for his companion wanted no other society, and had no other desire than to live this kind of life permanently.

But Cosimo, who by his senseless method of treatment had already driven one son into reckless and dissolute courses, now proceeded to do the same with the other. It was no doubt desirable that Gian Gastone should marry, and that he should be induced to lead a less retired life; but Cosimo's methods for attaining these objects were the worst that could have been employed. Fired with the idea of planting a branch of the Medici in Germany, Cosimo arranged, through his daughter the Electress Palatine, when Gian Gastone was twenty-four, that the latter should be married to Anne of Saxe-Lauenburg, daughter of the deceased Duke of Saxe-Lauenburg (who had left no son), and widow of the Count Palatine, Philip of Neuberg, "a lady of enormous weight, immense self-will, and no personal attractions."[19] She was coarse and unintellectual, was "more like a Bohemian peasant than a princess," cared only for field sports (which Gian Gastone detested), and considered her small patrimony of Reichstadt, a petty village in a secluded part of the mountains in Bohemia, the only place in the world worth living in. Gian Gastone strongly objected to the wife thus chosen for him, who was about as unsuitable to a man of his tastes as could have been found; but Cosimo would not listen to his protests, and after making him accompany him to Loreto to make numerous votive offerings, despatched him to Dusseldorf (the seat of the Elector Palatine), where in July 1697 the marriage was performed; after which Gian Gastone and his uncongenial consort proceeded to the remote Bohemian village which was in future to be his abode.

Arrived there, Gian Gastone found himself condemned to live in a small and mean castle in the midst of a village, without any intellectual society, with a wife altogether his inferior, in a country which was buried deep in snow for half the year, and where during the other half there was nothing to do but shoot. His wife cared only about horses and dogs, and spent most of her time "holding conversations in the stables"; she was capricious, hysterical, imperious, brainless, and apt to burst out suddenly in wrath or in tears, and her character and manners had after three years' experience caused her former husband to take to drink. Gian Gastone writes to his father that she "is nothing more than a contadina." Placed in such conditions, and saddled with a coarse and ill-favoured wife who offended his tastes at every turn, Gian Gastone stood it for a year and then fled to join his mother in Paris. Thence he was forced by Cosimo to return to his hated domicile in Bohemia; but the various miseries of his existence there began ere long to produce in him a settled melancholy. "Nevertheless from time to time Gian Gastone's keen and witty Tuscan spirit caused him to treat facetiously even the dismal circumstances in which he found himself," [20] and his letters to his father [21] occasionally de-

scribe the untoward conditions of his life with considerable
humour. After a time he tried to induce his wife to come
with him for the winter to Prague, but she utterly declined
to quit Reichstadt, and flew into a passion whenever the subject was mentioned; and at length the constant quarrels with
the vulgar and unrefined woman to whom he had been united,
the inclement climate, and disgust at his surroundings drove
Gian Gastone to remove to Prague, where he took to low society, intemperance, and a generally dissolute life. And henceforth he was more often at Prague than at Reichstadt.

By this time Cosimo (whose errors were all caused by
egregious vanity and want of wisdom rather than by deliberately malevolent intentions) began to perceive the mistake he had made; and seeing that his elder son's health was
failing, and that Gian Gastone would probably become ere
long the heir to the throne, desired that he should return to
Tuscany. But as he would not agree to Gian Gastone doing
so by himself, he turned all his efforts to induce Anne of
Saxe-Lauenburg to come, at all events for a time, to Tuscany.
Every power was brought to bear to effect this, and the
struggle continued for eight years without avail; urgent letters from Cosimo to Anne herself, the authority of her relative the Elector Palatine (who visited Reichstadt in person
with this object), even the commands of the Pope, all were
equally powerless to remove Anne of Saxe-Lauenburg from
Reichstadt.[22] Eventually in 1708 Cosimo gave it up as hopeless, and wrote to Gian Gastone to return to Florence leaving
her behind.[23] This Gian Gastone did, and henceforth they
lived apart.

In 1705 Prince Ferdinand's health began to decline; and
as he and the Princess Violante had no children, while the
same was the case as regarded Gian Gastone and his wife
Anne, the question of the succession began to be of primary
importance in the affairs of Tuscany. Cosimo, therefore, in
1709, compelled his brother Francesco Maria, who was now
nearly fifty, to resign his cardinal's rank and to marry Eleo-

nora Gonzaga, the young daughter of the Duke of Guastella;
but though they went through the marriage ceremony they
separated at once, and Francesco died in the following year
leaving no children.[24]

In view of the large families of three successive generations
it is remarkable that the Medici should have died out as they
did. Cosimo I had eight children (five sons and three daughters); in the next generation Ferdinand I had also eight
children (four sons and four daughters); and in the next
generation Cosimo II had again eight children (five sons and
three daughters). Yet from one cause or another descendants
failed to such an extent that in the fifth generation from
Cosimo I the family entirely died out.

For nearly twenty years the wars between France, Spain,
and Austria had threatened the independence of Tuscany.
That state under Cosimo's clerical administrators had become ready to be the prey of whoever marched an army into
its territory. All the strength it had possessed under Cosimo I
and Ferdinand I had departed. Forts had been allowed to
fall into disrepair, and their armaments to become obsolete;
the fleet had disappeared; the army was contemptible, wanting in men, arms, and equipment. Cosimo had only maintained
Tuscany's independence in the midst of these wars by the
usual resource of a weak state, that of siding first with one
and then with another of the combatants according to whichever at the moment was the strongest. Their armies had frequently invaded Lombardy, and Tuscany would have been
similarly overrun had it not been that each of the three powers
was determined to prevent the central state in Italy from
becoming the property of either of the others.

These conditions were now intensified by its becoming
apparent that at no distant date there would remain no
descendant of the Medici family to occupy the Tuscan throne,
none of Cosimo's three children having any children. Therefore, between the various powers who all cast greedy eyes

upon the most important State in Italy there now began a
political contest, which lasted for the next thirty years, as
to which of them should become the possessor of Tuscany
when that throne should be vacant, "the European monarchs
watching like wreckers the last moments of the foundering
Medici." [25] Meanwhile Cosimo protested furiously against
any such question being debated, declaring it to be his right
to nominate a successor to the throne after the demise of his
sons; and that even if this were disallowed the position reverted to that which had existed before Cosimo I created that
throne, the right to say by whom they would be governed
reverting to the Tuscan people.

In 1712 there was assembled the Congress of Utrecht, in
which almost every state in Europe took part, and at which
each had some claim to urge as a portion of the terms of any
general peace which might be effected. At this congress
Cosimo's right to nominate a successor to the throne of Tuscany on the death of his second son was practically acknowledged by the powers. Although not a final settlement of the
question, it was a matter of common knowledge that Cosimo
intended to nominate his daughter, the Electress Anna Maria
Ludovica, to succeed his second son if she outlived the latter;
and the Emperor Charles VI signified to her and to Cosimo
that he would be ready to give his sanction to this arrangement.

In 1713, when Cosimo was seventy-one, his eldest son,
Prince Ferdinand, died, at the age of fifty. [26] He was greatly
lamented in Tuscany, not only on account of his abilities,
his agreeable disposition (which caused the excesses of his
later years to be forgiven), and his constant opposition to the
foolish methods of government by which the country was
being brought to ruin, but also on account of the high hopes
which had been entertained of the complete change which it
was felt he would have introduced whenever he succeeded to
the throne.

Upon the death of Cosimo's eldest son the Florentine Sen-

ate was convened, and passed a decree,[27] which was confirmed by the Grand Duke, that on the death of Prince
Giovanni Gastone, his sister, the Electress Anna Maria Ludovica, should succeed to the throne. This decree was formally
promulgated and communicated to the various courts of
Europe, its promulgation in Florence being accompanied by
public festivities. Austria declined to agree, declaring that
the decree showed that Cosimo's ultimate intention was to
give Tuscany to a Bourbon; but Cosimo placed his chief
reliance on England and Holland, who were both ready to
withstand Austria in the matter, George I being specially
opposed to any foreign power obtaining a preponderating
influence in Italy. France also did not object to the decree,
Louis XIV only taking exception to its incompleteness, and
urging that prudence, policy, and national justice pointed
to the ultimate successor being the Princess Elizabeth of
Parma, through Margherita de' Medici, daughter of Cosimo
II.[28] Lastly, Philip V of Spain took a still more definite
course by promptly marrying the Princess Elizabeth, as a
preliminary to claiming Tuscany for Spain when the time
came. Meanwhile the Peace of Utrecht (1714) took place
without any opposition being made by any of the powers
to the Electress Anna Maria Ludovica being considered the
rightful successor to the throne of Tuscany after her brother,
Giovanni Gastone.

In 1715 Louis XIV died, his death causing important
changes in European politics; and in 1716 the Electress Anna
Maria Ludovica, now fifty years of age, became a widow,
and returned from Dusseldorf to Florence, where she immediately became the principal personage at the court. On
her arrival Ferdinand's widow, the Princess Violante, retired
to Siena, of which she was made Governor. The altered state
of European affairs caused by the death of Louis XIV led in
1718 to a quadruple alliance between England, Holland,
France, and Austria. And these powers in a treaty concluded
at London decided, without even consulting the Grand Duke

of Tuscany, that on the death of Cosimo's son, Gian Gastone, Tuscany should go to Don Carlos of Spain, the eldest son of Elizabeth of Parma, Queen of Spain; this being done in order to pacify Austria as to the chance of a Bourbon being allowed to obtain Tuscany. The article of this treaty which thus sacrificed Tuscany, trampled on a formal national decree, and excluded Cosimo's favourite child from the succession, was kept secret, but could not long be concealed; and when it became known it filled both the Florentines and the Grand Duke with unbounded indignation. The people hated Cosimo, but at the moment this feeling was swallowed up in their wrath against the four powers who had thus treated their country. Cosimo sent vehement protests to all the powers concerned; but each of them profited in various ways by other clauses in the treaty, and would do nothing to invalidate it; and Cosimo was informed that he must submit, and that if he did not, foreign troops would be sent into Tuscany to hold it for disposal in accordance with the treaty of London. Thus did Cosimo see himself insulted, his country sold, and the independence of Tuscany annihilated.

But at this juncture Cosimo, though he was now seventy-six years old, displayed an energy and vigour at variance with all his previous history. Troops were raised throughout Tuscany, the fortresses were repaired and their armaments brought up to date, the harbour defences of Porto Ferrajo and Leghorn were strengthened, and every arrangement made to resist to the uttermost. Tuscany, if it was to perish as an independent state, should die fighting. At the same time Cosimo drew up a formal declaration to the powers which stated that "no successor to the Medici could be recognised in the free and independent State of Tuscany unless approved by the people through their representative the Florentine Senate; therefore no power had a right to exclude the Electress Anna as chosen by that body and hailed with public acclamation; and that except by violence there was no way of making a free nation submit to feudal supremacy, a thing utterly at

variance with its nature and institutions; or of introducing
garrisons into a neutral and unoffending country which had
only been striving to preserve its own peace without molesting
any one." [29] By this time England and Holland were at war;
it was believed that Cosimo's determined attitude must be
supported secretly by some other power; while it seemed
probable that some new turn in international politics might
throw the whole question again into discussion. Cosimo's protest was consequently received with respect.

In 1720 peace was again restored, and a fresh congress
was assembled at Cambrai. At this congress the whole question of the Tuscan succession was argued out afresh, Cosimo's
ambassador being Corsini, who displayed much ability in
demonstrating the injustice to Tuscany of the proposed
course, and more particularly the certainty that any rule of
that country in Austrian hands (which the Florentines feared
was now contemplated) would be of a most tyrannical character; while in any case it was, he argued, most unfair not
to allow the rule of Tuscany to pass, after Prince Giovanni
Gastone's death, to his sister, the Electress Anna Maria Ludovica, she being eminently qualified, both in character and
ability, to govern the country well. These discussions at Cambrai continued all through the years 1721 and 1722, while
the negotiations, intrigues, and secret agreements between
the various powers over the bone of contention, Tuscany,
were interminable.

Meanwhile age began to tell upon Cosimo. Worn out by
these long contests over the independence of his country, and
with his strength failing now that he was approaching eighty
years of age, he abandoned the rule of the state entirely to
his capable daughter, with whose control of affairs her
brother, Gian Gastone (only anxious to be left in his beloved
seclusion), had no desire to interfere. She conducted all negotiations with foreign powers, showed a capable management
of home affairs, mitigated the harsher aspects of Cosimo's
laws, and spent much in works of public benefit. Her con-

duct was widely praised, and it became a general wish that she might survive her brother and succeed to the throne. So that her efforts to make other powers accept the decree of the Florentine Senate were vigorously supported by the people of Tuscany. The memory of her mother's youthful sorrows was revived in September 1721 by the death of the Grand Duchess Marguerite Louise at Paris at the age of seventy-six; and this increased the regard entertained for the daughter of a princess for whom the Florentines had always felt much sympathy.

In 1723, the discussions at Cambrai showing that whatever other arrangements were made between the leading powers of Europe they were determined to adhere to their unjust treatment of Tuscany, Corsini was instructed to lodge a final solemn protest, with the object of asserting the rights of Cosimo's successor and of making the act of violence on which the powers were bent more marked. This was the last public act of Cosimo's life; and on the 31st October 1723, after handing over the government to his son Gian Gastone, Cosimo III passed away,[30] after a reign of fifty-three years in which (with the best intentions) he had produced nothing but evil and the utmost national misery.

————————

Cosimo III is an example of how a character which in a private capacity would be unobjectionable may in the position of a ruler become a pattern of everything most baneful. In a private sphere he would have been a very ordinary person, and probably much respected, since the chief defects of his character would never in that case have had any opportunity of developing. Placed, however, on a throne, the combined effects of his want of wisdom, vanity, weakness, bigotry, and tyranny caused him to present an example of everything that is worst in a ruler. Under him joyous and light-hearted Tuscany became a vale of tears. Hating his sons, apparently for no other reason than that they were each in their different ways more capable than himself, he ruined both their lives by the most narrow-minded domestic tyranny. Lastly, Cosimo III was the first of his house who by his conduct as a ruler turned the poorer classes of the people against him, and thereby overthrew that which had always been the strongest bulwark of his family. Such was the result which had been produced by Ferdinand II's weakness in allowing his eldest son to be brought up by a foolish and incapable mother in the manner that he did, whereby evils were entailed for half a century, upon both the country and the family, which were appalling in their magnitude and deplorable in their consequences.

CHAPTER XXX

GIOVANNI GASTONE

Born 1671. (*Reigned* 1723-1737.) *Died* 1737

WE must not linger over the remaining years of the Medici, for their sun is setting fast, and setting in deepest gloom. From the effects of such a reign as that of Cosimo III they were not able to recover, and the fourteen years' reign of the last Medici Grand Duke has little to show us upon which it is pleasant to dwell.

Gian Gastone was fifty-two when in 1723 he succeeded to a throne which he looked upon by no means as an object of desire, but rather as a distasteful burden which he would have escaped from if he could, grievously interfering as it did with the seclusion to which, by being uniformly excluded by his father from all public affairs, he had grown accustomed.

Nevertheless Gian Gastone set himself with commendable perseverance to reform the many abuses which weighed upon the country. He dismissed at once all the spies, hypocrites, and sycophants who had surrounded his father; he annulled at a stroke the long list of pensions (called "Pensions on the Creed") paid to Jews, Turks, heterodox Catholics, heretical Protestants, and other so-called "converts," which had formed a heavy item in the national expenditure; and by other similar measures set himself resolutely to relieve taxation. He abolished the organised system of *espionage* which had so long been established over the domestic life of the citizens; the prison doors were opened, and prisoners (most of them under punishment for ecclesiastical offences) set at liberty; penalties were remitted, and exiles allowed to return. Imitating the example of his grandfather, Ferdinand II,

Gian Gastone mixed freely with his subjects; and to assist him in social matters—since his wife, Anne of Saxe-Lauenburg, refused to live in Tuscany, and he disliked his arbitrary sister, the Electress—he installed his widowed sister-in-law, the Princess Violante Beatrice, as dispenser of the hospitalities of the court. The Royal Palace re-awoke to life; the religious gloom which had long hung round it was swept away; and instead of the dark-robed monks who had pervaded its corridors and precincts, the youth and beauty of Florence were once more gathered within its walls.

The Princess Violante was the bright spot in Gian Gastone's reign. Her virtues, amiability, and good sense were invaluable to him. In a short time she became the chief influence, not only in social matters, but also in public affairs; an influence justly deserved, and followed by the best results. She was universally beloved; possessing considerable talents she was a zealous patroness of literature and of genius in every form, her sympathy for the poor and oppressed was continually manifested, cheerfulness followed wherever she appeared, and we are told, "she was equally liked by the learned, the friendless, and the gay." [1] Her many virtues were so generally acknowledged that Pope Benedict XIII (1724-1730) bestowed on her the Golden Rose. Nor were any found who did not consider this unusual honour deserved.

The intrigues of the chief powers of Europe, as to which of them should become the possessor of Tuscany on Gian Gastone's death, still continued; and, feeling himself powerless to oppose them, the latter turned his chief attention to securing that whenever the throne passed into other hands his sister's inheritance of the vast private property belonging to the family should be assured to her, and to obtaining compensation to her for territorial or other possessions of the State which had been purchased out of the family's private fortune. The former category included their various palaces and villas crowded with precious furniture and countless objects of art, which were all indisputably the private property of the family; while in the latter category were included the whole of the artillery, certain ports and fortresses, and the town and district of Pontremoli. In this endeavour Gian Gastone was to a large extent successful, it being conceded that the private property of the family would, of course, be inherited by his sister; while the question of compensation for possessions of the State which had been purchased out of their private fortune was left for future settlement; though in the end the Medici received no compensation on this account.

During the years 1724-1731 the discussions and negotiations between the leading powers of Europe over the Tuscan succession were endless, Austria refusing to consider any other question until this was settled, while Spain endeavoured in every way to compel Gian Gastone to accept Don Carlos as his successor, fear of Austria alone preventing her from sending troops into the country to enforce this. Meanwhile the condition of the people of Tuscany steadily improved; Gian Gastone's reduction of taxation, his abolition of the punishment of death, his destruction of the hated system of domestic *espionage,* and his efforts for the amusement of the people had brought about gaiety and light-heartedness in place of gloom and misery; commerce and agriculture began to revive; while the Princess Violante's cheerfulness spread itself everywhere, everything which could create happiness among the people being encouraged by her.

Nor did the gloomy prospects of Tuscany in the political sphere blacken the people's whole horizon. In those days Florence was accustomed from time to time to give itself up to a simple light-hearted enjoyment which helped not a little to ameliorate adverse political conditions. Thus at the time of the annual Carnival in particular there were not only processions of carriages (*corsi*) with battles of flowers and *confetti,* but also numerous masked balls, masquerades, and other diversions of the kind in which all classes joined. During

Carnival time masks were permitted to be worn both at the theatres and in the streets, any attempt to restrict this being much resented by the people. The Uffizi colonnade, known to us under such a different aspect, must have presented a singularly animated and picturesque appearance on an afternoon preceding one of these masked balls. For whenever a masked ball was to take place in the evening it was customary for this to be preceded in the afternoon by a promenade in masks and dominoes under this colonnade, such promenades being attended by all classes, and even the Grand Duke himself sometimes taking part in them.

But a shadow was cast over everything by the proceedings of the various powers who were anxious for Gian Gastone's death, each bent upon being the first in the field when that event occurred. A slight illness of his in 1728 was at once represented by Spain and Austria as a mortal sickness; whereupon an Imperial edict was issued calling on the Tuscans when Gian Gastone expired to acknowledge the successor appointed by Austria. The Grand Duke remonstrated against such a disturbance of his government, but his protests were ignored. In the following year, upon his dislocating his ankle by a fall, reports of his death were again spread. Spain assembled a fleet and army to take possession of Tuscany, while Austria sent thirty thousand men into Lombardy, commanded by Marshal Daun, who offered their services to the Grand Duke. But Gian Gastone was determined, if possible, to prevent Tuscany from being desolated by war; he declined the offer, and temporised with Spain, and the danger for the moment passed off, Gian Gastone agreeing to acknowledge Don Carlos as his successor, and Spain offering in return to consent to the Electress Anna Maria Ludovica being a member of the Cabinet with the title of Grand Duchess.

While all Europe resounded with preparations for war, the death of Pope Benedict XIII started a fresh series of negotiations. Austria demanded to be allowed to occupy

Milan, while the Spanish fleet threatened to seize Leghorn.
Gian Gastone still refused to agree to the occupation of any
part of Tuscany by either of the rival powers, but began to
be weary of this struggle against contending forces whom he
was powerless to resist. And the death of Princess Violante [2]
in 1731, amidst the tears of a whole nation, completed his
despair. He had never wholly relinquished the vices to which
he had taken during his father's lifetime, and these now
established a complete hold over him. He abandoned public
affairs almost entirely to his ministers; an infamous favourite,
Giuliano Dami, became the head of his household, the dispenser of honours, and the sole channel of access to him; and
retiring from public view Gian Gastone sank into absolute
degradation, becoming a drunken sensualist seen only by a
group of the vilest companions, "spending half his time in
bed to recover from the effects of the half ill-spent out of it,"
and seeking diversion in the company of buffoons.

Meanwhile Spain and Austria each took steps to obtain a
military hold of the country. A combined Spanish and British
fleet seized Leghorn, and landed an army of thirty thousand
Spaniards who were quartered in different parts of Tuscany.
Thereupon the Emperor Charles VI despatched an Austrian
army of fifty thousand men to enter Tuscany by Pontremoli;
and a struggle in Tuscany between the two powers was only
averted by Don Carlos being called away to lead a Spanish
army against Naples, Austria at the same time suffering a
defeat at the passage of the Po. The Emperor's intention was
to give Tuscany, if he obtained it, to his daughter, the celebrated Maria Theresa. The Florentines, on the other hand,
hated the idea of an Austrian ruler, and if they were not to
have one of their own race, infinitely preferred a Spanish to
an Austrian one. France looked only at what might best
assist her views in regard to Milan and Savoy; while England
and Holland desired peace in any way that it could be obtained, regardless of what consequences might result to
Tuscany.

At length, in October 1735, an agreement was made between Austria, France, England, and Holland, as the basis of a general peace, that the Grand Duchy of Tuscany should be given to the Emperor's daughter, Maria Theresa; that she should be married to Francis, Duke of Lorraine; and that the latter, in exchange for Tuscany, should resign Lorraine to France; Tuscany thus becoming, instead of Lorraine, an appanage of the house of Austria. Spain at first refused to agree, but having suffered reverses both in Lombardy and Naples, eventually did so on being given a *quid pro quo* elsewhere. And in January 1736 this agreement between the five powers was ratified at the Peace of Vienna.

The Florentines were furious at their country being thus deliberately sold by the powers of Europe, and the more so at being after all handed over to an Austrian ruler, predicting that they would be subjected to a grinding tyranny.[3] Gian Gastone sent urgent protests to London, Paris, and Vienna, but without any avail; he was looked on by the powers as "a mere object of sale." Weakened in mind and body by his excesses, plunged into deepest melancholy at the fate of his country and family, and sinking under an accumulation of miseries, he left his ministers to govern the country as they chose. On the 12th February 1736 Francis, Duke of Lorraine, was married to Maria Theresa,[4] and formally renounced the Duchy of Lorraine in exchange for the territories of the Medici whenever they should become vacant by Gian Gastone's death, the arrangement being guaranteed by France and Austria.

In January 1737, in accordance with the above convention, the Spanish garrisons throughout Tuscany were withdrawn and Austrian troops took their place, General Braitwitz at Florence and General Wachtendonk at Leghorn swearing allegiance to the Grand Duke on the 5th February 1737. But Gian Gastone was already dying of an accumulation of diseases, and past caring who had Tuscany. One last act his love of science prompted—the erection in Sta. Croce of the monument to Galileo and removal to it of the latter's remains from the Medici chapel attached to that church. The first public act of the first Medici had been that of taking a prominent part in the birthday of Art; the last public act of the last Medici Grand Duke was the erection of a due memorial to Science. On the 9th July 1737 Gian Gastone breathed his last at the age of sixty-six,[b] sincerely regretted by the people, who had greatly benefited by his principles of government, and only saw his vices dimly at a distance, while they mourned at the passing away of the last ruler over Tuscany belonging to their own race.

CHAPTER XXXI

ANNA MARIA LUDOVICA

("THE LAST OF THE MEDICI")

Born 1667. *Died* 1743

THE Electress Anna Maria Ludovica was seventy years old when her brother Gian Gastone died. Married at twenty-four to the Elector Palatine of the Rhine, she had filled an important position for twenty-six years up to the time of his death and her return as a widow to live with her father Cosimo. And during those years she had shown herself to be a woman of unusual ability. After her father's death she had, during the fourteen years of her brother's reign, lived more or less in retirement, not being on good terms with him, and feeling shame at the degradation into which he sank during the latter part of his reign. Endowed with more energy and force of character than either of her brothers, she had ruled well during the few years that her father had left the government in her hands, notwithstanding that she was considerably handicapped by the style of administration which he had established. As the result of her satisfactory control of affairs she had seen herself earnestly desired by the people of Tuscany as their future ruler, and had seen a decree passed by the Florentine Senate assuring the throne to her on her brother's death; and she had also seen that decree spurned and over-ridden by the chief powers of Europe, herself and her ancient family insulted, and the independence of her country trampled upon. She was now to see the final stage in that process, and the inauguration of a foreign rule over Tuscany; even the promise that in any new government established she should be a member of the Council and have the rank and title of Grand Duchess being set aside.

It would all have been hard enough for an exceptionally proud woman like the Electress Anna to endure if the Austrian Grand Duke had proceeded to occupy in person the throne which her grandfather's great-grandfather had created. It was made many times worse by the kind of rule which was set up.

Upon Gian Gastone's death the new Grand Duke, Francis II, came to Florence and formally took possession of the State, but after a month or two departed to Vienna, and thenceforth left the government of Tuscany to be permanently ¹ administered (or mal-administered) by an agent, a certain M. de Beauveu, who was given the title of Prince de Craon. Both he and his wife were persons of exceedingly low birth and manners; yet they assumed vice-regal airs, lived in the Royal Palace, and maintained a third-rate kind of court, the chief feature of which was its vulgarity. All posts in the new administration were speedily filled with Lorrainers, and the Tuscans had ocular demonstration at every turn that they were now under a foreign rule. The meanness, the corruption, and the degraded character of this collection of needy place-hunters are graphically described in the letters of the first English ambassador ever sent to the court of Tuscany,² which show that as far as corruption in the administration was concerned, the country had gained nothing by the change.

With a court of this description established in the Palace, there ensued a total decline in the dignity which even in the worst days of Cosimo III and Gian Gastone had ever been accustomed to reign there. Horace Mann remarks on the entire inability of the new *régime* to maintain a due ceremony even on grand occasions, and says:—"They seem to forget the example of the Medici, the ceremony of whose court put it in their power to make a figure in things of more importance." Added to this the ignorance and want of taste of the newcomers in all matters relating to Art was colossal; and this, while specially irritating to the Florentines, often had the most ridiculous results. Among other demonstrations of this want of a quality which every Medici had possessed, the arrangement of the pictures in the Palace offered a conspicuous example. These were rearranged on a new principle, the two guiding rules of which were, first, the degree of freshness of the gilding on the frames, and, second, the position of the figures in the picture, *which figures must not turn their backs towards the throne.*

It was no wonder, the new Government being of this description, that the Electress Anna (the descendant of a race which even in their decay had still been distinguished) kept herself aloof from such a company. She occupied her own separate portion of the Palace, and had no relations with the new Grand Duke's agent and his wife.

"She lived retired; but it was a retirement of the utmost splendour. All that art and ingenuity could supply and money purchase the aged daughter of Cosimo gathered round her —jewels, precious metals, costly attire—the mass of these was immense." [3]

Moreover, she still continued to add pictures to the Uffizi Gallery. As a child she had known her great-uncle, Cardinal Leopold, and had imbibed some of the ideals which animated him, and nearly all the pictures of the Flemish and German schools which the Uffizi Gallery possesses were added to it by her. [4]

The amount that this daughter of the Medici spent in charity astounded the English ambassador; "1,000 zechins a month, often more." [5] As three zechins made £1 sterling, this represented £4,000 a year, equal at the present value of money to considerably more; and even this, he says, she often exceeded. No wonder the poor wept inconsolably when she died. She continued to maintain to some extent the state to which she had been accustomed in former days. The poet Gray, who was presented to her in 1740, describes her as receiving him "with much ceremony, standing under a huge black canopy," and as "never going out but to church, and then with guards and eight horses to her coach."

Thus did Anna Maria Ludovica de' Medici maintain in all ways the name of her family. However much that name had suffered discredit through others, it suffered none through her. And whether in regard to ruling with ability, the encouragement of all forms of art, a generous liberality to the poor, or the maintenance of a proper dignity, she showed herself a worthy descendant of the best of those who had gone before.

The object, however, which chiefly engaged both her time and her money was the completion of the family mausoleum. The work had somewhat languished during the reigns of Cosimo III and Gian Gastone, but Anna Maria Ludovica applied all her energies and the greater part of her large income to completing it as far as possible during the few years of life that remained to her. Her health was failing; she knew she had but a short time; and she pressed on this work vigorously, giving to it as much as "1,000 crowns a week," [6] and in her will leaving a large sum to be invested in order to provide a regular income for the completion of the building according to the original design.[7] There is something both pathetic and fine in the sight of this lonely and childless woman, the last of her race, steadily labouring in the midst of disappointment, sorrow, and ill-health, to complete the mausoleum of her ancestors before death should call her away to follow them.

But Anna Maria Ludovica did something more noteworthy than this. Her chief act was one as fine under the circumstances as anything the Medici did throughout their history. And by it she caused their sun, so long enveloped in dark clouds and impenetrable gloom, to shine out, as it sank, in

one departing ray of most resplendent glory. She hated the
new dynasty; she felt that her family had been grievously
treated by not being allowed to leave the throne of Tuscany
to whomsoever they considered had the best right to it; she
felt herself still more grievously ill used in not being allowed
to succeed her brother as Grand Duchess in her own right;
while the sore feelings thus created were daily kept alive by
the conduct of the ignoble court occupying the palace which
had been built by her family and been their home for two
hundred years. But at the same time she loved Tuscany; she
was keenly mindful of her family's long and honourable connection with that country; and she was determined that,
whatever her father and brother had been, she at least would
support that connection with honour to the very end. And
so she made that splendid gift which should make her name
ever honoured in Florence.

Far-reaching memories and mingled feelings must have
filled the mind of Anna Maria Ludovica as, last solitary
owner of the greatest collection of art treasures in the world,
she wandered through the long galleries of the Uffizi and the
Pitti surrounded by this mass of pictures, statues, bronzes,
rare gems, and other works of art, the earliest of them executed for Cosimo, Piero, and Lorenzo, the latest added to the
collection by herself, and thought over what she had determined on doing with this great inheritance.

The convention between the powers which had assigned
the throne to a foreign prince had not touched the vast private
property of the family, including the countless objects of
art and other valuable things with which their palaces, villas,
and picture-galleries were crowded; and to all these she had
succeeded on her brother's death. The whole of this invaluable
collection of treasures Anna Maria Ludovica now gave to the
State of Tuscany for ever, in the person of the new Grand
Duke and his successors, *on condition that none of it should
ever be removed from Florence, and that it should be for
the benefit of the public of all nations.*[8]

What the value in money of this truly royal gift may be is probably beyond computation. It included, with much besides: [9]—

(*a*) The whole of the pictures and statues which were in the Uffizi Gallery, the Royal Palace, the Villa Medici at Rome, and the other villas of the family, and now forming the Uffizi and Pitti Galleries.

(*b*) The rare collection of gems and other objects of art, now in the Gem Room of the Uffizi Gallery.

(*c*) A great collection of cameos, engraved gems, and similar articles, now in the museum of the Bargello, and including the celebrated collection of coins and medallions of Lorenzo the Magnificent, the oldest in Europe.

(*d*) Statues and busts by Donatello, Verrocchio, Mino da Fiesole, and other notable sculptors, now in the museum of the Bargello.

(*e*) A great collection of bronzes, now in the museum of the Bargello.

(*f*) The New Sacristy, with the masterpieces of Michelangelo.

(*g*) The whole of the contents of the Library of the Palace, and the Medici Library in San Lorenzo.

(*h*) A large and important collection of Egyptian and Etruscan antiquities, now forming the chief part of the Egyptian and Etruscan Museums, the Etruscan portion being specially valuable.

(*i*) A valuable collection of majolica, Urbino-ware, Faenza-ware, rare suits of armour, and curious and valuable arms, now in the museum of the Bargello.

(*j*) A large collection of valuable tapestries, now forming the Galleria degli Arazzi.

(*k*) The valuable tables of *pietra dura* work, cabinets, and other precious furniture, now in the Uffizi and Pitti Galleries.

(*l*) The inlaid tables, valuable cabinets, tapestry, and
other similar articles, now in the Royal apartments
of the Pitti Palace.

(*m*) The gold dessert service, gold and silver ornaments,
rare china, valuable plate, croziers and crucifixes
in ivory and amber, the mitre with miniatures made
of humming-birds' feathers which had belonged to
Clement VII, priceless works in *niello*, handsome
goblets and vases by Benvenuto Cellini, and many
other heirlooms of the family, all now in the Treasure Room of the Pitti Palace.

(*n*) The reliquaries and other ornaments of the Grand
Ducal chapel in the Pitti Palace.

(*o*) The immense Medicean wardrobe of costly robes and
dresses for state occasions.[10]

From Poggio Imperiale, from Castello, from Petraia, from
Cafaggiolo, from Poggio a Caiano, from the Villa Medici at
Rome, from every habitation that the Medici had occupied,
poured in for many years afterwards this great collection of
objects of art to be gathered in the galleries and museums
of Florence in accordance with the terms of this gift; terms
to which Florence owes it that these treasures have not been
long since either dispersed,[11] or removed to Vienna or Rome.
The Medici themselves have passed away, but their works
live on. And of all that they have left behind them as a record
of the spirit which animated them, nothing can surpass that
which a whole world enjoys through the gift which was their
last act, and which the traditions of their house and the
principles implanted long before by its founder caused them
to present to their nation, even when smarting under a sense
of injustice and disappointment.

Speaking of this action, an Italian writer of the present
day has said:—

"By this act the Princess Anna Maria, in securing to the
country so much that was most notable of its art, acquired

a truly imperishable title to the gratitude of Italy, and one which deserved to outweigh and make forgiven many faults of her ancestors." [12]

It is when one looks at the Florence of to-day, without manufactures or the business of a seaport and yet so prosperous a city, that one realises what this gift (with all the others previously given by the Medici) has meant to her. That prosperity entirely depends on Florence's power to attract visitors from other countries; without that power she, the second city of Italy, would sink back at once to the level of her ancient rival Lucca. And were all that the Medici gave to Florence taken away [13] the whole of that influx of visitors from other countries would cease. For her three great churches would not by themselves attract it; and even San Marco would be gone.[14] So that Anna Maria Ludovica, little as she could have realised all that its consequences would be, by this parting gift in the name of her family did the very best thing she could have done to ensure the future prosperity of Florence. Yet in the city which her action has thus enriched her very name is almost unknown. No statue of her adorns any of its open spaces; no gallery or museum of all those which she has to a great extent filled, and protected from having their contents removed to other cities, has her name written over its doors or any bust or picture of her placed in honour on its walls. And thousands interested in art pass through Florence every season, or even leave that city after long residence there, without ever having heard her name.

Of the items included in this gift the last, the Medicean wardrobe, was not permanently retained.[15] Some thirty years afterwards, in the time of the Grand Duke Pietro Leopoldo (the first of the Austrian Grand Dukes who was a resident ruler of Tuscany) it was broken up and sold. And some idea of the magnificence customary in what we now know as the Pitti Palace in the time of the Medici Grand Dukes is given us by the details of this sale, which on account of the mass of valuable things to be disposed of continued monthly for ten years. Napier says:—

"Nor was the ancient Medicean wardrobe, which had long reposed in idle splendour, more spared by the stern frugality of Leopold.... Almost every residence of the Medici throughout Tuscany had its peculiar wardrobe, independent of the great magazine of Medicean splendour in Florence, and all were now exposed to public sale. Velvets, damasks, gold embroideries, chairs and mirror frames of massive silver, gold brocades, rich lace, fringes, and costly silken fabrics, were either sold to the public or condemned to the crucible. Gian Gastone's state bed, embroidered throughout with a profusion of beautiful pearls and other gems, was picked to pieces, and many exquisite works in jewellery and precious metals, the symbols of Medicean taste and magnificence, were all broken up or otherwise disposed of to the amount of half a million of crowns." [16]

Anna Maria Ludovica had not to endure for many years the daily mortifications resulting from the establishment of a foreign rule over her country. In 1742, five years after that rule had been set up, her health began to give way. She suffered much from dropsy, and felt that she had not much longer to live. Having still a large amount of personal property to dispose of, including her own wearing jewels, the contents of her wardrobes, the furniture of her rooms, china, plate, and nearly £2,000,000 sterling in money, she set about adding various codicils to the will which she had made some three years before. And desiring to leave some portion of her property to her next-of-kin, whoever he might be, she had drawn up for her a genealogical tree showing, not only the historic Medici, the descendants of Giovanni di Bicci, of whom she was the last, but also the collateral branches of the family. By its means, retracing her family for some four hundred and fifty years, back to Salvestro, the grandfather of Giovanni di Bicci. she discovered that a descendant of Salvestro's brother Giovenco, a certain Pietro Paolo de'

Medici, was her nearest of kin, though not, of course, a descendant of the historic Medici; whereupon she added a clause to her will declaring him her heir and leaving him a portion of her property. She only lived a few months after completing these final testamentary dispositions; and on the 18th February 1743, at the age of seventy-six, Anna Maria Ludovica, the last remaining descendant of Giovanni di Bicci, passed away,[17] and the family which he had founded, and which had had such a long and eventful history, was extinct.

The chief provisions of Anna Maria Ludovica's will and its codicils are briefly detailed by the English Ambassador, Horace Mann, as follows:—

(1) All her courtiers and servants to have their salaries for life.

(2) Pensions to her four executors.

(3) To pay the above pensions and salaries, a large sum of money deposited in the bank of Sta. Maria Nuova.

(4) To the Marquis Rinuncini (the principal executor) her lands in the State of Urbino, and a considerable legacy of much of the rich furniture in her Audience Room.

(5) Her china, half to young Rinuncini, and half to Coroni.

(6) To the Marquis Guadagni, to Siristori, and to Bardi (her other three executors) besides their pensions, very rich presents in silver.

(7) To Madame Uguccioni, her mistress of the robes, the whole of the contents of a room containing, besides many other things, velvet brocades, linen, etc., valued at 10,000 crowns, and a toilet service of gold.

(8) To all her maids-of-honour presents, and the usual fortunes in case of marriage.

(9) To the Austrian Grand Duke she left the whole of

her own wearing jewels, "annexing them to those of the State of Tuscany, with which they are to descend. Their value in present money is supposed about £500,000. Besides this the Grand Duke is left heir to a thousand other things." [18]

(10) To her "più prossimo agnato" (nearest of kin), Pietro Paolo de' Medici, 30,000 crowns; and as other pensioners die off, their pensions to go to him and his heirs till the sum is made up to 100,000 crowns. Also jewels and plate valued at about 150,000 crowns.

(11) Presents in jewels to the Queen of Hungary (Maria Theresa), to Prince Charles, and to several princes of Germany.

(12) Also a very large legacy to the Prince of Salzbach (Elector Palatine).

A codicil, dated 7th October 1739, provided that on the death of legatees who were given pensions under the will, "the portions of the estate set free by their death are to be invested by the executors in sound securities, and the interest of such investments to be devoted to carrying on, finishing and perfecting the Royal Mausoleum situated behind the choir of the venerable church of San Lorenzo with the same excellence and preciousness employed up to the present, and on the plan of the models and designs which have been made." [19]

On the night of the 22nd February a stately funeral, accompanied by every accessory which could heighten its melancholy grandeur, and surrounded by so great a mass of torches that they lighted up the entire street as the procession moved along,[20] left the Royal Palace, and passed slowly down the Via Maggio, over the Ponte Sta. Trinità, and along the Via Tornabuoni to the mausoleum behind San Lorenzo. "The body was conveyed in a sort of coach, quite open, and with a canopy over the head." [21] It was the funeral given by the orders of the Austrian Grand Duke to her who had hoped to die Grand Duchess of Tuscany in her own right. Thus with solemn pomp, and amidst the tears of the many poor whom she had assisted, was laid with her ancestors in that mausoleum where none any more were to be buried, one who had maintained not unworthily the honour of her family, and whose tomb bears the inscription, "The last of the royal race of the Medici."

CHAPTER XXXII

AND so the long story of the Medici closes; and closes where it began, in that "venerable church of San Lorenzo," which they built and endowed, and which gathers in itself all the threads of their chequered history during the three hundred and forty-three years which lie between the tomb of Giovanni di Bicci in the Old Sacristy and that of Anna Maria Ludovica in the crypt of the mausoleum behind the choir. In this church they were baptised as children, married as young men and girls, and buried when their lives came to an end; for family tradition required that they should all be laid at last in San Lorenzo. And here the black threads of tragedy and sorrow, the blue ones of love and happiness, and the golden ones of gratified ambition mingle and cross each other in the great tapestry of this family's long romance.

Here in this church of San Lorenzo, soon after its rebuilding was finished, was seen the first great mourning of the family, when Cosimo's favourite son, Giovanni, died; soon followed by the funeral of Cosimo himself (1464). Here four years later took place the splendid marriage of the young Lorenzo to Clarice Orsini, when the whole city gave itself up to feasting and delight. A few years later we have a far different scene in San Lorenzo; it is after the murder at High Mass of the people's favourite, Giuliano, and the huge black catafalque surrounded with tall candles in the centre of the nave, the solemn music, and the weeping crowd, attest a whole city's grief (1478). Then come other scenes; the Medici are in exile, and every inch of standing space in the church is occupied by a deeply-moved crowd listening to the great preacher Savonarola, who delivered some of his most impressive sermons from the carved black marble pulpit which stands in the north aisle (1496). Four years after the return of the Medici comes the funeral of Giuliano (Duc de Nemours), the first of the family to be buried in the New Sacristy, then just added to the church (1516). And this is followed three years later by the pompous funeral of his nephew, Lorenzo (Duke of Urbino). Then after Florence's struggle for liberty is over, and Alessandro has been installed as Duke, we have another imposing scene in San Lorenzo. It is the marriage of Alessandro to Margaret, daughter of Charles V, the last step in a scheme which had subjected the city to a tyrant's rule, and the crowd which looks on is a sullen and dispirited one (1536). Six months later we have again a burial in San Lorenzo; but it is a very different one from any which have preceded. In the dead of night, with as few lights as possible, in silence and secrecy, the murder being still unknown to the city, is hurriedly borne into San Lorenzo by a few hired servants the body of the detested Alessandro. The lid of the sarcophagus of Lorenzo (Duke of Urbino) in the New Sacristy is forced open, the body unceremoniously placed therein, the sarcophagus again closed, and the small band of servants depart as secretly as they have come (1537). This is followed two years afterwards by the marriage of Duke Cosimo to Eleonora di Toledo, in the presence of her father, the Viceroy of Naples, and a numerous retinue of Spanish nobles. Twenty-three years later San Lorenzo witnessed those two sad funerals when Cosimo buried within one month his wife Eleonora and his two sons, Giovanni and Garzia (1562). And then, after the Medici had become Grand Dukes, San Lorenzo saw a long succession of splendid marriages and pathetic funerals, beginning with the marriage of Cosimo's son Francis to the Archduchess Joanna, the sister of an Emperor, and ending with the funeral of Anna Maria Ludovica, when San Lorenzo witnessed for the last time the burial of one of the house of Medici.

The plain, severe style of the church, with its columns of grey *pietra serena* ("the quiet stone"), has an indescribably peaceful effect. In the Old Sacristy (at the end of the south transept) lie Giovanni di Bicci, his wife Piccarda, and his two grandsons, Piero il Gottoso and Giovanni. In front of the high altar of the church lies Cosimo Pater Patriae. At the end of the north transept we have the New Sacristy,

> "... That Chamber of the Dead,
>   Where the gigantic shapes of Night and Day,
>   Turned into stone, rest everlastingly !" [1]

Here, where so many of the house of Medici have at different times been interred,[2] there still rest the remains of Lorenzo the Magnificent, his brother Giuliano, Lorenzo's son Giuliano (Duc de Nemours), Lorenzo's grandson Lorenzo (Duke of Urbino), and Alessandro. Then comes a gap, Pietro (buried at Monte Cassino), Leo X and Clement VII (buried in Rome) and Catherine (buried in France) being absent. Lastly, in the mausoleum behind the choir [3] lie Giovanni delle Bande Nere and his wife Maria, with the thirty-two remaining members of the family.

In the case of the Old and New Sacristies the sarcophagi contain the remains of those to whom they refer; but in the case of the mausoleum all the tombs are in the crypt,[4] the sarcophagi in the upper portion of the mausoleum being only intended as monuments. As the church of San Lorenzo stands on a height, and as the floor of the mausoleum is on a level with that of the church, it results that the crypt of the mausoleum is above ground, being on the ground level of the Piazza Madonna, from which there is now an entrance to the crypt. As originally built there was no entrance from the Piazza Madonna, and the crypt could only be reached by the staircase leading down into it from the floor of the mausoleum. It was therefore a place where it was easy to keep the coffins secure from all danger of depredation by thieves who might seek to plunder them of the jewels which they contained. And in this crypt the coffins (standing in the places marked by the respective tombstones) remained for about one hundred years.

But in 1791 the Austrian Grand Duke Ferdinand III decided to remove them from this situation. A mortuary chapel for the Austrian Grand Dukes had been constructed in part of the vault of the church of San Lorenzo; and to reach it more conveniently this Grand Duke made an entrance from the Piazza Madonna into the crypt of the Medici mausoleum, so as to reach, by passing through the latter, the mortuary chapel which lies beyond it.[5] This throwing open of the crypt of the mausoleum made it necessary to remove the Medici coffins elsewhere. Beneath this upper crypt there is a lower (subterranean) one, of exactly the same size and shape; and to this the Grand Duke Ferdinand III removed the Medici coffins.

Either during this removal of the coffins to the lower crypt in 1791, or during the sixty years after it (owing to want of due guard over them after they were placed in the lower crypt), thieves obtained access to the coffins,[6] plundering a number of them of their jewels, and creating considerable disorder.

In 1856, to remedy this state of things, it was decided to institute an official examination of the whole of the coffins, to open and examine each carefully, and to rearrange them in due order. Before this took place, the Pope, Pius IX, visited the mausoleum, and after holding a service in the crypt gave his authority for this examination of the bodies, ordering it to be conducted with due reverence for the dead. This was then carried out by a Commission appointed by the Government in 1857. The coffins, to the number of forty-nine, were in turn opened and examined, and the condition of the bodies, their dress, and ornaments were minutely detailed in an official report. The report showed (as will be seen by the details which have been given in the footnotes on the subject) that the bodies of all those who were cardinals had been left untouched by the thieves; but that all others [7] had been robbed of most of their jewels. The examination being concluded, the coffins were again closed, and were arranged in the lower crypt in the same situations as they had occupied in the upper crypt, each being placed immediately under the tombstone in the upper crypt having reference to it. And this done the entrance to the lower crypt (at the bottom of the flight of steps which leads down to it) was then walled up.[8]

Thus each tombstone in the upper crypt is over the coffin to which it refers. In the centre, buried in his black armour, lies Giovanni delle Bande Nere (with on his tombstone the words *Cognomento Invictus*), and by his side his wife, Maria Salviati. Around them, in the various "bays" and other parts of the crypt, lie their descendants of six generations.[9] Anna Maria Ludovica, the last of them, rests near one of the centre pillars. Each of the first four Grand Dukes is interred in one of the "bays" with his wife and two of his children. Similarly in the upper part of the mausoleum each monument stands over the spot in the crypt which holds the tomb of that Grand Duke.

The three places of sepulture, the Old Sacristy at the end of the south transept,[10] the New Sacristy at the end of the north transept, and the mausoleum adjoining the choir, serve to mark the stages through which the Medici passed. We see them first as careful and assiduous men of business, prudent, generous of their wealth, and unflinching defenders of the poorer classes against tyranny; then as far-sighted and capable statesmen, heavily burdened with public affairs, and steadily raising the power and prosperity of their country above all her former rivals, and at the same time spending both efforts and wealth on the advancement of learning and the encouragement of all forms of art; lastly, we see them as crowned heads, ruling over a state which had been made by   m the most important in Italy. And in each of these stages we see them (until their decay) incontestably superior to all their contemporaries similarly situated.

Nor should the evils of one reign be allowed to occupy all the foreground of the picture to the exclusion of everything else. Many other Medici had governed Tuscany before Cosimo III; and a single bad reign should not be suffered to do more than balance a single good one. The evil effects of Cosimo III's reign have long since passed away; the lasting benefits to Tuscany brought about by Cosimo I, Ferdinand I, Cosimo II, and Ferdinand II (not to mention Cosimo Pater Patriae and Lorenzo the Magnificent) remain for all time.

Lastly, they were as a family justly to be called great. Great in their extraordinary ability; great in their large-mindedness; great in their generosity of character; great in their unparalleled love for Learning and Art; great in their abounding energy, vitality, and many-sidedness; great, above all, in their peculiar gift for pouring oil on troubled waters and allaying fierce political passions which no others could pacify. Speaking of their attainments and the causes to which their success was due, Yriarte says:—

"The grasp, the varied capacity, and the enterprising spirit of the Medici may be gathered from the specimens of their correspondence preserved in the archives of Florence. They are equally at home in the most contrasted topics; in war, in diplomacy, in domestic administration, in foreign policy, in literature, and in the fine arts. . . . Their success was due in no small degree to the grandeur of conception, liberality, and nobility of mind that seemed natural to this family."

Looked at as a whole, they stand out as worthy reflectors of the glory of Tuscany.

The Medici, whatever else they may have been, were at all events thorough Florentines, and loved Florence with an ardour which none can surpass. When they became Grand Dukes they did not (as might have been the case) rule from a distance, receiving the surplus revenue of the State, spending their wealth elsewhere, and interesting themselves but little in the welfare of Florence. Instead of this, they so thoroughly made themselves one with Florence that her history and theirs are bound up together. They gloried in her glory; they increased it in countless ways; and they so completely identified themselves with all that does honour to Florence that it is herself she would most honour in honouring them.

To obliterate their memory from Florence is impossible. Well chosen was their motto *"Semper"* which the earlier members of the family adopted.[11] Wherever we turn in that city reminiscences of them confront us. The Medici Palace, the home of their earlier days, still stands, solemn and grand, as when it was "the hotel of the princes of the whole world" and memorable for much else besides. Castello speaks to us of Maria Salviati and her gallant soldier husband. The Piazza Sta. Trinità with its grave column of Justice, the Ponte Vecchio with its strange "Passaggio," and the broad sweep of the Ponte Sta. Trinità, bring to our minds the iron-handed but capable ruler Cosimo I. The Boboli gardens are eloquent of Eleonora di Toledo and her band of healthy children. The spacious Pitti Palace, the home of the family's later days, is still the royal residence of Tuscany as when the beautiful Isabella danced and sang and led all social functions there. The great mausoleum reminds us of Ferdinand I and his prophetic speech. Poggio Imperiale, and the pictures in the long gallery over the Arno, recall Maria Maddalena, with her accomplished sisters-in-law Eleonora, Caterina, and Claudia, and her lively daughters, Maria Cristina, Margherita, and Anna. In the Uffizi and Pitti Galleries we are surrounded by mementoes of the three talented brothers, Ferdinand II, Giovanni Carlo, and Leopold. And everywhere in crowded museums and galleries we see pictures, statues, bronzes, gems, vases, inlaid tables, costly cabinets, and other objects of art innumerable, every one of which has been examined with interest and eventually purchased by some member of this family.

As we stand in the magnificent mausoleum where their line comes to an end, and, surrounded by their great porphyry monuments, finished with the workmanship given to a costly gem, think of this family's long history; their gifts to their country [12] and to Europe, and their last gift to Florence of so much that is precious to all the world, we realise something of what the Medici were and did, and feel that they were indeed no ordinary people, and that their works were of the kind that "survives the funeral fires" and endures when tombs and monuments have crumbled into dust.

EPILOGUE

It has been said by one who felt the grandeur of their history, "Let the Medici rest in peace in their tombs of marble and porphyry; for they have done more for the glory of the world than any king, prince, or emperor." [1] But they did more than that; and we must not in their case say: "Sic transit gloria mundi." While other rulers of their time have left nothing but a memory of their own personal glory, that glory which we know passes so utterly away, the Medici have left something more lasting than that.

They are all past and gone now, all these Medici whose lives we have been following, and those also whose story intermingles with theirs: Pico della Mirandola, the bright and beautiful sunbeam; Savonarola, the martyred reformer; Bourbon, the sad and ruined soldier; the three great antagonists, Charles, Francis, and Henry; all that "glorious company" of the great in Art, and many other distinguished names; all their hopes, ambitions, wrong-doings, and sorrows are in the grave now. Some, setting before them a purely selfish aim and striving after nothing really great, have left nothing behind them except it be a name on which men cast contempt. Others (whether as artists, scholars, or rulers), aspiring after some aim higher than this, have left behind them things which still shed a blessing of one kind or another on mankind, and so their memory is honoured. Of all those whose names have passed before us the great in Art, at any rate, have left behind them works which are still a source of good to mankind, giving it its highest form of enjoyment, and ever drawing it upwards from all that is trivial and ignoble. That we still possess these is due in large measure to the Medici. And greater even than this is their other work, the resuscitation of Learning, which has spread knowledge far and wide, with benefits to mankind that are immeasurable. *This* is the glory that the Medici have; and this glory will not pass away.

FINIS

NOTES

PREFACE

1. Amongst writers on the subject Mr. Hyett and Mr. Armstrong are almost the solitary exceptions to this blinding partisanship.

2. *E.g.* Roscoe.

3. The well-balanced and careful writer Mr. Hyett, in speaking of those "who seem unable to write the name of *Medici* without having first dipped their pens in gall," includes in this class Cavalcanti, Sismondi, Perrens, Napier, Trollope, and to a considerable extent also Symonds.—(*Florence,* by F. A. Hyett, 1903, p. 289.)

4. Such facts, for instance, as that when Cosimo returned to power in 1434 none of those who had attempted to take his life and ruin his family were put to death, or that Piero put down an armed rebellion without the loss of a single life and turned his enemies into friends, or that Lorenzo saved the life of the Cardinal Riario who had just attempted to murder him, are seen in their true significance when looked at apart from all such comments.

5. Excepting those which are frescoes.

PROLOGUE

        Died

1. NICCOLÒ PISANO. The father of modern art 1278
    DANTE. The immortal poet who recreated intellectual life in Western Europe. 1321
    GIOTTO. The father of modern Painting. *"He by whom dead painting was restored to life."* 1337
    PETRARCH. The father of modern Learning, who first taught men to study the classical writings of Rome. . 1374

CHAPTER I

1. The word "Renaissance" must not be allowed to be ousted in favour of a new fashion. The term "Renascence," which a certain school of writers are anxious to introduce with an idea that it is English, appears both pedantic and incorrect; there is no such word as "nascence" in the English language.

2. The "Duomo," the cathedral of Florence.

3. Giotto's campanile.

4. The Palazzo della Signoria (Palazzo Vecchio).

5. Sta. Maria Novella (with Giotto's and Orcagna's frescoes, and the Spanish chapel).

6. The Uffizi colonnade.

7. San Lorenzo (with the New Sacristy, and the Medici Mausoleum). The dome is that of the mausoleum.

8. *Florentine Life during the Renaissance,* by Walter Scaife.

9. *The Makers of Venice,* by Mrs. Oliphant.

CHAPTER II

1. *See* page 655.

2. There were two other Popes who also had this name of Medici, but they did not belong to this family: viz., Pius IV (Johannes Angelus Medici of Milan), who was Pope from 1559 to 1565, and Leo XI (Alessandro Medici), who was Pope for a month in 1605. The former belonged to an obscure family in Milan and took this name; and the latter belonged to the Medici of Naples, and was therefore not a descendant of the historic Medici; though he was a distant connection, being descended from a brother of the grandfather of Giovanni di Bicci.

3. The murder of Ippolito de' Medici by his so-called cousin Alessandro "the Moor," who was either the illegitimate son of an illegitimate son, or else not of the Medici blood at all (*see* chapter xviii).

4. The eighth generation is that of Cosimo I, and the ninth that of his sons. Most of these charges are now known to have been false accusations due to political animosity, and are rejected by modern historians, in the fuller light now available, as untrue (*see* pages 577, 582-585, 621-622, 647).

CHAPTER III

1. From 1400 to 1743, in which latter year Anna Maria Ludovica, the "last of the Medici," died. On her death no one of Giovanni di Bicci's blood remained. Any of this name now existing in Italy are not descendants of the historic Medici, but are descended from one or other of the above-mentioned collateral branches.

2. There is no foundation for the story that the Medici were originally doctors (*medici*). That story seems to have originated in two ways. First, with the mediæval love of a play upon words, Cosimo, Giovanni's eldest son, chose for the patron saints of himself and his family, St. Cosmo and St. Damian, the two doctor saints, and these were in his time generally introduced into pictures painted for him or in his honour. Secondly, when the wits of Paris, in the days of Catherine de' Medici (always so hated in France on account of her *bourgeois* origin), desired to hold her up to contempt, they concocted the story that the Medici were originally apothecaries (*medici*), and that the family arms, the celebrated *palle* (or balls) represented the

pills which they made. The story is an entire fable; the Medici can be traced back for two hundred years before Giovanni di Bicci's time, and throughout this period were merchants and bankers, not doctors. They did not belong, for instance, to the doctors' guild, but to the guild of bankers. The precise signification of the Medici arms, the red balls on a field of gold, is unknown.

3. The *dei*, written *de'*, customary in the case of the Medici and other families in Florence, had no significance similar to the French *de*, not denoting high birth or nobility, but seems simply to have originated from the correctness of the Tuscan mode of speech. It appears to have been employed without any rule that is discoverable; so that while we always find, *e.g.*, Vieri dei Cerchi, Lorenzo de' Medici, or Alessandra de' Mozzi, we also find Filippo Strozzi, Baccio Valori, and Francesco Guicciardini.

4. Dante in the *Inferno* (Canto x. ver. 91) alludes to this act, which occurred only five years before he was born.

5. The height of the tower is 330 feet; it commanded all the main streets of the city.

6. Thus the ancient connection of Florence with England in commerce is still kept in memory by our English silver coin of this name. The gold florin continued to hold its credit in Europe until the Republic was destroyed in 1530.

7. The whole of our modern system of banking was originated by the Florentine bankers, which Florence's widespread trade enabled them to carry out.

8. Macaulay's Essay on Machiavelli. The equivalent would be considerably higher now.

9. From the Greek words καλὸs μαλλόs—"beautiful white," or "beautiful fleece."

10. Their emblem of the lamb may be seen on the cathedral walls.

11. Also begun in 1298, as can be seen by its foundation stone near the campanile; not in 1294, as nearly always stated.

12. Since this was written, this interesting old building has received a modern dress. Its restorers have, however, been careful to maintain the character of the building as little impaired as possible.

13. With Giotto must be coupled his Sienese contemporary Duccio. But Duccio's influence throughout Italy was so infinitesimal compared with that of Giotto that the latter takes entire precedence.

14. Boccaccio had also died within a year of Petrarch.

15. For a full account of the political history of Florence during the time of Giovanni di Bicci, *see* Hyett's *Florence* (chapter xi).

16. Throughout this history of the Medici, wherein contemporary historical events must frequently be mentioned (more particularly in the earlier portion of their story), it is not attempted to do more than indicate, as briefly as will suffice for the purpose, such principal events as have a bearing on the history of the Medici.

17. Sigismund, in opening the Council, and speaking, of course, in Latin, used a feminine adjective to a noun which is neuter. He said, "Date operam ut illa *nefanda* schisma eradicetur." A trembling eccle-

siastic behind him whispered to him, "Pardon, your Majesty, but 'schisma' is of the neuter gender." Whereupon the Emperor loftily replied, "Ego Imperator Romanus sum, et *super grammaticam*" (I am the Roman Emperor, and above grammar).

18. The Church of England sent six bishops to this Council: viz., those of London, Salisbury, Bath, Chester, Norwich, and Lichfield. The most celebrated of them was Robert Hallam, Bishop of Salisbury. They were sent with specific instructions from the King of England, Henry V. We are told that on one occasion they threw themselves in a body at the feet of the Emperor Sigismund, as the successor of Constantine and of Charlemagne, and entreated him "to pull the Pope out of his seat"; and that "The bold English bishop, the Bishop of Salisbury, told the Pope to his face that the Council was superior to the Pope."

19. "Donatello did not compete, being only a boy, but he must have been familiar with every stage in the contest, which excited the deepest interest in Tuscany."—(Lord Balcarres.)

20. Ruskin has found fault with them on this very ground, as trenching on the sphere belonging properly to painting and to sculpture. But it was just thus that this work became the invaluable school which it did for both the painter's and the sculptor's art.

21. *Women of Florence*, by Isidoro del Lungo.

22. When the inscription was put up (after Giovanni's death) Pope Martin V objected to the words "Quondam Papa," and wrote to the Signoria demanding that they should be erased. The reply was a refusal, written by Cosimo, and couched in the words of Pontius Pilate, saying, "Quod scripsi, scripsi." And there they still remain.

23. One or two modern writers, in the endeavour to detract from any credit due to the Medici, have attempted to maintain that Giovanni di Bicci was not the author of this tax at all, though even they have had to admit that he was universally held to be so by his countrymen, and have been unable to mention the name of any one else as its author. Even, however, were there not ample evidence of his authorship, the above fact alone would suffice; for in such a government as that of Florence, it would have been impossible that this universal credit should be given him by the people at the time it took place, for an important measure of which, not he, but some one else, was the author. Such writers are, moreover, refuted by those on their own side who attribute unworthy motives to him for the act.

24. It is said to have taken place in the church of Santo Stefano, near the Por Sta. Maria.

25. The guild of the apothecaries was an important one, as their chemical knowledge was required in the preparation of the dyes on which the wool trade so largely depended. And the painters similarly needed their assistance in connection with the preparation of their colours.

26. For many interesting details regarding the Florentine guilds, see *Florence*, by F. A. Hyett, pp. 32-37.

27. It was at one of these stormy meetings that Brunelleschi's illus-

tration of his point by the problem of making an egg stand on its end occurred. When all had tried it and failed, Brunelleschi simply cracked the end of the egg and so made it stand; whereupon they said: "But we could all have done that." To which he replied: "Yes, and so it would be if I told my design for building the dome." On another occasion Brunelleschi's temper became so unbearable to the Board that he was by their orders forcibly carried out of the house and deposited on his back in the street.

28. The dome of St. Peter's at Rome, built more than a hundred years later, and for which it formed the model, is 1 foot less in diameter, the respective diameters being: Duomo at Florence (inside measurement), 138½ feet; St. Peter's at Rome, 137½ feet. The Pantheon is larger than either, being 142 feet in diameter. Both are, however, much larger than the Pantheon when viewed from outside, being double cupolas, and the above measurements being those of the inner dome only.

29. The other two being the dome of the cathedral and that of the church of Santo Spirito.

30. It was dedicated in 393 to St. Lawrence in memory of Laurentius, the son of a rich widow, Giuliana, at whose expense the church was built. St. Ambrose's sermon on the occasion of its consecration is still in existence.

31. Seven other families joined with him; but Giovanni initiated the proposal, chose the architect, and gave the bulk of the money.

32. *Renaissance of the Fine Arts.*

33. Brunelleschi's other principal buildings are, the Pazzi Chapel in the cloisters of Sta. Croce (considered "a jewel of classic architecture adapted to the Renaissance spirit"), Palazzo Pazzi (now Quaratesi), Palazzo Busini, and Palazzo Barbadori.

34. Especially in these days, when the great Chancellor, Lord Eldon's, motto, *"Sat cito, si sat bene"* (Quick enough, if well enough, done) is so little in favour.

35. In the best of these, the fresco of *The Tribute Money,* Masaccio has given us a portrait of himself in the young Apostle standing on the right of the tax-gatherer, next to the portico.

36. The register of the *catasto* for the year 1427 shows that he was in great destitution.

37. One other fresco of his has in recent years been discovered on the entrance wall of Sta. Maria Novella, till now hidden under a painting by another artist, but it is in a much ruined state.

38. It is recorded of Raphael that he copied these frescoes of Masaccio's no less than seven times.

39. It was in this chapel that Michelangelo obtained his broken nose; insulting another artist, the latter knocked him down, breaking his nose.

40. Rogers' *Italy.*

41. In recent years part of the work in the Brancacci chapel hitherto attributed to Masaccio has been thought to be by another artist, Masolino. But this, even if the case, makes no difference to

Masaccio's fame, as sufficient of his work would still remain to maintain it. The share attributed to Masolino is denied by Cavalcaselle.

42. Called the "Old Sacristy" from the time when, nearly a hundred years later, the "New Sacristy" was built.

43. Often said to be by Donatello, but, though much in his manner, it is considered by some critics not to be by him.—(Lord Balcarres.)

CHAPTER IV

1. Contessina was, of course, her Christian name, not a title. One of the daughters of Lorenzo the Magnificent had the same name.

2. Now No. 21 Via de' Bardi.

3. *See* note 23 of chapter iv.

4. In the Medici arms eight balls, all of them red, indicate the time of Giovanni di Bicci (*see* page 134).

5. This academy had been started in the fourteenth century for the study of Greek and Latin by the learned Neapolitan monk Ambrogio Traversari, afterwards Prior of the Order. Landino, Pucci, and many others afterwards famous in different branches of learning, were all educated with Cosimo and his brother Lorenzo at this academy.

6. Besides other cities, Cosimo had banks at Paris, London, Bruges, Lyons, Venice, Genoa, Rome, and Naples.

7. Now the Via Cavour.

8. *See* note 15 of chapter viii.

9. *See* page 80.

10. Vasari.

11. He lived in the palace in the Via de' Bardi which is now the Capponi palace. His daughter Ginevra married one of the Capponi family.

12. He was subsequently permitted to move from Padua to Venice.

13. Some have held that this was Donatello's second visit to Rome, and that he had accompanied Brunelleschi thither in 1403; but this is not believed by most modern critics (*see* M. Raymond's *La Scultura Fiorentina*).

14. Poggio, writing at this time about the ruins of Rome, speaks of a statue with a head as though that were something quite extraordinary.

15. Machiavelli informs us that the most eminent of these were Rinaldo degli Albizzi, Ridolfo Peruzzi, Palla Strozzi, Niccolò Barbadori, and members of the Guicciardini, Guadagni, Uzzani, and Gianni families.

16. That Cosimo, when subsequently he gained complete power, did not annul this banishment of the Albizzi and their adherents was surely natural enough. To have allowed them to return would only have again plunged Florence into that faction-fighting which had ever been the chief obstacle to her welfare. An exception might apparently have been made in the case of the noble-hearted Palla Strozzi; but it is possible that Cosimo knew more on that point than we do, and may have known that however peaceable a man Palla Strozzi him-

self was, he would inevitably become a cause of such disturbances. Palla Strozzi retired to Padua, and remained there for the rest of his life, dying in 1464 at the age of ninety-two.

17. It has been said:—"All men and women who are of any use to the world in which they live are ambitious."

18. It demonstrates both the aim which was in view in these costly searchings for ancient documents, and the spirit in which they were undertaken, when we find Cyriac of Ancona, in starting for the East on one of these quests, saying, "I go to awake the dead."

19. Always in Florence called the "Duomo."

20. The campanile ("Giotto's tower") was not completed until fifty years after Giotto's death.

21. Antonio Pierozzi, better known to us as St. Antonino, was, on account of the various qualities which he showed as Prior of San Marco, made Archbishop of Florence by Pope Eugenius IV in 1445. His statue is the only one of an ecclesiastic which has been placed among those in the Uffizi colonnade.

22. The church of Santo Spirito was built by the parishioners of that quarter of the city, the four chief families who paid for it being the Frescobaldi, the Capponi, the Ridolfi, and the Corbinelli.

23. The Peruzzi were another great banking family, who, with the Bardi, were ruined by Edward III (see p. 45). These two families lent him a large sum of money with which to fight the battle of Crécy; Professor Villari says that the sum thus lent to Edward III—and the loss of which, by his never repaying the debt, ruined these two families—was 1,365,000 gold florins, equal in our present money to nearly £7,000,000 sterling.

24. The effect of the "New Learning" in producing the Reformation has not been generally recognised to the full extent that it deserves (see pages 306-308).

25. The earliest of these "Fathers of the Church" of course all wrote in Greek; Tertullian (third century) was the first of them who wrote in Latin.

26. The number of the Eastern bishops was twenty-three; all except one were Metropolitans of important provinces; they were accompanied by a large number of theologians and other learned men.

27. Symonds' *Renaissance in Italy*.

28. The Council closed its sittings on the 6th July.

29. This interesting document is still preserved in the Medici Library (now called the Laurentian Library), with the original signatures, including those of the Emperor and the Pope.

30. A marble tablet recording this agreement may be seen on the wall of the choir of the cathedral. It was, however, null and void from the first.

31. Giovanni Cavalcanti, an anti-Medicean, wrote a history of his time (1420-1455), which has been the chief mine whence statements against Cosimo have been drawn.

32. Gino Capponi, ii. 277.

33. Who, for instance, related what passed at this chance meeting

in the street? Cosimo is not likely to have done so, and Baldaccio had not time to do so.

34. Alberti, writing seven years later, declares that he had seen there twelve hundred churches in ruins.

35. Cosimo's library was open to all scholars.

36. It is now called the Library of San Lorenzo, or the Laurentian Library. But it would be well done to cause it to revert to its own proper name, seeing that both the building itself and nearly all the treasures it contains were provided by this family.

37. This original copy of the Pandects of Justinian is practically priceless in value. It is considered to be probably the sole authentic source from which all other remaining copies of the Roman law have been taken. It is said to have been discovered by the Pisans at Amalfi, when the fleet of Pisa captured that town in 1137. It was captured by the Florentine army from the Pisans when Pisa was taken in 1406, was considered by the Florentines their greatest treasure, and was closely guarded in the Palazzo della Signoria. Pope Leo X, in his desire to collect everything of that kind at Rome, carried it off thither in the year 1516, but after remaining there for about two hundred and seventy years it was restored to its proper home in Florence. The Emperor Justinian, when completing it, ordered that a list of names of the authors consulted in drawing up this code of the Roman law, and of their works, should be prefixed by Tribonian (his minister who had helped him in this great work) to the Pandects; and this list being found at the beginning of the Florentine manuscript is called the Florentine Index. The rich binding which this valuable book originally had was, after the Medici had passed away, stripped off by the Austrian Grand Duke of Tuscany, Pietro Leopoldo, and sold to the mint for "thirty gold deniers."

38. This library was paid for twice over by the Medici. Confiscated by the Signoria when the family were banished in 1494, it was re-purchased twenty years afterwards by Leo X, was transported by him to Rome, and was again returned to Florence by Clement VII.

39. Brunelleschi's last work was to design for the Milan cathedral the vault crowned with a marble spire which covers the nave at the intersection of the nave and transept.

40. Equal in our present money to two millions sterling.

41. See page 506.

42. Donatello, by Hope Rea.

43. He was not helped by any preceding intermediate period, leading gradually to this change. For the sculptures of Niccolò Pisano, much as they were in advance of all that had gone before, still appertained essentially to the mediæval method: as decorations to architecture, not as isolated statues with an independent message of their own.

44. Vasari says that it was finished before Cosimo's exile in 1433.

45. Donatello, by Lord Balcarres.

46. Donatello's favourite subject was undoubtedly St. John the Baptist. He had sculptured him in boyhood, youth, and manhood, in relief, bust, and full-length statue, in marble and in bronze; and there

are more than twenty of his works on this one subject alone in the various galleries of Europe.

47. Lord Balcarres considers it "was probably made shortly before Donatello's journey to Padua," which took place in 1443.

48. Giotto no doubt had vaguely felt this, and striven after it so far as his limited powers of technique permitted; but his successors had none of his spirit, and had been mainly occupied in copying only his manner.

49. *See* the reliefs on the helmet of Goliath in his bronze statue of *David* in the Bargello.

50. Perkins' *Tuscan Sculptors.*

51. His Christian name was Guido; on becoming a friar he took the name of Giovanni; his family name is unknown. He was born at Vicchio, in the Mugello. He was fifty years old when he began painting in Florence.

52. *The Painters of Florence,* by Mrs. Ady.

53. *Modern Painters.*

54. In the picture Michelozzo is the man in the black *capuchon.* with his foot on the third rung of the ladder.

55. Dr. Wilhelm Bode.

56. *Luca e Andrea della Robbia,* by Miss Cruttwell.

57. Donatello executed the other. Both are now in the Opera del Duomo, Florence.

58. There is a copy of this work in the South Kensington Museum

59. *Luca della Robbia,* by the Marchesa Burlamacchi.

60. Ruskin's *Stones of Venice.*

61. Ghiberti's workshop was in the house which is now No. 29 Via Bufalini, opposite the hospital of Sta. Maria Nuova.

62. It was not an easy thing to get any work out of Lippi. There is an amusing story of how, when he was painting this picture for Cosimo, the latter being at last in despair (owing to Lippi's lazy ways) of ever seeing the picture finished, had him locked up in the room in the Medici Palace where it was being painted, declaring that he should not be let out until the work was done. Whereupon Lippi tied his bed-clothes into a rope, let himself down from the window into the street, and disappeared into the slums of Florence, not to be found again for many days.

63. His words are:—

> "We've a youngster here,
>
>   .   .   .   .   .
>
> His name is Guidi,—he'll not mind the monks;
> They call him Hulking Tom, he lets them talk;—
> He picks my practice up. He'll paint apace;
> I hope so, though I never live so long,
> I know what's sure to follow."

All of which is, of course, an exact reversal of the position.

64. Tommaso Guidi was Masaccio's name. The other youths who

were his companions gave him the nickname of "Masaccio" (Clumsy Tom), by which he is known in Art.

65. Perkins' *Tuscan Sculptors*.

66. This bust is now at Berlin.

67. Luca Pitti was Gonfaloniere in 1460.

68. A position such that it has given rise to a Tuscan proverb, "So you think yourself a Cosimo de' Medici"; a retort used to a presumptuous person.

69. Without being Gonfaloniere; an office which Cosimo only held twice, once in 1434 and once in 1439.

70. The "New Sacristy," begun in 1516 by Leo X, was intended by him as a second mausoleum for the house of Medici. To it was again added in 1604 (by Ferdinand I) a third and yet more sumptuous mausoleum for the later members of the family. The entrance to both these from the church is now closed, and a separate entrance to them provided from the cloisters.

71. Donatello himself was then dead.

72. *See* page 38.

73. *See* below.

74. Burckhart, referring to Symonds' sneer at Cosimo for being *"bourgeois,"* remarks:—"A man of Cosimo's position—a great merchant and party leader, the first of Italians by culture, who also had on his side all the thinkers, writers, and investigators,—such a man was to all intents and purposes already a prince."

75. Symonds ii. 168.

CHAPTER V

1. *See* pages 21-22.

2. Now the Royal Palace in Florence.

3. It is now the official residence of the Prefect of Florence. But in view of its importance architecturally, historically, and in connection with the culture of the Renaissance it would add greatly to the memorials of Florence if some successful effort could be made by those Florentines who take so much public-spirited interest in the memorials of their city to rescue it from its present condition of a public office. No single building could be so just a focus of the sentiment which takes pride in the Renaissance. And, as the first of all museums of Art, it might well be converted into a museum connected specially with the age of Cosimo, Piero, and Lorenzo; of which time it still possesses one unique treasure in the chapel on its first floor.

4. The arches of this *loggia* were afterwards filled in by Michelangelo, who here first invented the particular pattern of curved barred windows often seen in Florence, which he called *"inginocchiate"* (kneeling), though these have since been changed for the more ordinary pattern. The iron rings seen along the lower storey were for holding banners and torches, and for tying up horses. And the stone seats were for retainers who might have to wait outside, and as a convenience to the people generally.

5. Here the number of balls, which had previously been eight, is for the first time reduced to seven, the number always used by Cosimo (*see* page 134).

6. These lamps are nowadays often spoken of as "Strozzi lamps," because the Strozzi Palace bears one, but that on the, much older, Medici Palace is considered by connoisseurs to be more perfect in its design, and the best specimen in existence.

7. The well-known Strozzi Palace, for instance, probably the finest of these, was not built until sixty years after the Medici Palace. The Pitti Palace (built by the Medici still later) is, of course, much larger, but it is not so perfect in its architecture as this palace.

8. In length it is about 300 feet, in depth 150 feet, and in height 90 feet. Nearly one-third of this length was added by the Riccardi family when, about two hundred and thirty years afterwards, they bought the palace (*see* note 82 of chapter xxviii). When sold to them it was made a condition of the sale that any additions they might make should be of the same style and design as the main portion of the palace.

9. The Pitti Palace. It is strange that this latter, built by the Medici, and their residence for two hundred years, is given a name which it never bore in their time (*see* note 20 of chapter xxiv), and that neither of the palaces built and inhabited by the Medici through three centuries bears their name.

10. Excepting those connected with Savonarola.

11. *Firenze Città Nobilissima*, by Migliore (1684).

12. It was sold to the Riccardi family in 1659, but re-bought by the State about a hundred years afterwards.

13. Put up long after the Medici had passed away.

14. Beyond the *cortile* there was originally a garden, in the space between the back of the palace and the Via de' Ginori.

15. One of these ancient Roman sarcophagi formerly contained the remains of Guccio de' Medici, who was Gonfaloniere in 1299.

16. *See* page 158.

17. *See* page 252.

18. *See* page 337.

19. Lord Lindsay's *Sketches of the History of Christian Art*.

20. Perhaps the finest example of this which Art can show is to be seen in Raphael's fresco pictures in the *Camera della Segnatura* in the Vatican (*see* page 275).

CHAPTER VI

1. Both of them represent the iris, but whereas the French one has only the leaves, the Florentine one has both the leaves and the flowers.

2. During this period, and while Piero was still in ignorance of Dietisalvi Neroni's real character, and following the counsel of Cosimo made him his chief adviser, Neroni took every opportunity of trying to lead Piero into measures calculated to undermine his popularity with

the people. It was probably partly in order to give this artifice time to work that the rebellion was so long delayed.

3. Regarding the pictorial record of this episode, *see* page 128.

4. *See* page 338.

5. *See* page 415.

6. This tournament in 1469 was called Lorenzo's; that held in 1475 being called Giuliano's.

7. We have all these, as well as Lorenzo's own dress, reproduced in Gozzoli's fresco in the chapel of the Medici Palace, painted a few months afterwards (*see* chapter vii).

8. Armstrong.

9. Equal to about £50,000 sterling of our present money.

10. "It is evidently modelled with the intention of casting in bronze, and the clay has been painted in imitation, either by Antonio himself or subsequently."—(Miss Cruttwell.)

11. The artists Pollajuolo, Verrocchio, and Botticelli worked at this time almost entirely for the Medici.

12. *See* Mr. Armstrong's words (page 176).

13. Possibly in the sack of the Medici Palace in 1494, and just because it represented one of the Medici; or else in the second sack of the palace in 1527, when intensified animosity would naturally connect it with the hated Clement VII, Giuliano's son (*see* chapter xv).

14. *Antonio Pollajuolo,* by Miss M. Cruttwell.

15. *See* page 194.

16. *Florentine Life during the Renaissance,* by Walter Scaife.

17. The olive branch exposed at the window of a palace denoted a marriage in the family.

18. *Women of Florence,* by Isidoro del Lungo.

19. *Luca della Robbia,* by the Marchesa Burlamacchi.

20. *See* page 675.

21. His earliest known work is his series of frescoes in the church of San Francesco at Montefalco, painted in 1452.

22. His proper name was Sandro Filipepi, the cognomen "Botticelli" being a nickname. The register of the *catasto* tax for 1458 shows that he was born in 1444, not 1446 as often stated.

23. Up to this time Botticelli had been merely an assistant of Filippo Lippi, to whom he was apprenticed in 1460 when he was sixteen, and whom he accompanied to Prato in 1464, when Lippi proceeded there to finish his frescoes in the cathedral. Returning thence in 1465 Botticelli was soon taken up by Piero il Gottoso, and thenceforth until the latter's death in 1469 was employed almost entirely in his service.

24. *See* page 81.

25. *See* his *Madonna of the Magnificat,* and his period (III. p. 256).

26. *See* his period (II. p. 207).

27. Except the *Fortitude,* the commission for which was obtained for Botticelli by him.

28. *See* Ruskin's *Mornings in Florence,* chapter iii.

29. Its over-bright colouring is due to its having been much damaged and repainted.

30. *See* page 257.

31. *The Painters of Florence,* by Julia Cartwright (Mrs. Ady).

32. This has always been the traditional account handed down. And that account is very remarkably corroborated by the internal evidence of the picture; as is shown below (pp. 128-130). The new theory that it was painted for a certain unknown Giovanni Lami, put forward in Mr. Horne's recent work on Botticelli, appears to the present writer impossible, in view both of the historical evidence and the internal testimony of the picture itself.

33. Not necessarily in all cases *portraits* of those concerned, but representations of them.

34. The figure in the right-hand corner, wearing a yellow robe and looking towards the spectator, is generally declared to be Botticelli himself, though doubts have been thrown upon this.

35. Vasari has interchanged the two figures noted as representing Giovanni and Giuliano, and different opinions have been held on the point. It is in reality immaterial to the meaning of the picture which of the two figures represents Giovanni and which Giuliano; and it was no doubt for this reason that Botticelli took no trouble to give portraits in their case.

36. This figure can scarcely have been intended by Botticelli to represent Giuliano, since the latter was *four years younger than Lorenzo,* whereas this figure is that of an older man.

37. Ruskin's *Mornings in Florence,* chapter iii.

38. It is really a mace.

39. Vasari says that the St. Sebastian was painted some three or four years later for Lorenzo the Magnificent, but it is considered more probable that it was painted during this period.

40. One seldom sees this tomb properly as the front of it is towards the chapel of the Madonna, and is often obscured from view by a wooden screen which fills the archway during the winter months.

41. They were, however, beginning. It was in the year that Piero died that the artist Piero della Francesca painted the portraits of the Duke and Duchess of Urbino; while, as we have seen, Botticelli had painted a portrait of Lucrezia Tornabuoni.

42. Those of Giovanni di Bicci and Cosimo being both by Bronzino (1512-1572) and taken from older representations of them.

43. Chapter vii.

44. It was this family who shortly afterwards, at Lorenzo's instigation, caused the choir of Sta. Maria Novella to be decorated with Ghirlandajo's well-known frescoes. The principal street in modern Florence preserves their name in memory. Their palace was at the corner where that street is joined by the Via dei Corsi.

45. *Histoire des Papes,* by Dr. Louis Pastor, vol. v, p. 33.

46. *Opera a ben vivere,* edited by Francesco Palermo (Florence, 1858).

47. It was the practice of that time, especially among the great families, for a married woman to retain her own family name, instead of changing it for that of her husband; or sometimes to add the latter

to the former, as Maria Salviati does in signing herself in her letter, "Maria Salviati de' Medici" (page 549). The latter method is still the custom in Italy.

48. It probably found its way to Berlin owing to the plundering of the Medici Palace in 1494.

CHAPTER VII

1. It is now in the Accademia delle Belle Arti.

2. Ruskin's *Modern Painters*.

3. Even Ruskin dismisses it with merely a similar remark.

4. The five great *patriarchates* which embraced all Christendom having been (1) Antioch, (2) Alexandria, (3) Jerusalem, (4) Constantinople, as being the imperial capital, and (5) Rome, "in consequence of its having been the former capital." And "Patriarch" (Chief Father) and "Papa" (Holy Father) being respectively the Greek and Latin forms of the same title and office.

5. He had not yet, of course, gained the name of Lorenzo the Magnificent; nor, in fact, was Lorenzo ever called so by his contemporaries, the name being applied to him after his death. Neither in his case, nor in that of any other member of the Medici family, does Gozzoli consider it necessary to give a *portrait* of the person represented. He indicates by the dress and other accessories who is meant.

6. Possibly as a distinguishing sign alluding to his being always an invalid. Whether for this reason or not, in no case is Piero il Gottoso ever represented wearing anything on his head.

7. Most of these wear the peculiar cap which we always associate with Cosimo Pater Patriae, as he is always shown wearing it. Probably it either denoted a scholar, or perhaps signified a member of Cosimo's Platonic Academy.

8. A leopard was the crest of his house.

9. Except those *in mosaic* at Ravenna of the Emperors Justinian and Constantine IV, which are scarcely portraits in the same sense.

10. *See* page 115.

11. Not yet changed to six, because we are still in Piero's time (page 134).

12. *The Painters of Florence,* by Mrs. Ady.

13. He writes reporting his progress with the frescoes in this chapel, says he requires some more of the (expensive) ultramarine colour, and complains of the great heat in working in the summer weather in this chapel.

14. Besides the Emperor and the Patriarch, the two figures about whom there can be no question are those of Lorenzo and Cosimo, on account both of their dress and the insignia on the trappings of their chargers, Cosimo's three peacock feathers and Lorenzo's tournament dress fixing these two figures with absolute certainty.

CHAPTER VIII

1. *Lorenzo de' Medici*, by E. Armstrong, M.A.
2. *See* page 240.
3. *See* pages 232-235.
4. Machiavelli's *History of Florence* was written about 1513, and "is a vivid picture of the life of the Florentine Republic drawn with simplicity and vigour." (*Florence*, by F. A. Hyett.)
5. Guicciardini says that he came to be styled "the needle of the Italian compass."
6. Actually he was only a very little over twenty.
7. *See* page 197.
8. *See* page 90.
9. Nevertheless Marietta did not marry the hero of this snowballing match. She married in 1471 one of the Calcagrini family of Ferrara, and left Florence for the city of which Leonora of Arragon became two years later the Duchess.
10. *Women of Florence*, by Isidoro del Lungo.
11. "How beautiful is youth
    Which yet flies quickly away.
    Who has a mind to be joyous, let him be so;
    For of to-morrow there is no certainty."
12. Roscoe.
13. Marsilio Ficino, in a letter to Bracciolini, describes one of these birthday feasts.
14. The name is a corruption of *Dio ti salvi* ("God save thee").
15. During this visit, at the performance of a miracle play, the church of Santo Spirito caught fire and was burnt down. Until recently there has been confusion among writers over this burning of Santo Spirito in 1471, since Brunelleschi's celebrated masterpiece, which still stands, was known to have been begun in 1430. The matter has now been cleared up by Moreni in his *Due Vite,* in which he quotes the writings of Bandinucci, who tells us that the fire of 1471 took place in the *old* church of Santo Spirito, and that the new church (Brunelleschi's), which had been begun in 1430 and was, when the fire occurred, nearly completed, stood next to it, and was not touched by the fire.
16. A fact which incidentally shows how far Lorenzo's position was from that of a sovereign ruler, notwithstanding all his power.
17. "He personally visited the town, distributed relief among the sufferers, reassured the inhabitants, and during the rest of his life spent liberally on estates which he had purchased in the neighbourhood."—(Armstrong.)
18. Afterwards the mother of Isabella and Beatrice d'Este.
19. On a wooden stage erected for the occasion on the side of the piazza towards the Via Condotta.
20. Her charms and goodness were the favourite theme of Politian and all the poets of the time.

21. Politian, when he wrote this poem, was only twenty-one years old.

22. Roscoe's *Life of Lorenzo the Magnificent.*

23. It was in these words that Politian had spoken of Lorenzo the Magnificent and his works as a poet. The laurel grove is a conspicuous feature of the picture, spreading right out from the shore over Venus as if protecting her.

24. *Sandro Botticelli,* by Mrs. Ady (1903).

25. *See* also Walter Pater's comments on this picture in *The Renaissance.*

26. This true meaning of the *Primavera,* and Botticelli's deliberate intention to make it speak of Lorenzo, his tournament motto, and how during the six years that had since passed he had carried it out, has apparently not hitherto been noticed.

27. *See* page 116.

28. Always representing Lorenzo, from the play on the Latin form of his name, Laurentius.

29. So constantly associated with the season of spring by the classic poets of antiquity.

30. These pictures relating to Giuliano's tournament could not have been painted until some time afterwards, as in any case they could not have been so until after Politian's poem had appeared; and they may have been executed at any time during Lorenzo's life. If painted, as is most probable, subsequently to Giuliano's death in 1478, they would remind Lorenzo of a time of bygone joys; and would be all the more prized by him on that account.

31. The picture in the Pitti Gallery of the very plain-looking, elderly person which was long put down as a portrait of Simonetta is now acknowledged not to refer to her.

32. *Women of Florence,* by Isidoro del Lungo.

33. Walking shortly afterwards in his garden, Lorenzo called attention to a sun-flower "which at evening remains with its face turned towards the western horizon which has taken from it the vision of the sun," and declared it a symbol of ourselves when we lose one whom we love, "for we remain," said he, "with the thought turned towards the last impression of the lost vision." (*Women of Florence.*)

34. *See* page 516.

35. Jacopo de' Pazzi's reluctance to join the plot until he was assured that it had the Pope's concurrence, Montesecco's confession before his execution regarding what passed at the interview with the Pope to which he was taken by Girolamo Riario, the preparation of troops, and lastly, the behaviour of Pope Sixtus when the plot failed, all make it impossible to doubt this, notwithstanding Bishop Creighton's desire to absolve the Pope from complicity in the matter.

36. Armstrong.

37. This villa still exists. After having been called, first the Villa Mozzi, and then the Villa Spence, it has now happily by its present owner been made to revert to its original and proper name of the Villa Medici.

38. The choir and high altar are under the dome, not at the east end of the church.

39. *See* also page 178.

40. This account of the affair is that given by Filippo Strozzi (the elder), who was an eye-witness.

41. *Palle,* the balls—the arms of the Medici.

42. Renato knew of the plot, but is reported to have refused to take part in it; and Lorenzo has been severely, and apparently justly, blamed for not intervening to save his life, as he did in the case of Renato's cousin Guglielmo. It is possible, however, that Lorenzo knew more than transpired, while he may easily not have felt inclined to do for other members of the family what he did for his sister's husband.

43. Armstrong.

44. Known to us as the Palazzo Quaratesi.

45. It was many years before it was re-established.

46. Executed by Bertoldo.

47. This, by the way, admits the Pope's full complicity in the matter: thus fully refuting those who have desired to absolve him thereof.

48. *Florence,* by F. A. Hyett.

49. Against Cosimo in 1433, Piero in 1466, Lorenzo in 1470, and now again against Lorenzo in 1478.

50. *Lorenzo de' Medici,* by E. Armstrong, M.A.

51. His mother was Antonia Gorini.

52. *See* note 75 of chapter ix.

53. Before the skulls and bones were placed in fresh coffins and the tomb again closed photographs of the two skulls were taken; and that of Giuliano's shows very distinctly the great sword-cut above referred to.

CHAPTER IX

1. English writers constantly speak of Ferdinand, King of Naples, and Ferrante, King of Naples, as though these were two different men, which is not the case. The two forms of the name are used indiscriminately by the Italian writers of the time.

2. It will be found published in full in the *Life of Lorenzo the Magnificent,* by Roscoe, who calls it "one of the most extraordinary specimens of priestly arrogance that ever insulted the common-sense of mankind."

3. The Pope managed to deprive Florence of her former ally Milan, which, afraid of Papal censures, remained neutral, as did also Venice.

4. *Italy and her Invaders,* by Professor Hodgkin.

5. Laurentius Valla was a native of Pistoia, and became a professor of law at Pavia. He critically examined the so-called *Donation of Constantine,* and pronounced it to be an obvious forgery, and openly declared that the Popes "had no right to their position." Professor Villari says:—"To him we owe the thorough demolition of the false document."

6. Hodgkin's *Italy and her Invaders,* ix. 273.

7. The first printing press established in Florence had been set up there one year previously (*see* note 33 of chapter ix).

8. The Papal authorities subsequently hunted out and destroyed all copies of the document published by the Church of Tuscany (entitled *Contrascommunica del clero Fiorentina fulminata contro il sommo Pontefice Sisto IV*) on which they could lay their hands. With the result that in after years it came to be questioned whether so remarkable a sentence as that of the Tuscan bishops had ever been promulgated. But the learned historian and antiquary, Lami (1697-1770), has placed the matter beyond all doubt, he having himself seen copies of the document which still existed in his time.

9. "No reliance could be placed on the word or clemency of the man who had enticed Piccinino to Naples, and caused him to be secretly murdered."—(Hyett.)

10. Roscoe i. 220.

11. In this result Lorenzo's long-standing friendship from boyhood with Federigo, the King's second son, and with Ippolita, Duchess of Calabria, whom he had known when she was Ippolita Sforza, much assisted him.

12. *See* also page 188.

13. The large jar which she carries is probably meant to signify the arts of peace.

14. This picture after being lost for many years was rediscovered in 1894 by the late Mr. W. Spence, being found rolled up and hidden away in a disused apartment of the Pitti Palace.

15. Referring to the Pope having confiscated the Medici bank in Rome, which caused Lorenzo severe loss.

16. Referring to the intrigues which throughout the war were sedulously instigated by the Riario to undermine Lorenzo's influence with his countrymen.

17. By drawing the husband of his favourite sister into a plot against his life, by which her affection as a wife and as a sister became opposed.

18. Girolamo Riario made two other attempts on Lorenzo's life (*see* page 514).

19. *See* page 151.

20. "Florence at peace, and the calm studious heads
    Come out again, the penetrating eyes;
    As if a spell broke, all resumed
    Each art you boast."—BROWNING.

21. Presumably this refers to the *Cappella Medici* in Santa Croce, built for Cosimo Pater Patriae by Michelozzo, and from time to time enriched by the family with many beautiful works, including panel paintings by the artists of the school of Giotto, and various fine works of Mino da Fiesole and Luca della Robbia, some which still remain.

22. Giovanni was, of course, not "made an archbishop," as Trollope and others have said. Moreover, it is sufficiently evident that he could not be made such by the King of France. He was, as Lorenzo's letter says, admitted to minor orders (by receiving the tonsure) and "ren-

dered capable of holding a benefice." The tonsure was given to all persons performing minor offices about the church (readers, acolytes, etc.), and did not involve any pledge to proceed to holy orders afterwards; and, as a matter of fact, Giovanni was not ordained a priest until after his election as Pope. What happened when he was seven years old was that he was rendered capable of receiving the income of an abbey and an archbishopric, a deputy performing the duties. This abuse was common in that age, and Montalembert, in his *Monks of the West*, speaks of it as one of the chief causes of the disorders in the French Church before the Revolution.

23. Those who under other circumstances would have been the leaders of faction-fighting naturally called Lorenzo's rule a tyranny. But we find even Savonarola declared by his opponents to have made himself "tyrant of Florence." (Villari's *Savonarola*, ii. 71.)

24. Guicciardini.

25. *See* page 196.

26. Roscoe says:—"Before adopting an ecclesiastical life Giambattista Cibò was married and had several children, the eldest of whom, Francesco Cibò, was married to Maddalena, Lorenzo's daughter."

27. Or perhaps rather for the betrothal; the actual marriage took place at Rome.

28. A portrait of Pietro at the age of seventeen is to be seen in the copy of Homer printed in 1488 (now in the National Library of the Uffizi), and given to Pietro on the occasion of his marriage (*see* page 699).

29. In this same year Filippo Strozzi (the elder) began to build a new palace for his family, the present Strozzi Palace. He relates how he had a careful horoscope drawn out, and in accordance with it laid the foundation-stone at sunrise on the 6th August 1489. Though inferior in its architecture to the palace of the Medici, built sixty years before, it followed the general style of the latter. It was designed by Benedetto da Maiano, an artist who had by this time gained a considerable reputation both as a sculptor and an architect.

30. The Pope stipulated that in view of Giovanni's age it should remain a secret for three years; though it soon became an open one.

31. *See* Gibbon's words (page 56).

32. *Florentine Life during the Renaissance,* by Walter Scaife.

33. Florence (owing to the feeling of disdain for printed, as compared with manuscript, books which prevailed amongst scholars) was the last of the great cities to establish a printing press, being surpassed even by London. Following Mayence in 1450, Naples established printing in 1465, Rome in 1467, Venice and Milan in 1469, Paris, Nuremberg, and Verona in 1470, and London (under the auspices of Caxton) in 1476. And it was not until 1477 that Florence produced a printed book, brought out by the printing press set up by Bernardo Cennini. In Mayence the *Gothic* type was used; the *Roman* type was introduced by Seveynheim and Pannartz at Rome in 1467; and the *Italic* by Aldus Manutius at Venice in 1500.

34. The first printed edition of the works of Homer was brought out

at Florence in 1488, by Demetrius Chalcondylas and Demetrius Cretensis.

35. Thomas Linacer, or Linacre, was one of the most eminent physicians and scholars of England. He was born about 1460, and was the first Englishman who studied Aristotle and Galen in the original Greek. He taught Greek at Oxford and gave lectures on physic. Henry VII called him to court and entrusted to him the education of Prince Arthur. In 1518 Linacre became the founder of the College of Physicians in London, obtaining letters patent for it from Henry VIII. He died in 1524, and was buried in St. Paul's.

36. *See* page 220.

37. *The Cambridge Modern History,* vol. iii. chap. xiv ("The Italian Renaissance," by A. J. Butler, M.A.).

38. *Florence,* by F. A. Hyett.

39. Lorenzo's well-known song, "O chiara stella, che co' raggi tuoi," has always been much admired.

40. *Lorenzo de' Medici,* by E. Armstrong, M.A.

41. Symonds says that for fertility of conception and mastery of metre, Politian's Latin poems have never been surpassed by any modern writer. His full name was Angelo Ambrogini of Montepulciano, but he was always known as Poliziano. Mr. Armstrong says of him:—"The classics were absorbed into his system and became a part of himself. Latin and Greek sprang naturally to his lips, there was no inward process of translation; he thought with the thoughts of the ancients. . . . Hence Politian's Latin writings live, and deserve to live. . . . His poem on the Violet, and an elegy on the death of Albiera degli Albizzi, are still treasured gems of Latin poetry."

42. Pico della Mirandola and Politian are both buried in the church of San Marco, where their monuments are to be seen one below the other.

43. In addition to the works of sculptors and painters Lorenzo's collections of works belonging to the minor arts—vases, gems, and valuable objects of art of all kinds—were immense. His collection of cameos, coins, and medallions (now in the Bargello Museum in Florence) is the oldest in Europe.

44. *I.e.,* in 1490.

45. Painting in oils on canvas was introduced at Venice about the year 1478, and all artists soon began to follow the Bellini brothers in using this method.

46. *See* page 81.

47. For Botticelli's first period, *see* pages 124-132.

48. Pages 162-165.

49. Until recently these were supposed to have all perished, but a few years ago the present owner of the villa (Signor Lemmi) discovered under the whitewash several of these frescoes, painted in reference to the marriage of Lorenzo Tornabuoni and Giovanna degli Albizzi in 1486. These fine frescoes are now in the Louvre.

50. For Botticelli's third and fourth periods, *see* pages 256-262.

51. As Mrs. Ady says:—"The natural bent of his mind led him to

paint every vein and wrinkle in the faces of his personages, and every brooch and jewel in their robes, with the same minute realism."

52. So said by Vasari; now said to be Gentile de' Becchi, Bishop of Arezzo.

53. One of the shepherds is a portrait of himself.

54. Cafaggiolo, like so many of these great country villas of the time, was practically a castle.

55. Being the last words from Lorenzo's pen, it has been called his "Swan Song."

56. Some of the medical remedies given him were better calculated to hasten his end than to effect his recovery. Ludovico Sforza had sent him a very famous Lombard doctor, Lazaro of Pavia; but the chief remedy which he prescribed was a mixture of pulverised diamonds and pearls. Whether owing to jealousy of the Lombard physician, sorrow at Lorenzo's death, or the result of foul play, the body of his most eminent Florentine physician, Pier Leoni, was on the morning after Lorenzo's death found at the bottom of a well in the garden of the villa.

57. Politian's account is corroborated to some extent by a letter written by Benedetto Dei only a week after Lorenzo's death (*see* Armstrong's *Lorenzo de' Medici*, p. 310).

58. This was a Government Insurance Fund, in which by regular subscriptions parents could provide marriage portions for their daughters. In 1485 the Signoria, being much pressed to repay the expenses of the late war, decided, instead of increasing taxation, that only one-fifth of the sum insured for in this fund should be paid to the girl on her marriage, and that the remainder should be retained by the State as a Government debt, bearing interest at seven per cent. This was a most unpopular measure, but not on account of the arrangement itself, for it obviously assisted economy, while it was preferred to increased taxation, but because it was considered that the interest of seven per cent. was too low. In any case it can scarcely be called a misappropriation, even by the State. Still less was it a misappropriation of State funds to his own use by Lorenzo or a ground for the statement made by one modern writer that "He had seized on the dowries of Florentine maidens to pay for his own pleasures."

59. Creighton iv. 341.

60. Any examination of Lorenzo's personal money transactions will show that he always erred on the side of over-payment, and that anything in the nature of an endeavour to get the best of a bargain was abhorrent to him.

61. Creighton's *History of the Papacy*, iv. 340-343.

62. Now in the Uffizi Gallery.

63. Whether this is intentional it is impossible to say, but it may have been so. The younger branch of the family bore no good-will to the elder branch, and in particular to Lorenzo and his son Pietro (*see* chapter x), and Vasari, as the court painter of Cosimo I (of the younger branch), had every inducement to represent Lorenzo in no flattering manner.

64. Bertoldo was a pupil of Donatello, and died the year before Lorenzo. The still more celebrated Pollajuolo died in 1498.

65. *Verrocchio*, by Miss M. Cruttwell.

66. *Lorenzo de' Medici*, by E. Armstrong, M.A.

67. *Lorenzo de' Medici*, by E. Armstrong, M.A.

68. *Life of Lorenzo de' Medici*, by William Roscoe.

69. This resolution was voted for by 483 out of 546 senators.

70. Sismondi vii. 290; Perrens' *History of Florence*, i. 431; Symonds ii. 315, 318, iii. 264, iv. 369, 386, Symonds' *Sketches and Studies in Italy* (1879), 144, 145; Villari's *Savonarola*, i. 36, 39, 45; Trollope iii. 469.

71. Hallam's *Europe during the Middle Ages*, i. 542.

72. *See* pages 212-213, 219.

73. *See* page 218.

74. There is an able defence of Lorenzo's character by Ernesto Masi in *La Vita Italiana nel Rinascimento*, pp. 1-30.

75. It was in recent times long disputed exactly where in the New Sacristy Lorenzo and Giuliano lay buried; but this question was set at rest in October 1895, when, by order of the Government, the end wall of this sacristy was opened and their bodies found buried there in coffins which, though much broken, had their names on them. Their remains were put into new coffins and re-interred in the same spot.

76. A single line at the foot might record that Giuliano was also buried there.

77. It was Lorenzo who placed on the walls of the cathedral the marble slab to the memory of Giotto, and who wrote the words thereon.

CHAPTER X

1. Several poems written by him are still preserved in the Medici Library in San Lorenzo.

2. Pope Innocent VIII, on hearing of Lorenzo's death, exclaimed: "The peace of Italy is at an end!"

3. *See* page 188.

4. For a description of the composition of this army, *see* page 245.

5. Authorities differ much as to the strength of Charles's army; it is variously stated at 15,000, 20,000, 30,000, and 40,000 men. Various circumstances, however, seem to show that it could scarcely have much exceeded 20,000.

6. Roscoe says that the rate of interest was even as much as cent. per cent.

7. Not far from Spezia.

8. The *condottieri* troops employed by Florence and other Italian states in the wars of that time were inferior in power to such a force as Charles commanded in two respects. First, and chiefly, because an army is not merely a collection of regiments, and because, therefore, of the immense difference in military power between a force which possesses all the organisation and coherence of an army as compared with a collection of troops (even though equal in training and discipline) which is without that organisation. And secondly,

because the *condottieri* troops of Italy had not in 1494 the degree of discipline which would have made them equal, in that particular at all events, to those of an organised army. Thirty years later Giovanni delle Bande Nere, the greatest *condottieri* leader of his age, introduced a great change in this respect; and his troops were highly disciplined. The altogether superior power which an organised army possessed over a collection of the kind of troops hitherto employed in Italy was demonstrated only seven months later at Fornovo, when Charles's army (though then in by no means the same state of fitness) attacked and beat off a force of the above description which was more than four times stronger numerically and had every advantage of position (*see* pages 247-248).

9. What this meant was seen a few years later at Prato (*see* pages 239-240).

10. All places on Charles's line of march. He had already taken three of the four fortresses.

11. It is significant on this point that the deputation sent by the citizens themselves a few days afterwards did not attempt to do otherwise than agree to the same concession (*see* page 244).

12. Pietro fled by the Porta San Gallo; his brother, the young Cardinal Giovanni, disguised himself as a Dominican monk, conveyed as many as possible of their most valuable literary possessions to the monastery of San Marco, and then fled and joined Pietro at Venice.

13. Equal in our present money to about £300,000.

14. Though their gold and silver stands, and the pearls and rubies with which they were encrusted, have disappeared.

15. The statue, with the inscription placed upon it by the Signoria, still stands in the Loggia de' Lanzi, facing the Palazzo Vecchio, and is the memorial of an important episode in the history of Florence. In after years, when Cosimo I ruled Florence with a rod of iron from that palace, the inscription must have had a strangely sarcastic flavour.

16. The illegitimate son of Lorenzo's brother Giuliano, *see* page 177.

17. Pietro's body was subsequently recovered, and was buried in the abbey of Monte Casino, where in 1552 Cosimo I erected a handsome monument to his memory.

18. It would seem as though Antonio Pollajuolo also gives us a contemporary likeness of Pietro, corroborating that by Botticelli. There is in the Kaiser Friedrich Museum at Berlin a picture by Pollajuolo of *David,* in which the latter, represented in the dress of a young Florentine noble, and with the active athletic figure which all accounts record of Pietro, has a face extraordinarily like that of Botticelli's *Pietro the Unfortunate.* Miss Cruttwell, in her *Antonio Pollajuolo,* draws attention to the similarity between the two pictures: —"The features are identical. In both paintings we see the same delicate face with prominent cheek-bones, the same heavy-lidded. pale grey eyes, the same shock of brown hair growing low on the broad forehead, the same curved, melancholy mouth." Pollajuolo, as we know from a letter of his, paid a visit to Florence from Rome in July 1494, and had some communication with Pietro.

19. *Sandro Botticelli,* by H. P. Horne, p. 27.

20. The gold medallion is very peculiarly executed. Instead of being painted, it is *an actual cast,* taken from the medal itself, and inserted into the material of the picture, the cast being then gilded all over by the painter.

21. *See* page 11.

22. Yet these troops had already seen Milan, Pavia, Piacenza, Pisa, and various other cities of Italy.

23. *See* pages 196-200.

24. *See* page 67.

25. Milan, Rome, Naples, Venice, Ferrara, Mantua, Rimini, and many others.

26. In the Este family at Ferrara, for instance, such murders were incessant during this very period.

27. *E.g.,* the Tudors in England, and the Sforza, Riario, and many others in Italy.

28. Amassed in a banking business which covered all Europe.

29. We have, for instance, seen the *Libro di Ragione* testifying that Cosimo's charitable expenditure amounted to a sum more than double the entire income of the Florentine state (*see* page 77).

30. *Siena,* by Langton Douglas.

CHAPTER XI

1. *Storia di Firenze,* by Cerretani.

2. There is a bust of Charles VIII in the Bargello Museum.

3. Its sound was compared to the lowing of a cow, and when its deep voice was heard, men said, "La vacca muggia" ("the cow is lowing"), meaning that there was a general summons. It could be heard in every part of Florence.

4. The above episode, in which his bravery saved Florence at so critical a juncture, has caused the statue of Piero Capponi to find a place in the gallery of honour in the Uffizi colonnade.

5. Writers (Symonds included) have universally misrepresented this battle to the disparagement of the French; besides failing altogether to notice the important military point which gives it special interest.

6. Symonds.

7. Though not in the courtyard of the Bargello, as depicted in George Eliot's *Romola* (see note 6 of chapter xxiv).

8. The great hall in the Palazzo della Signoria (Palazzo Vecchio) was constructed by Savonarola in order to accommodate this *Consiglio Maggiore.*

9. *See* Mrs. Oliphant's *Makers of Florence,* Professor Villari's *Life of Savonarola,* and George Eliot's *Romola.*

10. The Signoria, in a letter to the Pope, who had complained of the delay, stated:—"Even by long and arduous examination, continued for many days, and with the aid of torture, we could barely extort anything from him."

11. *Florence,* by F. A. Hyett.

12. *Botticelli,* by Steinmann

13. With golden lilies on a light blue ground. This picture is in much better preservation than the *Madonna of the Magnificat,* which has had many travels and suffered much therefrom.

14. The pomegranate is a symbol of the Church, but the *bitten* pomegranate is the emblem of the Fall of Man.

15. Botticelli's somewhat different treatment of the subject can be seen by comparing his picture with the engraving representing the *Calumny* of Apelles taken from Lucian's description, to be seen in the collection of engravings in the Uffizi Gallery, No. 59.

16. *Botticelli,* by Steinmann.

17. Within the last five years there has been placed on the spot where Savonarola was burnt (replacing the former small plain slab) a larger one, bearing the following inscription: "Qui, dove con i suoi confratelli Fra Domenico Buonvicini e Fra Silvestro Maruffi il XXIII Maggio del MCCCCIXVIII per iniqua sentenza fu impiccato ed arso Fra Girolamo Savonarola, dopo quattro secoli fu collocata queta memoria." (Here, where with his brethren, Fra Domenico Buonvicini and Fra Silvestro Maruffi, on the 23rd May 1498, by an iniquitous sentence Fra Girolamo Savonarola was hanged and burnt, after four centuries has been placed this memorial.) And there it is customary with the Florentines on the 23rd May to lay bouquets of flowers to Savonarola's memory.

18. Botticelli was buried with extreme secrecy (probably because he was a noted partisan of Savonarola), and his tomb still remains without any tombstone.

19. Lorenzo di Credi and Andrea del Sarto were the only two first-class painters of the Tuscan school who survived him; Andrea del Sarto by seven years, and Lorenzo di Credi by thirteen years.

20. *Perugino,* by G. C. Williamson.

21. Alexander VI's death, believed at the time to be due to poison, is now considered to have been due to natural causes.

22. Part of the army was sent back to France by sea, and part by land.

23. His portrait by Raphael hangs in the Uffizi Gallery, and is thoroughly characteristic. There is a replica of it also in the Pitti Gallery, and another in the National Gallery, London.

24. It was at this time that Giovanni formed the great friendship of his life, that with Galeotto della Rovere, nephew of Julius II. Giovanni was devotedly fond of him, and when after a year or two Galeotto died, was for long inconsolable; and in after years as Pope he never heard the name of Galeotto mentioned without showing his affectionate remembrance.

25. Michelangelo's statue of *David* had been finished the previous year. Perugino and Lorenzo di Credi were called upon to advise as to where it should be placed.

26. It is disputed whether Raphael painted the whole of the fresco, or only the portion signed by him.

27. *Modern Painters,* vol. iii.

28. The block of marble from which this statue was carved on its

way to Bandinelli's workshop fell into the Arno. When the statue was set up the Florentine wits of the day declared that the marble had tried to drown itself to avoid the disgrace which was in store for it.

29. *The Cambridge Modern History*, vol. ii. chap. i.

30. The learned writer of chap. i. vol. ii. of *The Cambridge Modern History*, the late Dr. Kraus, is firmly of opinion that the fundamental idea underlying this general scheme is to be attributed to none other than Pope Julius II himself. At the same time it was, of course, not entirely original, the same idea having been propounded in different forms by Clement, Origen, John Scotus, Dante, and St. Thomas Aquinas and specially dwelt upon by Pico della Mirandola.

31. *See* page 106.

32. He intended that it should occupy the apse of the new St. Peter's, when it would have dominated the whole interior of the church. After all, however, the tomb never got into St. Peter's at all, while it hung like a millstone round Michelangelo's neck for about forty years. Only one side of it was ever completed, and this portion (containing the celebrated statue of *Moses*) was deposited in the church of San Pietro in Vincoli, where it still remains.

33. Ranke's *History of the Popes*.

34. A monument to his memory stands on the site of the battle.

35. *Florence,* by F. A. Hyett.

36. Giovanni Ridolfi was appointed Gonfaloniere.

37. Professor Villari's *Life and Times of Machiavelli.*

38. Soderini was afterwards, when Giovanni became Pope, given by him a home in Rome, and settled there permanently.

CHAPTER XII

1. Her sister-in-law, Isabella d'Este, was the first.

2. His portrait was evidently painted at a later date (*see* page 289).

3. Niccolò Machiavelli (1469-1527) is generally completely misunderstood by popular writers. Professor Villari in his *Life of Machiavelli* has pointed out that *The Prince* was written with a very noble object, and has effectually refuted "the base assertion that it was written to curry favour with the Medici."

4. *See* pages 292 and 351.

5. A curious detail is that the top of the first finger of the left hand seems to have been cut off. The same detail occurs in Allori's picture.

6. This valuable picture is now the property of Herr Oscar Huldschinsky, Berlin, having been bought for the sum of £17,700.

7. During this campaign he was dangerously wounded in the head at the attack on the castle of Mondolfo.

8. Cambi.

9. It was only two years after this that he arranged the sumptuous pageant which received the name of "The Field of the Cloth of Gold," at which he entertained Henry VIII.

10. There is no record as to where Madeleine de la Tour d'Auvergne was buried.

11. In particular on account of the four allegorical figures reclining on the two sarcophagi (*see* page 351).

12. Giuliano is represented wearing his uniform as Gonfaloniere of the Papal forces.

13. That which has been called *Il Pensieroso*. It was for many years debated which of the two tombs was Giuliano's and which Lorenzo's, and writers before 1875 have taken opposite views; but in that year the question was set at rest by the opening of the sarcophagus over which this figure sits, the result of which showed it to be Lorenzo's (*see* page 375).

14. Thus Rogers writes:—
"That is Duke Lorenzo; mark him well;
His mien most noble, most majestical."
While another writer considers Lorenzo's statue to denote a character showing "self-devoted absorption in noble designs."

CHAPTER XIII

1. Elected Pope on the 11th March, he was ordained a priest on the 15th March, and a bishop on the 19th March.

2. From 11th March 1513 to 1st December 1521.

3. *The Cambridge Modern History*, vol. ii. chap. i.

4. It was he who thus obtained the copy of the first five books of Livy, now in the Medici Library in San Lorenzo, Florence.

5. Leo's creating Giulio a cardinal was entirely illegal, the latter being barred by the canons of the Church on account of the illegitimacy of his birth. The historian of Leo's life says:—"The Pope got over the difficulty by simply declaring him legitimate."

6. It was in the hope of inducing Henry VIII also to join this alliance that Leo X created Wolsey a cardinal.

7. Maximilian Sforza (the eldest son of Il Moro) was driven out, and Milan was placed under the government of Odet de Foix, Maréchal de Lautrec.

8. In Raphael's fresco in the Vatican of *The Coronation of Charlemagne,* commemorating this event, portraits of Leo X (as Leo III), of Francis I (as Charlemagne), and of Giuliano's little son Ippolito (as a page) are all given.

9. The marriage of Giuliano with Philiberte of Savoy having been the first.

10. This action, abominable as it was, was not exceptional in that age. Mr. Marion Crawford, in his *Sketches from Venetian History,* speaking generally of such cases, remarks that in that age a safe conduct seemed so invariably the prelude to a political assassination that the extraordinary thing is that men should have continued to put any faith in such promises.

11. A portion of these were commanded by the young Giovanni delle Bande Nere, Leo's distant relative belonging to the younger branch of the family (chapter xxiii).

12. Roscoe's *Life of Leo X.*

13. The personal character given to Leo by Erasmus, Sarpi, and so many other writers (including such an authority as Dr. Kraus), could scarcely have been given if this was not the case.

14. There was already a printing press at Rome for works in the Latin character, but none hitherto for the Greek character.

15. *The Medici Popes*, by H. M. Vaughan.

16. He pointed out that this was particularly objectionable, in that it prevented the people from kissing the Pope's toe. But Leo does not seem to have considered the argument one carrying much weight.

17. For a graphic account of the mode of life at the court of Leo X, *see* Mr. Herbert Vaughan's *The Medici Popes*.

18. Ranke's *History of the Popes*.

19. We get a curious light thrown on the way the Papacy was hastening to its doom when we find Julius II in 1510 excommunicating "every town in which a General Council shall assemble"; and also when we find it said during Leo X's life, that "the bare mention of such a Council is equivalent to a declaration of war."

20. St. Peter's is said to have cost from first to last £10,000,000 sterling.

21. Various contemporary authorities have given credit to the rumour that he was poisoned at the instance of Francis I, but there is no evidence whatever to support this.

CHAPTER XIV

1. Nardi.

2. It was this which had originated his advancement in his own country, and which later on caused him to be selected as tutor to the future Charles V.

3. He was only actually in Rome a year, as he did not reach there from Spain till the 29th August 1522.

4. "Alas what grief! Of how great importance it is in what times the excellence of each exalted man falls."

CHAPTER XV

1. The greater part of the votes were divided between Giulio de' Medici and Wolsey, while the Cardinal Farnese offered 200,000 ducats to either side in his own behalf.

2. *See* page 293.

3. The Giuliano killed in the Pazzi conspiracy (Clement's father), and the Giuliano, brother of Leo X (Ippolito's father), must here be distinguished.

4. "His mother was a mulatto slave, and he had the dark skin, thick lips, and curly hair of a negro." (GINO CAPPONI.)

5. There is now no doubt of this, though none cared at the time to contradict the Pope's assertion that he was the son of Lorenzo (Duke of Urbino), and as such he has generally been mentioned in history, historians contenting themselves with saying that he was

reputed to be so, but was more probably Clement's own son. Not only was the fact generally known in the family, but also Clement's subsequent conduct in so persistently, in spite of many obstacles, pushing forward this detested, incapable and vicious youth in place of the capable and universally liked Ippolito, would alone suffice to prove it. Moreover, the historian Ammirato states that afterwards, when Clement and Alessandro were both dead, Cosimo I told him positively that Alessandro was Clement's son. Lorenzino said that he was not of the Medici blood at all (*see* note 5 of chapter xviii).

6. *Sommario della Storia d'Italia,* by Francesco Vettori. Vettori was himself one of the envoys on this occasion, and one of those who gave this advice.

7. *History of the Commonwealth of Florence,* by Adolphus Trollope.

8. The husband of Vittoria Colonna.

9. *See* chapter xxiii.

10. One exception was the Duc d'Alençon (the husband of Francis's sister, Marguerite), who disgracefully fled from the field, and whose flight was partly the cause of the defeat. He died two months later.

11. He was created a Duke by Charles V in 1530.

12. The copy of Andrea del Sarto is now at Naples.

13. *See* chapter xxiii.

14. The historian Guicciardini, writing some fifteen years afterwards, called Clement's conduct during the years 1524-1526 an *"eterna infamia."*

15. One of these hostages was Filippo Strozzi, who nearly lost his life in consequence of the Pope's action (*see* page 336).

16. The story of France's great soldier, Charles, Duke of Bourbon, is one of the saddest in history. His soldiers buried him at Gaeta, where they erected a noble monument to his memory and that of his wife, Susanne de Bourbon.

17. *Charles V,* by W. Robertson.

18. The portraits of Francesco della Rovere, Duke of Urbino, and of his wife, Eleonora Gonzaga (the daughter of Isabella d'Este), are to be seen in the Uffizi Gallery.

19. *See* chapter xvi.

CHAPTER XVI

1. *See* page 329.

2. Ippolito, aged seventeen, Alessandro, aged fifteen, and the little "Duchessina," Catherine, aged eight.

3. Referring to the time when Pope Sixtus IV had demanded the surrender to him of Lorenzo, and when the Florentines had refused to give him up.

4. Referring to the illegality of his creation as cardinal (*see* page 297).

5. Excepting Catherine, kept as a prisoner by the Republic (*see* chapter xix).

6. Roscoe justly remarks:—"It was not by the continuance of, but

by the departure from, the system of government which the earlier Medici had established, that the Florentine Republic sank under the degrading yoke of despotic power."

7. Clarice's husband was much alarmed at her action; he apologised for it to the Signoria, and, by way of keeping friends with both sides, accompanied Ippolito to Pisa.

CHAPTER XVII

1. *See* page 344.

2. De Lautrec had died of the plague in August 1528.

3. The Treaty of Cambrai was the first great settlement of the affairs of Europe. Being concluded by Margaret of Austria and Louise of Savoy, it is often called the "Ladies' League."

4. The second son of Il Moro.

5. The Pope's entry into Bologna for this conference with the Emperor was made in great state, but it was remarked that there were none of the usual acclamations from the people.

6. Chapter xviii.

7. Even here Clement found scope for his favourite artifices. Charles V only agreed to the Medici being restored to their former position, that position being, however, made hereditary; and the Emperor's Diploma accordingly only made Alessandro hereditary head of the Republic. Clement did not press for more than this at the time, but he found means later on to convert this into a formal abolition of the Republic, and the conversion of Alessandro into Duke of Florence (*see* page 350).

8. A populous suburb, all of which had to be destroyed, extended from the Porta alla Croce Beccaria almost up to this monastery, a distance of nearly half a mile.

9. Giulio on becoming Pope took the name of Clement, "to signify his merciful disposition."

10. Michelangelo (not for the first time in his life) fled in a panic of fear a few days before the Imperial army reached Florence. He was outlawed and his property confiscated, but was urged to return; which he did about the end of November.

11. Niccolò Capponi, who was Gonfaloniere from May 1527 until within a few months of the city being besieged, was worthy of the best days of Florence's history, and by far the ablest man that she possessed. He was the eldest son of Piero Capponi, Charles VIII's opponent. When the storm began to gather which, had his advice been followed, would have been prevented, the citizens deprived him of his office, charged him with treason, and threatened to take his life; but he still continued to serve his country. He formed one of the embassy sent to Rome to plead with the Pope at the beginning of the siege, and died on the journey back to Florence, broken down at his country's misfortune. Symonds says that the final blow which caused his death was the news, brought to him by Michelangelo, that Malatesta Baglioni was a traitor.

12. Gino Capponi, iii. 241.

13. It was called an *incamiciata,* because Colonna's force all wore white shirts over their armour.

14. Francesco Ferrucci's house is still to be seen in the Via Santo Spirito. A tablet on it recording his death at the battle of Gavinana says, "With him fell Florentine liberty." His devoted struggle in defence of his country has earned his statue a place in the Uffizi colonnade.

15. "Although the submission of Florence had been nominally to the Emperor, it was practically to the Pope. It was the Pope, and not the Emperor, who reconstructed the Florentine Government. Ferrante Gonzaga acted for the Emperor, and Baccio Valori for the Pope."— (Hyett.)

16. Varchi.

17. It is stated by Varchi that Fra Benedetto was sent to Rome, and there by the Pope's own orders cruelly starved to death in the castle of St. Angelo.

18. Clement had also the private reason that to make the announcement as to Alessandro's future position before he had disposed of Ippolito would be inconvenient.

19. Most of the money for its construction was lent by Filippo Strozzi. It was predicted at the time that he would live to rue it (*see* page 554).

20. Varchi says it weighed 22,000 lbs.

21. The name which has ever since been given to the villa at which the terms of the capitulation were signed is significant, the *Villa delle Bugie* (the villa of lies). It stands a short distance beyond the Torre del Gallo. It was an unfortunate name for the house to have at which Guicciardini afterwards wrote his celebrated history of Italy.

22. Michelangelo, referring to the statue of *Night,* wrote:—

> "Ah, glad am I to sleep in stone, while wrong
> And dire disgrace rage unreproved near;
> A happy chance to neither see nor hear;
> Oh then wake me not! Hush! whisper low!"

23. It came to be called the Confession of Augsburg.

24. In this same year (1532) the conquest of Peru added still further to Charles's dominions.

25. Clement never once ventured to enter Florence after the siege of 1530 and his repudiation of the terms on which the city surrendered, often proceeding by the most difficult routes in order to avoid that city. On this occasion the intense hardships which the Pope and the small band of cardinals whom he took with him suffered in this journey to Bologna by the rough road which passed through Perugia are vividly described by Dr. Edmund Bonner (afterwards Bishop of London), who says that the journey was "wondrous painful to the Pope," and speaks of the various "unfortunable accidents," of the "evil lodging," and of the Pope having often to go on foot for several miles "by reason of th' foulness and danger of the way."

26. *See* pages 355-356.

27. The grounds on which Henry claimed that his marriage to Katharine had been illegal, and the arguments for and against it, do not concern this history, and are to be found in histories of England. Though spoken of as a divorce it was, technically speaking, not a divorce, but a decree of nullity, which Henry desired from the Pope.

28. In the documents of the time she is constantly called the Pope's niece; whereas she was of course only his very distant cousin, he being the first cousin of her grandfather, Pietro.

29. During subsequent years the same test was applied to points of doctrine, and one by one all doctrines that would not bear the test of the first six centuries were gradually wiped off.

30. Not in consequence of it, as nearly always stated.

31. Clement VII cannot be credited with any reason based on religious grounds for refusing to annul Henry's marriage to Katharine of Arragon. His action was throughout due to his fear of offending Charles V, a fear which the latter had increased by his threats when they met at Bologna in December 1532.

32. Strangely enough on the death of Clement VII there appear to have been none of the usual rumours that death was due to poison.

33. "To him more than to any other man is due the success of the Reformation as a movement antagonistic to Rome." (*The Cambridge Modern History*, vol. ii.)

34. An incident cited by Ranke speaks volumes on this point, and shows how, not only Clement, but all interested in the vast Papal system, dreaded the very name of a General Council. The writer whom he quotes tells his correspondent, an Archbishop, "that the mere rumour of the probability of a General Council *had so depreciated the value of all offices in Rome that no money was to be got for them.*"

35. Catherine was always called the "Duchessina" in Rome, in consequence of her father having been for a time Duke of Urbino; and Clement's use of the term when speaking of her shows that although he had pretended to acquiesce when Adrian VI gave back that Duchy to its rightful Duke, he had not really done so.

36. *See* note 28 of this chapter.

CHAPTER XVIII

1. Ippolito and Alessandro both died at the age of twenty-six; Catherine lived to the age of seventy, and Margaret to the age of sixty-five.

2. His mother was a lady of Urbino, Pacifica Brandano.

3. *See* page 346.

4. As distinguished from the crown worn by the Grand Dukes.

5. Lorenzino in his defence (*see* page 373) denied that *any* Medici blood flowed in Alessandro's veins; he stated that though Clement VII believed the latter to be his son, it was not so.

6. Except her short one year's experience under Walter de Brienne two hundred years before.

7. It was while this orgy of crime was going on in the world outside

that, in the quiet monastery of San Marco, Sogliano, a pupil of Lorenzo di Credi, was painting in the refectory his well-known fresco, which bears on it the date 1536.

8. Napier.

9. Varchi here refers to the marriage of Alessandro to the Emperor's daughter, which it was now known had been arranged and that it would take place ere long; though it did not actually do so until after Ippolito's death.

10. As a means of bringing about peace between them, the Pope urged Charles to consent to give Milan to Francis's second son, Henry; but Charles refused "in view of the precarious health of the Dauphin," since, if the latter died, this would result in Milan becoming permanently a possession of the French crown.

11. Signifying "those who have gone out."

12. Known as the Council of Trent.

13. So called on account of his small, slight figure. His proper name was Lorenzo.

14. It was formerly asserted that the lady whom Alessandro expected to meet at Lorenzino's house was Caterina de' Ginori, Lorenzino's aunt; but M. Gautier, in his recent life of Lorenzino, contradicts this, and shows that it was Laudomia.

15. Lorenzino afterwards wrote the full details of the murder, and these may be read in full in the accounts of this affair given by Varchi and other writers. Varchi's account was received by him from Lorenzino's own lips.

16. He had previously obtained an order for post horses.

17. This latter view was in after years much in vogue, being considerably assisted by the fact that it was the one which Cosimo I (and his descendants, the Grand Dukes of Tuscany) desired should be held, Lorenzino being descended from the eldest son of Pier Francesco the elder, while Cosimo was only descended from the latter's second son (*see* page 562). Professor Del Lungo calls the former "the unfortunate Lorenzino."

18. Cosimo, the son of Giovanni delle Bande Nere.

19. *Apologia di Lorenzo di Pier Francesco de' Medici.*

20. The view which has taken pleasure in stigmatising him as "Lorenzaccio," and holding him up to general execration, is not one which is endorsed by that of the Florentines of his own time. It is the growth of a later age; and had, as has been shown, a definite motive.

21. *See* chapter xxiv.

22. Except for a short time by Cosimo I (*see* page 558).

CHAPTER XIX

1. Salmon's *Infallibility of the Church*.

2. Catherine received a double portion of this, according as her policy brought her into collision, now with one and now with the other of the two religious parties. While again in other cases the

Roman Catholic party falsified her words and actions in order to show that in what they did they had the Queen on their side.

3. *Women of the Valois Court,* by Imbert de Saint-Amand (1900).

4. *See* note 5. The information furnished by these State papers has been the chief source relied upon in this history of Catherine de' Medici. (*See* also note 20 of chapter xx.)

5. The chief information of the above kind which has in recent years become available is that furnished by the following:—

Spanish State Papers (1558-1603), 7 vols.; published in 1894.

Venetian State Papers (1202-1607), 10 vols.; published in 1900.

Foreign State Papers, London (1558-1580), 13 vols.; published in 1903.

Catherine de' Medici's letters (largely from the Russian State Papers). Edited by Count Hector de La Ferrière and G. Baguenault de Puchesse; published in 1903.

6. *See* Miss Sichel's *Catherine de' Medici,* p. 5.

7. *Ibid.,* p. 5.

8. *Ibid.,* pp. 15 and 19.

9. *See* pages 216-218.

10. *See* page 410.

11. *See* page 393.

12. Often written in cipher.

13. Chapter xx.

14. It is stated that when Lorenzo was dying at the Medici Palace his mother was unable to go to him as she was herself on her death-bed at Careggi, so that they were unable to see each other.

15. *See* page 93.

16. Ariosto had come to Florence in 1513 to study the Tuscan idiom.

17. "A soliary branch becomes green with a few leaves;
And I am in suspense between fear and hope
Whether winter will spare it to me, or tear it from me."

18. *See* pages 509-510.

19. Though, of course, she had no right to the title, the rightful Duke of Urbino having regained his duchy five years before.

20. The name was due to the ceremony with which each of the nuns was admitted, viz., by a portion of the wall of the convent being opened for her entrance, and bricked up again behind her. But it was, of course, purely a symbolical ceremony, and the convent had its regular doorway: as, in fact, we see from the narrative of Catherine's removal thence. So that the whole of what Trollope says on this point, and as to there being "other entrances known to the initiated," and its inculcation of duplicity, and so on, is entirely erroneous and misleading.

21. "Glorious mountains, whose Alp-like summits
Make against the winds a barrier and defence!
Happy valleys, through which in wave on wave
The Arno with lordly step takes his way!"

22. Leonardo Bertolini.

23. Clement himself went by sea in order to avoid passing through Florence (*see* note 25 of chapter xvii).

24. Afterwards so well known in the time of Cosimo I as painter, architect, and the historian of the lives of the painters.

25. Evidently some portrait of her was to be kept in Florence, and Vasari was painting it. But this portrait has apparently been lost.

26. In all the State documents connected with her marriage Catherine is always called by the French King and the French historians "the Duchess of Urbino," which much irritated the real Duke of Urbino.

27. It is significant that Alessandro was not present at Catherine's marriage. Had he *really* been her half-brother he would have been her nearest relative, and his presence at her marriage almost imperative. But Clement VII had no intention of parading such a connection as Alessandro before the eyes of the French; so, while he insisted on Ippolito being present, he took good care that Alessandro should not be so.

28. Unfortunately the *pyx* which it contained was stolen in 1860.

29. *See* note 10 of chapter xviii.

30. All the accounts of Catherine's appearance in her girlhood and at the time of her marriage mention that she had fair hair. This she inherited from her mother, Madeleine de la Tour d'Auvergne. Later on in her life black or dark hair became greatly in fashion in France; and it is probable that when this occurred she dyed her hair dark to accord with the prevailing fashion. This would account for the discrepancy in this particular between her earlier portraits and her later ones by Clouet and others in France.

31. *Women of the Valois Court,* by Imbert de Saint-Amand.

32. *Guerres de religion,* by Michelet.

33. At Chaumont may still be seen her bedroom, with her bed, toilet table, and *prie dieu,* with on the latter her "Book of the Hours." In this book are prayers for various persons, each with a miniature of the person prayed for, and prayers to God to "have mercy on this country over which Thou hast permitted me to rule, and deal not punishment upon it on account of wrongdoings of mine."

34. Francis, the eldest son, succeeded his father as Duke of Guise. His brother Charles became Cardinal of Lorraine. The third son, Claude, Duke of Mayenne, was married to Diane de Poictiers' daughter.

35. Diane de Poictiers taught the little Mary, Queen of Scots, to call Catherine behind her back, "La fille de marchands," and was never tired of making joking allusions to this topic. It was at this period that to please Diane the wits of Paris invented the fable that the Medici were originally doctors (or rather apothecaries), and that their family arms, the six balls, represented the pills they made; an ill-natured joke which has had a longer life than it deserved.

36. There were a few who pitied Catherine and were indignant at the treatment she received. On one occasion Maréchal Tavannes, incensed at the insults so constantly shown her, made an offer to Catherine to cut off the nose of the Duchess of Valentinois, which would, he said, put an end to all Catherine's troubles on this score.

37. *Lettres de Diane de Poictiers,* edited by M. Georges Guiffrey.

38. *See* pages 633-634.

39. *See* page 413.

40. *Lettres de Catherine de Medicis,* edited by Count Hector de la Ferrière and G. Baguenault de Puchesse (1903).

41. *Ibid.*

42. Except, of course, the accusation made against her when the Dauphin died (page 401).

43. *La Diplomatie Vénitienne,* by M. Armand Baschet.

44. The French *Parlement* must not be confounded with the English *Parliament,* from which it differed both in constitution and functions.

45. Venetian State Papers: *Secret Records.* Despatches of the ambassador, Giacomo Soranzo.

46. *La Diplomatie Vénitienne,* by Armand Baschet.

47. Dumas in his novels (which, of course, contain nothing belonging to history but their framework and local colouring) represents Catherine as bringing up her sons to be vicious and incapable in order that the real power might be hers; but this has no historical foundation. Catherine had no idea that her husband would die while her sons were young enough for such a plan to be of any use; while Francis, the most incapable of them, was brought up under tutors appointed by Henry II, who would certainly never have permitted anything of the kind. And similar instructors had charge of Catherine's other sons, the second, Charles, having as the superintendent of his education the Prince de la Roche sur Yonne, who appointed Amyot as the boy's tutor.

48. *Histoire d'Elizabeth de Valois,* by the Marquis du Prat.

49. *Archives de l'Histoire de France,* and *Recueil de fragments historiques sur les derniers Valois,* by M. Armand Eudel.

50. Then a widower through the death in 1558 of Mary of England.

51. Montgomery was Captain of the King's Scottish Guard. They numbered a hundred men, all of them gentlemen.

52. To which Catherine had a prior claim (*see* page 434).

CHAPTER XX

1. *Histoire Universelle,* by I. A. d'Aubigné.

2. *Women of the Valois Court,* by Imbert de Saint-Amand.

3. *See* pages 380-381.

4. *Guerres de religion,* by Michelet.

5. *La Diplomatie Vénitienne,* by M. Armand Baschet.

6. *See* Miss Sichel's *Catherine de' Medici,* pp. 6-7.

7. Though the Reformation did not in France so soon develop into a conflict, its doctrines had been promulgated there as early as they were in Germany, Jacques Lefèvre, of Etaples in Picardy (who had been a scholar of the Renaissance in Italy), even forestalled Luther, publishing in 1512 a commentary on St. Paul's Epistles in which he enunciated two of the main doctrines afterwards put forward by Luther. It was

Picardy also which produced Calvin (born 1509), who, establishing himself at Geneva, made that city the headquarters of French Protestantism, from whence he issued his orders to the Protestants in France as autocratically as did the Pope from Rome to the Roman Catholics.

8. There were again and again attempts to seize the person of the King, and keep him a prisoner, in order that the party which had possession of him might be able to use the weight of his authority against their opponents, and show the throne as on their side.

9. A diplomatic term for "malice of the Guises."

10. *Lettres de Catherine de Medicis,* edited by the Comte de la Ferrière.

11. Perhaps one of the most amusing of these tales is that of *the pink candles,* which on being lighted filled the room with poisonous vapour; by which means, according to the story, Charles IX (having on that night unexpectedly changed rooms with his brother Henry) was poisoned in mistake for Henry; a story which not long ago formed the subject of a play at a Continental theatre. Since Henry was Catherine's favourite son, the story is all the more piquant.

12. *History of the Papacy,* by Mandell Creighton.

13. As an example of the length to which that age could go in their credulous belief in the use of subtle poisons, we find even an historian like Jovius attributing the death of Cardinal Bibbiena in 1520 to a poison administered to him *in new laid eggs,* the hen having been made to imbibe the poison.

14. Fresh stories of this kind are continually being invented, the race of custodians in charge of historical buildings throughout Europe having long since discovered that such stories connected with the buildings which they show to visitors have a distinct pecuniary value.

15. *See* also page 472, regarding Charles IX's window in the Louvre

16. *La Diplomatie Vénitienne,* by M. Armand Baschet.

17. *Guerres de religion,* by Michelet.

18. *Marie de Medicis and her Court,* by Louis Battifol.

19. *Dames illustrées,* by Brantôme.

20. In narrating the history of this third period of Catherine's life the authorities chiefly relied upon have been the reports of the Venetian and other ambassadors, and Catherine's own letters (*see* pages 380 and 422). To quote them too frequently would grievously encumber the text for the general reader. References have therefore mainly been confined to those required in denoting the source from which some extract illustrating a point has been taken, or in quoting some statement of a modern writer (such as Miss Sichel) which it was desired to refute. Beyond the authorities mentioned in note 5 of chapter xix, the chief authority followed has been *The Cambridge Modern History,* which is itself based upon the results of all the most recent research, and is in my opinion a much more reliable guide than, for instance, Professor Mariéjol (in *The Lavisse History of France*), who with all his learning is still in the thraldom of those contemporary French writers who, as I have shown (pages 379, 458 and 463), are not to be depended upon. It is almost needless to say that the present book

takes an exactly opposite view of the character and conduct of Catherine de' Medici to that taken by Miss Sichel in her recent book *Catherine de' Medici and the French Reformation*, with its sequel, *The Later Years of Catherine de' Medici*.

21. Brothers of her mother, Mary of Lorraine.

22. We see this brought out very clearly by what happened a year later, on the death of Francis II, in the case of the Prince of Condé and the King of Navarre, whose lives were only able to be saved by Catherine, because, by Francis II's death, the power of the Guises came to an end.

23. Thus depriving of his office the deservedly honoured Montmorency, Constable of France, who had given long and good service to Francis's father, Henry II.

24. Louis XIII.

25. *Lettres de Catherine de Medicis*, edited by the Comte de la Ferrière.

26. The promise obtained from the Guises that the persecutions should be discontinued was communicated to the Protestants; when in spite of it the persecutions continued, they put it down to duplicity on Catherine's part.

27. *See* Miss Sichel's *Catherine de' Medici*, p. 109.

28. It was this same Duchess of Guise, however, who twelve years later took a very different attitude, and was the chief instigator of her son Henry, Duke of Guise, to murder Coligny and execute the massacre of St. Bartholomew's Day.

29. The highest authority has said that Catherine de' Medici "had no natural tendency to cruelty." (*The Cambridge Modern History*, vol. iii, chap. i.)

30. Many of them saluted him before laying their heads on the block.

31. The Guises.

32. Among other communications of a similar kind a celebrated pamphlet was sent to the Cardinal of Lorraine, entitled *A Letter to the Tiger of France*.

33. *See* Miss Sichel's *Catherine de' Medici*, p. 113.

34. *See* pages 444-445 as regards Condé.

35. This letter Miss Sichel takes as evidence that Catherine was plotting Condé's death. Not only, however, does Catherine's conduct a few days later entirely disprove this, but also it is to be noted that the latter writes in exactly the same strain (using almost the identical words) about her own son, the Duc d'Alençon, when, about twelve years afterwards, she kept him temporarily a prisoner at Amboise, to keep him out of mischief, on which occasion she writes to Guise: "The place is strong and massive, and the little frog (her name for Alençon) cannot possibly get away from it."

36. *The Cambridge Modern History*, vol. iii. chap. i.

37. *The Cambridge Modern History*, vol. iii. chap. i. It took the Church of England exactly one hundred years to find (in 1661) peace at last (after her long conflict) on the same basis.

38. Elizabeth of England, for instance, could not have done so; and if she could not, it is certain that none other could.

39. It is consequently known as the Council of Poissy.

40. Francis I divided France into provinces, each of which had its *Parlement*.

41. About ten miles.

42. *The Châteaux of Touraine*, by M. H. Lansdale.

43. See Miss Sichel's *Later Years of Catherine de' Medici*, pp. 19-21.

44. Spanish State Papers: *Secret Records*. Despatches of the Duke of Alva.

45. The palace of the Tuileries, after being greatly enlarged by successive sovereigns of France, was in 1871 entirely destroyed by the Communists, and only its beautiful gardens now remain.

46. From *tuile*, a tile. For the reason for the name *see* pp. 120-121.

47. It was just at this time (December 1564) that in Florence Cosimo I was constructing his similar but much longer gallery, the "Passaggio," through a portion of that city to connect the Ducal palace with the Palazzo Vecchio, in the same manner as Catherine connected the Tuileries with the Louvre.

48. Calvin himself had died in 1564.

49. Not to be confounded with the Duke of Alva.

50. Spanish State Papers.

51. Of all the Venetian ambassadors during these thirty years M. Armand Baschet singles out as by far the most distinguished Giovanni Correr, who came as ambassador to France during the Second Religious War, and who, he says, "writes with a talent which reveals a profound insight." Giovanni Correr was on more intimate terms with Catherine than any of his successors, and so largely did she discuss all affairs with him that M. Baschet considers that "to obtain a just idea of Catherine de' Medici during this period it is entirely necessary to study the remarkable pages of this most capable ambassador." (*La Diplomatie Vénitienne*, by M. Armand Baschet.)

52. *Lettres de Catherine de Medicis*.

53. Her Edict of January, 1562.

54. *Lettres de Catherine de Medicis*.

55. The Guises.

56. *Lettres de Catherine de Medicis*.

57. Jeanne d'Albret was the daughter of Francis I's sister Marguerite, who had married Henri d'Albret. Jeanne herself married Antoine de Bourbon, Duc de Vendôme, and was Queen of Navarre in her own right, her son Henry only becoming King of Navarre at her death.

58. *The Cambridge Modern History*, vol. iii. chap. i.

59. Salviati asserts that Guise had wished that his mother should herself fire the shot.

60. Lord Acton after careful computation considered that the number of persons slain in this massacre was rather over 2,000.

61. *See* page 428.

62. *See* also pages 428, 469, 470 and 476.

63. Notwithstanding this, the custodians who show the building to visitors still continue to repeat this story, and so to perpetuate false "history" (*see* note 14 of this chapter).

64. As, for instance, the assertion of her having assembled "a Council of murder" in the gardens of the Tuileries on the 23rd August, at which the massacre is said to have been decided upon. (*See* Miss Sichel's *The Later Years of Catherine de' Medici*, p. 167.)

65. All the authorities who hold her to have been responsible for the massacre admit this.

66. The Venetian ambassadors were under compulsion not to allow any bias to enter into their official despatches to their Government, since this might mislead the latter.

67. *Chronique du temps de Charles IX*, by M. Merimée.

68. We have also to remember that even Michelet, with all his hatred of her, considered that she was not guilty, either of instigating Coligny's death, or of responsibility for the massacre on St. Bartholomew's Day.

69. But while the responsibility for the massacre on St. Bartholomew's Day, 1572, must be borne by the French people themselves, it would be quite a mistake to suppose that the English can cast any stones at them in this respect. Seven years later there occurred in Ireland a massacre of the Roman Catholic population of the province of Munster, carried out by English Protestant troops under the special orders of Queen Elizabeth, which was greater in degree and not in any way less revolting in character than the massacre in Paris; while it had far less excuse. We have the crime of these Roman Catholics stated by a certain Sir William Drury to be that they had "infinite Masses in their churches every morning without any fear. I spied them, for I chanced to arrive last Sunday at five in the morning and saw them resort out of the churches by heaps. This is shameful in a reformed city." It is strange that while the French massacre is copiously commented on, this English one is seldom, if ever, mentioned. But the fair-minded Ranke sees no reason for any such distinction, and relates what took place as follows:—"The English Protestants ... punished their opponents with fearful cruelty. Men and women were driven into barns and there burnt to death; children were strangled; all Munster was laid waste; and English (Protestant) colonists took possession of the depopulated province." Well, therefore, may we bear in mind with reference to the Paris massacre, that it was not only in France, or by one religious party, that at this period such tragedies were enacted.

70. *See* page 454.

71. *Guerres de religion*, by Michelet.

72. The story that Charles IX died through remorse for the massacre of St. Bartholomew's Day, a story sedulously propagated by the Protestants, is not corroborated by any evidence, and does not now obtain any credit among historians.

73. This daughter died at the age of five.

74. "His secretary opened and closed the puncture whenever it was necessary to fill the pen."

75. So called because they struck their backs and shoulders with whips in penance for their sins.

76. *See* Miss Sichel's *Catherine de' Medici*, p. 23.

77. Clement VII had largely altered this tradition; but Catherine had no respect for Clement VII, and did not agree with any of his ideas, though as a girl she had been forced to obey him.

78. Chapter xxiv.

79. Miss Sichel's *The Later Years of Catherine de' Medici*, p. 256.

80. *Ibid.*

81. *Histoire Universelle*, by I. A. d'Aubigné.

82. *Lettres de Catherine de Medicis.*

83. *Ibid.*

84. Miss Sichel's *The Later Years of Catherine de' Medici*, p. 313.

85. *Lettres de Catherine de Medicis.*

86. *Ibid.*

87. Proverbial for his stout and unwieldy figure.

88. *Lettres de Catherine de Medicis.*

89. *Ibid.*

90. Called "Le Balafré," from a scar on the left cheek received in battle.

91. She was executed on 18th February 1587.

92. *Recit d'un Bourgeois de Paris*, by Dupuy.

93. Said to have been designed for Francis by Leonardo da Vinci from the model of a spiral shell.

94. As a consequence of this deed Henry III was himself murdered by the League six months afterwards.

95. *See* page 458.

96. *The Cambridge Modern History*, vol. iii. chap. i.

97. We may well ask whether it is likely that persons like Louise de Vaudemont would have been fond of Catherine if the latter had been keeping a poison cupboard in the apartments in which Louise nursed her. *See* also chapter xxvi.

98. *See* page 382.

99. *See* page 422.

CHAPTER XXI

1. *See* page 127.

2. No portrait exists of Lorenzo di Pier Francesco (Lorenzo the Younger).

3. *See* page 252.

4. Lorenzo's brother Giovanni, then on his way from Forlì to Pisa, appears to have taken part with his brother in this matter, as he is mentioned as being the principal instigator of the attack on San Marco.

5. *See* pages 526-529.

6. *See* page 531.

7. Born in 1515.
8. *See* pages 372-373.

CHAPTER XXII

1. The marriage of Giuliano (Duc de Nemours) to the aunt of the King of France did not take place until eighteen years later.
2. *See* pages 233-234.
3. *See* page 70.
4. She was an illegitimate daughter.
5. *See* page 135.
6. At whose marriage to the Duke of Calabria in Milan in 1465 Lorenzo the Magnificent, then sixteen, was present.
7. *The Ladies of the Italian Renaissance,* by Mrs. Ady.
8. *See* page 157.
9. In those days fifteen was the fashionable age for a girl to be married. Speaking of the fourteenth century, Professor Del Lungo says:—"It came to be considered late if a girl married at twenty, or even at eighteen; fifteen was the 'age of beauty.' "—(*Women of Florence,* by Isidoro del Lungo.)
10. A fresco transferred to canvas.
11. *See* pages 166-175.
12. The second of these attempts was the more disgraceful in that it was made in May 1481, notwithstanding that peace had been made by the Pope in the previous year (page 184). It was a plot to assassinate Lorenzo in the church of the Carmine, which Girolamo Riario got Battista Frescobaldi to engage to do. On the discovery of the plot Frescobaldi and all his fellow-conspirators were hanged from the windows of the Bargello.
13. A fourth son had been born in December 1485.
14. On her coins at this time she calls herself "Catharina Sfortia Vicecomes," ignoring the Riario connection altogether.
15. The year after the elder branch of the Medici had been driven out of Florence, and that period had begun there which has been called the "interregnum" (*see* chapter xi).
16. *Life of Catherine Sforza,* by Count Pasolini.
17. From this time she calls herself on her coins "Catharina Sfortia Medices."
18. Savonarola had been put to death in Florence three months before.
19. *Life of Niccolò Machiavelli,* by Tomasini.
20. Though other accounts say that she wore chain armour at this time.
21. *Life of Catherine Sforza,* by Count Pasolini.
22. *Ibid.*
23. Her house (which had been the property of her husband, Giovanni) is now No. 5 Via Cavour. It is a small house standing next to the northern end of the Medici Palace. In her time between her house and the Medici Palace intervened the house of her enemy, Pier Francesco

the Younger, which at his death passed to his son Lorenzino, and was afterwards destroyed, the addition to the Medici Palace being built on its site (page 374).

CHAPTER XXIII

1. It stands near the corner where the Corso joins the Via del Proconsolo, and now forms part of the schools of the Padri Scolopi.

2. His portrait, by Titian, is to be seen in the Pitti Gallery.

3. As was also evidenced by the ragged bone, from the rough saw, seen many years afterwards when his coffin was opened.

4. "His remains were in a coffin covered with black velvet enclosed in another coffin of red wood. The bones were fallen apart, but were enclosed in his black armour, the helmet having the visor closed. The right leg had been amputated, the bone showing how badly it was sawn, and making it well able to be understood why this caused his death. A leaden plate at the head bore an inscription giving his name, and the date and manner of his death, and detailing his great deeds in war." (*Official Report on the examination of the Tombs in the Medici Mausoleum*, 1857.)

5. As the greatest soldier which Florence has produced, his statue has been placed in the gallery of honour in the Uffizi colonnade.

6. It has often been said that had Giovanni delle Bande Nere lived only a year longer the capture and sack of Rome in 1527 would by him have been prevented. And this is almost certainly correct. For if upon Bourbon's undisciplined horde of ragged soldiery, as they streamed through Umbria on their way to Rome, had been brought an attack from the strictly disciplined Bande Nere led by their celebrated commander, not all Bourbon's great talent as a general could have saved his army from destruction. In which case the whole subsequent course of events, and the position of Clement VII towards Charles V, would have been altered.

7. Although the fighting of that age was child's play compared to the warfare of the present day, this axiom of war has only become more intensified.

8. *Jean des Bandes Noires,* by M. Pierre Gautier.

9. It is a pity that Maria's excellent suggestion was not carried out.

10. *See* page 371.

11. *See* page 352.

12. *See* page 717.

13. "The body was found embalmed, and was dressed in black as a nun. The head rested on two bricks. Upon the coffin among many crosses was inscribed the name 'Maria.'" (*Official Report on the examination of the Tombs in the Medici Mausoleum.* 1857.)

CHAPTER XXIV

1. *See* page 350.

2. Francesco Guicciardini did not join the rest, but retired from

Florence in disgust to his villa in Arcetri, and occupied himself in writing his celebrated history.

3. It was erected about twenty-five years afterwards. The column came from the Baths of Caracalla in Rome, and was presented to Cosimo by Pope Pius IV, who was Pope from 1559-1565.

4. Its trap-door is near the central pillar of the hall. Out of it were taken a large number of human bones.

5. Whence George Eliot describes Romola watching the execution of her godfather.

6. This applies to the period of the Podestà (1200-1494), and of his successor, the Bargello, or head of the police (1537-1782), from whom the building takes its present name; but does not apply to the years 1494-1537, during which period the Bargello (or Executor of Justice) resided, and carried out executions and torture, in a building which now forms the back part of the Palazzo Vecchio, and had its entrance in the Via de' Gondi. And it was in this latter building, and not in the present Bargello, that in 1497 Bernardo del Nero was put to death. Cosimo I removed the Executor of Justice (the Bargello) to the old citadel of the Podestà, which thus again became the chief prison and place of execution, and remained so during the rest of Florentine history. The scaffold was by the well in the centre of the courtyard. It and all the instruments of torture were burnt by the Grand Duke Pietro Leopoldo in 1782.

7. There is a fine portrait of Filippo Strozzi by Titian at Vienna.

8. He returned the palace to the family before his death.

9. There is a portrait in fresco of Cosimo as a boy on the wall of the Sala di Giovanni delle Bande Nere in the Palazzo Vecchio, painted by his contemporary Vasari.

10. It was on this occasion that the well-known "Spanish chapel" (formerly the chapter-house) in the Green Cloister of Santa Maria Novella obtained its name, owing to its being made over for the use of the Viceroy of Naples and his numerous suite during their stay in Florence.

11. From which it is noticeable how exactly opposite were the aims of Cosimo I to those, e.g., of Lorenzo the Magnificent, to whose principles nothing would have been more repugnant than conduct of this character; witness his dying advice to his son Pietro.

12. They lived in barracks situated in the small street immediately behind Orcagna's Loggia, the Via Lambertesca.

13. Maria, their eldest child, was born in the Medici palace in the Via Larga.

14. See page 369.

15. See page 587.

16. Henry VIII died in January, and Francis I in March. Luther died in the same year.

17. The Cambridge Modern History, vol ii. p. 82.

18. See page 374.

19. See page 46.

20. The name "Pitti Palace" is an invention of modern times. The

palace was of course never called by this name in the time of the Medici. Throughout their time their palace was called the Ducal Palace, the Grand Ducal Palace, or latterly (in the time of Cosimo III and Gian Gastone) the Royal Palace.

21. All three of these were at that time *doorways;* the only *windows* on the ground floor were the four small square barred ones.

22. *See* page 679 and note 31 of chapter xxviii.

23. *See* pages 650 and 677-680.

24. The palace continued of these same dimensions during the reigns of Francis I and Ferdinand I, and as a matter of fact this lady is evidently of the time of Ferdinand I. For she wears the same very marked shape of dress noted as being worn by Christine of Lorraine and other ladies of that time (*see* page 629). This makes the error of supposing that the palace in the background had any connection with the Pitti family still more marked.

25. Their eighth child (Pietro) was born four years afterwards.

26. The oldest botanical gardens in Europe.

27. Owing to their situation on the slope of a hill, their great extent, the care with which they have been planned, and the beauty of the views which they command over the country surrounding Florence, the Boboli gardens have a charm which few others possess.

28. Chapter xxv.

29. *See* page 741.

30. The beautiful bronze statue worshipped in the third century before Christ as Apollo, and now called the *Idolino,* though found in Cosimo's time, did not come into this collection until 1779.

31. Because, being a lion wounded by Bellerophon, a connection was traced between it and the *Marzocco* of Florence, and to some evil portended to Florence.

32. It is now, with all the rest, in the Etruscan Museum.

33. Giorgio Vasari (1511-1576), the historian of the painters, sculptors, and architects, and himself also a painter and an architect, was Cosimo's right-hand man in all matters relating to art. Bronzino (1502-1572) was Cosimo's chief painter.

34. *See* page 233.

35. Vasari was occupied among other things in painting in fresco the walls of the rooms in the Palazzo Vecchio, including the Sala di Leone X, Sala di Clemente VII, Sala di Giovanni delle Bande Nere, and the great hall.

36. He died in Florence, and is buried in the cathedral. His portrait is in the Uffizi Gallery.

37. A medal was struck on the occasion by Cosimo, which shows him wearing the Order of the Golden Fleece; it is to be seen in the Florentine collection of coins and medals in the Bargello Museum, Florence.

38. To commemorate this victory Cosimo afterwards erected a column in the Piazza San Felice, Florence; but it was removed in the time of the Austrian Grand Dukes. A tablet on one of the adjacent houses records its having stood there.

39. Montalcino also surrendered four years later, and was incorporated with Cosimo's dominions.

40. On its being subdued Charles V granted to his son Philip II the investiture of the fief of Siena; and theoretically Cosimo held Siena by sub-investiture from Philip II.

41. *See* pages 658, 691 and 724.

42. *The Cambridge Modern History,* vol. iii. chap xii.

43. Cosimo built the Mercato Nuovo, which was the principal mart for silk. The fine bronze boar in front of it was executed by Tacca, being a copy of the ancient one in marble in the Uffizi Gallery.

44. In this fortress was found by the Grand Duke Pietro Leopoldo the huge brass cannon, weighing 27,000 lbs., the work of Michelangelo, and called "Saint Paul" because the brazen head of the apostle formed the cascabel. It had been left there by the Medici as a curious object of art. Pietro Leopoldo was declared by his detractors to have destroyed it for the sake of the brass, an accusation which even Napier repeats (vol. vi. p. 198); nevertheless it is now in the Bargello Museum.

45. The olive has been called the "tree of civilisation," since it requires tending for about eighteen years before it yields any return.

46. One of these tapestries is to be seen in the Municipal Council hall in the Palazzo Vecchio bearing Van der Roost's signature, a piece of meat roasting on a spit.

47. *See* page 741.

48. The collection includes the three large Flemish tapestries representing the festivities at Marseilles at the marriage of Catherine de' Medici, which were sent by her as a present to Cosimo at the time of his own marriage in 1539.

49. Now Ponte alle Grazie.

50. The architect was Ammanati.

51. This is rendered perfectly certain by Cosimo's letter to Oradini, in which in full detail he orders Oradini to arrange for the assassination of Piero Strozzi, saying that he is to engage two or more assassins for the purpose, and that he (Cosimo) will bear all the expenses.

52. Alfonso himself became Duke of Ferrara in the following year on the death of his father.

53. *See* page 415.

54. The four marriages of Philip II were:—

(i) Maria of Portugal.	Married	1543.
(ii) Mary of England.	"	1554.
(iii) Elizabeth of France.	"	1559.
(iv) Anna of Austria.	"	1570.

55. His father was a petty shopkeeper in Milan.

56. The family of Pius IV could not, and never did, claim any relationship with the Medici of Florence until his elevation to the Papacy. Giacomo Medichino, the brother of Giovanni Angelo, was a corsair, and was made by force Marquis of Marignano; he then took service under Spain, and became general of the league of the Emperor

Charles V and Clement VII. In the war with Siena Cosimo employed
Giacomo to command his army, and his brother Giovanni Angelo
shortly afterwards becoming Pope, the two brothers claimed a relationship to Cosimo, which, though entirely without any foundation, it
suited the latter at the time not to contest; and the genealogist thereupon inserted a new branch into the family tree of that portion of the
Medici who were descended from Giambuono, son of Chiarissimo,
bearing the names of Giovanni Angelo and his brother Giacomo.
Symonds, in his *Sketches in Italy*, gives an amusing account of the
transaction.

57. Catherine and Cosimo had each a common great-grandfather in
Lorenzo the Magnificent, thus:—

LORENZO THE MAGNIFICENT.

PIETRO	LUCREZIA
LORENZO	MARIA
CATHERINE	COSIMO

58. The dates of birth of Cosimo's and Eleonora's eight children
were:—

MARIA	born	1540	LUCREZIA	born	1544
FRANCIS	"	1541	GARZIA	"	1547
ISABELLA	"	1542	FERDINAND	"	1549
GIOVANNI	"	1543	PIETRO	"	1554

59. The Order came to an end in 1859.

60. *The Cambridge Modern History*, vol. iii. chap. xii.

61. Thus Giustiniano, a Venetian, says it is so reported in the Roman
newspapers; and Muratori, after relating the story, says: "If this be
the truth or a lie I do not know." Galluzi (writing about two centuries
after the event) says that he considers it would have been almost
impossible for Cosimo to have treated the widespread report with the
indifference that he did if it had been true. Lastly Botta, a strong
anti-Medicean, severe in condemning the faults of that family, but a
man very anxious to be just and upright, states that he considers it was
simply an invention of Cosimo's enemies.

62. *See* page 647.

63. More particularly the painstaking labours of the late Signor
Saltini, the results of which were published in his *Tragidie Medicee*
(1898), in which book the documents in the State archives which refute
the story are quoted in full.

64. *The Cambridge Modern History*, vol. iii. chap. xii.

65. *See* page 750.

66. The former name for the Uffizi Gallery; *see* page 636.

67. *Official Report of the examination of the Tombs in the Medici
Mausoleum*. 1857.

68. *See* page 317.

69. The remains of these frescoes are still to be seen.

70. Now the Via della Ninna.

71. This church stood at the corner of the present Uffizi building, and was partially demolished when in 1561 Cosimo built this range of public offices. Its very old and interesting pulpit is to be seen in the little church of San Leonardo in Arcetri.

72. Now Ponte alle Grazie.

73. This *loggia* opens into the church above its west door, and thus formed a means for the members of the family to be present at Mass in this church.

74. The subsequent extension of the Ducal Palace made this no longer necessary, and the corridor now issues direct into the eastern end of the palace.

75. *Miscellanea Fiorentina di Erudizione e Storia,* by Signor Jodico del Badia.

76. *The Cambridge Modern History,* vol. ii.

77. Pope Pius V died two years afterwards. He was succeeded by Gregory XIII (1572-1585).

78. The iris.

79. Usually heavily jewelled.

80. She was the daughter of Antonio Martelli, a man in humble circumstances living in the Via de' Servi.

81. "First Grand Duke of Etruria."

82. *See* page 751.

83. *Official Report on the examination of the Tombs in the Medici Mausoleum.* 1857.

CHAPTER XXV

1. Napier's *Florentine History,* v. 326.

2. In this same year died Giorgio Vasari, historian, painter, and architect, and author of the *Lives of the Painters, Sculptors, and Architects.*

3. Now closed.

4. The palace which stands at the end of the Via Tornabuoni (nearly opposite the church of San Gaetano), and is now Messrs. Haskard's bank.

5. *See* page 506.

6. It was asserted that this murder of his sister-in-law was executed by Francis's order

7. That relating the deaths of Bernardino Antinori and Eleonora.

8. Either the crypt of the mausoleum then being constructed (*see* pages 636-637), or more probably the adjoining crypt of the church of San Lorenzo.

9. This shows that there was no hurried burial, time having been given for the body to be embalmed.

10. *Diario del Settimanni,* State Archives, Florence.

11. When in 1857 his coffin was opened the body was found "clothed in white velvet embroidered with gold thread, and having on the head a little cap of black velvet surrounded with a circlet of flowers in metal filigree-work. On a tablet of silver fixed behind the head was an

inscription saying, 'Cosimo, son of Pietro, and grandson of the Grand Duke Cosimo I, called away at four years old. Snatched from a great fortune. Born into this world in February 1571. Alas how quickly commanded to leave it, September 1576.'"

12. Francesco Settimanni himself was a strong anti-Medicean.

13. He died in Spain in 1604.

14. *See* page 612.

15. *Origine e Descendenza de' Medici,* State Archives, Florence.

16. The room, with the hole in the ceiling, and a rope showing how the crime was executed, is still to be seen in the villa of Ceretto Guidi.

17. She was buried in San Lorenzo, but there is no tablet to her memory in the family mausoleum. The diary of interments kept in that church mentions that the body when brought for burial was disfigured (*sfigurato*) owing to the manner of her death.

18. The Pope who reformed the calendar. The new calendar (involving the dropping of ten days) came into operation in January 1582.

19. The account of the later stages of this affair is drawn from Mr. Marion Crawford's *Ave Roma Immortalis.*

20. Eleonora di Toledo was never Grand Duchess, her husband gaining the rank of Grand Duke after her death.

21. As can be seen by the dates on their respective tombs in the family mausoleum, Filippo being born in June 1577, and his mother dying in April 1578.

22. "Her blonde hair was dressed in the fashion of the time; in her ears were gold ear-rings with small gold clasps; her dress, on which were fixed a number of gold orange leaves, was of crimson satin, with a wide band of velvet of the same colour, embroidered with gold, running along the petticoat, as well as along its inside edge. She had also a bodice of rose colour, stockings of red silk, and velvet shoes, embroidered with gold, cut in a peculiar fashion and with very high heels. On a leaden plate behind her head was her name and title as Grand Duchess, stating that she was the daughter of the Emperor Ferdinand I, and giving the date of her decease." (*Official Report on the examination of the Tombs in the Medici Mausoleum.* 1857.)

23. "Who does not know the Mercury of Gian Bologna, that airy youth with winged feet and cap, who with the *caduceus* in his hand, and borne aloft upon the head of Æolus, seems bound upon some Jove-commissioned errand? Who has not admired its lightness and truth of momentary action, which none but an artist skilful in modelling and well versed in anatomy could have attained? Since, Mercury-like, it has winged its way to the museums and houses of every quarter of the globe." (Perkins' *Tuscan Sculptors.*)

24. Among those who worked here for Cosimo were Benvenuto Cellini.

25. *See* page 591.

26. There is a portrait of him in the Uffizi Gallery.

27. *See* page 620.

28. Napier.

29. Formerly in the Torre del Gallo, Florence.

30. The house was in the Piazza San Marco, on the south side, facing the church.

31. Trollope.

32. Bianca Capello's house is still to be seen in the Via Maggio (an abbreviation for Via Maggiore) with her strange uncouth coat of arms over the entrance, the front of the house being profusely decorated with frescoes. There is an underground passage from it to the Pitti Palace, now closed.

33. It is noticeable that though there are so many pictures of her there are none in court dress or with the crown of Tuscany displayed by her side, as in the case of every other Grand Duchess.

34. There is a cameo of Bianca, by Bernardo di Castel Bolognese, in the Bargello Museum, Florence, which many consider to give a superior idea of her beauty to any portrait which exists.

35. See page 622.

36. See page 626.

37. The year that Mary, Queen of Scots, was put to death.

38. It is now a royal villa of the King of Italy.

39. It still contains a few reminiscences of her, including the room in which she died, a pleasing portrait of her by Bronzino, and a pretty portrait of a girl about fourteen who was Bianca's adopted daughter.

40. The chief of these was a medicine called *Bezzuar* (a secretion formed in the biliary ducts of certain animals, particularly the crocodile, the porcupine, the Peruvian goat, and the Indian gazelle) which was supposed by the Arabian doctors to be a general cure for every malady, and which in consequence of its high estimation by them was sold at an immense price.

41. That which is now shown to visitors as the room of Bianca Capello, with a stone tablet on the wall to that effect. Though this is an error, it was in this room that their two bodies were laid side by side and together prepared for burial; which is perhaps the reason that it became called by Bianca's name.

42. The above account of the deaths of Francis and Bianca is taken from the records contained in Doc. I, III, IX, and XVI, *Archivio Storico Italiano*, State Archives, Florence.

43. One thing, however, this story incidentally shows, namely, the certainty universally felt of Bianca's undying affection for Francis.

44. When in 1857 the Medici coffins were opened the body of Francis was found, like that of Joanna, completely preserved by the very effective embalming process that had been employed. "The face accorded in every way with the numerous portraits of him; the hands were curled up and contracted, seeming to accord with the stories related of his death which assert that he died in the spasms of poisoning. [This in 1857 was still the accepted theory.] The body was clothed in a plain black garment of camel-hair, without any distinguishing sign of his high rank. His name and titles as Grand Duke, and date of his death,

were on a small leaden plate behind the head." (*Official Report on the examination of the Tombs in the Medici Mausoleum*. 1857.)

45. The family mausoleum not being as yet in existence, Francis, Joanna, and their children were buried at first in the New Sacristy. Their remains were subsequently removed to the mausoleum when it was afterwards built (page 717).

46. Napier.

CHAPTER XXVI

1. Especially was this the case in regard to Pius V (1565-1572), who deliberately got rid of the art collections of the Vatican.

2. The great collection of sculpture which now forms the chief possession of the Vatican was practically begun, nearly a hundred years later, by Pope Clement XIV (1769-1775).

3. "O Niobe, con che occhi dolenti
   Vedev' io te, segnata in su la strada,
   Tra sette e sette tuoi figliuoli spenti."
                              —Dante, *Purgatorio,* xii. 37.

4. Galuzzi, Lib. v. cap. i.

5. For the dowry given her by Catherine de' Medici on her marriage, *see* page 664.

6. *See* page 596.

6a. "By dignity alone" (not force, understood).

7. It was not, however, until two hundred years later, under the Austrian Grand Duke Pietro Leopoldo, that the great difficulties of this engineering problem were finally overcome.

8. Pope Sixtus V died in 1590. He was followed in rapid succession by Urban VII (1590), Gregory XIV (1590-1591), Innocent IX (1591-1592), and Clement VIII (1592-1605).

9. Henry IV's portrait is also to be seen in the Uffizi Gallery, his robes being embroidered in the same manner as his wife's dress, with *fleur-de-lys* in gold.

10. *See* note 11 of chapter xxix.

11. The year after the death of Queen Elizabeth in England.

12. *Diario del Settimanni,* State Archives, Florence.

13. *See* page 639.

14. Or, more correctly speaking, practically finished; for work on it even still continues (*see* page 746).

15. The jewelled cushion on the tomb of Cosimo II, which cost 70,000 francs (£2,800), was stolen about twenty-five years ago. An imitation of it has been placed on the tomb in the present year.

16. Forsyth.

17. But *see* page 746.

18. *Intarsiatura, intarsia,* or *intarsio* properly means any inlay work. While generally applied to works executed in wood, it is also used technically in regard to inlay work in stone.

19. This still exists. On the staircase is a bust of its founder, Ferdinand I.

20. In the Gem Room of the Uffizi Gallery are to be seen various

costly articles of this *pietra dura* work, in jasper, amethyst, lapis-lazuli, and topaz, inlaid with diamonds, rubies, and pearls, which were all made for the altar of the mausoleum when it should be set up.

21. In these operas the Florentines also invented the methods of scoring, barring, and figuring in the writing of operatic music which have ever since been adopted.

22. *Ordine e Descendenza de' Medici,* State Archives, Florence.

23. Now a royal villa of the King of Italy.

24. Both Ferdinand's own statue in Florence and that of Henry IV in Paris were completed by Gian da Bologna's pupil, Pietro Tacca.

25. *See* page 681.

26. When in 1857 Ferdinand's coffin was opened the body was found clothed in a black doublet ornamented with stripes of velvet and satin, with over this the robes of the Grand Master of the Order of Santo Stefano. There were also two handsome gold medallions, one of them bearing his likeness and name, with, on the reverse, the cross of Santo Stefano, and the other also bearing his likeness and name, with, on the reverse, his emblem and motto. The fine bronze statue over his monument in the mausoleum is by Pietro Tacca.

27. From the time of Cosimo Pater Patriae to that of Francis I, viz., in 1433, 1466, 1470, 1478, 1494, 1527, 1537, and 1575, including three banishments of the family.

28. B.C. 28 to A.D. 14.

29. It is not generally realised that these stories were not rumours which obtained at the time that these deaths occurred, but stories which made their first appearance long afterwards (in some cases as much as a hundred years' or more afterwards), and in every case from a doubtful source.

30. It will scarcely be believed (in view of the circumstances under which the murder in question occurred, and of Ferdinand's undoubted character), but it is a fact that those interested in fabricating stories of crime against Cosimo's house declared in after years that the murder of Isabella by her husband Orsini had been instigated by her brother Ferdinand and was carried out with the full concurrence of her brother Francis.

31. The late Signor G. E. Saltini, in his *Tragidie Medicee* (1898), has taken in turn each of these stories against Cosimo I and his sons, and (assisted by the almost unique knowledge of the archives of Tuscany which he possessed) has subjected each of these stories to a searching analysis, with the result that the whole are shown to be entirely false. Such a testimony from such a source is conclusive. Though even without it the fact would be certain, on the grounds which have already been mentioned.

32. In the foregoing chapters every case attributed to them has been mentioned; so that the above statement can easily be verified.

33. Prominent instances are, the first palace built by them given the name of the Riccardi Palace, the second palace built by them given the name of the Pitti Palace, the important library collected by them given the name of the Laurentian Library, the great galleries of art

collected by them, and given by them to the nation, called only the Uffizi or the Pitti Galleries, and with no sign of their name upon doors or walls, the tomb of the great Lorenzo the Magnificent (the most prominent Florentine in Europe) left without even a tombstone, with other similar instances. There is not a single palace, art gallery, or public building called by their name. And it would be quite possible for a foreign visitor to see all the sights of Florence without ever knowing that the Medici had anything to do with any one of them.

CHAPTER XXVII

1. The twins, Lorenzo and Maddalena, were nine, while their little sister Claudia was five.

2. *See* pages 658 and 665.

3. On the terrace the beautiful fountain (with marble Cupids in graceful attitudes on its edge), though it is a part of the extension of the palace by Cosimo II, was designed by Ammanati, Cosimo I's architect. The sound of its water has a delicious effect in the cool and shady courtyard below the terrace.

4. The walls are adorned with numerous frescoes, one of which shows the open space in front of the building as it was in Cosimo's time, and another gives a picture of the Medici villa of Cafaggiolo in the Mugello. Some of the rooms still contain portraits of various members of the Medici family.

5. *See* page 653.

6. *See* pages 694-696.

7. Equal nowadays to a salary of over £2,000 a year.

8. *See* pages 671-674.

9. Galileo's original telescope, with many of his other instruments, is still to be seen in the Museum of Natural Science, Florence. Besides it and the pendulum, he invented the thermometer, the hydrostatic balance, and the proportional compass, discovered the laws of weight, and was the first experimental philosopher.

10. Galileo's statue has consequently received a place in Florence's gallery of honour in the Uffizi colonnade beside Petrarch, Dante, Leonardo da Vinci, and Michelangelo.

11. The "Torre del Gallo."

12. *Pascarel*, by Ouida.

13. *Il Giojello*.

14. Rogers' *Italy*.

15. *See* also pages 694-696.

16. Henrietta Maria's son, Charles II, with his dark hair and swarthy complexion, showed traces of the Medici blood.

17. She was married to him at Innsbruck in 1622. There are two portraits of Eleonora Gonzaga at Florence, one a pretty picture of her as a child (in the Pitti Gallery), and the other when she was grown up (in the Uffizi Gallery), the latter by Sustermans.

18. *See* page 10.

19. Marie's escape from the castle of Blois had in it a decidedly comic

element. She was imprisoned in the suite of apartments which had
been those of Catherine de' Medici. Cardillac and the Count de Brenne,
who assisted her to escape, decided that as all the doors and passages
were carefully guarded she must drop from one of her windows on to
the terrace (which at that time extended half way up to the first floor)
overlooking the town, and from the terrace to the street. But the
Queen was fat and unwieldy, and looked with terror at the slender
rope-ladders provided, while she declared that for her to be seen swinging about in such a position would be exceedingly undignified. However, there was no other way, and finally, on the night of the 21st
February 1618, she had to attempt it. With great difficulty they got
her down the first ladder to the terrace, but in such a terrified state
that she refused altogether to face the second ladder. It seemed that
the attempt must fail. But eventually they discovered a narrow gully
in the walls; they tied her up in a heavy cloak, and Cardillac guiding
her course from above, and De Brenne dragging from below, she was
tobogganned down to the street, more like a bale of goods than a queen
of France. There she was placed in a carriage, which conveyed her
in safety to Loches.

20. The two large pictures by Rubens in the Sala di Rubens of the
Uffizi Gallery, representing Henry IV at the battle of Ivry, and his
triumphant entry into Paris, were painted for Marie de' Medici, and sent
by her as a present to her uncle Ferdinand I. They are a portion of
a set the remainder of which are in the Louvre.

21. Son of the Earl of Leicester by a previous marriage to that with
Amy Robsart.

22. He is buried in the family mausoleum. When in 1857 his coffin
was opened the body was found "dressed in a doublet of white satin,
with lace ruffles on the wrists, and a large cloak, also of white satin,
extending down to the knees; and with stockings of silk, and long
leather boots. Fixed inside the coffin was a plate of gilded bronze
with his name, age, and the date of his death."

23. She is buried in the family mausoleum. When her coffin was
opened in 1857 "the body was found clothed in a dress of silver and
gold tissue, of violet colour, with large open sleeves, and with a very
large ruff of the most beautiful lace round the neck. The skirt of the
dress was covered all over with artificial flowers, and a garland of
artificial flowers on the head. On the breast was a leaden plate bearing
her name, age, and the date of her death."

24. She is buried in the family mausoleum.

25. She was buried by her own desire in the convent of the Crocetta,
but in 1810 her remains were removed to the family mausoleum.
When in 1857 her coffin was opened, the body was found, not clothed
as a nun, but "in a dress of violet-coloured brocade, with many
flowers of silver sewn on the skirt of the dress, and scattered round
the head, perhaps having originally formed a garland. The shoes
were of velvet in good preservation, with very high heels of cork.
Inside the coffin was a leaden plate with her name, age, and the
date of her death."

26. *See* page 664.

27. The Emperor Rudolph II, son of Maximilian II, died in 1612, and was succeeded by his brother Matthias, who died in 1619. Ferdinand II was their first cousin, the son of the Archduke Charles who was the brother of Maximilian II.

28. The bronze statue over his tomb is by Tacca, and is a splendid piece of work. The bronze under-robe is made to resemble gold, while the upper robe is made to resemble dark green velvet. The crown and jewelled cushion stolen about twenty-five years ago from the top of the sarcophagus have recently been replaced (1907). When in 1857 the Medici coffins were opened the body of Cosimo II was found "reduced to bones, the head being covered wtih three hoods, one of silk, one of oil-cloth, and one of velvet. The body was clothed in the great cloak of Grand Master of the Order of Santo Stefano, worn over a doublet of black silk richly embroidered in black, with long hanging sleeves, and a collarette of lace; the leather belt was fastened with a clasp of oxidised iron; black Spanish breeches, black silk stockings, and cloth shoes. Under the shoulders were found two gold medallions which had escaped the greed of those who had rifled the coffin; these had on one side his likeness, with his name and title written round it, and on the other the Medicean balls, surmounted with the crown with the sceptre passing through it, and the motto *Virtutis proemia*, and date of his death, 28th February 1620. On the breast was a leaden plate with the inscription 'Cosimo Medici II, fourth Grand Duke of Tuscany, died 28th February 1620, at the age of thirty.' The coffin was very large, but entirely broken, and rifled of all precious things except the two gold medallions, which had slipped behind the shoulders. The remains were placed in a new coffin and re-buried." (*Official Report on the examination of the Tombs in the Medici Mausoleum.* 1857.)

29. *See* Napier's *Florentine History*, vol. v. pp. 393 and 421.

CHAPTER XXVIII

1. *Diario della Città di Firenze, dall'anno 1613 fino all'anno 1635.* State Archives of Tuscany.

2. We are given ample opportunity of realising how magnificent were the costumes of both the men and the ladies who took part in these assemblies from the numerous portraits belonging to this time to be seen in the long corridor between the Uffizi and Pitti Galleries.

3. In all her portraits Maria Maddalena has reddish hair.

4. Regarding the character and achievements of Maria Maddalena, *see* also page 669.

5. *See* page 315.

6. It was in this year that in England Charles I succeeded his father, James I.

7. At the Schloss Amras, the residence of the Archdukes of Tyrol,

Claudia collected round her many portraits of her family, which are still to be seen there.

8. *See* page 684.

9. There is a portrait of Margherita's husband, Eduardo Farnese, Duke of Parma, in the Uffizi Gallery.

10. *See* pages 724-725.

11. *Relazione del Contagione dell' anni 1630 e 1633,* by Rondinelli.

12. *Relazione del Contagione dell' anni 1630 e 1633,* by Rondinelli. Francesco himself died of the plague five years afterwards.

13. She is buried in the family mausoleum. When her coffin was opened in 1857 the body was found clothed in black velvet and reduced to bones. On her coffin was a leaden plate bearing her name and titles, and a long inscription detailing without exaggeration her many virtues. On the breast, hung round the neck by a chain, was a gold medallion bearing her portrait and name, and on the reverse a bird of Paradise in flight and the motto *Ethera.*

14. She is buried in the family mausoleum. She was evidently buried splendidly dressed and adorned with many jewels, for when in 1857 the Medici coffins were examined hers was found to have been entirely rifled by thieves, and only a garland of artificial flowers round her head remained, even her dress being torn to pieces.

15. Philip IV had succeeded his father, Philip III, in 1621.

16. *See* page 686.

17. It was in this year that Galileo discovered the rings of the planet Saturn.

18. As he rose from his knees Galileo is said to have whispered to a friend "Eppur si muove" ("Nevertheless it does move").

19. There is a good portrait of Galileo by Sustermans in the Uffizi Gallery. It was presented to the gallery by Ferdinand's brother, Prince Leopold, who was one of Galileo's most promising pupils.

20. There is a likeness of him painted in fresco on the front of the house.

21. A tablet over the door, put up by a subsequent generation, states in grandiloquent language that here the majesty of the Grand Duke did not disdain to do honour to the glory of Science in the person of Galileo.

22. Galileo's great successor, Newton, was born in the same year that Galileo died.

23. It is fitting that Florence, "the home of all who live by thought," should be the city to hold that shrine.

24. "The church of Santa Croce would disappoint you as much inside as out if the presence of great men did not always cast a mingled shadow of the awful and the beautiful over our thoughts" (Leigh Hunt).

25. She is buried in the family mausoleum. When her coffin was opened in 1857 "the body was found clothed in a dress of plain black cloth covered with a very large black veil, and completely wrapped in a black silk sheet. On the feet were shoes with immensely thick cork soles, two fingers thick. On the breast was a gold medallion with a

triple chain, bearing on one side a portrait of her husband, Ferdinand I, and on the other her own portrait and name." (*Official Report on the examination of the Tombs in the Medici Mausoleum.* 1857.)

26. A melancholy reminiscence of this celebrated trial remains in the Pitti Gallery in the portrait of this Canon Pandolfo Ricasoli, painted with a devil whispering into his ear; this latter detail having been added to his portrait after this trial.

27. The title of "Prince" and "Princess" had by this time become customary in the case of the younger members of the family.

28. *See* page 593.

29. For instance in the case of the Royal Palace at Munich, and the Luxembourg Palace at Paris.

30. *History of Architecture,* by Fergusson.

31. With the usual curious suppression of the Medici, even in regard to the palace which they built, this supposed intention is always attributed, not to the Medici, but to Luca Pitti. It is unfortunate for this version of the story that the Strozzi palace *was not built until after Luca Pitti was dead.*

32. The name does not refer to treasure in money and jewels, which were kept in the fortress of San Giorgio (page 641).

33. *See* page 742.

34. Beneath each window on the ground floor along the façade is a large lion's head wearing the crown of Tuscany. From the mouth of the one nearest to the archway at the eastern end leading into the Boboli gardens issues a fountain of water, said to be the purest in Florence, which is brought all the way from the mountains near Pratolino (nine miles north of Fiesole), being carried over the river by a pipe laid over the Ponte Vecchio.

35. The present Throne Room is in another apartment.

36. Died 1612.

37. Died 1608.

38. *See* note 18 of chapter xxxi.

39. Along the whole front of the building at the top of each of the three stories run stone balconies. They add much to the general effect in looking at it from below.

40. *See* page 638.

41. Many of these, all the property of Ferdinand or his brothers, are still to be seen in the Pitti and the Uffizi Galleries.

42. The name given to this superior kind of mosaic.

43. "The large tables in the Pitti Gallery with a porphyry ground-work, and with representations of shells and flowers delicately shaded, are all the work of Luigi and Carlo Siriès" (Horner).

44. Her tombstone has on it in Latin the words, "You who read ask not my name. I was a little daughter of Ferdinand II, Grand Duke of Tuscany, and having entered this life and been duly baptized then gladly sought the heavenly life."

45. *See* page 665. Claudia died in 1648, after resigning the government of Tyrol to her son, Ferdinand Karl, in 1646.

46. There is a portrait of Claudia Felicitas (in the character of

Galla Placidia) in the Uffizi Gallery, holding a crucifix in her hand, and with a broken idol on the table before her.

47. The Emperor Ferdinand II died in 1637, and was succeeded by Ferdinand III (1637-1658).

48. He is buried in the family mausoleum. When in 1857 his coffin was opened the body was found "dressed in clothes made in the Spanish fashion, with a doublet of violet-coloured velvet embroidered in gold, and a felt cap with plumes; on the boots were spurs of oxidised iron." A leaden plate fixed inside the coffin bore his name, and a long eulogy of some twenty lines detailing his many talents.

49. They are those in square frames at the northernmost end of the gallery. The set (more satisfactorily painted) in oval frames, nearer to the Pitti end of the gallery, are those of the maids-of-honour of the next Grand Duchess, during the reign of Cosimo III.

50. The population of India now is three hundred millions.

51. Public Audience Hall.

52. The Peacock Throne was made by the Emperor Shahjehàn, and valued at £2,500,000. It was set with an enormous profusion of rubies, emeralds, topaz, and diamonds, and included two peacocks (the work of Austin de Bordeaux) made entirely of precious stones. It was eventually carried off by Nadir Shah when he invaded India in the eighteenth century. Bernier, the French physician, who saw it in 1663, wrote a long description of it.

53. "If there be an Elysium on earth,
        It is this, it is this."

54. Private Audience Hall.

55. Of the *Diwàn-i-Khàs* at Agra, Bernard Taylor says:—"The three white pavilions overhanging the river are like precious caskets of marble, inlaid with precious stones and topped with golden domes. Balustrades of marble, wrought in open patterns of such rich design that they resemble fringes of lace, extend along the edge of the battlements. The Jumna washes the walls seventy feet below, and from the balconies the eye looks out upon the gardens and palm groves on the opposite bank, and on the Tàj, like a palace of ivory and crystal, about a mile down the stream."

56. Private Apartments.

57. Jasmine Tower.

58. The Tàj, the tomb of Urjummund Bànu Begum, Shahjehàn's favourite wife, and in which he and she lie buried side by side, took twenty years to build, and its cost is variously estimated from £2,000,000 to £4,000,000 sterling for materials alone, nothing being paid for the labour except the food for the workmen.

59. It is impossible to use any other word for this architecture than Saracenic; but except in so strong a resemblance, this style of architecture has no connection with that developed by the Saracen Turks. It was an entirely independent style developed by the Chaghtai Turks, whom we know as the Moguls. Its best name seems, therefore, "Indian Saracenic."

60. It is of course not the architecture of these buildings, but only

their decoration, which is referred to as showing this influence; and this only to the extent mentioned.

61. Moore.

62. The architect of the Tàj was a Turk named Eesa Effendi.

63. Ferdinand was probably placed in communication with the Mogul Emperor through the Augustinian monks in India.

64. Austin de Bordeaux was eventually poisoned at Delhi by some of those who were jealous of his influence with the Emperor Shahjehàn.

65. Napier.

66. He did not become a cardinal until three years before the end of Ferdinand II's reign.

67. Thus this society was formed by Ferdinand even before Pope Urban VIII's death relieved him from the antagonism which that Pope showed to all such enquiries.

68. Galileo after his condemnation was only allowed to have one pupil at a time, and Viviani was this pupil at the time of Galileo's death, being then about twenty years old.

69. There is a second set of their portraits in a book of portraits in the Marucellian Library.

70. Magalotti, the secretary, when the society broke up became a member of the Royal Society of England, then just founded.

71. Napier's *Florentine History*, vol. v. p. 486.

72. To it the Magliabecchian Library (chapter xxix) was afterwards added, the two together forming the present National Library. But the Magliabecchian Library only added thirty thousand out of the total of two hundred thousand printed books, and none of the manuscript books.

73. The official designation of the Pitti Gallery is still the "Galleria Palatina" (Gallery of the Palace), which name may be seen over several of the doors.

74. Spacious as the Pitti Palace is it did not suffice in the reigns of the later Medici Grand Dukes, and the Palazzo della Crocetta, in the Via Colonna (which now contains the Egyptian, the Etruscan, and the Tapestry Museums) was maintained as a guest-house in which guests at the court were lodged when the Grand Ducal palace was too full to receive them.

75. Since then painters have considered it an honour to be asked to send their portraits to this gallery, so that the collection is steadily increasing.

76. More pictures were afterwards added by Cosimo III, and later on also those obtained from churches pulled down; but the great bulk of the pictures in the Uffizi and Pitti Galleries still remain those collected there by Leopold and Giovanni Carlo and their brother Ferdinand II.

77. So called from the two small pillars of Oriental alabaster placed in it.

78. Certainly as regards quality, if not also as regards number of pictures.

79. *See* page 740.

80. Written before the recent unfortunate alteration in the arrangement of the rooms containing the portraits of the painters (1910).

81. The persecution which called forth Milton's well-known poem.

82. In the previous year Ferdinand sold the Medici Palace in the Via Larga to the Riccardi family.

83. There is a portrait of Prince Charles of Lorraine (at a later age) by Sustermans in the Uffizi Gallery.

84. Cardinal Mazarin died after the marriage had been settled upon, but before it had taken place; but this did not stop the marriage, as Marguerite Louise and her mother had at first hoped it might do.

85. He is buried in the family mausoleum. When his coffin was opened in 1857 it was found perfectly undisturbed by any thieves, as also was the case with all those of the family who had been cardinals. "The body was dressed in the pontifical vestments, with an alb trimmed with rich lace, and a chasuble of cloth of gold and violet silk; on the head the mitre, and at the feet the cardinal's red hat; on the breast was a gold cross set with emeralds and rubies, and a rosary of blood-red jasper; by his side a staff covered with red velvet and having tassels of gold." A leaden plate at his head bore a long Latin inscription of twenty-eight lines, giving his name and detailing his great talents and many good qualities. (*Official Report on the examination of the Tombs in the Medici Mausoleum.* 1857.)

86. He is buried in the family mausoleum. When in 1857 his coffin was opened, the body was found "vested as a cardinal in a crimson satin robe, with on the head his cardinal's mitre, and the red hat at his feet. On the breast was a handsome cross, which opened in the middle with a spring, and contained various relics; it was enamelled on the back in white, with the figure of the Redeemed in black, and on the front was set with five topaz and eight emeralds; this was a masterpiece of enamel work. On the finger of the right hand was a large episcopal ring with an oval-shaped emerald, and round the ring white enamel inside, and outside small green and red flowers. This also was an admirable piece of work." (*Official Report on the examination of the Tombs in the Medici Mausoleum.* 1857.)

87. He is buried in the family mausoleum. When in 1857 his coffin was opened, the body was found "clad in the great cloak of a Knight of Malta, and below this a doublet of black velvet, cloth breeches, and velvet boots laced with many ribbons. At his feet was his felt hat with a high crown and broad brim. Sewn on the breast of the doublet was a gold medallion, on which was on one side the effigy of Pope Clement IX, and on the other the Paschal Lamb and the Holy Spirit, with the words, *Ipse dominus possessio ejus.*" A leaden plate inside the coffin bore his name and titles, and stated that he was a general, and had won much distinction in the Thirty Years' War, and in the campaigns in Italy. (*Official Report on the examination of the Tombs in the Medici Mausoleum.* 1857.)

88. He is buried in the family mausoleum. When in 1857 his coffin was opened, the body was found "clothed in the great cloak of Grand Master of the Order of Santo Stefano, and under this a velvet coat orna-

mented with rich lace; at his feet a large hat with high crown and a broad brim; and at his right side a sceptre of gilded wood, his crown having been stolen. On the cloak and on the breast of the coat were fastened two gold medallions, both of them bearing on the front his portrait and name, and on the reverse the branch of a rose-tree with three roses, which was his special emblem, and the motto *Gratia obvia, ultio quaesita.* In his hand was a rosary, and to it was attached another small gold medallion with a representation of the Saviour on one side and of the Blessed Virgin on the other." Near his head was a leaden plate with a long inscription giving his name and titles, and detailing his deeds and virtues. (*Official Report on the examination of the Tombs in the Medici Mausoleum.* 1857.)

CHAPTER XXIX

1. The maids-of-honour of the Grand Duchess, chosen from all the first families of Florence, presented a numerous and imposing array. A complete series of their portraits is to be seen in the long corridor between the Pitti Palace and the Uffizi Gallery. They are those in *oval* frames in the portion of the corridor which adjoins the church of Sta. Felicità. There are twenty-five of them; and among them many faces of much beauty.

2. He is buried in the family mausoleum. When in 1857 his coffin was opened, the body was found "dressed in a purple chasuble, an alb adorned with rich lace, and a cope of violet-coloured silk richly embroidered with gold; on the head the scarlet cap, and at the feet the mitre and cardinal's hat. On the breast was a gold cross set with five amethysts; and on the finger a ring enamelled with flowers on a white ground and bearing a jacinth. In the hands was held a cross of ebony with a handsome crucifix of gilded silver." Behind the head was a leaden plate bearing his name and rank, with a long inscription in Latin describing his many attainments, his various works in the cause of Learning and Art, and his high character. (*Official Report on the examination of the Tombs in the Medici Mausoleum.* 1857.)

3. Galuzzi viii. ii.

4. Several of Marguerite Louise's letters are to be seen in the Florentine archives.

5. One of Cosimo's most hated measures was his causing executions to be carried out in the public streets, in order to terrify the people, which struck them with horror.

6. Galuzzi viii. ii.

7. It was on this occasion that, in order to make space for an increased number of singers, Luca della Robbia's and Donatello's reliefs of the *Cantorie* were removed from the two organ-lofts, and have never since been replaced in the position for which they were designed.

8. One of the learned men of the time, Francesco Marucelli, who had collected about twelve thousand books, founded the present Marucellian Library, bequeathing it at his death in 1703 to the city of

Florence. Another passionate lover of books, Antonio Magliabecchi, who was librarian of the Palatine Library, collected about thirty thousand books which at his death in 1714 he likewise bequeathed to his native city (*see* note 72 of chapter xxviii).

9. *See* note 26 of chapter xxix.

10. Francesco Redi was celebrated as the first physician of his day, as a writer on Natural History, and as a poet. He foreshadowed many of the modern discoveries of bacteriology and the means of obtaining immunity from various diseases by inoculation. He founded the Florentine Museum of Natural History. His poem *Bacco in Toscana* has obtained a wide celebrity. His renown in medical science has caused his statue to be placed in the Uffizi colonnade.

11. For some reason the group of *Niobe and her Children,* and the *Apollino,* were still left in the Villa Medici at Rome, and were not brought thence and placed with the rest of the Medicean art possessions until 1772, under the Austrian Grand Duke Pietro Leopoldo.

12. *Firenze Città Nobilissima,* by Ferdinando Leopoldo del Migliore (1684).

13. *See* page 752.

14. Louis XIV at this period dominated all European politics, and the principal events of this portion of his stirring reign were—

War with Holland	1672.
Victories of Turenne	1674–1675.
Peace of Nymwegen	1678.
Occupation of Luxembourg . .	1682.
Revocation of the Edict of Nantes .	1685.
Devastation of the Palatinate . .	1688.
Victories of Marshal Luxembourg .	1690–1693.
Peace of Ryswyck	1697.
War of the Spanish Succession . .	1701.
Victories of Vendôme and Tallard .	1702–1703.
Battle of Blenheim	1704.
" Ramillies	1706.
" Oudenarde . . .	1708.
" Malplaquet . . .	1709.
Peace of Utrecht	1714.
Death of Louis XIV . . .	1715.

15. Hence the alteration in the shape of the crown of Tuscany from that worn by previous Grand Dukes.

16. She is buried in the crypt of the family mausoleum. When in 1857 her coffin was opened, the body was found "clothed in a handsome dress of black silk, ornamented with black and white lace at the neck, on the sleeves, and at the hem of the skirt. On the breast was a large gold medallion, having on one side her likeness and name, and on the other her crest, the birth of the pearl, that is, Oceanus, Tritons, and Galatea, who holds in her hand an open shell, with the motto *Dos in candore*." A parchment enclosed in a leaden tube bore her name

and titles, and a long and fulsome eulogy, ascribing to her all possible virtues.

17. The small circular building in a retired part of the Boboli gardens was built as a studio for Gian Gastone.

18. Afterwards chief Librarian of the Vatican Library.

19. Letters of Horace Mann, English Ambassador at the court of Tuscany.

20. *Gli ultimi dei Medici*, by Emilio Robiony (1905).

21. All Gian Gastone's letters to his father Cosimo are preserved in the Florentine archives.

22. The numerous letters on this subject which passed during the years 1698-1708 are to be seen in the Florentine archives.

23. Cosimo's letter says that evidently his own sins have prevented his obtaining his desire in this matter.

24. He is buried in the crypt of the family mausoleum. He was probably buried wearing many jewels, for when in 1857 his coffin was opened it was found to have been entirely ransacked by thieves, nothing remaining except the skeleton, the shoes with gold buckles, and a long Latin inscription inside the coffin giving his name and titles and a fulsome eulogy on his character.

25. Napier.

26. He is buried in the family mausoleum. When in 1857 his coffin was opened, the body was found "dressed in the costume of the time, wearing a breast-plate over a brocaded coat embroidered in silver. The breeches were fastened at the knee with buckles, each having five diamonds. The stockings were of silk, and the shoes ornamented with large roses of lace. The ruffles of the shirt sleeves were fastened with links made of two small gold buttons with his own initials on them. His sword, with the hilt entwined with a gold sword knot, lay by his side broken. Near his head was a gold medallion, and another similar to it on the breast, bearing on one side his likeness and name, and on the other a thunderbolt issuing from the clouds and the motto *Et lucet et terret*." But the most remarkable thing about this coffin (showing also that it must have been opened again on a subsequent occasion) was that it contained the embalmed heart of Ferdinand's wife, the Princess Violante, who died many years after him. For the same report says:—"In this coffin was also found, enclosed in a vase of majolica, the heart of the Princess Violante Beatrice of Bavaria, his wife." The vase had an inscription giving her name, titles, and amiable qualities, and stating that "this truly royal heart, which in life was full of all virtues, has in accordance with her dying will and testament been placed in this coffin of her husband." (*Official Report on the examination of the Tombs in the Medici Mausoleum*. 1857.)

27. Dated November 1713.

28. *See* page 667.

29. Napier's *Florentine History*, vol. v. p. 550.

30. Owing to the darkness and general confusion in the lower crypt, and to his coffin having no distinguishing marks on the outside, the thieves failed to discover it, and when opened in 1857 it still contained

the jewelled crown and sceptre buried with him. "The body was
clothed in the great cloak of Grand Master of the order of Santo
Stefano, and by his side the sceptre. On the head was the royal
crown, worn over a velvet cap. Under the cloak the body was
wrapped in a black silk sheet, and had near the head a large gold
medallion, and another similar to it on the breast. These medallions
had on one side his likeness and name, and on the reverse a female
figure representing Tuscany seated in front of a temple inscribed 'Paci,'
with the Grand Duke clad in armour standing before her and making
a sign that it should remain closed, with the motto 'Sic stabis.'"
(*Official Report on the examination of the Tombs in the Medici
Mausoleum.* 1857.)

CHAPTER XXX

1. Napier.
2. She was buried by her own desire in the convent of Sta. Teresa.
But during the time of the French occupation of Florence at the
beginning of the nineteenth century her remains were brought thence
and interred in the Medici mausoleum. When in 1857 the Medici
coffins were examined, hers "was found bound with a red cord and
stamped with the seal of the French Emperor, but it contained only
bones intermingled with fragments of lead. On the night of the
26th February 1858, her remains were again restored to the convent of
Sta. Teresa, being borne thither in the royal hearse with all honour, and
laid at rest in the nuns' cemetery." (*Official Report on the examination
of the Tombs in the Medici Mausoleum,* 1857.) It has already been
noted how her embalmed heart was found in another coffin, being
placed by her desire in that of her husband (*see* note 26 of chapter xxix).
3. This expectation was falsified by subsequent events, the Austrian
rule over Tuscany proving a lenient and beneficent one.
4. By this marriage Francis nine years later became Emperor.
5. He is buried in the family mausoleum. As in the case of that of
his father, his coffin escaped discovery by the thieves who subsequently
plundered the Medici coffins (*see* page 752), and when opened in
1857 was found unrifled. "The body was dressed in black velvet, with,
over this, the great cloak of Grand Master of the order of Santo
Stefano. On the head was the Grand Ducal crown, worn over a cap;
and by his side the sceptre. But the crown and sceptre were corroded
by the acids which had been used in embalming the body. Round the
neck was a rosary with a gold filigree medal. On the breast and near the
head were two great gold medallions, each weighing twelve ounces.
These had on one side a symbolical temple in ruins, with female figures,
representing Art and Science, weeping; and on the reverse a funeral
urn with, resting upon it, his bust, and a figure representing Hope
letting another similar bust fall. Round the border was his name."
(*Official Report on the examination of the Tombs in the Medici
Mausoleum.* 1857.)

CHAPTER XXXI

1. Tuscany continued to be ruled in this way, as a mere province of Austria, for the whole of the next twenty-eight years; until in 1765 the Empress Maria Theresa's third son, Pietro Leopoldo, was at the age of eighteen made Grand Duke of Tuscany, and came to conduct the government in person.

2. Horace Mann was sent as the first English ambassador to the court of Tuscany in 1741, four years after Gian Gastone's death. His copious letters to Horace Walpole (which begin at once on his arrival at Florence) are therefore the best available evidence as to the social and political conditions which succeeded those which had existed under the Medici Grand Dukes.

3. Horace Mann's letters to Horace Walpole.

4. "She was herself an artist, something more than an amateur, and had added a picture by herself to the masterpieces in the great gallery."
—(Mann).

5. Horace Mann's letters to Horace Walpole.

6. Mann.

7. See the codicil added for this purpose to her will (page 746).

8. Article III of the document in which Her Serene Highness the Electress Anna Maria Ludovica makes this gift to Tuscany.

9. It is not meant to imply that there have not been other works of art added to these galleries and museums since, but these additions are in proportion insignificant.

10. See page 743.

11. In the same manner as the valuable collections once possessed by Modena, Mantua, and Ferrara have been.

12. Gli ultimi dei Medici, by Emilio Robiony (1905).

13. Libraries, museums, and galleries of art, with much more besides.

14. See page 57.

15. The terms of the gift had specially allowed this item to be at the free disposal of the Austrian Grand Duke.

16. Napier's Florentine History, vol. vi. p. 197.

17. When in 1857 her coffin was opened, the body was found "wrapped in a silk sheet, under which was a handsome dress of violet-coloured velvet. On the head was the Electoral crown, which was fixed to the head with a long silver pin. On the breast was a large gold medallion, with on one side her likeness and name, and on the other the sun irradiating the world, with the motto Diffuso lumine." Behind the head, engraved on a plate of copper, was a long Latin inscription of forty-four lines describing her good deeds and high character, the sorrow she had had to bear in seeing all of her family die before her and their line brought to an end, her splendid gift to Tuscany of all the art collections of the family, and the fortitude with which she had endured her disappointments and sorrows. (Official Report on the examination of the Tombs in the Medici Mausoleum 1857.)

18. One of these was the large and richly ornamented cabinet which was presented to Anna Maria Ludovica by the city of Paris, and is now to be seen in the hall in the Pitti Palace which was the Throne Room of the Medici Grand Dukes. It contains in the center compartment a statuette of her husband, the Elector William, and the two side compartments when opened disclose two miniature ball-rooms, their walls lined with looking-glasses, and in the centre of each little ball-room a group of Cupids dancing, giving a very pretty effect.

19. This, however, was not done so far as the interior decoration of the dome was concerned (*see* pages 637-638).

20. Mann says that the number of torches was so great that their cost amounted to 12,000 crowns.

21. Horace Mann's letters.

CHAPTER XXXII

1. Rogers' *Italy*.

2. *See* page 717.

3. By a new arrangement, which has greatly improved the approach to these buildings, the entrance to the mausoleum and to the New Sacristy is now through the cloisters of San Lorenzo, instead of from the Piazza Madonna into the crypt as formerly.

4. On the arch of the crypt furthest from the altar are the Medici arms, with the name of Ferdinand I, and the date of the commencement of the mausoleum, 1604.

5. A small door at the end of the crypt opens into a passage which leads into this mortuary chapel of the Austrian Grand Dukes.

6. It is asserted that this happened during the French occupation of Tuscany (1801-1814); and this is most probably the time when this plundering of the Medici coffins occurred.

7. Except those of Cosimo III and Gian Gastone, which the thieves had not discovered.

8. The whole work of this Commission was conducted with great care; each of the workmen employed to assist the Commission worked with two sentries over him to ensure that none of the jewels still left should be stolen; and the bodies remain with the dresses and ornaments which have been detailed in the various footnotes on the subject in chapters xxiii to xxxi.

9. In several cases the few words on the tombstone, when studied in connection with the history, are very pathetic.

10. The church of San Lorenzo is not orientated; the choir and high altar are at the western end.

11. *See* page 135.

12. Seen best when the Florence of to-day is compared with Ferrara, Mantua, Parma, and other capitals of former rival states.

EPILOGUE

1. Alexandre Dumas.